Queensland & the Great Barrier Reef

Cairns & the Daintree Rainforest p247

Townsville to Mission Beach p217

Whitsunday Coast p194

Capricorn Coast & the Southern Reef Islands p178

Fraser Island & the Fraser Coast p157

Noosa & the Sunshine Coast p134

Brisbane & Around p50

The Gold Coast p115

THIS EDITION WRITTEN AND RESEARCHED BY

Charles Rawlings-Way, Meg Worby, Tamara Sheward

PLAN YOUR TRIP

ON THE ROAD

PETER CADE /GETTY IMAGES ©

SNORKELLING, GREAT BARRIER REEF P241

RICHARD I'ANSON /GETTY IMAGES ©

GOLD COAST P115

HOLGER METTE /GETTY IMAGES ©

Contents

JEFF HUNTER/GETTY IMAGES ©

CLOWNFISH, GREAT BARRIER REEF P241

SAILING THROUGH THE WHITSUNDAYS P203

ON THE ROAD

TJAKUPAI DANCER, KURANDA P264

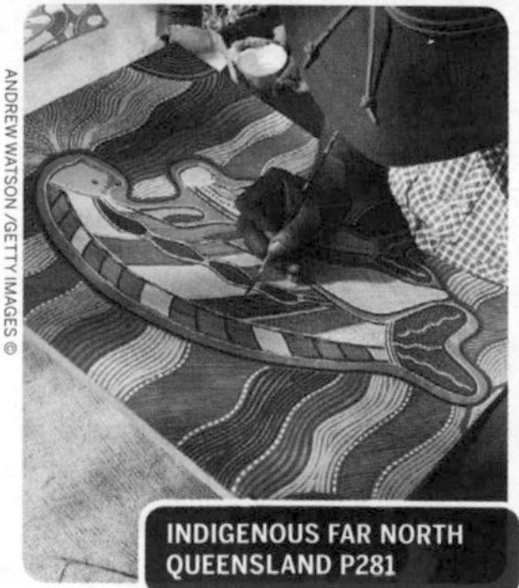

INDIGENOUS FAR NORTH QUEENSLAND P281

Contents

KOALA, HORSESHOE BAY P227

Welcome to Queensland

Let it all hang out in Queensland: Australia's holiday haven offers beaches, reefs, jungles, cheery locals and a laid-back tropical pace of life.

Changing Landscapes

Queensland's most famous 'landscape' is actually underwater: the astonishing 2000km-long Great Barrier Reef. Also offshore are hundreds of islands, harbouring giant dunes and surreal forests growing in the sand. Back on the mainland, bewitching national parks protect lush rainforests, sparkling lakes and wildlife that ranges from cute and cuddly (koalas) to downright fearsome (crocs). Skyscrapers define the landscape in Surfers Paradise and Brisbane: everywhere else you'll find laid-back beach towns and sugar-cane fields rattling under the Queensland sun.

Big Adventures

Outdoor Queensland is truly 'great'. Take the Great Barrier Reef for starters: slip on some goggles and ogle one of the most amazing underwater landscapes on Earth. There's also white-water river rafting or easygoing kayaking along the coast. Bushwalking here is first-rate: propel yourself along a multiday 'Great Walk', or take a shorter hike through a rainforest gorge or up a mountainside. Sail across the azure Whitsunday waters, or tackle a 4WD adventure along Fraser Island's 'beach highway'. There's also surfing, skydiving, mountain-biking, fishing and hang-gliding.

Eat, Drink & Be Merry

With a hip coffee-bean scene, rambling farmers markets and fabulous riverside restaurants, Brisbane has redefined itself as a foodie destination. The city's alter ego shows up at sunset, when nightclubs, pubs and small city bars light up the night. Elsewhere in the state – including foodie haunts such as Noosa, Cairns and Port Douglas – you'll find culinary rewards great and small, from fish and chips to sizzling steaks. Wash it down with Queensland's ubiquitous XXXX beer, or hunt down some fine wine from the little-known Granite Belt wine region.

Urban Delights

Wrapped around river bends, boom town Brisbane is a glamorous patchwork of neighbourhoods, each with a distinct cultural flavour: bohemian West End; party-central Fortitude Valley; affluent Paddington; exclusive New Farm...explore and soak up the vibes. The Gold Coast should also be high on your list: nightclubs and surf clubs in equal measure. Other hubs include Cairns (gateway for the Daintree and Great Barrier Reef), Noosa (on the Sunshine Coast), and Airlie Beach (to access the Whitsundays). Urban essentials abound: cafes, bars, restaurants, galleries, shops and more.

Why We Love Queensland

By Charles Rawlings-Way & Meg Worby, Authors

Growing up in chilly southern Australian towns, the very notion of Queensland – with its beaches, islands, sunshine and swaying palms – was irresistible in our imaginations. Towns like Mission Beach, Noosa and Port Douglas assumed near-mythical status, demanding to be investigated at the first opportunity. Then, when the time came to actually explore the Sunshine State, the reality didn't disappoint. And we haven't stopped exploring since! From the tropical north to the booming southeast, Queensland is an essential Australian destination.

For more about our authors, see page 336

Above: Exploring the Great Barrier Reef (p241)

Queensland & the Great Barrier Reef

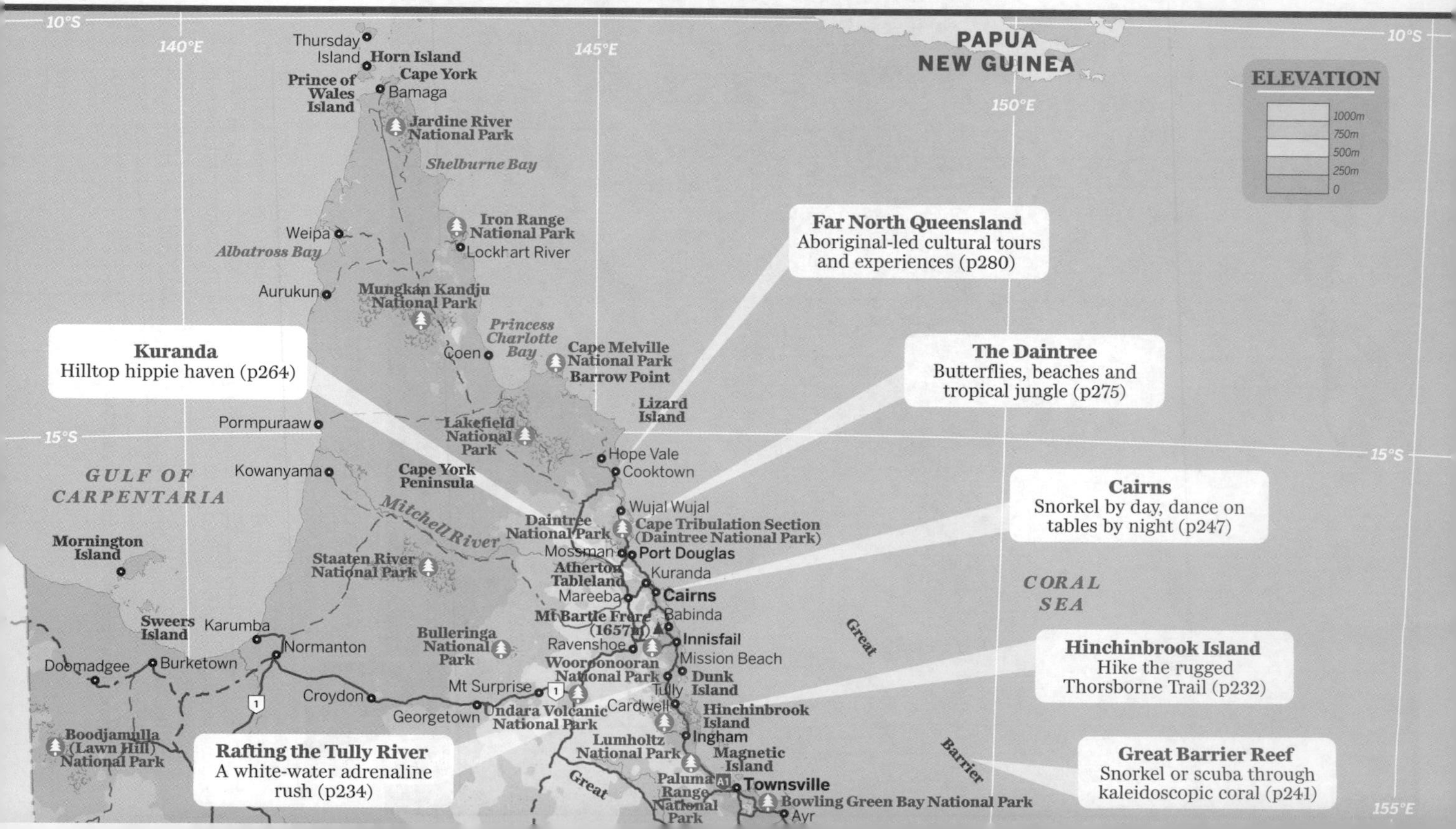

0 — 400 km
0 — 200 miles

Far North Queensland
Aboriginal-led cultural tours and experiences (p280)

Kuranda
Hilltop hippie haven (p264)

The Daintree
Butterflies, beaches and tropical jungle (p275)

Cairns
Snorkel by day, dance on tables by night (p247)

Hinchinbrook Island
Hike the rugged Thorsborne Trail (p232)

Rafting the Tully River
A white-water adrenaline rush (p234)

Great Barrier Reef
Snorkel or scuba through kaleidoscopic coral (p241)

ELEVATION
1000m
750m
500m
250m
0

10°S
140°E
145°E
150°E
15°S
155°E
PAPUA NEW GUINEA
Thursday Island
Horn Island
Cape York
Prince of Wales Island
Bamaga
Jardine River National Park
Shelburne Bay
Iron Range National Park
Weipa
Lockhart River
Albatross Bay
Aurukun
Mungkan Kandju National Park
Princess Charlotte Bay
Coen
Cape Melville National Park
Barrow Point
Lizard Island
Pormpuraaw
Lakefield National Park
Hope Vale
Cooktown
GULF OF CARPENTARIA
Kowanyama
Cape York Peninsula
Mitchell River
Wujal Wujal
Daintree National Park
Cape Tribulation Section (Daintree National Park)
Mossman
Port Douglas
Mornington Island
Staaten River National Park
Atherton Tableland
Kuranda
Cairns
Mareeba
CORAL SEA
Mt Bartle Frere (1657m)
Babinda
Sweers Island
Karumba
Bulleringa National Park
Innisfail
Ravenshoe
Normanton
Mission Beach
Doomadgee
Burketown
Wooroonooran National Park
Dunk Island
Great
Mt Surprise
Tully
Croydon
Cardwell
Undara Volcanic National Park
Hinchinbrook Island
Georgetown
Ingham
Boodjamulla (Lawn Hill) National Park
Lumholtz National Park
Magnetic Island
Barrier
Paluma Range National Park
Townsville
Great
Bowling Green Bay National Park
Ayr

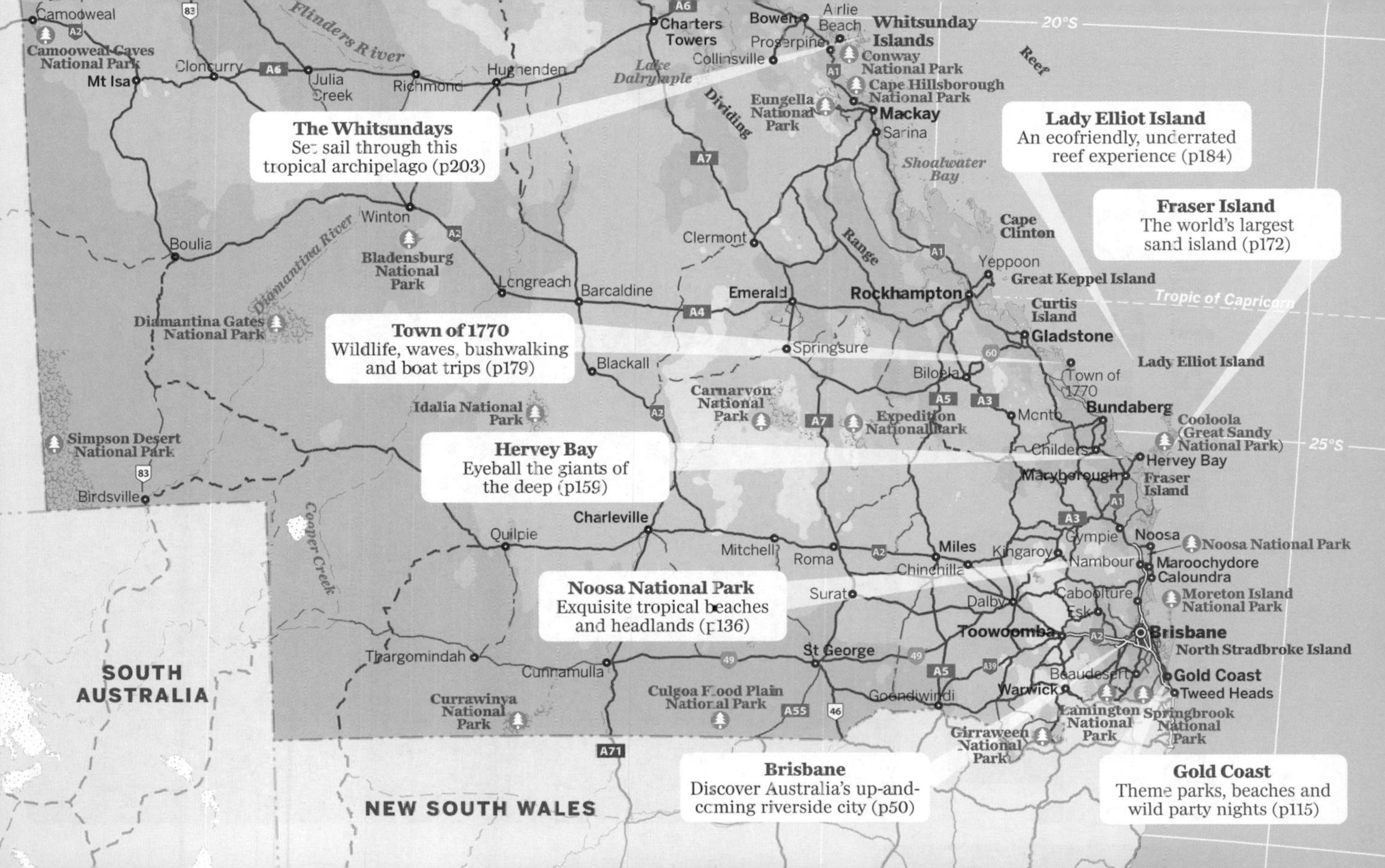

The Whitsundays
Set sail through this tropical archipelago (p203)
Town of 1770
Wildlife, waves, bushwalking and boat trips (p179)
Hervey Bay
Eyeball the giants of the deep (p159)
Noosa National Park
Exquisite tropical beaches and headlands (p136)
Brisbane
Discover Australia's up-and-coming riverside city (p50)
Gold Coast
Theme parks, beaches and wild party nights (p115)
Fraser Island
The world's largest sand island (p172)
Lady Elliot Island
An ecofriendly, underrated reef experience (p184)
Camooweal
Camooweal Caves National Park
Mt Isa
Cloncurry
Julia Creek
Richmond
Hughenden
Flinders River
Charters Towers
Lake Dalrymple
Collinsville
Bowen
Proserpine
Airlie Beach
Whitsunday Islands
Conway National Park
Cape Hillsborough National Park
Eungella National Park
Mackay
Sarina
Dividing
Range
Shoalwater Bay
Reef
20°S
Winton
Bladensburg National Park
Boulia
Diamantina River
Diamantina Gates National Park
Clermont
Cape Clinton
Yeppoon
Great Keppel Island
Rockhampton
Curtis Island
Gladstone
Tropic of Capricorn
Longreach
Barcaldine
Emerald
Springsure
Blackall
Biloela
Town of 1770
Bundaberg
Monto
Carnarvon National Park
Expedition National Park
Idalia National Park
Simpson Desert National Park
Birdsville
Cooloola (Great Sandy National Park)
25°S
Childers
Hervey Bay
Maryborough
Fraser Island
Charleville
Quilpie
Mitchell
Roma
Miles
Chinchilla
Kingaroy
Gympie
Noosa
Noosa National Park
Nambour
Maroochydore
Caloundra
Caboolture
Moreton Island National Park
Surat
Dalby
Esk
Toowoomba
Brisbane
North Stradbroke Island
Cooper Creek
Thargomindah
Cunnamulla
St George
Gold Coast
Beaudesert
Tweed Heads
Warwick
Goondiwindi
Currawinya National Park
Culgoa Flood Plain National Park
Lamington National Park
Springbrook National Park
Girraween National Park
SOUTH AUSTRALIA
NEW SOUTH WALES

Queensland & the Great Barrier Reef's Top 15

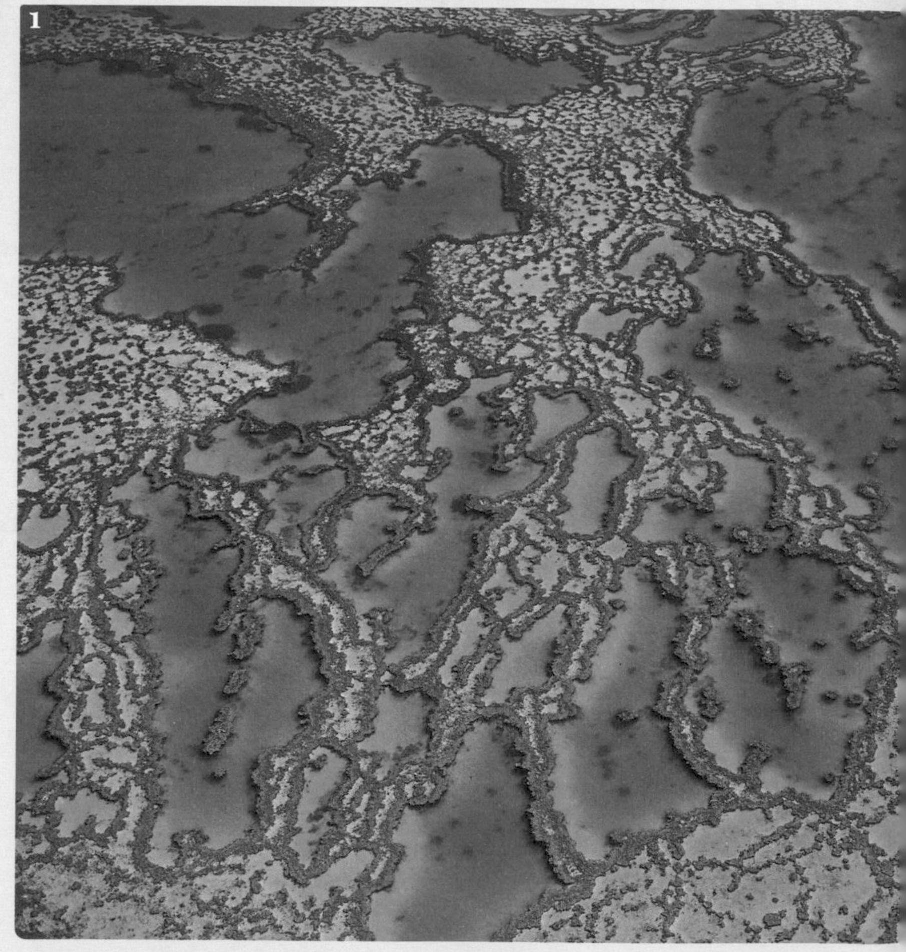

Great Barrier Reef

1 Stretching more than 2000km along the Queensland coastline, the reef (p241) is a complex ecosystem populated by dazzling coral, languid sea turtles, gliding rays, timid reef sharks and tropical fish of every colour and size. Whether you dive on it, snorkel over it, explore via scenic flight or glass-bottomed boat, linger in an island resort, or camp on a remote coral-fringed atoll, this vivid undersea kingdom and its coral-fringed islands is unforgettable.

Daintree Rainforest

2 Lush green rainforest tumbles down towards brilliant white-sand coastline in the ancient, World Heritage–listed Daintree Rainforest (p275). Upon entering this extraordinary wonderland – home to 3000 or so plant species including fan palms, ferns and mangroves – you'll be enveloped by birdsong, the buzz of insects and the constant commentary of frogs. Continue exploring via wildlife-spotting tours, mountain treks, interpretive boardwalks, tropical-fruit orchard tours, canopy walks, 4WD trips, horse riding, kayaking and cruises.

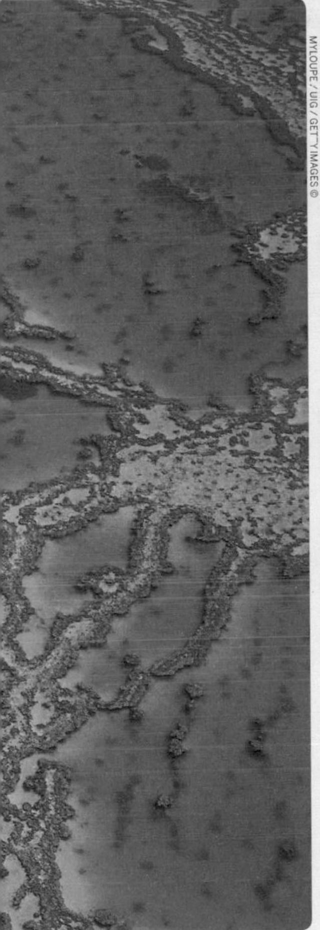

MYLOUPE / UIG / GETTY IMAGES ©

2

NIGEL PAVITT / GETTY IMAGES ©

3

4

RICHARD I'ANSON / GETTY IMAGES ©

Sailing the Whitsundays

3 You can hop around an entire archipelago of tropical islands in this seafaring life and never find anywhere with the sheer tropical beauty of the Whitsundays (p203). Travellers of all monetary persuasions launch yachts from party town Airlie Beach and drift between these lush green isles in a slow search for paradise (you'll probably find it in more than one place). Wish you were here?

Above: Whitehaven Beach

Gold Coast

4 Brash, trashy, hedonistic, over-hyped...Queensland's Gold Coast (p115) is all of these things, but if you're looking for a party, bring it on! Beyond the bling is the beach – an improbably gorgeous coastline of clean sand, warm water and peeling surf breaks. Australia's bronzed surf life-savers patrol the sands and pit their skills against one another in surf carnivals – gruelling events involving ocean swimming, beach sprints and surf boat racing that put the rest of us limp squids to shame. Also here are Australia's biggest theme parks – rollercoaster nirvana.

Noosa National Park

5 Cloaking the headland beside the stylish resort town of Noosa itself, Noosa National Park (p136) features a string of perfect bays fringed with sand and pandanus trees. Surfers come here for the long, rolling waves; walkers make the trip for the unspoilt natural vibes. Lovely hiking trails criss-cross the park: our pick is the scenic coastal trail to Hell's Gates on which you might spy sleepy koalas in the trees around Tea Tree Bay, and dolphins swimming off the rocky headland.

Brisbane

6 If you've never been to Australia's river city (or, like many Aussies, you haven't been in a while) you're in for a surprise. Billing itself as Australia's new 'World City', Brisbane (p52) has shed its redneck undertones in favour of simmering coffee culture, boutique bookshops, fabulous museums and festivals, and a hip small-bar scene that, per capita, compares with Melbourne and Sydney. Inner-city neighbourhoods each have a distinct flavour: follow the bends of the Brisbane River and spend some time exploring each one.

Right: Riverfire Festival

SIMON DIETE PHOTOGRAPHY / GETTY IMAGES ©

7

8

Rafting the Tully River

7 You won't find a wilder ride in all of Australia than down the Tully River, smack bang in the wettest part of the country. (Check out the towering gumboot at the entrance to Tully town: the 7.9m structure represents the amount of rain that fell in 1950.) Rafting trips (p234) are timed to coincide with the release of the river's hydroelectric floodgates, so even if it's not raining, adrenaline hounds are guaranteed thrills – and possibly spills – on Grade 4 rapids all year round.

Indigenous Far North Queensland

8 The human history of Far North Queensland is as dramatic as its natural surrounds. Indigenous people have called the region's rainforests and beaches home for more than 40,000 years, and a boom in indigenous-led tours and experiences (p280) makes it easier than ever for visitors to see it all through native eyes. Throw a spear, make a boomerang, sample bush tucker, try to interpret rock art, go on a rainforest walk, dig the didgeridoo: a world of new – yet incredibly old – adventures awaits.

Cairns

9 It's early morning in Cairns (p250) and you're boarding a boat out to the reef. By mid-morning you're snorkelling or diving around the colorful coral; by late afternoon you're heading back to shore after an action-packed day. But it's not over yet: you order a cold sundowner and decide on one of Cairns' myriad restaurants for an alfresco dinner. Then you're ready to hit this hedonistic city's bars, pubs and clubs, and you end up dancing till 4am. Suddenly the sun is coming up. Do it all again?

Top: Cairns Esplanade Lagoon

Fraser Island

10 Fraser Island (p172) is an ecological wonderland created by drifting sand, where wild dogs roam free and lush rainforest grows in the sand. It's a primal island utopia, home to a profusion of wildlife including the purest strain of dingo in Australia. The best way to explore the island is in a 4WD – cruising up Seventy-Five Mile Beach and bouncing along sandy inland tracks. Tropical rainforest, freshwater pools and beach camping under the stars will bring you back to nature.

Bottom: Dingo on Fraser Island

Hinchinbrook Island

11 Queensland has plenty of resort islands where you can sprawl on a sunlounge and do very little. But if you're up for something more active, consider hiking the Thorsborne Trail (p232) on Hinchinbrook Island. Tracking north–south along the island, the Thorsborne isn't for the faint-hearted – prepare to cross creeks, draw water and protect your food from ravenous rats. End-to-end, allow three nights at bush camp sites along the ungraded 32km-long track. Hiker numbers are limited, so book ahead.

Whale Watching at Hervey Bay

12 For most of the year, Hervey Bay (p159) is a sleepy seaside village with a remarkably long beach and a flat, shallow sea. That all changes in mid-July, when migrating humpback whales cruise into the bay, and thousands of tourists cruise out to watch them play. It's one of the top whale-watching regions in the world, and seeing these aqua-acrobats waving, blowing, breaching and cavorting is a guaranteed breathtaker.

WALTER BIBIKOW / GETTY IMAGES ©

RICHARD I'ANSON / GETTY IMAGES ©

BOB CHARLTON / GETTY IMAGES ©

Town of 1770

13 Built on the site of Captain Cook's first Queensland landing (in 1770), this idyllic village (p179) and the wildlife-rich peninsula surrounding it remain largely unspoilt. Outdoor adventures abound, from sea kayaking to surfing great breaks off nearby Agnes Water. Four national parks in the area offer superb bushwalking, and 1770 also makes a fine base for boat trips out to dive or snorkel the southern Barrier Reef. The sleepy township is dotted with prime lookouts, perfect for watching the prettiest sunsets on the East Coast.

Kuranda

14 You can drive or catch a bus from Cairns to the hinterland rainforest village of Kuranda (p264) in around half an hour. But that would be missing the point! Kuranda is as much about the journey as it is the destination. Hop into a gondola on the 7.5km-long Skyrail Rainforest Cableway, browse Kuranda's markets for arts, crafts and gourmet goodies, then wind your way back down to Cairns through picturesque mountains, 15 tunnels and across 37 bridges on the Kuranda Scenic Railway.

Top right: Kuranda Scenic Railway

Lady Elliot Island

15 This ecofriendly resort island (p184) is one of the loveliest and most underrated places to experience the Great Barrier Reef. Snorkel straight off the beach: the reef surrounding the tiny coral cay is teeming with tropical fish, turtles and resident manta rays. At hatching time (January to April) you can see baby turtles scamper across the sand, while humpback whales cruise past between June and October. Getting to the island is equally memorable, with a scenic flight over the turquoise reef-filled waters.

Bottom right: Green turtle on Lady Elliot Island

Need to Know

For more information, see Survival Guide (p305)

Currency
Australian dollar ($)

Language
English

Visas
All visitors to Australia need a visa, except New Zealanders. Apply online for an ETA or eVisitor visa, each allowing a three-month stay.

Money
ATMs widely available. Credit cards accepted at most hotels, restaurants and shops.

Mobile Phones
European phones will work on Australia's network, but most American or Japanese phones will not. Use global roaming or a local SIM card and pre-paid account.

Time
Queensland is on Australian Eastern Standard Time (AEST) which is GMT/UCT plus 10 hours.

When to Go

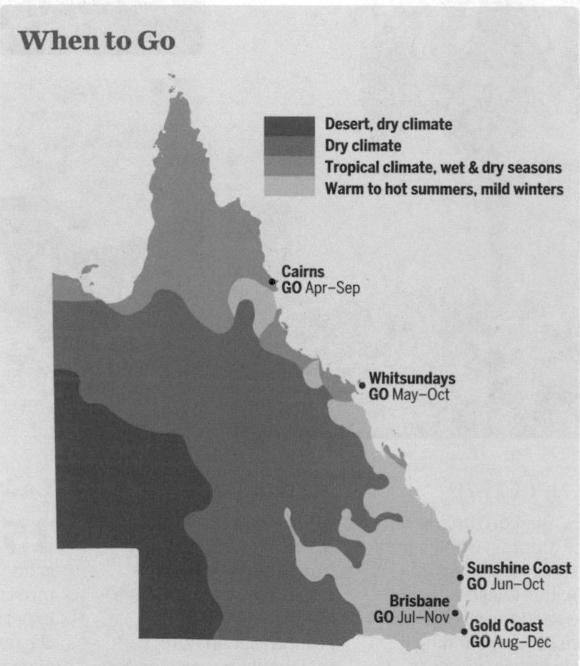

High Season
(Jun–Sep)

➡ Crowds and lofty accommodation prices in the north; a bit more wintry in the southeast, but still fine and mild.

➡ Best time to see migrating whales.

➡ Good visibility at Great Barrier Reef.

Shoulder
(Apr & May, Oct & Nov)

➡ Warm, pleasant temperatures, with long beach days.

➡ Fewer crowds, and resort prices come down slightly.

Low Season
(Dec–Mar)

➡ Wet season: hot and humid with torrential rain in the north.

➡ Party season on the Gold Coast; accommodation books out quickly.

➡ Unsafe swimming north of Agnes Water from November to May (jellyfish).

Websites

Lonely Planet (www.lonelyplanet.com/queensland) Destination information, hotel bookings, traveller forum and more.

Queensland Holidays (www.queenslandholidays.com.au) Extensive Queensland coverage: accommodation and attractions.

Courier Mail (www.couriermail.com.au) Brisbane's daily paper: current affairs and rugby league.

Queensland Department of National Parks, Recreation, Sport & Racing (www.nprsr.qld.gov.au) National parks info.

Important Numbers

Australian landline phone numbers have a two-digit area code followed by an eight-digit number. Drop the initial 0 in the area code if calling from abroad.

Emergency	☎000
Country Code (Australia)	☎61
International Access Code	☎0011
Queensland Area Code	☎07
Reverse Charges	☎1800-REVERSE (738 3773)

Exchange Rates

Canada	C$1	$0.96
China	Y1	$0.17
Euro Zone	€1	$1.47
Japan	¥100	$1.05
New Zealand	NZ$1	$0.92
South Korea	W100	$0.10
UK	UK£1	$1.78
USA	US$1	$1.06

For current exchange rates see www.xe.com.

Daily Costs

Budget: Less than $100

➡ Dorm bed: $25–$35

➡ Double room in a hostel: from $80

➡ Simple pizza or pasta meal: $10–$15

➡ Short bus ride: $4

Midrange: $100–280

➡ Double room in a midrange hotel: $100–$200

➡ Cafe breakfast or lunch: $20–$40

➡ Short taxi ride: $25

➡ Car hire per day: from $35

Top End: More than $280

➡ Double room in a top-end hotel: from $200

➡ Three-course meal in a classy restaurant: from $80

➡ Adventure activities: sailing the Whitsundays from $300 per night; diving course $650

➡ Flight from Brisbane to Cairns: from $110

Opening Hours

Opening hours vary seasonally (eg Cooktown is quiet during the Wet), but use the following as a general guide:

Banks 9.30am–4pm Monday to Friday; some 9am–noon Saturday

Cafes 8am–5pm

Clubs 10pm–4am Thursday to Saturday

Pubs & Bars noon–midnight; bars often later

Restaurants noon–2.30pm and 6.30–9pm

Shops 9am–5pm Monday to Saturday

Supermarkets 7am–8pm

Arriving in Queensland

Brisbane Airport (p94) Airtrain trains run into Brisbane's city centre every 15 to 30 minutes from 5.45am to 10pm. Prebooked shuttle buses service city hotels. A taxi into the city costs $35 to $45 (30 minutes).

Gold Coast Airport (p117) Prebooked shuttle buses service Gold Coast hotels. Public bus 702 runs from the airport along the coast to Surfers Paradise and beyond. A taxi to Surfers Paradise costs around $35 (25 minutes).

Cairns Airport (p259) Sun Palm shuttles meet arriving flights and can deliver you to Cairns, Mission Beach or Port Douglas. A taxi into central Cairns costs around $25 (15 minutes).

Getting Around

Queensland is a massive state: getting from A to B requires some thought.

Car Travel at your own tempo, explore remote areas and visit regions with no public transport. Hire cars in major towns; drive on the left.

Plane Fast-track your holiday with affordable, frequent, fast domestic flights. Carbon offset your flights if you're feeling guilty.

Bus Reliable, frequent long-haul services around the country (not always cheaper than flying).

Train Reliable, regular services up and down the coast. Opt for a sleeper carriage rather than an economy seat.

For much more on **getting around**, see p317

What's New

Brisbane Bars
Brisbane has twigged to small-bar culture: there's a slew of sassy new booze rooms here. Top of our list are Super Whatnot in the city and The End in the West End. (p83) (p84)

Magnetic Island Snorkelling
Self-guided snorkelling tours have opened up off Nelly Bay and Geoffrey Bay. They are accessed from the beach, and explore shipwrecks and reefs.

Port Douglas Moonlight Cinema
The latest addition to Australia's outdoor movie scene. Kick back in the tropical night with contemporary and classic flicks. (p274)

Dunk Island
Travellers can now return to glorious Dunk for the first time since Cyclone Yasi. The resort remains closed, but the walking trails and campsite have reopened. Water taxis run from Mission Beach. (p239)

Gold Coast Rapid Transit
The long-awaited Gold Coast tram system just may be up and running by the time you read this, shunting people between Southport and Broadbeach. (p117)

Airlie Beach Upgrade
Airlie Beach has shifted from trashy to flashy, with a multimillion-dollar revamp of its infamously tacky main drag. Don't worry: the backpacker bars are still there. (p208)

Granite Belt Brewery
Queensland's emerging Granite Belt wine region now has an excellent microbrewery to accompany all the chardonnay and shiraz. (p105)

Sir Thomas Brisbane Planetarium
On the slopes of Mt Coot-tha, Brisbane's planetarium has reopened after extensive refurbishments. The new 'optical star projector' screens impressive stellar scenes. (p60)

Brisbane City Hall
Wow! The renovations are complete, and the auditorium has never looked so good. The observation tower and Museum of Brisbane are open again too. (p53)

Fitzroy Island Turtle Rehabilitation Centre
This new facility rescues and rehabilitates sick and injured sea turtles, before sending them back to the ocean. Take a tour of the 'turtle hospital'. (p264)

Mossman Gorge Centre
The stylish new gateway to Mossman Gorge has a tour bookings desk, art gallery and bush-tucker restaurant. (p274)

Helmet Diving from Cairns
Explore the Great Barrier Reef without the snorkels, scuba gear or saturated hairdos: get amongst it with air hoses and submerged walking platforms. (p251)

For more recommendations and reviews, see lonelyplanet.com/queensland

If You Like...

Beaches

Surfers Paradise The brash, buzzy heart of the Gold Coast is a beacon for young sun-worshippers (and the surf is heavenly). (p117)

Rainbow Beach This aptly named surf spot dazzles with its ancient, multicoloured sand cliffs and dunes. (p164)

Whitehaven Beach The jewel of the Whitsundays, with powdery white sand and gin-clear waters. (p215)

Four Mile Beach Reach for your camera: backed by palms, this long, photogenic Port Douglas beach is one for the holiday album. (p269)

Cape Tribulation The rainforest sweeps down to smooch the reef at these empty stretches of sand. (p276)

Islands

North Stradbroke Island Take a quick trip from Brisbane for whale-watching, surfing, long beach walks and swimming in forest-ringed lakes. (p98)

The Whitsundays Book in at one of the archipelago's top resorts, or board a sailboat and explore as many of these pristine islands as you can. (p203)

Dunk Island Recent cyclones didn't spare gorgeous Dunk and its butterflies, bushwalks and birdlife, but take a daytrip or camp overnight and see how the rebuild is shaping up. (p239)

St Helena Island Engaging convict history a short hop from Brisbane in Moreton Bay. (p97)

Lady Musgrave Island Ringed by reef, this secluded island is a great place to play castaway. (p185)

Indigenous Culture

Kuku-Yalanji Dreamtime Walks Guided walks through Queensland's Mossman Gorge with knowledgeable Indigenous guides. (p274)

Ingan Tours Aboriginal-operated rainforest tours from Mission Beach. (p234)

Tjapukai Cultural Park Interactive tours and vibrant performances in Cairns by local Tjapukai people. (p250)

Bama Way Experience Far North Queensland on Indigenous-run tours: sacred sites, bush tucker and boomerang throwing. (p259)

Fireworks Gallery Brisbane gallery showcasing eye-popping contemporary indigenous art from around Queensland and beyond. (p86)

Food & Drink

Jan Powers Farmers Market Next to the Brisbane Powerhouse, this fabulous farmers market is the place for brilliant local food. (p98)

Noosa Food & Wine Festival This lovely Sunshine Coast town serves up a gluttonous eat-drink-and-be-merry festival in May. (p137)

Granite Belt Wineries Surprise! Queensland has vineyards! Tour the low-key cellar doors in this cool mountainous region and sample some top drops. (p104)

Atherton Tableland The volcanic soil of the Tableland yields exotic fruits, strong coffee, surprising wines and lush dairy products. (p264)

Bundaberg Rum Distillery Visit the home of Queensland's iconic (and eye-smarting) firewater, squeezed from local sugar cane. (p169)

Scenic Journeys

Sailing the Whitsundays Set sail in this magical Queensland archipelago. (p203)

Cairns to Kuranda Sail above the rainforest on a cable car to Kuranda, then take the scenic old-fashioned railway back. (p266)

Seaplane to Lizard Island Take a seaplane to this remote Queensland island, splashing down on Watson's Bay. (p282)

Atherton Tableland Travel the inland route between Cairns and Mission Beach (via Mareeba) and scan the scenic Atherton Tableland. (p264)

Luxury Stays

Daintree Eco Lodge & Spa A rainforest retreat with it all – boutique villas, spa and guided walks led by members of the Kuku Yalanji community. (p276)

Mouses House In Springbrook National Park, behind the Gold Coast, you'll find private cedar cottages in the misty forest. (p133)

Paradise Bay This eco-resort on South Long Island in the Whitsundays has just 10 beautifully sited bungalows: luxury without compromising the environment. (p212)

Latrobe Apartment A flashy, exclusive apartment in Brisbane's flashy, exclusive Paddington. (p75)

Limes A slick slice of boutique accommodation in Brisbane's Fortitude Valley (not that anyone comes to the Valley to sleep...). (p74)

HARVEY LLOYD / GETTY IMAGES ©

ANDREW WATSON / GETTY IMAGES ©

(Top) Tjakupai dancer, Kuranda (p264)
(Bottom) Wooroonooran National Park (p261)

Month by Month

TOP EVENTS

Brisbane Festival, September

Cairns Festival, August

Woodford Folk Festival, December

Noosa Food & Wine Festival, May

Coolangatta Gold, October

January

January yawns into action as Queensland recovers from its Christmas hangover, but then everyone realises: 'Hey, it's summer!'. Be prepared for heat and humidity all along the coast, and monsoonal rains up north. The Daintree region virtually shuts down.

Big Day Out

This touring one-day rock festival rolls into the Gold Coast. It features a huge line-up of big-name international artists (think Metallica, Pearl Jam, Blur) and plenty of home-grown talent. There's much moshing, sun and beer. (www.bigdayout.com)

Australia Day

Australia's 'birthday' (when the First Fleet landed in 1788) is 26 January: Queenslanders celebrate with picnics, barbecues, fireworks and, increasingly, nationalistic chest-beating. In less mood to celebrate are Indigenous Australians, who refer to it as 'Invasion Day'. (www.australia-day.com)

February

High temperatures and frown-inducing humidity continue. It's still the cyclone season (from December to April) anywhere north of the tropic line. Brisbanites flock to the Gold Coast or Sunshine Coast beaches on weekends.

Chinese New Year

Brisbane's sizeable Chinese community celebrates the new year in Fortitude Valley's Chinatown Mall (Duncan St). Expect cacophonous firecrackers, gyrating dragons, martial-arts displays and (of course) fabulous food. (www.chinesenewyear.com.au)

March

Heat and humidity ease in Queensland's south – crowds dissipate and resort prices drop. Meanwhile, high temperatures and general irritability prevail in the north.

Brisbane Comedy Festival

Feeling blue? Check yourself into this month-long laugh-fest at the re-energised Brisbane Powerhouse arts hub on the banks of the Brisbane River. Local and international acts. (www.briscomfest.com)

April

April is arguably the best time to visit Queensland. The weather is fine north and south, crowds are thin on the ground, and you can usually land a decent deal on accommodation.

Gold Coast Film Festival

Around 75% of the Queensland film industry centres on the Gold Coast – so let's throw a festival! Independent, local and international films all get a screening, plus there are free outdoor flicks and film-making workshops. (www.gcfilm festival.com)

Surfers Paradise Festival

Four weeks of good times in Surfers (...as distinct from the 48 other good-time weeks that happen here every year). Expect fine food, fireworks, buskers, arts and lots of live music. (www.surfers paradisefestival.com)

May

The end of the Wet up north brings folks outdoors, while in the southeast they get their last full beach days before cooler weather rolls in. You can find good deals on accommodation all around.

Noosa Food & Wine Festival

One of Australia's best regional culinary festivals, with cooking demonstrations, wine tasting, cheese exhibits, feasting on gourmet fare and live concerts at night. Held over three days in mid-May. (www. noosafoodandwine.com.au)

Wintermoon Music Festival

On the edge of Eungella National Park, 70km north of Mackay, Wintermoon is a family-friendly folk and world music festival. Most people camp, and impromptu performances happen all around the grounds. Held on the Labour Day long weekend. (www.winter moonfestival.com)

June

The tourist season kicks into gear as visitors from southern states head to Queensland's warm, stinger-free waters. Prices are higher and accommodation fills quickly. Southeast Queensland has cooler, mild temperatures.

Cooktown Discovery Festival

This event commemorates Captain Cook's landing in 1770, with a re-enactment by costumed local performers, both of Aboriginal and European ancestry. Highlights include fireworks, tug-of-war competitions and Indigenous heritage activities – campfire yarns, performances, and food stalls, including bush tucker. (www.cooktowndiscovery festival.com.au)

Laura Aboriginal Dance Festival

Sleepy Laura, 330km north of Cairns in Far North Queensland, hosts the largest traditional indigenous gathering in Australia. Communities come together for dance, song and ceremony. The Laura Races and Rodeo happen the following weekend. (www. lauradancefestival.com)

July

July sees even bigger numbers of out-of-state visitors fleeing the cold southern drear. Expect crowded markets, tours and accommodation in the far north.

Mareeba Rodeo & Festival

A fixture since 1949, this two-week event is one of Australia's biggest rodeos. It has all the crowd favourites – bull riding, steer wrestling, cattle shows – plus sideshows, rides, stalls and plenty of big hats. Mareeba is an hour's drive west of Cairns. (www. mareebarodeo.com.au)

August

Peak season continues in northern Queensland, where temperatures remain mild and rainfall is minimal. In the south, cooler weather continues, making for brisk, sunny days on the beach.

'Ekka' Royal Queensland Show

The Royal Queensland Show (formerly the Brisbane Exhibition, shortened to 'Ekka') brings the country to Brisbane in a festive 10-day event. Fireworks, concerts, fashion parades, theme-park rides, show bags, junk food and prize-winning livestock by the truck load. (www.ekka. com.au)

Cairns Festival

Running for three weeks from late August into September, this massive art-and-culture festival brings a stellar program of music, theatre, dance, comedy, film, indigenous art and public exhibitions to Cairns. Lots of outdoor events. (www.cairns.qld. gov.au/festival)

Hervey Bay Whale Festival

One of the world's best whale-watching towns pays homage to its favourite cetacean in this early-August event. Attractions include an illuminated evening street parade, a kids' festival and free seafront concerts. (www.herveybaywhalefestival.com.au)

September

Peak northern tourist season begins to tail off in September, as the weather generally remains mild across the country.

Brisbane Festival

One of Australia's largest and most diverse arts festivals runs for 22 days in September. The impressive schedule includes concerts, plays, dance and fringe events. It finishes off with 'Riverfire', an elaborate fireworks show over the Brisbane River. (www.brisbanefestival.com.au)

Wallaby Creek Festival

In late September, this three-day festival features blues, roots and world sounds. There are kids activities, workshops, performance artists and acrobats. It all happens in a lush tropical setting near Rossville, 40km south of Cooktown. (www.wallabycreekfestival.org.au)

Carnival of Flowers

This 10-day flora-fest in Toowoomba celebrates the return of spring to south-east Queensland. The highlight is the Floral Parade featuring flower-bedecked floats. There's also a food-and-wine component, concerts, garden tours, open-air cinema and blooming displays all over the 'garden city'. (www.tcof.com.au)

Noosa Jazz Festival

Affluent Noosa can get a bit self-centred and uptight at times, but this jazz fest gives the locals permission to let it all hang out. Over 90 different performances hit town, at both indoor and outdoor venues. Some events are free. (www.noosajazz.com.au)

NRL Grand Final

The culmination of the annual National Rugby League competition – which features the Brisbane Broncos, North Queensland Cowboys and Gold Coast Titans amongst 13 other teams – is the Grand Final in late September. Get to a barbecue, drink some beer and yell at the TV with the locals. (www.nrl.com.au)

October

October brings the tail end of the dry season in the north, with temperatures on the rise. Warmer weather blankets the south though beach days remain few and nights remain cool.

Coolangatta Gold

The epic Coolangatta Gold is a test of surf-lifesaving endurance that includes a 23km surf-ski paddle, a 3.5km swim and various beach runs – adding up to 41.5km in all. The event is open to the public, so anyone can enter (see the 1984 movie of the same name for inspiration). (www.sls.com.au/coolangattagold)

November

Northern beaches may close due to 'stingers' (jellyfish) in the shallows north of Agnes Water. The surf life-saving season flexes its muscles on beaches everywhere. With the beginning of the Wet, the Cooktown area has limited services until April.

Noosa Triathlon Multi Sport Festival

More than 50,000 folks flock to Noosa on the Sunshine Coast for this three-day event which extols the virtues of fitness and healthy living. Fun runs, bike races and triathlons are the big lures, plus live music, cooking demos and kids activities. (www.usmevents.com.au)

December

Holidays begin two weeks before Christmas. Cities are packed with shoppers and the weather hots up. North of Townsville, monsoon season is underway. The beaches are busy down south.

Woodford Folk Festival

On the Sunshine Coast, the Woodford Folk Festival stages a diverse collection of performers playing folk sounds from across the globe. Runs from 27 December to 1 January. (www.woodfordfolkfestival.com)

Itineraries

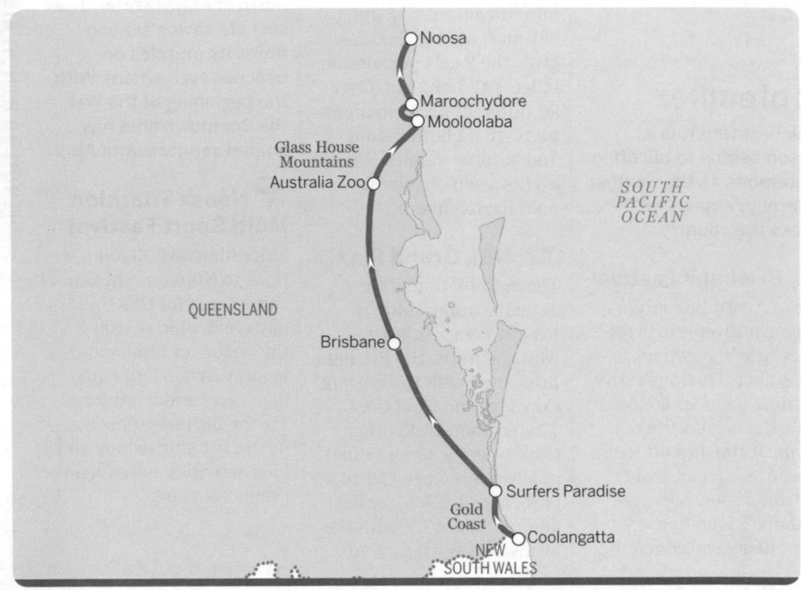

5 DAYS Gold Coast to Noosa

Kick off your trip on the **Gold Coast**, stopping in laid-back **Coolangatta** and the party-prone pleasure dome of **Surfers Paradise**. If you have a couple of days to spare, let loose your inhibitions (and your stomach) at the Gold Coast theme parks. To sample some culture head north to **Brisbane**, taking in the superb Gallery of Modern Art, some bars and live tunes in the West End, and a night on the tiles in Fortitude Valley.

Truck north to the **Glass House Mountains** for some breathtaking panoramas and rock-climbing. Nearby is the superb **Australia Zoo** – brilliant if you have the kids in tow (and even if you don't). Next up, sunny **Mooloolaba** has solid surf and a super-friendly beach vibe; its northern neighbour **Maroochydore** is just as surf-centric. Another half-hour north and you'll reach **Noosa**, a classy resort town with sublime beaches, a lush national park (home to sometimes-sighted koalas) and a first-class foodie scene.

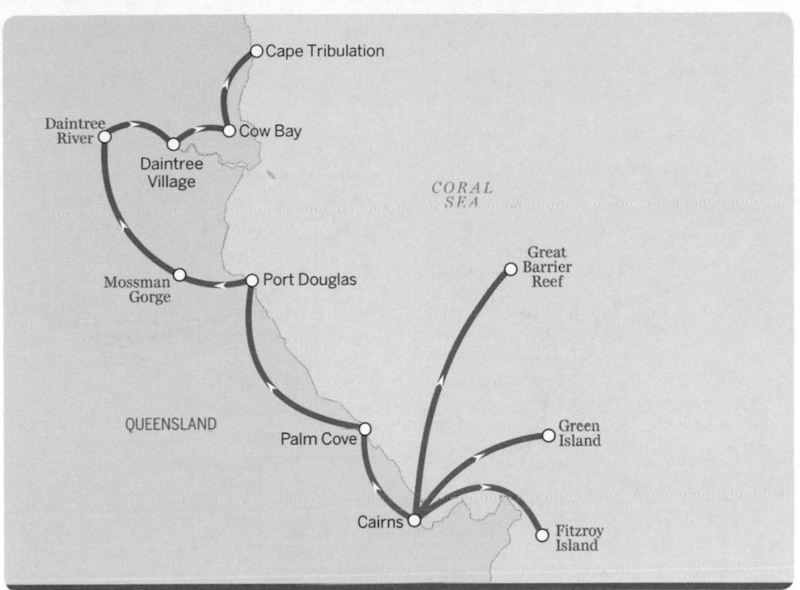

Cairns to Cape Tribulation

Australia's reef-diving capital and gateway to the Daintree Rainforest, **Cairns** is an obligatory Queensland destination. Spend your time here pinballing between botanic gardens, hip restaurants and buzzy watering holes. A short hop offshore, reef-trimmed **Green Island** and **Fitzroy Island** have verdant vegetation and lovely beaches. Further afield, a snorkelling or dive trip to the **Great Barrier Reef** is essential. With more time, you could plan a few days on a live-aboard expedition to Cod Hole, one of Australia's best dive spots.

A short drive north of Cairns, treat yourself to a stay in a plush resort at **Palm Cove**. An hour further north is **Port Douglas**, an up-tempo holiday hub with fabulous eateries, bars, and a beaut beach. It's also a popular base for boat trips to the outer reef.

Tracking north, next stop is **Mossman Gorge**, where lush lowland rainforest surrounds the photogenic Mossman River. Take a guided walk and cool-off in a waterhole.

Further north is the **Daintree River**, where you can go on a crocodile-spotting cruise, then stop for lunch at **Daintree Village**. Afterwards, continue back to the river, where you'll cross by vehicle ferry to the northern side. From here continue driving north (easy does it – this is cassowary country!) to the Daintree Discovery Centre – a great place to learn about this magnificent jungle wilderness. The beach at nearby **Cow Bay** is perfect for a few hours of beach-combing.

Last stop is **Cape Tribulation**, a magnificent natural partnership between rainforest and reef. If you have a couple of extra days, spend a few nights taking in the splendour at one of the upmarket lodges tucked into the rainforest.

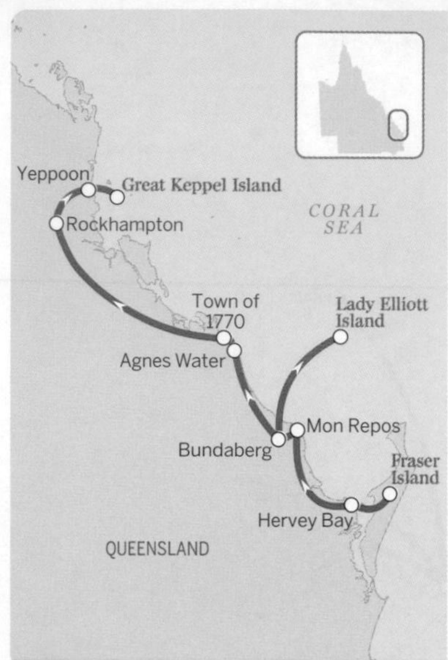

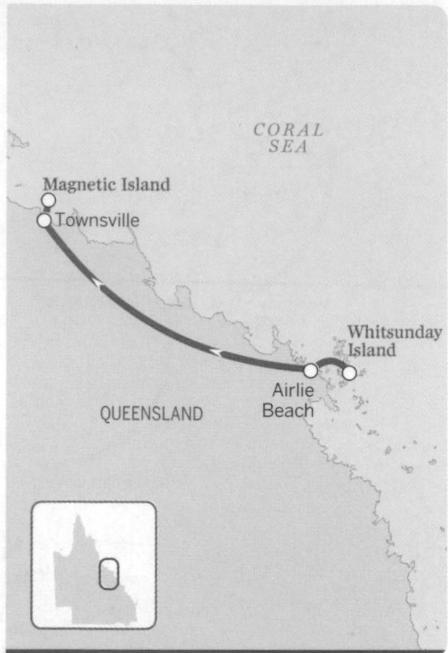

Hervey Bay to Great Keppel Island

Start your Tropic of Capricorn explorations in **Hervey Bay**, with great swimming beaches and whale-watching cruises in season (July to October). From here, hire a 4WD or join a tour to **Fraser Island**, with its massive dunes, beach 'highways', bushwalks and shimmering lakes.

Back on the mainland, head north to **Mon Repos** where massive loggerhead turtles nest and new hatchlings dash into the sea (November to March). Old-fashioned, country **Bundaberg** is next; don't miss a tour of the iconic Bundaberg Rum Distillery. From Bundaberg, hop a flight to low-key **Lady Elliott Island**, with super snorkelling and diving through coral gardens rich in marine life.

After Lady Elliott, head north to **Agnes Water** and the **Town of 1770** for white-sand beaches, top fishing and the last accessible surf breaks as you continue your run north. Motor on to **Rockhampton** for a taste of the outback, and the seaside village of **Yeppoon**. From there, launch yourself to **Great Keppel Island**, a stunning spot with fine beaches and forest-clad hills.

Airlie Beach to Magnetic Island

Fly into **Airlie Beach** where there are two must-dos: cut loose after dark with scores of other travellers, and book a boat trip out to the **Whitsunday Islands**. There are myriad day-trip options, but a multiday sail will let you explore remote islands with no one else on them. Make sure your itinerary includes **Whitsunday Island** for a memorable swim off sublime **Whitehaven Beach**, oft touted as the prettiest beach in Australia. After cruising the islands, book a night or two at a swish island resort. Feeling more adventurous? Consider signing up for an overnight kayaking trip to one of the islands.

Back in Airlie, pack yourself up and track north around three hours to **Townsville**, Queensland's third-biggest city. Promenade along the waterfront, check out the excellent Reef HQ Aquarium, clamber up Castle Hill and enjoy the first-rate local dining scene. Experienced divers might want to book a dive on the famous wreck of the *SS Yongala* offshore. Wind up your journey on **Magnetic Island**, an unpretentious isle with easygoing beach villages, plenty of wildlife and scenic bushwalking tracks.

Plan Your Trip

Your Reef Trip

The Great Barrier Reef, stretching over 2000km from just south of the Tropic of Capricorn (near Gladstone) to just south of Papua New Guinea, is the most extensive reef system in the world, and made entirely by living organisms. There are numerous ways to see the magnificent spectacle of the Reef. Diving and snorkelling are the best methods of getting up close and personal with the menagerie of marine life and dazzling corals. You can also surround yourself with fabulous tropical fish without getting wet on a semi-submersible or glass-bottomed boat, which provide windows to the underwater world below.

When to Go

High season is from June to December. The best overall visibility is from August to January.

From December to March northern Queensland (north of Townsville) has the wet season, bringing oppressive heat and abundant rainfall; from July to September it's drier and cooler.

Anytime is generally good to visit the Whitsundays. Winter (June to August) can be pleasantly warm, but you will occasionally need a jumper. South of the Whitsundays, summer (December to March) is hot and humid.

Southern and central Queensland experience mild winters – pleasant enough for diving or snorkelling in a wetsuit.

Picking Your Spot

There are many popular and remarkable spots from which to access the Reef but bear in mind that individual areas change over time, depending on the weather or any recent damage.

Best Wildlife Experiences

Sea turtles hatching on Lady Elliot Island or Heron Island; looking out for reef sharks, turtles and rays while kayaking off Green Island; spotting koalas on Magnetic Island; and Fraser Island wildlife.

Best Snorkelling Experiences

Head to Knuckle, Hardy and Fitzroy Reefs, Magnetic Island or the Whitsunday Islands.

Best Views from Above

Scenic chopper or plane ride from Cairns, Hamilton and the Whitsunday Islands. Skydiving over Airlie Beach.

Best Sailing Experiences

Sailing from Airlie Beach through the Whitsunday Islands; exploring Agincourt Reef from Port Douglas.

Useful Websites

Dive Queensland (www.divequeensland.com.au)

Great Barrier Reef Marine Park Authority (www.gbrmpa.gov.au)

Queensland Department of National Parks (www.nprsr.qld.gov.au)

Mainland Gateways

There are several mainland gateways to the Reef, all offering slightly different experiences or activities. Here's a brief overview, ordered from south to north.

Agnes Water & Town of 1770 are small towns and good choices if you want to escape the crowds. Tours head to Fitzroy Reef Lagoon, one of the most pristine sections of the Reef, where visitor numbers are still limited. The lagoon is excellent for snorkelling but also spectacular viewed from the boat.

Gladstone is a slightly bigger town but still a relatively small gateway. It's an exceptional choice for avid divers and snorkellers, being the closest access point to the southern or Capricorn reef islands and innumerable cays, including Lady Elliot Island.

Airlie Beach is a small town with a full rack of sailing outfits. The big attraction here is spending two or more days aboard a boat and seeing some of the Whitsunday Islands' fringing coral reefs. Whether you're a five- or no-star traveller, there'll be a tour to match your budget.

Townsville is a renowned gateway among divers. A four- or five-night live-aboard around the numerous islands and pockets of the Reef is a great choice. In particular, Kelso Reef and the wreck of the SS *Yongala* are teeming with marine life. There are also a couple of day-trip options on glass-bottomed boats. **Reef HQ**, which is basically a version of the Reef in an aquarium, is also here.

Mission Beach is closer to the Reef than any other gateway destination. This small, quiet town offers a few boat and diving tours to sections of the outer reef. Although the choice isn't huge, neither are the crowds.

Cairns is the main launching pad for Reef tours with a bewildering number of operators offering relatively inexpensive day trips on large boats to intimate five-day luxury charters. The variety covers a wide section of the Reef, with some operators going as far north as Lizard Island. Inexpensive tours are likely to travel to inner, less pristine reefs. Scenic flights also operate out of Cairns.

Port Douglas is a swanky resort town and a gateway to the Low Isles and Agincourt Reef, an outer ribbon reef featuring crystal-clear water and stunning corals. Diving, snorkelling and cruising trips tend to be classier, pricier and less crowded than in Cairns. You can also take a scenic flight from here.

Cooktown is close to Lizard Island but the town and its tour operators shut down between November and May for the wet season.

Islands

Speckled throughout the Reef are a profusion of islands and cays that offer some of the most stunning access to the Reef. Here is a list of some of the best islands, travelling from south to north.

For more information on individual islands, take a look at areas around the Whitsunday Coast, Capricorn Coast, Townsville to Mission Beach, Cairns and Port Douglas to Cooktown.

Lady Elliot Island has a coral cay that is awe-inspiring for birdwatchers, with some 57 species living on the island. Sea turtles also nest here and it's possibly the best location on the Reef to see manta rays. It's also a famed diving spot. There's a resort here, but you can also visit Lady Elliot on a day trip from Bundaberg.

Heron Island is a tiny, tranquil coral cay sitting amid a huge spread of reef. It's a diving mecca, but the snorkelling is also good and it's possible to do a reef walk from here. Heron is a nesting ground for green and loggerhead turtles and home to some 30 species of birds. The sole resort on the island charges accordingly.

Hamilton Island, the daddy of the Whitsundays, is a sprawling family-friendly resort laden with infrastructure. While the atmosphere isn't exactly intimate, there is a wealth of tours going to the outer reef. It's also a good place to see patches of the Reef that can't be explored from the mainland.

Hook Island is an outer Whitsunday island surrounded by reefs. There is excellent swimming and snorkelling here, and the island offers good bushwalking. There's affordable accommodation on Hook and it's easily accessed from Airlie Beach, making it a top choice for those on a budget.

Orpheus Island is a national park and one of the Reef's most exclusive, tranquil and romantic hideaways. This island is great for snorkelling – you can step right off the beach and be surrounded by the Reef's colourful marine life. Clusters of fringing reefs also provide plenty of diving opportunities.

Green Island is another of the Reef's true coral cays. The fringing reefs here are considered to be among the most beautiful surrounding any island, and the diving and snorkelling are quite spectacular. Covered in dense rainforest, the entire island is a national park. Bird life is abundant.

Reef Highlights

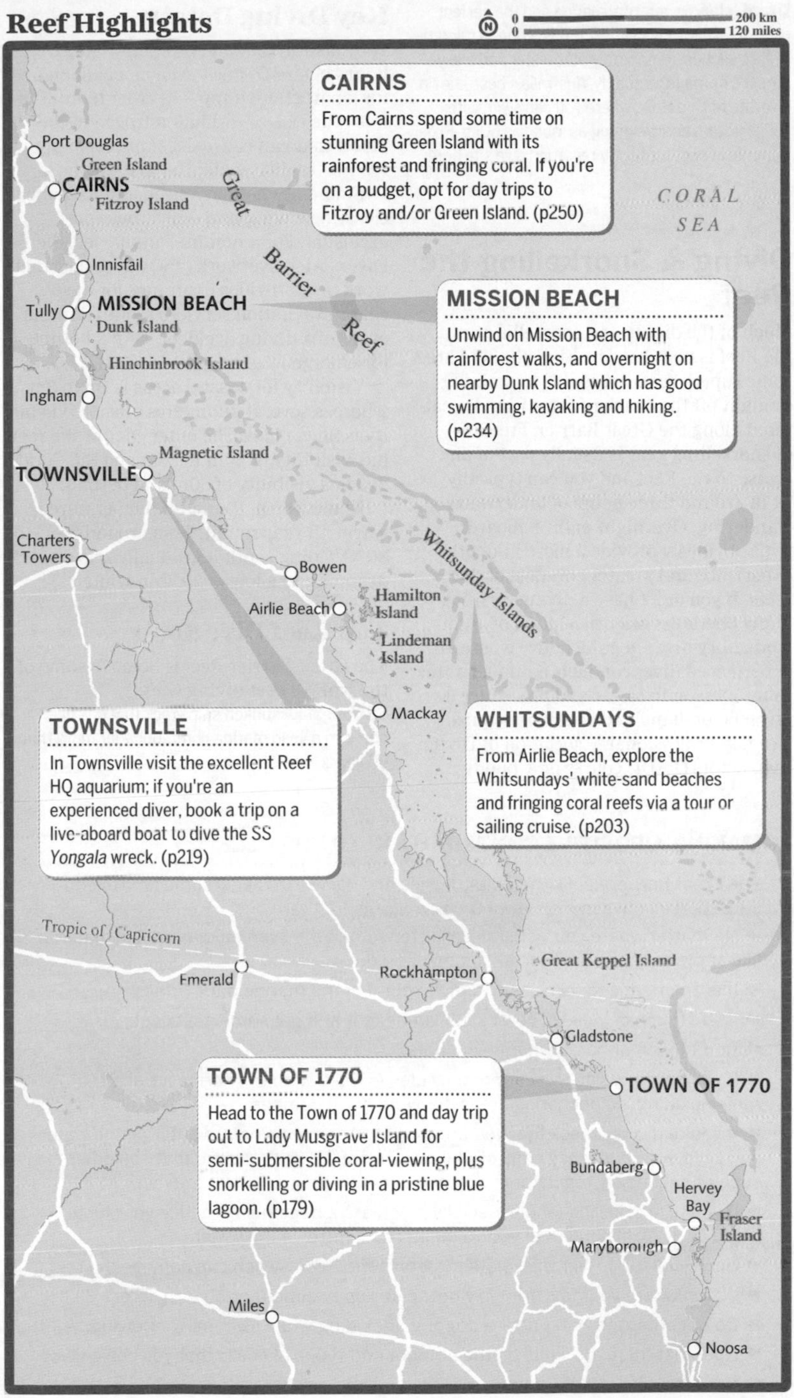

0 200 km
0 120 miles

CAIRNS

From Cairns spend some time on stunning Green Island with its rainforest and fringing coral. If you're on a budget, opt for day trips to Fitzroy and/or Green Island. (p250)

MISSION BEACH

Unwind on Mission Beach with rainforest walks, and overnight on nearby Dunk Island which has good swimming, kayaking and hiking. (p234)

TOWNSVILLE

In Townsville visit the excellent Reef HQ aquarium; if you're an experienced diver, book a trip on a live-aboard boat to dive the SS *Yongala* wreck. (p219)

WHITSUNDAYS

From Airlie Beach, explore the Whitsundays' white-sand beaches and fringing coral reefs via a tour or sailing cruise. (p203)

TOWN OF 1770

Head to the Town of 1770 and day trip out to Lady Musgrave Island for semi-submersible coral-viewing, plus snorkelling or diving in a pristine blue lagoon. (p179)

Port Douglas
Green Island
CAIRNS
Fitzroy Island
Great Barrier Reef
CORAL SEA
Innisfail
Tully
MISSION BEACH
Dunk Island
Hinchinbrook Island
Ingham
Magnetic Island
TOWNSVILLE
Charters Towers
Bowen
Whitsunday Islands
Airlie Beach
Hamilton Island
Lindeman Island
Mackay
Tropic of Capricorn
Emerald
Rockhampton
Great Keppel Island
Gladstone
TOWN OF 1770
Bundaberg
Hervey Bay
Fraser Island
Maryborough
Miles
Noosa

Lizard Island is remote, rugged and the perfect place to escape civilisation. It has a ring of talcum-white beaches, remarkably blue water and few visitors. It's home to, arguably, Australia's best-known dive site at Cod Hole, where you can swim with docile potato cod weighing as much as 60kg. Pixie Bommie is another highly regarded dive site here.

Diving & Snorkelling the Reef

Much of the diving and snorkelling on the Reef is boat-based, although there are some superb reefs accessible by walking straight off the beach of some islands scattered along the Great Barrier. Free use of snorkelling gear is usually part of any cruise to the Reef and you can typically fit in around three hours of underwater wandering. Overnight or 'live-aboard' trips obviously provide a more in-depth experience and greater coverage of the reefs. If you don't have a diving certificate, many operators offer the option of an introductory dive – a guided dive where an experienced diver conducts an underwater tour. A lesson in safety and procedure is given beforehand and you don't require a five-day Professional Association of Diving Instructors (PADI) course or a 'buddy'.

Key Diving Details

Your last dive should be completed 24 hours before flying – even in a balloon or for a parachute jump – in order to minimise the risk of residual nitrogen in the blood that can cause decompression injury. It's fine to dive soon after arriving by air.

Find out whether your insurance policy classifies diving as a dangerous sport exclusion. For a nominal annual fee, the Divers Alert Network (www.diversalertnetwork.org) provides insurance for medical or evacuation services required in the event of a diving accident. DAN's hotline for emergencies is ☎919 684 9111.

Visibility for coastal areas is 1m to 3m whereas several kilometres offshore visibility is 8m to 15m. The outer edge of the reef has visibility of 20m to 35m and the Coral Sea has visibility of 50m and beyond.

In the north, the water temperature is warm all year round, from around 24°C to 30°C. Going south it gradually gets cooler, dropping to a low of 20°C in winter.

Top Reef Dive Spots

The Great Barrier Reef is home to some of the world's best diving sites.

SS Yongala A sunken shipwreck that has been home to a vivid marine community for more than 90 years.

MAKING A POSITIVE CONTRIBUTION TO THE REEF

The Great Barrier Reef is incredibly fragile and it's worth taking some time to educate yourself on responsible practices while you're there.

- No matter where you visit, take all litter with you – even biodegradable material like apple cores – and dispose of it back on the mainland.
- It is an offence to damage or remove coral in the marine park.
- If you touch or walk on coral you'll damage it and get some nasty cuts.
- Don't touch or harass marine animals.
- If you have a boat, be aware of the rules in relation to anchoring around the reef, including 'no anchoring areas' to avoid coral damage.
- If you're diving, check that you are weighted correctly before entering the water and keep your buoyancy control well away from the reef. Ensure that equipment such as secondary regulators and gauges aren't dragging over the reef.
- If you're snorkelling (and especially if you are a beginner) practice your technique away from coral until you've mastered control in the water.
- Hire a wetsuit rather than slathering on sunscreen, which can damage the reef.
- Watch where your fins are – try not to stir up sediment or disturb coral.
- Do not enter the water near a dugong, including when swimming or diving.
- Note that there are limits on the amount and types of shells that you can collect.

TOP SNORKELLING SITES

Some nondivers may wonder if it's really worth going to the Great Barrier Reef 'just to snorkel'. The answer is a resounding yes. Much of the rich, colourful coral lies just underneath the surface (as coral needs bright sunlight to flourish) and is easily accessible. Here's a round-up of the top snorkelling sites:

- Fitzroy Reef Lagoon (Town of 1770)
- Heron Island (Capricorn Coast)
- Great Keppel Island
- Lady Elliot Island (Capricorn Coast)
- Lady Musgrave Island (Capricorn Coast)
- Hook Island (Whitsundays)
- Hayman Island (Whitsundays)
- Lizard Island (Cairns)
- Border Island (Whitsundays)
- Hardy Reef (Whitsundays)
- Knuckle Reef (Whitsundays)
- Michaelmas Reef (Cairns)
- Hastings Reef (Cairns)
- Norman Reef (Cairns)
- Saxon Reef (Cairns)
- Green Island (Cairns)
- Opal Reef (Port Douglas)
- Agincourt Reef (Port Douglas)
- Mackay Reef (Port Douglas)

Cod Hole Go nose-to-nose with a potato cod.

Heron Island Join a crowd of colourful fish straight off the beach.

Lady Elliot Island 19 highly regarded dive sites.

Pixie Bommie, Delve into the after-five world of the Reef by taking a night dive.

Boat Excursions

Unless you're staying on a coral-fringed island in the middle of the Great Barrier Reef, you'll need to join a boat excursion to experience the Reef's real beauty. Day trips leave from many places along the coast, as well as from island resorts, and typically include the use of snorkelling gear, snacks and a buffet lunch, with scuba diving an optional extra. On some boats a marine biologist presents a talk on the Reef's ecology.

Boat trips vary dramatically in passenger numbers, type of vessel and quality – which is reflected in the price – so it's worth getting all the details before committing. When selecting a tour, consider the vessel (motorised catamaran or sailing ship), the number of passengers (from six to 400), what extras are offered and the destination. The outer reefs are usually more pristine. Inner reefs often show signs of damage from humans, coral bleaching and coral-eating crown-of-thorns starfish. Some operators offer the option of a trip in a glass-bottomed boat or semi-submersible.

Many boats have underwater cameras for hire – although you'll save money by hiring these on land (or using your own waterproof camera or underwater housing). Some boats also have professional photographers on board who will dive with you and take high-quality shots of you in action.

Live-Aboards

If you're eager to do as much diving as possible, a live-aboard is a good option as you'll do three dives per day, plus some night dives, all in more remote parts of the Great Barrier Reef. Trip lengths vary from one to 12 nights. The three-day/three-night voyages, which allow up to 11 dives, are among the most common.

Check out the various options as some boats offer specialist itineraries following marine life, such as minke whales or coral spawning, or offer trips to remote spots like the far northern reefs, Pompey Complex, Coral Sea Reefs or Swain Reefs.

It's recommended to go with operators who are Dive Queensland members: this ensures they follow a minimum set of guidelines. Ideally, they are also accredited by **Ecotourism Australia** (www.ecotourism.org.au).

Popular departure points for live-aboard dive vessels, along with the locales they visit are:

Bundaberg The Bunker Island group, including Lady Musgrave and Lady Elliot Islands, possibly Fitzroy, Llewellyn and rarely visited Boult Reefs or Hoskyn and Fairfax Islands.

1770 Bunker Island group.

Gladstone Swain and Bunker Island groups.

Mackay Lihou Reef and the Coral Sea.

Airlie Beach The Whitsundays, Knuckle Reef and Hardy Reef.

Townsville *Yongala* wreck, plus canyons of Wheeler Reef and Keeper Reef.

Cairns Cod Hole, Ribbon Reefs, the Coral Sea and the far northern reefs.

Port Douglas Osprey Reef, Cod Hole, Ribbon Reefs, Coral Sea and the far northern reefs.

Dive Courses

In Queensland there are numerous places where you can learn to dive, take a refresher course or improve your skills. Dive courses are generally of a high standard, and all schools teach either PADI or Scuba Schools International (SSI) qualifications. Which certification you choose isn't as important as choosing a good instructor, so be sure to seek local recommendations and meet with the instructor before committing to a program.

A popular place to learn is Cairns, where you can choose between courses for the budget-minded (four-day courses from around $490) that combine pool training and reef dives, to more intensive courses that include reef diving on a live-aboard (five-day courses including three-day/two-night live-aboard start from $700).

Other places where you can learn to dive, and then head out on the Reef include Airlie Beach, Bundaberg, Hamilton Island, Magnetic Island, Mission Beach, Port Douglas and Townsville.

Camping on the Great Barrier Reef

Pitching a tent on an island is a unique and affordable way to experience the Great Barrier Reef. Campers enjoy an idyllic tropical setting at a fraction of the price of the five-star island resort that may be located down the road from the camp ground. Camp site facilities range from virtually nothing to showers, flush toilets, interpretive signage and picnic tables. Most islands are remote, so ensure you are adequately prepared for medical and general emergencies.

Wherever you stay, you'll need to be self-sufficient, bringing your own food and water (5L per day per person). Weather can often prevent planned pick ups, so have enough supplies to last an extra four days in case you get stranded.

Camp only in designated areas, keep to marked trails and take out all that you brought in. Fires are banned so you'll need a gas stove or similar.

National park camping permits need to be booked in advance online through Queensland Department of National Parks (www.nprsr.qld.gov.au). Our top picks:

Whitsunday Islands Nearly a dozen beautifully sited camping areas, scattered on the islands of Hook, Whitsunday and Henning.

Capricornia Cays Camping available on three separate coral cays including Masthead Island, North West Island and Lady Musgrave Island – a fantastic, uninhabited island that's limited to a maximum of 40 campers.

Dunk Island Equal parts resort and national park with good swimming, kayaking and hiking.

Fitzroy Island Resort and national park with short walking trails through bush and coral just off the beaches.

Frankland Islands Coral-fringed island with white-sand beaches off Cairns.

Lizard Island Stunning beaches, magnificent coral and abundant wildlife, but visitors mostly arrive by plane.

Orpheus Island Secluded island (accessible by air) with pretty tropical forest and superb fringing reef.

Clownfish, Great Barrier Reef (p241)

Plan Your Trip

Queensland Outdoors

Ancient rainforests, magnificent islands, point breaks and the Great Barrier Reef: Queensland is tailor-made for outdoor action. Scuba diving and snorkelling are daily indulgences, while the surfing is world-class. There's also whale-watching, sailing, kayaking and other watery pursuits. Back on dry land you can go on a bushwalk, try hang-gliding or do some wildlife spotting. For an adrenaline rush, hire a 4WD, try white-water rafting or go skydiving.

Best Outdoor Experiences

Best Wildlife Spotting

Whales off Hervey Bay

Koalas on Magnetic Island

Cassowaries in the Daintree Rainforest

Platypuses in Eungella National Park

Dingoes on Fraser Island

Top Five Aquatic Activities

Diving on the Great Barrier Reef

Surfing at Burleigh Heads

Kayaking at North Stradbroke Island

Sailing around the Whitsundays

Fishing on Lake Tinaroo

Best National Parks for Bushwalking

Wooroonooran

Carnarvon

Lamington

Springbrook

Girraween

On the Land

Bushwalking

Despite the heat and humidity, bushwalking happens in Queensland year-round, from short 1km ambles to multiday treks with camping along the way.

There are some celebrated, rugged tracks for experienced walkers in Queensland: one of the most famous is the 32km ungraded Thorsborne Trail on Hinchinbrook Island in northern Queensland. With limited walker numbers, the Thorsborne traverses a range of environments – including remote beaches, rainforests and creeks – amid spectacular mountain scenery.

When to Walk

The accommodating climate in southeast Queensland makes hiking feasible year round. But regardless of the season, you should always take plenty of drinking water with you: the Queensland sun kicks like a mule.

North of the Capricorn Coast, the best time to hike is from April to September – things can get pretty hot and sticky during the summer season (November to March). Longer walking tracks are often closed over summer, and even shorter tracks require advance planning to take into account the harsher conditions. Summer is also the most dangerous period for bushfires: the Department of National Parks, Recreation, Sport & Racing ((www.nprsr.qld.gov.au) in Queensland can advise on current alerts.

Resources

A sociable way to explore the region is by contacting a local bushwalking club, such as **Brisbane Bushwalkers** (www.bbw.org.au), which welcomes like-minded interlopers to join group outings. **Bushwalking Queensland** (www.bushwalkingqueensland.org.au) can advise on other club contacts around the state.

On the bookshelves, look for the following books:

- Lonely Planet's *Walking in Australia* details 60 walks of different lengths and difficulty in various parts of the country, including walks through three of Queensland's World Heritage–listed sites.
- *Take a Walk in South-East Queensland* (John & Lyn Daly; 2009) covers more than 170 walks, including overnight treks as well as easy, moderate and hard day hikes in 22 national parks in Brisbane, the Gold Coast, Sunshine Coast and Fraser Coast regions. See www.takeawalk.com.au.
- *Tropical Walking Tracks* (Kim Dungey & Jane Whytlaw; 2007) Includes dozens of walks outside Cairns, Kuranda and Cooktown, in the Daintree area and in the Atherton Tableland. See www.footloosebooks.com.au.

Cycling & Mountain Biking

Queensland gets hot and humid, but during the winter plenty of two-wheelers go touring for days, weekends or even weeks. The landscape is (mostly) low-lying and mountain-free, and the sun is usually shining. Or you can just rent a bike for a few hours and wheel around a city.

Rates charged by rental outfits for road or mountain bikes range from $10 to $15 per hour and $25 to $50 per day. Security deposits range from $50 to $200, depending on the rental period. For more information, contact **Bicycle Queensland** (www.bq.org.au) or see Lonely Planet's *Cycling Australia*.

Paragliding, Hang-Gliding & Parasailing

You'll see paragliders circling the skies over plenty of places along the Queensland coast, but one of the best spots is above the Carlo Sandblow at Rainbow Beach, where championship competitions happen every January.

Tandem paragliding flights there generally last around 20 to 30 minutes and cost around $180.

If you're keen to try hang-gliding, **South East Queensland Hanggliding** (www.hangglidequeensland.com.au) runs tandem flights at Mt Tamborine in the Gold Coast hinterland. Flights last around 20 minutes and cost $275. Paragliding is also offered from the same steep launchpad by **Paragliding Queensland** (www.pgqld.com.au; tandem flights $260).

Parasailing (dangling below a parachute-like canopy while being dragged along by a boat) is another heart-starting way to get the most from the coast. There are beachside operators on the Gold Coast and many other beach resorts along the coast.

GREAT WALKS OF QUEENSLAND

The 'Great Walks of Queensland' project is a $16.5 million undertaking to create a world-class set of 10 multiday walking tracks. For complete track descriptions, maps and campsite bookings, visit www.nprsr.qld.gov.au/experiences/great-walks.

GREAT WALK	DIFFICULTY	DISTANCE	DURATION	WHAT YOU'LL SEE
Carnarvon	hard	86km	6-7 days	Dramatic sandstone gorges, Aboriginal rock paintings, panoramic ridgelines
Conondale Range	hard	56km	4 days	Valleys, gorges, forests, waterfalls, ridges and 360-degree views inside Conondale National Park
Cooloola	moderate	102km	5 days	Rainforest, tall eucalypt forest, dry coastal woodland, heath plains and sea views in Cooloola Recreation Area
Fraser Island	hard	90km	up to 8 days	Rainforests, coloured sands, picturesque lakes, towering sand dunes
Gold Coast Hinterland	moderate	55km	3 days	Palm-filled valleys, mist-covered mountains, clifftop views, waterfalls, crystal-clear rivers
Mackay Highlands	moderate	50km	4-6 days	Rainforest, gorges, steep escarpments, rolling farmlands
Sunshine Coast Hinterland	moderate	58km	4 days	Scenic Blackall Range, waterfalls, eucalypt forest, subtropical rainforest and fine views
Wet Tropics	moderate	100km	6 days	Waterfalls, gorges, views and World Heritage rainforest at Girringun National Park
Whitsunday	hard	30km	3 days	Lowland tropical rainforest, rocky creeks, lush palm valleys, views, rugged Conway Range (inside Conway National Park)
Whitsunday Ngaro Sea Trail	moderate	200m to 7km	up to 4 days	Series of walking and sea kayaking trails around Whitsunday, South Molle and Hook Islands in the Whitsunday archipelago

Koala, Horseshoe Bay (p227)

Wildlife Watching

Native wildlife is one of Queensland's (and indeed Australia's) top selling points. National parks are your best bet for the greatest concentrations of species, although many native critters are nocturnal (bring a torch). Queensland is also a bird-watching nirvana, with a wide variety of habitats and species, particularly water birds.

As well as the national parks, wildlife hot spots include Cape Tribulation and the Mareeba Wetlands for birds; Magnetic Island for koalas; Fraser Island for dingoes; Hervey Bay for whales; Mon Repos, near Bundaberg, for sea turtles; North Stradbroke Island for dolphins, sea turtles and rays; and the Daintree for crocodiles and cassowaries. And, as the precautionary road signs attest, the rainforest around Mission Beach is also home to cassowaries.

On the Water

Diving & Snorkelling

The Queensland coast boasts enough spectacular dive sites to make you blow bubbles and gasp for breath. The Great Barrier Reef offers some of the world's best diving and snorkelling, and there are dozens of operators vying to teach you how to scuba dive or provide you with the ultimate dive safari. There are also around 1600 shipwrecks along the Queensland coast, putting a man-made spin on the marine metropolis concept.

You can snorkel just about everywhere along Queensland's coast, which requires minimum effort and no experience. Many dive spots are also popular snorkelling sites.

Diving is generally good year-round although during the wet season – December to March – floods can wash a lot of mud out into the ocean and visibility is sometimes poor. Aside from the myriad diving and snorkelling reef tours available in Cairns and Port Douglas, other top dive spots include the following:

Bundaberg Wreck dives, gropers, turtles and rays.

Hervey Bay Shallow caves, schools of large fish, wreck dives, turtles, sea snakes, stone fish, rays and trevally,

Snorkelling, Great Barrier Reef (p241)

Mooloolaba Pristine reefs and wreck diving on the sunken warship HMAS *Brisbane*.

Moreton Island Tangalooma wrecks, nudibranches, urchins, sponges and coral, plus good snorkelling.

North Stradbroke Island Manta rays, leopard and grey nurse sharks, humpback whales, turtles, dolphins, and hard and soft corals.

Rainbow Beach One of Australia's top diving destinations, with grey nurse sharks, turtles, manta rays and giant gropers amid volcanic pinnacles.

Southport Abundant marine life including rays, sharks, turtles and 200 fish species.

Diving Courses & Prices

Every major town along the Queensland coast has a dive school, but standards and dive options vary – it's worthwhile doing some research before signing up. Many budget courses only offer shore dives, which can be less interesting than open-water dives out on far-flung sections of the reef. At the other end of the scale, some of the more expensive courses enable you to live aboard a boat or yacht for several days far from the mainland, with all your meals included in the price.

Multiday PADI open-water courses cost anywhere from $400 to $800; one-day introductory courses start at around $200. Normally you have to show that you can tread water for 10 minutes and swim 200m before you can start a course. Many schools will also require that you undertake a medical, which usually costs extra (around $80). For certified divers, renting gear and going on a two-tank day dive generally costs between $150 and $200. Snorkellers can hire a mask, snorkel and fins from a dive shop for around $30 to $50.

Surfing

From a surfer's perspective, Queensland's Great Barrier Reef is one of nature's tragic errors – it's effectively a 2000km-long breakwater! Mercifully, there are some pumping surf beaches along the coast in southern Queensland. The Gold Coast has great breaks, as does virtually the entire shoreline of the Sunshine Coast. Get your hands on a copy of Mark Warren's definitive *Atlas of Australian Surfing* for the low-down on the best breaks.

You can hire boards from almost any surf shop along the coast, and op shops in surf towns are usually full of used boards. But unless you're taking lessons, it's best to start off with boogie boarding and work your way up – surfing isn't as easy as it looks! Always ask locals and lifesavers about the severity of breaks, rips and hazards – broken boards, noses and egos are not uncommon, particularly among inexperienced surfers with lofty ambitions.

BUNGEE JUMPING & SKYDIVING

Brave? Lose a bet? Just plain crazy? Cairns is the place to try bungee jumping, with multiperson 'jungle swings' for those not willing to go it alone. If you'd rather jump out of a plane, sign up for some skydiving at Caloundra, Surfers Paradise, Brisbane, Airlie Beach, Mission Beach or Cairns. Most folks start with a 9000ft jump, with around 30 seconds of freefall – or up the ante to 14,000ft with up to a minute of pant-wetting plummeting. Prices start at around $300 for a skydive, and $100 for a bungee jump.

MARCOS WELSH / GETTY IMAGES ©

Above: White-water rafting, Wooroonooran National Park (p261)

Left: Surfing, Gold Coast (p115)

Top Surf Spots

Agnes Water & Town of 1770 Pretty much the last place on the coast heading north where you can catch a wave (north of here the Great Barrier Reef intercepts the ocean swells). The breaks here are strictly for old hands, though: the waves can get fast and steep, you have to paddle well out from shore, and you may be sharing your personal space with the odd reef shark.

Burleigh Heads The point break here is magnificent, peeling in from the national park on the headland to the main beach – but it does require some experience.

Caloundra to Mooloolaba A very popular strip of sandy suburban shoreline with fine beach breaks.

Coolangatta An essential surf haunt for Gold Coasters, particularly Kirra Beach. The Superbank is here too – a 2km-long sandbar stretching from Snapper Rocks to Kirra Point.

Noosa Popular with longboarders, with good wave action at Sunshine Beach and the point breaks around the national park, especially during the cyclone swells of summer (December to February).

North Stradbroke Island Harder to get to, but has fabulous surf beaches that are always less crowded than the Gold Coast and Sunshine Coast beaches.

Surfing Lessons

If you're new to the beach, the best way to find your feet is with a few lessons, and there are dozens of surf schools in southeast Queensland. Two of the best spots to learn – mostly because the waves are kind to beginners – are Surfers Paradise and Noosa. Two-hour group lessons typically cost around $60, with five-day courses for the super-keen costing around $250.

White-Water Rafting

The mighty cascades of the Tully, North Johnstone and Russell Rivers between Townsville and Cairns are renowned white-water-rafting locations, benefiting from extraordinarily high rainfall in the area (the town of Tully received 7.9m of rain in 1950!). The Tully is the most popular of the three with moderate Grade III to IV rapids, which means the rapids are moderate but rafts require continuous manipulation to stay upright. The Tully also receives regular hydro-electric dam

KAYAKING & CANOEING

Kayaking and canoeing are brilliant in Queensland. Numerous outfits along the coast offer paddling expeditions along calm waterways and lakes, or out through the protected Barrier Reef waters – sometimes from the mainland to offshore islands.

SITE	OPERATOR	WHAT YOU'LL SEE
Caloundra	Blue Water Kayak Tours (www.bluewaterkayaktours.com)	Tours out to Bribie Island
Great Sandy National Park	Elanda Point (www.elanda.com.au)	High-backed dunes, wildflowers, mangroves, rainforests
Magnetic Island	Magnetic Island Sea Kayaks (www.seakayak.com.au)	Photogenic bays, island coastline
Mission Beach	Coral Sea Kayaking (www.coralseakayaking.com)	Day paddles to Dunk Island; multiday trips to Hinchinbrook Island
Moreton Bay	Redlands Kayak Tours (www.redlandskayaktours.com.au)	Mangroves, sealife, creeks, islands
Noosa	Noosa Ocean Kayak (www.noosakayaktours.com)	Dolphins and turtles on Laguna Bay, river kayaking on Noosa River
North Stradbroke Island	Straddie Adventures (www.straddieadventures.com.au)	Mangroves and island coastline, dolphins, sea turtles, rays
Southport	Adventure Outlet (www.adventureoutlet.com.au)	Trips to South Stradbroke Island, wildlife
Whitsunday Islands	Salty Dog (www.saltydog.com.au)	One-day and multiday trips exploring South Molle Island, coral reefs, dolphins, turtles, sea eagles

Sailing the Whitsundays (p203)

water releases, with rafting trips timed to coincide with the increased flow.

Most of the guides who operate tours here have internationally recognised qualifications and safety is high on their list of priorities. This said, you don't need any experience to take part, just a need for speed. You also need to be older than 13 on the Tully (or age 10 on the Russell). Rafting day-trips cost around $200, including transfers.

Sailing

Queensland's waters are pure utopia for salty sea-dogs of all levels of ability, with some of the most spectacular sailing locations in the world. The hands-down winner of the state's many picture-postcard sailing spots is the Whitsunday Islands – 74 idyllic gems surrounded by a translucent blue sea that, at times, has a seamless and uninterrupted horizon. There are myriad charters, tours and boat operators based at Airlie Beach, the gateway to the islands. There's also a sizeable local sailing scene around Manly, just outside Brisbane, or you can explore some of the islands off the Far North Queensland coast on board a chartered boat or cruise from Port Douglas.

Whitsunday Sailing Tours

You'll find plenty of day tours that hop between two or three islands, but three-day/two-night all-inclusive cruises are better value and provide a deeper appreciation of the area's assets. You can also choose between tours that sleep their passengers on board, or ones that dock at island resorts for the night.

The main benefit of joining a tour is that you don't require any sailing expertise – some outfits will get you to participate under guidance, but you can be a complete landlubber and still enjoy a true sailing experience. The range of tours is huge and, as with most activities, the smaller the number of passengers the greater the price. As a general guide, day tours cost around $160 for adults and $60 for children. Three-day, two-night sailing packages typically start from around $500 per person.

Chartering a Boat

It's fairly easy to charter your own boat at Airlie Beach, but be warned: that glassy

Fishing, Noosa (p136)

sea has the potential to turn nasty and, regardless of what operators say, braving the ocean solo should only be attempted by sailors with some experience.

If you're lacking the skills but still want a far more intimate experience than a tour, consider chartering your own boat and hiring a skipper to do the hard work for you. The cost of a 'bareboat' (unskippered) charter will set you back somewhere between $600 and $1200 per day, depending on the size of the boat. With a skipper you're looking at upwards of $1500 per day.

Fishing

Fishing in all its formats is incredibly popular in Queensland, especially in coastal areas. More than a few Queensland families spend entire summers living out of the back of their 4WDs while trying their luck in the surf breaks. There are also plenty of dams, rivers, lakes and jetties that are perfect for dangling a line. Some of our favourite fishing spots include North Stradbroke Island, Fraser Island, Rainbow Beach, Lake Tinaroo and Lakefield National Park.

STINGER WARNING

All water activities, including diving and snorkelling, are affected by stingers (box jellyfish), which can be found at any time of year off the Queensland coast and in river mouths, from Agnes Water north. They are dangerous and should not be taken lightly. Look for the stinger-resistant enclosures at beaches during the peak stinger season, which runs from November to May. Never enter the water at beaches that have been closed due to stingers, and consider using a full-body lycra suit if you must swim in the water during stinger season.

There are local fishing shops in most coastal towns where you can get advice on what's biting where and get set up with a rig. Fishing charters are also big-business in Queensland: hook yourself onto a tour in places like North Stradbroke Island, Caloundra, Rainbow Beach, Port Douglas, Hamilton Island and Maroochydore. The heavy-tackle game-fishing season runs from September to December.

Information & Resources

The Great Barrier Reef has traditionally been a popular fishing ground (so many fish!), but zoning laws introduced in 2004 in response to concerns about environmental damage and overfishing have tightened the area of reef that can be fished. There are also limitations on the number of fish you can catch and their size, and restrictions on the type of gear you can use. You also need to be aware of which fish are protected entirely from fishing.

To find out what you can catch, where and how, contact the Department of National Parks, Recreation, Sport & Racing ((www.nprsr.qld.gov.au)) or swing into a local fishing shop. For information on weather and tide conditions and what's biting, tune in to local radio stations. For weekly reports on fishing spots along the coast see www.fishingmonthly.com.au.

Plan Your Trip

Travel with Children

If you can survive the longhaul distances between cities, travelling around Queensland with the kids can be a real delight. There is oodles of interesting stuff to see and do, both indoors and outdoors, including beaches, zoos, theme parks and adventures on the Great Barrier Reef. Lonely Planet's Travel with Children contains plenty of useful information.

Best Regions for Kids

Brisbane

Big-city kiddie adventures: ferry rides, an artificial riverside swimming beach, hands-on museums and galleries, and a koala sanctuary.

Gold Coast

The beaches here are great, but there are five massive rollercoaster-wrapped theme parks just north of Surfers Paradise.

Noosa & the Sunshine Coast

Don't miss Noosa National Park, the native critters at Australia Zoo, and a visit to Mooloolaba's bedazzling Underwater World.

Fraser Island & the Fraser Coast

Go eye-to-eye with some giant mammals on a whale-watching cruise from Hervey Bay, or careen around the beach in a 4WD on Fraser Island.

Cairns & Hinterland

Rainforest walks, a swimming lagoon, playgrounds and boat trips to the reef or islands. Don't miss the scenic railway to Kuranda in the hinterland.

Queensland for Kids

Accommodation

Many Queensland motels and caravan parks have playgrounds and swimming pools, and can supply cots and baby baths. Some motels also have in-house children's videos and child-minding services.

Top-end hotels and many (but not all) midrange hotels are well versed in the needs of guests with children. B&Bs, on the other hand, often market themselves as child-free. It pays to check before booking.

Babysitting

Some of Queensland's licensed child-care agencies have places set aside for casual care: check under Baby Sitters and Child Care Centres in the phone directory, or phone local councils for child care provider lists. Avoid unlicensed operators. Day-care or babysitting options with rates starting at around $25 per hour include:

Busy Bees Babysitting (☎0417 794 507; www.busybeesbabysitting.com.au) Gold Coast, Cairns and Port Douglas.

Care4Kidz (☎07-3103 0298; www.careforkidz.com.au) Brisbane

Dial an Angel (☎07-3878 1077, 1300 721 111; www.dialanangel.com) Brisbane.

Change Rooms & Breastfeeding

Queenslanders are relaxed about breast-feeding and nappy (diaper) changing in public. All cities and most major towns also have centrally located public rooms (often in shopping centres) where parents can go to nurse their baby or change a nappy; check with the local tourist office.

Discounts

Child concessions (and family rates) often apply to accommodation, tours, admission fees and transport around the state, with some discounts as high as 50% of the adult rate. However, the definition of 'child' varies from under-5s to under 18 years. Accommodation concessions generally apply to children under 12 years sharing the same room as adults. Kids under two-years-old receive discounts on many flights across Australia (they are seatbelted onto a parent's lap and thus don't occupy a seat).

Eating Out

Many cafes, restaurants, surf clubs and pubs offer kids' meals, or will provide small serves from the main menu. Some also supply high chairs. Many fine-dining restaurants, however, don't welcome small children. If all else fails, grab some fish-and-chips and head for the beach. There are also plenty of free or coin-operated barbecues in parks around the state.

Necessities

Queensland has high-standard medical services and facilities, and items such as baby formula and disposable nappies are widely available.

Major hire-car companies will supply and fit child safety seats, charging a one-off fee of around $25. Taxi companies aren't legally required to supply child seats, but may be able to organise one if you call in advance.

Children's Highlights

Outdoor Adventures

➡ Sea kayaking along the Noosa River or around Dunk Island off Mission Beach.

➡ Horse riding through the Gold Coast hinterland or along the beach near Noosa.

➡ Snorkelling the Great Barrier Reef on a boat trip from Port Douglas.

➡ Taking a 4WD camping adventure on Fraser Island.

Theme Parks

Dreamworld (p123) – Roller coasters, IMAX movies and Bengal tigers.

Sea World (p123) – Performing seals and dolphins, plus sharks, dugongs and polar bears up close.

Warner Bros Movie World (p123) – Movie-themed rides and wandering VIP cartoon characters.

Wet'n'Wild (p123) – It's wet, and it's wild: pools, slides and aquatic mayhem.

WhiteWater World (p123) – Cool off on a humid Gold Coast afternoon.

Rainy-Day Activities

➡ Exploring museums and galleries in Brisbane: Queensland Museum & Sciencentre (p57); Queensland Maritime Museum (p57), and the kids' galleries and installations at the Gallery of Modern Art (p57).

➡ Watching sharks, seals and other marine life at Underwater World (p146) on the Sunshine Coast.

➡ Visiting Townsville's Reef HA Aquarium (p219) for a look at the wonders of the reef.

When to Go

The southeast (Brisbane, Gold Coast, Sunshine Coast) can be great fun any time of year, though it does get chilly during the winter (June to August), making for unpredictable beach days.

Winter is the best (but busiest) time to visit Far North Queensland, with clear nights, stinger-free beaches and an absence of summer's oppressive heat, humidity and monsoonal downpours.

Travelling during Australian school holidays can be maddening and expensive – particularly on the Gold Coast and Sunshine Coast.

Regions at a Glance

Brisbane & Around

Neighbourhoods
Drinking
Islands

Brisbane's West End

Divided by the meandering Brisbane River, Brisbane is a tight-knit web of distinct neighbourhoods: our favourite is the bohemian West End, where you'll find bookshops, bars, live music rooms and myriad cheap eats.

Cafes & Bars

Brisbane is hot! But that doesn't mean the locals don't enjoy a steaming cup of java. Cool cafes abound, plus a clutch of quality bean roasters. Brisbane has also joined the Australia-wide boom in small bars, found down laneways and in compact shopfronts.

Moreton Bay Islands

In Moreton Bay you'll find the underrated North Stradbroke Island, with excellent surfing, sea-kayaking and beach walks, and Moreton Island, which has a full-kit resort and loads of activities. You can also visit the former prison island of St Helena.

p50

The Gold Coast

Surfing
Nightlife
Wilderness

Surfers Paradise

They don't call it Surfers Paradise for nothing! The beach here is one of the best places in Australia to learn to surf, or head south for the more challenging breaks around Burleigh Heads and Kirra.

Clubs, Pubs & Bars

All along the Gold Coast – from the throbbing clubs in Surfers Paradise to the brawling surf-side pubs in Coolangatta – you'll never be far from a cold aprés-surf beer (or tequila, champagne or poolside daiquiri).

National Parks

Ascend the winding roads into the Gold Coast hinterland to discover some brilliant national parks: Springbrook, Lamington and Tamborine feature waterfalls, hikes and the constant trill of native birdsong.

p115

Noosa & the Sunshine Coast

Surfing
Food
Nature

Sunshine Coast Surf

Blonde, bronzed and waxy – the relaxed surfer ethos of the Sunshine Coast permeates the back streets and beaches, with reliable breaks and warm waves all the way along the coast.

Noosa Dining Scene

You know you're *really* on holiday when you wake up in your hotel/hostel/resort and the choice of where to have breakfast, lunch and dinner is the most important item on the day's agenda. Welcome to Noosa!

Noosa National Park

Bathed by the South Pacific, with photogenic beaches reaching up to hillsides awash with dense subtropical bush – accessible Noosa National Park is perfect for bushwalking, swimming or just chilling out in the sun.

p134

Fraser Island & the Fraser Coast

Islands
Marine Life
Small Towns

Fraser Island

Fraser Island – the largest sand island in the world – a unique subtropical ecosystem that's pretty darn close to paradise. A day tour merely whets the appetite; camp overnight and wish upon a thousand shooting stars.

Whale Watching

Off Hervey Bay, migrating humpback whales breach, blow and tail-slap. When they roll up alongside the tour boat with one eye peeking above the water, you've got to wonder who's watching who.

Rainbow Beach & Childers

One on the coast and one inland, these two little towns are absolute beauties: Rainbow Beach for its magnificent cliffs and beach, and Childers for its country vibe and historic architecture.

p157

Capricorn Coast & the Southern Reef Islands

Diving & Snorkelling
Islands
Accessible Outback

Southern Reef

From the Town of 1770, book a snorkelling cruise out to the southern Great Barrier Reef or a bunk on a live-aboard dive vessel. In this psychedelic underwater world, tropical fish flit through a coloured landscape of coral, anemones and marine life.

Lady Elliot Island

Tiny, coral-ringed Lady Elliot is superb for snorkelling, with reefs accessible by merely wading in directly off the beach. The island resort is unpretentious and eco-friendly, and the flight here is akin to a scenic tour.

Rockhampton

Just 40km from the coast, Australia's 'beef capital' Rockhampton gives visitors a true taste of the bush, with buckin' broncos, big hats and loads of bulldust. Further west, cattle station stays offer full immersion into outback living.

p178

Whitsunday Coast

Islands
Sailing
Nightlife

The Whitsundays

With 74 tropical beauties to choose from, the Whitsunday Islands archipelago is truly remarkable. There are plenty of ways to experience them: bushwalking, kayaking, staying in resorts or just lounging around on a yacht.

Island-hopping

The translucent seas around the Whitsundays would seem incomplete without the snow-white billows of sails in the picture. The wind, the sea, the beckoning sandy bays… Climb aboard a yacht as a crew member or just for a fun day trip, and find your perfect isle.

Airlie Beach

The main jumping-off point for trips around the Whitsundays, Airlie Beach is a party town full of party people. Join the thirsty throngs in the bars after dark.

p194

Townsville to Mission Beach

Coastline
Nature
Architecture

Beautiful Beaches

The coastline between Townsville's palm-shaded Strand and Flying Fish Point near Innisfail shelters both vast, sandy expanses and intimate coves. Offshore, you'll find stand-out beaches on the wild Hinchinbrook Island and lovable Dunk.

National Parks

Hiking, camping, swimming and picnicking opportunities abound in the national parks. Weird wildlife, such as flightless prehistoric-looking cassowaries, roam the rainforest. Top picks include the bushwalking paradise Hinchinbrook Island and the rainforest-cloaked peaks of Paluma Range National Park.

Historic Buildings

Old-time architecture includes the gold-rush era streetscapes of Charters Towers, beautiful 19th-century buildings in Townsville, and Australia's highest concentration of art-deco architecture in Innisfail.

p217

Cairns & the Daintree Rainforest

Diving & Snorkelling
Nightlife
Indigenous Culture

Reef Trips

Every day from Cairns and Port Douglas a flotilla of boats ferries passengers out to experience the bedazzling underwater world of the Great Barrier Reef. To sidestep the crowds, join a live-aboard vessel and explore more remote sections of the reef.

Cairns after Dark

There are so many backpackers and international tourists in Cairns that it's sometimes hard to spot a local. But you can usually find one or two in the city's boisterous pubs and bars – great fun after dark.

Daintree Tours

Several excellent Aboriginal-led tour companies can take you on a cultural journey through the timeless Daintree Rainforest and Mossman Gorge, offering an insight into the area's rich indigenous heritage.

p247

On the Road

Brisbane & Around

Includes ➡

Best Places to Eat

- Brew (p76)
- Gunshop Café (p79)
- George's Seafood (p78)
- Varias (p109)
- Oceanic Gelati (p101)

Best Places to Stay

- Latrobe Apartment (p75)
- Limes (p74)
- Bowen Terrace (p75)
- Stradbroke Island Beach Hotel (p101)
- Vacy Hall (p111)

Why Go?

Australia's most underrated city? Booming Brisbane is an energetic river town on the way up, with an edgy arts scene, pumping nightlife and great coffee and restaurants. Lush parks and historic buildings complete the picture, all folded into the elbows of the meandering Brisbane River.

Brisbanites are out on the streets: the weather is brilliant and so are the bodies. Fit-looking locals get up early to go jogging, swimming, cycling, kayaking, rock climbing or just to walk the dog. And when it's too hot outside, Brisbane's subcultural undercurrents run cool and deep, with bookshops, globally inspired restaurants, cafes, bars and band rooms aplenty.

East of 'Brizzy' is Moreton Bay, with its low-lying sandy isles, beaches and passing parade of whales, turtles and dolphins. To the west is the rural inland hub of Toowoomba (also underrated) and the surprising Granite Belt Wine Region, which bottles up some impressive drops.

When to Go

Brisbane

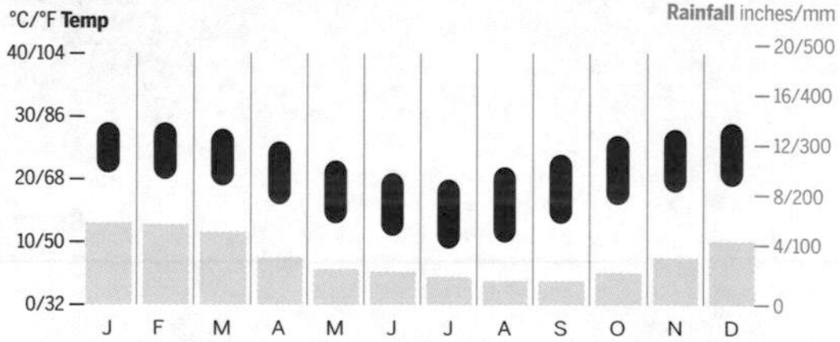

Jan Brisbane swelters during summer, the perfect time to head to North Stradbroke Island.

May–Aug Cool, mild temperatures (bring a jacket) and clear skies – Brisbane at its best!

Sep Spring has sprung. Warm temperatures and the very arty Brisbane Festival.

Brisbane & Around Highlights

1. Exploring the cavernous volumes of Brisbane's **Gallery of Modern Art** (p57).
2. Finding a patch of lawn at Streets Beach in Brisbane's **South Bank Parklands** (p57).
3. Catching some live comedy at the **Brisbane Powerhouse** (p59).
4. Checking out some bookshops and bars in Brisbane's **West End** (p84).
5. Spending a night on the tiles in **Fortitude Valley** (p84).
6. Roaming along the **North Gorge Headlands Walk**, spotting turtles offshore (p99).
7. Going bush in the city: hiking up bushy slopes to the **Mt Coot-tha Lookout** (p60).
8. Chugging up, down or across the **Brisbane River** on a ferry (p95).
9. Meandering between cellar doors in the **Granite Belt Wine Region** (p104).

BRISBANE

POP 2.15 MILLION

Brisbane's charms are evident: the arts, the cafes, the bars, the weather, the old Queenslander houses, the go-get-'em attitude. But perhaps it's the Brisbane River itself – which broke so many hearts when it flooded in 2011 and 2013 – that gives the city its edge. The river's organic convolutions carve the city into a patchwork of urban villages, each with a distinct style and topography: bohemian, low-lying West End; hip, hilltop Paddington; exclusive, peninsular New Farm; prim, pointy Kangaroo Point. Move from village to village and experience Queensland's diverse, eccentric, happening capital.

History

The first settlement in the Brisbane area was established at Redcliffe on Moreton Bay in 1824 as a penal colony for Sydney's more recalcitrant convicts. After struggling with inadequate water supplies and hostilities from the displaced local Aboriginal population, the colony was relocated to the banks of the Brisbane River, the site of the city centre today. The new site suffered at the hands of numerous crooked warders and was abandoned in 1839. Subsequently, the Moreton Bay area was thrown open to free settlers in 1842, marking the beginning of Brisbane's rise to prominence.

By the time of Queensland's separation from New South Wales in 1859, Brisbane had a population of around 6000. Huge wealth flowed into the city from the new pastoral and gold-mining enterprises in the Darling Downs, and grandiose buildings were erected to reflect this new-found affluence. The frontier-town image was hard to shake off, however, and it wasn't until the 1982 Commonwealth Games and Expo '88 that Brisbane's reputation as a cultural centre came into being.

Sights

Most of Brisbane's major sights are in the CBD or inner-city suburbs. A walk through the city centre will reveal Brisbane's colonial history and architecture, while a ferry ride or bridge walk across the river lands you in South Bank, home to both stellar art museums and peaceful parklands (complete with artificial swimming lagoon).

City Centre

★City Hall LANDMARK

(Map p58; ☎07-3403 8463; www.brisbane.qld.gov.au; King George Sq; ⏰10am-5pm) FREE Overlooking King George Sq, this fine 1930s sandstone edifice is fronted by a row of sequoia-sized Corinthian columns and has an 85m-high clocktower with a fabulous lookout, from which bells peal across the city rooftops. In 2013 the hall opened up again after three-year renovation. Free guided tours run hourly from 10.30am to 3.30pm; free clocktower tours run every 15 minutes from 10.45am to 4.45pm. The excellent Museum of Brisbane (p53) is also located here.

The results of the renovations are spectacular, with the building's best features – ceilings, lavishly tiled lobbies and art-deco light fittings – all brought to the fore. The domed auditorium itself is truly magnificent – a cavernous volume (Australia's version of the Hagia Sophia?) with a 4300-pipe organ, 1644 seats and mahogany-and-bluegum floors. The Rolling Stones played their first-ever Australian gig here in 1965. Phone for guided tour bookings; clocktower tours are on a first-come, first-served basis.

Commissariat Store Museum MUSEUM

(Map p58; www.queenslandhistory.org; 115 William St; adult/child/family $5/3/10; ⏰10am-4pm Tue-Fri) Built by convicts in 1829, this former

WHEN IT RAINS, IT POURS

Imagine the shocked faces in 2011 when Aussies flicked on the nightly news and saw swirls of brown river water flowing through downtown Brisbane! Wild weather across the Sunshine State caused major inundations, with Australia's third-largest city recording its biggest flood since 1974. Boats, pontoons, ferry docks, the city's excellent Riverwalk walkway network and even a riverside restaurant were all picked up and carried off downstream. More than 30,000 homes in low-lying suburbs were swamped. The clean-up was quick, but then in 2013 it happened again – not as severe this time, but still devastating for locals who had just finished scraping the river mud out of their houses from 2011. The Brisbane River: defining and defiling the city all at once.

BRISBANE IN...

Two Days

Start with breakfast in Brisbane's boho **West End** (we like Gunshop Café (p79) and the Burrow (p78)) then saunter across to the South Bank Parklands (p57). Spend a few hours swanning around at the Gallery of Modern Art (p57), then grab some lunch at a riverside eatery and cool off with a swim at Streets Beach (p65). As the evening rolls in, jump on a ferry to the Brisbane Powerhouse (p59) in New Farm for a bite, a drink or perhaps a show.

On day two head downtown for a gander at the mix of old and new architecture, visiting the newly renovated City Hall (p52; don't miss the Museum of Brisbane (p53) on the third floor) and the Treasury Building (p56), before ambling through the lush City Botanic Gardens (p53). Finish the day in **Fortitude Valley**: a brew at Alfred & Constance (p84), a noodle soup in Chinatown (p59), and a night of indulgences in the bars and clubs.

Four Days

On day three check out the rather French cafes in **New Farm**. Cafe Bouquiniste (p81) and Chouquette (p81) are are hard to beat. Next scoot over to Paddington to check out the retro shops. Take a drive up to the lookout on top of Mt Coot-tha Reserve (p60) then meander away an hour or two in the Brisbane Botanic Gardens (p60). Dress up for dinner and drinks in the city: slake your thirst at Super Whatnot (p83) then eat in style at E'cco (p77).

On day four take a river cruise to Lone Pine Koala Sanctuary (p61). Recount the day's wildlife encounters over a beer and a steak at the Breakfast Creek Hotel (p86) then head back to the West End for beers at the Archive Beer Boutique (p84) and a live band at Lock 'n' Load (p88).

government storehouse is the oldest occupied building in Brisbane. Inside is an immaculate little museum devoted to convict and colonial history. Don't miss the convict 'fingers' and the exhibit on Italians in Queensland.

Roma Street Parkland PARK

(Map p58; www.romastreetparkland.com; 1 Parkland Blvd; ⌚24hr) FREE This beautifully maintained, 16-hectare, 16-precinct downtown park is one of the world's largest subtropical urban gardens. Formerly a market and a railway yard, the park opened in 2001 and features native trees, a lake, lookouts, waterfalls, a playground, barbecues and many a frangipani. It's something of a maze: easy to get into, hard to get out.

Adjacent to the Roma Street Parkland is the **Old Windmill** (Map p58; Wickham Tce) – reputedly the oldest surviving building in Queensland (1828). Due to a design flaw, the windmill sails were too heavy for the wind to turn, and a convict-powered treadmill was briefly employed before the mill was abandoned. The building was converted into a signal post and later a TV broadcast site and meteorological observatory.

City Botanic Gardens PARK

(Map p58; www.brisbane.qld.gov.au; Alice St; ⌚24hr; 📶) FREE On the river, Brisbane's favourite green space is a mass of lawns, tangled Moreton Bay figs, bunya pines and macadamia trees descending gently from the Queensland University of Technology campus. Free guided tours leave the rotunda at 11am and 1pm Monday to Saturday. (Is it just us, or are things looking a tad shabby here? New signage please!).

Also in the gardens is a sculpture known as *Jemmy Morrill & the Brolgas*. Morrill was the sole survivor of an 1846 shipwreck on the Great Barrier Reef. Some local Aborigines found him and he lived with them for 17 years before returning to the new European colony in Queensland. He went on to play a pivotal role in improving relations between Aborigines and white colonists in the new state.

Museum of Brisbane MUSEUM

(Map p58; ☎07-3339 0800; www.museumofbrisbane.com.au; Level 3, Brisbane City Hall, King George Sq; ⌚10am-5pm) FREE Inside Brisbane's renovated City Hall, this great little museum illuminates the city from a variety of viewpoints, with interactive exhibits

Greater Brisbane

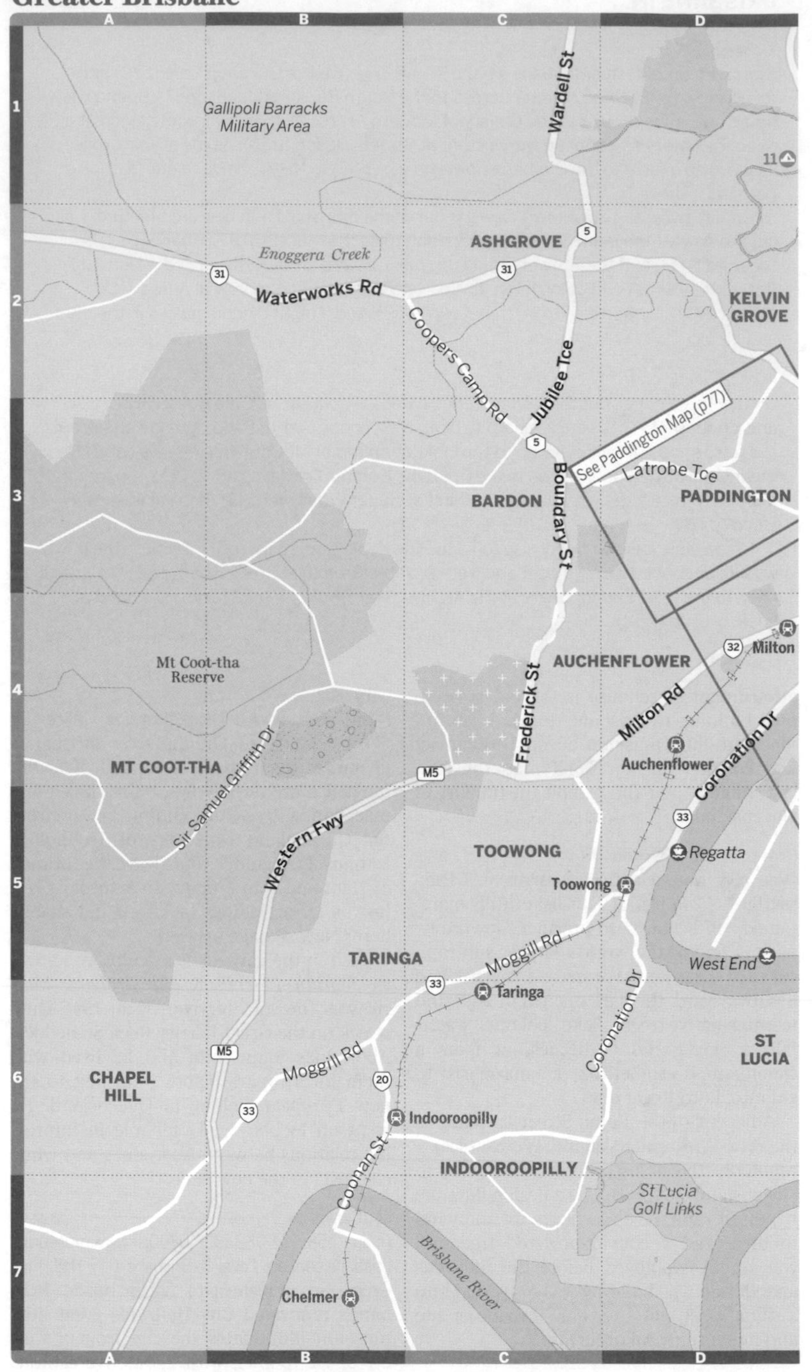

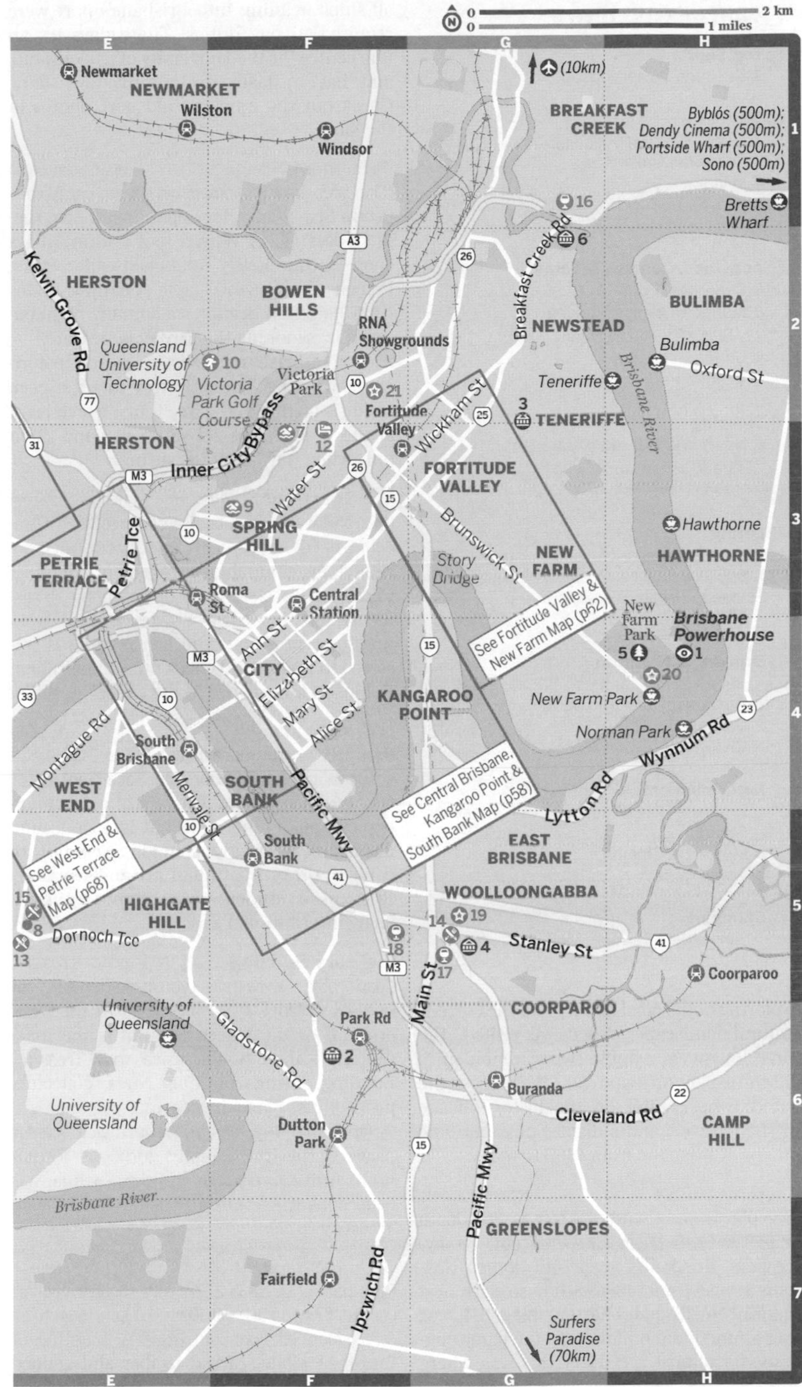

NEWMARKET
Newmarket
Wilston
Windsor
BREAKFAST CREEK
Byblós (500m); Dendy Cinema (500m); Portside Wharf (500m); Sono (500m)
(10km)
Bretts Wharf
16
6
Breakfast Creek Rd
HERSTON
BOWEN HILLS
BULIMBA
Kelvin Grove Rd
RNA Showgrounds
NEWSTEAD
Bulimba
Oxford St
Queensland University of Technology
10
Victoria Park
Victoria Park Golf Course
21
Teneriffe
Brisbane River
Fortitude Valley
3
TENERIFFE
HERSTON
7
12
Inner City Bypass
Wickham St
FORTITUDE VALLEY
Water St
9
SPRING HILL
Brunswick St
Hawthorne
HAWTHORNE
PETRIE TERRACE
Petrie Tce
Story Bridge
NEW FARM
Roma St
Central Station
See Fortitude Valley & New Farm Map (p62)
New Farm Park
Brisbane Powerhouse
5
1
Ann St
CITY
Elizabeth St
20
Mary St
Alice St
KANGAROO POINT
New Farm Park
Norman Park
Wynnum Rd
Montague Rd
South Brisbane
Merivale St
WEST END
SOUTH BANK
Pacific Mwy
See Central Brisbane, Kangaroo Point & South Bank Map (p58)
Lytton Rd
EAST BRISBANE
See West End & Petrie Terrace Map (p68)
South Bank
WOOLLOONGABBA
15
8
13
HIGHGATE HILL
Dornoch Tce
14
19
18
4
17
Stanley St
Main St
Coorparoo
COORPAROO
University of Queensland
Gladstone Rd
Park Rd
2
Buranda
Cleveland Rd
University of Queensland
Dutton Park
CAMP HILL
Pacific Mwy
Brisbane River
GREENSLOPES
Fairfield
Ipswich Rd
Surfers Paradise (70km)
2 km
1 miles

Greater Brisbane

exploring both social history and the current cultural landscape. When we visited, the three long-term exhibits were a fabulously kitsch display on Expo '88 ('We'll show the world!'); an exhibit on the history of the Brisbane River; and a display of panoramic photos of Brisbane from 1860 to today.

Customs House HISTORIC BUILDING

(Map p58; www.customshouse.com.au; 399 Queen St; 9am-5pm) FREE Crowded out by skyscrapers, Brisbane's lovely old domed Customs House (built 1886–89) is so darn aesthetically pleasing it's hard to imagine it was ever a functional building. As the name suggests, for almost a century this was where all ships heading into Brisbane's port were required to pay duties. These days it's an info centre for the University of Queensland, and has a flashy restaurant downstairs. Check out the amazing old port photos in the lobby.

Parliament House HISTORIC BUILDING

(Map p58; www.parliament.qld.gov.au; cnr Alice & George Sts; tours 1pm, 2pm, 3pm & 4pm non-sitting days) FREE With a roof clad in Mt Isa copper, this lovely blanched-white stone French Renaissance–style building dates from 1868 and occupies a suitably regal position overlooking the City Botanic Gardens: it's one of Brisbane's most treasured historical landmarks. The only way to get a peek inside is on one of the free tours, which leave at the times listed above on demand (2pm only when parliament is sitting).

Old Government House HISTORIC BUILDING

(Map p58; www.ogh.qut.edu.au; George St; 10am-4pm Sun-Fri) FREE This 1862 gem was designed by estimable government architect Charles Tiffin, as an appropriately plush residence for Sir George Bowen, Queensland's first governor. Tour the lavish innards (restored in 2009), and check out some William Robinson landscapes in the gallery upstairs.

QUT Art Museum MUSEUM

(Map p58; www.artmuseum.qut.edu.au; 2 George St; 10am-5pm Tue-Fri, noon-4pm Sat & Sun) FREE On the Queensland University of Technology campus is this excellent little museum, displaying regularly changing exhibits of contemporary Australian art and works by Brisbane art students, plus temporary exhibits by international artists.

Treasury Building HISTORIC BUILDING

(Map p58; www.treasurybrisbane.com.au; cnr Queen & William Sts; 24hr) FREE At the western end of the Queen St Mall is the magnificent Italian Renaissance–style Treasury Building, dating from 1889. No tax collectors inside – just Brisbane's casino.

Opposite the casino fronting a grassy plaza stands the equally gorgeous former **Land Administration Building**, which has been converted into a five-star hotel called Treasury (p72).

St John's Cathedral CHURCH

(Map p58; 07-3835 2222; www.stjohnscathedral.com.au; 373 Ann St; 9.30am-4.30pm, tours 10am & 2pm Mon-Sat, 2pm Sun) FREE A magnificent fusion of stone, carved timber and stained glass just west of Fortitude Valley, St John's Cathedral is a beautiful piece of 19th-century Gothic Revival architecture. The building is a true labour of love: construction began in 1906 and wasn't finished until 2009, making it one of the world's last cathedrals of this architectural style to be completed.

Mansions HISTORIC BUILDING
(Map p58; cnr George & Margaret Sts) South along George St from the Commissariat Store building, on the right at the junction with Margaret St, is the Mansions, an unusual three-storey, red-brick Romanesque terrace built in 1890. Look for the cats atop the parapets at each end of the building.

Around the corner facing Alice St and fronted by palms is the opulently styled Greek-revival **Queensland Club** (Map p58; www.queenslandclub.com; cnr George & Alice Sts).

South Bank

On South Bank, just over Victoria Bridge from the CBD, the **Queensland Cultural Centre** is the epicentre of Brisbane's cultural life. It's a huge compound that includes concert and theatre venues, four museums and the Queensland State Library.

★**Gallery of Modern Art** GALLERY
(GOMA; Map p58; www.qagoma.qld.gov.au; Stanley Pl; ⏲10am-5pm Mon-Fri, 9am-5pm Sat & Sun; ⓦ) FREE All angular glass, concrete and black metal, must-see GOMA focuses on Australian art from the 1970s to today. Continually changing and often confronting, exhibits range from painting, sculpture and photography to video, installation and film. There's also an arty bookshop here, kids' activity rooms, a cafe and free guided tours at 11am and 1pm. Brilliant!

South Bank Parklands PARK
(Map p58; www.visitsouthbank.com.au; Grey St; ⏲dawn-dusk) FREE This beautiful smear of green – technically on the western side of the Brisbane River – is home to performance spaces, sculptures, buskers, eateries, bars, pockets of rainforest, BBQ areas, bougainvillea-draped pergolas and hidden lawns. The big-ticket attractions here are Streets Beach (p65), a kitsch artificial swimming beach resembling a tropical lagoon (packed on weekends); and the London Eye–style **Wheel of Brisbane** (Map p58; www.thewheelofbrisbane.com.au; Grey St; adult/child/family $15/10/42; ⏲11am-9.30pm Mon-Thu, 10am-11pm Fri & Sat, 10am-10pm Sun), which offers 360-degree views from its 60m heights. Rides last around 10 minutes and include audio commentary (and air-con!).

Also in the parklands is **Stanley St Plaza**, a renovated section of historic Stanley St lined with kitschy, mainstream cafes, shops, restaurants and a pub. The touristy/New Age South Bank Lifestyle Markets (p91) happen here on Friday nights and on Saturdays and Sundays.

Not far away, **Courier-Mail Piazza** is an outdoor performance space that screens big-ticket sporting events and movies during school holidays, both for free.

Queensland Museum & Sciencentre MUSEUM
(Map p58; www.southbank.qm.qld.gov.au; cnr Grey & Melbourne Sts; Sciencentre adult/child/family $13/10/40; ⏲9.30am-5pm) FREE Queensland's history is given the once-over here, with interesting exhibits including a skeleton of the state's own dinosaur *Muttaburrasaurus* (aka 'Mutt'), and the *Avian Cirrus*, the tiny plane in which Queenslander Bert Hinkler made the first England-to-Australia solo flight in 1928. Have a snack to a whale soundtrack in the outdoor 'Whale Mall'.

Also here is the Sciencentre, an educational fun house with over 100 hands-on, interactive exhibits that delve into life science and technology. Expect long queues during school holidays.

Queensland Art Gallery GALLERY
(QAG; Map p58; www.qagoma.qld.gov.au; Melbourne St; ⏲10am-5pm Mon-Fri, 9am-5pm Sat & Sun) FREE Duck into the QAG to see the fine permanent collection. Australian art dates from the 1840s to the 1970s: check out works by celebrated masters including Sir Sydney Nolan, Arthur Boyd, William Dobell and George Lambert. Free guided tours are available at 1pm.

Queensland Centre for Photography GALLERY
(Map p58; www.qcp.org.au; cnr Russell & Cordelia Sts; ⏲10am-5pm Wed-Sat, 11am-3pm Sun) FREE Beat the street heat with a detour into this cool little gallery to check out some ace Australian contemporary photography. It's an artist-run affair, showing about 10 exhibitions per year.

Queensland Maritime Museum MUSEUM
(Map p58; www.maritimemuseum.com.au; Stanley St; adult/child/family $12/6/28; ⏲9.30am-4.30pm) On the southern edge of the South

Central Brisbane, Kangaroo Point & South Bank

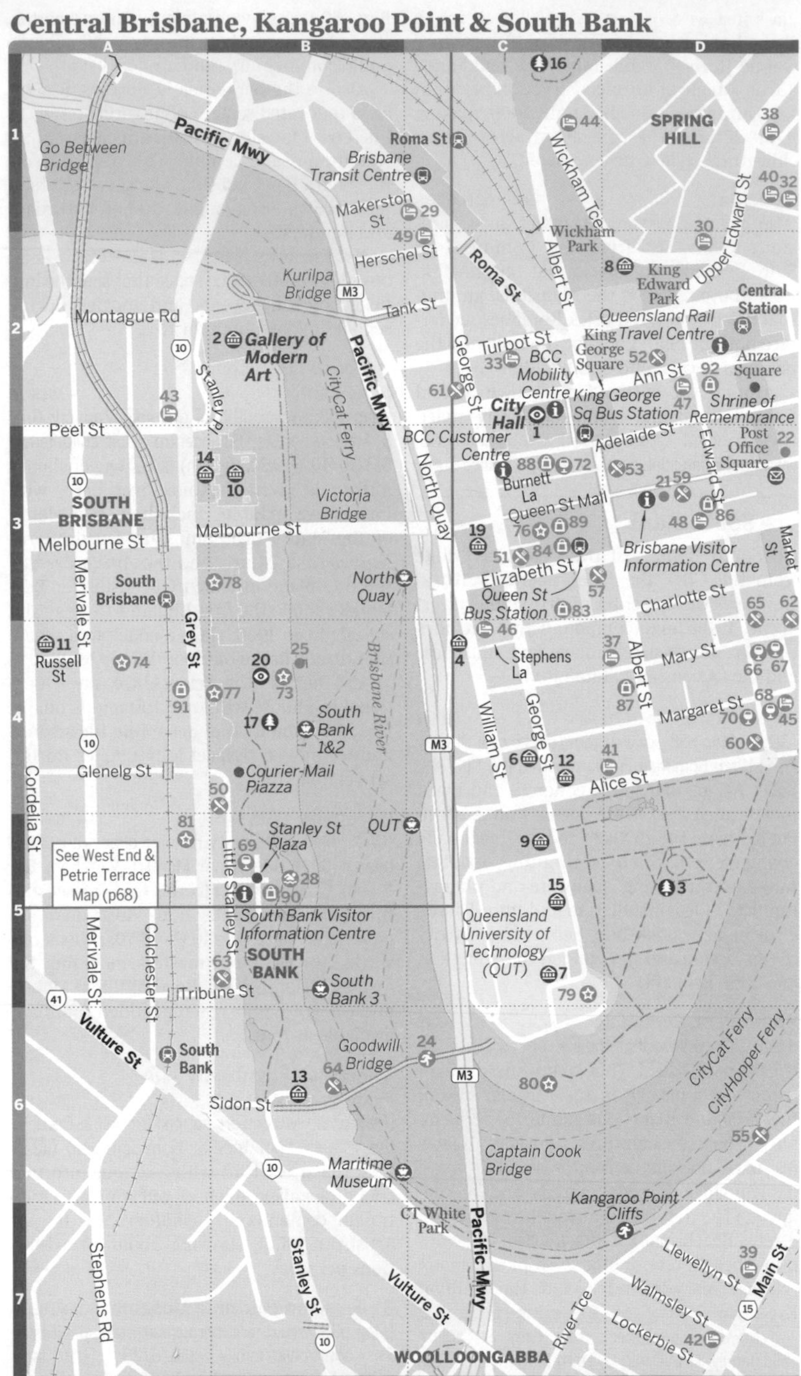

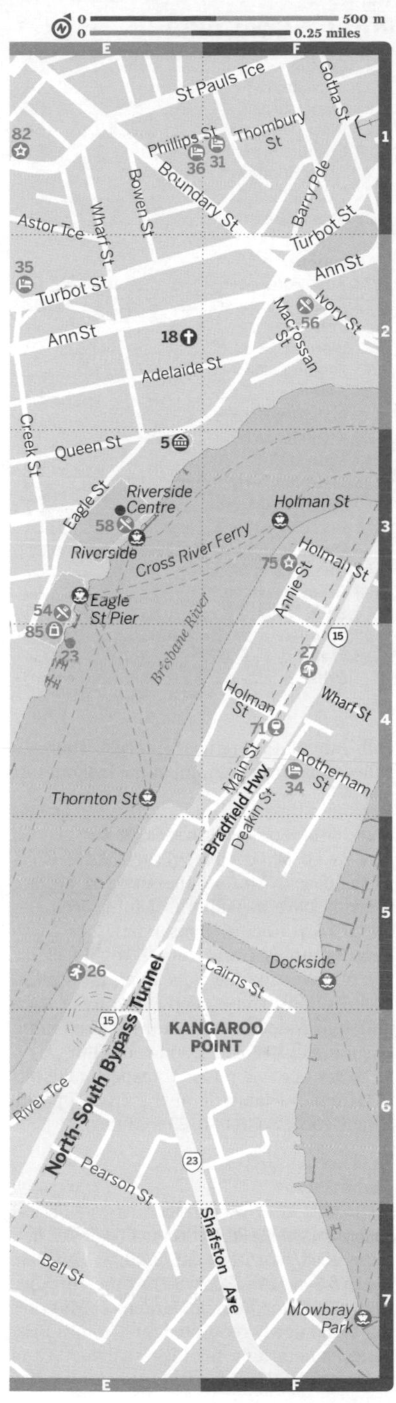

Bank Parklands is this quaint old museum, the highlight of which is the gigantic HMAS *Diamantina,* a restored WWII frigate that you can clamber aboard and explore.

Fortitude Valley & New Farm

★Brisbane Powerhouse ARTS CENTRE

(Map p54; www.brisbanepowerhouse.org; 119 Lamington St, New Farm; ⊙9am-5pm Mon-Fri, 10am-4pm Sat & Sun) FREE On the eastern flank of New Farm Park stands the Powerhouse, a once-derelict power station that's been superbly transformed into a contemporary arts centre. Inside the brick husk are graffiti remnants, pieces of old industrial machinery and randomly placed headphones offering sonic soundgrabs. The Powerhouse hosts a range of visual arts, comedy and music performances (many free), and has two restaurants with killer river views.

Chinatown NEIGHBOURHOOD

(Map p62; Duncan St, Fortitude Valley) Brisbane's Chinatown occupies only one street (check out the Tang dynasty archway and the lions at the Ann St end), but it's just as flamboyant and flavour-filled as its Sydney and Melbourne counterparts. Glazed flat ducks hang behind steamy windows; aromas of Thai, Chinese, Vietnamese, Laotian and Japanese cooking fill the air. There are free outdoor movies during summer, and the whole place goes nuts during Chinese New Year festivities.

New Farm Park PARK

(Map p54; www.newfarmpark.com.au; Brunswick St, New Farm; ⊙24hr;) New Farm Park, off the tail end of Brunswick St by the river, is a large, open parkland with picnic areas and gas barbecues, jacaranda trees, rose gardens and free wif-fi. The playground here – a Crusoe-esque series of platforms amongst some vast Moreton Bay figs trees – is a hit with the kids. Jan Powers Farmers Market (p91) and Moonlight Cinema (p89) are held here too.

Brunswick Street Mall LANDMARK

(Map p62; Brunswick St, Fortitude Valley; ⊙24hr) In Fortitude Valley during the day the action focuses on Brunswick Street Mall, a pedestrianised arcade full of pavement cafes, bars and shops. The mall is a tad seedy, although it is slated for a $4-million makeover in 2014: James St and Brunswick St are probably better places to begin your explorations.

Central Brisbane, Kangaroo Point & South Bank

Top Sights
1 City Hall ... C2
2 Gallery of Modern Art ... B2

Sights
3 City Botanic Gardens ... D5
4 Commissariat Store Museum ... C4
5 Customs House ... E3
6 Mansions ... C4
Museum of Brisbane ... (see 1)
7 Old Government House ... C5
8 Old Windmill ... D2
9 Parliament House ... C5
10 Queensland Art Gallery ... B3
11 Queensland Centre for Photography ... A4
12 Queensland Club ... C4
13 Queensland Maritime Museum ... B6
14 Queensland Museum & Sciencentre ... A3
15 QUT Art Museum ... C5
16 Roma Street Parkland ... C1
17 South Bank Parklands ... B4
18 St John's Cathedral ... E2
19 Treasury Building ... C3
20 Wheel of Brisbane ... B4

Activities, Courses & Tours
21 Brisbane Greeters ... D3
22 CitySights ... D3
23 Kookaburra River Queens ... E4
24 Planet Inline ... C6
25 River City Cruises ... B4
26 Riverlife Adventure Centre ... E5
27 Story Bridge Adventure Climb ... F4
28 Streets Beach ... B5

Sleeping
29 Abbey on Roma ... C1
30 Astor Metropole ... D2
31 Dahrl Court ... F1
32 Diamant Hotel ... D1
33 Explorers Inn ... C2
34 Il Mondo ... F4
35 Inchcolm Hotel ... E2
36 Kookaburra Inn ... E1
37 M on Mary ... D4
38 Metropolitan Motor Inn ... D1
39 Paramount Motel ... D7
40 Punthill Brisbane ... D1
41 Quay West Suites Brisbane ... D4
42 Queensland Motel ... D7
43 Riverside Hotel ... A2
44 Soho Motel ... C1
45 Stamford Plaza Brisbane ... D4
46 Treasury ... C4
Urban Brisbane ... (see 44)

Greater Brisbane

Mt Coot-tha Reserve OUTDOORS
(www.brisbane.qld.gov.au; Mt Coot-tha Rd, Mt Coot-tha; 24hr) FREE A 15-minute drive or bus ride from the city, this huge bush reserve is topped by 287m Mt Coot-tha (more of a hill, really). On the hillsides you'll find the Brisbane Botanic Gardens, the Sir Thomas Brisbane Planetarium, walking trails and the eye-popping **Mt Coot-tha Lookout** (www.brisbanelookout.com; 1012 Sir Samuel Griffith Dr; 24hr) FREE. On a clear day you can see the Moreton Bay islands.

To get here via public transport, take bus 471 from Adelaide St in the city, opposite King George Sq ($4.80, 25 minutes). The bus drops you off at the lookout and stops outside the botanic gardens and planetarium en route.

Just north of the road to the lookout, on Samuel Griffith Dr, is the turn-off to **JC Slaughter Falls**, 700m along a walking track; plus a 1.5km **Aboriginal Art Trail**, which takes you past eight art sites with works by local Aboriginal artists. You can also hike to the lookout from JC Slaughter Falls (about 4km return – steep!). There's a cafe and flashy restaurant at the lookout too.

Brisbane Botanic Gardens GARDENS
(www.brisbane.qld.gov.au/botanicgardens; Mt Coot-tha Rd, Mt Coot-tha; 8am-5.30pm) FREE At the base of Mt Coot-tha, these 52-hectare gardens have a plethora of mini ecologies on display: cactus, bonsai and herb gardens, rainforests, arid zones… You'll feel like you're traversing the globe in all its vegetated splendour! Free guided walks are at 11am and 1pm Monday and Saturday; free minibus tours at 10.45am Monday to Thursday.

To get here via public transport, take bus 471 from Adelaide St in the city, opposite King George Sq ($4.80, 25 minutes).

Sir Thomas Brisbane Planetarium PLANETARIUM
(07-3403 2578; www.brisbane.qld.gov.au/planetarium; Mt Coot-tha Rd, Mt Coot-tha; admission free, shows adult/child/family $15/9/40; 10am-4pm Tue-Fri & Sun, 11am-7.30pm Sat) At the entrance to the Brisbane Botanic Gardens at Mt Coot-tha is the newly renovated Sir Thomas Brisbane Planetarium, the biggest planetarium in Australia. The observatory has a variety

47 X-Base Brisbane Central D2
48 X-Base Brisbane Embassy D3
49 X-Base Brisbane Uptown C2

Eating
50 Ahmet's B4
51 Bean C3
52 Bleeding Heart Gallery D2
53 Brew D3
54 Cha Cha Char E3
55 Cliffs Cafe D6
56 E'cco F2
57 Govindas C3
58 Groove Train E3
59 Hanaichi D3
60 Il D4
61 Java Coast Cafe C2
62 Merlo Coffee D4
63 Piaf B5
64 Stokehouse B6
65 Verve Cafe & Bar D3

Drinking & Nightlife
66 Belgian Beer Cafe D4
67 Laneway D4
68 Moo Moo D4
69 Plough Inn B5
70 Port Office Hotel D4
71 Story Bridge Hotel F4
72 Super Whatnot C3

Entertainment
73 Ben & Jerry's Openair Cinemas B4
74 Brisbane Convention and Exhibition Centre A4
75 Brisbane Jazz Club F3
76 Event Cinemas C3
Metro Arts Centre .... (see 65)
77 Queensland Conservatorium B4
78 Queensland Performing Arts Centre B3
79 QUT Gardens Theatre C5
80 Riverstage C6
81 South Bank Cinema A5
82 Sportsman's Hotel E1
Ticketek .... (see 51)

Shopping
83 Archives Fine Books C3
84 Australian Geographic C3
85 Brisbane Riverside Markets E4
86 Dogstar D3
87 Folio Books D4
88 Record Exchange C3
89 RM Williams C3
90 South Bank Lifestyle Markets B5
91 Title A4
92 World Wide Maps & Globes D2

of telescopes, and there are 10 regular outer-space shows inside the **Cosmic Skydome**, narrated by the likes of Harrison Ford and Ewan McGregor (bookings advised).

To get here via public transport, take bus 471 from Adelaide St in the city, opposite King George Sq ($4.80, 25 minutes).

Lone Pine Koala Sanctuary WILDLIFE RESERVE
(☎07-3378 1366; www.koala.net; 708 Jesmond Rd, Fig Tree Pocket; adult/child/family $33/22/80; ⏰9am-5pm) About 12km south of the city centre, Lone Pine Koala Sanctuary occupies a patch of parkland beside the river. It's home to 130 or so koalas, plus kangaroos, possums, wombats, birds and other Aussie critters. The koalas are undeniably cute – most visitors readily cough up the $16 to have their picture snapped hugging one. There are animal presentations scheduled throughout the day.

To get here catch bus 430 ($6.70, 45 minutes) from the Queen St bus station. Alternatively, **Mirimar II** (☎0412 749 426; www.mirimar.com; incl park entry per adult/child/family $65/38/190) cruises to the sanctuary along the Brisbane River, departing from the Cultural Centre Pontoon on South Bank next to Victoria Bridge. It departs daily at 10am, returning from Lone Pine at 1.45pm.

Boggo Road Gaol HISTORIC BUILDING
(Map p54; ☎0411 111 903; www.boggoroadgaol.com; Annerley Rd, Dutton Park; historical tours adult/child/family $25/12.50/50, ghost tours adult/child over 12 $40/25; ⏰historical tours 11am & 1pm Tue-Fri, 11am, 1pm & 3pm Sat, hourly 10am-1pm & 3pm Sun, night tours 7pm Thu, ghost tours 7.30pm Wed & Sun) Tours of old Victorian prisons have a grim appeal: it's part morbidly fascinating 'dark tourism'; part architectural heritage appreciation; part 'Look how far we've come' social commentary; and part just plain spooky. This version takes you through the notorious Boggo Road Gaol a couple of kilometres south of the city centre, which was a working prison from 1883 to 2002.

Newstead House HISTORIC BUILDING
(Map p54; www.newsteadhouse.com.au; cnr Breakfast Creek Rd & Newstead Ave, Newstead; adult/child/family $6/4/15; ⏰10am-4pm Mon-Thu, 2-5pm Sun) On a breezy hill overlooking the river, Brisbane's oldest house dates

Fortitude Valley & New Farm

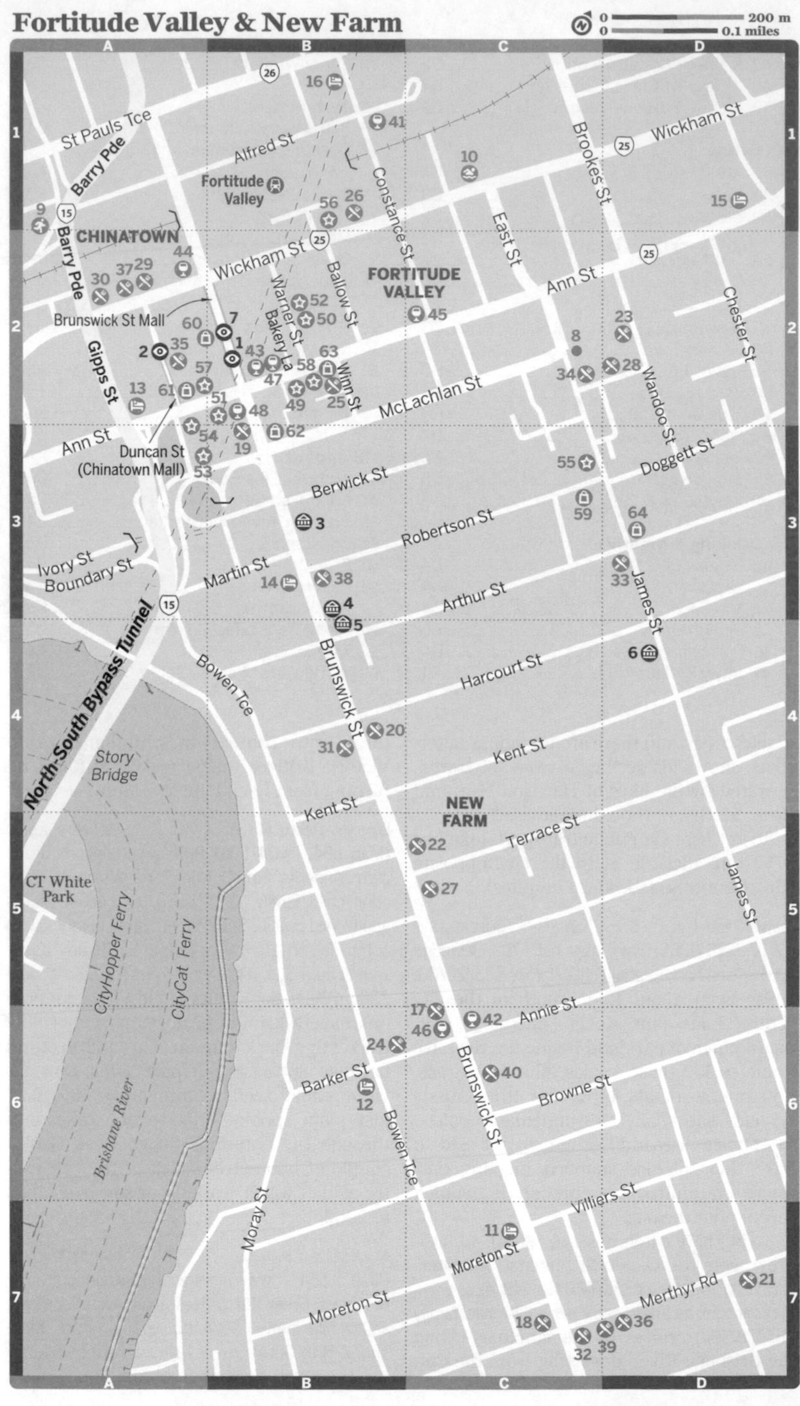

Fortitude Valley & New Farm

Sights
1 Brunswick Street Mall ... B2
2 Chinatown ... A2
3 Institute of Modern Art ... B3
4 Jan Murphy Gallery ... B3
5 Philip Bacon Galleries ... B4
6 Suzanne O'Connell Gallery ... D4
7 Valley Walk of Fame ... B2

Activities, Courses & Tours
C!RCA ... (see 3)
8 James St Cooking School ... C2
9 Rocksports ... A1
10 Valley Pool ... C1

Sleeping
11 Allender Apartments ... C7
12 Bowen Terrace ... B6
13 Bunk Backpackers ... A2
14 Central Brunswick Apartments ... B3
15 Emporium ... D1
16 Limes ... B1

Eating
17 Anise ... C6
18 Arriva ... C7
19 Brunswick Social ... B3
20 Burger Urge ... B4
Buzz ... (see 15)
21 Cafe Bouquiniste ... D7
22 Café Cirque ... C5
23 Campos ... D2
24 Chouquette ... B6
25 Flamingo ... B2
26 Garuva ... B1
27 Himalayan Cafe ... C5
28 James St Market ... D2
29 Kuan Yin Tea House ... A2
30 Lust For Life ... A2
31 Pintxo ... B4
32 Siam Square Thai ... C7
33 Sitar ... D3
34 Spoon Deli Cafe ... C2
35 Thai Wi-Rat ... A2
36 The Smoke BBQ ... D7
37 The Vietnamese ... A2
38 Tibetan Kitchen ... B3
39 Vue ... D7
Wagamama ... (see 15)
40 Wok on Inn ... C6

Drinking & Nightlife
41 Alfred & Constance ... B1
42 Alibi Room ... C6
43 Bowery ... B2
Cru Bar & Cellar ... (see 34)
44 Elephant Arms ... A2
45 Fringe Bar ... C2
46 Gertie's ... C6
47 La Ruche ... B2
48 Press Club ... B2

Entertainment
49 Beat MegaClub ... B2
Birdees ... (see 13)
50 Church ... B2
51 Cloudland ... B2
52 Electric Playground ... B2
53 Family ... A3
Judith Wright Centre of Contemporary Arts ... (see 3)
54 Oh Hello ... A3
55 Palace Centro ... C3
56 Wickham Hotel ... B1
57 X&Y Bar ... A2
58 Zoo ... B2

Shopping
59 Blonde Venus ... C3
60 Brisbane Valley Markets ... A2
61 Butter Beats ... A2
Emporium ... (see 15)
62 in.cube8r gallery ... B3
63 Maiocchi ... B2
64 Title ... D3
Trash Monkey ... (see 61)

from 1846 and is beautifully fitted out with Victorian furnishings, antiques, clothing and period displays. It's a modest, peach-coloured L-shaped affair, surrounded by manicured lawns with lovely river views. Wedding photographers do their best to avoid the big brick electrical substation in the gardens. Free Sunday afternoon concerts.

Alma Park Zoo ZOO
(☎07-3204 6566; www.almaparkzoo.com.au; 18 Alma Rd, Dakabin; adult/child/family $37/27/105; ⏰9am-4pm) Bond with a multicultural mix of furred and feathered brethren at Queensland's oldest zoo, 28km north of the city. Inhabiting 16 hectares of subtropical gardens is a large brood of native birds and mammals, including koalas, kangaroos, emus and dingoes (plus some international interlopers). You can touch many of the animals; feeding times are all between 10.30am and 3pm.

To get here via public transport take the Caboolture line from Roma St Station ($7.50, 45 minutes). The zoo is a 1.8km walk from the station.

Daisy Hill Koala Centre WILDLIFE RESERVE
(☎07-3299 1032; www.ehp.qld.gov.au/wildlife/daisyhill-centre; Daisy Hill Rd, Daisy Hill Conserva-

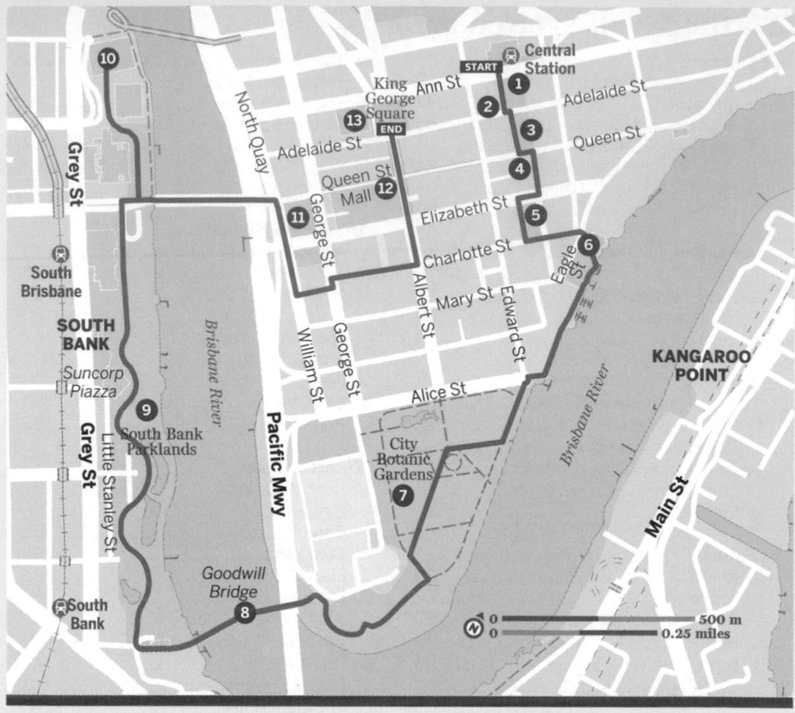

City Walk
CBD & South Bank Circuit

START CENTRAL STATION
FINISH KING GEORGE SQ
LENGTH 5KM; TWO HOURS

Cross Ann St south of Central Station to the sobering **1 Shrine of Remembrance** above the northern edge of **2 Anzac Sq**, with its bulbous boab trees and wandering ibises. At the southern side of the square, scale one of the pedestrian bridges over Adelaide St, which lead to the elevated, manicured **3 Post Office Sq**. The square is fronted at its southern end by Brisbane's stately stone **4 GPO**. Take the alley between the wings of the post office through to Elizabeth St. Cross the road and stick your head into beautiful white-stone **5 St Stephen's Cathedral**.

Walk through the grassy courtyard behind the cathedral until reaching Charlotte St. Take a left, cross Eagle St and duck through **6 Eagle St Pier** on the river. Check the Story Bridge views to your left, then go down the steps to the riverside boardwalk and truck south.

At Edward and Alice Sts, detour through the **7 City Botanic Gardens** (p53). Cast an eye across the river to the Kangaroo Point cliffs, then skirt around the back of the Brisbane Riverstage to the pedestrian-only **8 Goodwill Bridge**: check out HMAS *Diamantina* in the Queensland Maritime Museum to your left. From here, jag north into the **9 South Bank Parklands** (p57).

If time is your friend, duck into the outstanding **10 Gallery of Modern Art** (p57). Otherwise, cross Victoria Bridge back into central Brisbane. Just south of the gorgeous **11 Treasury Building** (p56) on William St, an unnamed alley cuts through to George St. Dogleg across George into Charlotte St, continue along Charlotte then turn left into Albert St in Brisbane's modern CBD.

Continue along Albert St, cross **12 Queen St Mall** and then Adelaide St into King George Sq, with towering **13 City Hall** (p52) anchoring the southwest side. After taking in the scene, back-track to the mall for a much-deserved pick-me-up.

tion Park, Daisy Hill; ⌚10am-4pm) FREE About 25km southeast of the city, Daisy Hill offers informative displays and a number of fat and happy-looking koalas – but it's no zoo. The surrounding area is an important koala habitat and part of a 435-hectare conservation park. The centre is designed to acquaint visitors with koalas on a much more comprehensive level than just a cuddle and photo encounter (no koala touching involved). There are also some beaut picnic and bushwalking spots here, plus plenty of opportunities to see bird life and other fuzzy natives on the loose.

Activities

Walking

Feel like stretching your legs? Pick up the self-guided *Brisbane City Walk* brochure from info centres, which weaves you through Roma Street Parkland, South Bank Parklands and the City Botanic Gardens.

Sadly the city's excellent **Riverwalk** pathway was destroyed in the 2011 floods, but a stroll along the riverbanks remains rewarding. The new, more flood-resistant Riverwalk – including a section linking New Farm with the CBD – is being built at a cost of $72 million, and at the time of writing is expected to open in 2014.

Cycling

Brisbane is hilly but it's still one of Australia's most bike-friendly cities, with over 900km of bike paths, including tracks along the Brisbane River. A good starter takes you from the City Botanic Gardens, across the Goodwill Bridge and out to the University of Queensland. It's about 7km one way and you can stop for a beer at the Regatta pub in Toowong en route.

Bicycles are allowed on Brisbane's trains, except on weekdays during peak hours. You can also take bikes on CityCats and ferries for free.

CityCycle BICYCLE RENTAL
(☎1300 229 253; www.citycycle.com.au; hire per hour/day $2.20/165, first 30min free; ⌚hire 5am-10pm, return 24hr) Brisbane's public bike-share program has had a rocky start, but it's starting to win over the locals. Basically you subscribe via the website (per day/week/three months $2/11/27.50), then hire a bike (additional fee) from any of the 100-plus stations around central Brisbane. Good for short hops; pricey by the day. BYO helmet and lock (see the website for a list of bike shops where you can buy them).

Bicycle Revolution BICYCLE RENTAL
(Map p68; www.bicyclerevolution.org.au; 294 Montague Rd, West End; per day/week $35/100; ⌚9am-5pm Mon, 9am-6pm Tue-Fri, 8am-2pm Sat) This friendly community shop has a handsome range of recycled bikes assembled by staff with reconditioned parts. Very 'hipster'.

Gardens Cycle Hire BICYCLE RENTAL
(☎0408 003 198; www.brisbanebicyclehire.com; hire per day/week $40/90) Bikes delivered to your door.

Swimming

Streets Beach SWIMMING
(Map p58; www.visitsouthbank.com.au; ⌚daylight hours) FREE A central spot for a quick (and free) dip is the artificial, riverside Streets Beach at South Bank. Lifeguards, hollering kids, beach babes, strutting gym-junkies, ice-cream carts – it's all here.

Centenary Pool SWIMMING
(Map p54; ☎1300 332 583; www.brisbane.qld.gov.au; 400 Gregory Tce, Spring Hill; adult/child/family $5/3.60/15.20; ⌚5.30am-8pm Mon-Thu, 5.30am-7pm Fri, 7am-4pm Sat, 7am-2pm Sun) This is the best pool in town and has been recently refurbished, with an Olympic sized lap pool, a kids pool and diving pool with a high tower.

Spring Hill Baths SWIMMING
(Map p54; www.bluefitbrisbane.com.au; 14 Torrington St, Spring Hill; adult/child/family $5/3.60/15.20; ⌚6.30am-7pm Mon-Thu, 6.30am-6pm Fri, 8am-5pm Sat & Sun) Opened in 1886, this quaint heated 25m pool is encircled by cute timber change rooms. It's one of the oldest public baths in the southern hemisphere.

Valley Pool SWIMMING
(Map p62; www.valleypool.com.au; 432 Wickham St, Fortitude Valley; adult/child/family $5/3.60/15.20; ⌚5.30am-7.30pm Mon-Fri, 7.30am-6pm Sat & Sun) Big clean outdoor pool, popular with glam, gym-going types (of both genders).

Climbing & Abseiling

You can make like Spiderman at the **Kangaroo Point Cliffs**, on the southern banks of the Brisbane River at Kangaroo Point. These pink volcanic cliffs are around 200 million years old and, regardless of your level of expertise, joining the other scrambling figures is exhilarating! The cliffs are floodlit until midnight or later.

OFF THE BEATEN TRACK

D'AGUILAR NATIONAL PARK

Suburban malaise? Slake your wilderness cravings at this 50,000-hectare **national park** (www.nprsr.qld.gov.au/parks/daguilar; 60 Mount Nebo Rd, The Gap), just 10km north-west of the city centre but worlds away. At the entrance the **Walkabout Creek Visitor Information Centre** (07-3512 2300; www.walkaboutcreek.com.au; wildlife centre adult/child/family $6.40/4.35/16; 9am-4.30pm) has maps. Also here is the **South East Queensland Wildlife Centre** where you can see a resident platypus, plus turtles, lizards, pythons and gliders. There's also a small walk-through aviary, and a cafe.

Walking trails in the park range from a few hundred metres to 13km, including the 6km Morelia Track at Manorina day-use area and the 4.3km Greene's Falls Track at Mt Glorious. Mountain biking and horse riding are also options. You can camp in the park too, in remote, walk-in bush **camp sites** (13 74 68; www.qld.gov.au/camping; per person $5.45). There are a couple of walks (1.5km and 5km) kicking off from the visitor centre, but other walks are a fair distance away (so you'll need your own wheels).

To get here catch bus 385 ($6.70, 30 minutes) from Roma St Station; the last bus back to the city is at 4.48pm (3.53pm on weekends).

Riverlife Adventure Centre ROCK CLIMBING
(Map p58; 07-3891 5766; www.riverlife.com.au; Naval Stores, Kangaroo Point Bikeway, Kangaroo Point; 9am-5pm) Near the 20m Kangaroo Point Cliffs, Riverlife runs rock-climbing sessions (from $49) and abseiling exploits ($39). It also offers kayaking river trips (from $39) and hires out bikes (per four hours $30), kayaks (per two hours $33) and in-line skates (per four hours $40).

Story Bridge Adventure Climb ADVENTURE TOUR
(Map p58; 1300 254 627; www.sbac.net.au; 170 Main St, Kangaroo Point; adult/child from $99/85) A Brisbane must-do, the bridge climb offers unbeatable views of the city – at dawn, day, twilight or night. The 2½-hour climb scales the southern half of the bridge, taking you 80m above the twisting, muddy Brisbane River below. Minimum age 10. Bridge abseiling expeditions are also available.

Urban Climb ROCK CLIMBING, ABSEILING
(Map p68; 07-3844 2544; www.urbanclimb.com; 2/220 Montague Rd, West End; adult/child $18/16; noon-10pm Mon-Thu, noon-9pm Fri, 10am-6pm Sat & Sun) A large indoor climbing wall with 200-plus routes.

Rocksports ROCK CLIMBING
(Map p62; 07-3216 0462; www.rocksports.com.au; 224 Barry Pde, Fortitude Valley; climbing from $17; 10am-9.30pm Mon-Fri, 10am-5pm Sat & Sun) Thirty ropes and 100 different indoor climbs on the industrial side of Fortitude Valley.

Adventures Around Brisbane ROCK CLIMBING, ABSEILING
(1800 765 494; www.adventuresaroundbrisbane.com.au; climbing & abseiling 2/3hr from $79/89) Climb the Kangaroo Point Cliffs or abseil down them: either way it's a lot of fun! Also runs trips into the Glass House Mountains.

In-Line Skating

You can hire skates and equipment from Riverlife Adventure Centre (p66).

Planet Inline SKATING
(Map p58; 07-3217 3571; www.planetinline.com; Goodwill Bridge; tours $15) Skaters reclaim the streets on Wednesday night with Planet Inline skate tours starting at 7.15pm from the top of the Goodwill Bridge ($15). It also runs a Saturday-morning breakfast-club tour ($15), and Sunday-afternoon tours that differ each week and last about three hours ($15).

Skydiving & Ballooning

Jump the Beach Brisbane SKYDIVING
(1800 800 840; www.jumpthebeachbrisbane.com.au; skydives from $344) This company picks up from the CBD and offers tandem skydives over Brisbane, landing on the sand in Redcliffe.

Fly Me to the Moon BALLOONING
(07-3423 0400; www.brisbanehotairballooning.com.au; per person $299) One-hour hot-air balloon trips over Brisbane. Pick-up and breakfast included.

Golf

Victoria Park Golf Course GOLF

(Map p54; ☎07-3252 9891; www.victoriaparkgolf-complex.com; Herston Rd, Herston; 18 holes Mon-Fri $28, Sat & Sun $34, club hire $50; ⏰6am-10pm Sun-Thu, 6am-11pm Fri & Sat) Brisbane's most central public course, immediately north of Spring Hill. The floodlit driving range is open late.

Indooroopilly Golf Club GOLF

(☎07-3721 2173; www.indooroopillygolf.com.au; Meiers Rd, Indooroopilly; 18 holes Mon-Fri $65, club hire $30; ⏰6am-5pm Mon-Fri) About 8km south of the city centre. Weekends are members-only.

Courses

Mondo Organics Cooking School COOKING COURSE

(Map p54; ☎07-3844 1132; www.mondo-organics.com.au; 166 Hardgrave Rd, West End; 3hr class $110-140) Award-winning chefs teach a wide range of skills at these hands-on classes. You can master the nuances of cooking Japanese, Italian, Persian, modern Spanish, classic French, vegetarian and other styles. Wine appreciation classes also make the grade.

James St Cooking School COOKING COURSE

(Map p62; ☎07-3252-8850; www.jamesstcookingschool.com.au; 22 James St; 3hr class $135-155) Upstairs at the James St Market is this fab cooking school, offering both hands-on and demonstration classes. Three-hour courses cover the likes of modern Australian, French, Thai, seafood and 'beer and BBQing'. Lots of fresh produce from the market downstairs.

Tours

There are all sorts of organised tours of Brisbane and the surrounding areas on offer – the visitor information centres in the city or South Bank can help with bookings. And if all else fails, jump on a ferry!

CityCat BOAT TOUR

(☎13 12 30; www.translink.com.au; one-way $5.60; ⏰5.25am-11.50pm) Ditching the car or bus and catching a sleek CityCat ferry along the river is the Brisbane sightseeing journey of choice. Stand on an open-air deck and glide under the Story Bridge to South Bank and the city centre. Ferries run every 15 to 30 minutes between the University of Queensland in the southwest to Apollo Road terminal north of the city, stopping at 14 terminals in between, including New Farm Park, North Quay (for the CBD), South Bank and West End.

CitySights GUIDED TOUR

(Map p58; www.citysights.com.au; day tickets per adult/child/family $35/20/80; ⏰9am-3.45pm) This hop-on-hop-off shuttle bus wheels past 19 of Brisbane's major landmarks, including the CBD, Mt Coot-tha, Chinatown, South Bank and Story Bridge. Tours depart every 45 minutes from Post Office Sq on Queen St. The same ticket covers you for unlimited use of CityCat ferry services.

XXXX Brewery Tour TOUR

(Map p68; ☎07-3361 7597; www.xxxxbrewerytour.com.au; cnr Black & Paten Sts, Milton; adult/child $25/16; ⏰hourly 11am-4pm Mon-Fri, 12.30pm, 1pm & 1.30pm Sat, 11am, noon & 12.30pm Sun) Feel a XXXX coming on? Grown-up entry to this brewery tour includes a few humidity beating ales, so leave the car at home. Also on offer are beer-and-barbecue tours on Wednesday nights and Saturday during the day (adult/child $38/29), which include lunch. Book all tours in advance, online or by phone. There's also an alehouse here if you feel like kicking on. The brewery is a 20-minute walk west from Roma St Station, or take the train to Milton Station. Wear enclosed shoes.

Brisbane Greeters GUIDED TOUR

(Map p58; ☎07-3006 6290; www.brisbanegreeters.com.au; Brisbane Visitor Information Centre, Queen St Mall; ⏰10am) FREE Free, small-group, hand-held introductory tours of Brizzy with affable volunteers. Tours are themed: public art on Monday, Queenslander architecture in Tuesday, churches on Wednesday, the river on Sunday etc. Call to see what's running, or to organise a customised tour. Bookings essential.

Brisbane Lights Tours GUIDED TOUR

(☎07-3822 6028; www.brisbanelightstours.com; adult/child from $65/30) Three-hour nocturnal tours departing at 6.30pm nightly (hotel pick-ups included), covering a dozen city landmarks, with dinner (or a snack) at Mt Coot-tha Lookout and a 20-minute CityCat cruise.

Araucaria Ecotours ECOTOUR

(☎07-5544 1283; www.learnaboutwildlife.com; tours from $99) A range of day tours ex-Brisbane with a very green bent: birdwatching, rainforests, bushwalking and glow-worms all get some attention. Within

West End & Petrie Terrace

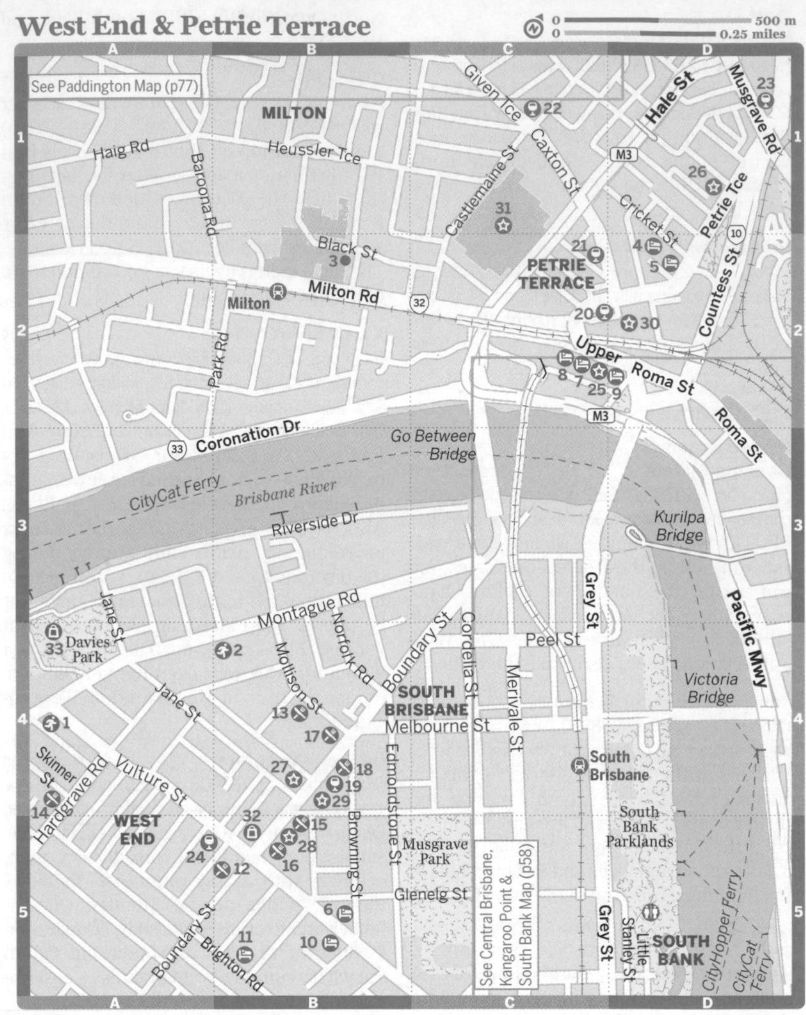

the city there's the 'Bushwaking in Brisbane' day tour, traipsing through the surrounding bushland. Three-day tours also available.

River City Cruises CRUISE
(Map p58; ☎0428 278 473; www.rivercitycruises.com.au; South Bank Parklands Jetty A; adult/child/family $25/15/60) River City runs 1½-hour cruises with commentary from South Bank to New Farm and back. They depart from South Bank at 10.30am and 12.30pm (plus 2.30pm during summer).

Ghost Tours TOUR
(☎0401 666 441; www.ghost-tours.com.au; walking/coach tours from $30/50) 'Get creeped' on these 90-minute guided walking tours or 2½-hour bus tours of Brisbane's haunted heritage: murder scenes, cemeteries, eerie arcades and the infamous Boggo Road Gaol (p61). Offers several tours a week; bookings essential.

Steam Train Sunday TOUR
(☎07-3432 5100; www.theworkshops.qm.qld.gov.au; adult/child/family $21/12/62) One Sunday a month, beautifully restored steam trains chug out of Roma St Station for a one-hour

West End & Petrie Terrace

Activities, Courses & Tours
1 Bicycle Revolution ... A4
2 Urban Climb ... B4
3 XXXX Brewery Tour ... B2

Sleeping
4 Aussie Way Backpackers ... D2
5 Banana Benders Backpackers ... D2
6 Brisbane Backpackers Resort ... B5
7 Brisbane City Backpackers ... C2
8 Brisbane City YHA ... C2
9 Chill Backpackers ... D2
10 Gonow Family Backpacker ... B5
11 Somewhere to Stay ... B5

Eating
12 Blackstar Coffee Roasters ... B5
13 Burrow ... B4
14 Cafe Checocho ... A4
15 Forest ... B5
16 George's Seafood ... B5
17 Gunshop Café ... B4
18 Little Greek Taverna ... B4

Drinking & Nightlife
19 Archive Beer Boutique ... B4
20 Cabiria ... C2
21 Caxton Hotel ... C2
22 Dowse Bar ... C1
Iceworks ... (see 22)
Lychee Lounge ... (see 19)
23 Normanby Hotel ... D1
24 The End ... A5

Entertainment
25 Beetle Bar ... C2
26 Brisbane Arts Theatre ... D1
27 Hi-Fi ... B4
28 Lock 'n' Load ... B5
29 Loft West End ... B4
30 Palace Barracks ... D2
31 Suncorp Stadium ... C1

Shopping
32 Avid Reader ... B5
Barracks ... (see 20)
33 Davies Park Market ... A4
Egg Records ... (see 24)

tour around town. Go online for the latest schedule.

Kookaburra River Queens CRUISE
(Map p58; ☎07-3221 1300; www.kookaburrariverqueens.com; Eagle St Pier; lunch/dinner cruises per person from $42/79) Chug up and down the river on a wooden paddle steamer. Meals are three-course seafood and carvery buffet affairs; there's live jazz on the Sunday lunch cruise.

Carlton Brewhouse TOUR
(☎07-3826 5858; www.carltonbrewhouse.com.au; Cuthbert Dr, Yatala; 1hr tours $25, 4hr with bus transfers $60; ⊙10am & noon Wed-Sat) This big Melbourne brewer has made a move into Queensland, pumping out three million bottles of the good stuff a day. Seeing this much liquid gold in one spot is awe-inspiring (do your best Homer Simpson drool) – and you get to taste some at the end of the tour. It's a half-hour drive south of Brisbane. Four-hour bus tours from the Gold Coast are also an option.

Festivals & Events

Check out www.visitbrisbane.com.au for full listings of what's happening around town.

Brisbane International TENNIS
(www.brisbaneinternational.com.au) This pro tennis tournament attracts the world's best players. It's held in January at the Queensland Tennis Centre just prior to the Australian Open (in Melbourne).

Australia Day Cockroach Races QUIRKY
(www.cockroachraces.com.au) An Australia Day (January 26) tradition at the Story Bridge Hotel in Kangaroo Point. BYO roach, or you can choose from the house stable. Proceeds go to charity.

Chinese New Year CULTURAL EVENT
(www.chinesenewyear.com.au) Held in Fortitude Valley's Chinatown Mall (Duncan St) in January/February. Firecrackers, dancing dragons and fantastic food.

Brisbane Comedy Festival COMEDY
(www.briscomfest.com) Four-week festival in March featuring local and international laugh-mongers at the Brisbane Powerhouse.

Urban Country Festival MUSIC
(www.urbancountry.com.au) Four-day country-music fest in May with up to 500 guitar twangers and nasally bards. Held 45 minutes north of Brisbane in Caboolture (where Keith Urban grew up…nothing to do with the festival name though).

Paniyiri Festival GREEK CULTURE
(www.paniyiri.com) Greek cultural festival with dancing, food and music. Held in late May at Musgrave Park in the West End.

Brisbane Winter Carnival HORSE RACING
(www.queenslandracing.com.au) The state's major horse-racing carnival, held in May and June. The biggest day is the Stradbroke Handicap in early June.

Out of the Box ARTS
(www.outoftheboxfestival.com.au) Six-day biennial festival of performing and visual arts for kids, with lots of interactive and free events. Held in June in even-numbered years.

Brisbane Pride Festival GAY & LESBIAN
(www.brisbanepridefestival.com.au) Brisbane's annual gay and lesbian celebration is held over four weeks in September (some events in June, including the fab Queen's Ball).

Queensland Music Festival MUSIC
(QMF; www.queenslandmusicfestival.org.au) Statewide festival with styles ranging from classical to contemporary, held over two weeks in July in odd-numbered years. Most events are free.

'Ekka' Royal Queensland Show AGRICULTURAL
(www.ekka.com.au) Country and city collide in August for Queensland's largest annual event, the Ekka (formerly the Brisbane Exhibition, which was shortened to 'Ekka'). Baby animals, showbags, spooky carnies, shearing demonstrations, rides and over-sugared kids ahoy!

Brisbane Writers Festival ARTS
(BWF; www.brisbanewritersfestival.com.au) Queensland's premier literary event has been running for 50 years: words, books, and people who put words in books. Held in September.

Brisbane Festival ARTS
(www.brisbanefestival.com.au) Brisbane's major festival of the arts, held over three weeks in September.

Valley Fiesta MUSIC
(www.valleyfiesta.com.au) Rock bands and DJs take over Fortitude Valley's Brunswick St and Chinatown malls for three days in October: Brisbane's biggest free music fest.

Great Brisbane Duck Race QUIRKY
(www.duckrace.org.au) Raising money for cancer studies, this kooky October event involves 40,000 individually sponsored rubber ducks floating down the Brisbane River. The first bird to cross the finish line wins its owner a new car. There's lots of family fun peripheral to the main event.

Brisbane International Film Festival FILM
(www.biff.com.au) Twelve days of quality films flicker across Brisbane screens in November.

Sleeping

Brisbane has an excellent selection of accommodation options that will suit any budget. Many are beyond the business beds of the city centre, but they're usually within walking distance or have good public-transport connections.

Head for Spring Hill for peace and quiet; Fortitude Valley for party nights; Paddington for cafes and boutiques; Petrie Terrace for hostels; gay-friendly New Farm for restaurants; and West End for bars and bookshops.

There's a strange dearth of quality motels in Brisbane, but at a pinch, Kangaroo Point has a string of cheapies lining the busy highway feeding into the Story Bridge.

City Centre

X-Base Brisbane Uptown HOSTEL $
(Map p58; ☎07-3238 5888; www.stayatbase.com; 466 George St; dm $22-36, d & tw $130-140; ❄@🛜) This purpose-built hostel near

BRISBANE FESTIVAL

In September, Brisbane's streets become a hurly-burly of colour, flair, flavour and fireworks during the city's biggest annual arts event – the Brisbane Festival. Running over three weeks, the festival involves over 300 performances and 60-odd events, enticing 2000-plus artists from across the planet. Art exhibitions, dance, theatre, opera, symphonies, circus performers, buskers and vaudeville acts generate an eclectic scene, with many free street events and concerts around town.

The festival is opened each year with a bang – literally. Staged over the Brisbane River, with vantage points at South Bank, the city and West End, **Riverfire** is a massive fireworks show with dazzling visual choreography and a synchronised soundtrack.

For more info see www.brisbanefestival.com.au.

TOP FIVE WILDERNESS DAY TRIPS

If Brisbane is getting too hectic and you want to reacquaint yourself with nature, consider these easy day trips out of the city:

North Stradbroke Island (p98) An idyllic and little-developed island with super surfing, coastal walks, whale watching, diving and bushwalking.

Gold Coast Hinterland (p131) This rangy sea of forest with waterfalls, lookouts and walks makes a great antidote to urban grit. Springbrook National Park (p133) is our pick.

Glass House Mountains (p143) Volcanic cones sprout from humid green surrounds, with hikes to their craggy summits. Australia Zoo (p144) is here too.

D'Aguilar National Park (p66) A well-managed park barely outside the Brisbane city limits, with walking tracks and wildlife.

Girraween National Park (p108) Wander amid towering boulders, bewitching forests and colourful spring wildflowers.

Roma St Station flaunts its youth with mod interiors, decent facilities and overall cleanliness. Each room has air-con, a bathroom and individual lockers, and it's wheelchair-accessible. The bar downstairs is one big party place with live bands, DJs and open-mic nights.

X-Base Brisbane Central HOSTEL $
(Map p58; ☎07-3211 2433; www.stayatbase.com; 398 Edward St; dm $27-33, s/d/tw $55/70/70; ❄@📶) This colossal backpackers has basic rooms in a lace-fringed heritage building (once a Salvation Army budget hotel). There's a rooftop terrace with city views, a rickety old elevator and a bar downstairs. Not all rooms have air-con, but the location couldn't be more central

X-Base Brisbane Embassy HOSTEL $
(Map p58; ☎07-3014 1715; www.stayatbase.com; 214 Elizabeth St; dm $31-35, d with/without bathroom $99/79; ❄@📶) Another city branch of the X-Base chain, this spruced-up place is quieter than other hostels, but feels a bit soulless. There's a large screening room for films, and a sun deck with BBQ and city views.

Diamant Hotel BOUTIQUE HOTEL $$
(Map p58; ☎07-3009 3400; www.8hotels.com; 52 Astor Tce; d from $149; P❄📶) Behind an ultramod black-and-white facade, seven-storey Diamant has compact, contemporary rooms with natty wallpaper and thoughtful touches (original artwork, iPod docks, free wi-fi). The bigger suites have kitchenettes and lounge areas, and there's a bar-restaurant on the ground floor. Parking $28.

Urban Brisbane HOTEL $$
(Map p58; ☎07-3831 6177; www.hotelurban.com.au; 345 Wickham Tce; d from $150; ❄@📶🏊) Still looking sexy after a recent $10-million makeover, the Urban has stylish rooms with masculine hues, balconies and high-end fittings (super-comfy beds, big TVs, fuzzy bathrobes). There's also a heated outdoor pool, a bar, and lots of uniformed flight attendants checking in and out. Parking $15.

M on Mary APARTMENT $$
(Map p58; ☎07-3503 8000; www.monmary.com; 70 Mary St; 1-/3-bedroom apt from $180/499; P❄📶) A stone's throw from the botanic gardens, this 43-storey tower has modern, comfortably furnished one- and three-bedroom apartments (pricey, but with more affordable long-term rates). The best apartments have balconies; the not-so-good ones are a bit gloomy. Parking $30.

Inchcolm Hotel HISTORIC HOTEL $$
(Map p58; ☎07-3226 8888; www.theinchcolm.com.au; 73 Wickham Tce; r $160-250; P❄📶🏊) Built in the 1930s as doctors' suites, the heritage-listed Inchcolm (pronounced as per 'Malcolm') retains elements of its past (love the old elevator!), but the rooms have been overhauled. Those in the newer wing have more space and light; in the older wing there's more character. There's also a rooftop pool and in-house restaurant. Parking $30.

Soho Motel MOTEL $$
(Map p58; ☎07-3831 7722; www.sohobrisbane.com.au; 333 Wickham Tce; r $115-160; P❄@📶) This bricky 50-room joint a short hop from Roma St Station is better inside than it looks from the street, with smart, compact rooms

with little balconies. The owners are friendly and savvy, and pay attention to the little things: free wi-fi, 11am check-out, free parking, custom-made furniture and plush linen. Good value for money.

Abbey on Roma APARTMENT **$$**
(Map p58; ☎07-3236 0600; www.abbeyonroma.com.au; 160 Roma St; 1-bedroom apt from $180; P ❄ ≋) Across the street from Roma St Station, the better apartments here have been refurbished, with a clean, contemporary feel, spacious bedrooms, washing machines, driers and comfy lounge suites. The older standard rooms were in the process of being tarted-up at the time of research: ask what you're getting when you book.

Explorers Inn HOTEL **$$**
(Map p58; ☎07-3211 3488; www.explorers.com.au; 63 Turbot St; d from $100; ❄ @ ☜) This old-time red-brick number is central, clean, friendly and surprisingly quiet inside, but the rooms are tiny (the shower nooks are barely big enough to get wet in). But who wants to be swanning around a spacey hotel suite when the Brisbane sun is shining? If you're just here to sleep, you'll be fine.

Astor Metropole HOTEL **$$**
(Map p58; ☎07-3144 4000; www.astorhotel.com.au; 193 Wickham Tce; r $99-170; P ❄ ☜) Part of the Best Western chain, there's something vaguely American about the facade of this place, which disguises a 15-storey tower of hotel rooms set back from the street. The best rooms have great city views and all are immaculately clean, however the interior design is chintzy and mismatched. But hey, the price is right, and how about them views?

Treasury LUXURY HOTEL **$$$**
(Map p58; ☎07-3306 8888; www.treasurybrisbane.com.au; 130 William St; r from $230; P ❄ @ ☜) Brisbane's most lavish hotel is behind the equally lavish exterior of the former Land Administration Building. Each room is unique and awash with heritage features, with high ceilings, framed artwork, polished wood furniture and elegant furnishings. Perfect if plush and a little bit chintzy floats your boat. The best rooms have river views. Super-efficient staff; parking $20.

Quay West Suites Brisbane APARTMENT **$$$**
(Map p58; ☎07-3853 6000; www.quaywestbrisbane.com; 132 Alice St; 1-/2-/3-bedroom ste from $275/385/695; P ❄ ☜ ≋) Part of the national Quay West chain and festooned with balconies, this apartment hotel has lovely self-contained units with modern kitchens, fully equipped laundries, myriad TVs and stereos, and spectacular views. Refined interiors aim for luxury, and staff are down-to-earth. Parking $35.

Stamford Plaza Brisbane HOTEL **$$$**
(Map p58; ☎07-3221 1999; www.stamford.com.au; cnr Edward & Margaret Sts; r from $269; P ❄ @ ☜ ≋) In the southern CBD, the towering Stamford has classical music in the lobby and rows of Mercedes in the driveway. Opulent rooms are a tad antiquey (not that there's anything wrong with that...), but have huge beds, and there are multiple on-site bars, eateries and salons. Park your Merc for $40.

South Bank

Riverside Hotel HOTEL **$$**
(Map p58; ☎07-3846 0577, 1800 301 101; www.riversidehotel.com.au; 20 Montague Rd, South Bank; d/1-bedroom apt from $109/149; P ❄ ☜ ≋) This huge place spreads out over several taupe-coloured buildings, and has surprisingly friendly staff for such a big outfit. Right across the road from GOMA and South Bank, location is why you're here: don't expect too much from the motel-style rooms and you'll be fine.

West End

Gonow Family Backpacker HOSTEL **$**
(Map p68; ☎07-3846 3473; www.gonowfamily.com.au; 147 Vulture St, West End; dm $18-30, d $69; P ☜) These have to be the cheapest beds in Brisbane, and Gonow – only months old when we visited – is doing a decent job of delivering a clean, respectful, secure hostel experience despite the bargain-basement pricing. It's not a party place by any means: you'll be better off elsewhere if you're looking to launch drunken forays into the night. The upstairs rooms have more ceiling height.

Brisbane Backpackers Resort HOSTEL **$**
(Map p68; ☎07-3844 9956, 1800 626 452; www.brisbanebackpackers.com.au; 110 Vulture St, West End; dm $27-34, tw/d/tr $110/120/135; P ❄ @ ☜ ≋) Is there such a thing as 'backpacker kitsch'? If so, this hulking hostel probably qualifies, with dubious marketing relating to 'bad girls' and what they do and don't do...But if you're looking to party, you're in

the right place. There's a great pool and bar area, and rooms are basic but generally well maintained.

Somewhere to Stay HOSTEL $
(Map p68; ☎07-3846 2858, 1800 812 398; www.somewheretostay.com.au; 47 Brighton Rd, West End; dm $19-27, s $49-54, d $59-79; P @ 🛜 🏊) An enormous white Queenslander (actually, a couple of buildings) with more than 50 rooms and a very laid-back vibe. Cheap, casual and grungy: not for the pernickety.

Petrie Terrace

Aussie Way Backpackers HOSTEL $
(Map p68, ☎07-3369 0711; www.aussiewaybackpackers.com; 34 Cricket St; dm/s/d/f/q $26/55/68/78/104; ❄ 🛜 🏊) Set in a photogenic, two-storey timber Queenslander on the appealingly named Cricket St, Aussie Way feels more like a homely guesthouse than a hostel, with spacious, tastefully furnished rooms and a fab pool for sticky Brisbane afternoons. The doubles in the second building out the back are just lovely. All quiet after 10.30pm.

Brisbane City YHA HOSTEL $
(Map p68; ☎07-3236 1004; www.yha.com.au; 392 Upper Roma St; dm from $39, tw & d with/without bathroom from $122/103, f from $160; P ❄ @ 🛜 🏊) This immaculate, well-run hostel has a rooftop pool and a sundeck with incredible river views. The maximum dorm size is six beds (not too big); most have bathrooms. Big on security, activities, tours and kitchen space (lots of fridges). The cafe/bar has trivia nights and happy hours, but this is a YHA, not party central. Parking $10.

Chill Backpackers HOSTEL $
(Map p68; ☎07-3236 0088, 1800 851 875; www.chillbackpackers.com; 328 Upper Roma St; dm $29-35, d/tr $89/105; P ❄ @ 🛜) This garish aqua building on the CBD fringe has small, clean, modern rooms, and there's a roof deck with fab river views (just like the YHA up the road, but from a slightly reduced altitude). There are 150 beds here, but if they're full the affiliated Brisbane City Backpackers is a couple of doors away.

Brisbane City Backpackers HOSTEL $
(Map p68; ☎07-3211 3221, 1800 062 572; www.citybackpackers.com; 380 Upper Roma St; dm $21-33, s/tw/d/tr from $79/79/105/105; P ❄ @ 🛜 🏊)

BRISBANE FOR CHILDREN

From toddlers to teenagers, there's no shortage of options to keep kids busy (and parents happy) in Brisbane. For info on current happenings pick up the free monthly magazine *Brisbane's Child* (www.brisbaneschild.com.au). During school holidays the Brisbane City Council runs the 'Chill Out' activities program for 10- to 17-year-olds: see www.brisbane.qld.gov.au/whats-on/type/recreation-programs/chill-out.

Out and about, swing by the South Bank Parklands (p57), which has lawns, BBQs, playgrounds and the slow-spinning Wheel of Brisbane (p57) – a real mind-blower for anyone under 15. The lifeguard-patrolled Streets Beach (p65) is here too, with a shallow section for really small swimmers. New Farm Park (p59) is another lovely spot by the river, with a series of treehouse-like platforms interlinking huge (and shady) Moreton Bay fig trees.

The Brisbane River is a big plus. Take a ferry ride around the bends of central Brisbane, or chug further afield to the Lone Pine Koala Sanctuary (p61) where the kids can cuddle up to a critter. If you're heading out Mt Coot-tha way, catch a starry show at the Sir Thomas Brisbane Planetarium (p60).

Too humid to be outside? Head for the air con at the Queensland Cultural Centre on South Bank. Here the Queensland Museum (p57) runs some fab, hands-on programs for little tackers during school holidays. The incorporated **Sciencentre** has plenty of push-this-button-and-see-what-happens action. The Queensland Art Gallery (p57) has a Children's Art Centre which runs regular programs throughout the year, as does the State Library of Queensland (p93) and the Gallery of Modern Art (p57). Over in Fortitude Valley at the Judith Wright Centre of Contemporary Arts, **C!RCA** (Map p62; ☎07-3852 3110; www.circa.org.au; Level 3, 420 Brunswick St, Fortitude Valley) offers action-packed 'circus classes' (tumbling, balancing, jumping, trapeze work) for budding young carnies.

Day-care or babysitting options include Dial an Angel (p44) and Care4Kidz (p44).

On the Upper Roma St hostel row, this hyperactive party palace makes good use of its limited outdoor space, including a viewing tower, pool and barbecue area. Rooms and dorms are generally well kept, and the on-site bar has something happening every night: DJs, pool comps, quiz nights, karaoke... Free wi-fi too.

Banana Benders Backpackers HOSTEL $
(Map p68; 07-3367 1157, 1800 241 157; www.bananabenders.com; 118 Petrie Tce; dm $27-30, d & tw $70-76, apt per 2 weeks from $400;) This downbeat, banana-coloured backpackers has basic rooms and a great little deck out the back. It's a bit out of the way, a 10-minute uphill slog from Roma St Station. One-bedroom apartments available for two-week minimum stays.

Spring Hill

Kookaburra Inn GUESTHOUSE $
(Map p58; 07-3832 1303, 1800 733 533; www.kookaburra-inn.com.au; 41 Phillips St; s/tw/d without bathroom from $65/80/80;) This small, simple two-level guesthouse has basic rooms with washbasin and fridge, and clean shared bathrooms. The building itself is unremarkable, but there's a lounge, kitchen and outdoor patio. A decent budget option if you've done dorms to death. Air-con in some doubles only.

Spring Hill Terraces MOTEL $
(Map p54; 07-3854 1048; www.springhillterraces.com; 260 Water St; d $95-145, unit $175;) Offering good old-fashioned service, security and a tiny pool (a pond?), Spring Hill Terraces has inoffensive motel-style rooms and roomier terrace units with balconies and leafy courtyards. A 10-minute walk from Fortitude Valley.

Punthill Brisbane HOTEL $$
(Map p58; 07-3055 5777, 1300 731 299; www.punthill.com.au; 40 Astor Tce, Spring Hill; 1-/3-bed apt from $150/180;) Melbourne's Punthill hotel chain has made a move north, serving up a slice of hip hotel style in Spring Hill. The lobby is full of retro bicycles and every balcony has a bird cage with a faux-feathered friend in it...but aside from these quirks, what you can expect is stylish suites (all taupe, charcoal, ivory and nice art) in a central location for competitive prices. A good option all-round. Parking is $25.

Dahrl Court APARTMENT $$
(Map p58; 07-3831 9553; www.dahrlcourt.com.au; 45 Phillips St; 1-/2-bedroom apt per week from $400/450;) Tucked into a quiet, leafy pocket of Spring Hill, this old-fashioned complex offers good value for its roomy accommodation. The sizeable apartments are fully self-contained with kitchens and heritage aesthetics throughout (two with balconies). Weekly stays are the norm.

Metropolitan Motor Inn MOTEL $$
(Map p58; 07-3831 6000; www.metropolitanmotorinn.com; 106 Leichhardt St, Spring Hill; r $139-225;) This renovated '70s number presides over a busy intersection and attracts business bods who just want somewhere central to lie down that won't break the bank. No frills, but trim and tidy. Free wi-fi and 24-hour reception.

Fortitude Valley

Bunk Backpackers HOSTEL $
(Map p62; 07-3257 3644, 1800 682 865; www.bunkbrisbane.com.au; cnr Ann & Gipps Sts; dm $21-33, s $60, d/apt from $80/180;) This old arts college was reborn as a backpackers in 2006 – and the party hasn't stopped! It's a huge, five-level place with 55 rooms (mostly eight-bed dorms), just staggering distance from the Valley nightlife. There's also an in-house bar (Birdees), a Mexican cantina, and a few awesome apartments on the top floor.

Central Brunswick Apartments APARTMENT $$
(Map p62; 07-3852 1411; www.centralbrunswickhotel.com.au; 455 Brunswick St; r $140-180;) Emerging from the husk of an old brick brewery building, these 60 mod studio apartments are a hit with business bods. All have fully equipped kitchens, and there's an on-site gym, free wi-fi and rooftop BBQ. Parking $10 per night.

★ **Limes** BOUTIQUE HOTEL $$$
(Map p62; 07-3852 9000; www.limeshotel.com.au; 142 Constance St; d from $230;) A slick slice of style in the Valley, Limes has 21 handsome rooms that make good use of tight space – each has plush furniture, kitchenettes and thoughtful extras (iPod docks, free wi-fi, free gym pass). The rooftop bar and cinema (!) are magic.

Emporium LUXURY HOTEL $$$
(Map p62; 07-3253 6999; www.emporiumhotel.com.au; 1000 Ann St; d from $299;)

A short hop to Brunswick St and James St, first-rate Emporium has uber-mod rooms with high-end fittings and creature comforts – luxe king-sized beds, Bose audio systems, marble kitchenettes – and there's a heated outdoor pool, cocktail lounge and swath of eating options in the same complex. All zebra-print, cherry-red leather and mirrors, the lobby is a stunner! Parking $35.

New Farm

★Bowen Terrace GUESTHOUSE $

(Map p62; ☎07-3254 0458; www.bowenterrace.com.au; 365 Bowen Tce; dm/s/d without bathroom $35/60/85, d/f with bathroom $99/145; P @ ≋) A beautifully restored, 100-year-old Queenslander, this quiet guesthouse offers TVs, bar fridges, quality bed linen and lofty ceilings with fans in every room. Out the back there's a deck overlooking the enticing pool. No air-con but real value for money, with far more class than your average hostel. The only downside is the walls between rooms are a bit thin (built before TV was invented).

Allender Apartments APARTMENT $$

(Map p62; ☎07-3358 5832; www.allenderapartments.com.au; 3 Moreton St; d $135, 1-bedroom apt $160-170; ❄ ≈) Allender's apartments are a mixed bag. In the plain yellow-brick building are simply furnished but clean rooms. More attractive are the heritage apartments in the adjoining Fingal House, a 1918 Queenslander with polished timber floors, oak furniture and access to a private verandah or courtyard.

Kangaroo Point

Il Mondo HOTEL $$

(Map p58; ☎07-3392 0111, 1300 665 526; www.ilmondo.com.au; 25 Rotherham St; r $160, 1-/3-bedroom apt $250/500; P ❄ @ ≈ ≋) In a beaut location near the Story Bridge, this post-modern-looking, seven-storey hotel has handsome rooms and apartments with minimalist design, high-end fixtures and plenty of space. The biggest apartments sleep six – good value for a full house.

Queensland Motel MOTEL $$

(Map p58; ☎07-3391 1061; www.queenslandmotel.id.au; 777 Main St; d/tr/f $120/150/185; P ❄ ≈ ≋) A no-frills, affable, old-school motel near 'the Gabba' cricket ground; it's 20 minutes' walk to the city. Shoot for a room on the top floor, with palm trees rustling outside your window.

Paramount Motel MOTEL $$

(Map p58; ☎07-3393 1444; www.paramountmotel.com.au; 649 Main St; d/tw/f from $115/135/180; P ❄ ≈ ≋) This basic roadside motel sure ain't flashy, but the rooms are big, clean and spartan and have kitchenettes. There's a barbecue by the pool and the staff are quick with a smile. Aim for a room at the back away from the street.

Paddington & Around

Newmarket Gardens Caravan Park CAMPGROUND $

(Map p54; ☎07-3356 1458; www.newmarketgardens.com.au; 199 Ashgrove Ave, Newmarket; unpowered/powered sites $39/41, on-site vans $56, budget r $66, cabins $125-150; P ❄ @ ≈) This upbeat caravan park doesn't have many trees (some of them are mangoes – beware falling fruit!), but it's just 4km north of the city, accessible by bus and train. There's a row of six simple budget rooms (no air-con), five tidy cabins (with air-con) and a sea of van and tent sites. Not much in the way of distractions for kids.

Casabella Apartment APARTMENT $$

(Map p77; ☎07-3217 6507; www.casabella-apartment.com; 211 Latrobe Tce, Paddington; apt $185; P ≈) The understorey of this fuschia-coloured house at the quiet end of Paddo's main drag has been converted into a very comfortable self-contained unit. There are two bedrooms (sleeps three), warm Mediterranean colour schemes, recycled timber floors and lots of louvres to let the cross-breeze through (no air-con). Lovely! Free street parking.

Fern Cottage B&B $$

(Map p77; ☎07-3511 6685; www.ferncottage.net; 89 Fernberg Rd, Paddington; s/d $139/169; P ❄ ≈) This renovated, mustard-coloured, three-suite Queenslander features splashes of chintzy ambience and a shared guest kitchen. The suites are cushy (two of which sleep three; plus one double), and there's a barbecue terrace out the back. Free street parking.

★Latrobe Apartment APARTMENT $$$

(Map p77; ☎0448 944 026; www.stayz.com.au/77109; 183a Latrobe Tce, Paddington; apt from $200; P ❄ ≈) Underneath a chiropractor in affluent Paddington is this excellent two-bedroom apartment, sleeping four, with two bathrooms, polished floorboards, sexy lighting and a fabulous BBQ deck. It's a sleek, contemporary design, with quality everything: linen, toiletries, kitchenware, TV, iPod dock, leather lounge... Cafes and free parking up at street level.

Eating

Like most things in Brisbane, dining experiences can be broadly defined by which neighbourhood you're in. The city centre is the place for fine dining and coffee nooks. In Fortitude Valley you'll find cheap cafes and Chinatown. Nearby, New Farm has plenty of multicultural eateries, French-styled cafes and award winners. Eclectic West End is littered with bohemian cafes and cheap multicultural diners. South Bank swings between mainstream and pricey eats. But no matter where you are, you'll always be able to eat outside! (Is 'Brisbane' actually Latin for 'alfresco'?)

City Centre

The food courts in the big downtown shopping malls offer quick multicultural eats for just a fistful of dollars. The best ones are between Queen and Elizabeth Sts on the ground floors of the Wintergarden Centre and the Myer Centre.

★Brew CAFE, WINE BAR $
(Map p58; 07-3211 4242; www.brewgroup.com.au; Lower Burnett La; mains $6-12; 7am-5pm Mon, to 10pm Tue & Wed, to 11.30pm Thu & Fri, 9am-11.30pm Sat, 9am-3pm Sun) You'd expect to find this kind of subcultural underground cafe in Seattle or Berlin...but Brisbane? Breaking new coffee-cultural ground in Queensland, Brew takes the caffeine into the alleyways, serving simple food (tapas, pastas, sandwiches) to go with the black stuff. Wines and bottled beers if you feel like a different kind of brew.

Bleeding Heart Gallery CAFE $
(Map p58; 07-3229 0395; www.bleedingheart.com.au; 166 Ann St; mains $5-10; 7am-5pm Mon-Fri;) Set back from hectic Ann St in an 1865 servants' home (Brisbane's third-oldest building!), this spacious cafe/gallery has hippie vibes and hosts art exhibitions, occasional concerts and other events. All profits go into funding charitable community enterprises.

Bean CAFE $
(Map p58; www.facebook.com/beanbrisbane; rear 181 George St; mains $9-15; 7am-6pm) Another of Brisbane's new breed of hip laneway coffee shops, Bean is down a grungy, graffiti-spangled driveway off George St, surrounded by fire escapes, air-con-units and construction cranes. You can grab a biscuit or a basic eggy breakfast here, but coffee is the main game. Live music Thursdays at 5pm.

Java Coast Cafe CAFE $
(Map p58; 07-3211 3040; www.javacoastcafe.com.au; 340 George St; mains $11-20; 6.30am-3pm Mon-Fri) Behind a grungy downtown rollerdoor, a skinny alleyway leads to a hidden cafe garden with a fountain, subtropical plants and Buddha statues. An oasis on the Java coast! Good coffee, teas, sandwiches, salads and light meals with Asian accents.

Govindas VEGETARIAN $
(Map p58; 07-3210 0255; www.brisbanegovindas.com.au; Level 1, 99 Elizabeth St; all-you-can-eat $13; 11am-3pm & 5-7.30pm Mon-Thu, 11am-8.30pm Fri, 11am-3pm Sat;) Vegetarian curries, vegie puffs, dahl-lentil soup, salads, pappadams, chutneys, fruit pudding... Grab a cheap vegetarian plateful at this this Hare Krishna–run eatery, up a nondescript stairwell behind a nondescript facade.

Merlo Coffee CAFE $
(Map p58; 07-3221 2616; www.merlo.com.au; 10 Market St; items $4-8; 6.30am-4pm Mon-Fri) Keeping the downtown business bods firing, this roaster/cafe is one of several Merlos around Brisbane (a local success story). The food is fine (croissants, cakes, sandwiches), but what you're here for is the coffee: strong enough to get you through the next meeting.

Groove Train CAFE $$
(Map p58; www.groovetrain.com.au; Riverside Centre, 123 Eagle St; mains $17-35; 7am-late) An orange and dark-wood bunker hunkered down by the Riverside ferry terminal, Groove Train is long, low, lean and groovy. Watch the boats chug to-and-fro as you tuck into woodfired pizzas, wok fry-ups, burgers, calzones, risottos and big salads. Gets moody and bar-like at night.

Verve Cafe & Bar ITALIAN $$
(Map p58; 07-3221 5691; www.vervecafe.com.au; 109 Edward St; mains $17-35; noon-late Mon-Fri, 5pm-late Sat & Sun) Subterranean Verve allegedly stocks Australia's biggest selection of ciders. But that's not why you're here. Well, it might be – but try some of the imaginative

Paddington

pastas, salads, risottos and pizzas before you start drinking. The sand crab and snapper risotto with lemon and fresh thyme is a winner. Radiohead on the stereo; arty, relaxed crowd.

Hanaichi JAPANESE **$$**

(Map p58; ☎07-3210 0032; www.hanaichisushibar.com.au; Level 1, Wintergarden Centre, 171 Queen St; sushi $3.50-8, mains $15-25; ⊙11.30am-10pm) Ride the sushi train out of Hunger Central at Hanaichi, where the revolving track packs in the lunchtime passengers shoulder-to-shoulder. Also on offer are bento boxes, soups and an à la carte menu if you'd rather take your time. Plenty of good Japanese beers available too.

★E'cco MODERN AUSTRALIAN **$$$**

(Map p58; ☎07-3831 8344; www.eccobistro.com; 100 Boundary St; mains $40-43; ⊙noon-3pm Tue-Fri, 6-10pm Tue-Sat; ✎) One of the finest restaurants in the state, award-winning E'cco is a culinary must. Menu masterpieces from chef Philip Johnson include liquorice-spiced pork belly with caramelised peach, onion jam and kipfler potatoes. The interior is suitably swish: all black, white and stainless steel.

Paddington

Sleeping
1 Casabella Apartment A1
2 Fern Cottage B2
3 Latrobe Apartment A1

Eating
4 Fundies Wholefood Market D3
5 Gelateria Cremona A3
6 Il Posto B2

Drinking & Nightlife
7 Lark C3

Entertainment
8 Paddo Tavern C3

Shopping
9 Paddington Antique Centre B1
10 Retro Metro C2

II MODERN AUSTRALIAN **$$$**

(Map p58; ☎07-3210 0600; www.two.com.au; 2 Edward St; mains $35-50; ⊙10am-midnight) Just landed a new job? Got an anniversary? Tuesday night? Special occasion or otherwise, II (aka Restaurant Two) is an elegant choice, located near the City Botanic Gardens. Delectable fare – most of it largely locally sourced – includes the likes of roast duck breast with caramelised pear, turnips, shallots, broccoli and mandarin jus, plus magical desserts and cheese boards. Service is first-rate, and the wine list is superb.

Cha Cha Char STEAKHOUSE **$$$**
(Map p58; ☎07-3211 9944; www.chachachar.com.au; Shop 5, 1 Eagle St Pier; mains $38-95; ⏰noon-11pm Mon-Fri, 6-11pm Sat & Sun) Wallowing in awards, this long-running favourite serves Brisbane's best steaks, along with first-rate seafood and roast game meats. The classy semicircular dining room in the Eagle St Pier complex has floor-to-ceiling windows and river views.

South Bank

Open-walled cafes and mainstream restaurants are scattered along the South Bank Parklands. On the edge of the greenery, Grey St is also packed with eating and snacking options.

Piaf FRENCH **$$**
(Map p58; ☎07-3846 5026; www.piafbistro.com.au; 5/182 Grey St; breakfast mains $7-16, lunch & dinner $18-26; ⏰7am-late) A chilled-out but still intimate bistro with a loyal following, Piaf serves a small selection (generally just five mains and a few salads and other light options) of good-value, contemporary French-inspired food. French wines by the glass. No sign of Edith...

Ahmet's TURKISH **$$**
(Map p58; ☎07-3846 6699; www.ahmets.com; Shop 10, 168 Grey St; mains $19-34, banquets per person $34-46; ⏰11.30am-3pm & 6pm-late; ☑) On restaurant-lined Grey St, Ahmet's serves delectable Turkish fare amid a riot of colours and Grand Bazaar/Bosphorus murals. Try a Sucuk *pide* (oven-baked Turkish bread with Turkish salami, egg, tomato and mozzarella). Deep street-side terrace and regular live music.

Stokehouse MODERN AUSTRALIAN **$$$**
(Map p58; ☎07-3020 0600; www.stokehouse.com.au; River Quay, Sidon St, South Bank; mains $34-62; ⏰10am-1am) Looking for a classy restaurant in which to pop the question? This angular, concrete and dark-timber bunker by the river is for you! Start with the spanner crab with apple jelly, then move on to the Daintree barramundi with white clams and sauerkraut. Flashy Stoke Bar is next door (for champagne after she/he says 'Yes!').

West End

Goths, hippies, skaters and hipsters shuffle between the restaurants, cafes and bars along Boundary St in the West End, which has a concentration of good options around both the Vulture St and Browning St intersections.

★**George's Seafood** FISH & CHIPS **$**
(Map p68; ☎07-3844 4100; 150 Boundary St; meals $8-10; ⏰9.30am-7.30pm Mon-Fri, 10.30am-7.30pm Sat & Sun) With a window full of fresh mudcrabs, Moreton Bay rock oysters, banana prawns and whole snapper, this old fish-and-chipper has been here forever. The $8 cod-and-chips is unbeatable.

Burrow CAFE **$**
(Map p68; ☎07-3846 0030; www.theburrowwestend.com.au; 37 Mollison St; mains $10-20; ⏰7am-late Tue-Sun; 📶) In the open-sided understorey of a shambling old Queenslander, casual Burrow is like a Baja California cantina crossed with a student share-house: laid-back and beachy with surf murals and wafting Pink Floyd. Try the hangover-removing El Desperados taco for breakfast – pulled pork, eggs and jalapeño salsa. There's good coffee, too.

Blackstar Coffee Roasters CAFE **$**
(Map p68; 44 Thomas St; mains $6-12; ⏰7am-3pm Mon, to 5pm Tue-Fri, to late Sat, 8am-3pm Sun) A neighbourhood fave, West End's own bean roaster has excellent coffee, a simple breakfast menu (wraps, avocado on toast, eggs Benedict), wailing Roy Orbison and live jazz on Saturday evening. Try one of their cold-pressed coffees on a hot day.

Forest VEGAN **$**
(Map p68; www.theforest.com.au; 124 Boundary St; mains $5-9; ⏰10am-9pm; ☑) Brisbane's dreadlocked collective trundles into this laid-back, no-fuss diner for curries, vegie burgers, 'no-bull' (meatless) pies, samosas and daily specials (oh that vegetable chilli!), plus desserts and organic beer and wine.

Cafe Checocho CAFE, PIZZERIA **$**
(Map p68; 69 Hardgrave Rd; mains $9-18; ⏰8am-10pm; 📶☑) Serving up chess, coffee, pizza and chocolate *(che-co-cho)* on a little suburban foodie strip (with Vietnamese, Indonesian, Italian and Tibetan stablemates), this charming, lived-in cafe also has occasional live music and lots of vegetarian and vegan options. Order a pumpkin, macadamia, olive

and fetta pizza to chew while you're reading one of the books from the bookshelf (all for sale – only $2).

★**Gunshop Café** CAFE, MODERN AUSTRALIAN $$
(Map p68; ☎07-3844 2241; www.thegunshopcafe.com; 53 Mollison St; mains $17-33; ⏰6.30am-2pm Mon, 6.30am-late Tue-Sat, 6.30am-2.30pm Sun) With cool tunes, interesting art and happy staff, this peaceably repurposed gun shop has exposed-brick walls, sculptural ceiling lamps and an inviting back garden. The locally sourced menu changes daily, but regulars include smoked chicken lasagne, a pulled-pork baguette and wild-mushroom risotto. Boutique beers, excellent Australian wines and afternoon pick-me-ups available.

Mondo Organics MODERN AUSTRALIAN $$
(Map p54; ☎07-3844 1132; www.mondo-organics.com.au; 166 Hardgrave Rd; mains $25-36; ⏰8.30-11.30am Sat & Sun, noon-2.30pm Fri-Sun, 6pm-late Wed-Sat) Using the highest-quality organic and sustainable produce, Mondo Organics earns top marks for its delicious seasonal menu. Recent hits include duck breast with fig, sage and strawberry; and potato and parmesan gnocchi with golden shallots, zucchini and salsa verde. See the website for details about the attached Mondo Organics Cooking School (p67).

Little Greek Taverna GREEK $$
(Map p68; ☎07-3255 2215; www.littlegreektaverna.com.au; Shop 5, 1 Browning St; mains $15-30, banquets per person $35-42; ⏰11am-9pm) Uptempo, eternally busy and in a prime West End location, the LGT is a great spot for a big Greek feast and some people watching. Launch into a prawn and saganaki salad or a classic lamb yiros, washed down with a sleep-defeating Greek coffee. It's kid-friendly, too.

Caravanserai TURKISH $$
(Map p54; ☎07-3217 2617; www.caravanserairestaurant.com.au; 1 Dornoch Tce; mains $25-35; ⏰noon-2.30pm Fri & Sat, 6pm-late Tue-Sun) Woven tablecloths, red walls and candlelit tables create a snug atmosphere at this standout Turkish restaurant. Share an Ottoman meze platter (halloumi, chorizo, almond-crusted goats cheese, garlic prawns and more good stuff), or tuck into the excellent braised lamb shank.

Fortitude Valley & Chinatown

Although better known for drinkin', dancin' and general nocturnal shenanigans, the Valley also has some brilliant places to eat, particularly around Chinatown (Duncan St) where steaming noodle soups, bowls of dumplings and exotic spice scents lure passers-by.

James St Market MARKET, SELF-CATERING $
(Map p62; www.jamesstmarket.com.au; 22 James St; ⏰8.30am-7pm Mon-Fri, 8am-6pm Sat & Sun) Paradise for gourmands, this small but

LOCAL KNOWLEDGE

PHILIP JOHNSON: HEAD CHEF AT E'CCO

Kitchens are great: there's always a melting pot of ideas. You work with different chefs, and things evolve over the years.

Claim to Fame?

Winning *Gourmet Traveller's* Restaurant of the Year award in 1997. Some people say that's what helped put Brisbane's restaurant scene on the map. I hate to look at it like that but I think the rest of the country took notice: 'There must be some decent places to eat up there in Brisbane'. A well-known food critic said you couldn't eat north of Paddington – as in Paddington, Sydney. That changed a bit that year.

Cooking Style?

Modern Australian, it has Italian influences, and there's always a bit of Asian in it owing to our proximity, plus a bit of Mediterranean.

Dining Scene in Brisbane?

It's amazing. Brisbane is a city that has grown up in the last 15 years. I think for years we were considered playing second fiddle to Sydney and Melbourne. Now I think we have great restaurants with top quality and service.

Other Favourite Restaurant?

Something casual I love is Bar Alto (p86) at the Powerhouse.

beautifully stocked market has gourmet cheeses, a bakery/patisserie, fruit and veg, flowers, and lots of quality goodies. The fresh seafood counter serves excellent sushi and sashimi. The James St Cooking School (p67) is upstairs.

The Vietnamese VIETNAMESE $
(Map p62; ☎07-3252 4112; www.thevietnameserestaurant.com.au; 194 Wickham St; mains $10-20; ⊙11am-3pm & 5-10pm) Aptly if unimaginatively named, this is indeed the place in town to eat Vietnamese, with exquisitely prepared dishes served to an always crowded house. Go for something from the 'Chef's Recommendation' list: crispy beef strips with honey and chilli, or clay-pot prawns with oyster sauce. Great value for money.

Campos CAFE $
(Map p62; www.camposcoffee.com; 11 Wandoo St; mains $9-17; ⊙6.30am-4pm) Campos is a Sydney-based company, but that doesn't seem to bother the regulars here, who sidestep milk crates and stacks of cardboard boxes down a little alley behind the James St Market for some of the best coffee in town. Food-wise it's substantial cafe fare (baked eggs; cherry, chocolate and coconut loaf; buttermilk pancakes). Takeaway bags of beans, too.

Brunswick Social DUMPLINGS, BAR $
(Map p62; ☎07-3252 3234; www.thebrunswicksocial.com; 351 Brunswick St; dumplings from $8; ⊙6pm-late Wed, Thu, Sat & Sun, from 5pm Fri) Beat a retreat from the street down the stairs and into this sociable, funky dumpling house and late-night bar. A hip crew of Valley vixens and voyeurs eye each other over tapas-style plates of prawn-and-mushrom dumplings and BBQ pork buns. Drinks-wise, it's cocktails and craft beers: the 'Nu School Gimlet' (vodka, lime juice, lime marmalade and absinthe) will put a kink in your reality.

Tibetan Kitchen TIBETAN $
(Map p62; ☎07-3358 5906; www.tibetankitchen.com.au/thevalley; 454 Brunswick St; mains $14-19; ⊙6-9pm; ✎) Tasty Tibetan fare beneath prayer flags, paper lanterns and a massive pair of Tibetan Buddhist horns suspended from the ceiling. Try the *Bakra ko Tihun* (goat curry on the bone with pumpkin and squash). And if you've never tasted Nepalese rice beer, here's your chance.

Lust For Life CAFE $
(Map p62; ☎07-3852 5048; www.lustforlifetattoo.com; 176 Wickham St; items $5-12; ⊙7am-3pm Mon-Fri, 10am-3pm Sat & Sun) Bagels, sandwiches, salads, organic juices, pastries, strong coffee and 'music your nanna hates' are on offer at Lust For Life, a quirky tattoo parlour that has morphed itself into a cafe and art gallery. Nibble a mango, almond and white-chocolate muffin as you wait to get inked.

Sitar INDIAN $
(Map p62; ☎07-3254 0400; www.sitar.com.au; 69 James St; mains $12-25; ⊙noon-2pm Sun-Fri, 6-9pm daily; ✎) Away from the fray on a quiet section of James St, Sitar occupies a lovely old white weatherboard Queenslander. Step inside for trad curries, dahls, naans and tandoori dishes, including plenty of gluten-free and vegetarian options. Love the psychedelic sitar player painting above the door.

Kuan Yin Tea House CHINESE, VEGETARIAN $
(Map p62; ☎07-3252 4557; www.kuanyinteahouse.blogspot.com.au; 198 Wickham St; mains $6-12; ⊙11.30am-7.30pm Mon, Wed & Thu, to 8pm Fri, to 5pm Sat, to 3pm Sun; ✎) Kuan Yin is a small, garish BYO place with faux-wood panelling

THE BARRACKS

Across a footbridge from Roma St Station or a short walk from Caxton St in Petrie Terrace, the **Barracks** (Map p68; www.thebarracks.info; 61 Petrie Tce, Petrie Terrace) once served as a gaol (1860 to 1883), then a police depot (until the 1940s), and sat derelict for decades before reopening as a mixed-use development in 2008, following a $120 million overhaul. Comprising three big heritage-listed buildings from its former days, the development was hailed an immediate success (and garnered national awards) in the realm of urban renewal, and Brisbanites have embraced it as their own – noir history and all.

The Barracks houses shops, cafes, bars, restaurants (both casual and high-end), the six-screen Palace Barracks (p89) cinema (our favourite cinema in Brisbane), a supermarket, a bookshop, a wine shop and plenty of speciality stores. The pick of the bars is moody Cabiria (p87), a New York–style cocktail bar. Perfect for a rainy afternoon!

and a bamboo-lined ceiling. Food-wise it's flavourful vegetarian noodle soups, dumplings and mock-meat rice dishes. Try the tofu salad. Great tea selection, too.

Flamingo CAFE $
(Map p62; ☎07-3252 7557; www.facebook.com/pages/flamingo-cafe/362822247134; 5b Winn St; mains $10-15; ⏰7.30am-4pm Mon-Sat, 8.30am-4pm Sun) Hiding down a tiny lane off Ann St, Flamingo is a buzzy little bolt-hole cafe with black and pink walls, a boho vibe and cheerfully profane wait staff. Winning vegie burgers and banana-and-date loaf.

Thai Wi-Rat THAI, LAOTIAN $
(Map p62; ☎07-3257 0884; 20 Duncan St; mains $11-18; ⏰10am-4pm & 5-9.30pm) This modest, brightly illuminated hole-in-the-wall on the main Chinatown drag cooks up solid, chilli-heavy Thai and Laotian, including *pla dook yang* (grilled whole catfish). Takeaways available.

Buzz CAFE $
(Map p62; www.buzzfood.com.au; Shop 22, Emporium, 1000 Ann St; mains $10-23; ⏰6.30am-3pm) There's a real buzz about this upmarket cafe in the flashy Emporium retail precinct, just away from the Valley fray. It's an open-walled design (like so many places in Brisbane), with fancy red-and-white awnings: inside, business conversations buzz over wagyu beef burgers, smoothies, gluten-free salads and decent coffee. Aim for the home-made savoury mince with poached egg and horseradish mayo.

Spoon Deli Cafe CAFE $$
(Map p62; ☎07 3257 1750; www.spoondeli.com.au; Shop B3, 22 James St; breakfast $7-20, mains $18-30; ⏰6.30am-6pm Mon-Fri, 7am-5pm Sat & Sun) Inside James St Market, this upscale deli serves gloriously rich pastas, salads, soups and colossal paninis and lasagne slabs. The fresh juices are a liquid meal unto themselves. Walls are lined with deli produce: vinegars, oils, herbs and hampers. You'll feel hungry as soon as you walk in!

Garuva ASIAN FUSION $$
(Map p62; ☎07-3216 0124; www.garuva.com.au; 324 Wickham St; mains $25-27; ⏰6pm-late Sun-Thu, 5.30pm-late Fri & Sat; ✍) There's no signage here – just a pair of black doors next to the Wickham Hotel leading into a rainforested foyer and a cushioned seating area draped with silk curtains (all rather romantically *Arabian Nights*). The menu traverses a geographically loose Asian realm from Japanese tempura vegetables to Thai chilli prawns and Turkish octopus. Bookings advised.

Wagamama ASIAN FUSION $$
(Map p62; ☎07-3252 8229; www.wagamama.com.au; Emporium, 1000 Ann St; mains $18-22; ⏰11am-9pm Sun-Thu, to 10pm Fri & Sat) Sure, it's a chain restaurant, but Wagamama, with its long communal tables and moody lighting, is still the pick of the eateries in the ritzy Emporium centre on Ann St. It's perpetually busy, serving quality, well-priced Japanese curries, salads, wok fry-ups and ramen noodle soups.

New Farm

Multicultural New Farm is one of Brisbane's most food-focused 'burbs, and has seen an explosion of new eateries in recent years. It has a certain self-inflated vibe, but genuine, creative, good-value options can still be found.

Cafe Bouquiniste CAFE $
(Map p62; 121 Merthyr Rd; mains $8-12; ⏰7.30am-5pm Mon-Fri, 8.30am-5pm Sat, 8.30am-1pm Sun; ✍) Filling a tiny old side-street shopfront, this boho cafe and bookseller has buckets of charm (if not much space). The coffee is fantastic, service is friendly, and the prices are right for breakfast fare, toasted sandwiches, savoury tarts and cakes. Try the pumpkin, goats cheese and sage tart.

Chouquette CAFE, FRENCH $
(Map p62; ☎07-3358 6336; www.chouquette.com.au; 19 Barker St; items $2-10, 10 chouquettes $3.50; ⏰6.30am-5pm Wed-Sat, to 12.30pm Sun; ✍) Some New Farmers say Chouquette is the best patisserie this side of Toulouse. We're not sure how many of them have actually been to Toulouse, but their argument holds up. Grab a nutty coffee and bag of the namesake *chouquettes* (small choux pastries topped with granulated sugar), a shiny slice of *tarte au citron* or a filled baguette. Sexy French-speaking staff.

Café Cirque CAFE $
(Map p62; 618 Brunswick St; mains $14-17; ⏰7am-4pm; ✍) One of the best breakfast spots (served all day) in town, buzzing Café Cirque serves rich coffee and daily specials, along with open-face sandwiches and gourmet salads for lunch. It's a skinny little room with foldback windows to the street.

Burger Urge BURGERS $
(Map p62; www.burgerurge.com.au; 542 Brunswick St; mains $10-21; noon-late Mon-Thu, 11.30am-late Fri-Sun) One of several Burger Urges around town, serving brilliant buns, with lamb, chicken, cheese, chilli, Greek, Turkish, steak and vegie options aplenty. Sit on the footpath under rock-blaring speakers, or inside with the comic-book wallpaper.

Wok on Inn ASIAN FUSION $
(Map p62; 728 Brunswick St; mains $10-14; noon-2.30pm Sun-Fri, 5-10pm daily) With a shady front courtyard this industrious noodle bar is the spot for some quick-fire carbs. Choose your noodle, your cooking style (including Mongolian, Thai, Malay, Chinese and Hong Kong styles) and your meat/veg combo. They also do a regular $8.50 lunch special and a decent prawn laksa.

Vue CAFE, MODERN AUSTRALIAN $
(Map p62; 07-3358 6511; www.vuelounge.com.au; 1/83 Merthyr Rd; mains $11-20; 7am-10pm Tue-Sat, to 6pm Sun & Mon;) Equal parts cafe, bistro and burger joint, Vue covers a lot of bases and covers them well. Footpath tables curl around a funky Miró-meets-Gaudí column out the front, leading into an airy interior. Menu highlights include a Corona-battered barramundi burger, a spicy cajun calamari salad, and pan-fried eggs, chorizo, halloumi and ratatouille on sourdough. A real New Farm fave.

PORTSIDE WHARF

A few ferry stops downriver from New Farm is **Portside Wharf** (07-3907 4111; www.portsidewharf.com.au; 39 Hercules St, Hamilton), Brisbane's cruise ship terminal, which has spawned a shopping-and-eating complex and a copse of apartment towers. The vibe is a little contrived and artificial, but some of the restaurants here are beautifully sited overlooking the river. Standouts include **Sono** (07-3268 6655; www.sonorestaurant.com.au; mains $19-55; noon-2.30pm Wed-Sun, 6-9.30pm Tue-Sun), one of Brisbane's best Japanese restaurants; and **Byblós** (07-3268 2223; www.byblosbar.com.au; mains $24-36; 4.30pm-late Mon & Tue, 11.30am-late Wed-Sun), a hip spot specialising in Lebanese and Mediterranean edibles. Also at Portside is the five-screen Dendy Cinema (p89) if you feel like dinner and a movie. To get here, take the CityCat ferry to Bretts Wharf, and follow the riverside path 500m further east.

Siam Square Thai THAI $
(Map p62; 07-3254 1884; www.siamsquarethai.com; 888 Brunswick St, New Farm; mains $13-18; 5-10pm Tue-Sun) Straight-up Thai classics in a prominent corner location in New Farm. Watch the eclectic local parade of gay guys, shuffling winos, hand-holding couples and old Italian nonnas wander past the window as you sweat it out over a prawn jungle curry or some stir-fried BBQ duck with soy and ginger.

Watt MODERN AUSTRALIAN $
(Map p54; 07-3358 5464; www.wattrestaurant.com.au; Brisbane Powerhouse, 119 Lamington St; mains $9-25; 9am-late Mon-Fri, 8am-late Sat & Sun) On the riverbank level of the Brisbane Powerhouse is casual, breezy Watt. Order up some duck salad with sweet chilli, rocket and orange, or a smoked ham-hock terrine with lentils and cornichons. Wines by the glass; DJ tunes on Sunday afternoons. The flood sculpture out the front has been a bit too relevant of late...

Himalayan Cafe NEPALESE $$
(Map p62; 07-3358 4015; 640 Brunswick St; mains $15-25; 5.30-10pm Tue-Sun;) Awash with prayer flags and colourful cushions, this karmically positive, unfussy restaurant serves authentic Tibetan and Nepalese fare such as tender *fhaiya darkau* (lamb with vegies, coconut milk and spices). Repeat the house mantra: 'May positive forces be with every single living thing that exists'.

The Smoke BBQ BARBECUE $$
(Map p62; 07-3358 1922; www.thesmokebbq.com.au; 85 Merthyr Rd; mains lunch $15-21, dinner $25-37; 11.30am-2pm & 6-9pm Tue-Sat) The smell of hickory hangs heavy in the air of this small, buzzy restaurant plating up American-style barbecue. The menu includes tender short ribs, pulled pork and charcoal chicken (with vodka barbecue sauce), along with requisite sides like coleslaw, mac-and-cheese and fries. In-house joke: 'The trouble with barbecue is two or three days later you're hungry again'.

Pintxo SPANISH $$
(Map p62; 07-3333 2231; www.pintxo.com; 561 Brunswick St; tapas $9-14, share plates $16-28; noon-3pm Sat & Sun, 5.30pm-late Wed-Sun)

Grab a seat at the bar and choose your freshly prepared tapas as it glides past at this casual, paprika-red Spanish spot on Brunswick St. Shared plates are made to order, with authentic standouts like pancetta-wrapped shrimp, grilled chorizo with sweet potato and beef meatballs with *manchego* polenta. Wash it down with Spanish sangria, beers and wines by the glass.

Anise FRENCH **$$**
(Map p62; ☎07-3358 1558; www.anise.com.au; 697 Brunswick St; mains $24-34; ⊙noon-2.30pm Thu-Sat, 6-9pm Mon-Sat) This uber-stylish 21-seat restaurant/wine bar features an award-winning menu of seasonally inspired Gallic fare. Patrons plant themselves around the narrow bar and feast on *amuse-bouches* (hors d'oeuvres) such as oysters and Alsace foie gras, followed by grass-fed Black Angus beef, fresh fish of the day or slow-braised spring lamb. The six-course degustation menu ($100, or $155 with dishes paired with wines) is perfect for a special occasion.

Arriva ITALIAN **$$**
(Map p62; ☎07-3254 1599; www.arrivarestaurant.com.au; 6/84 Methyr Rd; mains $17-23; ⊙11am-late Tue-Sat) This tiny neighbourhood Italian diner serves authentic pizza and pasta from an efficient kitchen. Loyal locals cram in for *penne puttanesca* (anchovies, olives, capers, chilli) and *porcini* ravioli (creamy mushrooms, truffle sauce and Italian sausage). Check your calorie concerns at the door.

Kangaroo Point & Around

Cliffs Cafe CAFE **$**
(Map p58; www.cliffscafe.com.au; 29 River Tce; mains $12-20; ⊙7am-5pm) A steep climb up from the riverside, this cliff-top cafe has superb river and city-skyline views. It's a casual, open-air pavilion: thick burgers, battered barramundi and chips, salads, desserts and good coffee are the standouts.

Enoteca ITALIAN **$$$**
(Map p54; ☎07-3392 4315; www.1889enoteca.com.au; 10-12 Logan Rd, Woolloongabba; mains $36-42; ⊙noon-2.30pm Tue-Fri & Sun, 6pm-late Tue-Sat) Simple and simply wonderful traditional Roman pasta, fish and meat dishes served in a gorgeous 1889 shopfront south of the city centre in Woolloongabba: one of the best restaurants in Brisbane. Even if you're not here for a meal (there's a little wine store here too) check out the lavish lead-lighting, marvellous marble bar and walk-around glass display cabinet fill of Italian vino vessels.

Paddington

Gelateria Cremona GELATI **$**
(Map p77; ☎07-3367 0212; 5/151 Baroona Rd, Rosalie; gelato from $4.80; ⊙5-10pm Mon, 2-10pm Tue-Fri, 1-10pm Sat & Sun;) Authentic Italian gelato in dinky little tubs or cones, perfect for a promenade on a humid Brisbane evening. Try the classic vanilla bean or Dutch chocolate, or a lighter fruit sorbet (terrific grapefruit!). It's down the hill from the main Paddington strip in the cute Rosalie shopping enclave.

Fundies Wholefood Market CAFE **$**
(Map p77; ☎07-3367 0293; www.fundies.com.au; 219 Given Tce; mains $10-14; ⊙9am-6pm Sun-Fri, 8.30am-6pm Sat;) An organic food store and hippie cafe combined, this is the place to stock up on wholesome groceries. On the food front, try the big breakfast with tofu scramble or the curry lentil burger for lunch.

Il Posto ITALIAN **$$**
(Map p77; ☎07-3367 3111; www.ilposto.com.au; 107 Latrobe Tce; mains $20-29; ⊙noon-4pm & 5.30pm-late Tue-Sun) Pizza and pasta just like they make in Rome, served on an outdoor piazza (or inside if it's too humid). Pizzas come either *rosse* or *bianche* (with or without tomato base), and are thin and crispy. Great staff, Peroni beer on tap, and kid-friendly too (also just like Rome).

Drinking & Nightlife

The prime drinking destination in Brisbane is Fortitude Valley, with its lounges, live-music bars and nightclubs (both straight and gay). Most clubs here are open Wednesday to Sunday nights; some are free, others charge up to $20. Dress nicely and bring your ID. In the CBD there's a bottoms-up after-work crowd, while the West End has cool bars full of inner-city funksters. New Farm has some hip bars, attracting a mostly neighbourhood crowd.

City Centre

★**Super Whatnot** BAR
(Map p58; www.superwhatnot.com; 48 Burnett La; ⊙3pm-late Tue-Sat) Trailblazing Super Whatnot is a funky, industrial laneway space, with a mezzanine floor and sunken lounge.

Drinks: bottled boutique Australian beers and cocktails (try the cure-all Penicillin). Food: American-inspired bar snacks (hot dogs, mini burritos, nachos). Tunes: vinyl DJs Thursday to Saturday spinning funk, soul and hip-hop; live acoustic acts Wednesday. Winning combo!

Belgian Beer Cafe BAR

(Map p58; www.belgianbeercafebrussels.com.au; cnr Mary & Edward Sts; ⏲11.30am-late) Wood-panelled walls and art-deco lights lend an old-world charm to this buzzing space. Out the back, the beer garden has big screens and big after-work egos. Lots of Hoegaarden and Leffe and high-end bistro fare. Ignore the '80s-era Stevie Wonder.

Laneway BAR

(Map p58; www.theeuro.com.au/laneway; 181 Mary St; ⏲noon-midnight Mon-Fri, 6pm-midnight Sat) Upstairs above the urbane Euro restaurant (walk through the restaurant to the stairs, or shuffle in the back door from the eponymous Spencer La), Laneway is a sassy cocktail bar full of upwardly mobile city fashionistas. Sip a Clementina (spicy mandarin and tequila) then order a wagyu burger to keep you upright.

Port Office Hotel PUB

(Map p58; www.portofficehotel.com.au; cnr Edward & Margaret Sts; ⏲11am-late Mon-Fri, noon-late Sat) An oval-shaped marble bar, black laquered floorboards and charcoal-coloured walls conjure up a delightfully sinister atmosphere here – enough of an excuse for the downtown corporate crowd to act naughty after work. There's also a wine bar, and, if you're hungry, a classy eatery called Fix Restaurant.

Moo Moo WINE BAR

(Map p58; www.moomoorestaurant.com; cnr Margaret & Edward Sts; ⏲11am-late) Inside the heritage Port Office building, this ritzy steak restaurant has an equally schmick open-air wine bar on the laneway out the back. Corporate bods swill away long afternoons in the company of 90-plus wines by the glass.

South Bank

Plough Inn PUB

(Map p58; www.ploughinn.com.au; Bldg 29, Little Stanley St; ⏲11am-late) You'd think South Bank would be littered with cool places for a cool beer, wouldn't you? Think again... Plenty of places to eat: not many places to drink. If you're getting dry and desperate, the old Plough offers a mainstream pubby experience: wailing '80s rock, hefty meals, a big beer terrace and plenty of XXXX. Plough on in.

West End

Archive Beer Boutique BAR

(Map p68; www.archivebeerboutique.com.au; 100 Boundary St; ⏲11am-late) Interesting beer, interesting people, interesting place: welcome to Archive, a temple of beer with many a fine frothy on tap (try the Evil Twin West Coast Red Ale). Check the bar made of books! Oh, and the food's good, too (steaks, mussels, pasta). Upstairs is **Loft West End** (Map p68; www.loftwestend.com), a sophisticated cocktail/food room.

The End BAR

(Map p68; www.73vulture.com; 1/73 Vulture St; ⏲3pm-midnight) This mod-industrial shopfront conversion is a real locals' hangout, with hipsters, cheese boards, Morrissey on the turntable, DJs and live acoustic troubadours. The Blackstar mocha stout (caffeine courtesy of the local roaster) will cheer up your rainy river afternoon.

Lychee Lounge COCKTAIL BAR

(Map p68; www.lycheelounge.com.au; 94 Boundary St; ⏲3pm-midnight Sun-Thu, 3pm-1am Fri & Sat) Sink into the lush furniture and stare up at the macabre doll-head chandeliers at this exotic Asian lounge bar, with mellow beats, mood lighting and an open frontage to Boundary St. Is this what a *real* opium den looks like?

Fortitude Valley

★**Alfred & Constance** BAR

(Map p62; www.alfredandconstance.com.au; 130 Constance St; ⏲10am-3am) Wow! Fabulously eccentric A&C occupies two old weatherboard houses away from the main Valley action. Inside, fluoro-clad ditch diggers, tattooed lesbians, suits and surfies roam between the tiki bar, rooftop terrace, cafe area and lounge rooms checking out the interior design: chandeliers, skeletons, surfboards, old hi-fi equipment... It's weird, and very wonderful.

Bowery COCKTAIL BAR

(Map p62; www.thebowery.com.au; 676 Ann St; ⏲5pm-late Tue-Sun) The exposed-brick walls, gilded mirrors, booths and foot-worn floorboards at this long, narrow bar bring a touch of substance to the Valley fray. The cocktails and wine list are top-notch (and priced accordingly), and there's live jazz/dub Tuesday to Thursday. DJs spin on weekends.

Press Club COCKTAIL BAR
(Map p62; www.pressclub.net.au; 339 Brunswick St; ⏲5pm-late Tue-Sun) Amber hues, leather sofas, ottomans, glowing chandeliers, fabric-covered lanterns... It's all rather glamorously Moroccan here (with a touch of that kooky cantina from *Star Wars*). Live music on Thursday (jazz, funk, rockabilly) and DJs on weekends.

La Ruche COCKTAIL BAR
(Map p62; www.laruche.com.au; 680 Ann St; ⏲5pm-3am Wed & Thu, 5pm-5am Fri & Sat, 7pm-3am Sun) French for 'the hive', La Ruche is indeed buzzing, with a dressed-up crowd bantering over bespoke cocktails and tapas plates. Interiors morph *Alice in Wonderland* with the Mexican Day of the Dead, while there's a smoking courtyard out the back and an intimate retreat upstairs.

Fringe Bar BAR, CLUB
(Map p62; www.fringebar.com.au; cnr Ann & Constance Sts; ⏲11.30am-midnight Wed & Thu, 11.30am-5am Fri, 4pm-5am Sat) This old art-deco charmer has its fingers in a lot of different nocturnal pies: live music, DJs, lots of bar areas, pub food, trivia nights, comedy nights... All scuttling over a weathered terrazzo floor beneath giant origami-style lights. A great place to launch your night in the Valley.

Cru Bar & Cellar WINE BAR
(Map p62; www.crubar.com; 22 James St; ⏲11am-late Mon-Fri, 10am-late Sat & Sun) A mind-pickling menu of hundreds of wines (by the glass, bottle or half-bottle) is on offer at this classy (and pricey) joint, with confidently strutting staff, a glowing marble bar and fold-back windows to the street.

Elephant Arms PUB
(Map p62; www.elephantarms.com.au; 230 Wickham St; ⏲11am-late) Not too Brit and not too Celtic (just enough of each), this vast elephant-coloured pub in the heart of Fortitude Valley does a little bit of everything: meals, live music (originals and covers) and trivia, with some decent beers on tap and a buzzy beer garden out the back. A solid place to launch your nocturnal Valley foray.

Cloudland CLUB
(Map p62; www.katarzyna.com.au/venues/cloudland; 641 Ann St; ⏲5pm-late Thu & Fri, noon-late Sat & Sun) Like stepping into a surreal cloud forest, this multilevel club has a huge plant-filled lobby with a retractable glass roof, a wall of water and wrought-iron birdcage-like nooks. Even if you're not a clubber, peek through the windows during the day: the interior design is astonishing!

Oh Hello CLUB
(Map p62; www.ohhello.com.au; 621 Ann St; ⏲9pm-5am Thu-Sat) Oh hello! Fancy seeing you here. This convivial club is perfect if you like the idea of clubbing but find the reality a bit deflating. It's unpretentious (you can wear a T-shirt), there's a great selection of craft beers, and the cool kids here don't think too highly of themselves.

Family CLUB, GAY
(Map p62; www.thefamily.com.au; 8 McLachlan St; ⏲9pm-5am Fri-Sun) One of Brisbane's biggest and best clubs, the music here is phenomenal, pumping through four levels with myriad dance floors, bars, funky themed booths and elite DJs from home and away. The 'Fluffy' gay dance party happens on Sundays.

Birdees CLUB
(Map p62; www.birdees.com.au; 608 Ann St; ⏲4pm-late Mon-Thu, noon-5am Fri & Sat, noon-late Sun) Part of the sprawling Bunk Backpackers complex, Birdees fills, predictably, with backpackers going berserk. Big fun. The Aviary room upstairs has comedy on Thursday nights.

Electric Playground CLUB
(Map p62; www.electricplayground.com.au; 27 Warner St; ⏲9pm-5am Fri & Sat) The 1906 foundation stone of this old church says 'To the glory of God', but the new signage says, 'It's all about the music'. If you're not sure which one to believe, join the line to get inside, where ungodly good times unwind late into Friday and Saturday nights.

Church CLUB
(Map p62; www.thechurchnightclub.com.au; 25 Warner St; ⏲9pm-5am Fri & Sat) Next door to Electric Playground.

Beat MegaClub CLUB, GAY
(Map p62; www.thebeatmegaclub.com.au; 677 Ann St; ⏲9pm-5am Mon & Tue, 8pm-5am Wed-Sun) Five rooms + seven bars + three chill-out areas + hard house/electro/retro/techno beats = the perfect place for dance junkies. It's big

with the gay and lesbian crowd, with regular drag performances.

Wickham Hotel GAY, PUB
(Map p62; www.thewickham.com.au; 308 Wickham St; 10am-late) Brisbane's most popular gay and lesbian venue, with rainbow flags, drag shows and blaring Gloria Gaynor.

New Farm & Around

Gertie's BAR
(Map p62; www.gerties.com.au; 699 Brunswick St, New Farm; 4pm-midnight Tue-Fri, 3pm-midnight Sat, 2pm-midnight Sun) A sophisticated New Farm affair, Gertie's always seems to have groups of good-looking city girls sipping cocktails inside the fold-back windows (...do you think management pays them to sit there?). But even without the eye-candy, Gertie's – a moodily-lit corner bar with old soul on the stereo and retro photos on the walls – is a great place for a low-key drink or a bowl of pasta and a glass of wine.

Bar Alto BAR
(Map p54; www.baralto.com.au; Brisbane Powerhouse, 119 Lamington St, New Farm; 11am-late Tue-Sun) Inside the arts-loving Powerhouse, this snappy upstairs bar/restaurant has an enormous balcony with chunky timber tables overlooking the river – a mighty fine vantage point any time of day.

Alibi Room BAR
(Map p62; www.thealibiroom.com.au; 720 Brunswick St, New Farm; 3.30pm-midnight Mon-Thu, noon-midnight Fri, 10am-midnight Sat & Sun;) A laid-back alternative to the Valley's chichi lounges, this quirky eat-drink spot draws an eclectic crowd most days, particularly on $2-taco Tuesday nights. Also on the cards are creative cocktails, a broad beer and wine menu, $10 meals (burgers, salads, schnitzels), free wi-fi, tasty snacks (plus breakfast all day) and breezy window seats fronting Brunswick St.

Breakfast Creek Hotel PUB
(Map p54; www.breakfastcreekhotel.com; 2 Kingsford Smith Dr, Albion; 10am-late) This historic

BRISBANE'S GALLERY SCENE

The Gallery of Modern Art (aka GOMA , p57) and the Queensland Art Gallery (p57) in South Bank steal the show, but Brisbane also has a growing array of smaller private galleries and exhibition spaces where you can get an eyeful of both the mainstream and the cutting-edge.

➡ **Institute of Modern Art** (IMA; www.ima.org.au; 420 Brunswick St, Fortitude Valley; 11am-5pm Tue, Wed, Fri, Sat, 11am-8pm Thu) FREE in the Judith Wright Centre of Contemporary Arts in Fortitude Valley is an excellent noncommercial gallery with an industrial vibe, and has regular showings by local names. With risqué, emerging and experimental art for grown-ups, it's GOMA's naughty little cousin.

➡ **Suzanne O'Connell Gallery** (Map p62; www.suzanneoconnell.com; 93 James St, New Farm; 11am-4pm Wed-Sat) FREE in New Farm specialises in Indigenous art, with brilliant works from artists all across Australia. Check the website for regular exhibition openings.

➡ **Milani** (Map p54; www.milanigallery.com.au; 54 Logan Rd, Woolloongabba; 11am-6pm Tue-Sat) FREE is a superb gallery with cutting-edge Aboriginal and confronting contemporary artwork. It's in an industrial area surrounded by car yards and hairdressing equipment suppliers – if it looks closed, just turn the door handle.

➡ The estimable **Philip Bacon Galleries** (Map p62; www.philipbacongalleries.com.au; 2 Arthur St, Fortitude Valley; 10am-5pm Tue-Sat) FREE has been around since 1974 and specialises in 19th-century and modern Australian paintings and sculpture.

➡ A fabulous warehouse space, **Fireworks Gallery** (Map p54; www.fireworksgallery.com.au; 52a Doggett St, Newstead; 10am-6pm Tue-Fri, 10am-4pm Sat) FREE specialises in both Aboriginal art and offbeat contemporary ceramics, sculpture, weavings and canvases. It's just a short stroll from James St in Fortitude Valley.

➡ Fronted by a strip of astroturf, the charcoal-grey **Jan Murphy Gallery** (Map p62; www.janmurphygallery.com.au; 486 Brunswick St, Fortitude Valley; 10am-5pm Tue-Sat) FREE is another leading exhibition space in the thick of Fortitude Valley's gallery district.

1889 pub is a Brisbane classic. Built in lavish French Renaissance style, it has various bars and dining areas (including a beer garden and an art-deco 'private bar' where you can drink beer tapped from a wooden keg). The stylish Substation No 41 bar serves cocktails and legendary steaks.

Petrie Terrace

Cabiria BAR

(Map p68; www.cabiria.com.au; 6 The Barracks, 61 Petrie Tce, Petrie Terrace; ⌚7-11am & noon-2.30pm Mon-Fri, 5pm-late Tue-Sat) Brisbane's old police barracks have been converted into a complex of quality bars and eateries, the pick of which is cool Cabiria. It's a skinny, dimly lit, moody room with big mirrors and shimmering racks of booze (35 different tequilas). Awesome New York–style sandwiches, too.

Normanby Hotel PUB

(Map p68; www.thenormanby.com.au; 1 Musgrave Rd; ⌚10am-3pm) A handsome 1889 redbrick pub on the end of Petrie Tce, with a beer garden under a vast fig tree. Goes nuts during 'Sunday Sessions' (boozy wakes for the weekend).

Caxton Hotel PUB

(Map p68; www.caxton.com.au; 38 Caxton St, Petrie Tce; ⌚11am-late) The Caxton St strip off Petrie Tce used to be hip, but it's become a trashy collection of hyped-up bars and cheap kebab joints. But if you're dying for a beer, the old yellow Caxton Hotel remains a reasonably grounded option, with mainstream music and non-stop rugby on the big screens.

Paddington

Lark BAR

(Map p77; ☎07-3369 1299; www.thelark.com.au; 1/267 Given Tce; ⌚4pm-midnight Mon & Wed-Fri, 1pm-midnight Sat, 1-10pm Sun) Inside an intimate, two-level brick terrace, Lark serves up artful drinks and inventive fusion fare. Tapas share plates ($11 to $28) involve hits like wagyu sliders and parmesan-crusted mushrooms, washed down with international wines, crafty beers and cocktails (go for the Cherry Bourbon Smash). What a lark!

Dowse Bar BAR, LIVE MUSIC

(Map p68; www.facebook.com/dowsebar; cnr Given Tce & Dowse St, Paddington; ⌚4pm-late Thu-Sun) Tucked underneath the bigger, flashier Iceworks bar, Dowse Bar is an intimate, retro-quirky booze room that brings a bit of bearded student/hipster vibe to Paddington. Live acoustic acts croon to the crowd, who sit on old couches amongst wacky lamps and murals.

Iceworks BAR

(Map p68; www.iceworks.com.au; cnr Given Tce & Dowse St, Paddington; ⌚11am-late) The former home of the Ithaca Iceworks, this splashy watering hole has a long, astroturf-fronted bar with $20 jugs of Pimms and an open-sided interior that packs crowds on weekends – particularly during Brisbane Broncos rugby games at Suncorp Stadium across the street. Dowse Bar downstairs is more subdued and arty.

Kangaroo Point & Around

Story Bridge Hotel PUB

(Map p58; www.storybridgehotel.com.au; 200 Main St, Kangaroo Point; ⌚9am-late) Beneath the bridge at Kangaroo Point, this beautiful 1886 pub and beer garden is perfect for a pint after a long day exploring. Live jazz on Sundays (from 3pm); lots of different drinking and eating areas.

Canvas WINE BAR

(Map p54; www.canvasclub.com.au; 16b Logan Rd, Woolloongabba; ⌚3pm-midnight Tue-Fri, 11.30am-late Sat & Sun) In the shadow of the Gabba cricket ground, Canvas is hip, compact and artsy. Step down off Logan St – an emerging eating/drinking/antiques hub – pause to ogle the kooky mural, then order a 'Guerilla Warfare' cocktail from the moustachioed bartender.

Chalk Hotel PUB

(Map p54; www.chalkhotel.com.au; 735 Stanley St, Woolloongabba; ⌚7am-late) This sprawling South Brisbane beer barn has something for everyone: seven bars, a beer garden, live bands on Fridays and Saturdays, rock trivia on Wednesdays, cheap burgers and pizzas and big-screen sports. And if you're a Brisbane Lions Aussie Rules football fan, you're on home turf.

Entertainment

Most big-ticket international bands have Brisbane on their radar, and the city's nightclubs regularly attract top-class DJs. Theatres, cinemas and other performing-arts venues are among Australia's biggest and best.

GAY & LESBIAN BRISBANE

Brisbane can't compete with the extravagent G&L scenes in Sydney and Melbourne, but what you'll find here is quality rather than quantity.

For current entertainment and events listings, interviews and articles, check out **Q News** (www.qnews.com.au) and **Queensland Pride** (www.gaynewsnetwork.com.au). Tune in to **Queer Radio** (www.4zzzfm.org.au; 9-11pm Wed), a radio show on 4ZZZ (aka FM102.1) – another source of Brisbane info. For lesbian news and views, **Dykes on Mykes** precedes it (7pm to 9pm).

Major events on the calendar include the **Queer Film Festival** (www.bqff.com.au) held in April at the Brisbane Powerhouse, which showcases gay, lesbian, bisexual and transgender films; and the Brisbane Pride Festival (p70), which happens in September. Pride attracts around 25,000 people every year and peaks during Pride Fair Day held at New Farm Park mid-festival.

Brisbane's most enduring/endearing G&L venue is the Wickham Hotel (p86) in Fortitude Valley, a classic old Victorian pub with good dance music, drag shows and dancers. The Wickham goes into hyperdrive for both the Brisbane Pride and Sydney Gay & Lesbian Mardi Gras festivals.

Other good options in the Valley include the gay-friendly clubs Beat MegaClub (p85) and Family (p85), the latter of which hosts 'Fluffy' on Sundays, Brisbane's biggest gay dance party. Closer to the city, the **Sportsman's Hotel** (Map p58; www.sportsmanhotel.com.au; 130 Leichhardt St; 1pm-late) is another perennially busy gay venue: a blue-collar, downtown, orange-brick pub with XXXX billboards, pool tables, drag shows and bar food.

Free entertainment street-press includes *Time Off* (www.timeoff.com.au) and *Scene* (www.scenemagazine.com.au). *Q News* (www.qnews.com.au) covers the gay and lesbian scene. The *Courier-Mail* (www.news.com.au/couriermail) newspaper also has daily arts and entertainment listings, or check the *Brisbane Times* (www.brisbanetimes.com.au).

Ticketek (Map p58; 13 28 49; www.ticketek.com.au; cnr Elizabeth & George Sts; 9am-5pm) is a central booking agency that handles major events, sports and performances. Try **Qtix** (13 62 46; www.qtix.com.au) for loftier arts performances.

Live Music

Brisbane's love affair with live music began long before three lanky lads from Redcliffe sang harmonies and called themselves the Bee Gees. In recent years successful acts, including Katie Noonan, Powderfinger and Pete Murray, have illustrated Brisbane's musical diversity and evolution. Cover charges start at around $5.

Lock 'n' Load LIVE MUSIC
(Map p68; www.locknloadbistro.com.au; 142 Boundary St, West End; 10am-late Mon-Fri, 7am-late Sat & Sun) This ebullient, woody, two-storey gastropub lures an upbeat crowd of music fans. Bands play the small front stage (jazz and originals). Catch a gig, then show up for breakfast the next morning (the grilled sardines go well with hangovers).

Hi-Fi LIVE MUSIC
(Map p68; www.thehifi.com.au; 125 Boundary St, West End) This mod, minimalist rock room has unobstructed sight lines and a great line-up of local and international talent (from the Gin Blossoms to Suicidal Tendencies). Retro Vinyl bar is out the front.

Zoo LIVE MUSIC
(Map p62; www.thezoo.com.au; 711 Ann St, Fortitude Valley; 7.30pm-late Wed-Sun) Going strong since 1992, the Zoo has surrendered a bit of musical territory to the Hi-Fi venue, but is still a grungy spot for rock, hip-hop, acoustic, reggae and electronic acts (lots of raw local talent).

Brisbane Jazz Club JAZZ
(Map p58; 07-3391 2006; www.brisbanejazzclub.com.au; 1 Annie St, Kangaroo Point; 6.30-11pm Thu-Sat, 5.30-9.30pm Sun) Straight out of the bayou, this tiny riverside jazz shack has been Brisbane's jazz beacon since 1972. Anyone who's anyone in the scene plays here when they're in town. Cover charge ranges from $12 to $20.

Riverstage LIVE MUSIC
(Map p58; www.brisbane.qld.gov.au/facilities-recreation/arts-and-culture/riverstage; 59 Gardens Point Rd) Riverstage is a fab outdoor arena on the southern tip of the downtown Brisbane peninsula. Big internationals like the Stone Roses and guitar-god Slash grace the stage.

X&Y Bar LIVE MUSIC, DJ
(Map p62; www.xandybar.com.au; 648 Ann St; ⌚9pm-5am Thu-Sat) This unpretentious music room attracts an eclectic crowd, courtesy of its nondiscriminatory door policy. On stage is a mix of live music (mostly local indie rock) and DJs, but regardless of who's playing it's always a cool spot for a beer.

Beetle Bar LIVE MUSIC
(Map p68; www.beetlebar.com.au; 350 Upper Roma St; ⌚7pm-late Thu-Sat) Usually full of boozy backpackers from the surrounding hostels, Beetle Bar is the spot for up-and-coming local and national alt-rock acts. Look for the reconfigured VW Beetle on the roof.

Tivoli MUSIC, COMEDY
(Map p54; www.thetivoli.net.au; 52 Costin St, Fortitude Valley) International notables (Nick Cave, Noel Gallagher) plus local success stories (Parkway Drive, The Cat Empire) regularly tread the boards at this elegant old art-deco stager built in 1917 (and tarted-up more recently). You're likely to catch some quality comedy here, too.

Brisbane Convention and Exhibition Centre CONCERT VENUE
(Map p58; www.bcec.com.au; cnr Merivale & Glenelg Sts, South Bank) When the big guns are in town they rock this 8000-seat auditorium in South Bank.

Cinemas

Palace Barracks CINEMA
(Map p68; www.palacecinemas.com.au; 61 Petrie Tce, Petrie Terrace; adult/child $17.50/13; ⌚10am-late) Near Roma St Station in the Barracks Centre, the plush, six screen Palace Barracks shows Hollywood and alternative fare, and has a bar.

Palace Centro CINEMA
(Map p62; www.palacecinemas.com.au; 39 James St, Fortitude Valley; adult/child $17.50/13; ⌚10am-late) Palace Centro on James St screens art-house films and has a French film festival in March/April.

Dendy Cinema CINEMA
(www.dendy.com.au; Portside Wharf, 39 Hercules St, Hamilton; tickets $17.50; ⌚9am-late) Shows mainstream fare at Portside Wharf (p82), a short ferry downstream from New Farm.

South Bank Cinema CINEMA
(Map p58; www.cineplex.com.au; cnr Grey & Ernest Sts, South Bank; adult/child from $9/5; ⌚10am-late) The cheapest complex for mainstream releases: wade through a sea of popcorn aromas and teenagers.

Event Cinemas CINEMA
(Map p58; www.eventcinemas.com.au; Level 3, Myer Centre, Elizabeth St; adult/child $17/12.50; ⌚10am-late) On Queen St Mall; shows mainstream blockbusters.

Performing Arts & Comedy

Brisbane Powerhouse PERFORMING ARTS
(Map p54; www.brisbanepowerhouse.org; 119 Lamington St, New Farm) Nationally and internationally acclaimed theatre, music, comedy, dance... There are loads of happenings at the Powerhouse – many free – and the venue, with its cool bar-restaurants, enjoys

DON'T MISS

OUTDOOR CINEMA

One of the best ways to spend a warm summer night in Brisbane is with a picnic basket and some friends at an outdoor cinema. **Moonlight Cinema** (Map p54; www.moonlight.com.au; Brisbane Powerhouse, 119 Lamington Rd, New Farm; adult/child $16/12; ⌚7pm Wed-Sun) runs between December and February at New Farm Park near the Brisbane Powerhouse. New releases, indies and cult classics all get a screening from Wednesday to Sunday, flickering into life around 7pm. Tickets go on sale in the first week of November.

A parallel option is **Ben & Jerry's Openair Cinemas** (Map p58; www.openaircinemas.com.au; Cultural Forecourt, South Bank Parklands, South Bank; adult/child online $17/12, at the gate $22/17; ⌚from 6pm Mon-Fri, from 4pm Sat & Sun) in South Bank, where from mid-October to late November you can watch big-screen classics under the stars (or clouds). Hire a beanbag or bring a picnic rug.

a gorgeous setting overlooking the Brisbane River.

Judith Wright Centre of Contemporary Arts PERFORMING ARTS
(Map p62; www.judithwrightcentre.com; 420 Brunswick St, Fortitude Valley;) A medium-sized creative space (300 seats max) for cutting-edge performances: contemporary dance and world music, Indigenous theatre, circus and visual arts.

Metro Arts Centre THEATRE
(Map p58; www.metroarts.com.au; Level 2, 109 Edward St) This artsy downtown venue hosts community theatre, local dramatic pieces, dance and art shows. It's an effervescent spot for a taste of Brisbane's creative talent, be it offbeat, quirky, fringe, progressive or just downright weird. Artists and performers give free evening talks on the first Friday of every month.

Queensland Performing Arts Centre PERFORMING ARTS
(QPAC; Map p58; www.qpac.com.au; Queensland Cultural Centre, cnr Grey & Melbourne Sts, South Bank; box office 9am-8.30pm Mon-Sat) Brisbane's main high-arts performance centre comprises three venues and features concerts, plays, dance and performances of all genres: anything from flamenco to the Australian Ballet and *West Side Story* revivals.

QUT Gardens Theatre THEATRE
(Map p58; www.gardenstheatre.qut.edu.au; 2 George St, Queensland University of Technology; box office 10am-4pm) On the university campus in the city, but with productions that are anything but amateur. Expect to see Australia's best professional stage actors.

Queensland Conservatorium OPERA, LIVE MUSIC
(Map p58; www.griffith.edu.au/music/queensland-conservatorium; 140 Grey St, South Bank; box office 7am-10pm Mon-Fri, 8am-6pm Sat & Sun) Part of Griffith University, the Conservatorium hosts opera, as well as touring artists playing classical, jazz, rock and world music.

Brisbane Arts Theatre THEATRE
(Map p68; www.artstheatre.com.au; 210 Petrie Tce, Petrie Terrace) Intimate community theatre built in 1936; catch improvisation troupes, children's theatre or classic plays.

Paddo Tavern COMEDY
(Map p77; www.standup.com.au; 186 Given Tce, Paddington; 10am-late) If a carwash married its supermarket cousin, their first-born would probably look like this ugly Paddington pub, which has incongruously adopted a Wild West theme inside (stetsons, saddle seats, old rifles on the wall). But it's one of the best places in Brisbane to see stand-up comedy: check the website for listings.

Sport

Like most other Australians, Brisbanites are sports-mad. You can catch some interstate or international cricket at the **Gabba** (Brisbane Cricket Ground; Map p54; www.thegabba.org.au; 411 Vulture St, Woolloongabba), south of Kangaroo Point. The cricket season runs from October to March: if you're new to the game, try and get along to a Twenty20 match – cricket at its most explosive.

The Gabba is also a home ground for the Brisbane Lions, an **Australian Football League** (AFL; www.afl.com.au) team which dominated the league in the early 2000s (lately, not so much). Watch them in action, often at night under lights, between March and September.

Rugby league is also a massive spectator sport in Brizzy. The Brisbane Broncos, part of the **National Rugby League** (NRL; www.nrl.com.au) competition, play home games over winter at **Suncorp Stadium** (Map p68; www.suncorpstadium.com.au; 40 Castlemaine St, Milton) in Milton (between Petrie Terrace and Paddington). In rugby union, the Queensland Reds in the Super Rugby comp and the national Wallabies team also play at Suncorp and have strong followings.

Also calling Suncorp home are the Queensland Roar football (soccer) team, part of the **A-League** (www.aleague.com.au), attracting fat crowds in recent years. The domestic football season lasts from August to February.

Shopping

Brisbane is home to some fabulous riverside markets, eye-catching boutiques and galleries, plus one-of-a-kind shops – particularly around Fortitude Valley and Paddington – selling everything from indie fashions to Indigenous artwork, vintage apparel, new and used books and rare vinyl. **Queen St Mall** and the **Myer Centre** in the CBD house big chain stores, upmarket outlets and the obligatory touristy trash.

City Centre

Archives Fine Books BOOKS
(Map p58; www.facebook.com/archivesfinebooks; 40 Charlotte St; ⏲10am-7pm Mon-Fri, 9am-5pm Sat, 11am-5pm Sun) You could get lost in here for hours: look out for rickety bookshelves, squeaky floorboards and upwards of half-a-million second-hand books.

Record Exchange MUSIC
(Map p58; www.recordexchange.com.au; Level 1, 65 Adelaide St; ⏲9am-5pm) This warren-like upstairs shop is home to an astounding collection of vinyl, CDs, DVDs, posters and other rock memorabilia. 'Brisbane's most interesting shop' (self-professed).

Dogstar CLOTHING
(Map p58; www.dogstar.com.au; 188 Edward St; ⏲10am-5.30pm Mon-Thu, 10am-9pm Fri, 10am-5pm Sat, 11am-4pm Sun) There's more than a touch of Japanese style evident at this hip city shop. Beautiful fabrics and fine details feature prominently in skirts, jackets, wraps, tunics, jewellery and retro winter knits.

Australian Geographic SOUVENIRS, GIFTS
(Map p58; www.australiangeographic.com.au; Level 2, Myer Centre, Queen St Mall; ⏲9am-5.30pm Mon-Thu, 9am-9pm Fri, 9am-5pm Sat, 10am-5pm Sun) Stocks everything from books and calendars on Australian flora and fauna to glow-in-the-dark dinosaurs and telescopes. A good one for the kids.

Folio Books BOOKS
(Map p58; www.foliobooks.com.au; 80 Albert St; ⏲8.30am-6pm Mon-Thu, to 8pm Fri, to 5.15pm Sat, 7.30am-5pm Sun) A small downtown book nook selling eclectic reads. Opens early to entice the business crowd on the way to work.

World Wide Maps & Globes BOOKS
(Map p58; www.worldwidemaps.com.au; Shop 30, Anzac Sq Arcade, 267 Edward St; ⏲9am-6pm Mon-Thu, 9am-8pm Fri, 10am-4pm Sat) A good assortment of maps and travel guides (including camping and hiking guides).

RM Williams CLOTHING
(Map p58; www.rmwilliams.com.au; Level 1, Myer Centre, Queen St Mall; ⏲9am-5.30pm Mon-Thu, 9am-9pm Fri, 9am-5pm Sat, 10am-5pm Sun) An iconic manufacturer of Aussie bush/farm gear, RM Williams stocks natty leather

MARKET-LOVERS' GUIDE TO BRISBANE

Jan Powers Farmers Market (Map p54; www.janpowersfarmersmarkets.com.au; Brisbane Powerhouse, 119 Lamington St, New Farm; ⏲6am-noon 2nd & 4th Sat of month) Fancy some purple heirloom carrots or blue bananas? This fab farmers market, with more than 120 stalls, coughs up some unusual produce. Also great for more predictably coloured flowers, cheeses, coffees and fish. The CityCat ferry takes you straight there.

Davies Park Market (Map p68; www.daviesparkmarket.com.au; Davies Park, West End; ⏲6am-2pm Sat) Under a grove of huge Moreton Bay fig trees in the West End, this hippie riverside market features organic foods, gourmet breakfasts, herbs and flowers, bric-a-brac and buskers.

Brisbane Valley Markets (Map p62; www.brisbane-markets.com.au/brisbane-valley-markets.html; Brunswick St & Duncan St Malls, Fortitude Valley; ⏲8am-4pm Sat, 9am-4pm Sun) These colourful markets fill the Brunswick St Mall and the Duncan St (Chinatown) Mall in Fortitude Valley with a diverse collection of crafts, clothes, books, records, food stalls and miscellaneous works by budding designers.

Brisbane Riverside Markets (Map p58; www.brisbane-markets.com.au/brisbane-riverside-markets.html; Eagle St Pier; ⏲7am-4pm Sun) Set along the pedestrian lanes hugging the river, the Sunday Riverside Markets have dozens of stalls selling glassware, handicrafts, art, juices, snacks and live tunes. The CityCat ferry stop is just a couple of inches away.

South Bank Lifestyle Markets (Map p58; www.southbankmarket.com.au; Stanley St Plaza; ⏲5-10pm Fri, 10am-5pm Sat, 9am-5pm Sun) It's a bit touristy, but this 80-stall riverside market has a great range of clothing, craft, art, hand-made goods and souvenirs (just ignore the lacquered boomerangs).

boots, hats, oilskin jackets, belts, jumpers and flannelette shirts: the kind of stuff your rich agricultural uncle would wear when he makes the trip into town.

West End

★Egg Records MUSIC

(Map p68; www.eggrecords.com.au; 79 Vulture St; ⌚9.30am-5.30pm Mon-Fri, 9.30am-4pm Sat & Sun) This well-organized collection of LPs, CDs and fantastically kitsch memorabilia is a must-see for anyone with even the slightest hint of 'collector' in their DNA. Loads of second-hand vinyl and CDs, plus heavy-metal T-shirts and a cavalcade of plasticky treasures featuring Doctor Who, Star Wars characters, Evel Knievel...awesome!

Avid Reader BOOKS

(Map p68; www.avidreader.com.au; 193 Boundary St; ⌚8.30am-8.30pm Mon-Fri, 8.30am-6pm Sat, 8.30am-5pm Sun) Diverse pages, a little cafe in the corner and frequent readings and bookish events: a real West End cultural hub.

South Bank

Title BOOKS

(Map p58; www.titlespace.com; 1/133 Grey St; ⌚10am-6pm Mon-Sat, 10am-4pm Sun) Offbeat and alternative art, music, photography and cinema books, plus vinyl, CDs and DVDs – a quality dose of subversive rebelliousness (just what South Bank needs!). Pick up that Woody Guthrie 100th-birthday Centennial Collection you've had your eye on. There's another branch in **Fortitude Valley** (Map p62; 60 James St; ⌚10am-6pm Mon-Sat, 10am-4pm Sun).

Fortitude Valley

★in.cube8r gallery GIFTS, GALLERY

(Map p62; www.incube8r.com.au; 648 Brunswick St; ⌚10am-5pm Tue & Wed, 11am-6pm Thu & Fri, 10am-6pm Sat, 11am-3pm Sun) Supporting local talent, this artists' co-op features the work of 90 creative types, all of whom rent a wedge of space here to display and sell their wares. Prints, kids' clothes, egg-carton lampshades, driftwood jewellery, ceramics, canvases, glasswear, earrings made of Lego – it's all here!

Trash Monkey CLOTHING, ACCESSORIES

(Map p62; www.trashmonkey.com.au; 9/8 Duncan St; ⌚10am-7pm Mon-Wed, 10am-9pm Thu-Sat, 10am-5pm Sun) Countercultural mayhem in the Valley! Goths, skaters, punks, alt-rockers and rockabilly rebels head here for their shoes, T-shirts, caps, nylon stockings, dress-up gear, socks, belts and beanies, much of which is spangled with tattoo-centric designs. Pick up a new pair of leopard-skin brothel creepers for your audition with the Stray Cats.

Maiocchi CLOTHING, GIFTS

(Map p62; www.maiocchi.com.au; 715 Ann St; ⌚10am-5pm Mon-Fri, 9.30am-5pm Sat, 11am-4pm Sun) This is a great little store for individual pieces without the price tags of its glamorous neighbours. Also stocks quirky lamps, shoes, bags, clocks, stuffed toys, jewellery...

Blonde Venus CLOTHING

(Map p62; www.blondevenus.com.au; Shop 3, 181 Robertson St; ⌚10am-6pm Mon-Sat, 11am-4.30pm Sun) One of the top boutiques in Brisbane, Blonde Venus has been around for 20-plus years, stocking a well-curated selection of both indie and couture labels.

Butter Beats MUSIC

(Map p62; www.butterbeatsrecordstore.com; 11/8 Duncan St; ⌚10.30am-6pm Mon-Fri, 10am-5pm Sat, noon-5pm Sun) Rare and collectible records in the Valley. If they don't have it, they'll find it for you. Also stocks street-art supplies if you're in the mood for some tagging.

Emporium SHOPPING CENTRE

(Map p62; www.emporium.com.au; 1000 Ann St; ⌚shops 9am-5pm) This manufactured, corporate retail and eating precinct at the bottom end of Ann St has about 35 upmarket boutiques and eateries. Grab some noodles at Wagamama (p81), bunk down in fine style at the Emporium (p74) hotel, or lose your traveller's locks at Toni & Guy.

Paddington

Retro Metro CLOTHING

(Map p77; 27 Latrobe Tce; ⌚10am-5pm Mon-Sat, 11am-4pm Sun) A highlight of Paddington's boutique-lined main street, Retro Metro stocks a brilliant selection of vintage gear: cowboy boots, suits, cocktail dresses, handbags, jewellery, vinyl, '80s rock T-shirts, sunglasses, vases, ashtrays and other interesting knick-knackery. It has a clearance shop (actually a garage) down the street at 297 Given Tce.

Paddington Antique Centre ANTIQUES
(Map p77; www.paddingtonantiquecentre.com.au; 167 Latrobe Tce; ⌚10am-5pm) The city's biggest antique emporium is inside a 1929 theatre, with over 50 dealers selling all manner of historic treasure/trash: clothes, jewellery, dolls, books, '60s Hawaiian shirts, lamps, musical instruments, toys, WWII German helmets...

Information

EMERGENCY

Ambulance, Fire, Police (☎000) Brisbane's police HQ is at 200 Roma St in the city. There's another 24-hour station at the corner of Wickham St and Brookes St in Fortitude Valley.

Lifeline (☎13 11 14; www.lifeline.org.au) Crisis counselling.

RACQ (☎13 11 11; www.racq.com.au) Automotive roadside assistance.

INTERNET ACCESS

Wireless internet access is widely available at many hotels, cafes and hostels (including Global Gossip outlets at several of the big backpackers), though the concept of *free* wi-fi hasn't really caught on everywhere.

Brisbane Square Library (www.brisbane.qld.gov.au/; 266 George St; ⌚9am-6pm Mon-Thu, 9am-7pm Fri, 10am-3pm Sat & Sun) Free internet terminals and wi-fi access.

IYSC (Level 1, 150 Adelaide St; ⌚8.30am-6.30pm Mon-Fri, 10am-5pm Sat) Cheap downtown terminals.

State Library of Queensland (www.slq.qld.gov.au; Stanley Pl, South Bank; ⌚10am-8pm Mon-Thu, 10am-5pm Fri-Sun) Quick 20-minute terminals or free wi-fi.

MEDICAL SERVICES

Brisbane Sexual Health Clinic (☎07-3837 5611; www.health.qld.gov.au/sexhealth/help/brisbane.asp; Level 1, 270 Roma St; ⌚8.15am-5pm Mon, Tue, Thu & Fri, 8.15am-noon Wed) Free nether-region check-ups.

CBD Medical Centre (☎07-3211 3611; www.cbdmedical.com.au; Level 1, 245 Albert St; ⌚7.30am-7pm Mon-Fri, 8.30am-5pm Sat, 9.30am-4pm Sun) General medical services and vaccinations.

Pharmacy on the Mall (☎07-3221 4585; www.pharmacies.com.au/pharmacy-on-the-mall; 141 Queen St; ⌚7am-9pm Mon-Thu, 7am-9.30pm Fri, 8am-9pm Sat, 8.30am-6pm Sun)

Queensland Statewide Sexual Assault Helpline (☎1800 010 120; www.health.qld.gov.au/sexualassault)

Royal Brisbane & Women's Hospital (☎07-3636 8111; www.health.qld.gov.au/rbwh; cnr Butterfield St & Bowen Bridge Rd, Herston) Has a 24-hour casualty ward.

Travellers' Medical & Vaccination Centre (TMVC; ☎07-3815 6900; www.traveldoctor.com.au; 75a Astor Tce, Spring Hill; ⌚8.30am-5pm Mon, Thu & Fri, 8.30am-8pm Tue, 9am-5pm Wed, 8.30am-noon Sat) Travellers' medical services.

MONEY

There are foreign-exchange bureaus at Brisbane Airport's domestic and international terminals, as well as ATMs that take most international credit cards. For after-hours foreign exchange, the tellers in the Treasury Casino are there 24 hours a day. ATMs are abundant throughout Brisbane.

American Express (☎1300 139 060; www.americanexpress.com; 260 Queen St; ⌚8.30am-4pm Mon-Thu, 9am-5pm Fri) Inside the Westpac bank.

Travelex (☎07-3210 6325; www.travelex.com.au; Shop 149F, Myer Centre, Queen St Mall; ⌚9am-5pm Mon-Thu & Sat, 9am-8pm Fri, 10am-4pm Sun) Money exchange.

POST

Main Post Office (GPO; Map p58; www.auspost.com.au; 261 Queen St; ⌚7am-6pm Mon-Fri, 10am-1.30pm Sat)

TOURIST INFORMATION

BCC Customer Centre (Map p58; ☎07-3407 2861; www.brisbane.qld.gov.au; 266 George St; ⌚9am-5pm Mon-Fri) This Brisbane City Council centre provides info on disabled access around Brisbane. In the same building as the Brisbane Square Library.

BCC Mobility Centre (Map p58; ☎07-3027 5471; www.brisbane.qld.gov.au; City Hall, King George Sq; ⌚9am-5pm Mon-Fri, 10am-5pm Sat & Sun) Disabled access information and free wheelchair and pram hire (book in advance).

Brisbane Visitor Information Centre (Map p58; ☎07-3006 6290; www.visitbrisbane.com.au; Queen St Mall; ⌚9am-5.30pm Mon-Thu, 9am-7pm Fri, 9am-5pm Sat, 10am-5pm Sun) Located between Edward and Albert Sts. One-stop info counter for all things Brisbane.

South Bank Visitor Information Centre (Map p58; www.visitsouthbank.com.au; Stanley St Plaza, South Bank; ⌚9am-5pm) The low-down on South Bank, plus tours, accommodation and transport bookings and tickets to entertainment events.

Getting There & Away

The Brisbane Transit Centre – which incorporates Roma St Station in the same complex – is about 500m northwest of the city centre, and is the main terminus and booking point for all long-distance buses and trains, as well as Citytrain services. Central Station is also an important hub for trains.

AIR

Brisbane Airport (www.bne.com.au) is about 16km northeast of the city centre at Eagle Farm. It has separate international and domestic terminals about 2km apart, linked by the Airtrain (p95), which runs every 15 to 30 minutes from 5.45am to 10pm (between terminals per person $5). It's a busy international arrival and departure point with frequent flights to Asia, Europe, the Pacific islands, North America and New Zealand.

Several airlines link Brisbane with the rest of the country. Typical destinations and flight times: Sydney (1½ hours), Melbourne (2½ hours), Adelaide (2½ hours), Canberra (two hours), Hobart (four hours), Perth (five hours), Darwin (four hours). The main players:

Qantas (www.qantas.com.au)
Virgin Australia (p291)
Jetstar (www.jetstar.com.au)
Tiger Airways (www.tigerairways.com.au)

Qantas, Virgin Australia and Jetstar all fly to towns and cities within Queensland, especially the more popular coastal destinations and the Whitsunday Islands. Tiger Airways flies between Brisbane and Melbourne and Sydney.

Skytrans (p291) is a smaller airline flying between Brisbane and regional hubs including Toowoomba, Charleville and Mt Isa.

BUS

Brisbane's main bus terminus and booking office for long-distance buses is the **Brisbane Transit Centre** (Map p58; www.brisbanetransitcentre.com.au; Roma St). Booking desks for **Greyhound** (www.greyhound.com.au) and **Premier Motor Service** (www.premierms.com.au) are here.

If you're up for a long haul, buses run between Brisbane and Sydney ($185, 16 to 18 hours), Melbourne ($210, 40 hours), Adelaide ($395, 45 to 55 hours) and Darwin ($585, 49 hours), although it's probably going to be just as affordable to fly (if not cheaper...and a LOT quicker and easier).

Heading south to Byron Bay, there are four daily buses from Brisbane airport ($52, three hours) and the Brisbane Transit Centre ($38) on **Byron Easy Bus** (www.byroneasybus.com.au).

North to Cairns, approximate fares and journey times to places along the coast are as follows:

DESTINATION	ONE-WAY FARE	DURATION
Cairns	$305	30hr
Hervey Bay	$69	5½hr
Noosa	$22	2½hr
Mackay	$215	17½hr
Rockhampton	$160	11½hr
Townsville	$265	23hr

Airport to the Gold Coast & Beyond

Con-x-ion (p95) operates direct shuttle bus services from Brisbane Airport to the Gold Coast ($49). Services meet every major flight and will drop you anywhere on the Gold Coast.

Airport to the Sunshine Coast

Sun-Air Bus Service (www.sunair.com.au) is one of several operators with direct services from Brisbane Airport to the Sunshine Coast. Con-x-ion (p95) plies the same route. One-way fares start at around $40 (to the southern Sunshine Coast areas; more expensive the further north you go).

CAR & MOTORCYCLE

Brisbane has five major motorways (M1 to M5) run by **Queensland Motorways** (☎13 33 31; www.qldmotorways.com.au). If you're just passing through from north to south or south to north, take the Gateway Motorway (M1), which bypasses the city centre ($4.13 toll at the time of writing; see the website for payment options, in advance or retrospectively).

Car Rental

The major car-rental companies – **Avis** (www.avis.com.au), **Budget** (www.budget.com.au), **Europcar** (www.europcar.com.au), **Hertz** (www.hertz.com.au), **Thrifty** (www.thrifty.com.au) – have offices at Brisbane Airport and in the city.

Smaller rental companies with branches near the airport (and shuttles to get you to/from there) include:

Ace Rental Cars (☎1800 620 408; www.acerentals.com.au; 330 Nudgee Rd, Hendra)
Apex Car Rentals (☎1800 121 029; www.apexrentacar.com.au; 400 Nudgee Rd, Hendra)
East Coast Car Rentals (☎1800 028 881; www.eastcoastcarrentals.com.au; 504 Nudgee Rd, Hendra)

TRAIN

Brisbane's main station for long-distance trains is Roma St Station (essentially the same complex as the Brisbane Transit Centre). For reservations and information contact the **Queensland Rail Travel Centre** (Map p58; ☎1800 872 467; www.queenslandrail.com.au; Concourse Level, 305 Edward St; ⊙8am-5pm Mon-Fri) at Central Station. See p323 for info on long-distance routes and services ex-Brisbane, including the following:

NSW TrainLink Brisbane to Sydney

Spirit of the Outback Brisbane to Longreach via Rockhampton

Spirit of Queensland Brisbane to Cairns

Sunlander Brisbane to Cairns via Townsville

Tilt Train Brisbane to Cairns

Westlander Brisbane to Charleville.

Getting Around

TO/FROM THE AIRPORT

Airtrain (www.airtrain.com.au) trains runs every 15 to 30 minutes from 5.45am to 10pm from Brisbane Airport to Fortitude Valley, Central Station, Roma St Station (Brisbane Transit Centre) and other key destinations (one-way/return $16/30). There are also half-hourly services to the airport from Gold Coast Citytrain stops (one-way $37).

If you prefer door-to-door service, **Con-x-ion Airport Transfers** (www.con-x-ion.com) runs regular shuttle buses between the airport and CBD hotels (one-way/return $20/36); it also connects Brisbane Airport to Gold Coast hotels (one-way/return $49/92).

A taxi into the centre from the airport will cost $35 to $45.

CAR & MOTORCYCLE

There is ticketed two-hour parking on many streets in the CBD and the inner suburbs. Heed the signs: Brisbane's parking inspectors can be ruthless. Parking is cheaper around South Bank and the West End than in the city centre, but is free in the CBD during the evening.

A GPS unit could be your best friend: Brisbane's streets are organically laid-out and convoluted.

PUBLIC TRANSPORT

Brisbane's excellent public-transport network – bus, train and ferry – is run by **TransLink** (☎13 12 30; www.translink.com.au). There's a Translink Transit Information Centre at Central Station (on the corner of Edward St and Ann St), and another one at Roma St Station (Brisbane Transit Centre). The Brisbane Visitor Information Centre (p93) can also help with public transport info.

Fares Buses, trains and ferries operate on a zone system: most of the inner-city suburbs are in Zone 1, which translates into a single fare of $5.20/2.60 per adult/child. If travelling into Zone 2, tickets are $6.10/3.10. A Go Card will save you some money.

NightLink In addition to the services described in the following sections, there are also dedicated nocturnal NightLink bus, train and fixed-rate taxi services from the city and Fortitude Valley: see www.translink.com.au for details.

Boat

In addition to the fast CityCat (p67) services, Translink runs Cross River Ferries, connecting Kangaroo Point with the CBD, and New Farm Park with Norman Park on the adjacent shore (and also Teneriffe and Bulimba further north).

Free (yes free!) CityHopper Ferries zigzag back and forth across the water between North Quay, South Bank, the CBD, Kangaroo Point and Sydney St in New Farm. These additional services start around 6am and run till about 11pm. For Cross River Ferries, fares/zones apply as per all other Brisbane transport.

Bus

Translink runs Brisbane's bus services, including the free City Loop and Spring Hill Loop bus services that circle the CBD and Spring Hill, stopping at key spots like QUT, Queen Street Mall, City Botanic Gardens, Central Station and Roma Street Parkland. The loop buses run every 10 minutes on weekdays between 7am and 6pm.

The main stops for local buses are the underground **Queen St Bus Station** (Map p58) and **King George Sq Bus Station** (Map p58). You can also pick up many buses from the stops along Adelaide St, between George and Edward Sts.

Buses generally run every 10 to 30 minutes Monday to Friday, from 5am till about 11pm, and with the same frequency on Saturday morning (starting at 6am). Services are less frequent at other times, and cease at 9pm Sunday and at midnight on other days. CityGlider and BUZ services are high-frequency services along busy routes.

Train

TransLink's fast Citytrain network has six main lines, which run as far north as Gympie on the Sunshine Coast and as far south as Varsity Lakes on the Gold Coast. All trains go through Roma St Station, Central Station and Fortitude

GO CARD

If you plan to use public transport for more than a few trips, you'll save money by purchasing a **Go Card** (starting balance $5). Purchase the card, add credit and then use it on city buses, trains and ferries, and you'll save over 30% off individual fares. Go Cards are sold (and can be recharged) at transit stations and newsagents, or by phone or online. See www.translink.com.au/tickets-and-fares/go-card for details.

Valley Station; there's also a handy South Bank Station.

The Airtrain service integrates with the Citytrain network in the CBD and along the Gold Coast line.

Trains run from around 4.30am, with the last train on each line leaving Central Station between 11.30pm and midnight. On Sunday the last trains run at around 10pm.

TAXI

In the city there are taxi ranks at Roma St Station and at the top end of Edward St, by the junction with Adelaide St. You might have a tough time hailing one late at night in Fortitude Valley: there's a rank near the corner of Brunswick St and Ann St, but expect long queues.

Black & White (☎13 32 22; www.blackandwhitecabs.com.au)

Yellow Cab Co (☎13 19 24; www.yellowcab.com.au)

AROUND BRISBANE

Redcliffe

POP 51,180

The site of Queensland's first European settlement, the Redcliffe Peninsula, jutting into Moreton Bay about 35km north of Brisbane, talks up its historical credentials. There's not a whole lot of 'ye olde' stuff to see here, however, with the local focus squarely on maintaining a relaxed pace of life: a laid-back, beachy suburban vibe permeates the shoreline and backstreets. In the family vein, the area has plenty of unpolished fish-and-chip joints and calm beaches that are right up kids' alleys.

Redcliffe is also the childhood home of the brothers Gibb – Barry, Robin and Maurice – better known as the Bee Gees. Win friends and influence people by humming *Stayin' Alive* as you strut up and down Redcliffe Pde.

Sights & Activities

If you have a bike, a pedestrian/cycle path hugs the peninsula's shore from Scarborough in the north to Redcliffe Point about half-way up the coastline. It's a scenic way to check out the area, and there are regular sets of stairs up the escarpment to the shops and cafes along the esplanade.

On the way you can stretch your legs on the sizeable **Redcliffe Jetty**, which has had several makeovers since its beginnings in 1885. South of the jetty is **Suttons Beach Lagoon**, a free artificial swim-spot with various pools, a playground, barbecues and fake lawns and palm-studded atolls (brilliant for families). Further south again, at the base of the peninsula on Clontarf Beach, staff from the Redcliffe Visitor Information Centre feed the voracious local **pelicans** every day at 10am.

Redcliffe Historical Museum MUSEUM
(www.moretonbay.qld.gov.au/culturalheart; 75 Anzac Ave, Redcliffe; ⏰10am-4pm Tue-Sun) FREE Inside a converted church, the spick-and-span Redcliffe Historical Museum details the peninsula's history through information boards, artefacts and a series of personal accounts from locals. If we were curating, we'd aim for a stronger representation of local Ningy Ningy Indigenous culture and history, and more info on the Bee Gees (c'mon, everybody loves the Bee Gees!).

Brisbane Whale Watching WHALE WATCHING
(☎07-3880 0477; www.brisbanewhalewatching.com.au; adult/child incl lunch $135/95) From July to October, Brisbane Whale Watching corrals passengers onto a high-speed catamaran and whizzes them out to see humpback whales as they pass by on their annual migration. Trips depart Redcliffe Jetty.

Dolphin Wild ADVENTURE TOUR
(☎07-3880 4444; www.dolphinwild.com.au; adult/child/family incl lunch $125/75/325, snorkelling tour per adult/child additional $20/10) For a scenic trip around Moreton Bay, sign up for a one-day Moreton Island cruise with Dolphin Wild. Tours include boating around the bay, stopping at Moreton Island for snorkelling at the Tangalooma wrecks, lunch and a bit of beach time. Oh, and some dolphins! Tours depart Newport Marina in Scarborough.

Floatin' Fun KAYAKING
(☎0447 136 647; www.floatinfun.com.au; Scarborough Beach, off Landsborough Ave, Scarborough; hire per 30min/1hr/2hr $15/25/35; ⏰6am-3pm Sat & Sun) Hire a kayak, stand-up paddle board or pedal boat and splash around in the sea off the beach at Scarborough.

Kitepower Australia KITE-SURFING
(☎07-3284 1186; www.kitepower.com.au; 146 Hornibrook Esp, Clontarf; ⏰9am-5pm) If you're feeling adventurous, sign up for an adrenalin-pumping kite-surfing lesson with these

guys. A two-hour session is $200; if your biceps can take it, six hours is $500.

Sleeping & Eating

Oaks Mon Komo Redcliffe HOTEL **$$**
(07-3283 9300; www.oakshotelsresorts.com/monkomo; 99 Marine Pde, Redcliffe; d from $140, 1-/2-/3-bedroom apt from $185/250/300;) Most accommodation around Redcliffe is a little 'daggy', to use an Australianism. But the brand-spankin' new, multi-storey Mon Komo remedies this with stylish hotel rooms and apartments and a brilliant dining/drinking terrace out the front, across the road from Suttons Beach. The best option on the peninsula by many a mile.

Suttons Beach Apartments APARTMENT **$$**
(07-3284 9141; www.redcliffefurnishedapartments.com.au; 1 Sydney St, Redcliffe; 1-/2-bedroom apt from $125/190;) This outfit offers a studio-style one-bedroom apartment and a two-bedroom apartment, next to each other in a high-rise block not far back from Suttons Beach. Both have a balcony, barbecue, leather lounges and mod-minimal decor; the two-bedroom unit sleeps five. Cheaper for stays of seven nights or more (if you're really in the mood to stay in one place and unwind for a week).

Morgans SEAFOOD **$$**
(07-3203 5744; www.morgansseafood.com.au; Bird O'Passage Pde, Scarborough; takeaway $8-18, mains $31-50; takeaway 10am-7.30pm Mon-Thu, 10am-8pm Fri & Sat, 9.30am-7.30pm Sun; restaurant noon-2.30pm Wed-Fri & Sun, 5.30-8pm Wed & Fri, 6-8pm Thu, noon-8pm Sat) A sprawling seafood empire on the northern side of the peninsula, Morgans comprises a swish seafood restaurant, a sushi bar, fish market and seafood takeaway. If you want the full splurge, the award-winning restaurant with verandah overlooking the marina is for you; otherwise line up at the takeaway and chow down with the healthy-looking seagulls at the outdoor tables.

Reef Point Café CAFE **$$**
(www.reefpoint.com.au; Reef Point Esp, Scarborough; mains $16-23; 7am-4pm) Next to the caravan park in Scarborough on the northern fringe of the peninsula, this open-sided cafe does wraps, salads, pies, burgers, cooked breakfasts and frittatas, plus a passable espresso. Expect a little deep-fry aroma if it's windy and the fold-up walls are down.

Information

Redcliffe Visitor Information Centre (1800 659 500; www.moretonbay.qld.gov.au; Pelican Park, Hornibrook Esp, Clontarf; 9am-4pm) At the base of the peninsula on the Brisbane side. There's another smaller Redcliffe branch (07-3283 3577; Redcliffe Jetty, Redcliffe Pde, Redcliffe; 9am-4pm) also.

Getting There & Around

Translink (13 12 30; www.translink.com.au) buses 310, 315, 680 and 690 service the Redcliffe area, including Scarborough, from Brisbane ($9.50, one hour). You can also do a train-bus combo, catching a train from Central Station to Sandgate station then bussing it.

Some vehicle ferries to Moreton Island leave from Scarborough at the northern tip of the headland.

Manly & St Helena Island

POP 4220

Just a few kilometres south of the mouth of the Brisbane River, seaside **Manly** has a busy marina that makes a good base for trips out onto Moreton Bay. Bunched-up at the base of a hillside, the town itself is an affluent, self-contained delight, with plenty of places to eat (seafood rules) and sunny seaside lawns along the Esplanade.

Manly is also the gateway to little **St Helena Island**, about 6km from the Brisbane River mouth. A grim high-security prison from 1867 till 1932, St Helena still has the remains of several prison buildings, plus parts of Queensland's first tramway, built in 1884. The old trams were pulled by horses, but these days a tractor drags the coaches along as part of the island tour.

Sights & Activities

St Helena Island RUIN, HISTORIC SITE
(1300 438 787; www.sthelenaisland.com.au; William Gunn Jetty, Wyvernleigh Cl, Manly; day tour adult/child/family $74/42/189, night tour $95/50/250; 5hr day tours 9.15am Wed & 10am Sun, 3hr night tours 7pm Sat) To visit St Helena Island, take a trip from Manly Harbour on the Cat-O'-Nine-Tails boat. The five-hour day tour includes a tramway ride and a 'dramatised tour' of the prison, complete with floggings if you so desire. A spooky three-hour ghost tour departs on Saturday evening.

Jan Powers Farmers Market MARKET
(www.janpowersfarmersmarkets.com.au; Esplanade, btwn Cambridge & Cardigan Pdes, Manly; 6am-noon 3rd Sat of the month) Get along to this great farmers market (an offshoot of the Brisbane market of the same name), down by the shore at Manly. Expect loads of fresh produce, cakes, breads, olive oil, seafood, meats, honey, jam…

Royal Queensland Yacht Squadron SAILING
(RQYS; 07-3396 8666; www.rqys.com.au; 578 Esplanade, Manly) The estimable Royal Queensland Yacht Squadron, south of the town centre, runs yacht races every Wednesday afternoon, and many of the skippers are happy to take visitors on board for the ride (for free!). Sign on at the club before noon. Ask about sailing lessons if you're interested in learning how to hoist a spinnaker and duck under a boom.

Manly Pool SWIMMING
(07-3396 3281; www.manlypoolbrisbane.com.au; 1 Fairlead Cres, Manly; adult/child/family $5/3.60/10.60; 5.30am-7pm Mon-Fri, 6am-6pm Sat, 8am-6pm Sun) Hot and bothered? Cool off with a dip in this 25m outdoor pool on the Manly foreshore.

Sleeping & Eating

Manly Harbour Backpackers HOSTEL $
(07-3396 3824, 1800 800 157; www.manlyharbourbackpackers.com.au; 1/45 Cambridge Pde, Manly; dm $25-30, d/tr $75/90;) Upstairs above a row of shops on Manly's main strip, this chilled-out hostel has homely common areas and lots of activities on offer. Music-themed dorms have six to eight beds; some are en suite. Also here is the **Manly Deck** (www.manlydeck.com.au; mains $10-15; noon-10.30pm Mon-Wed, noon-11.30pm Thu, 8am-midnight Fri & Sat, 8am-10pm Sun), a bar-restaurant that serves cheap backpacker meals with an Indian bent (curries, tandoori-chicken pizza) and a $17 all-you-can-eat buffet breakfast.

Manly Marina Cove Motel MOTEL $$
(07-3348 1000; www.manlymarinacove.com; 578a Royal Esplanade, Manly; d/f from $165/215;) Down by the namesake marina a short walk along the foreshore from Manly's main street, this flashy motel ticks all the boxes: water views, big comfy beds, mod interior design and an absolute absence of floral print. A bit pricey for a motel, but worth it.

Manly Hotel PUB $$
(07-3249 5999; www.manlyhotel.com; 54 Cambridge Pde, Manly; s $80-130, d $95-145;) Upstairs at this orange-brick behemoth on the main street are 18 tidy rooms, the priciest of which have bathrooms, little Juliet-style balconies over the street and plush faux-colonial trimmings. The cheaper rooms are perfectly decent – you'll just have to wander down the hall to use the bathroom. Cold beer, live bands, breakfast, lunch and dinner all happen downstairs in the pub (breakfast $6 to $20, lunch and dinner mains $22 to $36).

Fish Cafe SEAFOOD $$
(07-3893 0195; www.fishcafe.com.au; cnr Cambridge Pde & Esplanade, Manly; takeaway $7-21, mains $29-42; 10am-late Mon & Tue, 8am-late Wed-Sun) For the best fish and chips in town, grab some takeaway (try the local whiting), wander across the road and pull up a seat overlooking the marina. The bistro section next door is a classier affair, serving sand-crab lasagne, oysters, Szechuan pepper squid and a rich bouillabaisse.

Thai Boat THAI $$
(07-3396 1600; www.thaiboat.com.au; 1/99 Cambridge Pde, Manly; mains $18-24; 5-8.30pm) Spice up your night with dinner at this bright corner Thai joint with iridescent purple-and-orange tablecloths. The *gang penang* coconut-and-peanut curry with prawns is a winner. You can opt for Moreton Bay bugs, the local crustacean, in any curry for an extra $10 or so.

Information

Wynnum Manly Visitor Information Centre
(07-3348 3524; www.manlyharbourvillage.com; 43a Cambridge Pde; 9am-4pm Mon-Fri, 10am-3pm Sat & Sun) A helpful shopfront info hub on the main street.

Getting There & Away

If you're not driving, the easiest way to get to Manly is to catch the train, which departs from Brisbane's Roma St Station or Central Station ($7.50, 40 minutes) every 30 minutes or so. It's a 10-minute walk downhill from the station to the waterfront, along Cambridge Pde.

North Stradbroke Island

POP 2000

An easy 30-minute ferry chug from Cleveland, this unpretentious holiday isle is

Point Lookout

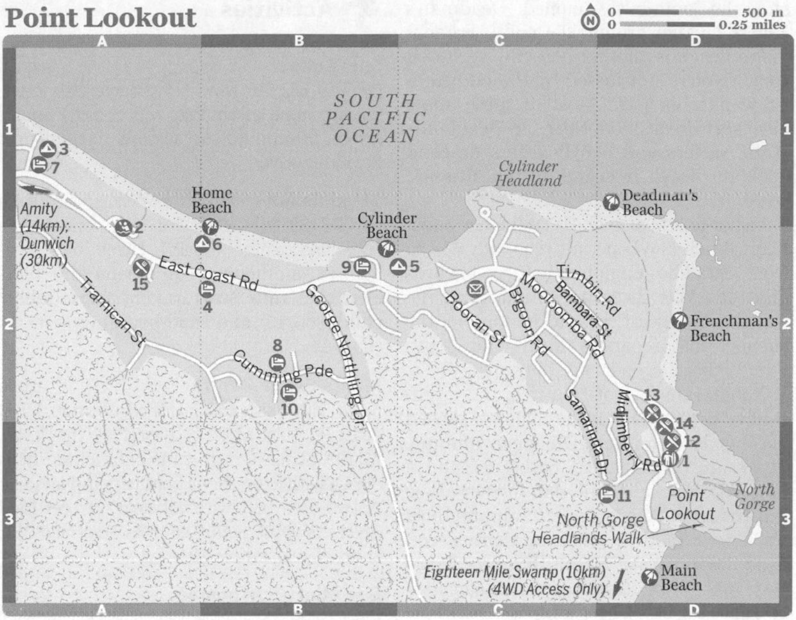

like Noosa and Byron Bay rolled into one. There's a string of glorious powdery white beaches, great surf and some quality places to stay and eat (catering to Brisbane's naughty-weekend-away set). It's also a hotspot for spying dolphins, turtles, manta rays and, between June and November, hundreds of humpback whales. 'Straddie' also boasts freshwater lakes and 4WD tracks.

There are only a few small settlements on the island, with a handful of accommodation and eating options – mostly near **Point Lookout** in the northeast. On the west coast, **Dunwich** is where the ferries dock. **Amity** is a small village on the northwestern corner. Much of the island's southern section is closed to visitors because of sand mining.

Interestingly, North and South Stradbroke Islands used to be one single island, but a savage storm blew through the sand spit between the two in 1896.

Point Lookout

Activities, Courses & Tours

1 Bob Minty Surfboards.......D3
Manta Scuba Centre.......(see 7)
2 Straddie Adventures.......A2

Sleeping

3 Adder Rock Campground.......A1
4 Allure.......B2
5 Cylinder Beach Campground.......C2
6 Home Beach Campground.......B2
7 Manta Lodge YHA.......A1
8 Pandanus Palms Resort.......B2
9 Stradbroke Island Beach Hotel.......B2
10 Straddie Views.......B2
11 Whale Watch Ocean Beach Resort.......D3

Eating

12 Fishes at the Point.......D3
13 Look.......D2
14 Oceanic Gelati.......D3
15 Point Lookout Bowls Club.......A2

Sights

At Point Lookout, the eye-popping **North Gorge Headlands Walk** is an absolute highlight. It's an easy 20-minute loop around the headland along boardwalks, with the thrum of cicadas as your soundtrack. Keep an eye out for turtles, dolphins and manta rays offshore. The view from the headland down Main Beach is a showstopper.

There are several gorgeous **beaches** around Point Lookout. A patrolled swimming area, Cylinder Beach is popular with families and is flanked by Home Beach and the ominously named Deadman's Beach. Further around the point, Frenchman's Beach is another peaceful, secluded spot if you're not fussed by the odd nudist wandering past. Most of these spots have surf breaks, too. Near the Headlands Walk, surfers and bodyboarders descend on Main Beach in search of the ultimate wave.

Fisher-folk take their 4WDs further down Main Beach (4WD permit required; $39.55 from Straddie Camping (p101)) towards **Eighteen Mile Swamp**, continuing all the way down the east coast to Jumpinpin, the channel that separates North and South Stradbroke, a legendary **fishing** spot.

About 4km east of Dunwich, the tanin-stained **Brown Lake** is the colour of stewed tea, but is completely OK for swimming. There are picnic tables, barbecues and a toilet at the lake. About 4km further along this road, take the 2.6km (40-minute) bush track to Straddie's glittering centrepiece, **Blue Lake**, part of **Naree Budjong Djara National Park** (www.nprsr.qld.gov.au/parks/naree-budjong-djara): keep an eye out for forest birds, skittish lizards and swamp wallabies along the way. There's a wooden viewing platform at the lake, which is encircled by a forest of paperbarks, eucalypts and banksias. You can cool off in the water, if you don't mind the spooky unseen depths. Further north towards Point Lookout, **The Keyholes** is a freshwater lake and lagoon system. There's 4WD access via the beach (permit required). Another happy diversion is a visit to **Myora Springs** – swimming holes surrounded by lush vegetation and walking tracks – near the coast about 4km north of Dunwich.

North Stradbroke Island Historical Museum MUSEUM
(07-3409 9699; www.stradbrokemuseum.com.au; 15-17 Welsby St, Dunwich; adult/child $3.50/1; 10am-2pm Tue-Sat, 11am-3pm Sun) Once the 'Dunwich Benevolent Asylum' – a home for the destitute – this small but impressive museum describes shipwrecks and harrowing voyages, and gives an introduction to the island's rich Aboriginal history (the Quandamooka are the traditional owners of Minjerribah, aka Straddie). Island artefacts include the skull of a sperm whale washed up on Main Beach in 2004, and the old Point Lookout lighthouse lens.

Activities

North Stradbroke Island Surf School SURFING
(0407 642 616; www.northstradbrokeislandsurfschool.com.au; lessons from $50; daily) Small-group, 90-minute surf lessons in the warm Straddie waves.

Straddie Adventures KAYAKING, SAND-BOARDING
(07-3409 8414, 0417 741 963; www.straddieadventures.com.au; daily) Hires out surfboards, snorkelling equipment and bicycles, and runs sea-kayaking trips (adult/child $60/45) and sand-boarding sessions ($30/25).

Manta Scuba Centre DIVING
(07-3409 8888; www.mantalodge.com.au; 1 East Coast Rd, Point Lookout) Based at the YHA, Manta Scuba Centre runs snorkelling trips ($85), with a two-hour boat trip and all gear. A two-dive trip with all gear for certified divers is $196. Scuba courses start at $253; snorkel gear hire is $25.

Bob Minty Surfboards SURFING
(07-3409 8334; www.bobmintysurfboards.com; 9 Mooloomba Rd, Point Lookout; per day surfboard/bodyboard $35/20; daily) Surfboard and bodyboard hire near Main Beach.

Straddie Super Sports BICYCLE RENTAL
(07-3409 9252; 18 Bingle Rd, Dunwich; 8.30am-4.30pm Mon-Fri, 8am-3pm Sat, 9am-2pm Sun) Hires out mountain bikes (per hour/day $6.50/30) and has a huge range of fishing gear for sale.

Tours

A number of tour companies offer 4WD tours of the island. Generally these take in a strip of the eastern beach and visit several freshwater lakes. All tour operators will collect you from either the ferry at Dunwich or your accommodation.

North Stradbroke Island 4WD Tours & Camping Holidays DRIVING TOUR
(07-3409 8051; www.stradbroketourism.com; adult/child half-day $35/20, full day $85/55) Offers 4WD tours around the Point Lookout area, with lots of bush, beaches and wildlife. Beach fishing is $45/30 per adult/child.

Straddie Kingfisher Tours DRIVING TOUR
(07-3409 9502; www.straddiekingfishertours.com.au; adult/child island pick-up $80/40, from Brisbane or Gold Coast $195/145) Operates six-hour 4WD and fishing tours; also has whale-

watching tours in season. Ask about kayaking and sand-boarding options.

Sleeping

Almost all of the island's accommodation is in Point Lookout, strung along 3km of coastline. Most places require stays of more than one night, but this is often negotiable outside of peak holiday times (but it's usually cheaper to book multiple nights).

Straddie Camping CAMPGROUND $
(07-3409 9668; www.straddiecamping.com.au; 1 Junner St, Dunwich; 4WD camp site from $16.50, unpowered/powered sites from $37/44, cabins from $115; booking office 8am-4pm) There are eight island campgrounds operated by this outfit, including two 4WD-only foreshore camps (permits required – $39.55 from Straddie Camping). The best of the bunch are grouped around Point Lookout: the campgrounds at **Adder Rock** and the **Home Beach** both overlook the sand, while the **Cylinder Beach** campground sits right on one of the island's best beaches. Book well in advance; good weekly rates.

Manta Lodge YHA HOSTEL $
(07-3409 8888; www.mantalodge.com.au; 1 East Coast Rd, Point Lookout; dm/d $32/82;) This three-storey, lemon-yellow hostel has clean (if unremarkable) rooms and a great beachside location (who wants to sit around in a dorm anyway?). There are jungly hammocks out the back plus a dive school downstairs.

Straddie Views B&B $$
(07-3409 8875; www.northstradbrokeisland.com/straddiebb; 26 Cumming Pde, Point Lookout; r from $150) There are two spacious downstairs suites in this B&B, run by a friendly Straddie couple. Cooked breakfast is served on the upstairs deck with fab sea views.

Whale Watch Ocean Beach Resort APARTMENT $$
(07-3409 8555, 1800 450 004; www.whalewatchresort.com.au; Samarinda Dr, Point Lookout; apt per 2 nights from $370;) On a spur of land high above Point Lookout are these roomy three-bedroom apartments with passably stylish furniture and large decks. Bring your binoculars to spot the namesake humpbacks. One-night stays possible but rates are *much* more expensive.

Stradbroke Island Beach Hotel HOTEL $$$
(07-3409 8188; www.stradbrokehotel.com.au; East Coast Rd, Point Lookout; d from $235;) Straddie's only pub has 12 cool, inviting rooms with shell-coloured tiles, blonde timbers, high-end gadgets and balconies. Walk to the beach, or get distracted by the open-walled bar downstairs en route (serving breakfast, lunch and dinner; mains $15 to $36). Flashy three- and four-bed apartments also available.

Allure APARTMENT $$$
(07-3415 0000, 1800 555 200; www.allurestradbroke.com.au; 43 East Coast Rd, Point Lookout; apt from $216;) These large ultramodern apartments are set in a leafy compound. Each villa (or 'shack' as the one-bedrooms are called) features lots of beachy colours, original artwork and an outdoor deck with barbecue. There isn't much space between villas, but they're cleverly designed with privacy in mind. Much cheaper rates for stays of more than one night.

Pandanus Palms Resort APARTMENT $$$
(07-3409 8106; www.pandanuspalmsresort.com; 21 Cumming Pde, Point Lookout; 2-/3-bedroom apt from $350/450;) High above the beach, the two- and three-bed townhouses here don't have air-con and are a bit '90s style-wise, but they're roomy and the best ones have ocean views, private yards and barbecues. There's a tennis court, too.

Eating

There are only a handful of dining choices around the island, mostly in Point Lookout. There are small supermarkets at Point Lookout and Dunwich, plus the excellent Island Fruit Barn, but if you're staying for more than a few days it makes sense to bring your food and drinks over from the mainland. Also check out the Stradbroke Island Beach Hotel (p101).

★**Oceanic Gelati** GELATI $
(07-3415 3222; 19 Mooloomba Rd, Point Lookout; gelati from $3; 9.30am-5pm) 'OMG! This is the best gelati ever.' So says one satisfied customer, and we're in complete agreement. Try the dairy-free tropical, cooling lemon or classic vanilla.

Island Fruit Barn CAFE $
(16 Bingle Rd, Dunwich; mains $10-14; 7am-5pm Mon-Fri, 7am-4pm Sat & Sun;) On the main road in Dunwich, Island Fruit Barn is a casual little congregation of tables with excellent breakfasts, smoothies, salads and sandwiches using top-quality ingredients.

Order a spinach-and-fetta roll, then stock up in the gourmet grocery section.

Point Lookout Bowls Club PUB $
(☎07-3409 8182; www.pointlookoutbowlsclub.com.au; East Coast Rd, Point Lookout; mains $9-25; ⏲11.30am-2pm & 6-8pm) For casual pub-grub meals that won't break the bank, head for the local bowls club. The chef is from France – could he be any further from home?

Seashells Cafe CAFE $
(☎07-3409 7886; 21 Ballow St, Amity; mains $10-24; ⏲10am-3pm Mon, 9am-9pm Wed-Sat, 9am-3pm Sun) The only eating option in Amity is this breezy, open-sided cafe/bar, with cold XXXX on tap and mainstay mains like seafood basket, veg fettuccine and lamb shanks, plus coffee and cake throughout the day.

Fishes at the Point SEAFOOD $
(www.fishesatthepoint.com.au; East Coast Rd, Point Lookout; mains $10-25; ⏲8am-8pm Sat-Thu, 8am-9pm Fri; 📶) True to form, Fishes offers fresh fish and chips, plus outdoor seating across the road from the North Gorge Headlands Walk. A bit heavy on the batter, but you need that after a surf.

Look MODERN AUSTRALIAN $$
(☎07-3415 3390; www.beachbarcafe.com; 1/29 Mooloomba Rd; mains $22-38; ⏲8am-3pm daily, 6-9pm Thu-Sat) The hub of the Point Lookout scene during the day, with funky tunes and breezy outdoor seating with water views. Lots of wines by the glass and smokin' chilli prawns.

ℹ Information

Although it's quiet most of the year, the island population swells significantly at Christmas, Easter and during school holidays: book accommodation or camping permits well in advance.

If you plan to go off-road, you can get information and buy a 4WD permit ($39.55) from Straddie Camping (p101).

ℹ Getting There & Away

The hub for ferries to North Stradbroke Island is the seaside suburb of Cleveland. Regular **Citytrain** (www.translink.com.au) services run from Brisbane's Central and Roma St stations to Cleveland station ($9.50, one hour); buses to the ferry terminal meet the trains at Cleveland station ($4.80, 10 minutes).

Big Red Cat (☎07-3488 9777, 1800 733 228; www.bigredcat.com.au; return per vehicle incl passengers $149, walk-on adult/child $20/10; ⏲5.15am-6pm Mon-Sat, 7am-7pm Sun) In a tandem operation with Stradbroke Ferries, the feline-looking Big Red Cat vehicle/passenger ferry does the Cleveland–Dunwich run around eight times daily (45 minutes).

Gold Cats Stradbroke Flyer (☎07-3286 1964; www.flyer.com.au; Middle St, Cleveland; return adult/child/family $19/10/50) Gold Cats Stradbroke Flyer runs around a dozen return passenger-only trips daily between Cleveland and One Mile Jetty at Dunwich (30 minutes).

Stradbroke Ferries (☎07-3488 5300; www.stradbrokeferries.com.au; return per vehicle incl passengers $149, walk-on adult/child $20/10; ⏲5.15am-6pm Mon-Sat, 7am-7pm Sun) Teaming up with Big Red Cat, Stradbroke Ferries' passenger and passenger/vehicle services run to Dunwich and back around 12 times daily (passenger ferries 25 minutes, vehicle ferries 45 minutes).

ℹ Getting Around

Straddie is big: it's best to have your own wheels to explore it properly. If not, **Stradbroke Island Buses** (☎07-3415 2417; www.stradbrokebuses.com) meet the ferries at Dunwich and run to Amity and Point Lookout (one-way/return $4.70/9.40). The last bus to Dunwich leaves Point Lookout at 6.20pm. There's also the **Stradbroke Cab Service** (☎0408 193 685), which charges around $60 from Dunwich to Point Lookout.

Straddie Super Sports (p100) in Dunwich hires out mountain bikes (per hour/day $6.50/30).

Moreton Island

POP 250

If you're not going further north in Queensland than Brisbane but want a slice of tropical paradise, slip over to blissful Moreton Island. You'll be reassured to learn that Moreton's cache of sandy shores, bushland, bird life, dunes and glorious lagoons are protected – 95% of the isle comprises **Moreton Island National Park & Recreation Area** (www.nprsr.qld.gov.au/parks/moreton-island). Apart from a few rocky headlands, it's all sand, with Mt Tempest, the highest coastal sand hill in the world, towering high at a lofty 280m. Off the west coast are the rusty, hulking Tangalooma Wrecks, which provide excellent snorkelling and diving.

The island has a rich history, from early Aboriginal settlements to the site of Queensland's first and only whaling station at **Tangalooma**, which operated between 1952 and 1962. These days, swimming, snorkelling and 4WD trails keep visitors occupied (in fact, the island is a 4WD-only domain).

Tangalooma now hosts the island's sole resort, and there are three other small settlements on the west coast: **Bulwer** near the northwestern tip, **Cowan Cowan** between Bulwer and Tangalooma, and **Kooringal** near the southern tip.

Sights & Activities

Check out the **dolphin feeding** which happens each evening around sunset at Tangalooma, halfway down the western side of the island. Around half a dozen dolphins swim in from the ocean and take fish from the hands of volunteer feeders. You have to be a guest of the Tangalooma Island Resort to participate, but onlookers are welcome. The resort also organises **whale-watching** cruises (from June to October). Also at the resort is the **Tangalooma Marine Education & Conservation Centre** (www.tangalooma.com/info/dolphin_feeding/tmecc; Tangalooma Island Resort; 10am-noon & 1-5pm), which has a display on the diverse marine and bird life of Moreton Bay. You can pick up a map of the island showing walking trails here.

Just north of the resort, off the coast, are the famous **Tangalooma Wrecks** – 15 sunken ships forming a sheltered boat mooring and a brilliant snorkelling spot. You can hire **snorkelling** gear from the resort, or **Tangatours** (07-3410 6927; www.tangatours.com.au) runs two-hour kayaking and snorkelling trips around the wrecks ($79) as well as guided **paddleboarding** ($49) and dusk **kayaking** tours ($69).

Island **bushwalks** include a desert trail (two hours) leaving from the resort, as well as the strenuous trek up Mt Tempest, 3km inland from Eagers Creek – worthwhile, but you'll need transport to reach the start.

Built in 1857 at the island's northern tip, **Cape Moreton Lighthouse** is the oldest operating lighthouse in Queensland, and is the place to come for great views if the whales are passing by.

Tours

Most day and two-day tours depart from Brisbane or the Gold Coast. For dolphin-spotting tours from Scarborough on the Redcliffe Peninsula north of Brisbane, see Dolphin Wild (p96).

SUNSET SCENES

For a flaming sunset view over Moreton Bay, head up to the top of the Tangalooma Island Resort complex on Moreton Island. This is one of the few places around Brisbane that faces west over the bay, which means you can watch the sun sink down over the water, with the Tangalooma Wrecks looking surreal in the foreground.

Adventure Moreton Island ADVENTURE TOUR
(1300 022 878; www.adventuremoretonisland.com; 1-day tour from $129) Operated in cahoots with Tangatours at Tangalooma Island Resort, these tours offer a range of activities (including paddle-boarding, snorkelling, sailing, kayaking and fishing), ex-Brisbane. Overnight resort accommodation packages also available (including tour from $288).

Moreton Bay Escapes ADVENTURE TOUR
(1300 559 355; www.moretonbayescapes.com.au; 1-day tour adult/child from $179/129, 2-day camping tour $309/179) A certified ecotour, this one day 4WD tour includes snorkelling or kayaking, sand-boarding, marine wildlife watching and a picnic lunch. Camp overnight to see more of the isle.

Sunrover Tours ADVENTURE TOUR
(07-3203 4241, 1800 353 717; www.sunrover.com.au; day tour adult/child $145/125, plus $30 park fees) A 4WD-tour operator with full-day and longer camping tours (two and three days). Snorkelling, shipwrecks, bushwalks and dolphin-spotting. Departs Brisbane.

Moreton Island Adventures DRIVING TOUR
(07-3909 3333; www.moretonislandadventures.com.au; 14 Howard Smith Dr, Port of Brisbane; 1-day tours adult/child from $159/130) Guided 4WD trips with either an eco or adventure bent, departing Port of Brisbane on the flashy Mical vehicle ferry.

Sleeping & Eating

Aside from the resort, there are a few holiday flats and houses for rent at Kooringal, Cowan Cowan and Bulwer: see listings at www.moretonisland.com.au.

There are also 10 national-park **camping grounds** (13 74 68; www.nprsr.qld.gov.au/experiences/camping; sites per person/family $6/21) on Moreton Island, all with water, toilets and cold showers; five of these are right on the beach. Book online or by phone before you get to the island.

There is a small convenience store plus cafes, restaurants and bars at the resort; plus (rather expensive) shops at Kooringal and Bulwer: otherwise, bring food and drink supplies along with you from the mainland.

Tangalooma Island Resort HOTEL, APARTMENT **$$$**
(☎07-3637 2000, 1300 652 250; www.tangalooma.com; 1-night packages from $370;) This beautifully sited place has the island accommodation market cornered. There are abundant sleeping options, starting with simple hotel rooms. A step up are the units and suites, where you'll get beachside access and more contemporary decor. The apartments range from two- to four-bedroom configurations. The resort also has several eating options. Accommodation prices generally include return ferry fares and transfers.

Information

There are no paved roads on Moreton Island, but 4WDs can travel along the beaches and cross-island tracks (regular cars not permitted) – seek local advice about tides and creek crossings before venturing out. You can pick up maps from the ferry operators. Permits for 4WDs cost $43.60, valid for one month, and are available through ferry operators, online or via phone from the Department of National Parks, Recreation, Sport & Racing (p282). Ferry bookings are mandatory if you want to take a vehicle across.

Online, see www.visitmoretonisland.com.

Getting There & Around

Several ferries operate from the mainland. To explore once you get to the island, bring a 4WD on one of the ferries or take a tour (most tours are ex-Brisbane, and include ferry transfers).

Micat (www.micat.com.au; 14 Howard Smith Dr, Port of Brisbane; return passenger adult/child $50/35, vehicle incl 2 people $195-230) Vehicle ferries from Port of Brisbane to Tangalooma around eight times weekly (75 minutes); see the website for directions to the ferry terminal.

Moreton Island Tourist Services (☎07-3408 2661; www.moretonisland.net.au) 4WD taxi transfers around the island; one-way trips range from $50 to $220.

Tangalooma Flyer (☎07-3268 6333, shuttle bus 07-3637 2000; www.tangalooma.com; return adult/child $80/45) Fast passenger catamaran operated by Tangalooma Island Resort. It makes the 75-minute trip to the resort three times daily from Holt St Wharf in Brisbane (see the website for directions). A shuttle bus (adult/child one way $21/10.50) scoots to the wharf from the CBD or airport; bookings essential.

Granite Belt

Dappling the western flanks of the Great Dividing Range about 210km southwest of Brisbane, the Granite Belt region features rolling hillsides lined with vine rows and orchards (apples, pears, plums, peaches) that thrive in the cool, crisp air here (Stanthorpe, the regional hub, sits at an altitude of 915m). This is Queensland's only real wine region of any size – the only place in the state where it's cool enough to grow commercial quantities of grapes. Further south, on the NSW border, balancing boulders and spring wildflowers attract bushwalkers to the photogenic Girraween National Park.

Stanthorpe & Ballandean

Queensland's coolest town (literally), **Stanthorpe** (population 4300) is one of the state's secret tourist hotspots. With a distinct four-season climate, the town is a winter retreat where normally sweltering Queenslanders can cosy up in front of an open fire with a bottle of *vino rosso* from one of the 50-plus local wineries. In 1860 an Italian priest planted the first grapevines here, but it wasn't until the influx of Italian immigrants in the 1940s (bringing with them a lifetime of viticultural nous) that the wine industry really took off. Today functional Stanthorpe and the tiny village of **Ballandean** (population 470), about 20km to the south, boast a flourishing wine industry, with cellar-door sales, on-site dining, vineyard events and boutique accommodation.

The Granite Belt's changing seasons also make it a prime fruit-growing area and there's plenty of fruit picking available for backpackers who don't mind chilly mornings.

Sights & Activities

Wine-tasting is a must-do in this neck of the woods, as is a drive through the boulder-strewn, vine-lined Granite Belt landscape. If you plan on swilling one too many, opt for a tour.

Weekenders come not only for the wine but also the food: across the Granite Belt region you'll find some brilliant boutique foodie businesses offering delectible edibles (and drinkables).

Stanthorpe Regional Art Gallery GALLERY
(☎07-4681 1874; www.srag.org.au; cnr Lock & Marsh Sts; ⌚10am-4pm Tue-Fri, to 1pm Sat & Sun) FREE The Stanthorpe Regional Art Gallery, northwest of the post office, has a small but surprisingly engaging collection of works by local artists – mostly canvases and ceramics. It makes a lovely rainy-day detour, or swing by on a Sunday lunchtime to check out some art with a live music soundtrack. One of Queensland's better regional art galleries.

Granite Belt Brewery BREWERY
(☎07-4681 1370; www.granitebeltbrewery.com.au; 146 Glenlyon Dr, Stanthorpe; ⌚10am-4pm) It's not just about the wine around here you know – there's a local brewery too. Swing into the bar at the Happy Valley accommodation/restaurant to sample a few brews. A $12 tasting paddle gives you a sample of each of the current offerings, which might include the Granite Pilsner, Poziers Porter or Irish Red Ale. Thirsty work.

Granite Belt Dairy FOOD
(☎07-4685 2277; cnr Amiens Rd & Duncan Ln, Thulimbah; ⌚10am-4pm) What's wine without cheese? The Granite Belt's leading cheesemaker delivers a tasty array of the good stuff, all available for sampling. Also on offer at the adjoining Jersey Girls Cafe are fantastic milkshakes and cheesecakes, Devonshire teas and light lunches, plus fresh-baked bread, chutneys and other picnic hamper-fillers. Don't leave without trying the whiffy Bastard Tail washed rind soft cheese.

Heavenly Chocolate FOOD
(☎07-4684 5121; www.heavenlychocolate.com.au; 2117 Pyramids Rd, Wyberba; ⌚10am-4pm Fri-Mon) There's no denying it: chocolate makes a punchy accompaniment to a full-bodied red, and Heavenly Chocolate prepares decadent hand-made chocolates and fudge – plus 21 different creamy hot chocolates for those cold winter days. Smells heavenly!

TOP FIVE GRANITE BELT WINERIES

With dozens of Granite Belt wineries offering free tastings, you could easily spend a week wading through the wines of the region and still only make a ripple on the surface. But if you've only got a day or two in the area, here's a roundup of our favourite spots. It's usually worth a phone call in advance to the smaller cellar doors to make sure they're open.

Ballandean Estate (☎07-4684 1226; www.ballandeanestate.com; 354 Sundown Rd, Ballandean; ⌚9am-5pm) One of Queensland's oldest and biggest wineries, with many award-winning vintages and an impressive cafe/restaurant called the Barrel Room Cafe (p109). Also offers free winery tours at 11am.

Boireann Wines (☎07-4683 2194; www.boireannwinery.com.au; 26 Donnellys Castle Rd, The Summit; ⌚10am-4pm Fri-Mon) Boireann's hand-made premium reds rank among the finest in the region (and have been awarded five stars by Aussie wine guru James Halliday). Small cellar door about 10km north of Stanthorpe.

Golden Grove Estate (☎07-4684 1291; www.goldengroveestate.com.au; 337 Sundown Rd, Ballandean; ⌚10am-3pm) Established family-run estate with many unique varieties, including an excellent Nero d'Avola red, a vine native to Sicily.

Ravens Croft (☎07-4683 3252; www.ravenscroftwines.com.au; 274 Spring Creek Rd, Stanthorpe; ⌚10.30am-4.30pm Fri-Sun) Highly respected winemaker producing superb reds (petit verdot, cabernet sauvignon and South African pinotage) and whites (including a top-notch verdelho). It's a modest cellar door in the backcountry west of Stanthorpe.

Robert Channon Wines (☎07-4683 3260; www.robertchannonwines.com; 32 Bradley Ln, Stanthorpe; ⌚11am-4pm Mon, Tue & Fri, 10am-5pm Sat & Sun) Lots of trophy-winning wines (it was the first winery in Queensland to be awarded five stars by James Halliday), and a buzzy weekend cafe with views over a pretty lake. Try the verdelho.

Bramble Patch FOOD
(☎07-4683 4205; www.bramblepatch.com.au; 381 Townsend Rd, Glen Aplin; ⏲10am-4pm) Follow the strawberry signs along Townsend Rd to this berry patch with a sense of humour – worth visiting for the ice cream with home-made berry compote, waffles with berries, jams, relishes, fortified berry wines, and of course fresh fruits (November to April).

Market in the Mountains MARKET
(☎0417 760 529; www.marketinthemountains.org; cnr Marsh & Lock Sts, Stanthorpe Civic Centre; ⏲8am-noon 2nd & 4th Sun of the month) Follow the locals into the Civic Centre for a Sunday morning artsy-craftsy hit: lots of hand-made trinkets, plus coffee, fresh local produce and the odd busker (...sometimes very odd).

Stanthorpe Heritage Museum MUSEUM
(☎07-4681 1711; www.halenet.com.au/~jvbryant/museum.html; 12 High St, Stanthorpe; adult/child/family $7/3.50/20; ⏲10am-4pm Wed-Fri, 1-4pm Sat, 9am-1pm Sun) The curio-crammed Stanthorpe Heritage Museum, on the town's northern outskirts, gives a comprehensive insight into Stanthorpe's tin-mining and grazing past. Well-preserved old buildings from the 1800s include a slab-timber jail, a shepherd's hut and a school house. There's a moving display on Stanthorpe's wartime losses, and home-made 'make-do' pieces – toys, kitchen items, pillow cases, curtains – showing local ingenuity during lean times.

Suttons Juice Factory FOOD
(☎07-4685 2464; www.suttonsfarm.com.au; 10 Halloran Dr, Thulimbah; ⏲9.30am-4.30pm) You can pick your own apples at Suttons (stock up for your road trip), or skip the hard work and sample their excellent apple cider, brandy, juices and syrups. The Shed Café here serves light lunches.

WHEN TO GO

If you plan on checking out a few vineyards around Stanthorpe and Ballandean, it's probably best to visit on a weekend. Accommodation prices are slightly higher from Friday to Sunday, but you'll have access to all the vineyards and restaurants, many of which close their doors during the working week.

Granite Belt Maze MAZE
(☎07-4683 2181; www.thegranitebeltmaze.com.au; 364 Old Warwick Rd, Glen Niven; admission $12; ⏲9.30am-4.30pm Fri-Mon, daily during school holidays) The timber-slatted Granite Belt Maze, 8.5km north of town, is as kitschy as a maze can be, but the kids will love it.

Tours

Filippo's Tours WINE
(☎07-4683 3130, 1800 020 383; www.filippostours.com.au; day tours ex-Stanthorpe/Brisbane from $85/145) Tours around the wineries and sights, including lunch. Also has overnight packages (per person from $305).

Granite Highlands Maxi Tours WINE
(☎07-4681 3969, 1800 852 969; www.maxitours.com.au; half-/full-day tours from $70/80) Offers good-value half- and full-day tours, plus overnight packages ex-Brisbane for groups (per person $275).

Stanthorpe Tours WINE
(☎0437 707 765; www.stanthorpetours.com.au; half-/full-day tours from $80/100) Upmarket half- and full-day tours in plush minibuses, with a heavy wine-and-cheese bent.

Wine Discovery Tours WINE
(☎0412 579 341; www.winediscoverytours.com.au; tours incl lunch from $120) Winery tours in a flashy 4WD, with detours to wilderness areas. Based in Ballandean.

Festivals & Events

Sicilian Vintage Lunch FOOD, WINE
(www.goldengroveestate.com.au) The Sicilian Vintage Lunch held in February at Golden Grove Estate (p105) celebrates the start of the vintage Italian-style with grape stomping, Italian music and a three-course Sicilian lunch.

Apple & Grape Festival FOOD
(www.appleandgrape.org) The Apple & Grape Festival is a three-day harvest festival held every even-numbered year in March. All hail the 37,000 tonnes of apples trucked out of here annually. Highlights range from a fun run to quilting exhibitions, grape crushes and a grand street parade.

Opera in the Vineyard OPERA
(☎07-4684 1226; www.ballandeanestate.com; Ballandean Estate, 354 Sundown Rd, Ballandean) Many of the wineries hold regular performances and events; check with the visitor

LOCAL KNOWLEDGE

MARK RAVENSCROFT, WINEMAKER & FOUNDER OF RAVENS CROFT WINES

What attracted you to the Granite Belt?

I came to this region 14 years ago. I had tasted the wines, seen the potential and land was cheap and the opportunity was there to start my own place.

What's unique about this growing region?

The area is one of the highest grape growing regions in Australia. It has really cool nights, which is great for natural acidity. Granite Belt wines can hold their own against any other Australian wines.

Any favourite wines from Queensland?

My favourite wine would have to be my 2002 Reserve Cabernet Sauvignon as it was my first trophy winner and gold medal at a national show. Other Granite Belt wines to look out for are wines from Pyramids Road winery – especially its Mourvèdre – and Boireann Wines.

What does the future hold for Granite Belt wineries?

As we have really only been recognised in the last 12 years I see a great future for GB wines.

What do you like to do in the area during your time off?

Time off – yeah right! I do a bit of bushwalking in Girraween National Park, but not enough.

Any tips for travellers coming here?

Try to go to as many of the smaller wineries as possible as they are mostly very individual wines. Use a car as the tour companies usually only visit the bigger ones.

information centre for details. One of the largest wineries, Ballandean Estate (p105), hosts regular cooking classes, themed degustation dinners and Opera in the Vineyard in May, all with copious amounts of food and wine.

Brass Monkey Season WINE, MUSIC
(www.granitebeltwinecountry.com.au/pages/winter-brass-monkey) The main event in the Granite Belt spans an entire season: winter (June to August) is Brass Monkey Season, with a parade of music events and food fiestas in town and at various wineries.

Sleeping

The Granite Belt high season is during the cooler months (May through September), when Queenslanders roll into the region for a dose of chilly temperatures and cosying up by the fire. Prices are higher over this period, and are higher on weekends year-round.

Top of the Town Tourist Park CARAVAN PARK $
(07-4681 4888; www.topoftown.com.au; 10 High St, Stanthorpe; powered sites $40, cabins from $110;) A bushy site on the northern side of Stanthorpe, this is a serviceable option if you're here for seasonal work in the vineyards and orchards. A snug six-person cottage costs $230 per night.

Backpackers of Queensland HOSTEL $
(0429 810 998; www.backpackersofqueensland.com.au; 80 High St, Stanthorpe; per week $195;) Something of a halfway house for young fruit pickers, this clean, efficient place has a minimum one-week stay in five-bed dorms with en suite bathrooms. No booze is allowed.

Diamondvale B&B Cottages COTTAGE $$
(07 4681 3367; www.diamondvalecottages.com.au; 26 Diamondvale Rd, Stanthorpe; d from $180;) In a bucolic bushland setting outside of Stanthorpe, Diamondvale is a friendly place with four private cottages (two one-bedroom and two two-bedroom), each with old-fashioned details, a wood-burning fireplace, kitchen and verandah. The communal barbecue hut is a winner, and you can walk along the creek 2km into town (or jump in for a swim).

WORTH A TRIP

GIRRAWEEN NATIONAL PARK

A short drive east of Ballandean, **Girraween National Park** (www.nprsr.qld.gov.au/parks/girraween) is home to some astonishing granite boulders, pristine forests and brilliant blooms of springtime wildflowers (Girraween means 'place of flowers'), all of which make a marvellous setting for a stroll. Wildlife is abundant and there are 17km of trails to take you around and to the top of some of the surreal granite outcrops. Short walks include the 1.6km return walk to the Granite Arch and a 3.6km return scramble up the Pyramid (1080m), while the granddaddy of Girraween walks is the 11km return trek to the top of Mt Norman (1267m).

Ballandean and Stanthorpe are a short drive away, but there are a couple of excellent places to stay in the area.

Girraween Environmental Lodge (07-4684 5138; www.girraweenlodge.com.au; Pyramids Rd, Ballandean; d $280, extra adult/child $60/30) is an ecofriendly bushland retreat set on 160 hectares adjacent to the national park. Made largely of recycled timber, the ten chic, self-contained timber cabins here sleep up to six people, are ultracomfy and have wood heaters and private decks with barbecues. There's also an outdoor spa and plunge pool. There's no restaurant at the lodge but you can buy a range of gourmet frozen meals, barbecue packs and breakfast baskets.

Wisteria Cottage (07-4684 5121; www.wisteriacottage.com.au; 2117 Pyramids Rd, Wyberba; d incl breakfast from $190) has three simple, tasteful and private timber cottages (one two-bedroom, two one-bedroom) in a large paddock with grazing cattle. The cabins have wide verandahs and cosy wood fires, and sleep up to six people. Breakfast comes in a big hamper, or there's the Heavenly Chocolate (p105) shop on site.

There are also two good drive-in **camping grounds** (13 74 68; http://parks.nprsr.qld.gov.au/permits; per person/family $5.60/22.40) in the park – **Castle Rock** and **Bald Rock Creek** – which teem with wildlife and have drinking water, barbecues and hot showers. Book online or via phone before you arrive.

The **visitor centre** at the end of Pyramids Rd has information on the park and walking tracks (opening hours hours vary, but map brochures should be available even if there's no one present). Although winter nights here can be cold, it's hot work scaling the boulders, so take plenty of water.

To reach the park, head 8km south of Ballandean, turn left on Pyramids Rd, and continue another 7km to the park entrance.

Murray Gardens MOTEL, CABIN **$$**
(07-4681 4121; www.murraygardens.com.au; 10 Pancor Rd, Stanthorpe; motel/cottages from $100/190;) This super-clean, well-managed and good-value option (pardon the plastic roses and chintzy cushions) is set on 7 bushy hectares on the outskirts of Stanthorpe. Choose between one of a row of motel rooms or a fully self-contained cottage with a fireplace or gas heating. Except for the local bird life, it's very quiet.

Apple & Grape Motel MOTEL **$$**
(07-4681 1288; www.appleandgrape.com.au; 63 Maryland St, Stanthorpe; d/f from $115/135;) There's a string of passable motels along Wallangarra Rd on the south side of Stanthorpe, but this one is a bit closer to the town centre. It's a two-storey affair set back from the street: the best rooms have been given a 2000s facelift, but some are still a bit '90s and bricky.

Briar Rose Cottages COTTAGE **$$**
(07-4683 6334; www.briarrosecottages.com.au; 66 Wallangarra Rd, Stanthorpe; 1-/2-bedroom cottage from $140/215) These two cottages on the eastern outskirts of Stanthorpe are small in size and perhaps too chintzy for some, but they're decent value and a two-minute drive into town. Both the two-bedroom front cottage and the one-bedroom back cottage have log fires, feather doonas and stacks of charm.

Azjure Studio Retreat BOUTIQUE HOTEL **$$$**
(0405 127 070; www.azjure.com.au; 165 Sundown Rd, Ballandean; 1-/2-bedroom studios from $320/460;) This much-awarded retreat

features three snappily designed, ultra-mod freestanding studios for two people (plus a villa for four) with sweeping views across the vines. Each has a roomy open-plan layout, huge windows, a verandah with barbecue and high-end fittings (including a spa tub with views). Kangaroos hop past in the twilight.

Vineyard Cottages & Restaurant COTTAGE **$$$**
(07-4684 1270; www.vineyardcottages.com.au; 28126 New England Hwy, Ballandean; cottages $230-375;) On the northern outskirts of Ballandean (about 20km south of Stanthorpe) you'll find these seven buttermilk-coloured brick cottages with spas and private verandahs overlooking English-style gardens. Inside a 100-year-old former church on the property is a decent restaurant (open for dinner nightly plus lunch on weekends; mains $28 to $38) with a fresh seasonal menu.

Eating

L'Aquila PIZZERIA, CAFE **$**
(07-4681 0356; 130 High St, Stanthorpe; mains $10-20; 9am-5pm Mon, to 8pm Tue-Thu, to 9pm Fri & Sat, 5-8pm Sun) It's hard to know what to make of this main-street Italian joint: it looks reasonably classy from the outside, but inside it's all cheap furniture and wailing '90s grunge. Still, if you're a fan of Alice In Chains, decent coffee and chunky pizzas (much better than the fast-food operators), you're in the right place.

★ **Varias** MODERN AUSTRALIAN **$$**
(07-4685 5050; www.varias.com.au; Queensland College of Wine Tourism, 22 Caves Rd, Stanthorpe; mains $28-32; 11am-3pm) This chic bistro features the delectable handiwork of student chefs at the adjunct Queensland College of Wine Tourism, a low-slung, angular, steel-and-stone construction just off the New England Hwy. Each course is paired with one of the college's excellent Bianca Ridge wines. It's an elegant and welcoming setting, with a flickering fire and floor-to-ceiling windows overlooking the vines: the classiest place to eat in Stanthorpe by a country mile.

Patty's on McGregor MODERN AUSTRALIAN **$$**
(07-4681 3463; www.pattysonmcgregor.com.au; 2 McGregor Tce, Stanthorpe; mains $30-38; 6.30pm-late Thu-Sat) A long-running Stanthorpe favourite, Patty's quirky backstreet shopfront serves a changing selection of beautifully prepared dishes with Eastern accents – perhaps a rogan josh curry with local organic lamb, or a za'atar-crusted pork loin cutlet with pear and garden honey, and always one vegetarian dish of the day. Black-and-white tile floors, candlelit tables and local artwork set the scene inside the cosy dining room.

Barrel Room Cafe MODERN AUSTRALIAN **$$**
(07-4684 1326; www.ballandeanestate.com/barrelroomcafe.aspx; Ballandean Estate, 354 Sundown Rd, Ballandean; mains $25-32; 10am-4pm Wed-Mon, 6pm-late Thu-Sun) This snug cafe/restaurant at Ballandean Estate (p105) winery, framed by massive 140-year-old wine barrels, is a beaut spot for a decadent meal and a bottle or two of the winery's excellent vintages. Organic lamb shoulder ragu, twice-cooked Tuscan pork belly and crispy-skinned duck breast with duck *tarte tatin* are a few recent hits from the seasonal menu.

Yim Thai THAI **$$**
(07-4681 0155; www.diningonthebelt.com.au/yim-thai-menu; 137a High St, Stanthorpe; mains $15-24; 11am-2.30pm Mon-Fri, 5.30pm-late daily) A surprising find on Stanthorpe's main street: Yim Thai's authentic Thai curries, soups and stir-fries, making an international fist of culinary life in agricultural inland Queensland.

Shiraz MODERN AUSTRALIAN **$$$**
(07-4684 1000; www.shirazrestaurantballandean.com; 28200 New England Hwy, Ballandean; mains $33-38; noon-2.30pm & 6pm-late Wed-Sun) Most food-focused locals rank Shiraz as the area's best restaurant, with a small warmly lit dining room and a tiny menu with exquisitely turned out fare – Black Angus rib fillet, rack of lamb, mouth-watering scallops and tender grilled barramundi. Small but well-chosen wine list. It's on the highway just north of Ballandean.

Information

Most of the Granite Belt wineries are located south of Stanthorpe around Ballandean. Pick up the *Granite Belt Wine Country* booklet from the **Stanthorpe Visitor Information Centre** (07-4681 2057, 1800 762 665; www.granitebeltwinecountry.com.au; 28 Leslie Pde, Stanthorpe; 9am-5pm). For alternative wine-tasting, grab the *Strange Bird Wine Trail* map listing the 20 or so wineries growing unusual varieties

(Tempranillo, Sylvaner, Viognier, Gewürztraminer, Malbec etc).

Getting There & Around

Greyhound Australia (www.greyhound.com.au) and **Crisps Coaches** (www.crisps.com.au) service Stanthorpe. There are buses to Warwick ($16, 45 minutes), Toowoomba ($44, 2½ hours), Brisbane ($56, 4½ hours) and Tenterfield in NSW ($20, 45 minutes), with connections to Byron Bay through **Northern Rivers Buslines** (www.nrbuslines.com.au).

To tour the Granite Belt wineries, either take a guided tour or bring your own set of wheels (plus a sober friend to do the driving).

Toowoomba

POP 157,030

Squatting on the edge of the Great Dividing Range, 700m above sea level, Toowoomba is a sprawling country hub with wide tree-lined streets, stately homes and down-to-earth locals. There's not a whole lot going on here from the travellers' perspective (in fact, when we asked a local friend 'What should we do when we get to Toowoomba?', his reply was 'Leave.'...): but if you've been darting across the state from end to end and need a break, it's not a bad spot to stop and chill out for a day or two.

The air is distinctly crisper up here on the range, and in spring the town's gardens blaze with colour. Not only is the 'Garden City' Queensland's largest and oldest inland city, it is also the birthplace of two national icons: the archetypal Aussie cake, the lamington, and Oscar-winner Geoffrey Rush.

Sights & Activities

Feel like stretching your legs? Take a walk through downtown Toowoomba and check out the stately late-19th-century sandstone buildings – including the **old post office**, **courthouse** and bedazzling 1911 Empire Theatre (p113), with its resplendent art-deco lobby. To assist your navigations the visitor centre publishes a series of *A Walk Through History* brochures. Or, for the ghoulishly inclined there's the *Tombstone Trails* brochure – a self-guided tour through Toowoomba's cemetery and early-pioneer graves.

Cobb & Co Museum MUSEUM
(07-4659 4900; www.cobbandco.qm.qld.gov.au; 27 Lindsay St; adult/child/family $12.50/6.50/32; 10am-4pm) How many school kids can you squeeze into one museum? Immediately north of Queens Park, the newly expanded (and rather good) Cobb & Co Museum houses an impressive carriage collection with hands-on displays depicting town life and outback travel back in horse-powered days. The museum also has a blacksmith forge, photographic displays of early Toowoomba and an Aboriginal collection – shields, axe heads, boomerangs – plus animated films relating Dreaming stories. Look for the half-dozen spinning windmills out the front.

Ju Raku En Japanese Garden GARDENS
(www.toowoombarc.qld.gov.au; West St; 7am-dusk) FREE Ju Raku En is a beautiful, Zen-like spot several kilometres south of the centre at the University of Southern Queensland. Designed by a Japanese professor in Kyoto, the 5-hectare garden has a rippling lake, carefully aligned boulders, conifers, bamboo stands, cherry blossom trees, photo-perfect bridges and wiggly paths.

Queens Park Gardens GARDENS
(www.toowoombarc.qld.gov.au; cnr Lindsay & Campbell Sts; 24hr) FREE These immaculate botanical gardens occupy the northeast corner of Queens Park, and blaze with colour in autumn. Plenty of parterre gardens, neat English flower beds, palms, conifers and canoodling teenagers.

Picnic Point PARK
(www.picnic-point.com.au; Tourist Rd; 24hr, cafe/restaurant 8.30am-5pm Mon-Thu, to 9pm Fri, 8am-9pm Sat, 8am-5pm Sun) FREE Riding high on the rim of the Great Dividing Range and strung along the eastern edge of town are Toowoomba's Escarpment Parks, the pick of which is Picnic Point. There are walking trails here, plenty of the namesake picnic spots and a cafe/restaurant (mains $10 to $28), but what everyone really comes for are the eye-popping views over the Lockyer Valley (Toowoomba really is quite lofty!).

Toowoomba Regional Art Gallery GALLERY
(07-4688 6652; www.toowoombarc.qld.gov.au/trag; 531 Ruthven St; 10am-4pm Tue-Sat, 1-4pm Sun) FREE The small Toowoomba Regional Art Gallery houses an interesting collection of paintings, ceramics and

drawings, plus rare books, maps and manuscripts in the library section. Regular touring exhibitions attract a few more visitors than usual.

Laurel Bank Park GARDENS

(www.toowoombarc.qld.gov.au; cnr Herries & West Sts; 24hr) FREE Test your senses at the beautifully manicured Laurel Bank Park, which has a scented garden full of pungent herbs and blooms for the visually impaired. Is there anything more perfect than a patch of jonquils in the springtime?

Festivals & Events

Carnival of Flowers HORTICULTURE

(www.tcof.com.au) Freesia fanatic? Daffodil devotee? Toowoomba's Carnival of Flowers is a hypercoloured spring fiesta held during the last week in September. It includes floral displays, a grand parade, exhibition gardens and a food and wine festival.

Sleeping

If you're trucking into town from the Brisbane direction without an accommodation booking, the Warrego Hwy (which turns into James St) is littered with serviceable motels.

Toowoomba Motor Village CARAVAN PARK $

(07-4635 8186; www.toowoombamotorvillage.com.au; 821 Ruthven St; unpowered/powered sites $27/33, cabins & units $75-112;) This trim-and-tidy hillside park is a 2.5km hike south of the centre, but is well equipped and has views over the suburbs.

★Vacy Hall GUESTHOUSE $$

(07-4639 2055; www.vacyhall.com.au; 135 Russell St; d $125-245;) Just uphill from the town centre, this magnificent 1873 mansion offers 12 heritage-style rooms with loads of authentic charm. A wide verandah wraps around the house, all rooms have en suites or private bathrooms, and some even have their own fireplaces. Super-high ceilings make some rooms taller than they are wide. Free wi-fi.

Central Plaza Hotel HOTEL $$

(07-4688 5333; www.toowoombacentralplaza.com.au; 523 Ruthven St; 1-/2-/3-bedroom apt from $170/415/525;) Flashy, corporate and an impressive nine floors high, the Central Plaza offers a modicum of urbane poshness in this big country town, where motels are many and most hotels are places you go to drink beer. Inside you'll find nice art, mod furniture and colourful, well-designed apartments with rooftop views. There's also a snazzy cocktail bar/cafe on the ground floor.

Park Motor Inn MOTEL $$

(07-4632 1011; www.parktoowoomba.com.au; 88 Margaret St; d/tr from $115/142;) Sometime around 2002, somebody made a mint selling multicoloured quilt covers to Australian motel owners. The quilt covers are still here, but the rooms are tidy and spacey, with big TVs, big mirrors and a big swimming pool. Great location too, across the road from Queens Park and away from the noisy motel strip on the road into town.

Eating

Metro Café CAFE $

(07-4632 0090; www.metrocafe.com.au; 15 Railway St; mains $13-19; 7am-4.30pm) Opposite the train station, this hip industrial cafe serves gourmet sandwiches, burgers and salads, vegetarian goodies (try the lentil burger), all-day breakfasts and super coffee. Outdoor seating in front, funky perspex lighting, cool contemporary art and happy staff (always a good sign) round out the experience. There's

FREAK OF NATURE: TOOWOOMBA'S INLAND TSUNAMI

On 10 January 2011 a wall of water raged through Toowoomba's town centre in an unprecedented weather event that has been likened to an inland tsunami. The wild weather that inundated Queensland in December 2010 and January 2011 caused floods throughout the state, including in Brisbane, and triggered a flash flood of epic proportions that took Toowoomba completely by surprise. Cars were tossed around like flotsam, people clung to trees and signposts, and houses were washed off their stumps. The torrential wall of water swept through the Lockyer Valley, devastating the small towns of Grantham and Murphys Creek. Despite its ferocity the flood left little lasting damage in Toowoomba, but ask any local about it and you'll still hear it described with shock, awe and wonderment.

Toowoomba

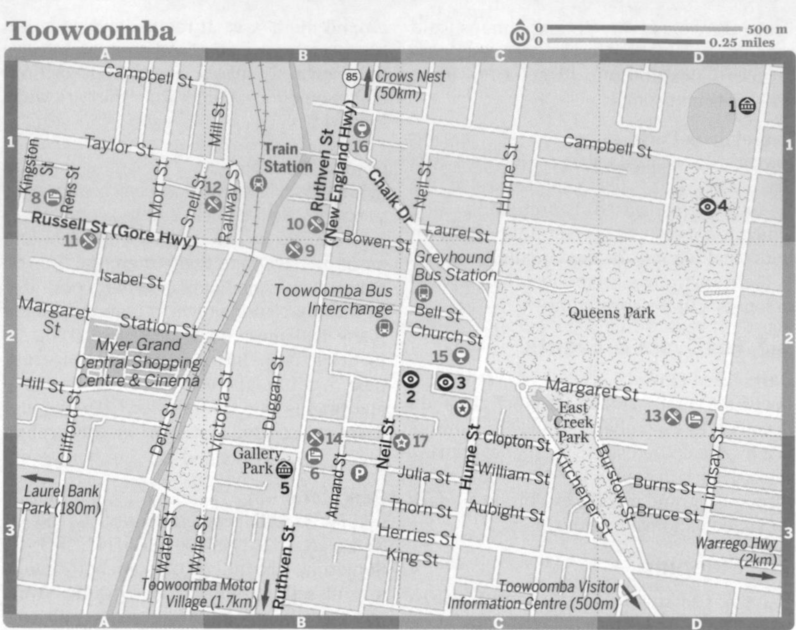

Toowoomba

Sights

1 Cobb & Co Museum D1
2 Courthouse C2
3 Old Post Office C2
4 Queens Park Gardens D1
5 Toowoomba Regional Art Gallery B3

Sleeping

6 Central Plaza Hotel B3
7 Park Motor Inn D2
8 Vacy Hall A1

Eating

9 Artisan B2
10 Chutney Mary's B1
11 Gip's A2
12 Metro Café B1
13 Park House Cafe D2
14 Phat Burger B3

Drinking & Nightlife

15 Fitzy's Fibber Magee C2
16 Spotted Cow B1

Entertainment

17 Empire Theatre C3

also a gallery and events space upstairs: check the website for happenings.

Artisan PIZZERIA $
(☎07-4638 0727; www.facebook.com/artisan-pizzaandsandwich; 41a Russell St; mains $8-20; ⏲11am-9pm Tue-Fri, 5-9pm Sat) Artisan is a hip, semi-industrial space with long, chunky-timber communal tables, stainless-steel chairs, old floorboards and art-deco ceilings. The busy open kitchen in the corner serves up simple pizzas, salads and flat-bread sandwiches. Good coffee too.

Park House Cafe MODERN AUSTRALIAN $
(☎07-4638 2211; www.parkhousecafe.com.au; 92 Margaret St; mains cafe $10-25, restaurant $29-35; ⏲7am-late) Facing Queens Park, this chic cafe has a lovely verandah and streetside patio, plus a new dining room being built when we visited. Gourmet sandwiches, hefty salads (try the seared lamb with fetta and roasted pumpkin), pastas, grilled meats and seafood lure pram-pushing mums from the park. At night the cafe vibe mutates into an upmarket restaurant scene, with generous pours of wine by the glass.

Phat Burger BURGERS $
(☎07-4638 4738; www.phatburgers.com.au; 520 Ruthven St; burgers $7-19; ⏰10am-9pm) Cheerful Phat plates up brilliant burgers with lurid orange napkins to mop up any spills. Top of the calorie charts is the Burghoffer, which is big enough to stop traffic (if you manage to eat one in its entirety at a single sitting, drop us a line). We love the home-made ground chilli paste.

Chutney Mary's INDIAN $$
(☎07-4638 0822; www.chutneymary.com.au; 335 Ruthven St; mains $17-20; ⏰noon-3pm & 5pm-late) Spice up your Toowoomba tenure with a visit to Chutney Mary's, where reliable curries, naans, tandoor and rice dishes accompany colourful dangling Indian trinkets.

Gip's MODERN AUSTRALIAN $$
(☎07-4638 3588; www.gipsrestaurant.com.au; 120 Russell St; mains $20-34; ⏰9am-9pm Mon-Fri, 11.30am-9pm Sat) Despite the slightly whacky name, Gip's is a classy set-up occupying the billiard room of historic Clifford House (1860). Regionally sourced delicacies dapple the menu: Moreton Bay bugs, Junee farm lamb rump, braised Bangalow pork belly. If the sun is shining, head for the jacaranda trees in the garden courtyard.

Drinking

Spotted Cow PUB
(www.spottedcow.com.au; cnr Ruthven & Campbell Sts; ⏰11am-3pm) A mustard-coloured pub with old blues on the stereo and regular live bands, the Spotted Cow is a Toowoomba institution. There are 70 different beers on offer if you've worked up a thirst, and tasty bistro meals (mains $12 to $28: go for the 1kg pot of mussels for $27). Trivia on Wednesday nights.

Fitzy's Fibber Magee PUB
(☎07-4631 3700; www.fibbers.com.au; 153 Margaret St; ⏰10.30am-late) If you fancy a cheeky pint, this affable Irish pub has myriad bars and eating areas, plus big steaks and rugby on the telly.

Entertainment

Empire Theatre THEATRE, LIVE MUSIC
(☎1300 655 299; www.empiretheatre.com.au; 56 Neil St; ⏰box office 9am-5pm Mon-Fri, 9am-1pm Sat) Toowoomba's cultural heart beats stridently inside the magnificent Empire Theatre, sections of which date back to 1911 (the art-deco facade is from 1933). Check out touring musical acts (Queensland musical hero Bernard Fanning was playing when we were in town), plus comedy festivals, opera and theatre, or just stick your head into the lobby and ogle the architectural details.

Information

Toowoomba Visitor Information Centre
(☎07-4639 3797, 1800 331 155; www.southernqueenslandcountry.com.au; 86 James St; ⏰9am-5pm; 📶) Located southeast of the centre, at the junction with Kitchener St. Peel yourself off a vast bed-sheet-sized map of town.

Getting There & Away

Toowoomba is 126km west of Brisbane on the Warrego Hwy. **Greyhound** (www.greyhound.com.au) provides regular daily services between Brisbane and Toowoomba ($35, two hours), and runs less frequently south to Stanthorpe ($44, 2½ hours).

If you're coming straight from Brisbane Airport, the **Airport Flyer** (☎07-4630 1444, 1300 304 350; www.theairportflyer.com.au; one-way/return $82/148) runs door-to-door services to/from Toowoomba (cheaper for more than one passenger).

Around Toowoomba

Crows Nest

POP 1450

North of Toowoomba the New England Hwy travels the ridges of the Great Dividing Range. It passes through a series of small settlements on the way to the cute town of Crows Nest, circulating around a village green about 50km north of Toowoomba.

Crows Nest hosts the **World Worm Races** (www.crowsnestfestival.com.au) as part of the Crows Nest Festival every October, but 6km east of town, **Crows Nest National Park** (www.nprsr.qld.gov.au/parks/crows-nest) is far more impressive, with a cascading waterfall and eucalypt forest punctuated by craggy granite outcrops and sheer 100m cliffs. There are some scenic walking tracks here (ranging from 2km to 4.5km) and cool-down swimming holes, plus there's a small bush camp site ($5.60 per person; book in advance online). For more weatherproof accommodation there's the **Crows Nest Caravan Park** (☎07-4698 1269; www.crowsnestcaravanpark.com.au; 7558 New England Hwy;

unpowered/powered sites $25/29, cabins $65-145;), with flocks of chattering parrots and neat cabins; and the excellent **Crows Nest Motel** (07-4698 1399; www.crowsnestmotel.com.au; 7547 New England Hwy; s/d/apt from $120/124/157;), a newish L-shaped arrangement with new bathrooms and TVs, quality linen and kangaroos bounding about in the back paddock. The apartments here are two-bedroom layouts with full kitchens, and are great value.

Also on offer in Crows Nest itself are the crafty **Crows Nest Village Markets** (0429 678 120; www.crowsnestvillagemarkets.com; Centenary Park; 7am-noon 1st Sun of the month), and the **Crows Nest Regional Art Gallery** (07-4698 1687; www.toowoombarc.qld.gov.au; New England Hwy; 10.30am-3.30pm Tue-Sat, 11.30am-3.30pm Sun) FREE inside the Shire Council building, which treads a path between contemporary abstract canvases, religious iconography and nature photography.

For local info, swing by the **Hampton Visitor Information Centre** (07-4697 9066, 1800 009 066; www.crowsnest.info; New England Hwy; 9am-5pm) 12km south of Crows Nest.

Woolshed at Jondaryan

Still fresh from a recent $2 million refurbishment, the huge **Woolshed at Jondaryan** (07-4692 2229; www.jondaryanwoolshed.com; 264 Jondaryan-Evanslea Rd, Jondaryan; adult/child/family $13/8/38; 9am-4.30pm) showcases the rich pastoral traditions of Queensland. Built in 1859, it's the state's (and possibly the world's) oldest operating woolshed and offers an engaging time-trip back to simpler (though more strenuous) days on the farm. It's located 45km northwest of Toowoomba on the Warrego Hwy.

The woolshed played a pivotal role in the history of the Australian Labor Party: it was here in 1890 that the first of the legendary shearers' strikes began. Today the woolshed is the centrepiece of a sprawling tourist complex with an interesting collection of rustic old buildings, antique farm and industrial machinery (including a mighty, steam-driven 'roadburner' which applied the first tarmac to many of Australia's roads) and weekend blacksmithing and shearing demonstrations.

Try to time your arrival for the daily 11am tour. Shearing in the woolshed, wagon rides, blacksmithing, sheepdogs working, wool spinning and the like happen thoughout the day.

There are also several rustic accommodation choices here, all organised through the Woolshed reception, ranging from basic shearers' quarters ($55 per night) to camp sites ($20 to $27) and cabins and cottages ($75 to $135).

Jondaryan hosts a string of annual events, including a nine-day **Australian Heritage Festival** in late August and early September, a **New Year's Eve Bush Dance** and an **Australia Day** celebration (book your accommodation well in advance).

The Gold Coast

Includes ➡

Best Places to Eat

- Providore (p125)
- Oskars (p129)
- BSKT Cafe (p126)
- Manolas Brothers Deli (p126)
- Borough Barista (p128)

Best Places to Stay

- Komune (p129)
- Vibe Hotel (p119)
- O'Reilly's Rainforest Retreat (p132)
- Mouses House (p133)
- Olympus Apartments (p118)

Why Go?

Boasting 35 beaches, 300 sunny days and four million visitors a year, the Gold Coast serves up a sexy Aussie cocktail of sun, surf and sand. It's no cliché to say that the beaches here are spectacular, with outstanding waves at Burleigh Heads, Currumbin and Kirra: it's one of the best places to learn to surf in Australia. Behind the beach is a shimmering strip of high-rise apartments, eateries, bars, clubs and theme parks. The party capital is Surfers Paradise, where the fun sucks you into a dizzying vortex and spits you back out exhausted. The hype diminishes drastically as you head south, with Broadbeach's sandy chic, Burleigh Heads' seaside charm and Coolangatta's laid-back surfer ethos. In the lush, subtropical hinterland, Lamington and Springbrook National Parks offer rainforest walks, waterfalls, sweeping views and cosy mountain retreats.

When to Go

Surfers Paradise

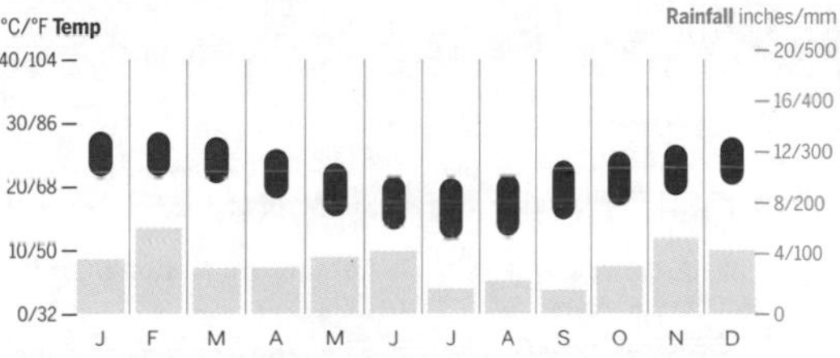

Jan Summer means sun, heat, busy beaches and the Big Day Out festival.

Jun–Aug Winter brings tourists from the chilly south chasing the sun.

Nov School-leavers ('schoolies') swarm into Surfers Paradise to party (avoid unless you're 18).

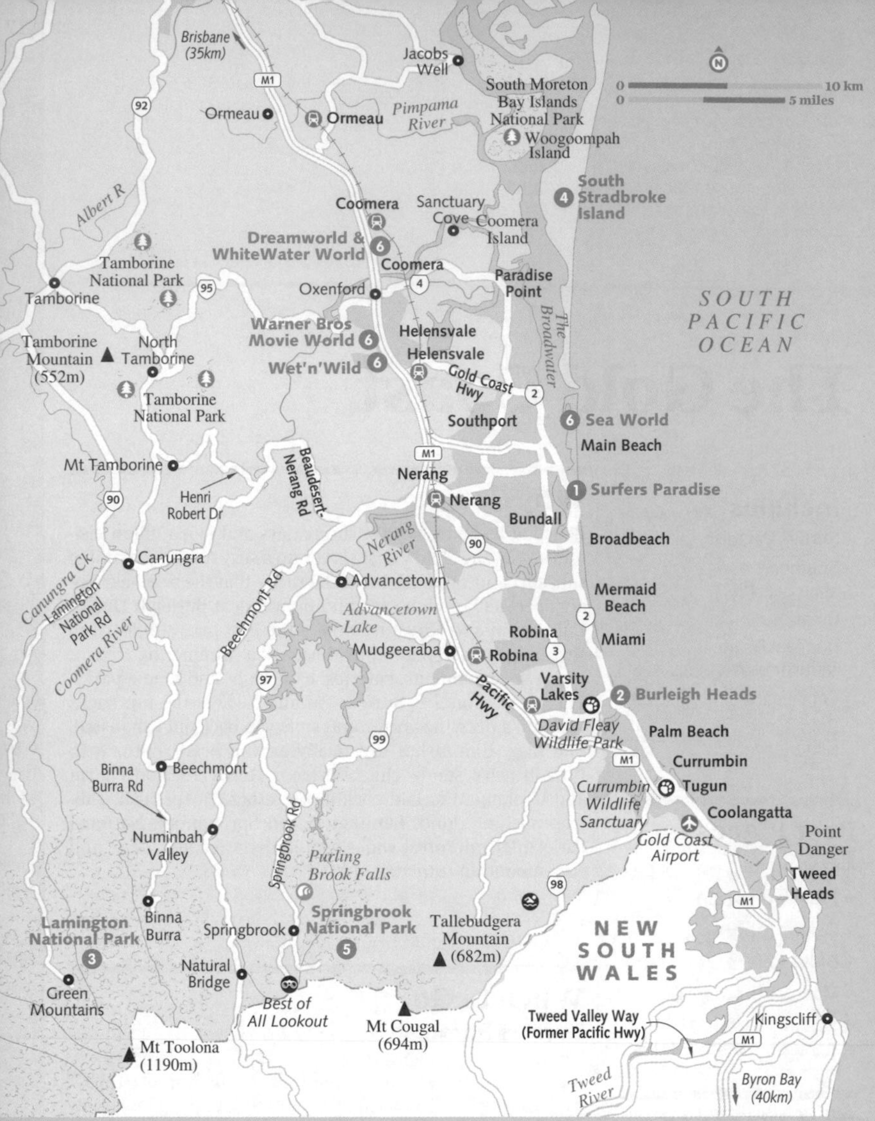

The Gold Coast Highlights

1 Drinking, dancing and watching the sun come up over the beach at **Surfers Paradise** (p117).

2 Getting up early to surf the point break at **Burleigh Heads** (p126).

3 Bushwalking through craggy gorges and rainforests in **Lamington National Park** (p132).

4 Beating a retreat from the crowds to a *looong* stretch of golden sand on **South Stradbroke Island** (p122).

5 Confirming the validity of the Best Of All Lookout's name in **Springbrook National Park** (p133).

6 Testing your nerve (and how long it's been since you had lunch) on the rollercoasters at the **Gold Coast theme parks** (p123).

Getting There & Away

AIR

Gold Coast Airport (www.goldcoastairport.com.au) is in Coolangatta, 25km south of Surfers Paradise. All the main Australian domestic airlines fly here, plus **Scoot** (www.flyscoot.com), **Air Asia** (www.airasia.com) and **Air New Zealand** (www.airnewzealand.com) flying in from overseas.

BUS

Greyhound (www.greyhound.com.au) and **Premier Motor Service** (www.premierms.com.au) run frequent daily services between Brisbane and the Gold Coast ($20, 1½ hours).

CAR & MOTORCYCLE

If you're driving, the Gold Coast is an easy one-hour hop south of Brisbane. Driving north, you'll cross the NSW/Queensland border at Tweed Heads: Coolangatta (the southern-most Gold Coast town) is immediately across the border.

TRAIN

Citytrain services run by TransLink (p296) connect Brisbane with Nerang, Robina and Varsity Lakes stations on the Gold Coast ($20.90, 75 minutes) roughly every half-hour. The same line extends north of Brisbane to Brisbane Airport (one-way Brisbane Airport to Varsity Lakes costs $36.10 and takes 1¾ hours).

Getting Around

TO/FROM THE AIRPORT

Gold Coast Tourist Shuttle (☎07-5574 5111, 1300 655 655; www.gcshuttle.com.au; one-way per adult/child $20/12) will meet your flight and drop you at most Gold Coast accommodation; book in advance. **Con-X-ion Airport Transfers** (☎1300 266 946; www.con-x-ion.com; one-way adult/child from $20/12) runs a similar service, with transfers available from Brisbane airport too (one-way adult/child $49/25). Both companies run transfers to the Gold Coast theme parks.

BUS

Surfside Buslines (www.surfside.com.au) – a subsidiary of Brisbane's main TransLink operation – runs regular buses up and down the Gold Coast, plus shuttles from the Gold Coast train stations into Surfers Paradise ($6.70) and beyond (including the theme parks).

Surfside (in conjunction with Gold Coast Tourist Shuttle) also offers a **Freedom Pass** including return Gold Coast Airport transfers and unlimited theme park transfers plus local bus travel for $71/36 per adult/child, valid for three days.

TAXI

Gold Coast Cabs (☎13 10 08; www.gccabs.com.au)

TRAM

By the time you read this, the new **Gold Coast Rapid Transit** (www.goldlinq.com.au) tram system might be operational, linking 16 stops over 13km between Southport and Broadbeach. Check the website for updates.

SURFERS PARADISE

POP 19,670

Some say the surfers prefer beaches elsewhere and paradise has been tragically lost, but there's no denying this wild and trashy party zone attracts a phenomenal number of visitors (20,000 per day!). Cashed-up tourists swarm to Surfers for a heady dose of clubs, bars, malls and maybe a bit of beachtime when the hangover kicks in. It's a sexy place: lots of shirtless, tattooed backpackers and more cleavage than the Grand Canyon. The beach itself is indeed a paradise, but if you're looking for cultural substance – with the notable exception of the Arts Centre – it's a case of 'Move along, nothing to see here'.

Sights

SkyPoint Observation Deck LOOKOUT
(www.skypoint.com.au; Level 77, Q1 Bldg, Hamilton Ave; adult/child/family $21/12.50/54.50; ⏲7.30am-8.30pm Sun-Thu, to 11.30pm Fri & Sat) Surfers' sights are usually spread across beach towels, but for an eagle-eye view, zip up to this 230m-high observation deck near the top of Q1, the 27th-tallest building in the world! You can also tackle the **SkyPoint Climb** up the spire to 270m high (adult/child from $69/49).

Infinity MAZE
(www.infinitygc.com.au; Chevron Renaissance, cnr Surfers Paradise Blvd & Elkhorn Ave; adult/child/family $25/17/70; ⏲10am-10pm) Lose the kids for an hour (literally) inside Infinity, a walk-through maze cunningly disguised with elaborate audiovisual displays.

Activities

Cheyne Horan School of Surf SURFING
(☎1800 227 873; www.cheynehoran.com.au; 2hr lesson $49, 3/5 lessons $129/189; ⏲10am & 2pm) Learn to carve up the waves with former pro surfer Cheyne Horan. Board hire $30 per day.

Whales in Paradise WHALE WATCHING
(☎07-5538 2111; www.whalesinparadise.com.au; cnr Cavill & Ferny Aves; adult/child/family

SCHOOLIES ON THE LOOSE

Every year in November, thousands of teenagers flock to Surfers Paradise to celebrate the end of their high-school education in a three-week party known as 'Schoolies Week'. Although local authorities have stepped in to regulate excesses, boozed-up and drug-addled teens are still the norm. Time for a trip to Noosa?

For more info see www.schoolies.com.

$95/60/250; Jun-Nov) Leaves central Surfers for 3½ hours of whale-watching action.

Jetboat Extreme BOATING
(07-5538 8890; www.jetboatextreme.com.au; Ferny Ave; 1hr ride adult/child $59/38) Slide and spin across the water in a turbo-charged, twin-jet-powered, custom-built jet boat.

Balloon Down Under BALLOONING
(07-5500 4797; www.balloondownunder.com; 1hr flights adult/child $299/240) Up, up and away on sunrise flights over the Gold Coast, ending with a champagne breakfast.

Tours

Bunyip Bike Tours CYCLING
(0447 286 947; www.bunyipbiketours.com.au; per person $49) Three-hour bike tours along Gold Coast beachfront trails. Hinterland tours also available.

Aqua Duck BOAT
(07-5539 0222; www.aquaduck.com.au; 36 Cavill Ave, Surfers Paradise; adult/child/family $35/26/95; 1hr tour every 75min 10am-5.30pm) Check out Surfers by land and water in a boat with wheels.

Festivals & Events

Big Day Out MUSIC
(www.bigdayout.com) Huge international music festival in late January.

Tropfest FILM
(www.tropfest.com/au/surfers-paradise) The biggest short film festival in the world hits screens in Surfers Paradise in February.

Quicksilver Pro Surfing Competition SURFING
(www.aspworldtour.com) The world's best surfers hit the waves in mid-March in the first comp of the annual world tour.

Surfers Paradise Festival FOOD, ARTS
(www.surfersparadisefestival.com) Food, wine and live music for four weeks in April.

Gold Coast Film Festival FILM
(www.gcfilmfestival.com) Mainstream and left-of-centre flicks from all over the world on outdoor screens. In April.

Gold Coast Marathon MARATHON
(www.goldcoastmarathon.com.au) Sweaty people running a really long way. In July.

Gold Coast 600 MOTORSPORTS
(www.surfersparadise.v8supercars.com.au) For three days in October the streets of Surfers are transformed into a temporary race circuit for high-speed V8 Supercars.

Sleeping

The **Gold Coast Accommodation Service** (07-5592 0067; www.goldcoastaccommodation-service.com) can arrange and book accommodation and tours.

Budds in Surfers HOSTEL $
(07-5538 9661; www.buddsinsurfers.com.au; 6 Pine Ave; dm/tw/d/q from $28/70/70/90; @) Laid-back Budds features tidy bathrooms, clean tiles, free wi-fi, a sociable bar and a beaut pool, all just a short hop from calm-water Budds Beach. Bike hire available.

Sleeping Inn Surfers HOSTEL $
(07-5592 4455, 1800 817 832; www.sleepinginn.com.au; 26 Peninsular Dr; dm $28-32, d & tw $68-114; @) This backpackers occupies an old apartment block away from the centre, so, as the name suggests, there's a chance you may get to sleep in. Pizza nights, barbecue nights and pick-ups in a vintage limo.

Backpackers in Paradise HOSTEL $
(07-5538 4344, 1800 268 621; www.backpackersinparadise.com; 40 Peninsular Dr; dm $25-33, d $80; @) If you're in Surfers to wage war against sleep, this party backpackers is for you. Encircling a courtyard carpeted with astroturf, most rooms are freshly painted and have bathrooms. The bar does cheap dinners – fuel-up before you hit the town.

★**Olympus Apartments** APARTMENT $$
(07-5538 7288; www.olympusapartments.com.au; 62 Esplanade; 1br $100-160, 2br $150-300;) Great value for money and directly opposite the beach, this friendly, smallish high-rise has well-kept, spacious apartments with one or two bedrooms: mod furnishings, nice art, super-clean, and all facing the sea.

Vibe Hotel HOTEL $$
(☎07-5539 0444, 13 84 23; www.vibehotels.com.au; 42 Ferny Ave; d $105-250;) Slick but affordable, this chocolate-and-green high-rise on the Nerang River is a vibrant gem amongst Surfers' bland plethora of hotels and apartments. The rooms are subtle-chic and the pool is a top spot for sundowners. The aqua-view rooms have Nerang River views.

Moorings on Cavill APARTMENT $$
(☎07-5538 6711; www.mooringsoncavill.com.au; 63 Cavill Ave; 1/2br from $128/168;) This roomy, 73-apartment tower at the river end of Cavill Ave is great for families: the vibe is quiet and respectful. The location is close to the beach, the shops and the restaurants. Super-clean and managed with a smile.

Chateau Beachside Resort APARTMENT $$
(☎07-5538 1022; www.chateaubeachside.com.au; cnr Elkhorn Ave & Esplanade; d/1-bedroom apt from $170/200;) Less Loire Valley, more Las Vegas, this seaside 'chateau' (actually an 18-storey tower) is an excellent choice. All the renovated studios and apartments have ocean views and the 18m pool is a bonus. Minimum two-night stay.

Artique APARTMENT $$$
(☎07-5564 3100, 1800 454 442; www.artiqueresort.com.au; cnr Surfers Paradise Blvd & Enderley Ave; 1-/2-bedroom apt from $240/290;) One of several slick new apartment towers at Surfers' southern end, Artique (certainly not antique) features a curvy facade, glazed balustrades, muted charcoal-and-cream tones, classy kitchens and fountains. Minimum stays apply (usually three nights).

Q1 Resort APARTMENT $$$
(☎1300 792 008, 07-5630 4500; www.q1.com.au; Hamilton Ave; 1-/2-/3-bedroom apt from $318/325/666;) Spend a night in the world's 27th-tallest building! It's a slick resort with a mod mix of metal, glass and fabulous wrap-around views. There's a lagoon-style pool and a fitness centre if the beach doesn't exhaust you. The very sassy French restaurant **Absynthe** (☎07-5504 6466; www.absynthe.com.au; mains $48; 6-10pm Tue-Sat) is here, too.

Eating

Self-caterers will find supermarkets in the **Chevron Renaissance Centre** (www.chevronrenaissancecentre.com; cnr Elkhorn Ave & Surfers Paradise Blvd; 7am-10pm Mon-Sat, 8am-8pm Sun) and **Circle on Cavill** (www.circleoncavill.com.au; cnr Cavill & Ferny Aves; 7am-10pm Mon-Sat, 8am-8pm Sun) shopping centres.

Bumbles Café CAFE $
(☎07-5538 6668; www.bumblescafe.com; 21 River Dr; mains $9-27; 7am-3pm Fri-Wed, to 10pm Thu) Chilled out, grey-painted corner cafe opposite shallow Budds Beach on the Nerang River. Order a FAT (fetta, avocado and tomato on toast) and enjoy a few minutes away from the fray.

Surfers Sandbar MODERN AUSTRALIAN $
(www.facebook.com/surferssandbar; cnr Elkhorn Ave & Esplanade; mains $12-32; 6.45am-late) The menu is predictable – burgers, fish and chips, pizza, steak sandwiches – but beachside prominence gives this cafe/bar the edge over most Surfers eateries. Forgo the pubby indoor space and chow-down on the terrace

THE GOLD COAST IN...

Two Days

Start with a beach swim before breakfast, then get dunked, rolled and spun a thousand different ways at one of the **Gold Coast theme parks**. Pull yourself together, grab some dinner in Surfers Paradise at Baritalia (p120) or Surfers Sandbar (p119) then hit the party scene along **Orchid Ave**.

Next day, hit the surf: book a lesson at Surfers Paradise or Currumbin, or head for the legendary big waves at Burleigh Heads or Coolangatta. Have lunch at Oskars (p129) overlooking Burleigh's beaut beach, then hang out with some native critters at Currumbin Wildlife Sanctuary (p127). Beachside beers at the Coolangatta Hotel (p131) await.

Three Days

With three days up your sleeve you can explore the hinterland. Skip Tamborine Mountain (unless Devonshire teas are your thing) and take a hike in Springbrook National Park (p133) (or just check out the waterfalls and lookouts you can drive right up to).

Surfers Paradise

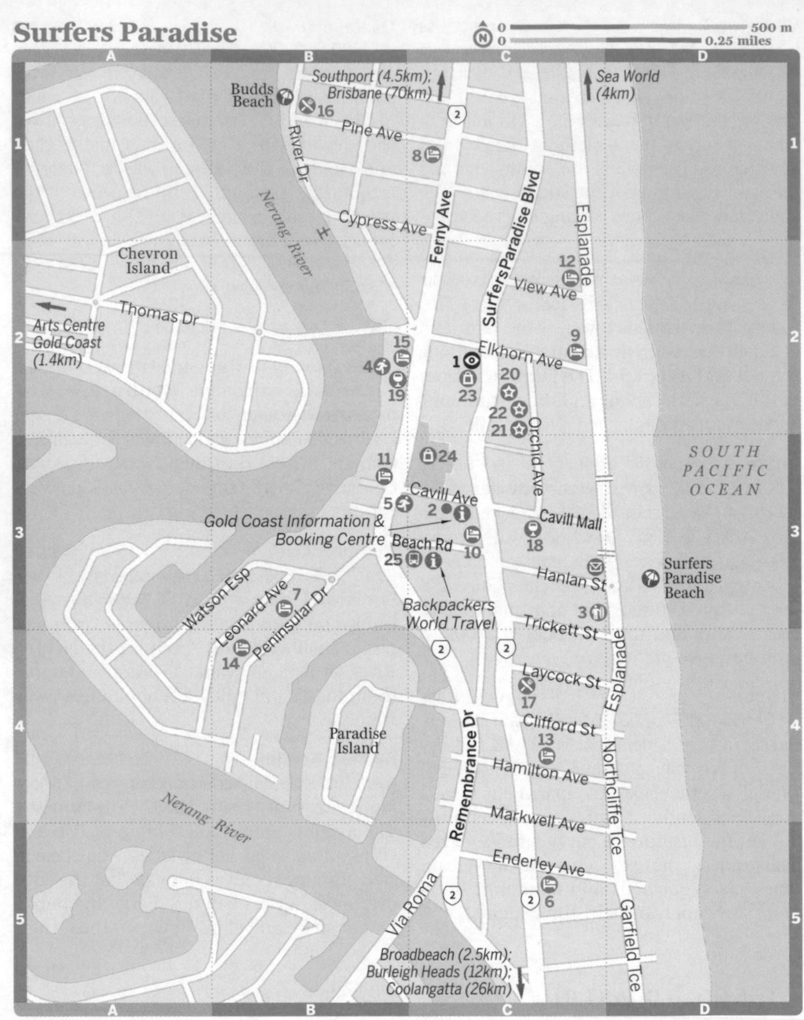

(you can hear lifesavers berating absent-minded swimmers across the street).

Baritalia ITALIAN **$$**
(☎07-5592 4700; www.baritaliagoldcoast.com.au; Shop 15, Chevron Renaissance Centre, cnr Elkhorn Ave & Surfers Paradise Blvd; mains $15-35; ⏲7.30am-late) This Italian bar and restaurant has a fab outdoor terrace and hip international staff. Go for the chilli seafood broth with Moreton Bay bugs, saffron and capers, or excellent pastas, pizzas and risotto. Decent wines by the glass and good coffee.

Matador SPANISH **$$**
(☎07-5570 2007; www.matadortapasbar.com; Chevron Renaissance Centre, cnr Elkhorn Ave & Surfers Paradise Blvd; tapas from $6.50, mains $18-40; ⏲4pm-late Mon-Fri, noon-late Sat & Sun) Small, bright and simple, this Spanish hole-in-the-wall is the pick of the Chevron Renaissance Centre eateries. It does a roaring trade in tapas (try the grilled prawns in serrano ham) and heftier mains, including an awesome Spanish marinara casserole.

Tandoori Place INDIAN **$$**
(☎07-5538 0808, 1300 082 636; www.tandooriplace.com; 30 Laycock St; mains $15-19, banquets

Surfers Paradise

Sights
1 Infinity ... C2
SkyPoint Observation Deck ... (see 13)

Activities, Courses & Tours
2 Aqua Duck ... C3
3 Cheyne Horan School of Surf ... C3
4 Jetboat Extreme ... B2
5 Whales in Paradise ... B3

Sleeping
6 Artique ... C5
7 Backpackers in Paradise ... B3
8 Budds in Surfers ... C1
9 Chateau Beachside Resort ... C2
10 Gold Coast Accommodation Service ... C3
11 Moorings on Cavill ... B3
12 Olympus Apartments ... C2
13 Q1 Resort ... C4
14 Sleeping Inn Surfers ... B4
15 Vibe Hotel ... B2

Eating
Absynthe ... (see 13)
Baritalia ... (see 1)
16 Bumbles Café ... B1
Matador ... (see 1)
Surfers Sandbar ... (see 9)
17 Tandoori Place ... C4

Drinking & Nightlife
18 Beergarden ... C3
19 Helm Bar & Bistro ... B2

Entertainment
20 Shuffle ... C2
21 Sin City ... C2
22 Vanity ... C2

Shopping
23 Chevron Renaissance Centre ... C2
24 Circle on Cavill ... C3

Transport
Bus Stop for Burleigh Heads ... (see 5)
Bus Stop for Southport ... (see 15)
25 Surfers Paradise Transit Centre ... C3

per person from $26; 11.30am-2.30pm & 5pm-late) One of 17 (yes 17!) Tandoori Place restaurants in the Gold Coast area, this burgundy food room thankfully doesn't feel like part of a chain. On the vast menu you'll find seafood, chicken, lamb, beef and hot, hot, *hot* vindaloo roo. Kids welcome ('Children are nature's gift').

Drinking & Nightlife

Orchid Ave is Surfers' club strip. Cover charges are usually $10 to $20; Wednesday and Saturday are the big party nights. You can tag along with other boozy backpackers on club crawls organised by **Plan B Party Tours** (1300 721 570; www.planbtours.com; tickets $60): tickets get you into five clubs and take the hassle out of the experience. **Big Night Out** (www.goldcoastbackpackers.net; tickets $30) and **Wicked Club Crawl** (07-5504 7025; www.wickedclubcrawl.com.au; tickets $30-50) are similar (but with four clubs).

Helm Bar & Bistro BAR
(www.helmbarsurfers.com.au; 30-34 Ferny Ave; 10am-9pm) Unless you like Irish pubs, this nautical-themed bar is the best drinking spot in town, perfect for a beer or six as the sun sets over the Nerang River. Good pizzas and steaks, too.

Beergarden BAR
(www.surfersbeergarden.com.au; Cavill Ave; 10am-5am) Not so much a garden – more of a black-painted beer barn overlooking Cavill Ave. Steel yourself with a few cold ones before you hit the clubs, or catch live bands on Saturday nights or reggae on Sunday afternoons.

Sin City CLUB
(www.sincitynightclub.com.au; 22 Orchid Ave; 9pm-late) This Vegas-style sin pit is the place for wrongdoings: sexy staff, big-name DJs and visiting celebs trying not to get photographed.

Shuffle CLUB
(www.platinumnightclub.com.au/shuffle-nightclub; Shop 15b, The Forum, 26 Orchid Ave; 9pm-5am Fri & Sat) Shuffle into Shuffle for an intimate club experience, with dirty underground house and a backpacker-heavy crowd (less red carpet, more downmarket).

Vanity CLUB
(www.vanitynightclub.com.au; 26 Orchid Ave; 5am-5pm) 'Because it's all about you' at Vanity, one of the glammest clubs in town, which digs deep into the sexy marketing book of tricks. Dress to the nines; no visible tatts.

☆ Entertainment

Arts Centre Gold Coast THEATRE, CINEMA
(☎07-5588 4000; www.theartscentregc.com.au; 135 Bundall Rd; ⏲box office 8am-9pm Mon-Fri, 9am-9pm Sat, 11am-7pm Sun) A bastion of culture and civility beside the Nerang River, the Arts Centre has two cinemas, a restaurant, a bar, the Gold Coast City Gallery and a 1200-seat theatre, which hosts productions (comedy, jazz, opera, kids' concerts etc).

ℹ Information

Backpackers World Travel (☎07-5561 0634; www.backpackerworldtravel.com; 6 Beach Rd; ⏲10am-6pm Mon-Fri, 10am-5pm Sat, to 4pm Sun) Accommodation, tour and transport bookings and internet access.

Gold Coast Information & Booking Centre (☎1300 309 440; www.visitgoldcoast.com; Cavill Ave; ⏲8.30am-5pm Mon-Sat, 9am-4pm Sun) The main GC tourist information booth; also sells theme-park tickets and has public transport info.

Post Office (www.auspost.com.au; Shop 165, Centro Surfers Paradise, Cavill Ave Mall; ⏲9am-5pm Mon-Fri)

Surfers Paradise Day & Night Medical Centre (☎07-5592 2299; 3221 Surfers Paradise Blvd; ⏲6am-11pm) General medical centre and pharmacy. Make an appointment or walk in.

ℹ Getting There & Away

Long-distance buses stop at the **Surfers Paradise Transit Centre** (10 Beach Rd). **Greyhound** (☎1300 473 946; www.greyhound.com.au) and Premier Motor Service (p117) have frequent services to/from Brisbane ($20, 1½ hours), Byron Bay ($30, 2½ hours) and beyond.

ℹ Getting Around

Car hire costs around $35 to $50 per day.

East Coast Car Rentals (☎07-5592 0444, 1800 028 881; www.eastcoastcarrentals.com.au; 80 Ferny Ave; ⏲7am-6pm Mon-Fri, 8am-5pm Sat, to 4pm Sun)

Red Back Rentals (☎07-5592 1655; www.redbackrentals.com.au; Surfers Paradise Transit Centre, 10 Beach Rd; ⏲8am-4.30pm Mon-Fri, to 4pm Sat)

Scooter Hire Gold Coast (☎07-5511 0398; www.scooterhiregoldcoast.com.au; 3269 Surfers Paradise Blvd; ⏲8am-5.30pm) Scooter hire (50cc) from around $65 per day.

SOUTHPORT & MAIN BEACH

POP 28,320 & 3330

The northern gateway to the Gold Coast, incongruously named Southport is a low-key residential and business district. It's sheltered from the ocean by a long sandbar called the Spit, which is is home to one of the big theme parks, Sea World.

Directly southeast is glorious, golden Main Beach, where the apartment blocks begin their inexorable rise towards Surfers.

◉ Sights

Main Beach Pavilion ARCHITECTURE
(Macarthur Pde, Main Beach; ⏲9am-5pm) The lovely Spanish Mission–style Main Beach Pavilion (1934) is a remnant from less hectic times. Inside are some fabulous old photos of the Gold Coast in pre-skyscraper days.

OFF THE BEATEN TRACK

SOUTH STRADBROKE ISLAND

This narrow, 21km-long sand island is largely undeveloped – the perfect antidote to the chaotic Gold Coast strip. At the northern end, the narrow channel separating it from North Stradbroke Island is a top fishing spot; at the southern end, the Spit is only 200m away. South Stradbroke was actually attached to North Stradbroke until a huge storm in 1896 blasted through the isthmus joining them. There's a resort here, plus three camping grounds, lots of wallabies and plenty of bush, sand and sea. And no cars!

The **Ramada Couran Cove Island Resort** (☎07-5597 9999; www.courancove.com.au; South Stradbroke Island; d/ste from $210/250; ❄🏊) is a luxe resort on the isle's northwest side, with rooms on stilts by the water, restaurants, a spa, a private marina and guided nature walks. Pre-booked ferry transfers (return adult/child $30/15) depart three times daily from Runaway Bay Marina on Bayview St, 7km north of Southport.

For details on camping on the island – at Tipplers, North Currigee and South Currigee camping grounds – incuding transport info, see www.mystraddie.com.au.

DON'T MISS

GOLD COAST THEME PARKS

The gravity-defying rollercoasters and waterslides at these American-style parks offer some seriously dizzy action – keeping your lunch down is a constant battle. Discount tickets are sold in most of the tourist offices on the Gold Coast; the VIP Pass (per person $110) grants unlimited entry to Sea World, Warner Bros Movie World and Wet'n'Wild.

A couple of tips: the parks can get insanely crowded, so arrive early or face a long walk from the far side of the car park. Also note that the parks don't let you bring your own food and drinks – load up on breakfast beforehand, or buy your lunch.

Dreamworld (1800 073 300, 07-5588 1111; www.dreamworld.com.au; Dreamworld Pkwy, Coomera; adult/child $95/75, online $90/70; 10am-5pm) Home to the 'Big 8 Thrill Rides', including the Giant Drop and Tower of Terror II. Lots of kid-centric rides too. Get your photo taken with Aussie animals or a Bengal tiger at Tiger Island. Access to WhiteWater World is included in the ticket price.

Sea World (07-5588 2222, 13 33 86; www.seaworld.com.au; Seaworld Dr, The Spit, Main Beach; adult/child $83/50; 9.30am-5.30pm) See polar bears, sharks, seals, penguins and performing dolphins at this aquatic park, which also has the mandatory rollercoasters and waterslides. Animal shows throughout the day.

Warner Bros Movie World (13 33 86, 07-5573 3999; www.movieworld.com.au; Pacific Hwy, Oxenford; adult/child $83/50; 9.30am-5pm) Movie-themed shows, rides and attractions, including the Batwing Spaceshot, Justice League 3D Ride and Scooby-Doo Spooky Coaster. Batman, Austin Powers, Porky Pig et al roam through the crowds.

Wet'n'Wild (13 33 86, 07-5556 1660; www.wetnwild.com.au; Pacific Hwy, Oxenford; adult/child $60/35; 10am-5pm) The ultimate waterslide here is the Kamikaze, where you plunge down an 11m drop in a two-person tube at 50km/h. This vast water park also has pitch-black slides, white-water rapids and wave pools.

WhiteWater World (1800 073 300, 07-5588 1111; www.whitewaterworld.com.au; Dreamworld Pkwy, Coomera; adult/child $95/75, online $90/70; 10am-4pm) Connected to Dreamworld; features waterslide rides like the Temple of Huey, the Green Room and the Cave of Waves. You can learn to surf here too! Ticket price includes entry to Dreamworld.

Gourmet Farmers Market MARKET
(07-5555 6400; www.facebook.com/marinamiragefarmersmarket; Marina Mirage, 74 Sea World Dr, Main Beach; 7-11am Sat) On Saturday mornings, the spaces between boutiques at this flashy mall fill with stalls selling seasonal fruit and veg, baked goods, pickles, oils, vinegars, seafood, pasta and more...

Produce by the Pier MARKET
(www.producebythepier.com.au; Broadwater Parklands, Southport; 8am-2pm Sat) Fresh fruit and veg, coffee, flowers, wine and deli goods in the park by the Broadwater Parklands pier.

Activities

Opposite the entrance to Sea World, in the car park of Phillip Park, is the start of the **Federation Walk**, a 3.7km trail through littoral rainforest and connecting to the **Gold Coast Oceanway** (www.goldcoastcity.com.au/oceanway), a 36km walking/cycling trail running from here to Coolangatta.

Mariner's Cove in Main Beach can book water activities. Sift through the plethora of operators here at the **Mariner's Cove Tourism Information & Booking Centre** (07-5571 1711; www.marinerscovemarina.com.au; Mariner's Cove, 60-70 Seaworld Dr, Main Beach; 8.30am-3.30pm Mon-Fri, 9.30am-2pm Sat & Sun).

Australian Kayaking Adventures KAYAKING
(0412 940 135; www.australiankayakingadventures.com.au; half-day tour adult/child $95/75, sunset tours $55/45) Paddle out to underrated South Stradbroke Island and spot some dolphins, or take a dusk paddle around Chevron Island in the calm canals behind Surfers.

Gold Coast Watersports PARASAILING
(0410 494 240; www.goldcoastwatersports.com; Mariner's Cove, 60-70 Sea World Dr, Main Beach; per person from $65) Daily parasailing jaunts.

Jet Ski Safaris JET-SKIING
(0409 754 538, 07-5526 3111; www.jetskisafaris.com.au; Mariner's Cove, 60-70 Sea World Dr,

Southport & Main Beach

Sights
1 Gourmet Farmers Market ... C2
2 Main Beach Pavilion ... D3
3 Mariner's Cove ... C3
4 Produce by the Pier ... B2
5 Sea World ... C1

Activities, Courses & Tours
6 Brad Holmes Surf Coaching ... D4
7 Broadwater Canal Cruises ... C3
Gold Coast Helitours ... (see 3)
Gold Coast Watersports ... (see 3)
Island Adventures ... (see 3)
Jet Ski Safaris ... (see 3)

Sleeping
8 Harbour Side Resort ... A1
9 Main Beach Tourist Park ... D4
10 Palazzo Versace ... C2
Surfers Paradise YHA at Main Beach ... (see 3)
11 Trekkers ... B3

Eating
12 Peter's Fish Market ... D2
Providore ... (see 1)
Sunset Bar & Grill ... (see 1)

Drinking & Nightlife
Fisherman's Wharf Tavern ... (see 3)

Information
Mariner's Cove Tourism Information & Booking Centre ... (see 3)

Main Beach; tour 30min/90min/2½hr per ski from $100/240/380) Jet-ski tours up and down the coast and out to South Stradbroke Island. No experience necessary; cheaper if you tandem on a ski with someone else.

Island Adventures WHALE WATCHING
(☎ 07-5532 2444, 1300 942 537; www.tallship.com.au; Mariner's Cove, 60-70 Sea World Dr, Main Beach; 3hr tour adult/child from $99/69) Cruises to South Stradbroke Island and beyond in search of big wet mammals. Lots of add-on options and longer tours also available.

Tours

Broadwater Canal Cruises CRUISE
(☎ 0410 403 020; www.broadwatercanalcruises.com.au; Mariner's Cove, 60-70 Sea World Dr, Main Beach; 2hr cruise adult/child/family $22/15/60; ⏲ 10.30am & 2pm) Runs slow-boat cruises around the Broadwater canals behind Surfers Paradise.

Gold Coast Helitours SCENIC FLIGHTS
(☎ 07-5591 8457; www.goldcoasthelitours.com.au; 5min ride adult/child $65/55, 20min $190/140) Runs a range of helicopter flights over the Gold Coast in black-and-orange choppers.

Sleeping

Surfers Paradise YHA at Main Beach HOSTEL $
(☎ 07-5571 1776; www.yha.com.au; 70 Sea World Dr, Main Beach; dm/d & tw $31/79; @ 📶) In a great first-floor position overlooking the marina. There's a free shuttle bus, barbecue nights every Friday, and the hostel is within wobbling distance of the Fisherman's Wharf Tavern. Sky-blue dorms; very well organised.

Trekkers HOSTEL $
(☎ 1800 100 004, 07-5591 5616; www.trekkersbackpackers.com.au; 22 White St, Southport; dm/d & tw $30/76; @ 📶 🏊) You could bottle the friendly vibes in this sociable old Queenslander and make a mint. The building is looking a bit tired, but the communal areas are homey and the garden is a mini-oasis.

Main Beach Tourist Park CARAVAN PARK $
(☎ 07-5667 2720; www.gctp.com.au/main; 3600 Main Beach Pde, Main Beach; powered sites/cabins & villas from $45/125; ❄ @ 📶 🏊) Just across the road from the beach and backed by high-rise apartments, this caravan park is a family favourite. It's a tight fit between sites, but the facilities are decent.

Harbour Side Resort APARTMENT $$
(☎ 07-5591 6666; www.harboursideresort.com.au; 132 Marine Pde, Southport; 1-/2-bedroom apt $130/170; ❄ @ 📶 🏊) 'Resort' is a bit of a stretch, and disregard the busy road: inside this facelifted, three-storey place you'll find motel-style units with well-equipped kitchens and a fab pool.

Palazzo Versace RESORT $$$
(☎ 07-5509 8000, 1800 098 000; www.palazzoversace.com; Sea World Dr, Main Beach; d/ste from $415/500; ❄ @ 🏊) A glitzy post-modern Roman apparition, the Palazzo Versace is pure extravagance, from the opulent rooms to the indulgent restaurants and bars. Everything, from the pool furniture to the bell-hops' belt buckles, is infused with over-the-top Versace glam. Staff are surprisingly un-snooty.

Eating

★ **Providore** CAFE $
(☎ 07-5532 9390; www.facebook.com/miragemarket; Shop 27, Marina Mirage, 74 Sea World Dr, Main Beach; mains $10-29; ⏲ 7am-6pm Sun-Wed, to 10pm Thu-Sat) Floor-to-ceiling windows rimmed with Italian mineral water bottles, inverted desk lamps dangling from the ceiling, good-looking Euro tourists, wines by the glass, bread racks, cheese fridges and baskets overflowing with fresh produce: this excellent deli/cafe gets a lot of things right. Order some polenta and eggs and start your day with aplomb.

Peter's Fish Market SEAFOOD, FISH & CHIPS $
(☎ 07-5591 7747; www.petersfish.com.au; 120 Sea World Dr, Main Beach; meals $9-16; ⏲ 9am-7.30pm, cooking from noon) A no-nonsense fish market selling fresh and cooked seafood in all shapes and sizes (and at great prices), fresh from the trawlers moored out the front.

Sunset Bar & Grill MODERN AUSTRALIAN $
(☎ 07-5528 2622; www.sunsetbarandgrill.com.au; Shop 31, Marina Mirage, 74 Sea World Dr, Main Beach; dishes $12-28; ⏲ 7am-6pm Mon-Fri, to 7pm Sat & Sun) This umbrella-shaded, family-friendly place by the water serves reasonably priced (if predictable) steaks, salads, burgers and seafood dishes.

Drinking

Fisherman's Wharf Tavern PUB
(☎ 07-5571 0566; Mariner's Cove, Main Beach; ⏲ 10am-midnight) This boisterous harbour side pub – on a pier out over the water – is a beers-from-10am kinda joint, and gets raucous on weekends (big Sunday sessions). The kitchen whips up reliable burgers and fish and chips, plus curries, steaks and salads.

Getting There & Away

Coaches stop at the **Southport Transit Centre** on Scarborough St, between North and Railway Sts. Catch local Surfside buses from outside the Australia Fair Shopping Centre on Scarborough St.

BROADBEACH

POP 4650

The decibel level tails off markedly directly south of Surfers Paradise in stylish Broadbeach, which offers chic cafes, shops and restaurants and a stretch of golden shore.

Activities

Brad Holmes Surf Coaching SURFING

(☎0418 757 539, 07-5539 4068; www.bradholmessurfcoaching.com; 90min lesson $75) Affordable one-on-one or group lessons at Broadbeach. Warm up with a t'ai-chi workout on the sand. Also caters to travellers with disabilities.

Sleeping

Hi-Ho Beach Apartments APARTMENT $$

(☎07-5538 2777; www.hihobeach.com.au; 2 Queensland Ave; 1-/2-bedroom apt from $100/130;) A top choice for location, close to the beach and cafes. You're not paying for glitzy lobbies here: it's standard, value-for-money, no-frills accommodation (a bit '90s decor-wise), but well managed, clean and quiet. Dig the Vegas-esque sign!

Wave APARTMENT $$$

(☎07-5555 9200; www.thewavesresort.com.au; 89-91 Surf Pde, Broadbeach; 1-/2-/3-bedroom apt from $290/405/480; @) Towering over glam Broadbeach, you can't miss this funky high-rise with its wobbly, wave-inspired facade. The plush pads here take full advantage of panoramic coastal views (especially good from the sky pool on the 34th floor). Minimum three-night stay.

Eating

★ **Manolas Brothers Deli** DELI, CAFE $

(MBD; www.m-b-d.com.au; 19 Albert Ave; dishes $8-21; 6.30am-5pm) Busy but strangely unhurried, MBD is a brilliant sidestreet deli-cafe. Ceiling-high shelves overflow with produce – vats of oil, Mediterranean sea salt, olives and pasta – and the counter is packed with gourmet pies, quiches, tarts, imported cheeses, antipasti and cakes. Park yourself at the long central table and sip a 'Flu Fighter' juice (orange, carrot, ginger and parsley).

★ **BSKT Cafe** CAFE $

(☎07-5526 6565; www.bskt.com.au; 4 Lavarack Ave, Mermaid Beach; mains $10-27; 7am-4pm Mon-Thu, to 10pm Fri-Sun;) This hip corner cafe is 100m from Mermaid Beach, a quick jaunt south of Broadbeach. The brainchild of four buddies who obsess over service and organic ingredients, it's a mod-industrial affair with chunky timber tables, super staff and adventurous mains: try the quesadilla with goats cheese and sesame, or the 18-hour sticky pork with sour herb salad. Great coffee, too.

Beer Thai Garden THAI $$

(☎07-5538 0110; www.beerthaigarden.com.au; 2765 Gold Coast Hwy; mains $18-23; 5.30-10pm;) With the best pad thai on the coast, Beer Thai Garden is right on the busy road but brims with atmosphere. Two affable elephants flank the entrance, and soft lighting brings an almost romantic vibe to the garden bar. Easy on the pocket, too.

Koi MODERN AUSTRALIAN, CAFE $$

(☎07-5570 3060; www.koibroadbeach.com.au; Wave Bldg, cnr Surf Pde & Albert Ave; mains breakfast $14-21, lunch & dinner $18-40; 7am-late) This cruisy cafe/bar is the pick of the eateries on Surf Pde. Fast-moving, black-clad wait staff shuffle out plates of risotto, pasta, gourmet pizza, tapas, seafood and Koi beans (with poached eggs, chorizo, crispy onion and balsamic reduction).

BURLEIGH HEADS & CURRUMBIN

POP 9200 & 2785

The true, sandy essence of the Gold Coast permeates the chilled-out surfie town of Burleigh Heads. With its cheery cafes and beachfront restaurants, famous right-hand point break, beautiful beach and little national park on the rocky headland, Burleigh charms everyone.

Beginner surfers should head to Currumbin Alley, 6km south of Burleigh. Currumbin itself is a sleepy little family-focused town, with safe swimming in Currumbin Creek.

Sights

Burleigh Head National Park PARK

(www.nprsr.qld.gov.au/parks/burleigh-head; Goodwin Tce, Burleigh Heads; 24hr) FREE A walk around the headland through Burleigh Head National Park is a must for any visitor – it's a 27-hectare rainforest reserve with plenty of bird life and several walking trails. Great views of the Burleigh surf en route.

David Fleay Wildlife Park WILDLIFE RESERVE

(☎07-5576 2411; www.nprsr.qld.gov.au/parks/david-fleay; cnr Loman La & West Burleigh Rd, West Burleigh; adult/child/family $19/9/48; 9am-5pm) Opened by the doctor who first succeeded

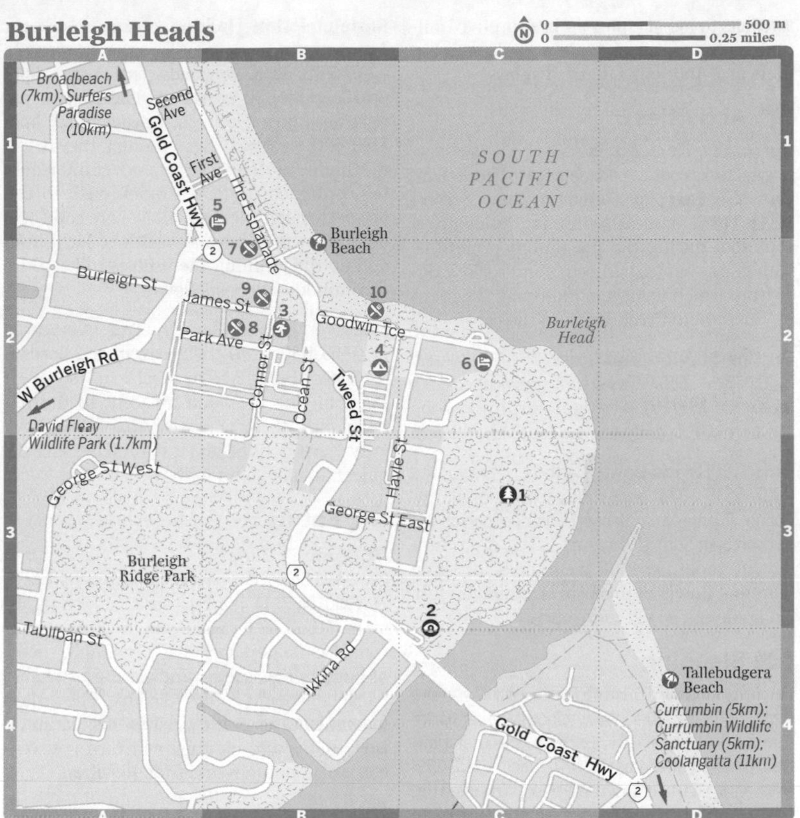

in breeding platypuses, this wildlife park has 4km of walking tracks through mangroves and rainforest and plenty of informative native wildlife shows throughout the day. It's around 3km inland from Burleigh Heads.

Currumbin Wildlife Sanctuary WILDLIFE RESERVE
(☎1300 886 511, 07-5534 1266; www.cws.org.au; 28 Tomewin St, Currumbin; adult/child/family $49/33/131; ⌚8am-5pm) Currumbin Wildlife Sanctuary has Australia's biggest rainforest aviary, where you can hand-feed a technicolour blur of rainbow lorikeets. There's also kangaroo feeding, photo ops with koalas and crocodiles, reptile shows and Aboriginal dance displays. It's cheaper after 3pm. Coach transfers available (return from $15).

Jellurgal Cultural Centre CULTURAL BUILDING
(☎07-5525 5955; www.jellurgal.com.au; 1711 Gold Coast Hwy, Burleigh Heads; ⌚8am-3pm Mon-Fri, 8am-4pm Sat, 9am-2pm Sun) FREE This new Aboriginal cultural centre at the base of Burleigh's headland sheds some light on life here hundreds of years ago. There's lots of art and

Burleigh Heads

Sights
1 Burleigh Head National Park C3
2 Jellurgal Cultural Centre C3

Activities, Courses & Tours
3 Burleigh Heads Bowls Club B2

Sleeping
4 Burleigh Beach Tourist Park B2
5 Burleigh Palms Holiday Apartments B1
6 Hillhaven Holiday Apartments C2

Eating
7 Borough Barista B2
8 Canteen Coffee B2
9 Fishmonger B2
10 Oskars B2

artefacts to look at, plus an interpretive multimedia boardwalk. Ask about daily walking tours and Aboriginal dance displays.

Activities

Currumbin Rock Pools SWIMMING
(www.gcparks.com.au/park-details.aspx?park=1751; Currumbin Creek Rd, Currumbin Valley; 24hr) FREE These natural swimming holes are a cool spot during the hot summer months, with grassy banks, barbecues and rocky ledges from which teenagers plummet. It's 14km up Currumbin Creek Rd from the coast.

Surfing Services Australia SURFING
(07-5535 5557; www.surfingservices.com.au; adult/child $35/25) Weekend surfing lessons at Currumbin (daily during school holidays).

Burleigh Heads Bowls Club LAWN BOWLS
(07-5535 1023; www.burleighbowls.org.au; cnr Connor & James Sts, Burleigh Heads; per person $4; noon-5pm Sun) If the surf is flat on a Sunday afternoon, kick off your shoes for some 'Barefoot Bowls' at the local lawn bowls club. No bookings, so get there early.

Sleeping

Burleigh Beach Tourist Park CARAVAN PARK $
(07-5667 2750; www.goldcoasttouristparks.com.au; 36 Goodwin Tce, Burleigh Heads; unpowered/powered sites from $30/41, cabins $151-219;) This council-owned park is snug, but it's well run and in a great spot near the beach. Aim for one of the three blue cabins at the front of the park.

Burleigh Palms Holiday Apartments APARTMENT $$
(07-5576 3955; www.burleighpalms.com; 1849 Gold Coast Hwy, Burleigh Heads; 1-bedroom apt per night/week from $150/550, 2-bedroom apt from $180/660;) Even though they're on the highway, these large and comfortable self-contained units – a quick dash to the beach through the back alley – are solid value. The owners have a wealth of local info, and do the cleaning themselves to keep the accommodation costs down.

Hillhaven Holiday Apartments APARTMENT $$
(07-5535 1055; www.hillhaven.com.au; 2 Goodwin Tce, Burleigh Heads; 2-bedroom apt from $180;) Right on the headland adjacent to the national park, these renovated apartments have great views of Burleigh Heads and the surf. It's quiet and only 150m to the beach.

Eating

★Borough Barista CAFE $
(www.facebook.com/pages/borough-barista/236745933011462; 14 The Esplanade, Burleigh Heads; mains $10-17; 6am-2.30pm) A little open-walled caffeine shack with a simple menu of burgers and salads and an unmistakable panache when it comes to coffee. The grilled haloumi burger with mushrooms, caramelised onions and chutney will turn you vegetarian. Cool tunes and friendly vibes.

Fishmonger SEAFOOD $
(07-5535 2927; 9 James St, Burleigh Heads; dishes $7-16; 10am-7.30pm) This low-key

LOCAL KNOWLEDGE

LUKE EGAN: FORMER PRO SURFER

The Gold Coast is one of the top five surfing destinations in the world. The most unique thing about the Goldy is that the waves break mostly on sand, so for sandy bottoms we get some of the most perfect waves in the world.

Best Surf Beaches

The length of ride on the famous points of Burleigh Heads, Kirra, Rainbow Bay and Snapper Rocks make the Goldy a must for every passionate surfer.

Where to Learn

The waves at Greenmount Point and Currumbin allow first-timers plenty of time to get to their feet and still enjoy a long ride. Learning to surf at these two places would be close to the best place to learn anywhere in Australia, and probably the world.

Best Experience

There isn't a better feeling than being 'surfed out' – the feeling you have after a day of surfing. Even though I no longer compete on the world surfing tour I still surf every day like it's my last.

fish-and-chip shop has been here since 1948. Grab some takeaway and head for the beach.

Canteen Coffee CAFE $
(☎0487 208 777; www.canteencoffee.com.au; 23 Park Ave, Burleigh Heads; items $3-8; ⏰7am-4pm Mon-Fri, to 3pm Sat & Sun) In a twin-business pairing with **Canteen Kitchen** next door (a larger cafe: mains $14 to $20), this caffeine cranny casts another vote for Burleigh Heads as the Gold Coast's coffee capital. A double-shot flat white and a slab of carrot cake will jump-start your afternoon.

Elephant Rock Café MODERN AUSTRALIAN, CAFE $$
(☎07-5598 2133; www.elephantrock.com.au; 776 Pacific Pde, Currumbin; mains $15-35; ⏰7am-late Tue-Sat, to 4pm Sun & Mon) On the refreshingly under-developed Currumbin beachfront you'll find this breezy, two-tier cafe, which morphs from beach-chic by day into ultra-chic at night. Great ocean views and even better seafood linguini.

Oskars SEAFOOD $$$
(☎07-5576 3722; www.oskars.com.au; 43 Goodwin Tce, Burleigh Heads; mains $38-43; ⏰10am-midnight) One of the Gold Coast's finest, this *ooh-la-la* restaurant right on the beach serves award-winning seafood and has sweeping views up the coast to Surfers. Try the spanner crab soufflé and the satay spiced green prawns.

Drinking

Currumbin Beach Vikings SLSC PUB
(☎07-5534 2932; www.currumbinslsc.com.au; 741 Pacific Pde, Currumbin; ⏰7.30am-9.30pm) In an incredible position on Currumbin beach below craggy Elephant Rock, this surf pavilion is perfect for an afternoon beer. The menu is predictable, but the view will knock your socks off.

COOLANGATTA

POP 5200

A down-to-earth seaside town on Queensland's southern border, Coolangatta has quality surf beaches (including the legendary 'Superbank' break) and a tight-knit community. The Coolangatta Gold surf-lifesaving comp happens here every October. Follow the boardwalk north around Kirra Point to the suburb of Kirra itself, with a long stretch of beach and challenging surf.

Activities

Cooly Surf SURFING
(☎07-5536 1470; www.surfshopaustralia.com.au; cnr Marine Pde & Dutton St, Coolangatta; ⏰9am-5pm) Cooly Surf hires out surfboards (half/full day $30/45) and stand-up paddleboards ($40/55), and runs two-hour surf lessons ($45).

Gold Coast Skydive SKYDIVING
(☎07-5599 1920; www.goldcoastskydive.com.au; tandem jump from $345) Plummet out of the sky from 12,000 feet up? Go on – you know you want to!

Tours

Rainforest Cruises CRUISE
(☎07-5536 8800; www.goldcoastcruising.com; 2hr cruise from $40) Cruise options ranging from crab-catching to surf 'n' turf lunches on rainforest cruises along the Tweed River.

Sleeping

★**Komune** HOTEL, HOSTEL $
(☎07-5536 6764; www.komuneresorts.com; 146 Marine Pde, Coolangatta; dm from $45, 1-/2-bedroom apt from $105/145, penthouse from $245; 📶🏊) With beach-funk decor, a Bali-esque pool area and an ultra laid-back vibe, this eight-storey converted apartment tower is the ultimate surf retreat. There are budget dorms, apartments and a hip penthouse begging for a party.

Kirra Beach Tourist Park CARAVAN PARK $
(☎07-5667 2740; www.goldcoasttouristparks.com.au; 10 Charlotte St, Kirra; unpowered/powered sites $30/37, cabins from $138; ❄@📶🏊) Large council-run park with plenty of trees, wandering ibises, a camp kitchen and a heated swimming pool. Good-value self-contained cabins (with or without bathroom), and a few hundred metres to the beach.

Coolangatta Sands Hostel HOSTEL $
(☎07-5536 7472; www.coolangattasandshostel.com.au; cnr Griffith & McLean Sts, Coolangatta; dm/d from $30/80; ❄@📶) Above the boozy Coolangatta Sands Hotel, this hostel is a warren of rooms and corridors, but there's a fab wraparound balcony above the street (no booze allowed unfortunately – go downstairs to the pub).

Coolangatta YHA HOSTEL $
(☎07-5536 7644; www.yha.com.au; 230 Coolangatta Rd, Bilinga; dm $27-34, s/d from $42/67; @📶🏊) A *looong* 4km haul from the action in an industrial pocket next to the noisy

Coolangatta

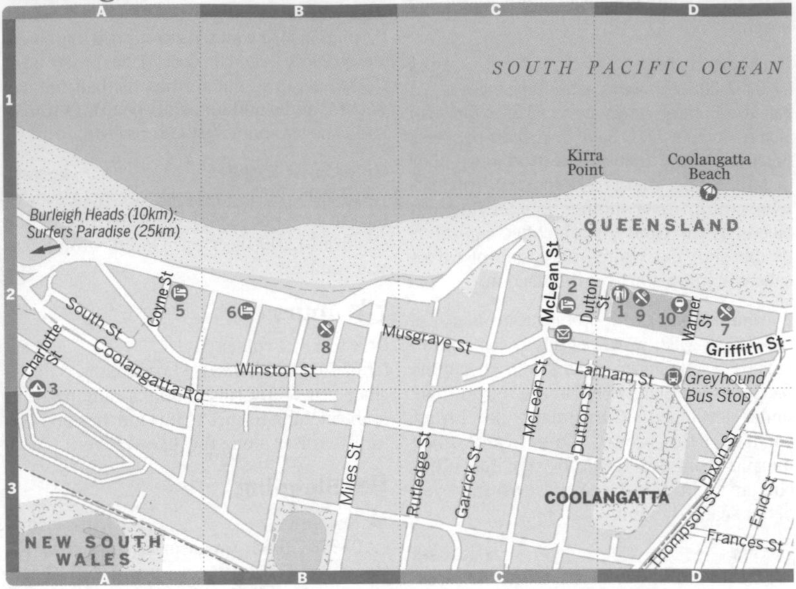

airport, this YHA is redeemed by free breakfast, free transfers to Coolangatta and the beach across the road. You can also hire surfboards ($20 per day) and bikes ($25).

Meridian Tower APARTMENT **$$**
(☎07-5536 9400; www.meridiantower.com.au; 6 Coyne St, Kirra; 1-/2-/3-bedroom apt per week from $815/930/1610; ❄📶🏊) This tall tower (the first in Kirra) opposite beautiful Kirra Beach has airy apartments with large north-facing balconies. It's a middle-of-the-road, family-friendly affair – not at all glam. Shorter stays possible outside of peak season.

Nirvana APARTMENT **$$$**
(☎07-5506 5555; www.nirvanabythesea.com.au; 1 Douglas St, Kirra; 2-/3-bedroom apt from $205/365) Attaining some sort of salty nirvana across from Kirra Beach, this sleek new apartment tower comes with all the whistles and bells: two pools, gym, cinema room, ocean views and sundry salons.

Eating

Burger Lounge BURGERS **$**
(☎07-5599 5762; www.burgerlounge.com.au; cnr Musgrave & Douglas Sts, Kirra; mains $10-17; ⏲10am-9pm Thu-Tue, 11am-9pm Wed) Awesome bun-fest in a triangular-shaped room at the base of the Nirvana apartment tower (fast-food nirvana?). The chicken-and-mango-chilli burger is a winner! Lots of good beers, cocktails and wines, too, and sangria by the jug.

Earth 'n' Sea PIZZERIA **$$**
(☎07-5536 3477; www.earthnseapizza.com.au; 72 Marine Pde, Coolangatta; mains $11-33; ⏲10am-9pm Mon-Fri, 8am-9pm Sat & Sun) An old-fashioned, family-friendly pizza and pasta restaurant on the main drag. Substance trumps style.

Bread 'n' Butter TAPAS **$$**
(☎07-5599 4666; www.breadnbutter.com.au; 76 Musgrave St; tapas $13-22, pizzas$19-25; ⏲5.30pm-late) Head upstairs to the Bread 'n' Butter balcony, where moody lighting and chilled tunes make this tapas bar perfect for a drink, some pizza or some tapas (or all three). Uses local and home-grown produce and recycles precisely 78% of waste. DJs spin on Friday and Saturday nights.

Bellakai MODERN AUSTRALIAN, CAFE **$$$**
(☎07-5599 5116; www.facebook.com/bellakai.coolangatta; 82 Marine Pde, Coolangatta; mains $30-37; ⏲5am-late) From 5am until late, Bellakai plates up fine food. Start with black-tiger-prawn dumplings, followed by the fish of the day with kipfler potatoes, sesame greens and miso butter.

Coolangatta

Activities, Courses & Tours
1 Cooly Surf D2

Sleeping
2 Coolangatta Sands Hostel C2
3 Kirra Beach Tourist Park A2
4 Komune E2
5 Meridian Tower A2
6 Nirvana B2

Eating
7 Bellakai D2
8 Bread 'n' Butter B2
Burger Lounge ....(see 6)
9 Earth 'n' Sea D2

Drinking & Nightlife
10 Coolangatta Hotel D2

Drinking

Coolangatta Hotel PUB
(www.thecoolyhotel.com.au; cnr Marine Pde & Warner St; 10am-late) The hub of Coolangatta's nocturnal scene, this huge pub right across from the beach has live bands (Grinspoon, The Rubens, The Cat Empire), sausage sizzles, pool comps, trivia nights, acoustic jam nights and pub meals. Big Sunday sessions.

Information

Coolangatta Tweed Medical Centre (07-5599 3010, after hours 0413 511 443; 2 Griffith St, Coolangatta; 8am-4.30pm Mon-Fri)

Post Office (www.auspost.com.au; cnr Griffith St & McLean St, Coolangatta; 9am-5pm Mon-Fri)

Getting There & Away

The **Greyhound** (1300 473 946; www.greyhound.com.au) bus stop is in Warner St; **Premier Motor Service** (www.premierms.com.au) coaches stop on Wharf St.

GOLD COAST HINTERLAND

Inland from the surf and sand of the Gold Coast, the forested mountains of the McPherson Range feel a million miles away. The national parks here have subtropical jungle, waterfalls and wildlife. Springbrook National Park is the wettest place in southeast Queensland, with cool air and dense forest. Lamington National Park attracts birdwatchers and hikers; Tamborine Mountain lures the cottage weekend set.

Tours

Bushwacker Ecotours ECOTOUR
(1300 559 355, 07-3848 8806; www.bushwacker-ecotours.com.au; tour adult/child from $125/95) Ecotours to the hinterland with rainforest walks in Springbrook National Park and around, departing the Gold Coast or Brisbane.

JPT Tour Group TOUR
(07-56301602; www.daytours.com.au; tour adult/child from $99/57) A variety of day tours ex-Brisbane or Gold Coast, including Lamington National Park via Tamborine Mountain and glow-worm tours to Natural Bridge.

Mountain Coach Company TOUR
(07-5524 4249, 1300 762 665; www.mountaincoach.com.au) Daily tours from the Gold Coast to Tamborine Mountain (adult/child $59/49), Lamington National Park ($84/54) and Springbrook National Park ($89/57). Transfer-only prices also available ex-Gold Coast (Tamborine Mountain adult/child $30/20; Lamington National Park $50/20).

Tamborine Mountain

This mountaintop rainforest community – comprising Eagle Heights, North Tamborine and Mt Tamborine – is 45km inland from the

WORTH A TRIP

LAMINGTON NATIONAL PARK

Australia's largest remnant of subtropical rainforest cloaks the deep valleys and steep cliffs of the McPherson Range, reaching elevations of 1100m on the Lamington Plateau. Here, the 200-sq-km **Lamington National Park** (www.nprsr.qld.gov.au/parks/lamington) is a Unesco World Heritage site and has over 160km of walking trails.

The two most accessible sections of the park are the **Binna Burra** and **Green Mountains** sections, both reached via long, narrow, winding roads from Canungra (not great for big campervans). Binna Burra can also be accessed from Nerang.

Sights & Activities

Bushwalks within the park include everything from short jaunts to multiday epics. For experienced hikers, the Gold Coast Hinterland Great Walk is a three-day trip along a 54km path from the Green Mountains section to the Springbrook Plateau. Other favourites include the excellent Tree Top Canopy Walk along a series of rope-and-plank suspension bridges at Green Mountains, and the 21km Border Track that follows the dividing range between NSW and Queensland and links Binna Burra to Green Mountains.

Walking guides are available from the **ranger stations** (7.30am-4pm Mon-Fri, 9am-3.30pm Sat & Sun) at Binna Burra and Green Mountains.

Sleeping & Eating

Green Mountains Campground (13 74 68; www.nprsr.qld.gov.au/parks/lamington/camping.html; site per person/family $5.50/22) There's a tiered national parks camping ground on the left as you head down the hill from O'Reilly's Rainforest Retreat. There are plenty of spots for tents and caravans (and a toilet/shower block); book in advance.

O'Reilly's Rainforest Retreat (07-5502 4911, 1800 688 722; www.oreillys.com.au; Lamington National Park Rd, Green Mountains; s/d from $163/278, 1-/2-bedroom villa from $400/435; @) This famous 1926 guesthouse has lost its original grandeur but retains a rustic charm – and sensational views! Newer luxury villas and doubles add a contemporary sheen. There are plenty of organised activities, plus a day spa, cafe, bar and **restaurant** (mains $25 to $40), open for breakfast, lunch and dinner.

Binna Burra Mountain Lodge (07-5533 3622, 1300 246 622; www.binnaburralodge.com.au; 1069 Binna Burra Rd, Beechmont; unpowered/powered site $28/35, safari tent from $55, d incl breakfast with/without bathroom $300/190, apt from $295) Stay in the lodge, in rustic log cabins, flashy new apartments or in a tent surrounded by forest in this atmospheric mountain retreat. The central **restaurant** (mains $20 to $40) serves breakfast, lunch and dinner, or there's a cafe-style **Teahouse** (mains $14 to $18) a few hundred metres up the road, open 9am to 3pm. Transport available.

Gold Coast, and has cornered the artsy-craftsy, Germanic-kitsch, chocolate/liqueur market in a big way. If this is your bag, **Gallery Walk** in Eagle Heights is the place to stock up.

Sights & Activities

Tamborine National Park PARK
(www.nprsr.qld.gov.au/parks/tamborine) Queensland's oldest national park comprises 13 sections stretching across the 8km plateau, offering waterfalls and super views of the Gold Coast. Accessed via easy-to-moderate walking trails are **Witches Falls**, **Curtis Falls**, **Cedar Creek Falls** and **Cameron Falls**. The visitor centre in North Tamborine has maps.

Skywalk WALKING
(07-5545 2222; www.rainforestskywalk.com.au; 333 Geissman Dr, North Tamborine; adult/child/family $19.50/9.50/49; 9.30am-4pm) Walk through the rainforest canopy at Skywalk, 30m above the ground. The path descends to the forest floor and leads to Cedar Creek. Look out for rare Richmond Birdwing butterflies.

Sleeping & Eating

Songbirds Rainforest Retreat HOTEL $$$
(07-5545 2563; www.songbirds.com.au; Lot 10, Tamborine Mountain Rd, North Tamborine; villas from $298) The classiest outfit on the hill. Each of the six plush Southeast Asian–inspired villas has a double spa with rainforest views.

St Bernards Hotel PUB $$
(☎07-5545 1177; www.stbernardshotel.com; 101 Alpine Tce, Mt Tamborine; mains $20-32; ⏰10am-midnight) A woody old mountain pub with a large terrace and sweeping views.

Mt Tamborine Brewery BREWERY $$
(☎07-5545 2032; www.mtbeer.com; 165 Long Rd, Eagle Heights; lunch mains $18-25; ⏰9.30am-5pm Mon-Thu, to late Fri-Sun) Beer boffins should head straight for this microbrewery for a Rainforest Lager or a tasting tray (four beer samples for $12). There's also a bistro.

Information

Tamborine Mountain Visitor Information Centre (☎07-5545 3200; www.tamborinemt-ncc.org.au; Doughty Park, Main Western Rd, North Tamborine; ⏰10am-4pm Mon-Fri, 9.30am-4pm Sat & Sun) Info on Tamborine National Park.

Springbrook National Park

About a 40-minute drive west of Burleigh Heads, **Springbrook National Park** (www.nprsr.qld.gov.au/parks/springbrook) is a steep remnant of the Tweed Shield volcano that centred on nearby Mt Warning in NSW more than 20 million years ago. It's a wonderland for hikers; trails through cool-temperate, subtropical and eucalypt forests offer a mosaic of gorges, cliffs and waterfalls.

The park is divided into four sections. The 900m-high **Springbrook Plateau** section houses the strung-out township of Springbrook along Springbrook Rd, and receives the most visitors: it's laced with waterfalls, trails and eye-popping lookouts. The scenic **Natural Bridge** section, off the Nerang–Murwillumbah road, has a 1km walking circuit leading to a huge rock arch spanning a water-formed cave – home to a luminous colony of glow worms. The **Mt Cougal** section, accessed via Currumbin Creek Rd, has several waterfalls and swimming holes (watch out for submerged logs and slippery rocks); while the forested **Numinbah** section to the north is the fourth section of the park.

Sights & Activities

Best of All Lookout LOOKOUT
(Repeater Station Rd, Springbrook) True to its name, the Best of All Lookout offers phenomenal views from the southern edge of the Springbrook Plateau to the lowlands below. The 350m trail from the carpark to the lookout takes you past a clump of gnarled Antarctic beech trees: you'll only find them around here and in northern NSW.

Purling Brook Falls WATERFALL
(Forestry Rd, Springbrook) Just off Springbrook Rd, the Purling Brook Falls drop a rather astonishing 109m into the rainforest: check them out from the vertigo-inducing lookout.

Canyon Lookout LOOKOUT
(Canyon Pde, Springbrook) Canyon Lookout affords views through the valley to Surfers Paradise. This is also the start of a 4km circuit walk to **Twin Falls**, which is part of Springbrook's longest trail, the 17km **Warrie Circuit**.

Goomoolahra Falls WATERFALL
(Springbrook Rd, Springbrook) At the end of Springbrook Rd there's a lookout beside the 60m Goomoolahra Falls, with views across the plateau and all the way back to the coast.

Sleeping & Eating

Settlement Campground CAMPGROUND $
(☎13 74 68; www.nprsr.qld.gov.au/parks/springbrook/camping.html; 52 Carricks Rd; per person/family $5.50/22) There are 11 grassy sites at this trim camping ground (the only one at Springbrook), which also has toilets and barbecues. Book ahead. The Gold Coast Hinterland Great Walk runs through here.

Mouses House CHALET $$$
(☎07-5533 5192; www.mouseshouse.com.au; 2807 Springbrook Rd, Springbrook; r from $250, 2 nights from $430; ❄📶) Linked by softly lit boardwalks, these 12 cedar chalets hidden in the misty woods are super-romantic mountain hideaways. Each has a spa and wood fire; breakfast, lunch and dinner hampers available.

Dancing Waters Café CAFE $
(☎07-5533 5335; www.dancingwaterscafe.com; 33 Forestry Rd, Springbrook; dishes $6-18; ⏰10am-4pm) Next to the Purling Brook Falls car park, this affable tearoom serves healthy salads and light meals (fab toasted chicken sandwiches and homemade scones).

Information

There's an unstaffed **visitor information centre** at the end of Old School Rd in the Springbrook Plateau section of the park, which has park maps.

Noosa & the Sunshine Coast

Includes ➡

Best Places to Eat

- ➡ Little Humid (p140)
- ➡ Berardo's (p140)
- ➡ Bohemian Bungalow (p155)
- ➡ Mooloolaba Fish Market (p149)
- ➡ Up Front Club (p156)

Best Places to Stay

- ➡ Secrets on the Lake (p153)
- ➡ Islander Noosa Resort (p138)
- ➡ YHA Halse Lodge (p138)
- ➡ Glass House Mountains Ecolodge (p143)
- ➡ Maroochydore Beach Motel (p148)

Why Go?

It's not called the Sunshine Coast for nothing: the 100 golden kilometres stretching from the tip of Bribie Island to the Cooloola Coast are aglow with glimmering coastlines, hot surf spots and a warm populace for whom smiles are de rigueur...and shoes démodé. Stylish Noosa boasts a sophisticated dining and resort scene, while Mooloolaba, with its popular beach, outdoor eateries and cafes, is a long-time favourite with holidaying Australian families.

The ethereal Glass House Mountains loom over the seascape, while further north, the Blackall Range offers a change of scenery with thick forests, lush pastures and quaint villages. The Sunshine Coast is also home to one of the world's great wildlife sanctuaries, the iconic Australia Zoo.

When to Go

Noosa

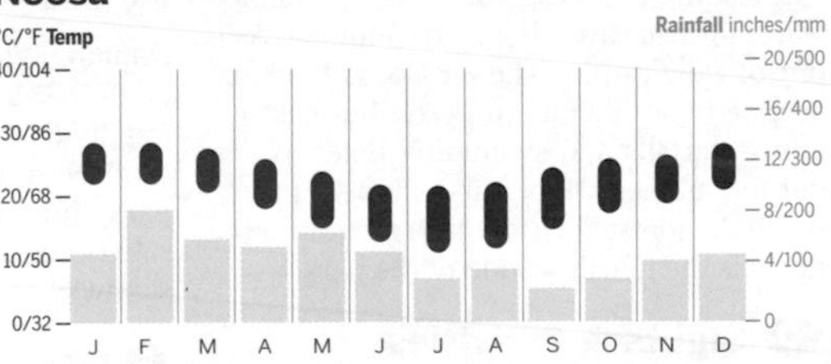

May Satisfy culinary cravings at the Noosa International Food & Wine Festival.

Sep Noosa's streets fill with music during the four-day Noosa Jazz Festival.

Dec Celebrate the end of the year with folks who like folk at the Woodford Folk Festival.

Noosa & the Sunshine Coast Highlights

1 Hiking the coastal track at **Noosa National Park** (p136).

2 Sampling gourmet beach fare in one of Noosa's **swish restaurants** (p138).

3 Surfing, sunning and lapping up the beach-cafe scene in **Mooloolaba** (p146).

4 Visiting the wild critters at **Australia Zoo** (p144).

5 Finding far-out treasures at the **Eumundi markets** (p154).

6 Donning flares, kaftans and wild, new-age hippie chic at the wonderful **Woodford Folk Festival** (p155).

7 Hiking to the summit of Mt Beerwah in the **Glass House Mountains National Park** (p143).

8 Canoeing and exploring the Cooloola Section of the **Great Sandy National Park** (p153).

Getting There & Away

AIR

The Sunshine Coast's airport (Sunshine Coast Airport) is at Marcoola, 10km north of Maroochydore and 26km south of Noosa. **Jetstar** (☎13 15 38; www.jetstar.com.au) and **Virgin Blue** (☎13 67 89; www.virginblue.com.au) have daily flights from Sydney and Melbourne. **Tiger Airways** (☎03-9034 3733; www.tigerairways.com) has less frequent flights from Melbourne.

BUS

Greyhound Australia (☎1300 473 946; www.greyhound.com.au) has several daily services from Brisbane to Caloundra ($17, two hours), Maroochydore ($20, two hours) and Noosa ($22, 2½ hours). **Premier Motor Service** (☎13 34 10; www.premierms.com.au) also services Maroochydore and Noosa from Brisbane.

Getting Around

Several companies offer transfers from the Sunshine Coast Airport and Brisbane to points along the coast. Fares from Brisbane cost $40 to $50 for adults and $20 to $25 for children. From Sunshine Coast Airport fares are around $20 to $30 per adult and $7 to $15 per child.

Sunbus (☎13 12 30; www.sunbus.com.au) buzzes frequently between Caloundra and Noosa, and has regular buses from Noosa to the train station at Nambour ($7, one hour) via Eumundi.

Col's Airport Shuttle (☎07-5450 5933; www.airshuttle.com.au)

Henry's (☎07-5474 0199; www.henrys.com.au)

Sun-Air Bus Service (☎07-5477 0888; www.sunair.com.au)

NOOSA

POP 14,000

Noosa is a swanky resort town with a stunning natural landscape of crystalline beaches and tropical rainforests. Designer boutiques and swish restaurants draw beach-elite sophisticates, but the beach and bush are still free, so glammed-up fashionistas simply share the beat with thongs, boardshorts and bronzed bikini bods baring their bits.

Noosa is undeniably developed but its low-impact condos and chichi landscape have been cultivated without losing sight of simple seaside pleasures. On long weekends and school holidays, however, bustling Hastings St becomes a slow-moving file of traffic.

The area has an amazing number of roundabouts and it's easy to get lost. Broadly speaking, Noosa encompasses three zones: Noosa Heads (around Laguna Bay and Hastings St), Noosaville (along the Noosa River) and Noosa Junction (the administrative centre).

Sights

One of Noosa's best features, the lovely **Noosa National Park** (Map p139; www.noosanationalpark.com/), covering the headland, has fine walks, great coastal scenery and a string of bays with waves that draw surfers from all over the country. The most scenic way to access the national park is to follow the boardwalk along the coast from town. Sleepy koalas are often spotted in the trees near Tea Tree Bay and dolphins are commonly seen from the rocky headlands around Alexandria Bay, an informal nudist beach on the eastern side. Pick up a walking track map from the **Noosa National Park Information Centre** (☎07-5447 3522; ⌚9.15am-4.45pm) at the entrance to the park.

For a panoramic view of the park, walk or drive up to **Laguna Lookout** from Viewland Dr in Noosa Junction.

The passage of the Noosa River that cuts into the **Great Sandy National Park** is poetically known as the 'river of mirrors' or the **Everglades**. It's a great place to launch a kayak and camp in one of the many **national park camping grounds** (www.nprsr.qld.gov.au; per person/family $5.45/21.80) along the riverbank.

Activities

Surfing & Water Sports

With a string of breaks around an unspoilt national park, Noosa is a fine place to catch a wave. Generally the waves are best in December and January but Sunshine Corner, at the northern end of Sunshine Beach, has an excellent year-round break, although it has a brutal beach dump. The point breaks around the headland only perform during the summer, but when they do, expect wild conditions and good walls at Boiling Point and Tea Tree on the northern coast of the headland. There are also gentler breaks on Noosa Spit at the far end of Hastings St, where most of the surf schools do their training.

Kite-surfers will find conditions at the river mouth and Lake Weyba are best between October and January, but on windy days the Noosa River is a playground for serious daredevils.

Merrick's Learn to Surf SURFING
(☎0418 787 577; www.learntosurf.com.au; 2hr lesson $60; ⏰9am & 1.30pm) Holds one-, three- and five-day surfing programs.

Adventure Sports Noosa KITE-SURFING
(Map p141; ☎07-5455 6677; www.kitesurfaustralia.com.au; 203 Gympie Tce, Noosaville; kite-surfing 2½hr lesson $250) Also hires kayaks ($35 per half-day) and bikes ($19 for two hours).

Go Ride A Wave SURFING
(☎1300 132 441; www.gorideawave.com.au; 2hr lesson $65, 2hr surfboard hire $25) Lessons and hire.

Noosa Stand Up Paddle WATER SPORTS
(☎0423 869 962; www.noosastanduppaddle.com.au; Group SUP lesson $55; ⏰lessons 9am, 11am, 1pm, 3pm) Learn stand-up paddling.

Noosa Longboards SURFING
(Map p139; ☎07-5447 2828; www.noosalongboards.com; 2/55 Hastings St, Noosa Heads; 2hr surfing lesson $60, surfboard hire from $40) Private and group lessons.

Canoeing & Kayaking

The Noosa River is excellent for canoeing; it's possible to follow it up through Lakes Cooroibah and Cootharaba and through the Cooloola Section of Great Sandy National Park.

Noosa Ocean Kayak Tours KAYAKING
(☎0418 787 577; www.noosakayaktours.com; 2hr tour $66, kayak hire per day $55) Tours around Noosa National Park and along the Noosa River.

Kayak Noosa KAYAKING
(Map p141; ☎07-5455 5651; www.kayaknoosa.com; 194 Gympie Tce, Noosaville; 2hr sunset kayak $55, half-/full-day guided kayak tour $90/145) Tours around Noosa National Park. Also hires out kayaks ($45 for two hours).

Adventure Activities

Noosa Ocean Rider BOATING
(Map p141; ☎0438 386 255; www.oceanrider.com.au; Jetty 17, 248 Gympie Tce, Noosaville ; 1hr per person/family $70/$250) Thrills and spills on a very fast and powerful speedboat.

Bike On Australia MOUNTAIN BIKING
(Map p139; ☎07-5474 3322; www.bikeon.com.au; tour from $80, bike hire per day $25) Hosts a variety of tours, including beach biking, self-guided and adventurous eco-jaunts.

Cruises

Gondolas of Noosa BOATING
(Map p139; ☎0412 929 369; www.gondolasofnoosa.com) Romantic day or moonlit cruises along the Noosa River leave from the Sheraton Jetty. Prices start from $150 for an hour.

Noosa Ferry CRUISE
(Map p139; ☎07-5449 8442; per person $20) This ferry service has informative 90-minute round-trip cruises that run to Tewantin from the Sheraton Jetty. Book ahead for the two-hour Biosphere Reserve cruise ($45).

Horse Riding

Noosa Horse Riding HORSE RIDING
(☎0438 710 530; www.noosahorseriding.com.au; Eumarella Rd, Lake Weyba; 1/2hr ride $65/95) Horse rides around (and in) Lake Weyba and the surrounding bush.

Tours

Fraser Island Adventure Tours ADVENTURE TOUR
(☎07-5444 6957; www.fraserislandadventuretours.com.au; day tour from $145) Popular day trips to Eli Creek and Lake McKenzie pack as much punch as a two-day tour.

Discovery Group DRIVING TOUR
(☎07-5449 0393; www.thediscoverygroup.com.au; day tour adult/child $175/120) Visit Fraser Island in a big black 4WD truck on tours that include a guided rainforest walk at Central Station and visits to Lakes Birrabeen and McKenzie. Also offers afternoon river cruises through the Everglades (from $79).

Offbeat Ecotours ECOTOUR
(☎1300 023 835; www.offbeattours.com.au; day tour adult/child $155/100) Spirited day trips into the magnificent Noosa Hinterland with waterfall swimming, intimate encounters with ancient flora and a gourmet lunch.

Festivals & Events

Noosa Festival of Surfing SURFING
(www.noosafestivalofsurfing.com/) A week of longboard action in March.

Noosa International Food & Wine Festival FOOD, WINE
(www.noosafoodandwine.com.au) A three-day tribute to all manner of gastronomic delights, held each May.

Noosa Long Weekend FOOD, FASHION
(www.noosalongweekend.com) Ten-day festival of arts, culture, food and fashion in June/July.

Noosa Jazz Festival JAZZ
(www.noosajazz.com.au) Four-day event in early September.

Sleeping

Accommodation prices can rise between 50% and 100% in peak season. During these times most places require a minimum two- or three-night stay. Low-season rates are quoted.

For an extensive list of short-term holiday rentals, try **Accom Noosa** (Map p139; ☎07-5447 3444; www.accomnoosa.com.au; Shop 5/41 Hastings St, Noosa Heads).

★**YHA Halse Lodge** HOSTEL $
(Map p139; ☎07-5447 3377; www.halselodge.com.au; 2 Halse Lane; members/non-members dm $29/32, d $78/96; @ 📶) This splendid colonial-era timber Queenslander is a legendary stop-over on the backpacker trail, and well worth the clamber up its steep drive. There are three- and six-bed dorms, doubles and a lovely wide verandah. The bar is a mix-and-meet bonanza and serves great meals ($10 to $15). Close to the Main Beach action.

Nomads Backpackers HOSTEL $
(Map p139; ☎07-5447 3355; www.nomadshostels.com; 44 Noosa Dr; dm from $26; @ 📶 🏊) One of the Nomad chain, this hostel has the usual trademarks: popular bar, central location and whoo-hoo atmosphere. You can't get less than an eight-bed dorm, but you'll be partying so hard it won't matter. If you remember to eat, Nomads do $5 meals that aren't as hideous as you might expect.

Noosa River Holiday Park CARAVAN PARK $
(Map p141; ☎07-5449 7050; www.sunshinecoastholidayparks.com; 4 Russell St; unpowered/powered site $34/42; 📶) In a lovely spot on the banks of the Noosa River, this park has the closest camping facilities to Noosa. Keep in mind that they do so love their rules and regulations here.

Anchor Motel Noosa MOTEL $$
(Map p141; ☎07-5449 8055; www.anchormotelnoosa.com.au; 223 Weyba Rd; r from $120; ❄ 📶 🏊) Ship-shape rooms with plenty of space and the porthole windows requisite for a marine-themed establishment. Unlike many motels, this is a social place, with guests mixing by the pool.

Noosa River Retreat APARTMENT $$
(Map p141; ☎07-5474 2811; www.noosariverretreat.com; 243 Weyba Rd; studios from $120; ❄ @ 📶 🏊) Your buck goes a long way at this orderly complex with spick, span and spacious units. There's a central barbecue and laundry, and the corner spots are almost entirely protected by small, native gardens; traffic can be noisy in other units.

Noosa Sun Motel APARTMENT $$
(Map p141; ☎07-5474 0477; www.noosasunmotel.com.au; 131 Gympie Tce, Noosaville; r $130-220; ❄ @ 📶 🏊) Uninspiring from the outside, but what lies within is most unexpected: modern, spacious and surprisingly stylish apartments replete with kitchenettes, free wi-fi and water views (cheaper units overlook the garden). Within walking distance of loads of eateries and shops.

Noosa Parade Holiday Inn APARTMENT $$
(Map p139; ☎07-5447 4177; www.noosaparadeholidayinn.com; 51 Noosa Pde; r from $110; ❄ 📶 🏊) The apartments are looking a little faded, but they're clean and comfortable, and a mere stroll from the treats of Hastings St.

Islander Noosa Resort RESORT $$$
(Map p141; ☎07-5440 9200; www.islandernoosa.com.au; 187 Gympie Tce; 2-/3-bedroom villas $210/260; ❄ @ 📶 🏊 🐾) Set on 4 acres of tropical gardens, with a central tropical pool and wooden boardwalks meandering through the trees, this resort is excellent value. It's bright and cheerful and packs a cocktail-swilling, island-resort ambience that sits well with poolside idlers and families alike. The onsite Moondoggy's Cafe-Bar (open from 7am to 6pm) is famous for its breakfasts.

Emerald APARTMENT $$$
(Map p139; ☎07-5449 6100; www.emeraldnoosa.com.au; 42 Hastings St; 2-bedroom apt from $270; ❄ @ 📶 🏊) The stylish Emerald has indulgent rooms bathed in ethereal white and sunlight. Expect clean, crisp edges and exquisite furnishings. All apartments are fully self-contained, but ask for a balcony with a view.

Eating

Noosa prides itself on being a foodie destination, with global and local flavours on offer everywhere from fine restaurants to

Noosa Heads

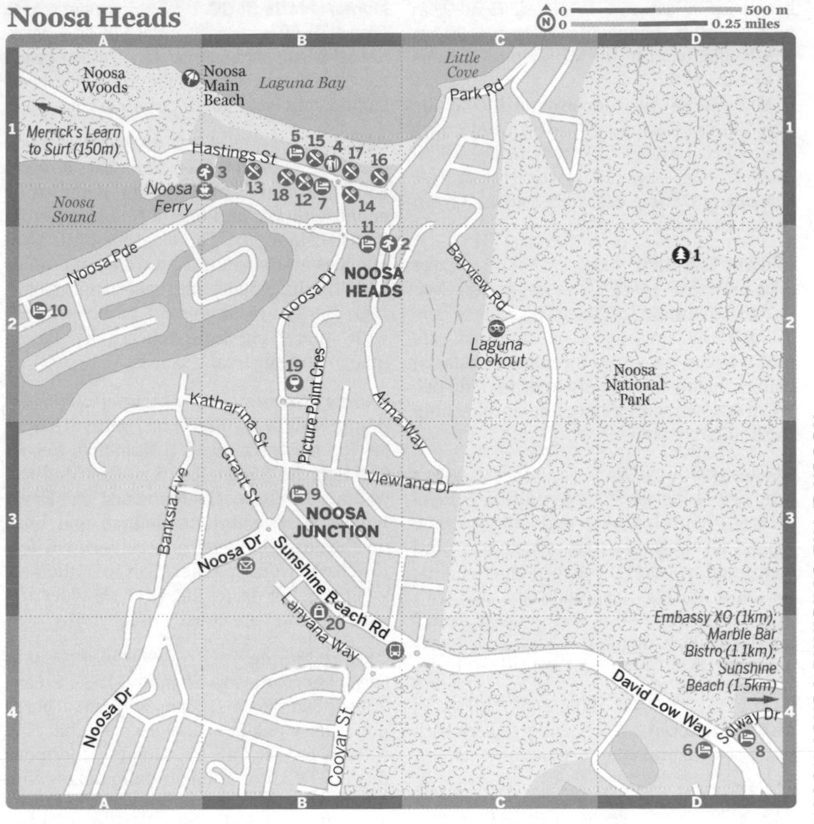

Noosa Heads

Sights

1 Noosa National Park D2

Activities, Courses & Tours

2 Bike On Australia B2
Gondolas of Noosa .... (see 3)
3 Noosa Ferry B1
4 Noosa Longboards B1

Sleeping

5 Accom Noosa B1
6 Chez Noosa D4
7 Emerald B1
8 Flashpackers D4
9 Nomads Backpackers B3
10 Noosa Parade Holiday Inn A2
11 YHA Halse Lodge B2

Eating

12 Aromas B1
13 Bay Village Shopping Centre Food Court B1
14 Berardo's B1
15 Bistro C B1
Cafe Le Monde .... (see 14)
Gaston .... (see 14)
Laguna Bakery .... (see 15)
16 Massimo's B1
17 Noosa Heads SLSC B1
18 Zachary's B1

Drinking & Nightlife

KB's .... (see 9)
19 Reef Hotel B2

Shopping

20 Noosa Fair Shopping Centre B3

Information

Noosa Visitor Centre .... (see 17)
Palm Tree Tours .... (see 13)

beachside takeaways. In Noosa Heads, eateries clutter happening Hastings St; in Noosaville, head to the strip along Thomas St or Gibson St.

You can eat well for around $10 at the **Bay Village Shopping Centre food court** (Map p139; Hastings St, Noosa Heads). Self-caterers can stock up at the **Noosa Fair Shopping Centre** (Map p139; Lanyana Way) in Noosa Junction.

Elegant Eggplant CAFE **$**
(Map p141; ☎07-5474 2776; www.eleganteggplant.com.au; 185 Gympie Tce, Noosaville; $9-15; ⏰7am-2.30pm) Delicious takes on standard cafe fare (sangas, salads, ginormous breakfasts) using mostly local, organic ingredients. Wash it down with a smoothie or refreshing fresh juice cocktail.

Burger Bar BURGERS **$**
(Map p141; 4 Thomas St; burgers $10-15; ⏰11am-9pm; ✎) This informal and quirky venue whips up hormone-free, vegetarian, and weird and wonderful between-bun delights; the lamb burgers (especially the one with brie cheese, lime slaw, and piccalilli sauce) are particularly divine.

Laguna Bakery BAKERY **$**
(Map p139; ☎07-5447 2606; 3/49 Hastings St; pastries $2.50, coffee $3) Friendly bakery with strong coffee and yummy pastries to go.

Massimo's GELATI **$**
(Map p139; 75 Hastings St; gelati $2-6; ⏰9am-10pm) Definitely one of the best *gelaterias* in Queensland.

★Little Humid MODERN AUSTRALIAN **$$**
(Map p141; ☎07-5449 9755; www.humid.com.au; 2/235 Gympie Tce, Noosaville; mains from $25; ⏰lunch Wed-Sun noon-2pm, dinner Tue-Sun from 6pm) Extremely popular eatery that many locals regard as the best in town. It lives up to the hype, with toothsome treats including crispy-skin confit duck leg, sticky-pork belly with calamari, and creative vegie options. Definitely book ahead.

Aromas CAFE **$$**
(Map p139; 32 Hastings St; breakfast $15-26, mains $13-36; ⏰ 7am-11pm) This European-style cafe is unashamedly ostentatious, with chandeliers, faux-marble tables and cane chairs deliberately facing the street so patrons can see and be seen. There's the usual array of panini, cakes and light meals, but most folk come for the coffee and the atmosphere.

Noosa Heads SLSC INTERNATIONAL **$$**
(Map p139; 69 Hastings St; mains $12-33; ⏰breakfast Sat & Sun, lunch & dinner daily) Perfect beach views from the deck make for idyllic beer-sipping and (very good) pub-food chomping.

Berardo's MODERN AUSTRALIAN **$$$**
(Map p139; ☎07-5447 5666; 52 Hastings St; mains $30-42; ⏰from 6pm) Beautiful Berardo's is culinary utopia and one of Noosa's most famous restaurants. The elegance of its food matches the surrounds, an all-white affair with tinkling piano and sun-dappled chic. Ingredients are almost all locally-sourced, with interesting little touches like green mango and sugarcane sauces.

Thomas Corner MODERN AUSTRALIAN **$$**
(Map p141; ☎07-5470 2224; cnr Thomas St & Gympie Tce; mains $16-33; ⏰11.30am-11pm Mon-Fri, 9am-11pm Sat, 8.30am-11pm Sun) Casual alfresco diner run by locally-renowned chef David Rayner that's short on flourish and huge on flavour. All kinds of local seafood feature here, from spanner crab to cuttle fish, while meatier dishes like lamb shoulder and wagyu brisket are equally droolworthy.

Cafe Le Monde MODERN AUSTRALIAN **$$**
(Map p139; 52 Hastings St; mains $15-39; ⏰6am-9.30pm Sun-Thu, to 11.30pm Fri & Sat) There's not a fussy palate or dietary need that isn't catered for on Cafe Le Monde's enormous menu. The large, open-air patio buzzes with diners digging into burgers, seared tuna steaks, curries, pastas, salads and plenty more. Come for daily happy-hour drinks between 4pm and 6pm.

Zachary's PIZZERIA **$$**
(Map p139; ☎07-5447 3211; www.zacharys.com.au; Upper Level, 30 Hastings St, Noosa Heads; pizzas from $16.50; ⏰noon-late) Award-winning local stayer dishing up pizzas like Hoisin duck and 'posh chicken' (with cranberries and camembert), and all the classic faves. They also have a surprisingly extensive cocktail list; it's a great place to kick off a night on the town.

Gaston MODERN AUSTRALIAN **$$**
(Map p139; 5/50 Hastings St; mains $17-25; ⏰7am-midnight) Unpretentious, but with a menu that's up there with the best of them, Gaston is a (beautiful-) people-watching paradise. Gawk at the passing parade over superb-value lunch specials ($17 for a main and a drink) or dinner deals ($50 for two mains and a bottle of wine).

Noosaville

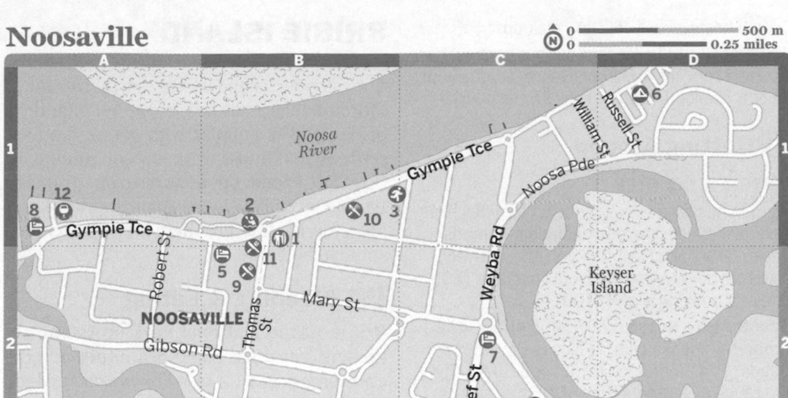

Noosaville

Activities, Courses & Tours
1 Adventure Sports Noosa ... B1
2 Kayak Noosa ... B1
3 Noosa Ocean Rider ... B1

Sleeping
4 Anchor Motel Noosa ... C2
5 Islander Noosa Resort ... B2
6 Noosa River Holiday Park ... D1
7 Noosa River Retreat ... C2
8 Noosa Sun Motel ... A1

Eating
9 Burger Bar ... B2
Elegant Eggplant ... (see 5)
10 Little Humid ... B1
11 Thomas Corner ... B2

Drinking & Nightlife
12 Noosa Yacht Club ... A1

Bistro C MODERN AUSTRALIAN $$
(Map p139; ☎07-5447 2855; Hastings St, On the Beach Resort; mains $19-40; ⌚7.30am-11.30pm) The menu at this beachfront brasserie is an eclectic and delectable blend of everything that seems like a good idea at the time. The legendary egg-fried calamari is always a hit; for breakfast, do not go past the corn-and-chive griddle cake with bacon, spinach and avocado salsa ($22).

Drinking

KB's BAR
(Map p139; 44 Noosa Dr, Noosa Junction; ⌚5pm-midnight) Noosa's backpackers and other free spirits start their nightly revelries at this popular hostel bar (attached to Nomads Backpackers). Live rock fills every crevice several nights a week.

Noosa Yacht Club YACHT CLUB
(Map p141; Gympie Tce; ⌚10am-late Mon-Sat, 8am-late Sun) Everything you'd expect from a yacht club: cheap grog, water views and sociable salts.

Reef Hotel PUB
(Map p139; ☎07-5430 7500; 19 Noosa Dr; ⌚11am-midnight Sun-Thu, to 3am Fri & Sat) A little on the soulless side, decor-wise, but live music and cold bevvies make it all okay.

Information

Noosa Visitor Centre (Map p139; ☎07-5430 5000; www.visitnoosa.com.au; 61 Hastings St, Noosa Heads; ⌚9am-5pm)

Palm Tree Tours (Map p139; ☎07-5474 9166; www.palmtreetours.com.au; Bay Village Shopping Centre, Hastings St; ⌚9am-5pm) Very helpful tour desk that's been on the scene for over 20 years. Can book tours, accommodation and bus tickets.

Post Office (Map p139; 91 Noosa Dr)

Getting There & Away

Long-distance bus services stop at the Noosa Junction station on Sunshine Beach Rd. **Greyhound Australia** (☎1300 473 946; www.greyhound.com.au) has several daily bus connections from Brisbane ($22, 2½ hours) while **Premier Motor Service** (☎13 34 10; www.premierms.com.au) has one ($23, 2½ hours).

Most hostels have courtesy pick-ups.

Sunbus (☎13 12 30; www.sunbus.com.au) has frequent services to Maroochydore ($7, one hour) and the Nambour train station ($7, one hour).

Getting Around

BICYCLE & SCOOTER

Bike On Australia (p137) rents out bicycles from several locations in Noosa including Nomads Backpackers and Flashpackers. Alternatively, bikes are delivered to and from your door ($35 or free if booking is over $100).

Scooter Hire Noosa (☎07-5455 4096; www.scooterhirenoosa.com; 13 Noosa Dr , Noosa Heads ; 2/4/24hr $35/45/59; ⊗8.30am-5pm) Big range of scooters from 50cc to 300cc in fun 'I'm on holiday!' colours.

BOAT

Noosa Ferry (Map p139; ☎07-5449 8442; www.noosaferry.com; Noosa Marina, Tewantin; one way adult/child/family $14/5/35, all-day pass $20/6/49) operates ferries between Noosa Heads and Tewantin every 30 minutes.

BUS

Sunbus has local services that link Noosa Heads, Noosaville, Noosa Junction and Tewantin.

CAR

All the big car-rental brands can be found in Noosa, or go with the locals at **Noosa Car Rentals** (☎0429 053 728; www.noosacarrentals.com.au). Car rentals in town start at about $50 per day.

BRIBIE ISLAND

POP 17,057

This slender island at the northern end of Moreton Bay is linked to the mainland by bridge and is popular with young families, retirees and those with a cool million or three to spend on a waterfront property. It's far more developed than Stradbroke or Moreton Islands, but there are still secluded spots to be found.

Sleeping & Eating

Bribie Island National Park on the northwestern coast has some beautifully remote **camping areas** (☎13 74 68; www.nprsr.qld.gov.au; person/family $5.45/21.80).

Sylvan Beach Resort RESORT **$$**
(☎07-3408 8300; www.sylvanbeachresort.com.au; 21-27 Sylvan Beach Esplanade; d from $175;) Cool and spacious beachside two- and three-bedroom units that all come with private balconies.

On The Beach Resort APARTMENT **$$$**
(☎07-3400 1400; www.onthebeachresort.com.au; 9 North St, Woorim; 2-/3-bedroom apt from $205/275;) Weird building, stunning views. Out-luxes anything else on the island with superb service and great facilities including a saltwater pool and huge sundeck.

BIG THINGS OF THE SUNSHINE COAST

Fans of kitsch (and gigantism) will adore Australia's (in)famous Big Things. Hulking in offbeat nooks and along lonely highways across the country, these wonderfully bad-taste monuments honour everything from bananas to boxing crocs in supersized novelty architecture. The Big Thing craze kicked off in the 1960s...and it shows, with many of them rusting and teetering in glorious abandonment. While every state in Australia has at least one Big Thing, there's an unusually high concentration of the gaudy goliaths dotted around the Sunshine Coast. Keen on a quirky quest? You won't have to look too hard to find the looming likes of...

The Big Pineapple Arguably the most famous of Queensland's Big Things; in Woombye, near Nambour. One of the few Big Things that you can go inside.

The Big Macadamia Nut Happily crumbling away in the shadow of the Big Pineapple; Woombye.

The Big Cow Looming awkwardly over Yandina, in the Sunshine Coast Hinterland.

The Big Mower Woe betide the grass that sprouts near this 7m-high monster; in Beerwah, not far from Australia Zoo.

The Big Pelican We dare you not to giggle at this guy's ginormous, goofball grin; in Noosaville on the Noosa River.

The Big Shell Frightful conch from the 1960s guarding a 'tropical lifestyle' store in Tewantin, Noosa.

UNEXPECTED TREASURE: ABBEY MUSEUM

The impressive art and archaeology collection in the **Abbey Museum** (07-5495 1652; www.abbeymuseum.com; 63 The Abbey Pl, Caboolture, off Old Toorbul Point Rd; adult/child/family $8.80/5/19.80; 10am-4pm Mon-Sat) spans the globe and would be at home in any of the world's famous museums. Once the private collection of Englishman John Ward, the pieces include neolithic tools, medieval manuscripts and even an ancient Greek foot-guard (one of only four worldwide), and will have you scratching your head in amazement. The church has more original stained glass from Winchester Cathedral than what is actually left in the cathedral. In June/July, make merry at Australia's largest medieval festival, held on the grounds.

The Abbey Museum is on the road to Bribie Island, 6km from the Bruce Hwy turn-off, where you'll find the **Caboolture Warplane Museum** (07-5499 1144; www.caboolturewarplanemuseum.com; McNaught Rd, Hangar 104, Caboolture Airfield; adult/child/family $10/5/20; 9am-3pm), with its collection of restored WWII warplanes, all in flying order.

Bribie Island SLSC AUSTRALIAN **$$**
(07-3408 2141; www.thesurfclubbribieisland.com.au; First Ave, Woorim; mains $14-29; 10am-10pm) Sit on the deck and shovel in some good pub grub. Be there between noon and 3pm (from 11.30am weekends) for filling, tasty lunch specials ($14).

Information

There is no 4WD hire on Bribie, and you'll need a **4WD permit** ($41.75 per week) to access the island's more off-track spots. Pick one up at **Gateway Bait & Tackle** (07-5497 5253; www.gatewaybaitandtackle.com.au; 1383 Bribie Island Rd, Ningi; 5.30am-5.30pm Mon-Fri, 4.30am-6pm Sat, 4.30am-5pm Sun) or online (www.nprsr.qld.gov.au).

Bribie Island Visitor Information Centre (07-3408 9026; www.bribie.com.au; Benabrow Ave, Bellara; 9am-4pm) Pick up 4WD maps and heaps of info.

Getting There & Away

Frequent Citytrain services run from Brisbane to Caboolture from where **Bribie Island Coaches** (www.bribiecoaches.com.au) connects to Bribie Island; regular Brisbane Translink fares apply (one-way $13.90).

GLASS HOUSE MOUNTAINS

The volcanic crags of the Glass House Mountains rise abruptly from the subtropical plains 20km northwest of Caboolture. In Dreaming legend, these rocky peaks belong to a family of mountain spirits. It's worth diverting off the Bruce Hwy onto the slower Steve Irwin Way to snake your way through dense pine forests and green pastureland for a close-up view of these spectacular volcanic plugs.

The **Glass House Mountains National Park** is broken into several sections (all within cooee of Beerwah) with picnic grounds and lookouts but no camping grounds. The peaks are reached by a series of sealed and unsealed roads that head inland from Steve Irwin Way.

Sights & Activities

A number of signposted walking tracks reach several of the peaks, but be prepared for some steep and rocky trails. **Mt Beerwah** (556m) is the most trafficked but has a section of open rock face that may increase the anxiety factor. The walk up **Ngungun** (253m) is more moderate and the views are just as sensational, while **Tibrogargan** (364m) is probably the best climb with a challenging scramble and several amazing lookouts from the flat summit. Rock climbers can usually be seen scaling Tibrogargan, Ngungun and Beerwah. **Mt Coonowrin** (aka 'crook-neck'), the most dramatic of the volcanic plugs, is closed to the public.

QPWS has compiled a list of organisations that offer eco-accredited tours of the Glass House Mountains; see www.nprsr.qld.gov.au/parks/glass-house-mountains/tour-operators.html.

Sleeping & Eating

★**Glass House Mountains Ecolodge** LODGE **$$**
(07-5493 0008; www.glasshouseecolodge.com; 198 Barrs Rd; r $112-185) This novel retreat overseen by a keen environmentalist is close

to Australia Zoo and offers a range of good-value sleeping options, including the cosy Orchard Room ($112) and the converted Church Loft ($175), each with polished floorboards and tremendous views of Mt Tibrogargan. Pick-ups available from Glass House Mountains station.

Glass on Glasshouse B&B $$$
(☎07-5496 9608; www.glassonglasshouse.com.au; 182 Glasshouse-Woodford Rd; cottages from $295) Luxury woodsy cottages that live up to their name with floor-to-ceiling glass walls; the views to Mt Beerwah and Mt Coonowrin are gasp-inducing. Pampering touches like spa baths, fireplaces and free breakfasts make temper tantrums inevitable when it's time to leave.

Glasshouse Mountains Tavern PUB $$
(10 Reed St, Glass House Mountains; mains $15-30; ⏲10am-9pm Sun-Thu, to midnight Fri & Sat) The 'Glassy' cooks up good pub nosh. The open fire keeps things cosy during winter and a peppering of outdoor seating is great for a midday middy on sunny days.

CALOUNDRA

POP 20,220

Straddling a headland at the southern end of the Sunshine Coast, Caloundra is slowly shedding its retirement-village image without losing its sleepy seaside charm. Excellent fishing in Pumicestone Passage (the snake of water separating Bribie Island from the mainland) and a number of pleasant surf beaches make it a popular holiday resort for families and water-sports fans.

Sights & Activities

Caloundra's beaches curve around the headland so you'll always find a sheltered beach no matter how windy it gets. **Bulcock Beach**, just down from the main street and pinched by the northern tip of Bribie Island, captures a good wind tunnel, making it popular with kite-surfers. There's a lovely promenade on the foreshore that extends around to **Kings Beach**, where there's a kiddie-friendly interactive water feature and a free saltwater swimming pool on the rocks. The coastal track continues around the headland towards **Currimundi**. Depending on the conditions, **Moffat Beach** and **Dickey Beach** have the best surf breaks.

Queensland Air Museum MUSEUM
(☎07-5492 5930; www.qam.com.au; Caloundra Airport; adult/child/family $13/7/30; ⏲10am-4pm) Plenty of planes to keep budding aviators happy for hours.

Caloundra Surf School SURFING
(☎0413 381 010; www.caloundrasurfschool.com; lessons per person from $45) The pick of the surf schools, with board hire also available.

Blue Water Kayak Tours KAYAKING
(☎07-5494 7789; www.bluewaterkayaktours.com; half-/full-day tours min 4 people $90/150, twilight tour $55) Energetic kayak tours across the channel to the northern tip of Bribie Island National Park.

Caloundra Cruise CRUISE
(☎07-5492 8280; www.caloundracruise.com; Maloja Jetty; adult/child/family $20/10/52) Cruises (90 minutes) on a 1930s-style boat into Pumicestone Passage.

DON'T MISS

CREATURE FEATURE: AUSTRALIA ZOO

Just north of Beerwah is one of Queensland's, if not Australia's, most famous tourist attractions. **Australia Zoo** (☎07-5436 2000; www.australiazoo.com.au; Steve Irwin Way, Beerwah; adult/child/family $59/35/172; ⏲9am-5pm) is a fitting homage to its founder, zany wildlife enthusiast, Steve Irwin. As well as all things slimy and scaly, the zoo has an amazing wildlife menagerie complete with a Cambodian-style Tiger Temple, the Asian-themed Elephantasia and the famous Crocoseum. There are macaws, birds of prey, giant tortoises, snakes, otters, camels and more crocs and critters than you can poke a stick at. Plan to spend a full day at this amazing wildlife park.

Various companies offer tours from Brisbane and the Sunshine Coast. The zoo operates a bus ($5) from towns along the coast, and a free bus from the Beerwah train station (bookings essential; see website).

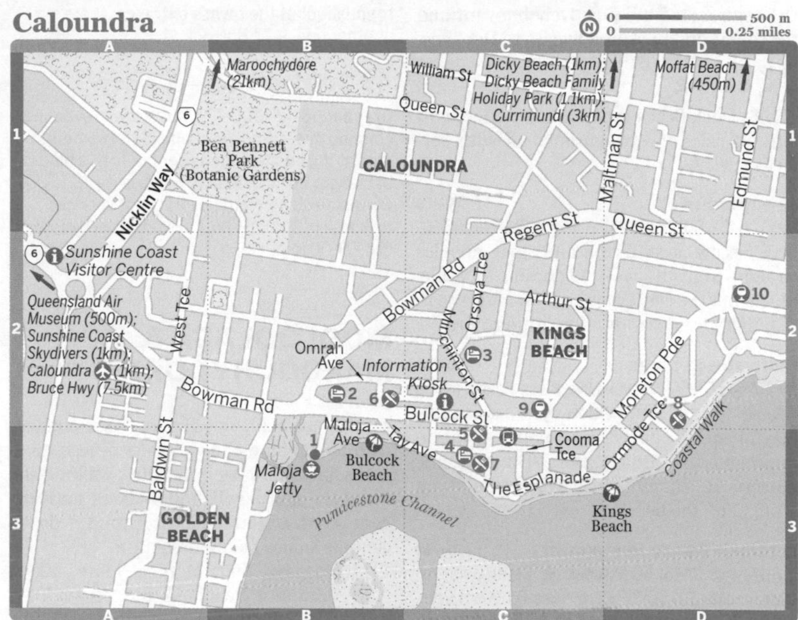

Sunshine Coast Skydivers SKYDIVING
(☎07-5437 0211; www.sunshinecoastskydivers.com.au; Caloundra Airport; tandem jumps from $249) Let your eyelids flap over stunning views of Caloundra from a brain-squeezing 15,000ft.

Sleeping

There's often a minimum three- to five-night stay in high season.

Caloundra Backpackers HOSTEL $
(☎07-5499 7655; www.caloundrabackpackers.com.au; 84 Omrah Ave; dm/d $28/70; @ 📶) Caloundra's only hostel, this is a no-nonsense budget option with a sociable courtyard, book exchange, and BBQ and pizza nights. Dorms aren't thrilling, but they're clean and peaceful.

Dicky Beach Family Holiday Park CARAVAN PARK $
(☎07-5491 3342; www.sunshinecoastholidayparks.com.au; 4 Beerburrum St; unpowered/powered site $37/41, cabin from $105; ❄ 📶 🏊) You can't get any closer to Dicky, one of Caloundra's most popular beaches. The brick cabins are as ordered and tidy as the grounds and there's a small swimming pool for the kids.

Caloundra

Activities, Courses & Tours
1 Caloundra Cruise B3

Sleeping
2 Caloundra Backpackers B2
3 City Centre Motel C2
4 Rumba Resort C3

Eating
5 Jerome's Family Restaurant C3
6 Jow Noodles B2
7 La Dolce Vita C3
8 Saltwater at Kings D2

Drinking & Nightlife
9 CBX C2
10 Kings Beach Tavern D2

City Centre Motel MOTEL $$
(☎07-5491 3301; www.caloundracitycentremotel.com.au; 20 Orsova Tce; s/d/f $85/120/145; P ❄ 📶) The closest motel to the city centre holds no surprises. It's a small complex and the rooms, although basic, are comfortable.

Rumba Resort RESORT $$$
(☎07-5492 0555; www.rumbaresort.com.au; 10 Leeding Tce; r from $240) This sparkling, resort-white five-star playground is ultra trendy for

Caloundra. Staff are positively buoyant and the rooms and pool area live up to the hype.

Eating

The Bulcock Beach esplanade is dotted with alfresco cafes and restaurants, all with perfect sea views.

Jow Noodles ASIAN $
(07-5437 0072; 105-111 Bulcock St; mains $10-18; lunch & dinner) Fresh and spicy noodles straight from the wok. It doesn't look like much, but the clattering kitchen and swarm of hungry traffic lends a fun atmosphere.

Saltwater at Kings CAFE $$
(07-5437 2260; 8 Levuka Ave, Kings Beach; mains $21-38; 8am-11pm) Oooh er! Saltwater's playful menu offers 'sexy salads', 'voluptuous' mains and 'little teasers'. The orgasmic desserts are equally saucy. Perfect for lunch straight off the beach.

Jerome's Family Restaurant ITALIAN $$
(07-5438 0445; 50 Bulcock St, Centrepoint Arcade; mains $14.50-27.50; Tues-Fri 10am-9pm, 5-9pm Sat & Mon) Old-school Italian joint in homey surrounds and a hearty, dependable menu with all the favourites: pizza, pastas, steaks and seafood. Nothing cutting-edge, but its traditional feel is what makes it a local favourite.

La Dolce Vita ITALIAN $$
(07-5438 2377; 10 Leeding Tce, Rumba Resort; mains $20-38; 7am-10pm Mon-Fri, 6.30am-11pm Sat & Sun) This modern Italian restaurant has a stylish black-and-white theme but it's best to sit outdoors behind the large glass-windowed booth for alfresco dining with gorgeous sea views.

Drinking & Nightlife

CBX PUB
(12 Bulcock St; 10am-midnight Sun-Thu, to 2am Fri & Sat) Live bands and DJs on weekends; pub meals available.

Kings Beach Tavern PUB
(www.kingsbeachtavern.com.au; 43 Burgess St, Kings Beach; 10am-midnight Sun-Thu, to 2am Fri & Sat) Beer! Bistro meals! The decor is mod-soulless, but the pub does host loads of Aussie alternative musical acts; check website for gig guide.

Information

Sunshine Coast Visitor Centre (07-5478 2233; 7 Caloundra Rd; 9am-5pm) On the roundabout at the town's entrance; there's another one at 77 Bulcock St.

Getting There & Away

Greyhound (1300 473 946; www.greyhound.com.au) buses from Brisbane ($17, two hours) stop at the **bus terminal** (Cooma Tce), a block back from Bulcock Beach. **Sunbus** (13 12 30; www.sunbus.com.au) has frequent services to Noosa ($8.20, 1½ hours) via Maroochydore ($4.60, 50 minutes).

MOOLOOLABA & MAROOCHYDORE

POP 11,064 & 16,757

Mooloolaba has seduced many a sea-changer with its sublime climate, golden beach and cruisy lifestyle. Take a morning walk on the foreshore and you'll find walkers and joggers, suntans and surfboards, and a dozen genuine smiles before breakfast.

Mooloolaba and Maroochydore, along with Alexandra Headland and Cotton Tree, are collectively known as 'Maroochy'. While Maroochydore takes care of the business end, Mooloolaba steals the show. Eateries, boutiques and pockets of resorts and apartments have spread along the Esplanade, transforming this once-humble fishing village into one of Queensland's most popular holiday destinations.

Sights & Activities

There are good surf breaks along the strip – one of Queensland's best for longboarders is the **Bluff**, the prominent point at Alexandra Headland. **Pincushion** near the Maroochy River mouth can provide an excellent break in the winter offshore winds.

Diving to the wreck of the sunken warship, the **ex-HMAS Brisbane**, is also incredibly popular. Sunk in July 2005, the wreck lies in 28m of water and its funnels are only 4m below the surface.

Underwater World AQUARIUM
(Map p147; 07-5458 6280; www.underwaterworld.com.au; The Wharf, Mooloolaba; adult/child/family $35/23/96; 9am-5pm) This is Queensland's largest tropical oceanarium, where you can swim with seals, dive with sharks or simply marvel at the ocean life outside the 80m-long transparent underwater tunnel. There's a touch tank, live shows and educational spiels to entertain both kids and adults.

Mooloolaba

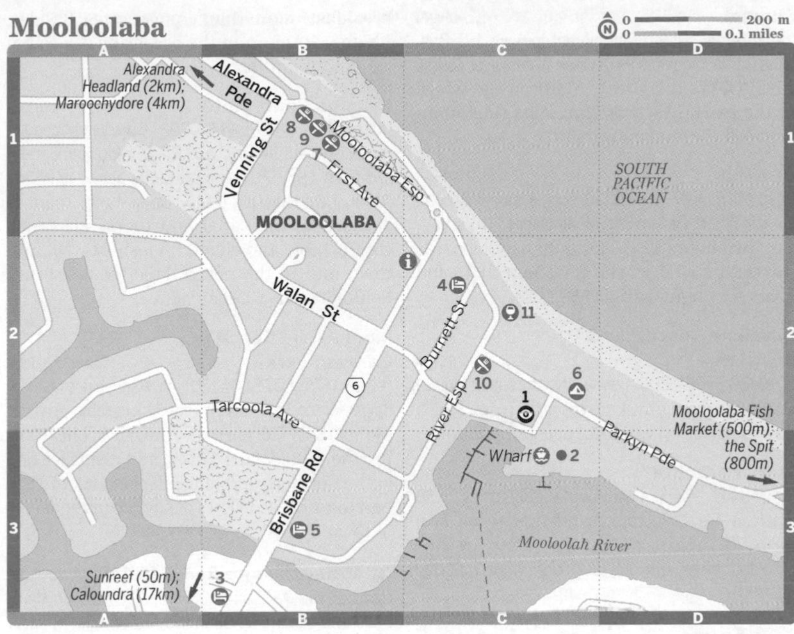

Mooloolaba

Big Pineapple LANDMARK

(www.bigpineapple.com.au; 76 Nambour Connection Rd, Woombye) FREE Just 10km west of Maroochydore lies (OK, sprouts) the 16m-high Big Pineapple, possibly the most iconic of all Queensland's Big Things (see p142). You can climb it, shop in its shadow (markets every Saturday from 6.30am to 1pm), or toot around it on a little train.

Scuba World DIVING

(Map p147; ☎1300 677 094; www.scubaworld.com.au; Mooloolaba Harbour (next to Underwater World); dives from $119; ⏰9am-5pm Mon-Sat, 10am-4pm Sun) Arranges shark dives (certified/uncertified divers $195/245) at Underwater World, coral dives off the coast and a wreck dive of the *Brisbane*. PADI courses available.

Robbie Sherwell's XL Surfing Academy SURFING

(☎07-5478 1337; www.robbiesherwell.com.au; 1hr lesson private/group $95/45) Dip a toe into Aussie surf culture at this long-established school.

Suncoast Kiteboarding KITE-BOARDING

(☎0422 079 106; www.suncoastkiteboarding.com.au; 2hr lesson $180) At Cotton Tree, Noosa and Caloundra.

Sunreef DIVING
(☎07-5444 5656; www.sunreef.com.au; 110 Brisbane Rd, Mooloolaba; PADI Open Water Diver course $595) Offers two dives ($150) on the wreck of the ex-HMAS *Brisbane*. Also runs night dives on the sunken warship.

Hire Hut WATER SPORTS
(Map p147; ☎07-5444 0366; www.oceanjetski.com.au; The Wharf, Parkyn Pde, Mooloolaba) Hires kayaks (two hours $25), stand-up paddleboards (two hours $35), jet skis (one hour $150) and boats (per hour/half-day $42/75).

Sunshine Coast Bike & Board Hire SURFING
(☎0439 706 206; www.adventurehire.com.au) Hires out bikes and surfboards from $30 a day. Free delivery to local accommodation.

Swan Boat Hire BOATING
(☎07-5443 7225; www.swanboathire.com.au; 59 Bradman Ave, Maroochydore; half-/full-day hire from $180/270; ⏲6am-6pm) On the Maroochy River. Also hires out kayaks (one hour/half-day $20/80).

Tours

Whale One WHALE WATCHING
(Map p147; ☎1800 942 531; www.whaleone.com.au; The Wharf, Mooloolaba; adult/child/family $119/79/320) Whale-watching cruises between June and November.

Canal Cruise BOAT TOUR
(Map p147; ☎07-5444 7477; www.mooloolabacanalcruise.com.au; The Wharf, Mooloolaba; adult/child/family $18/6/45; ⏲11am, 1pm & 2.30pm) These boat trips cruise past the McMansions preening beside the Mooloolah River.

Coastal Cruises BOAT TOUR
(Map p147; ☎0419 704 797; www.cruisemooloolaba.com.au; The Wharf, Mooloolaba) Sunset ($25) and seafood lunch cruises ($35) through Mooloolaba Harbour, River and canals.

Sleeping

During school holidays, rates can double and most places require a minimum two- or three-night stay.

Mooloolaba Beach Backpackers HOSTEL $
(Map p147; ☎07-5444 3399; www.mooloolababackpackers.com; 75 Brisbane Rd, Mooloolaba; dm/d $29/70; @☎≋) Some dorms have en suites, and although the rooms are a little drab, the amount of freebies (bikes, kayaks, surfboards, stand-up paddleboards and breakfast) more than compensates. Besides, it's only 500m from the beachside day activities and nightlife.

Kyamba Court Motel MOTEL $
(Map p147; ☎07-5444 0202; www.kyambacourtmotel.com.au; 94 Brisbane Rd, Mooloolaba; Sun-Fri s/d from $90/95, weekend tariffs apply; ❄☎≋) Although this motel is on a busy road, it also fronts the canal and rooms are large, comfortable and clean. It's a short walk into town and to the beach. Free breakfast and fishing rod use. Great value.

Mooloolaba Beach Caravan Park CARAVAN PARK $
(Map p147; ☎07-5444 1201; www.sunshinecoastholidayparks.com.au; Parkyn Pde, Mooloolaba; powered site from $41) The park runs two sites; one fronting the Mooloolaba Beach, and a smaller one at the northern end of the Esplanade, with the best location and views of any accommodation in town. Prices are for two people.

★**Maroochydore Beach Motel** MOTEL $$
(Map p149; ☎07-5443 7355; www.maroochydorebeachmotel.com; 69 Sixth Ave, Maroochydore; s/d/f from $115/130/170; P❄@≋) You've gotta love a theme motel, especially one as snazzy and spotless this one. There are 18 different rooms, including the Elvis Room (natch), the Egyptian Room and the Aussie room. The owners are lovely and helpful, and it's just 50m to the beach.

Maroochy River Resort BUNGALOW $$
(☎07-5448 4911; www.maroochyriverbungalows.com.au; 38-46 David Low Way, Maroochydore; 1-/2-bedroom bungalows from $120/150) About 5km out from the centre of town, this natty collection of bungalows sits right on Eudlo Creek, a calm waterway where you can kayak, stand-up paddle and canoe (all equipment available to rent from the resort). The bungalows are welcoming, and have sweet locations either tucked within the resort gardens or right on the water's edge. Superlative value that just gets better the longer your stay.

Landmark Resort RESORT $$
(Map p147; ☎07-5444 5555; www.landmarkresort.com.au; 11 Burnett St, Mooloolaba; studio/1-bedroom apt from $170/230; ❄@☎≋) Nothing compares to the ocean views from these breezy self-contained apartments. The resort sits above Mooloolaba's trendy eateries and is only 30m from the beach. There's a heated lagoon-style pool and a rooftop spa and barbecue.

Maroochydore

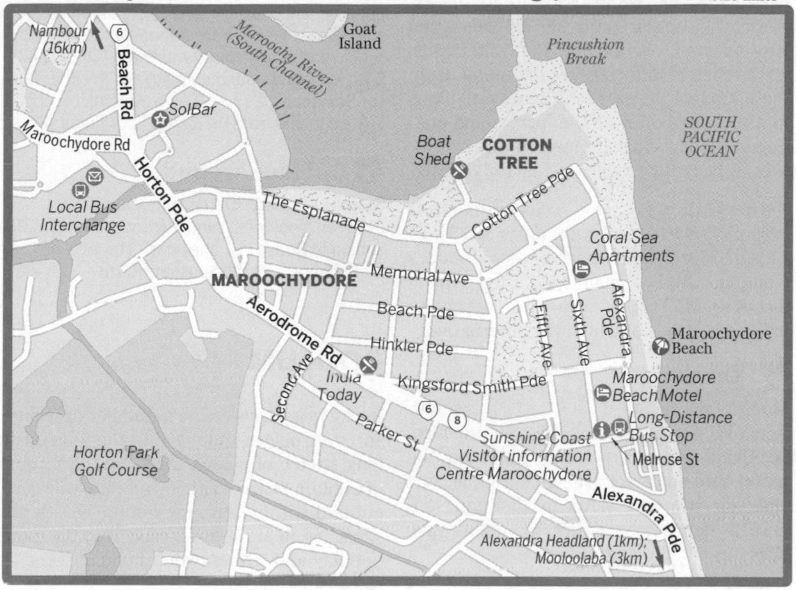

Coral Sea Apartments APARTMENT $$$
(Map p149; ☎07-5479 2999; www.coralsea-apartments.com; 35-37 Sixth Ave, Maroochydore; 1-/2-bedroom apt for 2 nights from $300/345;) These tastefully decorated apartments occupy a lovely spot close to Maroochy Surf Club and the beach. Balconies are big, breezy and have ocean views.

Eating

★Mooloolaba Fish Market SEAFOOD $
(Lot 201, Parkyn Pde, Mooloolaba; fish & chips from $10, seafood platters $55; ⏲7am-8pm) This splashy, stinky and altogether atmospheric fish market is home to a variety of restaurants and takeaways all selling the freshest of fresh seafood (what else?) at a miscellany of prices.

Thai Seasons THAI $
(Map p147; ☎07-5444 4611; 10 River Esplanade, Mooloolaba; mains $10-15; ⏲6-10pm) It's affectionately known as 'dirty Thai', but don't be put off by the plastic outdoor setting and grubby exterior; this unpretentious restaurant dishes out the very best Thai food in town. If it's crowded, order takeaway and head for the picnic tables overlooking Mooloolaba's main beach.

India Today INDIAN $
(Map p149; ☎07-5452 7054; 91 Aerodrome Rd, Maroochydore; mains $14-22; ⏲5-10pm Sun-Wed, 11.30am-2pm & 5-10pm Thu-Sat;) You can't miss the masses of fairy lights decorating this restaurant on Maroochydore's main drag. The menu is equally jazzy, with a humongous range of Indian favourites and lip-smacking regional specialties; there's also a very extensive vegetarian menu.

Bella Venezia ITALIAN $$
(Map p147; ☎07-5444 5844; 95 Esplanade, Mooloolaba; mains $25-42; ⏲noon-late) This understated, casually chic restaurant, with an all-Italian wine bar, spreads across an arcade cul-de-sac. The menu is high-end Oz-Italo and includes exquisite dishes such as Moreton Bay bug spaghetti.

Boat Shed SEAFOOD $$
(Map p149; ☎07-5443 3808; Esplanade, Cotton Tree; mains $21-37; ⏲9am-11.30pm Mon-Sat, to 5pm Sun) A shabby-chic gem on the banks of the Maroochy River, great for sunset drinks beneath the sprawling cotton tree. Seafood is the star of the menu; after dinner, roll back to the outdoor lounges for dessert and some seriously romantic stargazing.

Lot 104 FUSION $$

(Map p147; ☎07-5326 1990; 104/101-105 The Esplanade, Mooloolaba; mains $15-30; ⏲6pm-late) Hip hangout overlooking the water with all manner of munchies on the menu, from the addictive popcorn chicken share-plate, to the hands-off-it's-mine prawn-and-crab linguini. They're also renowned for their espresso; be ready to wait a while for your fix.

Karma Waters MODERN AUSTRALIAN $$

(Map p147; Mantra, Esplanade; mains $23-34; ⏲7.30am-10.30pm) Another outdoor eatery along the lively esplanade, Karma Waters dishes up Mod Oz cuisine with a Portuguese influence. Loads of gluten-free alternatives.

Drinking

Mooloolaba SLSC SURF CLUB

(Map p147; Esplanade, Mooloolaba; ⏲10am-10pm Sun-Thu, to midnight Fri & Sat) Right on the beach, Mooloolaba's true-blue Aussie surf club has stunning views by day and suntanned dance-floor antics by night. Also does top-notch pub grub.

SolBar CLUB

(Map p149; ☎07-5443 9550; 19 Ocean St, Maroochydore; ⏲7.30am-2pm Mon & Tue, 7.30am-2pm & 5pm-1am Wed & Thu, 7.30am-3am Fri, 5pm-3am Sat, 2pm-1am Sun) SolBar is a godsend for city-starved indie fans. A constantly surprising line-up takes to the stages here, while punters enjoy an array of international beers and a less-surfy atmosphere than most other joints in town.

Club WT CLUB

(Map p147; Wharf, Mooloolaba; ⏲10am-3am Thu-Sat) It's loud, tacky and incredibly popular with backpackers and locals. Inside the otherwise family-friendly Wharf Tavern.

Information

The Mooloolaba Esplanade seamlessly morphs into Alexandra Pde along the beachfront at Alexandra Headland ('Alex' to the locals), then flows into Aerodrome Rd and the main CBD of Maroochydore. Cotton Tree is at the mouth of the Maroochy River.

Sunshine Coast Visitor Information Centre (Map p147; ☎1300 847 481; www.visitsunshinecoast.com.au; cnr Brisbane Rd & First Ave, Mooloolaba; ⏲9am-5pm) Also has other branches throughout the region: Maroochydore (Map p149; cnr Sixth Ave & Melrose St; ⏲9am-4pm); Sunshine Coast Airport (Marcoola; ⏲airport hours)

Getting There & Away

Long-distance buses stop in front of the Sunshine Coast Visitor Information Centre in Maroochydore. **Greyhound Australia** (☎1300 473 946; www.greyhound.com.au) and **Premier Motor Services** (☎13 34 10; www.premierms.com.au) run to and from Brisbane ($20, 2 hours).

Getting Around

Sunbus (☎13 12 30) has frequent services between Mooloolaba and Maroochydore ($3.30) and on to Noosa ($7, one hour). The local bus interchange is at the Sunshine Plaza.

COOLUM

POP 7905

Rocky headlands create a number of secluded coves before spilling into the fabulously long stretch of golden sand and rolling surf of Coolum beach. With its budding cafe society, and within easy reach of the coast's hot spots, it's an attractive escape from the more popular and overcrowded holiday scene at Noosa and Maroochy.

Sights & Activities

For outstanding views of the coast, a hike to the top of **Mt Coolum**, south of town, is worth the sweat factor. Get all the details at the **visitor centre** (www.visitsunshinecoast.com.au; David Low Way, Coolum; ⏲9am-3pm).

Coolum Surf School SURFING

(☎0438 731 503; www.coolumsurfschool.com.au; 2hr lesson $55, 5-day package $200) Coolum Surf School will have you riding the waves in no time; they also hire out surfboards/bodyboards ($50/25 for 24 hours).

Skydive Ramblers SKYDIVING

(☎07-5448 8877; www.skydiveforfun.com; jump from 6000/15,000ft $299/429) Skydive Ramblers will throw you out of a plane at a ridiculous height. Savour the coastal view before a spectacular beach landing.

Sleeping

Villa Coolum MOTEL $

(☎07-5446 1286; www.villacoolum.com; 102 Coolum Tce, Coolum Beach; r $89-99; 🏊) Hidden behind a leafy verandah, these modest, good-value bungalows have spacious motel-style rooms; there's a large pool, and a pleasant garden to stroll through.

Coolum Beach Caravan Park CARAVAN PARK $
(☎07-5446 1474; 1827 David Low Way, Coolum; unpowered/powered site $37/41, cabin from $130) Location, location: the park not only has absolute beach frontage, but is also just across the road from Coolum's main strip.

Beach Retreat APARTMENT $$
(☎07-5471 7700; www.beachretreatcoolum.com; 1750 David Low Way, Coolum; d from $180-250;) With ocean views and within walking distance of the esplanade eateries, these spacious apartments are in a great spot. The central pool area is handy for rough beach weather. Rates get better the longer you stay.

Eating

Coolum's esplanade has sprouted a string of outdoor cafes and restaurants. It's fun to wander along the strip before deciding where to eat.

My Place INTERNATIONAL $$
(☎07-5446 4433; 1768 David Low Way, Coolum; mains $17-26; ⏲7am-11pm) Opposite the boardwalk and boasting sensational ocean views, My Place can't be beaten for sunset cocktails, shared meze plates or summer alfresco dining.

Sunrise CAFE $$
(☎07-5471 7477; 1748 David Low Way; mains $16-28; ⏲Wed-Sun 7am-9pm) A cafe that goes above and beyond the usual snackery, with scrumptious mains including crispy-skin salmon in chilli jam and mussels dripping with garlic and cream. The beachfront views are easy to swallow, too.

Castro's Bar & Restaurant ITALIAN $$
(☎07-5471 7555; cnr Frank St & Beach Rd; mains $19-30; ⏲5pm-late) Not even vaguely Cuban, but this popular spot does enjoy a FIdel-like longevity thanks to imaginative wood-fired pizzas and mains including salmon risotto and big-serve pasta classics.

PEREGIAN & SUNSHINE BEACH

POP 3519 & 2298

Fifteen kilometres of uncrowded, unobstructed beach stretch north from Coolum to Sunshine Beach and the rocky northeast headland of Noosa National Park.

Peregian is the place to indulge in long solitary beach walks, to surf the excellent breaks and take in fresh air and plenty of sunshine; it's not uncommon to see whales breaking offshore.

A little further north, the laidback latte ethos of **Sunshine Beach** attracts Noosa locals escaping the summer hordes. Beach walks morph into bush trails over the headland; a stroll through the **Noosa National Park** takes an hour to reach Alexandria Bay and two hours to Noosa's Laguna Bay. Road access to the park is from McAnally Dr or Parkedge Rd.

Sleeping

Flashpackers HOSTEL $
(Map p139; ☎07-5455 4088; www.flashpackers-noosa.com; 102 Pacific Ave, Sunshine Beach; dm from $27, girls' dorm $34, d from $70, includes breakfast;) Flashpackers challenges the notion of hostels as flea-bitten dives, with pristine dorm rooms and an airy tropical design. Thoughtful touches include full-length mirrors, ample wall sockets, free surfboard use and complimentary Friday night sausage sizzle.

Chez Noosa MOTEL $$
(Map p139; ☎07-5447 2027; www.cheznoosa.com.au; 263 Edwards St, Sunshine Beach; standard/deluxe unit from $110/120;) Right by Noosa National Park and set in aptly bushy gardens, the Chez is fantastic value for money. The self-contained units are basic but cute, and there's a heated pool and spa with an undercover BBQ area.

Peregian Court Resort APARTMENT $$
(☎07-5448 1622; www.peregiancourt.com; 380 David Low Way, Peregian Beach; 1/2 bedroom apt from $115/160, 2-night min stay;) It's just a minute's walk to the beach from these clean, airy and altogether comfy resort-style apartments. Each has a fully-equipped kitchen, but the onsite, seabreezy BBQ area encourages alfresco feasting.

Eating & Drinking

Baked Poetry Cafe CAFE $
(218 David Low Way, Peregian Beach Shopping Centre; dishes $10-16; ⏲9am-5pm Mon-Fri, to 4pm Sat & Sun) This minibakery and cafe is a local institution, known for great coffee and German sourdough bread. Try the *eier im glas*, a soft-boiled egg in a glass alongside a plate of bacon, grilled tomato and cheese.

Marble Bar Bistro BAR
(40 Duke St, Sunshine Beach; tapas $10-18.50; noon-late) Kick back in a cushioned lounge or perch yourself at one of the marble benches at this cruisy cocktail and tapas bar.

Embassy XO CHINESE $$
(07-5455 4460; 56 Duke St, Sunshine Beach; mains $25-39; 5-10pm Tue-Sun) This chic, ambient restaurant is *not* your suburban Chinese takeaway. Dive right in with the exquisite banquet (from $55 per person) or weekend yum cha, or linger over the inventive menu with a Chinese beer or Shanghai Mule.

COOLOOLA COAST

Stretching for 50km between Noosa and Rainbow Beach, the Cooloola Coast is a remote strip of long sandy beach backed by the Cooloola Section of the **Great Sandy National Park**. Although it's undeveloped, the 4WD and tin-boat set flock here in droves so it's not always as peaceful as you might imagine. If you head off on foot or by canoe along the many inlets and waterways, however, you'll soon escape the crowds.

From the end of Moorindil St in Tewantin, the **Noosa North Shore Ferry** (07-5447 1321; www.noosacarferries.com; one way per pedestrian/car $1/6; 5.30am-10.20pm Sun-Thu, 5am-12.20am Fri & Sat) shuttles across the river to Noosa North Shore. If you have a 4WD, you can drive along the beach to Rainbow Beach (and on up to Inskip Point to the Fraser Island ferry), but you'll need a permit (www.nprsr.qld.gov.au; per day/week/month $11/27.70/43.60). You can also buy a permit from the **QPWS office** (240 Moorindil St, Tewantin). Check the tide times!

On the way up the beach, you'll pass the **Teewah coloured sand cliffs**, estimated to be about 40,000 years old.

Lake Cooroibah

A couple of kilometres north of Tewantin, the Noosa River widens into Lake Cooroibah, which is surrounded by lush bushland. If you take the Noosa North Shore Ferry, you can drive up to the lake in a conventional vehicle and camp along sections of the beach.

Activities

Camel Company CAMEL RIDING
(0408 710 530; www.camelcompany.com.au; Beach Rd, Tewantin; safari adult/child from $60/45) Beach and bush safaris on board your very own dromedary.

Noosa Equathon HORSE RIDING
(07-5474 2665; www.equathon.com; Beach Rd, Noosa North Shore; 2hr beach ride $175) Intimate horse rides led by triple Olympian Alex Watson. Also runs overnight rides, starting at $350 per person.

Sleeping

Gagaju Bush Camp HOSTEL $
(07-5474 3522; http://gagaju.tripod.com; 118 Johns Rd, Tewantin; dm $15; @) The refreshingly feral Gagaju Bush Camp is a riverside eco-wilderness camp with basic dorms constructed out of recycled timber. There's a somewhat hands-off managerial approach, unless a good party is involved! Don't forget to bring food and mozzie repellent. A courtesy shuttle runs to and from Noosa twice a day.

Noosa North Shore Retreat RETREAT $
(07-5447 1225; www.noosanorthshoreretreat.com.au; Beach Rd; unpowered/powered site from $20/30, cabin/r from $75/145; @) They've got everything here, from camping and vinyl 'village tents' to shiny motel rooms and cottages. Ditch your bags, then head out for a paddle around the lake, a bushwalk or a bounce on the jumping pillow. The retreat also houses the **Great Sandy Bar & Restaurant**, open weekends for lunch and dinner (mains $15 to $25).

Lake Cootharaba & Boreen Point

Cootharaba is the biggest lake in the Cooloola Section of Great Sandy National Park, measuring about 5km across and 10km in length. On the western shores of the lake and at the southern edge of the national park, **Boreen Point** is a relaxed little community with several places to stay and to eat. The lake is the gateway to the **Noosa Everglades**, offering bushwalking, canoeing and bush camping.

From Boreen Point, an unsealed road leads another 5km to **Elanda Point**.

WORTH A TRIP

MONTVILLE & KENILWORTH

It's hard to imagine that the chintzy mountain village of **Montville** with its fudge emporiums, Devonshire tearooms and cottage crafts began life under the dramatic name of Razorback – until you arrive at the town's spectacular ridge-top location 500m above sea level. To work off that excess fudge, take a rainforest hike to Kondalilla Falls in **Kondalilla National Park,** 3km northwest of town. After a refreshing swim, check for leeches!

Secrets on the Lake (07-5478 5888; www.secretsonthelake.com.au; 207 Narrows Rd; midweek/weekend from $205/255;) is a romantic hideaway where boardwalks through the foliage lead to magical, wooden treehouses with sunken spas, log fires and stunning views of Lake Baroon.

From Montville, head to the tiny village of **Mapleton** and turn left on the Obi Obi Rd. After 18km, you reach **Kenilworth**, a small country town in the pretty Mary River Valley. **Kenilworth Country Foods** (07-5446 0144; www.kenilworthcountryfoods.com.au; 45 Charles St; 9am-4pm Mon-Fri, 10am-3pm Sat & Sun) is a boutique cheese factory with creamy yoghurt and wickedly good cheese. If you plan to camp in the Kenilworth State Forest or Conondale National Park you'll need a **permit** (13 74 68; www.nprsr.qld.gov.au; per person $5.45). The **Kenilworth Showgrounds** has camping (no permit required) for $15 per vehicle, with power, water and $1 showers.

Otherwise, head northeast on the Eumundi–Kenilworth Rd for a scenic drive through rolling pastureland dotted with traditional old farmhouses and floods of jacarandas. After 30km you reach the Bruce Hwy near Eumundi.

Activities

Kanu Kapers KAYAKING
(07-5485 3328; www.kanukapersaustralia.com; 11 Toolara St, Boreen Point; half-/full-day guided tour $155/185, 1-day self-guided tour $75) Paddle into the placid Everglades.

Discovery Group Canoe Safari BOATING
(07-5449 0393; www.thediscoverygroup.com.au; 3-day/2-night self-guided canoeing safari $155) Canoe and camp your way down the Everglades over three days. They also run afternoon cruises on-board a purpose-built boat ($79).

Sleeping & Eating

Lake Cootharaba Motel MOTEL $
(07-5485 3127; www.cootharabamotel.com; 75 Laguna St, Boreen Point; r $95-130;) A quaint and tidy spot that's less motel than lakeside retreat, this is a great base for visiting the Everglades or simply splashing about on Cootharaba. There are only five rooms; be sure to book ahead.

Boreen Point Camping Ground CAMPGROUND $
(07-5485 3244; Esplanade, Boreen Point; unpowered/powered site $22/28) On the river, this quiet, simple camping ground is dominated by large gums and native bush.

Apollonian Hotel PUB $
(07-5485 3100; 19 Laguna St, Boreen Point; mains $12-30; 10am-midnight) This is a gorgeous old pub with sturdy timber walls, shady verandahs and a beautifully preserved interior. The pub grub is tasty and popular. Plan to be there (and do book ahead) for the famous Sunday spit roast lunch.

Great Sandy National Park: Cooloola Section

The Cooloola Section of Great Sandy National Park covers more than 54,000 hectares from Lake Cootharaba north to Rainbow Beach. It's a varied wilderness area with long sandy beaches, mangrove-lined waterways, forest, heath and lakes, all featuring plentiful bird life, including rarities such as the red goshawk and the grass owl, and lots of wildflowers in spring.

The **Cooloola Way**, from Tewantin up to Rainbow Beach, is open to 4WD vehicles unless there's been heavy rain – check the situation with the rangers before you set out. Most people prefer to bomb up the beach, though you're restricted to a few hours either side of low tide. You'll need

WORTH A TRIP

THE MAJESTIC

About 10km northwest of Eumundi, the little village of **Pomona** sits in the shadow of looming Mt Cooroora (440m) and is home to the wonderful **Majestic Theatre** (☎07-5485 2330; www.majestictheatre.com.au; 3 Factory St, Pomona; ticket $15, meal deal $27; ⏰screening 7.30pm Tue-Fri), billed as the only authentic silent movie theatre in the world. It's one of the only places where you can see a silent movie accompanied by the original Wurlitzer organ soundtrack. They've been screening the iconic *The Son of the Sheikh* (first Thursday of each month) for the last 25 years!

a permit (www.nprsr.qld.gov.au; per day/week/month $11/27.70/43.60).

The best way to see Cooloola is by boat or canoe along the numerous tributaries of the Noosa River. Boats can be hired from Tewantin and Noosa (along Gympie Tce), Boreen Point and Elanda Point on Lake Cootharaba.

There are some fantastic walking trails starting from Elanda Point on the shore of Lake Cootharaba, including the 46km **Cooloola Wilderness Trail** to Rainbow Beach and a 7km trail to an unstaffed QPWS information centre at Kinaba.

The **QPWS Great Sandy Information Centre** (☎07-5449 7792; 240 Moorindil St, Tewantin; ⏰8am-4pm) can provide information on park access, tide times and fire bans within the park. The centre also issues car and camping permits for both Fraser Island and the Great Sandy National Park, but these are best booked online at www.nprsr.qld.gov.au.

The park has a number of **camping grounds** (☎13 74 68; www.nprsr.qld.gov.au; per person/family $5.45/21.80), many of them along the river. The most popular (and best-equipped) camping grounds are **Fig Tree Point** (at the northern end of Lake Cootharaba), **Harry's Hut** (about 4km upstream) and **Freshwater** (about 6km south of Double Island Point) on the coast. You can also camp at designated zones on the beach if you're driving up to Rainbow Beach. Apart from Harry's Hut, Freshwater and Teewah Beach, all sites are accessible by hiking or river only.

EUMUNDI

POP 1790

Sweet little Eumundi is a quaint highland village with a quirky New Age vibe greatly amplified during its famous market days. The historic streetscape blends well with modern cafes, artsy boutiques, silversmiths and crafty folk doing their thing. Once you've breathed Eumundi air, don't be surprised if you feel a sudden urge to take up beading or body painting.

Sights & Activities

★Eumundi Markets MARKET

(80 Memorial Dr; ⏰8am-1.30pm Wed, 7am-2pm Sat) The Eumundi markets attract thousands of visitors to their 300-plus stalls and have everything from hand-crafted furniture and jewellery to homemade clothes and alternative healing booths. Local produce and hot meals also go down a right treat.

Tina Cooper Glass GALLERY

(www.tinacoopergallery.com; 93 Memorial Dr; ⏰9am-4pm Wed & Sat, 10am-3pm Fri & Sun) Beautiful glass sculptures and other works of art are on display here. Often has in-shop glass-blowing exhibitions.

Murra Wolka Creations GALLERY

(☎07-5442 8691; www.murrawolka.com; 39 Memorial Dr; ⏰9am-4.30pm Mon-Fri) Buy boomerangs and didgeridoos hand-painted by Indigenous artists at this Aboriginal-owned-and-operated gallery.

Sleeping & Eating

Hidden Valley B&B B&B **$$**

(☎07-5442 8685; www.eumundibed.com; 39 Caplick Way; r $175-195; 📶❄) This not-so-hidden retreat is on 1.5 hectares of land, only 400m from Eumundi on the Noosa road. Inside this attractive Queenslander, you can choose a themed room to match your mood: Aladdin's Cave, the Emperor Suite or the Hinterland Retreat.

Harmony Hill Station B&B **$$**

(☎07-5442 8685; www.eumundibed.com; 81 Seib Rd; carriage $155; ❄) Perched on a hilltop in a 5-hectare property, this restored and fully self-contained 1912 purple railway carriage is the perfect place to relax or romance. Share the grounds with grazing kangaroos, watch the sunset from Lover's Leap, share a bottle of wine beneath a stunning night sky...or even get married (the owners are celebrants!).

Joe's Waterhole PUB $
(☎07-5442 8144; www.liveatjoes.com; 85 Memorial Dr; meals $10; ⏲10am-9pm Sun-Thu, to 11.30pm Fri & Sat) Pub grub and heaps of local/international music acts in down-home, knees-up surrounds.

Bohemian Bungalow INTERNATIONAL $$
(☎07-5442 8679; www.bohemianbungalow.com.au; 69 Memorial Dr; mains $19-30; ⏲8am-3pm & 5.30-9pm Thu-Sat, 8am-3pm Wed & Sun) Whimsical fare in this gorgeous white Queenslander includes hearty mains with oddball names like 'Flying South for the Winter' (homemade gnocchi with confit duck) and share plates like 'This Little Piggy Went to Paris' (pâté, pâté, pâté). They also whip up lovely coffees, gourmet pizzas and fine brekkies.

Imperial Hotel PUB $$
(☎07-5442 8811; Memorial Dr; mains $16-32; ⏲10am-7pm Mon & Tue, to 9pm Wed, to 11pm Thu-Sat, to 6pm Sun) This utterly gorgeous colonial-style pub serves up fine favourites (steak, local seafood) on back-in-time verandahs and classy dining rooms. Also has great beers on tap and live music.

Information

Discover Eumundi Heritage & Visitor Centre (☎07-5442 8762; Memorial Dr; ⏲10am-4pm Mon-Fri, 9am-3pm Sat, 10am-2pm Sun) Also houses the museum (admission free).

Getting There & Away

Sunbus (☎13 12 30; www.sunbus.com.au) runs hourly from Noosa Heads ($4.50, 45 minutes) and Nambour ($5.90, 40 minutes). A number of tour operators visit the Eumundi markets on Wednesdays and Saturdays.

SUNSHINE COAST HINTERLAND

Inland from **Nambour**, the Blackall Range forms a stunning backdrop to the Sunshine Coast's popular beaches a short 50km away. A relaxed half- or full-day circuit drive from the coast follows a winding road along the razorback line of the escarpment, passing through quaint mountain villages and offering spectacular views of the coastal lowlands. The villages (some suffering from an overdose of kitschy craft shops and Devonshire tearooms) are worth a visit, but the real attraction is the landscape, with its lush green pastures and softly folded valleys and ridges, and the waterfalls, swimming holes, rainforests and walks in the national parks. Cosy cabins and B&Bs are popular weekend retreats, especially during winter.

Tours

Plenty of tour companies operate through the hinterland and will pick up from anywhere along the Sunshine Coast.

Storeyline Tours TOUR
(☎07-5474 1500; www.storeylinetours.com.au; from $25) Runs small-group tours to the Eumundi Markets (Wednesdays and Saturdays, from $25) and various Hinterland villages.

WOODSTOCK DOWN UNDER

The famous **Woodford Folk Festival** (www.woodfordfolkfestival.com) features a huge diversity of over 2000 national and international performers playing folk, traditional Irish, Indigenous and world music, as well as buskers, belly dancers, craft markets, visual-arts performances, environmental talks and Tibetan monks. The festival is held on a property near the town of Woodford from 27 December to 1 January each year. Camping grounds are set up onsite with toilets, showers and a range of foodie marquees, but prepare for a mud bath if it rains. The festival is licensed so leave your booze at home. Tickets cost around $133 per day ($163 with camping) and can be bought online, at the gate or the **festival office** (☎07-5496 1066). Check online for updated programs.

Woodford is 35km northwest of Caboolture. Shuttle buses run regularly from the Caboolture train station to and from the festival grounds.

Boomerang Tours TOUR
(☎1300 287 626) Organises personalised tours of the Hinterland, taking in national parks, waterfalls and the Eumundi Markets. Includes sausage-sizzle lunch.

Maleny

POP 3442

Perched high in the rolling green hills of the Blackall Range, Maleny is an intriguing melange of artists, musicians and creative souls, the ageing hippie scene, rural 'tree-changers' and co-op ventures. Its bohemian edge underscores a thriving commercial township that has moved on from its timber and dairy past without yielding (much) to the tacky heritage developments and ye olde tourist-trap shoppes of nearby mountain villages. The town has a strong community and is heavily into all matters green.

Sights & Activities

Mary Cairncross Scenic Reserve OUTDOORS
(www.mary-cairncross.com.au; 148 Mountain View Rd) Mary Cairncross Scenic Reserve is a lovely rainforest shelter spread over 55 hectares just out of town. Walking tracks snake through the rainforest and there's a healthy population of bird life and unbearably cute pademelons.

Maleny Dairies TOUR
(☎07-5494 2392; www.malenydairies.com; 70 McCarthy Rd; $9; ⏲10.30am & 2.30pm Mon-Sat) Cute dairy tours that take in the milking pit, a handmilking demonstration, factory gawk and baby-calf-petting-fest; you get to sample the in-house delights at the end.

Sleeping

Morning Star Motel MOTEL $
(☎07-5494 2944; www.morningstarmotel.com; 2 Panorama Pl; r $88-110) The rooms at this comfortable and clean motel have outstanding coastal views and deluxe suites have spas. Wheelchair accessible.

Maleny Lodge B&B $$
(☎07-5494 2370; www.malenylodge.com.au; 58 Maple St; r from $159-260;) This B&B is a gracious 1905 residence with cushy, four-poster beds and lashings of stained wood and antiques. There's an open fire for cold winter days and an open pool house for warm summer ones. Prices include cooked breakfast.

Maleny Tropical Retreat B&B $$$
(☎07-5435 2113; www.malenytropicalretreat.com; 540 Maleny Montville Rd; cabin from $210, r from $235-275) Leafy and private, this is definitely one for the romantics. Choose between a self-contained cabin with fireplace and spa, or one of three luxurious B&B rooms with private verandahs and exquisite mountain views. There's a two-night minimum stay on weekends; breakfast is included.

Eating

Maple St is chockas with cafes, restaurants and cute little eating/drinking nooks. Almost everything everywhere will be organic, sustainable and sensitive to allergy and ethical concerns.

Up Front Club CAFE $
(☎07-5494 2592; 31 Maple St; dishes $12-26; ⏲7.30am-10pm) This cosy co-op cafe injects funk by the bucketful into Maleny's main strip, with organic breads, dahl, tofu and even something for the carnivores. Live music on the weekends includes reggae, folk and spontaneous jam-a-thons.

Monica's Cafe CAFE $
(11/43 Maple St; mains $8.50-20; ⏲7am-4pm Mon-Fri, 7.30am-2am Sat & Sun) Ever-changing blackboard specials boast hearty dishes and innovative salads. Sit outside to rubberneck at the fascinating parade, take a seat indoors at the long wooden table or clomp upstairs to the more private mezzanine.

Sweets on Maple DESSERTS $
(39 Maple St; home-made fudge 100g from $5; ⏲9.30am-4.30pm Mon-Fri, 10am-3.30pm Sat & Sun) There are a lot of ye olde lolly shops in this neck of the woods, but Sweets on Maple licks them all. The old-fashioned sweets parlour lures in passer-bys with the crazy-making smell of fresh-baking fudge, and keeps them there with flavours including chocolate chilli and Frangelico with lime. Divine.

Information

There's a small **visitor centre** (☎07-5429 6043; www.malenycommunitycentre.org; 23 Maple St; ⏲10am-3pm) at the Maleny Community Centre.

Fraser Island & the Fraser Coast

Includes ➡

Best Places to Eat

- Waterview Bistro (p166)
- Muddy Waters Cafe (p168)
- Bayaroma Cafe (p163)
- Rosie Blu (p171)
- Mammino's (p169)

Best Places to Stay

- Kingfisher Bay Resort (p175)
- Debbie's Place (p165)
- Beachfront Tourist Parks (p162)
- Flashpackers (p162)
- Colonial Village YHA (p162)

Why Go?

Nature lovers, rejoice! World Heritage–listed Fraser Island is the world's largest sand island, a mystical, at times eerie, land of giant dunes, ancient rainforests, luminous lakes and wildlife including Australia's purest strain of dingo. Across the calm waters of the Great Sandy Strait, the mellow coastal community of Hervey Bay is the gateway to Fraser Island. From July to October, migrating humpback whales stream into the bay before continuing on to Antarctica. Further south, tiny Rainbow Beach is a laid-back seaside village and an alternative launching pad to Fraser. Fishing, swimming, boating and camping are hugely popular along this stretch of coastline.

Inland, agricultural fields surround old-fashioned country towns steeped in history. Bundaberg, the largest city in the region, overlooks the sea of waving cane fields that fuel its eponymous rum, a fiery, gut-churning spirit guaranteed to scramble a few brain cells.

When to Go

Bundaberg

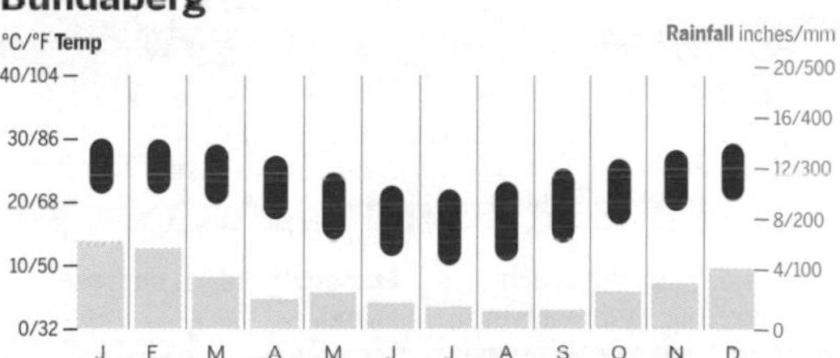

Jun–Jul Bring your brolly to Maryborough's Mary Poppins Festival.

Jul–Nov Watch humpback whales; optimal sighting time is August to October.

Nov–Mar Spy on turtles laying eggs in the sand at Mon Repos.

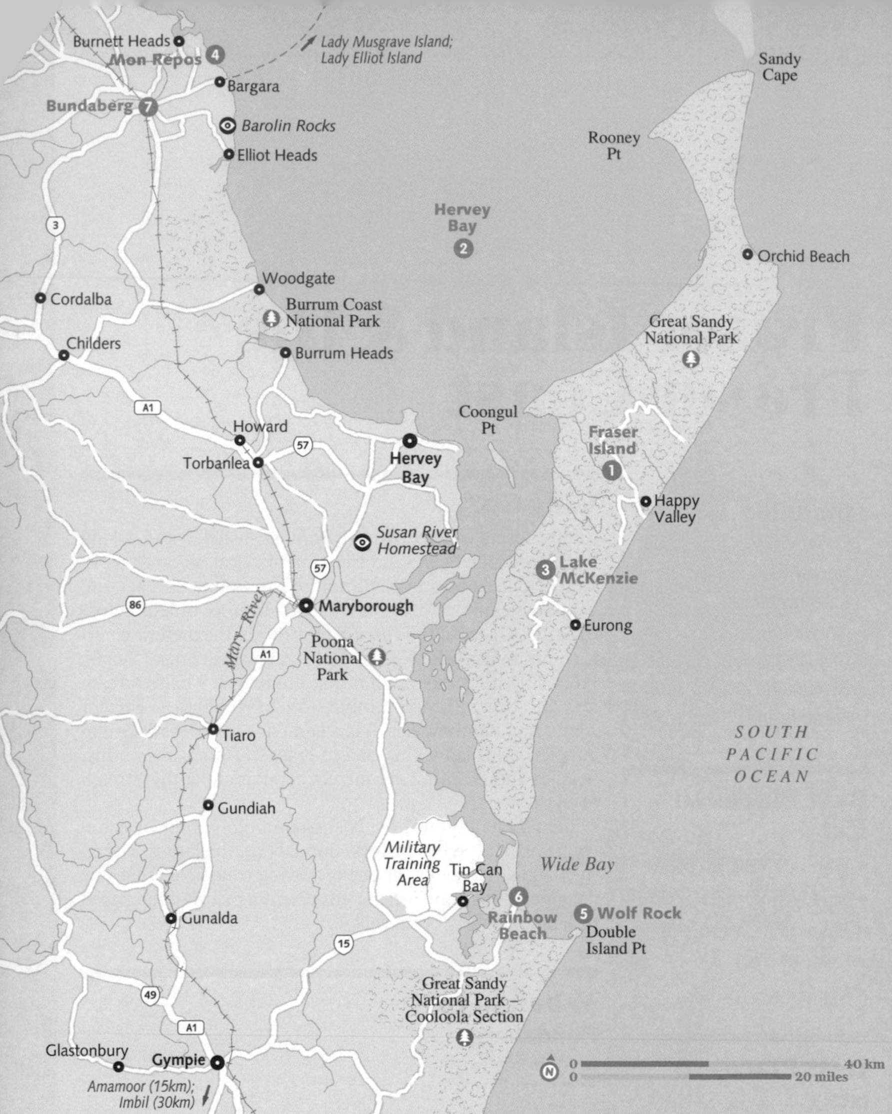

Fraser Island & the Fraser Coast Highlights

1 Cruising up the beach 'highway', hiking through the rainforest and camping under the stars on **Fraser Island** (p172).

2 Watching the whales play in **Hervey Bay** (p159).

3 Cooling off in the pristine, clear-blue water of the white-sand-fringed freshwater **Lake McKenzie** (p175) on Fraser Island.

4 Witnessing turtles take their first flipper-stumble down the beach at **Mon Repos** (p170).

5 Diving with sharks at **Wolf Rock** (p165) off Rainbow Beach.

6 Copping an eyeful of the coloured sand cliffs at **Rainbow Beach** (p164).

7 Sampling 'liquid gold' at the **rum distillery** (p169) in Bundaberg.

Getting There & Away

AIR

Qantas (13 13 13; www.qantas.com.au) and **Virgin Blue** (13 67 89; www.virginblue.com.au) fly to Bundaberg and Hervey Bay.

BUS

Greyhound Australia (1300 473 946; www.greyhound.com.au) and **Premier Motor Service** (13 34 10; www.premierms.com.au) both have regular coach services along the Bruce Hwy with stops at all the major towns. They also detour off the highway to Hervey Bay and Rainbow Beach.

TRAIN

Queensland Rail (1800 872 467; www.traveltrain.com.au) has frequent services between Brisbane and Rockhampton passing through the region. Choose between the high-speed *Tilt Train* or the more sedate *Sunlander*.

FRASER COAST

The Fraser Coast runs the gamut from coastal beauty, beachfront national parks and tiny seaside villages to agricultural farms and sugarcane fields surrounding old-fashioned country towns.

Hervey Bay

POP 76,403

Named after an English Casanova, it's no wonder that Hervey Bay's seductive charms are difficult to resist. Its warm subtropical climate, long sandy beaches, calm blue ocean and a relaxed and unpretentious local community lure all sorts of travellers to its shores, from backpacking travellers to families and sea-changing retirees. Throw in the chance to see majestic humpback whales frolicking in the water and the town's convenient access to the World Heritage–listed Fraser Island, and it's easy to understand how Hervey Bay has gone from sleepy fishing village to come-hither tourist hotspot.

Fraser Island shelters Hervey Bay from the ocean surf and the sea here is shallow and completely flat – perfect for kiddies and postcardy summer-holiday pics.

Sights

Reef World AQUARIUM
(07-4128 9828; Pulgul St, Urangan; adult/child $18/9, shark dive $50; 9.30am-4pm) A small aquarium stocked with some of the Great Barrier Reef's most colourful characters, including a giant 18-year-old groper. You can also take a dip with lemon, whaler and other non-predatory sharks.

Vic Hislop's Shark Show SHARK EXHIBIT
(07-4128 9137; 553 The Esplanade, Urangan; adult/child $17/8; 8.30am-5.30pm) For an informative, but slightly kitsch and often controversial peek at what hides beneath the sea visit the acclaimed Sharkman's collection of all things toothy. If the newspaper clippings of gruesome shark attacks don't make you shudder maybe the 5.6m frozen Great White in the freezer will!

Fraser Coast Discovery Sphere MUSEUM
(07-4197 4207; www.frasercoastdiscoverysphere.com.au; 166 Old Maryborough Rd, Pialba; adult/child/family $7.50/5.50/20.50; 10am-4pm) Loads of educational activities inspired by the region. Ideal for kids and curious adults.

Wetside Water Education Park PARK
(www.widebaywater.qld.gov.au/quicklinks/wetsidewatereducationpark; The Esplanade, Scarness; 10am-6pm daily, night show 7pm Sat) On hot days, this wet spot on the foreshore can't be beaten. There's plenty of shade, fountains, tipping buckets and a boardwalk with water infotainment. Opening hours vary so check the website for updates.

Activities

Whale Watching

Whale-watching tours operate out of Hervey Bay every day (weather permitting) during the annual migrations between late July and early November. Sightings are guaranteed from August to the end of October (with a free return trip if the whales don't show). Off season, many boats offer dolphin-spotting tours. Boats cruise from **Urangan Harbour** out to Platypus Bay and then zip around from pod to pod to find the most active whales. Most vessels offer half-day tours for around $120 for adults and $70 for children, and most include breakfast or lunch. Tour bookings can be made through your accommodation or the information centres.

Spirit of Hervey Bay WHALE WATCHING
(1800 642 544; www.spiritofherveybay.com; 8.30am & 1.30pm) The largest vessel with the greatest number of passengers.

MV Tasman Venture WHALE WATCHING
(1800 620 322; www.tasmanventure.com.au; 8.30am & 1.30pm) One of the best, with underwater microphones and viewing

Hervey Bay

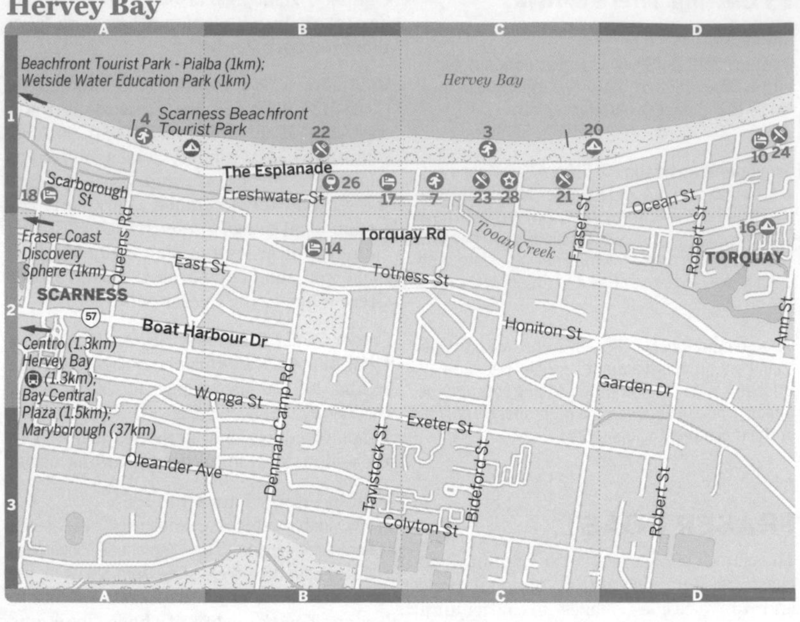

Hervey Bay

Sights

1 Reef World H2
2 Vic Hislop's Shark Show G1

Activities, Courses & Tours

3 Aquavue C1
Blue Dolphin Marine Tours .... (see 5)
Colonial Village YHA .... (see 13)
4 Enzo's on the Beach A1
5 Freedom Whale Watch H2
6 Krystal Klear H3
MV Tasman Venture .... (see 5)
7 Nomads C1
Spirit of Hervey Bay .... (see 5)

Sleeping

8 Alexander Lakeside B&B E1
9 Arlia Sands Apartments E1
10 Australis Shelly Bay Resort D1
11 Bay B&B F1
12 Boat Harbour Resort G3
13 Colonial Village YHA G3
14 Flashpackers B2
15 Grange Resort F1
16 Happy Wanderer Village D2
17 La Mer Beachfront Apartments B1
18 Mango Eco Hostel A1
19 Quarterdecks Harbour Retreat G3
20 Torquay Beachfront Tourist Park C1

Eating

21 Bayaroma Cafe C1
22 Black Dog Café B1
23 Café Tapas C1
24 Coast D1
Enzo's on the Beach .... (see 4)
25 Pier Restaurant G1
Simply Wok .... (see 23)

Drinking & Nightlife

26 Hoolihan's B1
27 Liquid Lounge G1

Entertainment

28 Viper C1

windows. Whale sightings are guaranteed during the high season; you will get a free subsequent trip if the whales don't show up.

Blue Dolphin Marine Tours WHALE WATCHING
(☎07-4124 9600; www.bluedolphintours.com.au) Skipper Pete has almost 30 years of marine mammal experience, making him the ideal receptacle for the many questions this up-close whale-watching trip will generate.

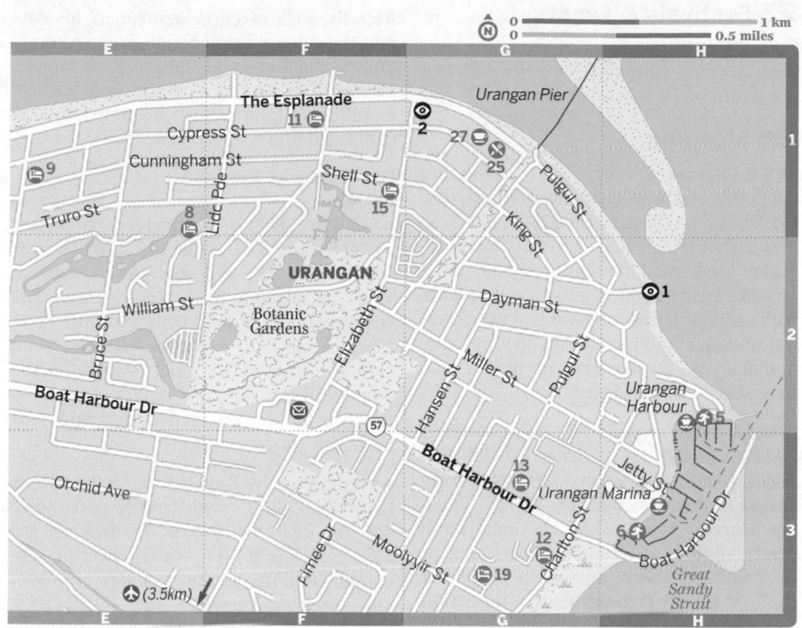

Freedom Whale Watch WHALE WATCHING
(☎1300 879 960; www.freedomwhalewatch.com.au) Watch the whales from three levels on a 58m catamaran.

Fishing

MV Fighting Whiting FISHING
(☎07-4124 3377; www.fightingwhiting.com.au; adult/child/family $70/35/175) Keep your catch on these calm water tours. Sandwiches, bait and all fishing gear included.

MV Princess II FISHING
(☎07-4124 0400; adult/child $150/100) Wet your hook with an experienced crew who've been trolling these waters for more than two decades.

Cruises

Krystal Klear CRUISE
(☎07-4124 0066; www.krystalkleer.com.au; 5hr tour adult/child $90/50) Cruise on a 40ft glass-bottomed boat, the only one in Hervey Bay. Includes snorkelling, coral viewing and an island barbecue.

Water Sports

Aquavue WATER SPORTS
(☎07-4125 5528; www.aquavue.com.au; The Esplanade, Torquay) Hires out paddle-boards, kayaks and aqua-trikes ($20 per hour), catamarans ($50 per hour) and jet skis ($50 per 15 minutes). Also runs guided Fraser Island jet-ski tours from $250.

Enzo's on the Beach WATER SPORTS
(☎07-4124 6375; www.enzosonthebeach.com.au; The Esplanade, Scarness) Kite-surfing (two-hour lesson $130) and paddle-boarding (per hour/two hours $30/40). Also hires out kayaks (from $20 per hour) and surf-skis ($15 per hour).

Scenic Flights

Fraser Coast Microlites SCENIC FLIGHT
(☎1800 811 728; flight from $125-250) Ditch the metal shell to soar over islands and lakes on 20-, 30-, 45- and 70-minute flights. Book ahead.

Other Activities

Skydive Hervey Bay SKYDIVING
(☎0458 064 703; www.skydiveherveybay.com.au) Tandem skydives from $325 at 12,000ft with up to 45 mouth-flapping seconds of freefall.

Susan River Homestead HORSE RIDING
(☎07-4121 6846; www.susanriver.com; Hervey Bay–Maryborough Rd) Horse-riding packages (adult/child $250/160) include accommodation, all meals and use of the on-site swimming pool and tennis courts. Day-trippers can canter off on two-hour horse rides (adult/child $85/75).

Festivals & Events

Hervey Bay Whale Festival WHALE
(www.herveybaywhalefestival.com.au) Celebrates the return of the whales in August.

Sleeping

★ **Flashpackers** HOSTEL $
(07-4124 1366; www.flashpackersherveybay.com; 195 Torquay Tce, Torquay; dm $25-30, d $70;) This is the new standard for backpacker accommodation in Hervey Bay. Comfortable, spacious dorm and en suite rooms, with reading lights, numerous power sockets, walk-in communal fridge, spotless communal areas and showers with power. Set a street back from the beach.

Beachfront Tourist Parks CARAVAN PARK $
(Pialba 07-4128 1399, Scarness 07-4128 1274, Torquay 07-4125 1578; www.beachfronttouristparks.com.au; unpowered/powered site $25/36) Fronting Hervey Bay's exquisitely long sandy beach, all three of these shady parks live up to their name, with fantastic ocean views; the Torquay site is in the heart of the action.

Colonial Village YHA HOSTEL $
(07-4125 1844; www.yha.com.au/hostels/qld/fraser-capricorn-coasts/hervey-bay; 820 Boat Harbour Dr, Urangan; dm/d/cabin from $27/56/72; @) This excellent YHA is set on eight hectares of tranquil bushland, close to the marina and only 50m from the beach. It's a lovely spot, thick with ambience, possums and parrots. Facilities include a spa, tennis and basketball courts and a sociable bar.

Mango Eco Hostel HOSTEL $
(07-4124 2832; www.mangohostel.net; 110 Torquay Rd, Scarness; dm/d $28/60; P) This small, locally-run hostel is an old-school travellers' haunt. Intimate and loaded with character, it sleeps guests in a four-bed dorm room and two very homey doubles. The wraparound verandah and outdoor dining area add to the cosy, tropical atmosphere.

Happy Wanderer Village CARAVAN PARK $
(07-4125 1103; www.happywanderer.com.au; 105 Truro St, Torquay; unpowered/powered site from $30/35, cabin/studio/villa from $69/89/121;) The manicured lawns and profuse gum-tree cover at this large park make for great tent sites.

Bay B&B B&B $$
(07-4125 6919; www.baybedandbreakfast.com.au; 180 Cypress St, Urangan; s $100, d $125-140; @) This great-value B&B is run by a friendly, well-travelled Frenchman, his wife and their dog... Guest rooms are in a comfy annexe out the back, and the Bay's famous breakfast is served in a tropical garden. Families can take over the separate fully self-contained unit.

Quarterdecks Harbour Retreat APARTMENT $$
(07-4197 0888; www.quarterdecksretreat.com.au; 80 Moolyyir St, Urangan; 1-/2-/3-bedroom villas $185/225/290;) These excellent villas are stylishly furnished with a private courtyard, all the mod cons and little luxuries such as fluffy bathrobes. Backing onto a nature reserve, it's quiet apart from the wonderful bird life, and only a cooee from the beach. The accommodation and tour packages are great value.

Australis Shelly Bay Resort APARTMENT $$
(07-4125 4533; www.shellybayresort.com.au; 466 The Esplanade, Torquay; 1-/2-bedroom unit $180/195; @) The bold, cheerful self-contained units at this complex are clean and spacious. All rooms have water views, and with the beach just across the road, this is one of the best options in town. Good discounts on multiple-night stays.

Alexander Lakeside B&B B&B $$
(07-4128 9448; www.herveybaybedandbreakfast.com.au; 29 Lido Pde, Urangan; r $140-150, ste $160-170; @) This warm and friendly B&B offers lakeside indulgence, where turtles come a-visiting in the morning. There's a heated lakeside spa, two spacious rooms with en suites and two luxury self-contained suites.

La Mer Beachfront A partments APARTMENT $$
(07-4128 3494; www.lamer.com.au; 396 The Esplanade, Torquay; 1/2 bedroom from $150/180;) With colours this bold, you'll think you're in the Med. The rainbow scheme continues indoors but it's actually quite pleasant. The apartments are large, comfortable and have fully equipped kitchens. Choose between poolside or beachfront units.

Arlia Sands Apartments APARTMENT $$
(07-4125 4360; www.arliasands.com.au; 13 Ann St, Torquay; 1/2 bedroom from $135/145;) These self-contained units may not be super-characterful, but they're comfortable, sport plush furniture and spacious modern bathrooms. It's off the main drag yet close to the beach and shops and is *très* quiet.

A WHALE OF A TIME

Every year, from July to early November, thousands of humpback whales cruise into Hervey Bay's sheltered waters for a few days before continuing their arduous migration south to the Antarctic. Having mated and given birth in the warmer waters off northeast Australia, they arrive in Hervey Bay in groups of about a dozen (known as pulses), before splitting into smaller groups of two or three (pods). The new calves utilise the time to develop the thick layers of blubber necessary for survival in icy southern waters, by consuming around 600L of milk daily.

Viewing these majestic creatures is simply awe-inspiring. You'll see these showy aqua-acrobats waving their pectoral fins, tail slapping, breaching or simply 'blowing', and many will roll up beside the whale-watching boats with one eye clear of the water...making those on board wonder who's actually watching whom.

Boat Harbour Resort APARTMENT $$
(07-4125 5079; www.boatharbourresort.net; 651-652 Charlton St, Urangan; studio from $120, bungalow from $150;) Close to the marina, these timber studios and cabins are set on attractive grounds. The studios have sizeable decks out the front and the roomy villas are great for families.

Grange Resort RESORT $$$
(07-4125 2002; www.thegrange-herveybay.com.au; 33 Elizabeth St, Urangan; 1-/2-bedroom villas $155/230;) Reminiscent of a stylish desert resort with fancy split-level condos and filled with life's little luxuries, this place is close to the beach and to town.

Eating

★ **Bayaroma Cafe** CAFE $
(07-4125 1515; 428 The Esplanade, Torquay; breakfast $10-22, mains $9.50-20; 6.30am-3.30pm) Famous for its coffee, all-day breakfasts and people-watching pole position, Bayorama has a jam-packed menu that truly has something for everyone (even vegetarians!). Attentive, chirpy service is an added bonus.

Enzo's on the Beach CAFE $
(www.enzosonthebeach.com.au; 351a The Esplanade, Scarness; mains $8-20; 6.30am-5pm) This shabby-chic beachside cafe is the place to fill up on sandwiches, wraps, salads and coffees before working it off on a hire kayak or kite-surfing lesson.

Café Tapas TAPAS $
(07-4125 6808; 417 The Esplanade, Torquay; tapas $9; 11am-midnight) This sleek venue has all the cool-kid accoutrements: upmarket artwork, dim lighting, red couches and low tables flickering with coloured lights. Come for Asian-inspired tapas; linger longer for cocktails and music.

Simply Wok ASIAN $$
(07-4125 2077; 417 The Esplanade, Torquay; mains $14-23; 7am-10pm) Noodles, stir-fries, seafood and curries will satisfy any cravings for Asian cuisine, and there's a nightly (from 5pm to 9pm) all-you-can-eat hot buffet for $16.90.

Black Dog Café FUSION $$
(07-4124 3177; 381 The Esplanade, Torquay; mains $15-37; lunch & dinner) Groovy, man. The very Zen menu features twists on sushi, Japanese pancakes, burgers, schnitzel, seafood salads and vegan options.

Coast FUSION $$
(07-4125 5454; 469 The Esplanade, Torquay; mains $21-60; Tues & Wed 5pm-late, Thurs-Sun 11.30am-late) Gourmet grub for the discerning diner prepared to splurge. Fancy meat and seafood dishes get the Asian/Middle Eastern fusion touch; desserts like the pumpkin cheesecake go beyond the realms of the superlative adjective.

Pier Restaurant SEAFOOD $$
(07-4128 9699; 573 The Esplanade, Urangan; mains $20-40; from 6pm Mon-Sat) Although sitting opposite the water, the Pier makes little use of its ocean views. But an interesting seafood menu – including macadamia/coconut crumbed prawns, chilli bugs and crabs – makes it a deservedly popular spot.

Drinking & Nightlife

Hoolihan's PUB
(382 The Esplanade, Scarness; 11am-2am) Like all good Irish pubs, Hoolihan's is wildly popular, especially with the backpacker crowd.

Liquid Lounge CAFE
(577 The Esplanade, Urangan; coffee from $3.50; ⏲Fri-Wed 8.30am-6.30pm, Thu 7.30am-4.30pm) Strong, good coffees and chatty service from passionate staff. Great location to boot.

Viper CLUB
(410 The Esplanade, Torquay; ⏲10pm-3am Wed, Fri & Sat) This new club is a rough diamond with cranking music and an energetic crowd, especially during summer.

Information

Hervey Bay covers a string of beachside suburbs – Point Vernon, Pialba, Scarness, Torquay and Urangan – but behind the flawless beachfront and pockets of sedate suburbia, the outskirts of town dissolve into a sprawling industrial jungle.

Hervey Bay Visitor Information Centre (☎1800 811 728; www.visitfrasercoast.com; Cnr Urraween & Maryborough Rds) Helpful and well-stocked with brochures and information. On the outskirts of town.

Getting There & Away

AIR

Hervey Bay airport is on Don Adams Dve, just off Booral Rd. **Qantas** (☎13 13 13; www.qantas.com.au) and **Virgin Blue** (☎13 67 89; www.virginblue.com.au) have daily flights to/from destinations around Australia.

BOAT

Boats to Fraser Island leave from River Heads, about 10km south of town, and Urangan's Great Sandy Straits Marina. Most tours leave from Urangan Harbour.

BUS

Buses depart **Hervey Bay Coach Terminal** (☎07-4124 4000; Central Ave, Pialba). **Greyhound Australia** (☎1300 473 946; www.greyhound.com.au) and **Premier Motor Service** (☎13 34 10; www.premierms.com.au) have several services to/from Brisbane ($69, 5½ hours), Maroochydore ($47, 3½ hours), Bundaberg ($24, 1½ hours) and Rockhampton ($87, six hours).

Tory's Tours (☎07-4128 6500; www.torystours.com.au) has twice daily services to Brisbane airport ($75).

Wide Bay Transit (☎07-4121 3719; www.widebaytransit.com.au) has hourly services from Urangan Marina (stopping along The Esplanade) to Maryborough ($8, one hour) every weekday, with fewer services on weekends.

Getting Around

CAR

Hervey Bay is the the best place to hire a 4WD for Fraser Island. Try any of the following for starters:

Aussie Trax (☎07-4124 4433; www.fraserisland4wd.com.au; 56 Boat Harbour Dr, Pialba)

Fraser Magic 4WD Hire (☎07-4125 6612; www.fraser4wdhire.com.au; 5 Kruger Ct, Urangan)

Safari 4WD Hire (☎07-4124 4244; www.safari4wdhire.com.au; 102 Boat Harbour Dr, Pialba)

Hervey Bay Rent A Car (☎07-4194 6626; www.herveybayrentacar.com.au; 5 Cunningham St, Torquay) Also rents out scooters ($30 per day).

Rainbow Beach

POP 1103

Gorgeous Rainbow Beach is a tiny town at the base of the Inskip Peninsula with spectacular multicoloured sand cliffs overlooking its rolling surf and white sandy beach. The town's friendly locals, relaxed vibe and convenient access to Fraser Island (only 10 minutes by barge) and the Cooloola Section of the Great Sandy National Park has made this a rising star of Queensland's coastal beauty spots.

Sights

The town is named for the **coloured sand cliffs**, a 2km walk along the beach. The cliffs arc their red-hued way around Wide Bay, offering a sweeping panorama from the lighthouse at Double Island Point to Fraser Island in the north.

A 600m track along the cliffs at the southern end of Cooloola Dr leads to the **Carlo Sandblow**, a spectacular 120m-high dune.

Activities

Bushwalking & Camping

The Cooloola Section of the **Great Sandy National Park** has a number of **national park camp sites** (www.nprsr.qld.gov.au; per person/family $5.45/21.80), including a wonderful stretch of beach camping along Teewah Beach. Book camping and **4WD permits** (www.nprsr.qld.gov.au; per day/week/month $11/27.70/43.60) online.

Bushwalking tracks in the national park (maps from the QPWS office on Rainbow Beach Rd) include the 46.2km **Cooloola Wilderness Trail**, which starts at Mullens car park (off Rainbow Beach Rd) and ends near Lake Cooloola.

Camping on the beach is one of the best ways to experience this part of the coast, but if you don't have camping gear **Rainbow Beach Hire-a-Camp** (07-5486 8633; www.rainbow-beach-hire-a-camp.com.au; per day/night from $30/50) can hire out equipment, set up your tent and camp site, organise camping permits and break camp for you when you're done.

Diving

Wolf Rock, a congregation of volcanic pinnacles off Double Island Point, is regarded as one of Queensland's best scuba-diving sites. The endangered grey nurse shark is found here all year round.

Wolf Rock Dive Centre DIVING
(0438 740 811, 07-5486 8004; www.wolfrockdive.com.au; 20 Karoonda Rd; double dive charter from $220) High-adrenalin dives for experienced divers at Wolf Rock.

Kayaking

Rainbow Beach Dolphin View Sea Kayaking KAYAKING
(0408 738 192; www.rainbowbeachsurfschool.com; Shop 1, 6 Rainbow Beach Rd; 3hr tour per person $70) Just like the name says, this mob offers dolphin-spotting kayak tours.

Skydiving & Paragliding

Skydive Rainbow Beach SKYDIVING
(0418 218 358; www.skydiverainbowbeach.com; 2400/4200m dives $299/369) Soft landings on the beach.

Rainbow Paragliding PARAGLIDING
(07-5486 3048, 0418 754 157; www.paraglidingrainbow.com; glides $180) Exhilarating tandem flights over the colourful cliffs.

Surfing

There's a good surf break at Double Island Point.

Rainbow Beach Surf School SURFING
(0408 738 192; www.rainbowbeachsurfschool.com; 3hr session $60) Surfing lessons.

Tours

Surf & Sand Safaris DRIVING TOUR
(07-5486 3131; www.surfandsandsafaris.com.au; per adult/child $75/40) Half-day 4WD tours through the national park and along the beach to the coloured sands and lighthouse at Double Island Point.

Dolphin Ferry Cruises CRUISE
(0428 838 836; www.dolphinferrycruises.com.au; 3hr cruise adult/child $30/15; departs 7am) Cruise across the inlet to Tin Can Bay to hand-feed wild Indo-Pacific dolphins and scout for dugong…all before checkout time.

Sleeping

★ **Debbie's Place** B&B $
(07-5486 3506; www.rainbowbeachaccommodation.com.au; 30 Kurana St; d/ste from $99/109, 3-bedroom apt from $260;) Inside this beautiful timber Queenslander dripping with pot plants, the charming rooms are fully self-contained, with private entrances and verandahs. The effervescent Debbie is a mine of information and makes this a cosy home away from home.

Pippies Beach House HOSTEL $
(07-5486 8503; www.pippiesbeachhouse.com.au; 22 Spectrum St; dm/d $22/65; @) With only 12 rooms, this small, relaxed hostel is the place to catch your breath between outdoor pursuits. Free breakfast, wi-fi and boogie boards sweeten the stay; be there Monday, Wednesday or Friday for a boomerang-painting workshop!

Dingo's Backpacker's Resort HOSTEL $
(1800 111 126; www.dingosresort.com; 20 Spectrum St; dm $24; @) This party hostel with bar has live music, karaoke and face-painting nights, a chill-out gazebo and cheap meals nightly.

Rainbow Sands Holiday Units MOTEL $
(07-5486 3400; www.rainbowsands.com.au; 42-46 Rainbow Beach Rd; d $95, 1-bedroom apt $125;) Perfectly pleasing low-rise, palm-fronted complex with standard motel rooms and self-contained units with full laundries for comfortable longer stays.

Fraser's on Rainbow HOSTEL $
(07-5486 8885; www.frasersonrainbow.com; 18 Spectrum St; dm/d from $25/75; @) Roomy dorms in a converted motel give you somewhere to sleep off any carousing at its popular outdoor bar.

Rainbow Beach Holiday Village CARAVAN PARK $
(07-5486 3222; www.rainbowbeachholidayvillage.com; 13 Rainbow Beach Rd; unpowered/powered site from $30/37, villa from $100;) Popular beachfront park.

Eating

Self-caterers will find a supermarket on Rainbow Beach Rd.

Waterview Bistro MODERN AUSTRALIAN $$
(07-5486 8344; Cooloola Dr; mains $26-35; 11.30am-11.30pm Wed-Sat, to 6pm Sun) Sunset drinks are a must at this swish restaurant with sensational views of Fraser Island from its hilltop perch. Get stuck into the signature seafood chowder ($22), or try the lunch special ($19, glass of wine included).

Rainbow Beach Hotel PUB $$
(1 Rainbow Beach Rd; mains $18-35; lunch & dinner) The spruced-up pub is bright, airy and brings to mind all things plantation, with ceiling fans, palm trees, timber floors and cane furnishings. The restaurant serves up traditional pub grub; scope the street scene from the upstairs balcony.

Information

QPWS (Rainbow Beach Rd; 8am-4pm)

Rainbow Beach Visitor Centre (07-5486 3227; www.rainbowbeachinfo.com.au; 8 Rainbow Beach Rd; 7am-5.30pm)

Shell Tourist Centre (36 Rainbow Beach Rd; 6am-6pm) Located at the Shell service station; tour bookings and barge tickets for Fraser Island.

Getting There & Around

Greyhound (1300 473 946; www.greyhound.com.au) has several daily services from Brisbane ($49, five hours), Noosa ($32, three hours) and Hervey Bay ($26, two hours). **Premier Motor Service** (13 34 10; www.premierms.com.au) has less-expensive services. **Cooloola Connections** (07-5481 1667; www.coolconnect.com.au) runs a shuttle bus to Rainbow Beach from Brisbane Airport ($135, three hours) and Sunshine Coast Airport ($95, two hours).

Most 4WD-hire companies will also arrange permits, barge costs (per vehicle $100 return) and hire out camping gear. Some recommended companies:

All Trax 4WD Hire (07-5486 8767; www.fraserisland4x4.com.au; Rainbow Beach Rd, Shell service station; per day from $170)

Rainbow Beach Adventure Centre 4WD Hire (07-5486 3288; www.adventurecentre.com.au; 66 Rainbow Beach Rd; per day from $180) Also rents trail bikes.

Maryborough

POP 26,000

Born in 1847, Maryborough is one of Queensland's oldest towns, and its port was the first shaky step ashore for thousands of 19th-century free settlers looking for a better life in the new country. Heritage and history are Maryborough's specialities, the pace of yesteryear reflected in its beautifully restored colonial-era buildings and gracious Queenslander homes.

This charming old country town is also the birthplace of Pamela Lyndon ('PL') Travers, creator of the umbrella-wielding Mary Poppins. The award-winning film *Saving Mr Banks* tells Travers' story, with early-1900s Maryborough in a starring role.

Sights

Portside HISTORIC SITE
(101 Wharf St; 10am-4pm Mon-Fri, to 1pm Sat & Sun) In the historic area beside the Mary River, Portside has 13 heritage-listed buildings, parklands and museums. Today's tidy colonial-era buildings and landscaped gardens paint a different story from Maryborough's once-thriving port and seedy streets filled with sailors, ruffians, brothels and opium dens. The **Portside Centre** (07-4190 5730; cnr Wharf & Richmond Sts; 10am-4pm), located in the former **Customs House**, has interactive displays on Maryborough's history. Part of the centre but a few doors down, the **Bond Store Museum** also highlights key periods in Maryborough's history. Downstairs is the original packed-earth floor and even some liquor barrels from 1864.

Mary Poppins Statue MONUMENT
On the street in front of the neoclassical **former Union Bank** (birthplace of Mary Poppins creator, PL Travers) is a life-size statue of the acerbic character Travers created rather than the saccharine Disney version.

Brennan & Geraghty's Store MUSEUM
(64 Lennox St; adult/family $5.50/13; 10am-3pm) This National Trust–classified store traded for 100 years before closing its doors. The museum is crammed with tins, bottles and packets, including early Vegemite jars and curry powder from the 1890s.

GOLD, WOOD, STEAM & SONG: GYMPIE & THE MARY VALLEY

Gympie's gold once saved Queensland from near-bankruptcy, but that was in the 1860s and not much has happened here since. History buffs will find a large collection of mining equipment and functioning steam-driven engines at the **Gympie Gold Mining & Historical Museum** (www.gympiegoldmuseum.com.au; 215 Brisbane Rd; adult/child/family $10/5/25; ⌚9am-3pm). There's also the **Woodworks Forestry & Timber Museum** (www.woodworksmuseum.com.au; cnr Fraser Rd & Bruce Hwy; admission $5; ⌚10am-4pm Mon-Sat) on the Bruce Hwy south of town. The highlight of the museum (and perhaps the lowlight of the logging industry) is a cross-section of a magnificent kauri pine that lived through the Middle Ages, Columbus' discovery of America and the Industrial Revolution, only to be felled in the early 20th century.

After the summer rains, the Mary Valley around here is lush and scenic. If you don't have a car, explore the valley on a 1923 steam train, the **Valley Rattler** (☎07-5482 2750; www.thevalleyrattler.com). Schedules and prices are ever-changing; see website for updates.

Amamoor is the site of the annual **Gympie Music Muster** (www.muster.com.au), a six-day country-music hoedown held annually in August.

Gympie Cooloola Tourism (www.cooloola.org.au; Lake Alford, Bruce Hwy, Gympie; ⌚9am-4.30pm) has a wealth of information on sights and activities along the entire Fraser Coast.

Greyhound (p122) and **Premier** (☎13 34 10; www.premierms.com.au) have numerous daily services to Gympie from Brisbane, Noosa, Bundaberg and Hervey Bay. **Traveltrain** (☎1800 872 467; www.traveltrain.com.au) operates the *Tilt Train* and the *Sunlander* from Brisbane to Gympie on their way to Rockhampton and Cairns.

Maryborough Military & Colonial Museum MUSEUM
(☎07-4123 5900; www.maryboroughmuseum.org; 106 Wharf St; adult/couple/family $5/8/10; ⌚9am-3pm) Check out the only surviving three-wheeler Girling car, originally built in London in 1911. There's also a replica Cobb & Co coach and one of the largest military libraries in Australia.

Queens Park PARK
With a profusion of glorious trees, including a banyan fig that's more than 140 years old, this is a pleasant spot for a picnic.

Maryborough Heritage City Markets MARKET
(cnr Adelaide & Ellena Sts; ⌚8am-1.30pm Thu) Market fun made all the more entertaining by the firing (1pm) of the historic Time Cannon, a town crier and rides (adult/child $3/2) on the Mary Ann steam loco through Queen's Park.

Activities

Tea with Mary TOUR
(☎1800 214 789; per person $13) Tour the historic precinct with a Mary Poppins–bedecked guide who spills the beans on the town's past; book through the visitor centre.

Guided Walks WALKING TOUR
(⌚9am Mon-Sat) FREE Free guided walks depart from the City Hall to take in the town's many sites.

Ghostly Tours & Tales TOUR
(☎1800 811 728; tours incl dinner $65; ⌚6pm, last Saturday of the month) Get spooked on a torch-lit tour of the city's grisly murder sites, opium dens, haunted houses and cemetery. Tours begin from the Maryborough Post Office in Bazaar St.

Festivals & Events

Mary Poppins Festival CULTURAL
(www.marypoppinsfestival.com.au) A supercalifragilisticexpialidocious festival celebrating PL Travers and the famous Miss Poppins. Every June/July over the school holidays.

Sleeping

Ned Kelly's Motel MOTEL $
(☎07-4121 0999; www.nedkellymotel.com.au; 150 Gympie Rd; s/d $49/79, cabins from $89; ❄🏊) Basic, budget and beside the highway. But there's a pool, laundry and mammoth Ned Kelly statue out the front: what more do you need?

Eco Queenslander BOUTIQUE HOTEL $$
(☎0438 195 443; www.ecoqueenslander.com; 15 Treasure St; per couple $140) You won't want to leave this lovely converted Queenslander with comfy lounge, full kitchen, laundry and a cast-iron bathtub. Sustainable features include solar power, rainwater tanks, energy-efficient lighting and bikes for you to use. Minimum two-night stay.

Tin Peaks B&B B&B $$
(☎07-4123 5294; www.tinpeaks.com.au; 54 Berallan Dve; d incl breakfast $135;) Spacious self-contained cottage that comes over all rustic (with a random hint of nautical), but has all the mod-cons you need. The huge verandah and warm furnishings make it just like home, but better. Six minutes from the CBD.

Eating & Drinking

Toast CAFE $
(☎07-4121 7222; 199 Bazaar St; dishes $6-12; 6am-4pm Mon-Sat, to 2.30pm Sun) Stainless-steel fittings, polished cement floors and coffee served in paper cups stamp a metro-chic seal on this groovy cafe.

★**Muddy Waters Cafe** SEAFOOD $$
(☎07-4121 5011; 103 Wharf St, Portside; mains $15-32; 9.30am-3pm Mon-Wed, 9.30am-9.30pm Thu, 9.30am-3pm & 6-9.30pm Fri & Sat) The shady riverfront deck and the summery menu at this classy cafe will keep you happy with tempting seafood dishes such as citrus-and-vodka-cured salmon and beer-battered fish.

Lounge 1868 BAR
(116 Wharf St; 6pm-late Fri & Sat) Ambient watering hole in the historic Customs House Hotel with a whopping great beer garden and small but sophisticated menu (mains are $12 to $17).

Information

The **Maryborough/Fraser Island visitor centre** (☎1800 214 789; www.visitfrasercoast.com; Kent St; 9am-5pm Mon-Fri, to 1pm Sat & Sun) in the 100-year-old City Hall is extremely helpful and has free copies of comprehensive self-guided walking tours. Speak with them about inclusive tickets to Portside's museums and attractions.

Getting There & Away

Both the *Sunlander* ($75, five hours) and the *Tilt Train* ($75, 3½ hours) connect Brisbane with the Maryborough West station, 7km west of the centre. It's connected to the centre via shuttle bus.

Greyhound Australia (☎1300 473 946; www.greyhound.com.au) and **Premier Motor Service** (☎13 34 10; www.premierms.com.au) have buses to Gympie ($29, one hour), Bundaberg ($39, three hours) and Brisbane ($65, 4½ hours).

Wide Bay Transit (☎07-4121 4070; www.widebaytransit.com.au) has hourly services (fewer on weekends) between Maryborough and Hervey Bay ($8, one hour), departing from outside City Hall in Kent St.

Childers

POP 1410

Surrounded by lush green fields and rich red soil, Childers is a charming little town, its main street lined with tall, shady trees and lattice-trimmed historical buildings. Backpackers flock here for fruit-picking and farm work. Sadly, Childers is best known for the 15 backpackers who perished in a fire in the Palace Backpackers Hostel in June 2000.

Sights & Activities

There is a moving memorial for the deceased backpackers and some fantastic art at the **Childers Palace Memorial & Art Gallery.** (72 Churchill St; 9am-5pm Mon-Fri, to 3pm Sat & Sun)

The Old Pharmacy (90 Churchill St; 9am-3.30pm Mon-Fri) was an operational apothecary's shop between 1894 to 1982, and also functioned as the town dentist, vet, optician and local photographer.

The lovely, 100-year-old **Federal Hotel** has swingin' saloon doors, while a bronze statue of two romping pig dogs sits outside the **Grand Hotel**.

On the last weekend in July, Childers' main street is swamped with street performers, musicians, dancers, and food and craft stalls during its annual **Festival of Cultures**, which draws over 50,000 people.

Sleeping & Eating

Sugarbowl Caravan Park CARAVAN PARK $
(☎07-4126 1521; www.sugarbowlchilders.com; Bruce Hwy; powered site $29, cabin $90;) A 10-minute walk out of town is this clean and green spot favoured by many seasonal pickers. The owners can help arrange work, and transport to job-sites. Rates are for two people; prices drop for longer stays.

Mango Hill B&B B&B $$
(☎07-4126 1311; www.mangohillcottages.com; 8 Mango Hill Dr; s/d incl breakfast $100/130;) For warm, country hospitality, the cute cane-cutter cottages at Mango Hill B&B, 4km south of town, are decorated with handmade wooden furniture, country decor and comfy beds that ooze charm and romance. There's an organic winery on-site.

Vietnamese Mini Resturant VIETNAMESE $
(☎07-4126 1144; 108 Churchill St; mains from $11; ⏲lunch & dinner) That there's a Vietnamese restaurant way out in Childers may come as a shock, but the fact that it's not half bad may be even more surprising. Definitely worth a stop.

Kapé Centro CAFE $
(65 Churchill St; mains $10-18; ⏲9am-3pm) Kapé Centro in the old post office building dishes up light meals, salads and pizzas.

Mammino's ICE CREAM $
(115 Lucketts Rd; ice-cream cups $5; ⏲9am-5pm) On your way out of town, take a detour to Mammino's for wickedly delicious, homemade macadamia ice cream. Lucketts Rd is off the Bruce Hwy just south of Childers.

Information

Childers Visitor Information Centre (☎07-4126 3886; ⏲9am-4pm Mon-Fri, to 3pm Sat & Sun) Beneath the Childers Palace Memorial & Art Gallery.

Getting There & Away

Childers is 50km southwest of Bundaberg. **Greyhound Australia** (☎1300 473 946; www.greyhound.com.au) and **Premier Motor Service** (☎13 34 10; www.premierms.com.au) both stop at the Shell service station north of town and have daily services to/from Brisbane ($86, 6½ hours), Hervey Bay ($17, one hour) and Bundaberg ($24, 1½ hours).

Burrum Coast National Park

The Burrum Coast National Park covers two sections of coastline on either side of the little holiday community of Woodgate, 37km east of Childers. The Woodgate section of the park begins at the southern end of The Esplanade, and has attractive beaches, abundant fishing and the **NPRSR camping ground** (www.nprsr.qld.gov.au; per person/family $5.15/20.60) at Burrum Point, reached by a 4WD-only track. Several walking tracks start at the camping ground or Acacia St in Woodgate. There are more isolated bush-camping areas in the Kinkuna section of the park, a few kilometres north of Woodgate; you'll need a 4WD to reach them. Book camping permits online at www.nprsr.qld.gov.au.

Woodgate Beach Tourist Park CARAVAN PARK $
(☎07-4126 8802; www.woodgatebeachtouristpark.com; 88 The Esplanade; unpowered/powered site $28/32, cabin $60-110, beachfront villa $135;) Close to the national park and opposite the beach.

Bundaberg

POP 69,805

Despite boasting a sublime climate, coral-fringed beaches and waving fields of sugar cane, 'Bundy' is still overlooked by most travellers. Hordes of backpackers flock here for fruit-picking and farm work; other visitors quickly pass through on their way to family summer holidays at the nearby seaside villages.

This is the birthplace of the famous Bundaberg Rum, a mind-blowingly potent liquor bizarrely endorsed by a polar bear but as iconically Australian as Tim Tams and Vegemite.

Sights & Activities

Bundaberg Rum Distillery DISTILLERY
(☎07-4131 2999; www.bundabergrum.com.au; Avenue St; self-guided tour adult/child $14/7, guided tour $25/12; ⏲10am-3pm Mon-Fri, until 2pm Sat & Sun; tours run on the hour) Bundaberg's biggest claim to fame is the iconic Bundaberg Rum – you'll see the Bundy Rum polar bear on billboards and bumper stickers all over town. Tours follow the rum's production from start to finish and include a tasting for the over-18s. Wear closed shoes.

Bundaberg Barrel BREWERY
(☎07-4154 5480; www.bundaberg.com; 147 Bargara Rd; adult/child $12/5; ⏲9am-4.30pm Mon-Sat, 10am-3pm Sun) Bundaberg Ginger Beer is not quite as famous as Bundy Rum, probably because it's nonalcoholic. Visit the Barrel to see how the ginger is mushed, crushed, brewed and fermented.

Bundaberg Regional Arts Gallery GALLERY
(07-4130 4750; www.brag-brc.org.au; 1 Barolin St; 10am-5pm Mon-Fri, 11am-3pm Sat & Sun) This small (and vividly purple) gallery has surprisingly good exhibitions.

Hinkler Hall of Aviation MUSEUM
(www.hinklerhallofaviation.com; Mt Perry Rd, Botanic Gardens; adult/child/family $18/10/38; 9am-4pm) This modern museum has multimedia exhibits, a flight simulator and informative displays chronicling the life of Bundaberg's famous son Bert Hinkler, who made the first solo flight between England and Australia in 1928.

Alexandra Park & Zoo PARK, ZOO
(Quay St) FREE Lovely sprawling park with plenty of shady trees, flower beds and swaths of green lawn for a lazy picnic, right beside the Burnett River. There's also a small zoo for the littlies.

Bundaberg Aqua Scuba DIVING
(07-4153 5761; www.aquascuba.com.au; 239 Bourbong St; diving courses from $349) Dive shop that runs courses.

Burnett River Cruises CRUISE
(0427 099 009; www.burnettrivercruises.com.au; School Lane, East Bundaberg; 2½hr tour adult/child $25/10) The *Bundy Belle,* an old-fashioned ferry, chugs at a pleasant pace to the mouth of the Burnett River. See website or call for tour times.

Sleeping

There are plenty of midrange motels on the Bundaberg–Childers Rd into town. Bundaberg's hostels cater to working backpackers, and most can arrange harvest work.

Bigfoot Backpackers HOSTEL $
(07-4152 3659; www.footprintsadventures.com.au; 66 Targo St; dm from $24; P) Comfortable and friendly central hostel that also runs fabulous turtle tours to Mon Repos. Fresh paint, happy staff and and a relaxed vibe raise this above its competitors. There are ample fruit-picking opportunities available.

Federal Backpackers HOSTEL $
(07-4153 3711; www.federalbackpackers.com.au; 221 Bourbong St; dm from $25) One for the workers, this hostel isn't exactly sparkling, but it is social. There's a lively bar on-site, and staff can help out with finding work and transport to jobs.

Cellblock Backpackers HOSTEL $
(07-4154 3210; cnr Quay & Maryborough Sts; dm per night/week from $28/165, d $70; @) Housed in a former jail – some might say aptly – this is a place for hardened travellers only. The rooms don't have windows (of course), but will do in a crisis. You'll forget about its shortcomings over a few drinks at the very happening poolside bar.

★**Inglebrae** B&B $$
(07-4154 4003; www.inglebrae.com; 17 Branyan St; r incl breakfast $120-150;) For old-world English charm in a glorious Queenslander, this delightful B&B is just the ticket. Polished timber and stained glass seep from the entrance into the rooms, which come with high beds and small antiques.

Bundaberg Spanish Motor Inn MOTEL $$
(07-4152 5444; www.bundabergspanishmotorinn.com; 134 Woongarra St; s/d $95/105;) In a quiet side street off the main drag, this Spanish hacienda–style motel is great value. Units are self-contained and all rooms overlook the central pool.

Burnett Riverside Motel MOTEL $$
(07-4155 8777; www.burnettmotel.com.au; 7 Quay St; d $150-200;) This modern pit stop is popular with conferences and travelling business folk, and the good facilities and popular H2O restaurant set it apart

TURTLE TOTS

Mon Repos, 15km northeast of Bundaberg, is one of Australia's most accessible turtle rookeries. From November to late March, female loggerheads lumber laboriously up the beach to lay eggs in the sand. About eight weeks later, the hatchlings dig their way to the surface, and under cover of darkness emerge en masse to scurry as quickly as their little flippers allow down to the water.

The **Mon Repos visitor centre** (07-4153 8888; 271 Bourbong St) has information on turtle conservation and organises nightly tours (adult/child $10.55/5.55) from 7pm during the season. Bookings are mandatory and can be made through the Bundaberg Visitor Centre (p172) or online at www.bookbundabergregion.com.au.

Bundaberg

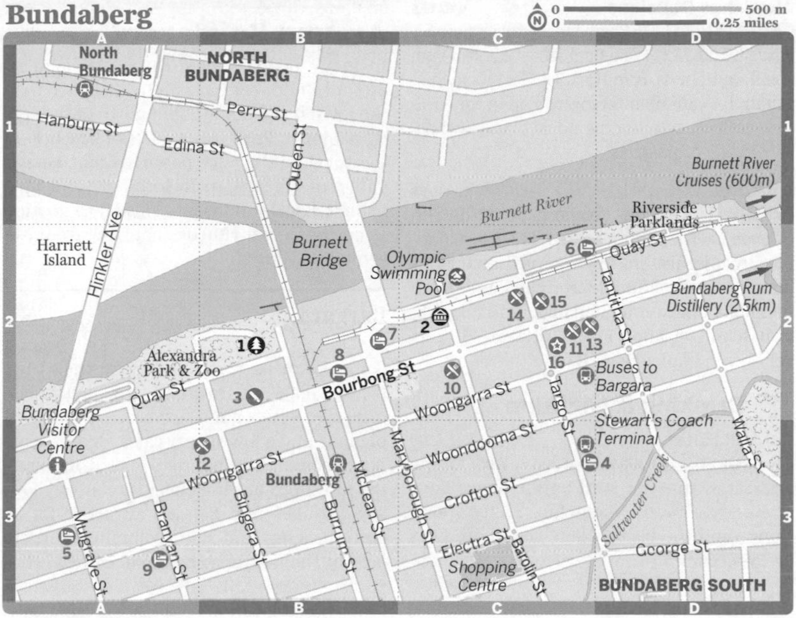

0 500 m
0 0.25 miles

North Bundaberg
NORTH BUNDABERG
Perry St
Hanbury St
Edina St
Queen St
Burnett River Cruises (600m)
Burnett River
Riverside Parklands
Quay St
Harriett Island
Hinkler Ave
Burnett Bridge
Olympic Swimming Pool
Tantitha St
Bundaberg Rum Distillery (2.5km)
Alexandra Park & Zoo
Quay St
Bourbong St
Buses to Bargara
Targo St
Woongarra St
Stewart's Coach Terminal
Walla St
Bundaberg Visitor Centre
Woondooma St
Woongarra St
Bundaberg
Saltwater Creek
Maryborough St
McLean St
Crofton St
Bingera St
Branyan St
Mulgrave St
Burrum St
Electra St
Barolin St
George St
Shopping Centre
BUNDABERG SOUTH

Bundaberg

Sights

1 Alexandra Park & Zoo B2
2 Bundaberg Regional Arts Gallery C2

Activities, Courses & Tours

3 Bundaberg Aqua Scuba B2

Sleeping

4 Bigfoot Backpackers C3
5 Bundaberg Spanish Motor Inn A3
6 Burnett Riverside Motel C2
7 Cellblock Backpackers B2
8 Federal Backpackers B2
9 Inglebrae A3

Eating

10 Alowishus Delicious C2
11 Indulge C2
12 Les Chefs B3
13 Rosie Blu C2
14 Spicy Tonight C2
15 Teaspoon C2

Entertainment

16 Central Hotel C2

from just about every other option in town. There's a gym, a sauna and fine river views.

Eating

Rosie Blu DELI $

(☎07-4151 0957; 90a Bourbong St; mains $9-19; ⊙8am-4pm Mon, 8.30am-4pm Tue-Fri, 8am-1.30pm Sat) Locals congregate en masse at this cute little spot, which isn't shy with its portions of gourmet sandwiches, salads and hot lunches dished up at lightning speed.

Spicy Tonight FUSION $

(☎07-4154 3320; 1 Targo St; dishes $12-20; ⊙11am-2.30pm & 5-9pm Mon-Sat, 5-9pm Sun) Bundaberg's saucy little secret combines Thai and Indian cuisine with hot curries, vindaloo, tandoori and a host of vegetarian dishes.

Teaspoon CAFE $

(10 Targo St; mains $5-10; ⊙8am-5pm Mon-Sat) Great coffee and astonishingly cheap breakfasts ($7!).

Indulge CAFE $

(80 Bourbong St; dishes $9-18; ⊙8.30am-4.30pm Mon-Fri, 7.30am-12.30pm Sat) Delicious pastries and a fancy menu built around local produce.

Alowishus Delicious CAFE $
(07-4154 2233; 176 Bourbong St; coffees from $3, mains $9.50-22; 7am-5pm Mon-Wed, 7am-9pm Thu, 7am-11pm Fri, 8am-11pm Sat, 9am-10pm Sun) Finally! A cafe open at night! Pop in for creative coffees, wholesome tucker and a massive range of pastries.

Les Chefs INTERNATIONAL $$
(07-4153 1770; 238 Bourbong St; mains $27; lunch Tue-Fri, dinner Mon-Sat) The most popular restaurant in town serves enormous plates of international fare. The large menu includes chicken enchiladas, grilled fish, veal schnitzel and yummy desserts. It gets very busy; book ahead. BYO.

Drinking & Nightlife

Central Hotel CLUB
(18 Targo St; 11.30am-9pm Tue & Wed, to 3am Thur-Sat) Strut your stuff on the dance floor at Bundy's hottest nightclub. Pretty young things and the backpackers crowd are here every weekend.

Information

Bundaberg Visitor Centre (07-4153 8888, 1300 722 099; www.bundabergregion.org; 271 Bourbong St; 9am-5pm)

Getting There & Around

AIR

The **Bundaberg Airport** (Airport Drive) is about 6km southwest of the centre. There are several daily flights to Brisbane with **Qantaslink** (13 13 13; www.qantas.com.au).

BUS

The coach terminal is on Targo St. Both **Greyhound Australia** (1300 473 946; www.greyhound.com.au) and **Premier Motor Service** (13 34 10; www.premierms.com.au) have daily services connecting Bundaberg with Brisbane ($87, seven hours), Hervey Bay ($24, 1½ hours) and Rockhampton ($50, four hours).

Duffy's Coaches (1300 383 397) have numerous services every weekday to Bargara ($5, 35 minutes), leaving from the back of Target on Woongarra St.

TRAIN

Run by **Queensland Rail** (1800 872 467; www.traveltrain.com.au), *Sunlander* ($89, seven hours, three weekly) and *Tilt Train* ($89, five hours, Sunday to Friday) travel from Brisbane to Bundaberg on their respective routes to Cairns and Rockhampton.

Around Bundaberg

In many people's eyes, the beach hamlets around Bundaberg are more attractive than the town itself. Some 25km north of the centre is **Moore Park** with wide, flat beaches. To the south is the very popular **Elliot Heads** with a nice beach, rocky foreshore and good fishing. Locals and visitors also flock to Mon Repos to see baby turtles hatching from November to March.

Bargara

POP 6893

Some 16km east of Bundaberg, the cruisy beach village of **Bargara** is a picturesque little spot with a good surf beach, a lovely esplanade and a few snazzy cafes. Recent years have seen a few high-rises sprout up along the foreshore but the effect is relatively low-key. Families find Bargara attractive for its clean beaches and safe swimming, particularly at the 'basin', a sheltered artificial rock pool.

In a great location opposite the esplanade, **Kacy's Bargara Beach Motel** (07-4130 1100; www.bargaramotel.com.au; 63 Esplanade; d from $139, 2-bedroom apt from $199;) offers a range of accommodation from pleasant motel rooms to self-contained apartments. Downstairs is the tropically themed **Kacy's Restaurant and Bar** (mains $17-40; breakfast & dinner daily, lunch Fri-Sun).

FRASER ISLAND

The local Butchulla people call it K'Gari or 'paradise', and not for no reason. Sculpted from wind, sand and surf, the striking blue freshwater lakes, crystalline creeks, giant dunes and lush rainforests of this gigantic sandbar form an enigmatic island paradise unlike any other in the world. Created over hundreds of thousands of years from sand drifting off the East Coast of mainland Australia, Fraser Island is the largest sand island in the world (measuring 120km by 15km), and the only place where rainforest grows on sand.

Inland, the vegetation varies from dense tropical rainforest and wild heath to wetlands and wallum scrub, with 'sandblows' (giant dunes over 200m high), mineral streams and freshwater lakes opening on to long sandy beaches fringed with pounding

SAND SAFARIS: EXPLORING FRASER ISLAND

The only way to explore Fraser Island (besides walking) is with a 4WD. For most travellers, there are three transport options: tag-along tours, organised tours or 4WD hire. This is a fragile environment; bear in mind that the greater the number of individual vehicles driving on the island, the greater the environmental damage.

Tag-Along Tours

Popular with backpackers, tag-along tours see groups of travellers pile into a 4WD convoy and follow a lead vehicle with an experienced guide and driver. Rates hover around $350to $400; be sure to check if yours includes food, fuel, alcohol, etc.

Advantages Flexibility; you can make new friends fast.

Disadvantages If your group doesn't get along it's a loooong three days. Inexperienced drivers get bogged in sand all the time, but this can be part of the fun.

Recommended operators include the following:

Colonial Village YHA (☎07-4125 1844; www.yha.com.au/hostels/qld/fraser-capricorn-coasts/hervey-bay) Hervey Bay.

Dropbear Adventures (☎1800 061 156; www.dropbearadventures.com.au) Ex-Hervey Bay, Rainbow Beach and Noosa.

Fraser Roving (☎07-4125 6386; www.fraserroving.com.au) Hervey Bay.

Fraser's on Rainbow (☎07-5486 8885; www.frasersonrainbow.com) Rainbow Beach.

Pippies Beach House (☎07-5486 8503; www.pippiesbeachhouse.com.au) Rainbow Beach.

Nomads (☎07-5447 3355; www.nomadsfraserisland.com) Noosa.

Organised Tours

Most organised tours cover Fraser's hotspots: rainforests, Eli Creek, Lakes McKenzie and Wabby, the coloured Pinnacles and the *Maheno* shipwreck.

Advantages Minimum fuss, expert commentary.

Disadvantages During peak season you could share the experience with 40 others.

Among the many operators:

Cool Dingo Tours (☎07-4120 3333; www.cooldingotour.com; 2-/3-day tour from $325/395) Overnight at lodges with the option to stay extra nights on the island.

Fraser Experience (☎07-4124 4244; www.fraserexperience.com; 1-/2-day tour $180/327) Small groups and more freedom with the itinerary.

Fraser Explorer Tours (☎07-4194 9222; www.fraserexplorertours.com.au; 1-/2-day tour $175/319) Highly recommended.

4WD Hire

You can hire a 4WD from Hervey Bay, Rainbow Beach or on Fraser Island itself. All companies require a hefty bond, usually in the form of a credit-card imprint, which you *will* lose if you drive in salt water – don't even think about running the waves!

When planning your trip, reckon on covering 20km an hour on the inland tracks and 40km an hour on the eastern beach. Most companies will help arrange ferries, permits and camping gear. Rates for multiday rentals start at around $185 a day.

Advantages Complete freedom to roam the island and escape the crowds.

Disadvantages You may tackle beach and track conditions that even experienced drivers find challenging.

There are rental companies in Hervey Bay (p159) and Rainbow Beach (p164). On the island, **Aussie Trax** (☎07-4124 4433; www.fraserisland4wd.com.au) hires out 4WDs from $230 per day.

Fraser Island

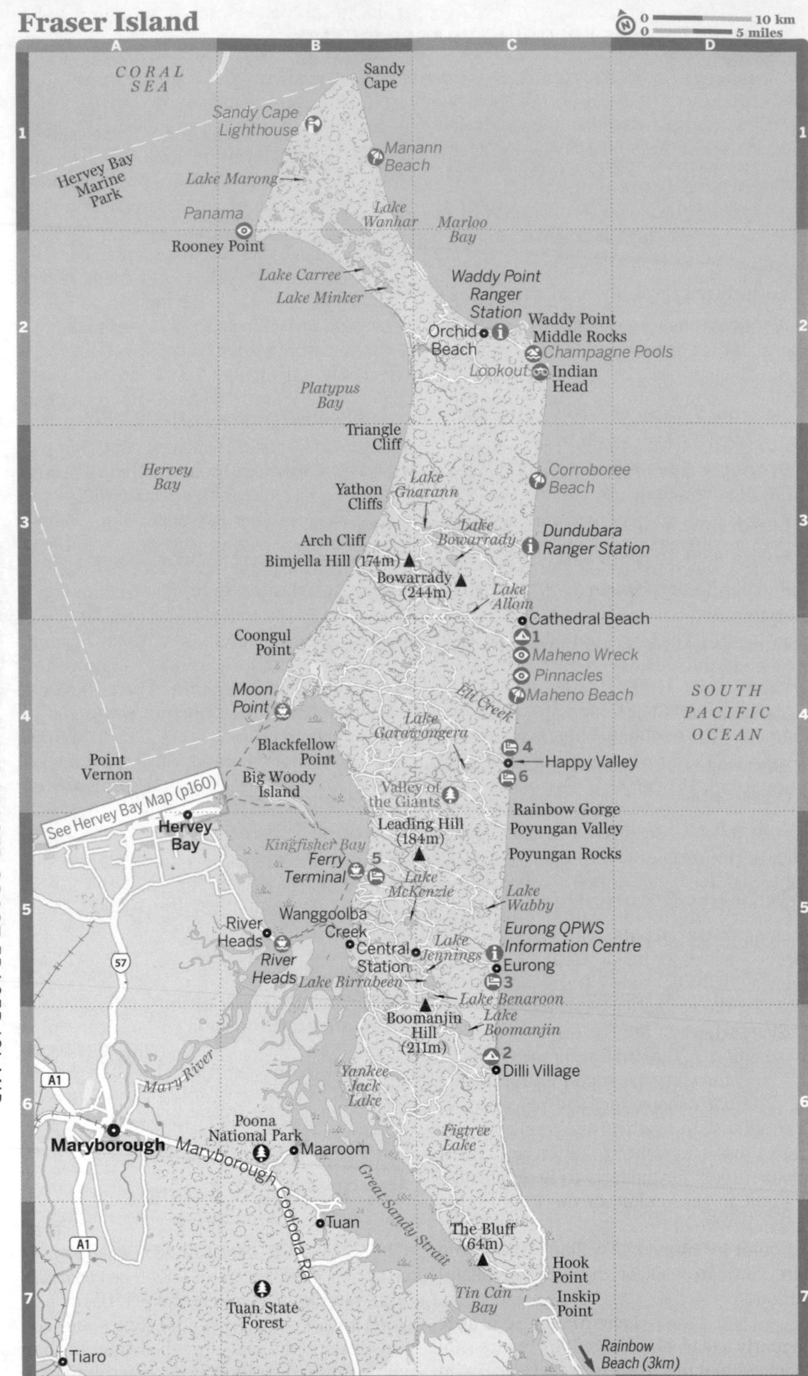

Fraser Island

Sleeping

1	Cathedrals on Fraser	C4
2	Dilli Village Fraser Island	C6
3	Eurong Beach Resort	C5
	Fraser Island Beachhouses	(see 3)
4	Fraser Island Retreat	C4
5	Kingfisher Bay Resort	B5
6	Sailfish on Fraser	C4

surf. The island is home to a profusion of bird life and wildlife including the famous dingo, while offshore waters teem with dugong, dolphins, sharks and migrating humpback whales.

Once exploited for its natural resources, sand and timber, Fraser Island joined the World Heritage list in 1992. The majority of the island is protected as part of the Great Sandy National Park.

This island utopia, however, is marred by an ever-increasing volume of 4WD traffic tearing down the beach and along sandy inland tracks. With over 360,000 people visiting the island each year, Fraser can sometimes feel like a giant sandpit with its own peak hour and congested beach highway.

Before crossing via ferry from either Rainbow Beach or Hervey Bay, ensure that your vehicle has suitably high clearance and, if camping, that you have adequate food, water and fuel. Driving on Fraser looks pretty relaxed in the brochures, but a sudden tide change or an unseen pothole can set your wheels spinning perilously.

Sights & Activities

Starting at the island's southern tip, where the ferry leaves for Inskip Point on the mainland, a high-tide access track cuts inland, avoiding dangerous Hook Point, and leads to the entrance of the Eastern Beach's main thoroughfare. The first settlement is **Dilli Village**, the former sand-mining centre; **Eurong**, with shops, fuel and places to eat, is another 9km north. From here, an inland track crosses to Central Station and Wanggoolba Creek (for the ferry to River Heads).

Right in the middle of the island is the ranger centre at **Central Station**, the starting point for numerous walking trails. From here you can walk or drive to the beautiful **McKenzie**, **Jennings**, **Birrabeen** and **Boomanjin Lakes**. Lake McKenzie is spectacularly clear and ringed by white-sand beaches, making it a great place to swim; Lake Birrabeen sees fewer tour and backpacker groups.

About 4km north of Eurong along the beach, a signposted walking trail leads across sandblows to the beautiful **Lake Wabby**, the most accessible of Fraser's lakes. An easier route is from the lookout on the inland track. Lake Wabby is surrounded on three sides by eucalypt forest, while the fourth side is a massive sandblow that encroaches on the lake at about 3m a year. The lake is deceptively shallow and diving is very dangerous.

As you drive up the beach, you may have to detour inland to avoid Poyungan and Yidney Rocks during high tide before you reach **Happy Valley**, with places to stay, a shop and bistro. About 10km north is **Eli Creek**, a fast-moving, crystal-clear waterway that will carry you effortlessly downstream. About 2km from Eli Creek is the rotting hulk of the **Maheno**, a former passenger liner blown ashore by a cyclone in 1935 as it was being towed to a Japanese scrap yard.

Roughly 5km north of the *Maheno* you'll find the **Pinnacles**, an eroded section of coloured sand cliffs, and about 10km beyond, **Dundubara**, with a ranger station and excellent camping ground. Then there's a 20km stretch of beach before you come to the rock outcrop of **Indian Head**. Sharks, manta rays, dolphins and (during the migration season) whales can often be seen from the top of this headland.

Between Indian Head and Waddy Point, the trail branches inland, passing **Champagne Pools**, which offers the only safe saltwater swimming on the island. There are good camping areas at **Waddy Point** and **Orchid Beach**, the last settlement on the island.

Many tracks north of this are closed for environmental protection.

Kingfisher Bay Resort (07-4194 9300; www.kingfisherbay.com) can organise scenic helicopter flights, or go for a jaunt with **Air Fraser Island** (07-4125 3600; www.airfraserisland.com.au; return flight from $135).

Sleeping & Eating

★**Kingfisher Bay Resort** RESORT $$
(07-4194 9300, 1800 072 555; www.kingfisherbay.com; Kingfisher Bay; d $188, 2-bedroom villa $228;) This elegant eco-resort has hotel rooms with private balconies and sophisticated two- and three-bedroom timber villas elevated to limit their environmental

impact. The villas and spacious holiday houses are gorgeous; some have spas on their private decks. There's a three-night minimum stay in high season. The resort has restaurants, bars and shops and operates daily ranger-guided, eco-accredited tours of the island (adult/child $160/110).

Fraser Island Beachhouses CABIN **$$**
(☎07-4127 9205, 1800 626 230; www.fraserislandbeachhouses.com.au; Eurong Second Valley; studio/house from $150/300; minimum stays apply;) Top option for those wanting their own space without sand or tents. The sunny, self-contained units are kitted out with polished wood, cable TVs and ocean views; there are four categories of beach house, with prices varying by size and location.

Eurong Beach Resort RESORT **$$**
(☎07-4120 1600, 1800 111 808; www.eurong.com.au; Eurong; r $135, 2-bedroom apt $185;) Bright, cheerful Eurong is the main resort on the East Coast and a solid option for most budgets. Choose from simple motel rooms and comfortable, self-contained apartments. There's a pub-style restaurant (open for breakfast, lunch and dinner; mains $18 to $40), a bar, two pools, tennis courts and a petrol station.

Fraser Island Retreat CABIN **$$**
(☎07-4127 9144; www.fraserisretreat.com.au; Happy Valley; cabin per 2 nights $330;) The retreat's nine timber cabins (sleeping up to four people) offer some of the best-value accommodation on the island. The cabins are airy, nestled in native foliage and close to the beach. There's a camp kitchen, restaurant and shop – which sells fuel – on-site.

Sailfish on Fraser APARTMENT **$$$**
(☎07-4127 9494; www.sailfishonfraser.com.au; d from $230-250, extra person $10;) Any notions of rugged wilderness will be forgotten quick smart at this plush, indulgent retreat. These two-bedroom apartments (which sleep up to six people) are cavernous and classy, with spas, mod cons, an alluring pool and 4WD washing area.

Camping

Supplies on the island are limited and costly. Before arriving, stock up well and be prepared for mosquitoes and March flies.

Camping permits are required at NPRSR camping grounds and any public area (ie along the beach). The most developed **NPRSR camping grounds** (☎13 74 68; www.nprsr.qld.gov.au; per person/family $5.45/21.80), with coin-operated hot showers, toilets and BBQs, are at Waddy Point, Dundubara and Central Station. Campers with vehicles can also use the smaller camping grounds with fewer facilities at Lake Boomanjin, Ungowa and Wathumba on the western coast. Walkers' camps are set away from the main camping grounds along the Fraser Island Great Walk trail. The trail map lists the camp sites and their facilities. Camping is permitted on designated stretches of the eastern beach, but there are no facilities. Fires are prohibited except in communal fire rings at Waddy Point and Dundubara – bring your own firewood in the form of untreated, milled timber.

Dilli Village Fraser Island CAMPGROUND **$**
(☎07-4127 9130; camp site per person $10, bunkroom/cabin $40/100) Managed by the University of the Sunshine Coast, Dilli Village offers good sites on a softly sloping camp ground.

Cathedrals on Fraser CARAVAN PARK **$**
(☎07-4127 9177; www.cathedralsonfraser.com.au; Cathedral Beach; 'wilderness site' $29, unpowered/powered site $39/45, cabin with/without bathroom $220/180;) Spacious, privately run park with abundant, flat, grassy sites that's a hit with families.

Information

A 4WD is necessary if you're driving on Fraser Island. General supplies and expensive fuel

FRASER ISLAND GREAT WALK

The Fraser Island Great Walk is a stunning way to experience this enigmatic island. The trail undulates through the island's interior for 90km from Dilli Village to Happy Valley. Broken up into seven sections of around 6km to 16km each, plus some side trails off the main sections, it follows the pathways of Fraser Island's original inhabitants, the Butchulla people. En route, the walk passes underneath the rainforest canopies, circles around some of the island's vivid lakes and courses through shifting dunes.

Visit **www.nprsr.qld.gov.au** for maps, detailed information and updates on the track.

DEALING WITH DINGOES

Despite its many natural attractions and opportunities for adventure, there's nothing on Fraser Island that gives a thrill comparable to your first glimpse of a dingo. Believed to be among the most genetically pure in the world, the dingoes of Fraser are sleek, spry and utterly beautiful. They're also wild beasts that can become aggressive at the drop of a hat (or a strong-smelling foodsack), and while attacks are rare, there are precautions that must be taken by every visitor to the island:

- However skinny they appear, or whatever woebegone look they give you, never feed dingoes. Dingoes that are human-fed quickly lose their shyness and can become combative and competitive. Feeding dingoes is illegal and carries heavy fines.
- Don't leave any food scraps lying around, and don't take food to the lakes: eating on the shore puts your food at 'dingo level', an easy target for scroungy scavengers.
- Stay in groups, and keep any children within arm's reach at all times.
- Teasing dingoes is not only cruel, but dangerous. Leave them alone, and they'll do same.
- Dingoes are best observed at a distance. Pack a zoom lens and practice some shush, and you'll come away with some brilliant photographs...and all your limbs intact.

are available from stores at Cathedral Beach, Eurong, Kingfisher Bay, Happy Valley and Orchid Beach. There are public telephones at those locations and at most camping grounds.

The main ranger station, **Eurong QPWS Information Centre** (07-4127 9128) is at Eurong. Others can be found at **Dundubara** (07-4127 9138) and **Waddy Point** (07 4127 9190). Offices are often unattended as the rangers are out on patrol.

The 4WD **Fraser Island Taxi Service** (07-4127 9188) operates all over the island. Bookings are essential, as there's only one cab for the whole island!

If your vehicle breaks down, call the **tow-truck service** (0428 353 164, 07-4127 9449) in Eurong.

PERMITS

You must purchase permits from **NPRSR** (13 74 68; nprsr.qld.gov.au) for vehicles (per day/week/month $11/27.70/43.60) and camping (per person/family $5.45/21.80) before you arrive. Permits aren't required for private camping grounds or resorts. Permit issuing offices:

Great Sandy Information Centre (07-5449 7792; 240 Moorinidil St; 8am-4pm) Near Noosa.

Marina Kiosk (07-4128 9800; Buccaneer Ave, Urangan Boat Harbour, Urangan; 6am-6pm)

Maryborough QPWS (07-4121 1800; Cnr Lennox & Alice Sts; 9am-4.30pm Mon-Fri)

Rainbow Beach QPWS (07-5486 3160; Rainbow Beach Rd; 8am-4pm)

River Heads Information Kiosk (07-4125 8485; 6.15am-12.30pm & 1.30-4pm) Ferry departure point at River Heads, south of Hervey Bay.

Getting There & Away

AIR

Air Fraser Island (07-4125 3600; www.airfraserisland.com.au) charges from $135 for a return flight (30-minute round trip) to the island's eastern beach, departing Hervey Bay airport.

BOAT

Vehicle ferries connect Fraser Island with River Heads, about 10km south of Hervey Bay, or further south at Inskip Point, near Rainbow Beach.

Fraser Island Barges (07-4194 9300, 1800 227 437; www.fraserislandferry.com.au) makes the crossing (vehicle and four passengers $160 return, 30 minutes) from River Heads to Wanggoolba Creek on the western coast of Fraser Island. It departs daily from River Heads at 8.30am, 10.15am and 4pm, and returns from the island at 9am, 3pm and 5pm.

Kingfisher Bay Ferry (07-4194 9300, 1800 227 437; www.fraserislandferry.com) operates a daily vehicle and passenger ferry (pedestrian adult/child return $50/25, vehicle and four passengers return $160, 50 minutes) from River Heads to Kingfisher Bay, departing at 6.45am, 9am, 12.30pm, 3.30pm, 6.45pm and 9.30pm (Friday and Saturday only) and returning at 7.50am, 10.30am, 2pm, 5pm, 8.30pm and 11pm (Friday and Saturday only).

Coming from Rainbow Beach, **Manta Ray** (07-5486 3935) has two ferries making the 15-minute crossing from Inskip Point to Hook Point on Fraser Island continuously from about 6am to 5.30pm daily (vehicle return $110).

Capricorn Coast & the Southern Reef Islands

Includes ➡

Best Places to Eat

- ➡ Ferns Hideaway (p191)
- ➡ Tree Bar (p181)
- ➡ Ginger Mule (p187)
- ➡ Saigon Saigon (p188)
- ➡ Megalomania (p190)

Best Places to Stay

- ➡ Svendsen's Beach (p192)
- ➡ LaLaLand Retreat (p181)
- ➡ Surfside Motel (p190)
- ➡ Criterion (p187)
- ➡ Workmans Beach Camping Area (p180)

Why Go?

The stretch of coastline that straddles the tropic of Capricorn is one of the quietest and most lovely lengths of the East Coast. While local families flock to the main beaches during school holidays, the scene is uncrowded for most of the year, and even in high season you needn't travel far to find a deserted beach.

The stunning powdery white sand and turquoise waters of the Capricorn Coast fit the holiday-brochure image perfectly. The pristine islands of the southern Great Barrier Reef offer some of the best snorkelling and diving in Queensland, and the opportunities for wildlife spotting – from turtle hatchlings to passing whales – are plentiful. Unspoilt beaches and windswept national parks can be found along the entire coastline.

Inland, you'll find bustling Rockhampton – Capricornia's economic hub and the capital of cattle country, with all the steakhouses, rodeos and gigantic hats to prove it.

When to Go

Rockhampton

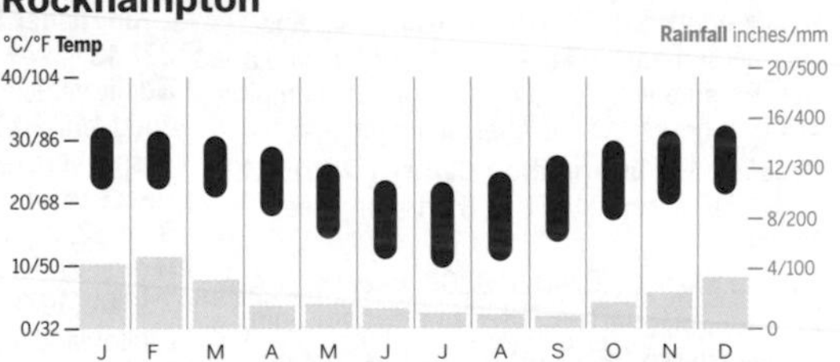

Feb The Agnes Blues & Roots Festival rocks the Discovery Coast.

Dec Nature puts on a stunning lightshow during summer solstice at Capricorn Caves.

Nov–Feb Temperatures soar and dangerous stingers are out.

AGNES WATER & TOWN OF 1770

POP 1815

Surrounded by national parks and the Pacific Ocean, the twin coastal towns of Agnes Water and Town of 1770 are among Queensland's most appealing – and least hectic – seaside destinations. The tiny settlement of Agnes Water has the East Coast's most northerly surf beach, while the even tinier Town of 1770 (little more than a marina!) marks Captain Cook's first landing in the state; the hamlet is known as 'The Birthplace of Queensland'. The 'Discovery Coast' is popular for surfing, boating, and fishing away from the crowds. To get here, turn east off the Bruce Hwy at Miriam Vale, 70km south of Gladstone. It's another 57km to Agnes Water and a further 6km to the Town of 1770.

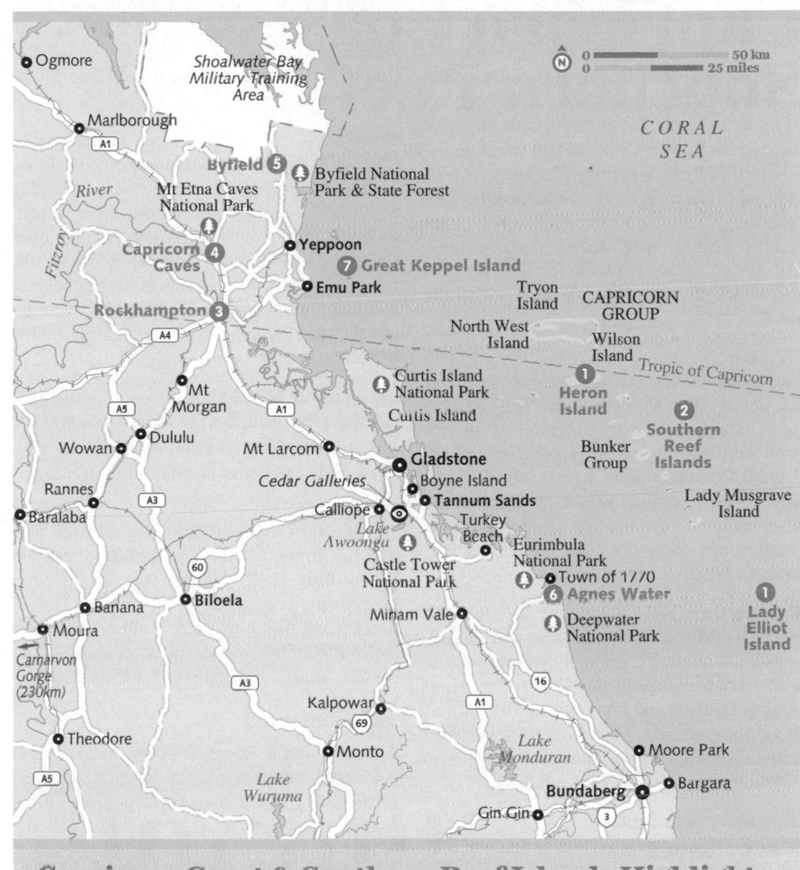

Capricorn Coast & Southern Reef Islands Highlights

1. Diving the spectacular underwater coral gardens of **Heron Island** (p185) and **Lady Elliot Island** (p184).
2. Playing castaway on the coral cays of the **Southern Reef Islands** (p184).
3. Tucking into a huge steak in Australia's beef capital, **Rockhampton** (p186).
4. Crawling through black holes and tight tunnels in the **Capricorn Caves** (p187).
5. Hiking through lush rainforest at **Byfield** (p191).
6. Surfing and chilling at Queensland's most northerly surf beach, **Agnes Water** (p179).
7. Claiming a tropical beach for the day on **Great Keppel Island** (p191).

Sights

Miriam Vale Historical Society Museum MUSEUM
(☎07-4974 9511; Springs Rd, near cnr Captain Cook Dr, Agnes Water; adult/child $3/free; ⏲1-4pm Mon & Wed-Sat, 10am-4pm Sun) The museum displays extracts from Cook's journal and the original telescope from the first lighthouse built on the Queensland coast.

Activities & Tours

The action around here happens on and in the water. Agnes Water is Queensland's northernmost **surf beach**. A surf life-saving club patrols the main beach and there are often good breaks along the coast. If you're looking for boating, Round Hill Creek at the Town of 1770 is a calm anchorage. There's also good **fishing** and **mudcrabbing** upstream, and the southern end of the Great Barrier Reef is easily accessible from here. Charter boats are available for fishing, surfing, snorkelling and diving trips out to the Reef.

1770 Larc Tours TOUR
(☎07-4974 9422; www.1770larctours.com.au; adult/child $155/95) Ride the world's most peculiar ecotourism chariot (a hot pink amphibious military vehicle) on adventurous seven-hour tours around Bustard Head and Eurimbula National Park. They also run hour-long afternoon tours (adult/child $38/17) and sandboarding safaris ($120).

ThunderCat 1770 ADVENTURE TOUR
(☎0411 078 810; tours from $70) Go wave-jumping on a surf-racing craft, slingshot over the waves on the Tube Rider Xpress or – best of all – bounce and spin through the water in a sumo suit. For those less in need of an adrenaline hit, explore calmer waterways on a Wilderness Explorer ecotour.

Lady Musgrave Cruises CRUISE
(☎07-4974 9077; www.1770reefcruises.com; Captain Cook Dr, Town of 1770; adult/child $185/85; ⏲departs daily 8.30am) This family-owned company has excellent day trips to Lady Musgrave Island. Groups spend five hours at the island, and cruises include coral viewing in a semi-submersible, lunch, morning and afternoon tea and snorkelling gear. For an extra cost you can go diving or reef fishing. Island camping transfers are also available for $340 per person.

Reef 2 Beach Surf School SURFING
(☎07-4974 9072; www.reef2beachsurf.com; Agnes Water Shopping Centre, Agnes Water) Learn to surf on the gentle breaks of the main beach with this highly acclaimed surf school. A three-hour group lesson is $17 per person; surfboard hire is $20 for four hours.

1770 Liquid Adventures KAYAKING
(☎0428 956 630; www.1770liquidadventures.com.au) Paddle off on a spectacular twilight kayak tour. For $55, you ride the waves off 1770, before retiring to the beach for drinks and snacks as the sun sets – keep an eye out for dolphins. You can also rent kayaks for $35 (two hours).

Scooteroo MOTORCYCLING
(☎07-4974 7697; www.scooterrootours.com; 21 Bicentennial Dr, Agnes Water; 3hr chopper ride $75) Straddle a chopper and vroom off on an irreverent and engaging 50km ride around the area. Anyone with a car licence can ride the gear-less bikes. Wear long pants and closed-in shoes; they'll supply the tough-guy leather jackets (with flames on them, of course).

Lazy Lizard Surf School SURFING
(☎0488 177 000; 31 Starfish St, Agnes Water) The Lazy Lizard offers lessons for smaller groups of up to 12 people ($22 for four hours).

Fishing FISHING
You can rent a dinghy (half day $75, full day $110) at Town of 1770's small marina; ask for Poppy Bob. He'll also get you set up with everything you need to dip a line. If you don't want to go it alone, **Hooked on 1770** (☎07-4974 9794; www.1770tours.com; half-/full-day tour $150/220) runs charter tours.

Festivals

Agnes Blues & Roots Festival MUSIC
(www.agnesbluesandroots.com.au; SES Grounds, Agnes Water) Top names and up-and-coming Aussie acts crank it up in the last weekend of February.

Sleeping

Workmans Beach Camping Area CAMPGROUND $
(Workmans Beach, Springs Rd, Agnes Water; sites per person $6) Why doesn't every coastal town have one of these? Workmans Beach is a council-run camping ground with spacious sites in gorgeous beachside surrounds; if you're really smitten, you can stay up to 44 days. Facilities are limited but for those

who can exist without whiz-bang mod-cons, you won't find anything lacking. You can't book sites; just turn up, and good-humoured council blokes will knock on your van/tent at an ungodly hour of the morning.

Cool Bananas HOSTEL $
(1800 227 660, 07-4974 7660; www.coolbananas.net.au; 2 Springs Rd, Agnes Water; dm $26, $140 weekly; @) This good-humoured, Balinese-themed backpackers has roomy six- and eight-bed dorms, open and airy communal areas, and is only a five-minute walk to the beach and shops. Otherwise, you can laze the day away in a hammock in the tropical gardens.

1770 Southern Cross Tourist Retreat HOSTEL $
(07-4974 7225; www.1770southerncross.com; 2694 Round Hill Rd, Agnes Water; dm/d incl breakfast $25/85; @) There's an enlightened approach to budget accommodation at this bushland retreat, with a fish-filled, swimmable lake, Buddhist statues and meditation areas ideal for pensive reflection (or sleeping off a hangover). The dorms are superb. It's 2.5km out of town, and is connected by a courtesy bus.

1770 Camping Ground CARAVAN PARK $
(07-4974 9286; www.1770campingground.com.au; Captain Cook Dr, Town of 1770; unpowered/powered site $33/37) A large but peaceful park with sites right by the beach and plenty of shady trees.

★**LaLaLand Retreat** RETREAT $$
(07-4974 9554; www.lalalandholiday.com.au; 61 Bicentennial Dve, Agnes Water; cottage $100-240; P) The colourful cottages at this vibrant guesthouse on the road into town are set in attractive bushland scrub and each sleeps up to five people. There is an excellent lagoon-style pool, wheelchair access and a sense of being removed from civilisation. Call for deals on rates.

Agnes Water Beach Club APARTMENT $$
(07-4974 7355; www.agneswaterbeachclub.com.au; 3 Agnes St, Agnes Water; 1-/2-bedroom apt from $145/200; @) Brand-new luxury apartments with excellent facilities in a great location.

Eating

Agnes Water Bakery BAKERY $
(Endeavour Plaza, Agnes Water; pies $5; from 6am) Do. Not. Miss. This. The pies here are above and beyond the offerings of most city bakeries, let alone those in a sleepy seaside village, with gourmet stuffings including the magnificent Tandoori chicken. Sweet treats and, surprisingly, coffees, are equally divine. It gets packed, so get in early.

Bustards CAFE $
(7 Agnes St, Agnes Water; mains $12-25; breakfast, lunch & dinner) The hottest breakfast spot in Agnes Water is close to the main beach and rightfully popular for its locally sourced seafood and light lunches. Charming and laid-back.

★**Tree Bar** MODERN AUSTRALIAN $$
(07-4974 7446; 576 Captain Cook Dr, Town of 1770; mains $19-34; breakfast, lunch & dinner) This little salt-encrusted waterfront diner has plenty of charm and an atmospheric bar. Local seafood is a winner here, though breakfasts (from $8) are pretty damned fine as well.

Deck INDIAN $$
(07-4974 9157; 384 Captain Cook Dr, Captain Cook Holiday Village, Town of 1770; mains $20-32; dinner Tue-Sun) Stupendous Indian fare that's not afraid to dip its toe in a vat of chillis. Lovely, palm-rustling surrounds make it even easier to swallow.

Yok Attack THAI $$
(07-4974 7454; Endeavour Plaza, Agnes Water; mains $17-25.50; lunch & dinner Mon-Sat) This simple Thai restaurant is very popular with the locals and is highly recommended by repeat customers.

Agnes Water Tavern PUB $$
(07-4974 9469; 1 Tavern Rd, Agnes Water; mains $15-30; lunch & dinner) Pleasant multipurpose pub with plenty of outdoor seating. Lunch and dinner specials daily.

Shopping

1770 Markets MARKET
(SES Grounds, Town of 1770) Mellow markets with chatty stallholders flogging everything from edibles to antiques. Held the second and fourth Sunday of the month from 8am to noon.

Information

The **Agnes Water visitor centre** (07-4902 1533; 71 Springs Rd, Town of 1770; 9am-5pm Mon-Fri, to 4pm Sat & Sun) is staffed by above-and-beyond volunteers who even leave information and brochures out overnight, just in case a lost soul blows into town. Next door, the **Agnes Water Library** (☎07-4902 1515; 71 Springs Rd, Town of 1770; ⌚9am-4.30pm Mon-Fri) has free internet access (half an hour, book in advance).

Getting There & Away

BUS

A handful of **Greyhound** (☎1300 473 946; www.greyhound.com.au) buses detour off the Bruce Hwy to Agnes Water; daily services include Bundaberg ($25, 1½ hours) and Cairns ($217, 21 hours). **Premier Motor Service** (☎13 34 10; www.premierms.com.au) also goes in and out of town.

EURIMBULA & DEEPWATER NATIONAL PARKS

South of Agnes Water is Deepwater National Park, an unspoiled coastal landscape with long sandy beaches, freshwater creeks, good fishing spots and two camping grounds. It's also a major breeding ground for loggerhead turtles, which dig nests and lay eggs on the beaches between November and February. You can watch the turtles laying and see hatchlings emerging at night between January and April, but you need to observe various precautions: the Agnes Water visitor centre has more info, or see www.nprsr.qld.gov.au/parks/deepwater.

The northern park entrance is 8km south of Agnes Water and is only accessible by 4WD. It's another 5km to the basic camping ground at Middle Rock (no facilities) and a further 2km to the Wreck Rock camping ground and picnic area, with rain and bore water and composting toilets. Wreck Point can also be accessed from the south by 2WD vehicles via Baffle Creek.

The 78-sq-km Eurimbula National Park, on the northern side of Round Hill Creek, has a landscape of dunes, mangroves and eucalypt forest. There are two basic camping grounds, one at Middle Creek with toilets only and the other at Bustard Beach with toilets and limited rainwater. The main access road to the park is about 10km southwest of Agnes Water.

You must obtain permits for all camping grounds from the **NPRSR** (☎13 74 68; www.nprsr.qld.gov.au; permit per person/family $5.45/21.80).

GLADSTONE

POP 31,778

Unless you've got an industry fetish, Gladstone, with its busy port, power station and alumina refineries, is rather uninspiring. You might want to head straight for the marina (Bryan Jordan Dr), the main departure point for boats to the southern coral cay islands of Heron, Masthead and Wilson on the Great Barrier Reef. If there's anything happening in town, it's on at the port end of Gondoon St.

Sights & Activities

If you have some time to spare before or after island hopping, drive up to the **Auckland Point Lookout** for views over Gladstone harbour, the port facilities and shipping terminals. A brass tablet on the lookout maps the harbour and its many islands.

ART DETOUR

Cedar Galleries (☎07-4975 0444; www.cedargalleries.com.au; Bruce Hwy, Calliope; ⌚9am-4pm Thu-Sat, 8am-4pm Sun) is a tranquil artists' bush retreat where you can watch painters and sculptors at work in the rustic slab-hut studios. To unleash your creative genius you can take **art & craft classes** with visiting artists (call ahead to book) or just browse the gardens and the gallery. There's also a cafe, a beautiful handcrafted wedding chapel, kids' jumping castle, a winery cellar door and a herd of friendly alpacas. The complex runs a weekly **farmers' market** every Sunday (from 8am to noon); the friendly bazaar is the ideal spot for stocking up on gourmet goodies, freshly baked bread, local wines and handmade gifts. Having too much fun to move on? Cedar Galleries has limited farmstay **accommodation** available (studio $100 first night, $60 subsequent nights).

This old-school Aussie artists' colony (25km south of Gladstone) is signposted off the Bruce Hwy, 7km southeast of Calliope.

WORTH A TRIP

CURTIS ISLAND

Curtis Island, just across the water from Gladstone, can't be confused with a resort island. Apart from swimming, fishing and lolling about on the dunes, its main drawcard is the annual appearance of rare flatback turtles on its eastern shores between October and January. Camping permits can be booked via **NPRSR** (☎13 74 68; www.nprsr.qld.gov.au; permit per person/family $5.45/21.80) or you can stay with the friendly folks at **Capricorn Lodge** (☎07-4972 0222; capricornlodge@bigpond.com; lodgings from around $80). They have a corner store and a liquor licence. Curtis Ferry Services (p184) connects the island with Gladstone every day bar Tuesday and Thursday.

Toondoon Botanic Gardens GARDENS
(☎07-4977 6899; Glenlyon Rd; ⊙7am-6pm Mon-Fri, 9am-6pm Sat & Sun Oct-Mar, 7am-5.30pm Mon-Fri, 8.30am-5.30pm Sat & Sun Apr-Sep) FREE More than 80 hectares of rainforest, lakes and Australian native plants. There's a visitor centre, an orchid house, and free guided tours between February and November. About 7km south of town.

Calliope River Historical Village HISTORIC SITE
(☎07-4975 7883; www.callioperiverhistoricalvillage.com; Dawson Hwy, Calliope; admission $5; ⊙10am-4pm) If you are in the area, **market days** (8am to 1pm, seven times a year; ask the visitor centre or see website for dates) at the Calliope River Historical Village, 26km south of Gladstone, are hugely popular, attracting over 3000 people. Wander around the village's restored heritage buildings and browse the 200-plus stalls of goodies.

Lake Awoonga LAKE
Created by the construction of the Awoonga Dam in 1984, Lake Awoonga is a popular recreational area 30km south of Gladstone. Backed by the rugged **Castle Tower National Park**, the barramundi-stocked lake has landscaped picnic areas, a cafe, barbecues, walking trails and bird life. You can hire watercraft from **Lake Awoonga Boat Hire** (☎07-4975 0930; tinnies half-day $80, kayaks per hour $15) and snooze lakeside at **Lake Awoonga Caravan Park** (☎07-4975 0155; www.lakeawoonga.net.au; Lake Awoonga Rd, Benaraby; 2 people unpowered/powered site $26/34, cabins from $70).

Tours

Gladstone's big-ticket industries, including the alumina refineries, aluminium smelter, power station and port authority, open their doors for free **industry tours**. The one- or 1½-hour tours start at different times on different days of the week depending on the industry. Book at the visitor centre.

Various charters offer fishing, diving and sightseeing cruises to the Swains Reef and Bunker Island groups. Try **MV Mikat** (☎0427 125 727; www.mikat.com.au), **Capricorn Star Cruises** (☎07-4978 0499; www.capricornstarcruises.citysearch.com.au) or **Kanimbla Charters** (☎1800 677 202; www.kanimblacharters.net.au).

Sleeping

Gladstone Backpackers HOSTEL $
(☎07-4972 5744; www.gladstonebackpackers.com.au; 12 Rollo St; dm/d $25/70; @) Friendly, family-run place in an old Queenslander, with a large kitchen, clean bathrooms and an airy outside deck. There's free use of bicycles and free pick-ups from the all transport depots.

Barney Beach Accommodation Centre CARAVAN PARK $
(☎07-4972 1366; www.barneybeachaccommodationcentre.com.au; 10 Friend St; powered site $39, cabin for 2 people $155-220; @) About 2km east of the city centre and close to the foreshore, this is the most central of the caravan parks. It's large and tidy, with a good camp kitchen and excellent self-contained accommodation. There are complimentary transfers to the marina for guests visiting Heron Island.

Harbour Sails Motel MOTEL $$
(☎07-4972 3456; www.harboursails.com.au; 23 Goondoon St; r from $150;) Sparkling, modern and central motel with the classy **Brass Bell Restaurant** attached (mains $22 to $34).

Auckland Hill B&B B&B $$$
(☎07-4972 4907; www.ahbb.com.au; 15 Yarroon St; s/d incl breakfast $175/235;) This sprawling, comfortable Queenslander has six spacious rooms with king-sized beds. Each is differently decorated: there's a spa suite and

one with wheelchair access. Breakfasts are hearty and the mood is relaxed.

Eating & Drinking

Gladstone Yacht Club PUB $$
(☎07-4972 2294; www.gyc.com.au; 1 Goondoon St; mains from $22; ⏰noon-2pm & 6-8.30pm Mon-Thu, 11.30am-2.30pm & 5.30-9pm Fri & Sat, 11.30am-2pm & 6-8.30pm Sun) The yacht club is a popular place for winin' and dinin', and with very good reason. The steak, chicken, pasta and seafood are tasty and generous, there are daily buffet specials and you can eat on the deck overlooking the water.

Tables on Flinders SEAFOOD $$$
(☎07-4972 8322; 2 Oaka La; mains from $38; ⏰lunch Tue-Fri, dinner Tue-Sat) If you feel like a Gladstone splurge, this is the place to do it, with exquisite local seafood including fresh mudcrab, bugs and prawns dominating the pricey menu.

Information

Gladstone City Library (☎07-4976 6400; 39 Goondoon St; ⏰9am-5.45pm Mon-Fri, to 3pm Sat & Sun) Free internet access but you must book in advance.

Visitor Centre (☎07-4972 9000; Bryan Jordan Dr; ⏰8.30am-4.30pm Mon-Fri, 9.30am-4.30pm Sat & Sun) Located at the marina, the departure point for boats to Heron Island.

Getting There & Away

AIR

Qantas (☎13 13 13; www.qantas.com.au) and **Virgin** (☎13 67 89; www.virginaustralia.com) operate flights to and from Gladstone Airport, which is 7km from the city centre.

BOAT

Curtis Ferry Services (☎07-4972 6990; www.curtisferryservices.com.au; return adult/child/family $30/22/from $84) has regular services to Curtis Island five days per week. The service leaves from the Gladstone marina and stops at Farmers Point on Facing Island en route. Transport to other nearby islands can be arranged on request.

You can also access the islands with various charter operators.

If you've booked a stay on Heron Island, the resort operates a launch (one way adult/child $50/25, two hours), which leaves the Gladstone marina at 11am daily.

BUS

Greyhound Australia (☎1300 473 946; www.greyhound.com.au) has several coach services from Brisbane ($143, 10 hours), Bundaberg ($44, 3 hours) and Rockhampton ($21, 1½ hours). The terminal is at the BP service station on the Dawson Hwy, about 200m southwest of the centre.

TRAIN

Queensland Rail (☎07-3235 1122, 1800 872 467; www.queenslandrail.com.au) has frequent north- and southbound services passing through Gladstone daily. The *Tilt Train* stops in Gladstone from Brisbane ($119, 5 hours) and Rockhampton ($39, one hour).

SOUTHERN REEF ISLANDS

If you've ever had 'castaway' dreams of tiny coral atolls fringed with sugary white sand and turquoise-blue seas, you've found your island paradise in the southern Great Barrier Reef islands. From beautiful Lady Elliot Island, 80km northeast of Bundaberg, secluded and uninhabited coral reefs and atolls dot the ocean for about 140km up to Tryon Island, east of Rockhampton.

Several cays in this part of the Reef are excellent for snorkelling, diving and just getting back to nature – though reaching them is generally more expensive than reaching islands nearer the coast. Some of the islands are important breeding grounds for turtles and seabirds, and visitors should be aware of precautions to ensure the wildlife's protection, outlined in the relevant NPRSR information sheets.

Camping is allowed on Lady Musgrave, Masthead and North West national park islands, and campers must be totally self sufficient. Numbers are limited, so it's advisable to apply well ahead for a camping permit. Contact **NPRSR** (☎13 74 68; www.nprsr.qld.gov.au; permit per person/family $5.45/21.80).

Access is from Town of 1770 and Gladstone.

Lady Elliot Island

On the southern frontier of the Great Barrier Reef, Lady Elliot is a 40-hectare vegetated coral cay popular with divers, snorkellers and nesting sea turtles and seabirds. Divers can walk straight off the beach to explore an ocean-bed of shipwrecks, coral gardens, bommies (coral pinnacles or outcroppings) and blowholes, and abundant marine life including barracuda, giant manta rays and harmless leopard sharks.

Lady Elliot Island is not a national park, and camping is not allowed; your only option is the low-key **Lady Elliot Island Resort** (☎1800 072 200; www.ladyelliot.com.au; per person $147-350). Accommodation is in tent cabins, simple motel-style units or more expensive two-bedroom, self-contained suites. Rates include breakfast and dinner, snorkelling gear and some tours.

The only way to reach the island is in a light aircraft. Resort guests are flown in from Bundaberg, the Gold Coast and Hervey Bay; flights are booked through the hotel. The resort also manages day trips; see their website for updates and info.

STINGERS

The potentially deadly chironex box jellyfish and irukandji, also known as sea wasps or marine stingers, occur in Queensland's coastal waters north of Agnes Water (and occasionally further south) from around October to April, and swimming is not advisable during these times. Fortunately, swimming and snorkelling are usually safe around the reef islands throughout the year; however, appearances of the rare and tiny (1cm to 2cm across) irukandji have been recorded on the outer Reef and islands. For more information on stingers and treatment, see p281.

Lady Musgrave Island

Wannabe castaways look no further. This tiny, 15-hectare cay, 100km northeast of Bundaberg, sits on the western rim of a stunning, turquoise-blue reef lagoon renowned for its safe swimming, snorkelling and diving. A squeaky white-sand beach fringes a dense canopy of pisonia forest brimming with roosting bird life, including terns, shearwaters and white-capped noddies. Birds nest from October to April while green turtles nest from November to February.

The uninhabited island is part of the Capricornia Cays National Park and there is a NPRSR camping ground on the island's west side; you must be totally self-sufficient and bring your own water. Numbers are limited to 40 at any one time, so apply well ahead for a permit with the **NPRSR** (☎13 74 68; www.nprsr.qld.gov.au; per person/family $5.45/21.80). Bring a gas stove; fires are not permitted on the island.

Day trips to Lady Musgrave depart from the Town of 1770 marina.

Heron & Wilson Islands

With the underwater reef world accessible directly from the beach, Heron Island is famed for superb scuba diving and snorkelling, although you'll need a fair amount of cash to visit. A true coral cay, it is densely vegetated with pisonia trees and surrounded by 24 sq km of reef. There's a resort and research station on the northeastern third of the island; the remainder is national park.

Heron Island Resort (☎1300 863 248; www.heronisland.com; d/suite/beach house from $419/669/909) has comfortable accommodation that is suited to families and couples; the Point Suites have the best views. Meal packages are extra, and guests will pay $50/25 (one way) per adult/child for launch transfer, $291 by seaplane, or $395 for helicopter transfer. All are from Gladstone.

Wilson Island (☎1300 863 248; www.wilsonisland.com; per couple $1100), also part of a national park, is an exclusive wilderness retreat with six permanent 'tents' and solar-heated showers. There are excellent beaches, superb snorkelling and, during the season, turtle-watching. The only access is from Heron Island and to get here, you'll need to buy a combined Wilson-Heron package and spend at least two nights on Wilson Island. Transfers between Wilson and Heron are included in the tariff.

North West Island

Behind North West's uninspiring name is a national park that's proving evermore popular with campers, walkers and those seeking a slice of seclusion. At 106 hectares, this is the second-biggest cay on the reef, and despite a dubious past (North West was once a guano mine and home to a turtle-soup cannery), is now an important site for nesting green turtles and birds; every October, hundreds of thousands of wedge-tailed shearwaters descend on the island to nest, squabble and scare the wits out of campers with their creepy nighttime howls.

There's a limit of 150 campers on the island at any one time; camping is closed from January 26 until Easter each year (day trips allowed year-round). There's no scheduled service to North West, but **Curtis Ferry Services** (07-4972 6990; www.curtisferryservices.com.au) can arrange a drop-off. **NPRSR** (13 74 68; www.nprsr.qld.gov.au) has more info on getting to the island, camping and essentials.

ROCKHAMPTON

POP 61,724

Welcome to Rockhampton ('Rocky' to its mates), where the hats, boots and utes are big…but the bulls are even bigger. With over 2.5 million cattle within a 250km radius of Rockhampton – it's called Australia's Beef Capital for a reason – it's no surprise the smell of bulldust hangs thick in the air. This sprawling country town is the administrative and commercial centre of central Queensland, its wide streets and fine Victorian-era buildings reflecting the region's prosperous 19th-century heyday of gold and copper mining and the beef-cattle industry.

Straddling the tropic of Capricorn, Rocky can be aptly scorching; it's 40km inland, lacks coastal sea breezes and summers are often unbearably humid. The town has a smattering of attractions but is best seen as the gateway to the coastal gems of Yeppoon and Great Keppel Island. Stay in the old part of town to enjoy some charming walks along the Fitzroy River.

Sights & Activities

★Botanic Gardens & Zoo GARDENS

(07-4932 9000; Spencer St; 6am-6pm) FREE Just south of town, these gardens are a beautiful oasis, with impressive figs, tropical and subtropical rainforest, landscaped gardens and lily-covered lagoons. The formal Japanese garden is a zen-zone of tranquillity, the **cafe** (open 8am to 5pm) serves tea and cakes under a giant banyan fig, and the awesome **free zoo** (open 8.30am to 4.30pm) has koalas, wombats, dingoes, apes, a walk-through aviary and tonnes more.

Tropic of Capricorn LANDMARK

(Gladstone Rd) Attitude on the latitude! Straddle the tropic of Capricorn at the visitor centre on Gladstone Rd; it's marked by a huge spire.

Quay Street STREET

In town, wander down this historic streetscape, with its grand sandstone Victorian-era buildings dating back to the gold-rush days. You can pick up leaflets that map out walking trails around Rockhampton from the visitor centres.

Rockhampton City Art Gallery GALLERY

(07-4936 8248; www.rockhamptonartgallery.com.au; 62 Victoria Pde; 10am-4pm) FREE Boasting an impressive collection of Australian paintings, this gallery includes works by Sir Russell Drysdale, Sir Sidney Nolan and Albert Namatjira. Contemporary Indigenous artist Judy Watson also has a number of works on display.

Dreamtime Cultural Centre CULTURAL CENTRE

(07-4936 1655; www.dreamtimecentre.com.au; Bruce Hwy; adult/child $14/6.50; 10am-3.30pm Mon-Fri, tours 10.30am) An easily accessible insight into Aboriginal and Torres Strait Islander heritage and history. The excellent 90-minute tours are hands on (throw your own boomerangs!) and appeal to all ages. About 7km north of the centre.

Heritage Village MUSEUM

(07-4936 8680; Bruce Hwy; adult/child/family $10.50/6.80/30.50; 9am-4pm) An active museum of replica historic buildings with townsfolk at work in period garb. There's also a visitor centre here. It's 10km north of the city centre.

Kershaw Gardens GARDEN

(07-4936 8254; via Charles St; 6am-6pm) FREE Just north of the Fitzroy River, this excellent botanical park is devoted to Australian native plants. Its attractions include artificial rapids, a rainforest area, a fragrant garden and heritage architecture.

Archer Park Rail Museum MUSEUM

(07-4922 2774; www.rockhamptonregion.qld.gov.au; Denison St; adult/child/family $8/5/26; 9am-4pm Sun-Fri) This museum is housed in a former train station built in 1899. Through photographs and displays it tells the station's story, and that of the unique Purrey steam tram. Take a ride on the restored tram (the only remaining one of its kind in the world!) every Sunday from 10am to 1pm.

Mt Archer MOUNTAIN

This mountain (604m) has walking trails weaving through eucalypts and rainforest abundant in wildlife. A brochure to the park is available from the visitor centres.

Tours

Little Johnny's Tours and Rentals TOUR
(☎ 0414 793 637; www.littlejohnnysrentals.com) Runs trips to many nearby attractions like Byfield and the Capricorn Caves, and also does minibus runs between Rockhampton Airport and Yeppoon.

Festivals & Events

Beef Australia AGRICULTURAL
(www.beefaustralia.com.au) Held every three years, this is a huge exposition of all things beefy.

Jazz on Quay Festival JAZZ
(www.jazzonquay.com.au) Held each spring along the Fitzroy River.

Sleeping

The northern and southern approach roads to Rocky are lined with numerous motels but if you want to stroll the elegant palm-lined streets overlooking the Fitzroy, choose somewhere in the old centre, south of the river.

Rockhampton Backpackers HOSTEL $
(☎ 07-4927 5288; www.rockhamptonbackpackers.com.au; 60 MacFarlane St; dm/d $22/60;) A YHA member, Rocky Backpackers has a spacious lounge and dining area, plus varied types of accommodation. They do it all, from arranging tours and courtesy pickups from the bus station to selling coach tickets. There's also free bike hire.

Southside Holiday Village CARAVAN PARK $
(☎ 07-4927 3013; www.sshv.com.au; Lower Dawson Rd; site unpowered/powered $30/38, cabin $72-93, villa $103-120;) One of the city's best caravan parks, with neat, self-contained cabins and villas, large grassed camp sites and a good kitchen. Prices are for two people. It's about 3km south of the centre on a busy main road.

Criterion HOTEL $$
(☎ 07-4922 1225; www.thecriterion.com.au; 150 Quay St; r $60-85, motel r $130-160;) The Criterion is Rockhampton's grandest old pub, with an elegant foyer and function room, a friendly bar and a great bistro (Bush Inn). Its top two stories have dozens of period rooms; the rooms have showers, although the toilets are down the hall. They also have a number of 4½-star motel rooms.

Coffee House MOTEL, APARTMENT $$
(☎ 07-4927 5722; www.coffeehouse.com.au; 51 William St; r $160-189;) The Coffee House features beautifully appointed motel rooms, self-contained apartments and spa suites. There's a popular, stylish cafe-restaurant–wine bar on site.

Eating & Drinking

★ **Ginger Mule** STEAKHOUSE $
(☎ 07-4927 7255; 8 William St; mains from $10; ⌚ 11.30am-midnight Wed & Thu, to 2am Fri, 4pm-2am Sat) Rocky's coolest eatery bills itself as a tapas bar, but everyone's here for one thing: steak! And bloody (or chargrilled) good steak it is too. They have regular

CAPRICORN CAVES

In the Berserker Range, 24km north of Rockhampton near the Caves township, the amazing **Capricorn Caves** (☎ 07-4934 2883; www.capricorncaves.com.au; 30 Olsens Caves Rd; adult/child $27/14; ⌚ 9am-4pm) are not to be missed. These ancient caves honeycomb a limestone ridge, and on a guided tour through the caverns and labyrinths you'll see cave coral, stalactites, dangling fig-tree roots and little insectivorous bats. The highlight of the one-hour 'cathedral tour' is the beautiful natural rock cathedral where a recording of 'Amazing Grace' is played to demonstrate the cavern's incredible acoustics. Every December, traditional Christmas carol singalongs are held in the cathedral. Also in December, around the summer solstice (1 December to 14 January), sunlight beams directly through a 14m vertical shaft into Belfry Cave, creating an electrifying light show. If you stand directly below the beam, reflected sunlight colours the whole cavern with whatever colour you're wearing.

Daring spelunkers can book a two-hour 'adventure tour' ($75) which takes you through tight spots with names such as 'Fat Man's Misery'. You must be at least 16 years old for this tour.

The Capricorn Caves complex has barbecue areas, a pool, kiosk, and **accommodation** (unpowered/powered site $30/35, cabin from $140).

late-week meals specials (including $10 steaks); pop down early or prepare to battle for a table. Morphs into a cocktail bar late in the evenings.

Saigon Saigon ASIAN $
(☎07-4927 0888; www.saigonbytheriver.com; Quay St; mains $12-20; ⏲11.30am-2.30pm & 5-9pm Wed-Mon) This two-storey bamboo hut overlooks the Fitzroy River and serves pan-Asian food with local ingredients like kangaroo and crocodile served in a sizzling steamboat. Not up for reptile? The menu is as intricate as the restaurant exterior's neon light display. There are lots of vegetarian options, too.

Steakhouse 98 SEAFOOD, STEAKHOUSE $$
(☎07-4920 1000; www.98.com.au; 98 Victoria Pde; mains $18-46; ⏲breakfast daily, lunch Mon-Fri, dinner Mon-Sat) In Rocky, it's all about the steak. And this licensed dining room doesn't disappoint with its Mod Oz takes on beef, as well as kangaroo, lamb and seafood. Sit inside or on the terrace overlooking the Fitzroy River. Attached to the Motel 98.

Pacino's ITALIAN $$
(☎07-4922 5833; cnr Fitzroy & George Sts; mains $25-40; ⏲dinner Tue-Sun) This stylish Italian restaurant oozes Mediterranean warmth with its wooden tables and potted fig trees. Pricey, though consistently popular for favourites such as osso bucco and pasta cooked a dozen different ways.

Heritage Hotel PUB $$
(☎07-4927 6996; www.theheritagehotel.com.au; cnr William & Quay St; meals $20-30; ⏲noon-3pm & 6-9pm Tue-Fri, 6-9pm Mon & Sat) This pub with sugarspun iron-lattice balconies has a cocktail lounge with river views and outdoor tables. The steak-heavy menu features other grilled meats billed under names like 'baaaah' and 'cluck cluck'. You'll work it out.

★ **Great Western Hotel** PUB
(☎07-4922 1862; www.greatwesternhotel.com.au; cnr Stanley & Denison Sts; ⏲10am-2am) Yeehaw! Looking like a spaghetti-western film set, this 1862 pub is home to Rocky's cowboys and 'gals. Out the back there's a rodeo arena where every Wednesday and Friday night you can watch brave cattlefolk being tossed in the air by bucking bulls and broncos. Touring bands occasionally rock here; you can get tickets online.

ℹ Information

Rockhampton Library (☎07-4936 8265; 230 Bolsover St; ⏲9am-5.30pm Mon, Tue, Thu, Fri, to 8pm Wed, to 4.30pm Sat) Free internet access, but you need to book.

Tropic of Capricorn Visitor Centre (☎1800 676 701; Gladstone Rd; ⏲9am-5pm) Helpful centre on the highway right beside the tropic of Capricorn marker, 3km south of the centre. Its sister branch is the Rockhampton visitor centre (☎1800 805 865; 208 Quay St; ⏲8.30am-

RINGERS & COWBOYS: FARM STAYS

Kick up some red dust on a fair-dinkum Aussie outback cattle station and find out the difference between a jackeroo, a ringer, a stockman and a cowboy. On a farm stay, you'll be immersed in the daily activities of a working cattle station, riding horses and motorbikes, mustering cattle, fencing, and cooking damper and billy tea over a campfire. Before you know it you'll find yourself looking for a ute and a blue dog to go with your RM Williams boots and Akubra hat.

Myella Farm Stay (☎07-4998 1290; www.myella.com; Baralaba Rd; 2/4 days $260/480, day trips $120; ❄@≋), 125km southwest of Rockhampton, gives you a taste of the outback on its 10.6-sq-km farm. The package includes bush explorations by horseback, motorcycle and 4WD, all meals, accommodation in a renovated homestead with polished timber floors and a wide verandah, farm clothes and free transfers from Rockhampton. You get to do bushie stuff like fix fences, dowse for water and help care for orphaned joeys at the station's kangaroo rehab centre.

The **Kroombit Lochenbar Cattle Station** (☎07-4992 2186; www.kroombit.com.au; dm $27, d with/without bathroom $86/78, 2-day & 2-night package per person incl room, meals & activities $280; ❄@≋) offers several farm-stay packages to choose from and you can pitch a tent or stay in bush-timber or upmarket cabins. While soaking up the Aussie experience you can learn to crack a whip, throw a boomerang or loop a lasso, and earn your spurs on a mechanical bucking bull. Rates include meals and pick-up from nearby Biloela.

4.30pm Mon-Fri, 9am-4pm Sat & Sun) in the beautiful former Customs House in central Rocky. Both centres also serve as branches for the NPRSR.

Getting There & Away

AIR

Qantas (13 13 13; www.qantas.com.au) and **Virgin** (13 67 89; www.virginaustralia.com) connect Rockhampton with various cities. The airport is about 6km from the centre of town.

BUS

Greyhound Australia (1300 473 946; www.greyhound.com.au) has regular services from Rocky to Mackay ($60, four hours), Brisbane ($155, 11 hours) and Cairns ($195, 17 hours). All services stop at the **Mobil roadhouse** (91 George St). **Premier Motor Service** (13 34 10; www.premierms.com.au) operates a Brisbane–Cairns service, stopping at Rockhampton.

Young's Bus Service (07-4922 3813; www.youngsbusservice.com.au; 171 Bolsover St) travels to Yeppoon and Mt Morgan ($6.40 one way) Monday to Friday. Buses depart from Bolsover St, outside the police station.

TRAIN

Queensland Rail (1800 872 467; www.queenslandrailtravel.com.au) runs the *Tilt Train*, which connects Rockhampton with Brisbane (from $135, 8 hours, Sunday to Friday) and Cairns (from $322, 16 hours, twice weekly). Rocky's a great gateway to Queensland's dusty interior: hop the twice-weekly *Spirit of the Outback* to bush towns including Longreach (from $145, 14 hours) or Emerald (from $75, five hours). The train station is 450m southwest of the city centre.

Getting Around

Sunbus (www.sunbus.com.au) runs a reasonably comprehensive city bus network operating all day Monday to Friday and Saturday morning; pick up a timetable at the visitor centre. Otherwise, there's always **Rocky Cabs** (13 10 08).

YEPPOON

POP 13,500

Pretty little Yeppoon is a small seaside town with a long beach, a calm ocean and an attractive hinterland of volcanic outcrops, pineapple patches and grazing lands. The handful of quiet streets, sleepy motels and beachside cafes attracts Rockhamptonites beating the heat, and tourists heading for Great Keppel Island only 13km offshore.

Sights & Activities

Cruises and the ferry to Great Keppel Island depart from the Keppel Bay Marina at Rosslyn Bay, just south of Yeppoon.

Cooberrie Park WILDLIFE RESERVE

(07-4939 7590; www.cooberriepark.com.au; Woodbury Rd; adult/child/family $25/15/65; 10am-3pm, animal show 1pm) About 15km north of Yeppoon, Cooberrie Park is a small wildlife sanctuary on 10 hectares of bushland. You can see kangaroos, wallabies and peacocks wandering freely through the grounds. You can also feed the critters and, for an extra cost, hold a furry koala or some slithering reptiles.

Funtastic Cruises CRUISE

(0438 909 502; www.funtasticcruises.com; full-day cruise adult/child/family $98/80/350) Funtastic Cruises operates full-day snorkelling trips on board its 17m catamaran, with a two-hour stopover on Great Keppel Island, morning and afternoon tea, and all snorkelling equipment included. It can also organise camping drop-offs to islands en route.

Sail Capricornia CRUISE

(0402 102 373; www.sailcapricornia.com.au; full day cruise incl lunch adult/child $115/75) Sail Capricornia offers snorkelling cruises on board the *Grace* catamaran, as well as sunset ($55) and three-day ($499) cruises.

Sleeping

There are beaches, caravan parks, motels and holiday units along the 19km coastline running south from Yeppoon to Emu Park. A fairly complete listing can be found at www.yeppooninfo.com.au.

Coral Inn Flashpackers HOSTEL $

(07-4939 2925; www.flashpackers.net.au; 14 Maple St; dm $29, d from $90;) Reef-bright colours and vibrant communal spaces make Coral Inn a difficult place to leave. All rooms have en suites, and there's a great communal kitchen. Parking is an extra $5, and there's absolutely no smoking anywhere on the property.

Beachside Caravan Park CARAVAN PARK $

(07-4939 3738; Farnborough Rd; unpowered/powered site $25/30-34) This basic but neat little camping ground north of the town centre commands a wonderful, totally beachfront location. It has good amenities and grassed sites with some shade but no cabins or on-site vans. Rates are for two people.

Surfside Motel MOTEL $$
(07-4939 1272; 30 Anzac Pde; r $110-140;) Across the road from the beach and close to town, this 1950s strip of lime-green motel units epitomises summer holidays at the beach. And it's terrific value – the rooms are spacious and unusually well equipped, complete with toaster, hair dryer and free wi-fi.

Driftwood Units UNIT $$
(07-4939 2446; www.driftwoodunits.com.au; 5-7 Todd Ave; unit $120-140;) Driftwood has huge self-contained units at motel prices with absolute beach frontage. Great for families, or anyone in need of a seaside slowdown. If you're too lazy to stagger a few steps to the beach, there's a nice saltwater pool on-site.

While Away B&B B&B $$
(07-4939 5719; www.whileawaybandb.com.au; 44 Todd Ave; s/d incl breakfast $115/140-155;) With four good-sized rooms and an immaculately clean house with wheelchair access, this B&B is a perfect, quiet getaway. There are complimentary nibbles, tea, coffee, port and sherry as well as generous breakfasts.

Eating & Drinking

Flour CAFE $
(07-4925 0725; 9 Normanby St; pastries $3.50, breakfast $8.50; 8am-3pm Mon-Fri, to 2pm Sat) Adorable smalltown cafe with big-city breakfasts and melt-in-mouth cakes. Loads of gluten-free options, and without a doubt the best coffee for miles.

Thai Take-Away THAI $$
(07-4939 3920; 24 Anzac Pde; mains $14-32; 6-10pm) A deservedly popular Thai BYO restaurant where you can sit outside on the sidewalk, catch a sea breeze, and satisfy those chilli and coconut cravings. There's a large selection of seafood dishes and snappy service.

Strand Hotel PUB $$
(07-4939 1301; Normanby St; mains from $14; 11.30am-2.30pm & 5.30-9pm Mon-Fri, 8am-9pm Sat & Sun) This is upmarket pub food with classic/exotic pizzas ($14 to $24) and fantastic steaks ($28 to $41). It's famous for its Sunday evening (6pm to 7.30pm) *parrilla*, an Argentinian barbecue, with music to match.

Megalomania FUSION $$
(07-4939 2333; Arthur St; mains $22-36; noon-3pm & 5.30-9pm Tue-Sat, to 3pm Sun) An urban-island feel permeates Yeppoon's best restaurant, which serves up Oz-Asian fusion cuisine with interesting takes on local seafood. Loll beneath the fig tree or clink silverware in the indoor woodsy surrounds.

Footlights Theatre Restaurant COMEDY
(07-4939 2399; www.footlights.com.au; 123 Rockhampton Rd; dinner & show $51) Footlights Theatre Restaurant hosts a three-course meal and a two-hour comedy-variety show every Friday and Saturday night.

Information

The **Capricorn Coast visitor centre** (1800 675 785; www.capricorncoast.com.au; Ross Creek Roundabout; 9am-5pm) has plenty of information on the Capricorn Coast and Great Keppel Island, and can book accommodation and tours.

Yeppoon library (07-4939 3433; 78 John St; 9am-5pm Mon, Tue, Thu & Fri, to 8pm Wed, to 4pm Sat) has free internet access; bookings essential.

Getting There & Away

Yeppoon is 43km northeast of Rockhampton. **Young's Bus Service** (07-4922 3813; www.youngsbusservice.com.au) runs frequent buses from Rockhampton ($6.40 one way) to Yeppoon and down to the Keppel Bay Marina.

If you're heading for Great Keppel or the Reef, some ferry operators will transport you between your accommodation and Keppel Bay Marina. If you're driving, there's a free day car park at the marina. For secure undercover parking, the **Great Keppel Island Security Car Park** (07-4933 6670; 422 Scenic Hwy; per day from $15) is on the Scenic Hwy south of Yeppoon, by the turn-off to the marina.

AROUND YEPPOON

The drive south from Yeppoon and Rosslyn Bay passes three fine headlands with good views: **Double Head**, **Bluff Point** and **Pinnacle Point**. After Pinnacle Point, the road crosses **Causeway Lake**, a saltwater inlet that's a top spot for estuary fishing. **Emu Park** (population 2021), 19km south of Yeppoon, is the second-largest township on the coast, but there's not much here, apart from more good views and the **Singing Ship**

WORTH A TRIP

BYFIELD

The staggeringly beautiful Byfield National Park is a diverse playground of mammoth sand dunes, thick semi-tropical rainforest, wetlands and rocky pinnacles. It's superb Sunday-arvo driving terrain, with plenty of hiking paths and isolated beaches to warrant a longer stay. There are five **camping grounds** (☎13 74 68; www.nprsr.qld.gov.au; per person/family $5.85/21.80) to choose from (pre-book). Nine Mile Beach and Five Rocks are on the beach and you'll need a 4WD to access them. When conditions are right, there's decent surf at Nine Mile.

Get to know the rainforest on a silent, electric boat cruise with **Waterpark Eco-Tours** (☎07-4935 1171; www.waterparkecotours.com; 201 Waterpark Creek Rd; 2-3hr tour $25, cabins $120), run out of a working tea-tree plantation.

Byfield Mountain Retreat (☎07-4935 1161; www.byfieldmountainretreat.com; 216 Arnolds Rd; per night/week $220/1200) is set on 66 acres of rich rainforest with heady hinterland views. The home sleeps 12, and there's a log fire, walking trails and king-sized beds. The retreat is attached to **Nob Creek Pottery** (☎07-4935 1161; www.nobcreekpottery.com.au; 216 Arnolds Rd; ⏲10am-4pm) FREE, a working pottery and gallery showcasing hand-blown glass, woodwork and jewellery; the handmade ceramics are outstanding.

Signposted just north of Byfield, **Ferns Hideaway** (☎07-4935 1235; www.fernshideaway.com; 67 Cahills Rd, Byfield; unpowered site per person $15, cabins $150; ❄🏊) is a secluded bush oasis with cabins, a camping ground, canoeing and nature walks. The homestead has a cosy **restaurant** (mains $20-38; ⏲lunch Fri & Sun, lunch & dinner Sat), replete with a log fire, hearty, heartwarming meals and live music on the weekends.

Byfield General Store (☎07-4935 1190; Byfield Rd; ⏲8am-6pm Wed-Mon) has fuel, basic grocery supplies and a simple courtyard cafe serving pies, sandwiches and highly recommended burgers. It doubles as an information centre.

The park is a 40km drive north from Yeppoon. North of Byfield, the Shoalwater Bay military training area borders the forest and park, and is strictly off limits.

memorial to Captain Cook – a curious monument of drilled tubes and pipes that emit mournful whistling and moaning sounds in the breeze. **Emus Beach Resort** (☎07-4939 6111; www.emusbeachresort.com; 92 Pattison St, Emu Park; dm $25-28, d/tr/q $80/95/105; ❄@🏊) is a superlative hostel, with a pool, kitchen, barbecue and a travel booking service; it also offers tours to the local crocodile farm. Otherwise, **Bell Park Caravan Park** (☎07-4939 6202; www.bellparkcaravanpark.com.au; Pattinson St; unpowered/powered site $25/30, cabin $107) is just stone's throw from the beach.

Emu Park Pizza & Pasta (☎07-4938 7333; Hill St; pizzas $12-24; ⏲ 4.30-9pm) is an unprepossessing place, but the pizzas attract locals from Yeppoon.

Situated 15km along the Emu Park–Rockhampton road, the **Koorana Crocodile Farm** (☎07-4934 4749; www.koorana.com.au; Coowonga Rd; adult/child $27/12; ⏲tours 10.30am & 1pm) can only be explored via the informative guided tours. After watching the man-eaters splash and dash frighteningly around, get your feeble human revenge by sampling croc kebabs, croc ribs or a croc pie at the restaurant.

GREAT KEPPEL ISLAND

Great Keppel Island is a stunning island with rocky headlands, forested hills and a fringe of powdery white sand lapped by clear azure waters. Numerous 'castaway' beaches ring the 14-sq-km island, while natural bushland covers 90% of the interior. A string of huts and accommodation options sits behind the trees lining the main beach but the developments are low-key and relatively unobtrusive. Only 13km offshore, and with good snorkelling, swimming and bush walking, Great Keppel is an easily accessible, tranquil island retreat.

The kiosk at Great Keppel Island Holiday Village has a few essentials, but if you want to cook, bring your own supplies.

Great Keppel Island

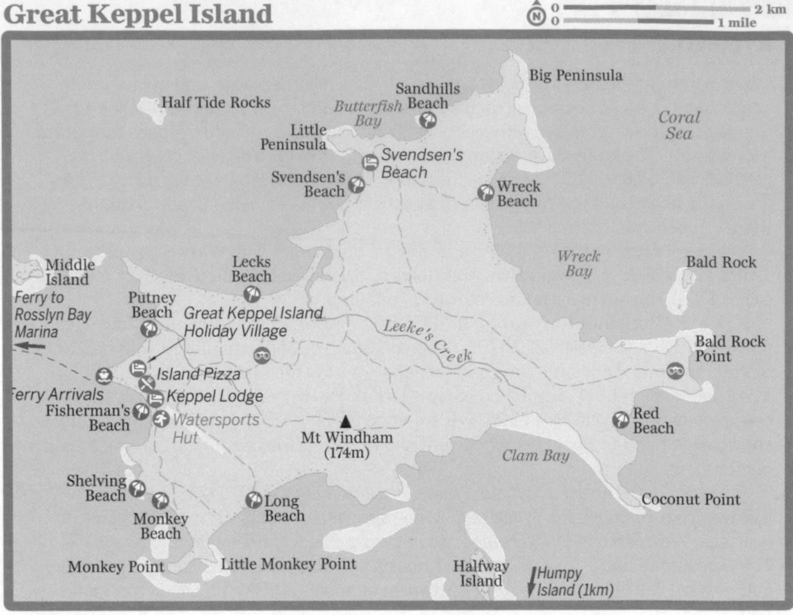

Sights

The beaches of Great Keppel rate among Queensland's best. Take a short stroll from **Fisherman's Beach**, the main beach, and you'll find your own deserted stretch of white sand. There is fairly good coral and excellent fish life, especially between Great Keppel and Humpy Island to the south. A 30-minute walk south around the headland brings you to **Monkey Beach**, where there's good snorkelling. A walking trail from the southern end of the airfield takes you to **Long Beach**, perhaps the best of the island's beaches.

There are several bushwalking tracks from Fisherman's Beach; the longest and perhaps the most difficult leads to the 2.5m 'lighthouse' near **Bald Rock Point** on the far side of the island. It's about three hours return.

Activities & Tours

Watersports Hut WATER SPORTS
(07-4925 0624; Putney Beach; Sat & Sun & school holidays) The Watersports Hut on the main beach hires out snorkelling equipment, kayaks and catamarans, and runs tube rides.

Freedom Fast Cats CRUISE
(07-4933 6888; www.freedomfastcats.com; Keppel Bay Marina, Rosslyn Bay; adult/child from $75/48) Operates a range of island tours, from glass-bottomed boat viewing to snorkelling and boom-netting.

Sleeping

★ **Svendsen's Beach** CABIN $$
(07-4938 3717; www.svendsensbeach.com; cabins per 3 nights per person $330) This secluded boutique retreat has two luxury tent-bungalows on separate elevated timber decks overlooking lovely Svendsen's Beach. It's an eco-friendly operation, run on solar and wind power; there's even a bush-bucket shower. It's the perfect place for snorkelling, bushwalking and romantic getaways. Transfers from the ferry drop-off on Fisherman's Beach are included in the tariff.

Great Keppel Island Holiday Village HOSTEL, CABIN $$
(07-4939 8655; www.gkiholidayvillage.com.au; dm $35, s & d tent $90, cabin $150, house from $230) The village offers various types of good budget accommodation (dorms, cabins, decked tents), as well as entire houses. It's a friendly, relaxed place with shared bathrooms, a decent communal kitchen and barbecue area.

Snorkelling gear is free and they run motorised canoe trips to top snorkelling spots.

Keppel Lodge GUESTHOUSE **$$**
(☎07-4939 4251; www.keppellodge.com.au; Fisherman's Beach; d per person $65-75, house $520-600; @) A pleasant open-plan house with four large bedrooms (with bathrooms) branching from a large communal lounge and kitchen. The house is available in its entirety – ideal for a group booking – or as individual suites.

Eating

Bring all supplies; there is only one restaurant and no supermarkets on the island.

Island Pizza PIZZERIA **$**
(☎07-4939 4699; The Esplanade; dishes $6-30; ⊙varies) This friendly place prides itself on its gourmet pizzas with plenty of toppings. Check blackboard for opening times.

Getting There & Away

Freedom Fast Cats (☎07-4933 6888; www.freedomfastcats.com) departs from the Keppel Bay Marina in Rosslyn Bay (7km south of Yeppoon) for Great Keppel Island each morning, returning that same afternoon (call ahead for exact times). The return fare is $52/33/150 per adult/child/family. If you've booked accommodation on the island, check that someone will meet you on the beach to help with your luggage.

OTHER KEPPEL BAY ISLANDS

Although you can make day trips to the fringing coral reefs of **Middle Island** or **Halfway Island** from Great Keppel Island (ask your accommodation or at Great Keppel Island Holiday Village), you can also camp (per person/family $5.85/21.80) on several national park islands, including **Humpy Island**, **Middle Island**, **North Keppel Island** and **Miall Island**. Take your own supplies and water. For information and permits contact the **NPRSR** (☎13 74 68; www.nprsr.qld.gov.au) or **Rosslyn Bay Marine Parks** (☎07-4933 6595).

The otherwise glamorous **Pumpkin Island** was temporarily renamed **XXXX Island**, after being leased until 2015 by the Queensland brewing giant; at the time of research unless you have any luck with a 'specially marked' box of beer, you are not allowed to visit.

From Rosslyn Bay, **Funtastic Cruises** (☎0438 909 502; www.funtasticcruises.com; cruise adult/child $98/80) offers day cruises exploring the islands and can also provide drop-offs and pick-ups for campers.

Whitsunday Coast

Includes ➡

Best Places to Eat

- Mr Bones (p211)
- Spice n Flavour (p198)
- Fish D'vine (p210)
- Jochheims Pies (p216)
- Kevin's Place (p199)

Best Places to Stay

- Qualia (p214)
- Whitsunday Island camping grounds (p216)
- Platypus Bushcamp (p202)
- Kipara (p208)
- Fernandos Hideaway (p200)

Why Go?

Speckling the calm waters of the Coral Sea, the superlative Whitsunday Islands are one of Australia's greatest natural attractions. Opal-jade waters and pure-white beaches fringe the forested domes of these 'drowned mountains', where you can camp in secluded bays, laze in resorts, snorkel, dive or island-hop through the archipelago. Beneath the shimmering seas, tropical fish swarm through the world's largest coral garden in the Great Barrier Reef Marine Park. The gateway to the islands, Airlie Beach, is a happening backpacker hub with a continuous parade of tanned, happy faces zinging between boats, beaches and banging nightclubs.

South of Airlie, Mackay is a typical coastal Queensland town with palm-lined streets framed by art deco buildings. There's not a lot to do here, but Mackay is a handy base for trips to Finch Hatton Gorge and Eungella National Park – lush hinterland oases where platypuses cavort in the wild. To the north, Bowen has secret beaches and historical street art.

When to Go

Mackay

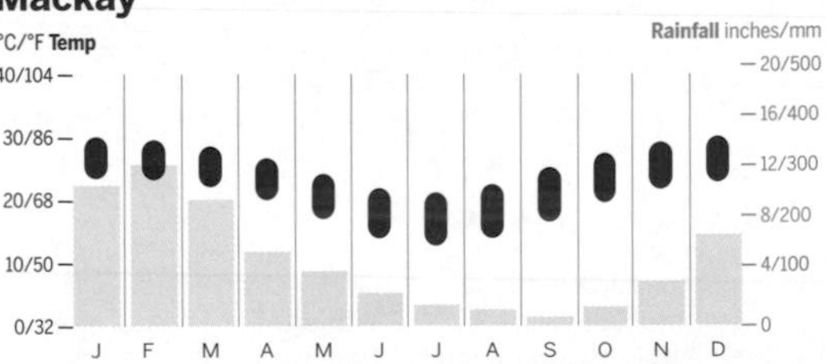

Jun–Oct The perfect time to enjoy sunny skies, calm days, mild weather and stinger-free seas.

Aug Sailboats skim across the water, and parties are held during Airlie Beach Race Week.

Sep–Oct Optimal conditions for kayaking around the islands.

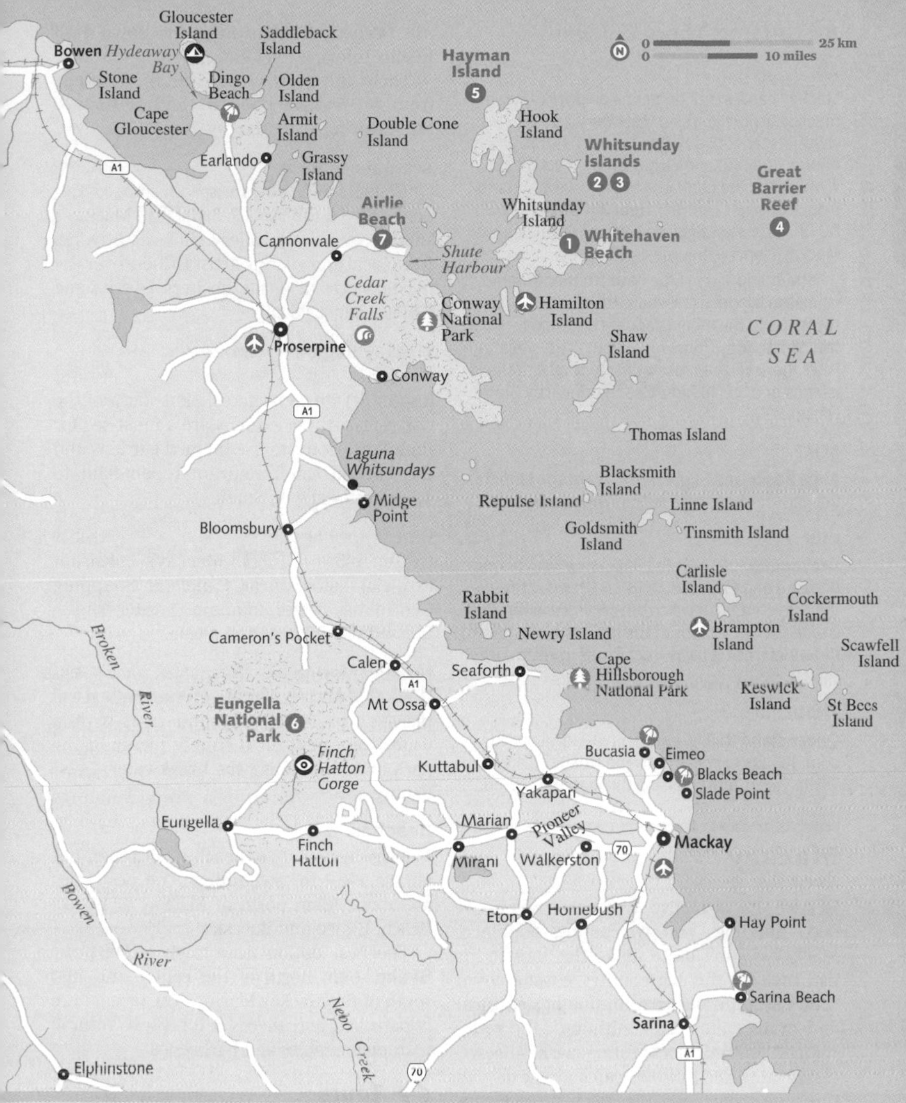

Whitsunday Coast Highlights

1 Being dazzled by the bright-white silica sand at stunning **Whitehaven Beach** (p215).

2 Sailing through the magnificent aquamarine waters of the **Whitsunday Islands** (p203).

3 Camping under the stars, hiking nature trails and making like an island castaway in the **Whitsunday Islands National Park** (p207).

4 Diving and snorkelling the fringing reefs or the outer **Great Barrier Reef** (p204).

5 Sipping cocktails by the pool at the luxurious tropical island resort of **Hayman Island** (p215).

6 Waiting patiently for a glimpse of a shy platypus and walking in the misty rainforest at **Eungella National Park** (p201).

7 Getting wet, swilling beer and partying hard in fun-lovin' **Airlie Beach** (p208).

Getting There & Away

AIR

Mackay has a major domestic **airport** (www.mackayairport.com.au). **Jetstar** (13 15 38; www.jetstar.com.au), **Qantas** (13 13 13; www.qantas.com.au) and **Virgin Blue** (13 67 89; www.virginblue.com.au) have regular flights to/from the major centres. **Tiger Airways** (02-8073 3421; www.tigerairways.com.au) flies to Mackay from Melbourne and Sydney.

Jetstar and Virgin Blue have frequent flights to Hamilton Island, from where there are boat/air transfers to the other islands. They also fly into the Whitsunday Coast Airport on the mainland; from there you can take a charter flight to the islands or a bus to Airlie Beach or nearby Shute Harbour.

BOAT

Airlie Beach and Shute Harbour are the launching pads for boat trips to the Whitsundays.

BUS

Greyhound (1300 473 946; www.greyhound.com.au) and **Premier** (13 34 10; www.premierms.com.au) have coach services along the Bruce Hwy with stops at the major towns. They detour off the highway from Proserpine to Airlie Beach.

TRAIN

Queensland Rail (www.queenslandrailtravel.com.au) has services between Brisbane and Townsville/Cairns passing through the region.

Mackay

POP 85,399

Despite its attractive tropical streets, art deco buildings and welcoming populace, Mackay doesn't quite make the tourist hit list. Instead, this big country coastal town caters more to the surrounding agricultural and mining industries. Although the redeveloped marina does entice with alfresco restaurants and outdoor cafes along its picturesque promenade, Mackay is more a convenient base for excursions out of town. It's only a 1½-hour drive to the Whitsundays, a short flight or charter boat to the pretty Cumberland Islands and a scenic jaunt past the sugar-cane fields to Pioneer Valley and Eungella National Park.

Sights

Mackay's impressive **art deco architecture** owes much to a devastating cyclone in 1918, which flattened many of the town's buildings. Enthusiasts should pick up a copy of *Art Deco in Mackay* from the Town Hall Visitor Information Centre.

There are good views over the harbour from **Mt Basset Lookout** and at **Rotary Lookout** in North Mackay.

Artspace Mackay GALLERY
(07-4961 9722; www.artspacemackay.com.au; Gordon St; 10am-5pm Tue-Sun) FREE Mackay's small regional art gallery showcases works from local and visiting artists. Chew over the masterpieces at onsite noshery **Foodspace** (9am-3pm Tue-Sun).

Mackay Regional Botanical Gardens GARDENS
(Lagoon St) On 33 hectares, 3km south of the city centre, these gardens are a must-see for flora fans. Home to five themed gardens and the Lagoon cafe/restaurant (open 9am to 4pm Wednesday to Sunday).

Bluewater Lagoon LAGOON
(9am-5.45pm) FREE Mackay's pleasant artificial lagoon near Caneland Shopping Centre has water fountains, water slides, grassed picnic areas and a cafe.

Mackay Marina MARINA
(Mackay Harbour) The lively marina is a pleasant place to wine and dine with a waterfront view, or to simply picnic in the park and stroll along the breakwater. Good fishing, too.

Beaches

Mackay has plenty of beaches, although not all are ideal for swimming. The best ones are about 16km north of Mackay at Blacks Beach, Eimeo and Bucasia.

The best option near town is **Harbour Beach**, 6km north of the centre and just south of the Mackay Marina. The beach here is patrolled and there's a foreshore reserve with picnic tables and barbecues.

Tours

Farleigh Sugar Mill TOUR
(07-4959 8360; 2hr tour adult/child $25/13; 9.30am & 1pm May-Dec) In the cane-crushing season, you can see how sugar cane is turned into sweet crystals. Dress appropriately for a working mill: long sleeves, long pants, enclosed shoes. Morning/afternoon tea included.

Reeforest Adventure Tours CULTURAL TOUR
(1800 500 353; www.reeforest.com) Offers a wide range of junkets, including a platypus

Central Mackay

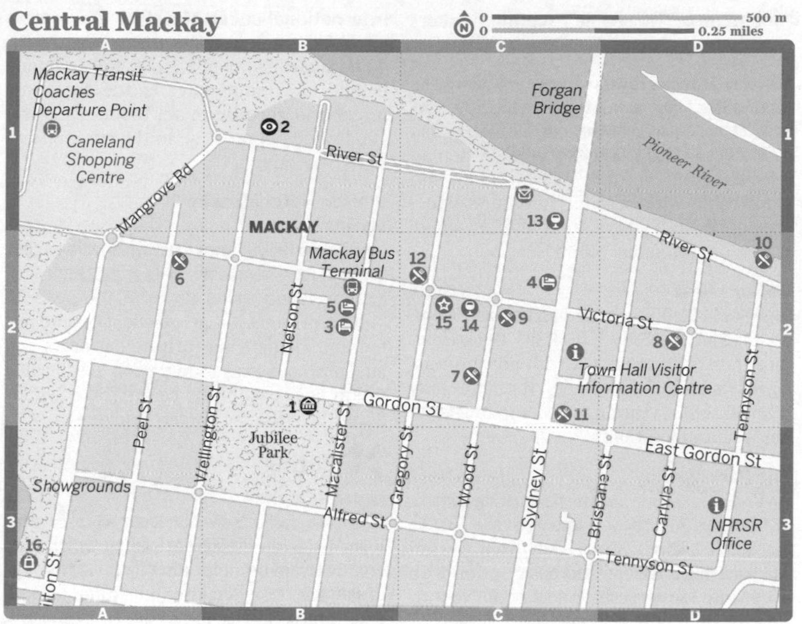

and rainforest ecosafari and two-day Eungella tours.

Heritage Walk WALKING
(☎07-4944 5888; ⌚9am Wed May-Sep) FREE Weekly wandering (1½ to two hours) that takes in the sights and secrets of ye olde Mackay. Leaves from the visitor centre at the Old Town Hall, Sydney St.

Festivals

Wintermoon Folk Festival MUSIC
(www.wintermoonfestival.com) Folk and world-music lovefest every May.

Sleeping

There are plenty of motels strung along busy Nebo Rd, south of the centre. The budget options (from around $110 for a double) post their prices out front and tend to suffer from road noise.

★**Stoney Creek Farmstay** FARM STAY $
(☎07-4954 1177; www.stoneycreekfarmstay.com; Peak Downs Hwy; dm/livery stable/cottage $25/100/145) This bush retreat (32km south of Mackay) is a down'n'dirty option in the best possible way. Stay in an endearingly ramshackle cottage, the rustic livery stable or the charismatic Dead Horse Hostel, and forget all about the mod-cons for a while: this is deadset bush livin'. Three-hour horse rides cost $95 per person. The owners will pick you up if you ring ahead

Central Mackay

Sights
1 Artspace Mackay ... B2
2 Bluewater Lagoon ... B1

Sleeping
3 Coral Sands Motel ... B2
4 Gecko's Rest ... C2
5 International Lodge Motel ... B2

Eating
6 Austral Hotel ... A2
7 Burp Eat Drink ... C2
8 Comet Coffee ... D2
Foodspace ... (see 1)
9 Kevin's Place ... C2
10 Maria's Donkey ... D2
11 Oscar's on Sydney ... C2
12 Spice n Flavour ... C2

Drinking & Nightlife
13 Ambassador Hotel ... C1
14 Gordi's Cafe & Bar ... C2

Entertainment
15 Tryst ... C2

Shopping
16 Markets ... A3

(minimum of two people). Willing Workers on Organic Farms (WWOOFs) welcome.

Mackay Marine Tourist Park CARAVAN PARK **$**
(07-4955 1496; www.mmtp.com.au; 379 Harbour Rd; unpowered/powered site $30/34, budget cabin $95, villa $110-150;) A step up from the usual caravan parks: all cabins and villas come with private patios and widescreen TVs, and you've gotta love anywhere with a giant jumping pillow.

Gecko's Rest HOSTEL **$**
(07-4944 1230; www.geckosrest.com.au; 34 Sydney St; dm/d/f $28/65/100;) Gecko's almost bursts at the seams with adventurous travellers and mine workers. It ain't exactly schmick, but it's the only hostel in town and has a central location.

The Park Mackay CARAVAN PARK **$**
(07-4952 1211; www.theparkmackay.com.au; 284 Farrellys Rd; unpowered/powered site $31/33, villa $85-120;) About 7km from central Mackay, this is a clean and basic option with an on-site kiosk, barbies and pool. No surprises – good or bad – here.

Coral Sands Motel MOTEL **$$**
(07-4951 1244; www.coralsandsmotel.com.au; 44 Macalister St; r $130-165;) One of Mackay's better midrange options, the Coral Sands boasts ultra-friendly management and large rooms in a central location. It's a bit tropi-kitsch, but with the river, shops, pubs and cafes so close to your doorstep, you won't care.

Ocean Resort Village RESORT **$$**
(1800 075 144; www.oceanresortvillage.com.au; 5 Bridge Rd; studio/family unit/2br unit from $90/100/135;) This is a good-value beachside resort set amid tropical gardens. The cool, shady setting has two pools, barbecue areas, half-court tennis and the occasional possum drop-in. The village is located 4km southeast of the town centre (take Gordon to Goldsmith to Bridge).

SUMMER STING: WHERE TO SWIM?

The presence of marine stingers means swimming in the sea isn't advisable between October and May unless you wear a stinger suit. In Airlie Beach, the gorgeous lagoon (p208) on the foreshore provides year-round safe swimming.

International Lodge Motel MOTEL **$$**
(07-4951 1022; www.internationallodge.com.au; 40 Macalister St; r from $120;) Hidden behind an unimpressive facade are clean, bright and cheerful motel rooms. This is a good-value option close to the city's restaurants and bars.

Clarion Hotel Mackay Marina LUXURY HOTEL **$$$**
(07-4955 9400; www.mackaymarinahotel.com; Mulherin Dr; d from $285;) This welcoming luxury hotel down at the peaceful marina precinct has an excellent on-site restaurant, kitchenettes, private balconies and an enormous swimming pool. It's located 6.5km northeast of the centre. Take Sydney St north across the Forgan Bridge.

Eating

Maria's Donkey TAPAS **$**
(07-4957 6055; 8 River St; tapas $8-15; noon-10pm Wed & Thu, to midnight Fri-Sun) Quirky, energetic riverfront joint dishing up tapas, jugs of sangria, occasional live music and general good times. Service is erratic, but somehow, that's part of the charm.

Comet Coffee CAFE **$**
(0423 420 195; 43 Victoria St; sandwiches $7-9; 5.30am-3pm Mon-Fri, 9am-noon Sat & Sun) Mackay's best drop is served in an old garage in the quiet end of town. Rifle through the magazine collection and munch on a magnificent muffin or pastrami-pickle-Swiss-cheese sanga.

Oscar's on Sydney FUSION **$**
(07-4944 0173; cnr Sydney & Gordon Sts; mains $10-23; 7am-5pm Mon-Fri, to 4pm Sat, 8am-4pm Sun) The delicious *poffertjes* (Dutch pancakes with traditional toppings) are still going strong at this very popular corner cafe, but don't be afraid to give the other dishes a go. Top spot for breakfast.

★ **Spice n Flavour** INDIAN **$$**
(07-4999 9639; 162 Victoria St; mains $15-25, banquets per person from $35; 11.30am-2.30pm Mon-Fri, 5.30pm-late daily) Chilli lovers disappointed by what passes for 'hot' in other Indian restaurants will get their fill of mouth-burning here (by request). All the favourites and some more exotic tastes are on the menu, and they offer drink-pairing advice for the unsure. Come what may, you must try the mango beer.

Kevin's Place ASIAN $$
(☎07-4953 5835; 79 Victoria St; mains $16-27; ⊙lunch & dinner Mon-Fri, dinner Sat) Sizzling, spicy Singaporean dishes and efficient, revved-up staff combine with the building's colonial ambience and the tropical climate to create a Rafflesesque experience.

Austral Hotel PUB $$
(☎07-4951 3288; 189 Victoria St; mains $19-36, steaks $24-47; ⊙noon-2.30pm & 6-9pm) So many steaks. Such little time.

Burp Eat Drink MODERN AUSTRALIAN $$$
(☎07-4951 3546; www.burp.net.au; 86 Wood St; mains from $33; ⊙11.30am-3pm & 6pm-late Tue-Fri, 6pm-late Sat) A swish Melbourne-style restaurant in the tropics, Burp has a small but tantalising menu. Sophisticated selections include pork belly with scallops, kaffir-lime-crusted soft shell crab, plus some serious steaks.

Drinking & Nightlife

Gordi's Cafe & Bar PUB
(85 Victoria St) Gordi's is a street-side watering hole known locally as the unrivalled pre-party or post-work meeting place.

Ambassador Hotel BAR
(☎07-4953 3233; www.ambassadorhotel.net.au; 2 Sydney St; ⊙5pm-late Thu, 4pm-late Fri-Sun) Art deco outside, wild'n'crazy inside. Multilevel carousing, including Mackay's only rooftop bar.

Sails Sports Bar BAR
(☎07-4955 3677; Mulherin Dr, Mackay Harbour; ⊙10am-midnight) This themed bar can get rowdy at night, but it's a great place on Sunday arvo with live music and a marina outlook.

Tryst CLUB
(99 Victoria St; ⊙10pm-4am Thu-Sat) Frenetic dance club hosting a mix of resident and guest-star DJs.

Shopping

Markets MARKET
They like their markets in Mackay, with a surprisingly varied bunch of bazaars selling everything from bric-a-brac to one-off duds to organic fruit. Try the **Mackay Showgrounds Markets** (Saturdays from 7.30am, Milton St), **Twilight Markets** (first Friday of the month from 5pm to 9pm, Mackay Surf Club) and the **Troppo Market** (second Sunday of the month from 7.30am, Mt Pleasant Shopping Centre carpark).

Information

The train station, airport, botanic gardens and visitor centre are about 3km south of the city centre. Mackay Harbour, 6km northeast of the centre, is dominated by a massive sugar terminal, while the adjacent marina has a smattering of waterfront restaurants.

Mackay Visitor Centre (☎1300 130 001; www.mackayregion.com; 320 Nebo Rd; ⊙9am-5pm Mon, 8.30am-5pm Tue-Fri, 9am-4pm Sat & Sun) About 3km south of the centre. Internet access.

NPRSR Office (☎07-4944 7818; www.nprsr.qld.gov.au; 30 Tennyson St; ⊙8.30am-4.30pm Mon-Fri) For camping permits.

Town Hall Visitor Information Centre (☎07-4957 1775; 63 Sydney St; ⊙9am-5pm Mon-Fri, to noon Sat) Info and internet access.

Getting There & Away

AIR

The airport is about 3km south of the centre of Mackay.

Jetstar (☎13 15 38; www.jetstar.com.au), **Qantas** (☎13 13 13; www.qantas.com.au) and **Virgin Blue** (☎13 67 89; www.virginblue.com.au) have flights to/from Brisbane. **Tiger Airways** (☎02-8073 3421; www.tigerairways.com.au) has direct flights between Mackay and Melbourne/Sydney.

BUS

Buses stop at the **Mackay Bus Terminal** (cnr Victoria & Macalister Sts), where tickets can also be booked. **Greyhound** (☎1300 473 946; www.greyhound.com.au) travels up and down the coast. Sample one-way adult fares and journey times: Airlie Beach ($30, two hours), Townsville ($67, 6 hours), Cairns ($113, 13 hours) and Brisbane ($213, 17 hours).

Premier (☎13 34 10; www.premierms.com.au) is less expensive than Greyhound but has less services.

TRAIN

The **Queensland Rail** (☎1800 872 467; www.traveltrain.com.au) *Tilt Train* connects Mackay with Brisbane ($260, 13 hours), Townsville ($125, 5½ hours) and Cairns ($200, 12 hours). The slower *Sunlander* does the same: Brisbane (economy seat/sleeper $140/240, 17 hours). The train station is at Paget, 5km south of the city centre.

Getting Around

Major car-rental firms have desks at the Mackay Airport: see www.mackayairport.com.au/travel/car-hire for listings.

Mackay Transit Coaches (07-4957 3330; www.mackaytransit.com.au) has several services around the city, and connects the city with the harbour and northern beaches; pick up a timetable from one of the visitor centres or look online. **Ocean Breeze Transfers** (www.ocean-breeze-transfers.com.au) run between the city and airport: book in advance.

For a taxi, call **Mackay Taxis** (13 10 08).

Mackay's Northern Beaches

The coastline north of Mackay is made up of a series of headlands and bays sheltering small residential communities with holiday accommodation.

At **Blacks Beach**, the beach extends for 6km, so stretch those legs and claim a piece of Coral Sea coast for a day. Of the several accommodation options, **Blue Pacific Resort** (07-4954 9090; www.bluepacificresort.com.au; 26 Bourke St, Blacks Beach; studio $165-180, 1-2br unit $180-265;) has bright, cheerful units directly on the beach. All rooms have self-catering facilities.

Close by is **Blacks Beach Holiday Park** (07-4954 9334; www.mackayblacksbeach-holidaypark.com.au; 16 Bourke St, Blacks Beach; unpowered/powered site $30/35, villa $140-180; P), with tent sites overlooking a gloriously long stretch of beach.

At the north end of Blacks Beach, the four-star **Dolphin Heads Resort** (07-4944 4777; www.dolphinheadsresort.com.au; Beach Rd, Dolphin Heads; d $160-220; @) has 80 comfortable, motel-style units overlooking an attractive (but rocky) bay.

North of Dolphin Heads is **Eimeo**, where the **Eimeo Pacific Hotel** (Mango Ave, Eimeo; 10am-10pm) crowns a headland commanding magnificent Coral Sea views. It's a great place for a beer.

Bucasia is across Sunset Bay from Eimeo and Dolphin Heads, but you have to head all the way back to the main road to get up there. The recently upgraded **Bucasia Beachfront Caravan Resort** (07-4954 6375; www.bucasiabeach.com.au; 2 The Esplanade; powered site $30-45;) has a selection of sites, some of which enjoy absolute beachfront views.

Sarina

POP 5730

In the foothills of the Connors Range, Sarina is a service centre for the surrounding sugarcane farms and home to CSR's Plane Creek sugar mill and ethanol distillery. It's also a nice little fishing spot: ask the locals for their favourite place to wet a hook.

The **Sarina Tourist Art & Craft Centre** (07-4956 2251; www.sarinatourism.com; Railway Sq, Bruce Hwy; 9am-5pm) showcases locally made handicrafts and assists with visitor information.

Sarina Sugar Shed (07-4943 2801; www.sarinasugarshed.com.au; Railway Sq; adult/child $21/11; tours 9.30am, 10.30am, noon & 2pm Mon-Sat) is the only miniature sugar-processing mill and distillery of its kind in Australia. After the tour, enjoy a complimentary tipple at the distillery.

The town centre straddles the Bruce Hwy. The **Tramway Motel** (07-4956 2244; www.tramwaymotel.com.au; 110 Broad St; d from $125, unit $180-200;), north of the centre, has clean, bright units. For a dining experience with a difference, head to the **Diner** (11 Central St; mains $4-6; 4am-6pm Mon-Fri, to 10am Sat), a rustic roadside shack that has served tucker to truckies and cane farmers for decades. Take the turn-off to Clermont in the centre of town and look for the tin shack on your left, just before the railway crossing.

Around Sarina

There are a number of low-key beachside settlements a short drive east from Sarina. Clean, uncrowded beaches and mangrove-lined inlets provide excellent opportunities for relaxing, fishing, beachcombing and spotting wildlife such as nesting marine turtles.

Sarina Beach

On the shores of Sarina Inlet, this laid-back coastal village boasts a long beach, a general store/service station and a boat ramp at the inlet.

★**Fernandos Hideaway** (07-4956 6299; www.sarinabeachbb.com; 26 Captain Blackwood Dr; s/d/ste $130/140/160;) is a Spanish hacienda–style B&B perched on a rugged headland. It offers magnificent coastal views and absolute beachfront. In the living room there's a stuffed lion, a suit of armour and an eclectic assortment of souvenirs from the eccentric owner's global travels.

Sarina Beach Motel (07-4956 6266; www.sarinabeachmotel.com; 44 Owen Jenkins Dve; d $135-160;) is located at the northern end of the Esplanade. Most rooms have beach frontage. Its restaurant is open nightly.

Armstrong Beach

Armstrong Beach Caravan Park (07-4956 2425; 66 Melba St; unpowered/powered site $21-50) is a lovely coastal spot just a few kilometres southeast of Sarina. Prices are for two people.

Pioneer Valley

Travelling west, Mackay's urban sprawl gives way to the lush greenness of beautiful Pioneer Valley, where the unmistakable smell of sugar cane wafts through your nostrils as loaded cane trains busily work their way along the roadside. The first sugar cane was planted here in 1867 and today almost the entire valley floor is planted with the stuff. The route to Eungella National Park, the Mackay–Eungella Rd, branches off the Peak Downs Hwy about 10km west of Mackay and follows the river through vast fields of cane to link up with the occasional small town or steam-belching sugar mill.

About 17km west of the small town of Mirani is the **Pinnacle Hotel** (www.pinnaclehotel.com.au; Eungella Rd , Pinnacle; mains $10-20). The pub has accommodation (camp sites $10 to $20, doubles $50), an outdoor cafe, and live music on Sunday afternoons. Try a Pinnacle Pie or regret it for the rest of your days.

Another 10km further down the road is the turn-off for Finch Hatton Gorge, part of Eungella National Park, and 1.5km past the turn-off is the pretty township of **Finch Hatton**.

From Finch Hatton, it's another 18km to Eungella, a quaint mountain village overlooking the valley. The last section of this road climbs suddenly and steeply with several incredibly sharp corners – towing a large caravan is not recommended.

Eungella

Pretty little Eungella (*young*-gulluh, meaning 'land of clouds') sits perched on the edge of the Pioneer Valley. There's a **general store** with snacks, groceries and fuel, plus a couple of accommodation and eating options. Lively **markets** are held on the first Sunday of each month (April to December) from 9am at the town hall.

The tidy little **Eungella Mountain Edge Escape** (07-4958 4590; www.mountainedgeescape.com.au; North St; 1/2br cabin $115/135;) has three self-contained wooden cabins perched on the edge of the escarpment. Wonderful views, predictably, are to be had here.

Eungella Chalet (07-4958 4509; www.eungellachalet.com.au; Chelmer St; 1/2br cabin $115/155;) exudes rustic charm in a once-grandiose kind of way. The chalet is perched on the edge of a mountain and the views are spectacular. The cabins are large and spacious but furnishings are quite dated. There's a small bar, a dining room and live music most Sunday afternoons.

Explorers' Haven (07-4958 4750; www.eungella.com; unpowered/powered site $25/30;) is a small and very basic camping ground located just north of the township, right on the edge of the escarpment. You'll need to self-register on arrival. Prices are for two people. Luxury cabin accommodation may be available; contact the park in advance.

If it's open, the **Hideaway Cafe** (07-4958 4533; Broken River Rd; dishes $4-10; 9am-4pm) is worth a stop; sit on the picturesque little balcony and enjoy a decent home-cooked dish.

Eungella National Park

Stunning Eungella National Park is 84km west of Mackay, covering nearly 500 sq km of the Clarke Range and climbing to 1280m at Mt Dalrymple. The mountainous park is largely inaccessible except for the walking tracks around Broken River and Finch Hatton Gorge. The large tracts of tropical and subtropical vegetation have been isolated from other rainforest areas for thousands of years and now boast several unique species including the orange-sided skink and the charming Eungella gastric-brooding frog, which incubates its eggs in its stomach and gives birth by spitting out the tadpoles.

Most days of the year, you can be pretty sure of seeing a platypus or two in the Broken River. The best times are the hours immediately after dawn and before dark, but you must remain patient, silent and still. Platypus activity is at its peak from May to August, when the females are fattening themselves up in preparation for gestating their young. Other river life you're sure to see are large northern snapping turtles and brilliant azure kingfishers.

Finch Hatton Gorge

About 27km west of Mirani, just before the town of Finch Hatton, is the turn-off to Finch Hatton Gorge. The last 2km of the 10km drive from the main road are on unsealed roads with several creek crossings that can become impassable after heavy rain. A 1.6km walking trail leads to **Araluen Falls**, with its tumbling waterfalls and swimming holes, and a further 1km hike takes you to the **Wheel of Fire Falls**, another cascade with a deep swimming hole.

A brilliantly fun and informative way to explore the rainforest here is to glide through the canopy with **Forest Flying** (☎07-4958 3359; www.forestflying.com; $60). The skyhigh guided tours see you harnessed to a 350m-long cable and suspended up to 25m above the ground; you control your speed via a pulley system. Bookings are essential, and you must weigh less than 120kg.

The following places are signposted on the road to the gorge:

Platypus Bushcamp (☎07-4958 3204; www.bushcamp.net; Finch Hatton Gorge; camp site $7.50, dm/d $25/75) is a true-blue bush retreat hand-built by Wazza, the eccentric owner. The basic huts have barely-there walls, with the rainforest at your fingertips. A creek with platypuses and great swimming holes runs next to the camp, and the big open-air communal-kitchen-eating area is the heart of the place. There are wonderful hot bush showers and a cosy stone hot tub. Bring your own food and linen. WWOOFers welcome.

The only luxury accommodation in Eungella National Park is the **Rainforest B&B** (☎07-4958 3099; www.rainforestbedandbreakfast.com.au; 52 Van Houweninges Rd; cabin $300). There's a touch of Balinese to this rainforest retreat with its garden sculptures, wooden cabin and romantic decor. A freshly-baked, complimentary afternoon tea awaits on your arrival. Rates go down the longer the stay.

The self-contained cabins at **Finch Hatton Gorge Cabins** (☎07-4958 3281; www.finchhattongorgecabins.com.au; d $95; ❄) are quite basic but have wonderful views of the forest. The cabins can sleep up to five people.

Broken River

Broken River, 5km south of Eungella, is home to a rightfully renowned **platypus-viewing platform** (near the bridge): it's reputedly one of the most reliable spots on earth to catch these meek monotremes at play. Bird life is also prolific. There are some excellent walking trails between the Broken River picnic ground and Eungella. Maps are available from the information office (by the platform), which is rarely staffed.

For accommodation, you have the choice of camping or cabins. **Broken River Mountain Resort** (☎07-4958 4000; www.brokenrivermr.com.au; d $130-190; ❄@🛜≋) has comfortable cedar cabins ranging from small, motel-style units to a large self-contained lodge sleeping up to six. There's a cosy guest lounge with an open fire and the friendly **Possums Table Restaurant & Bar** (mains $22.50-35.50; ⏲breakfast & dinner). The name is well-deserved: a family of possums dines on the balcony here every night. The resort organises several (mostly free) activities for its guests, including spotlighting, birdwatching and guided walks, and can arrange shuttle transfers for longer walks.

Fern Flat Camping Ground (www.nprsr.qld.gov.au; per person/family $5.45/21.80) is a lovely place to camp, with shady sites adjacent to the river where the platypuses play. Prepare to be spied on by nosy scrub turkeys, and serenaded by morning birds! This is a walk-in camping ground and is not vehicle accessible. Self-register camp sites are about 500m past the information centre and kiosk.

Crediton Hall Camping Ground (www.nprsr.qld.gov.au; per person/family $5.45/21.80), 3km after Broken River, is accessible to vehicles. Turn left into Crediton Loop Rd and turn right after the Wishing Pool circuit track entrance. The camping ground has toilets.

ℹ Getting There & Away

There are no buses to Eungella or Finch Hatton, but Reeforest Adventure Tours (p196) runs day trips from Mackay and will drop off and pick up those who want to linger; however, tours don't run every day and your stay may wind up longer than intended.

Cumberland Islands

There are about 70 islands in the Cumberland group, sometimes referred to as the southern Whitsundays. Almost all the islands are designated national parks. Apart from **Keswick Island** – home to the sophisticated and secluded **Keswick Island Guest House** (07-4965 8002; www.keswickislandguesthouse.com.au; s/d from $360/550;) – there's no formal accommodation in the Cumberlands.

Brampton Island is well-known for its nature walks, and was until recently the home of a posh resort. **Carlisle Island** is connected to Brampton by a narrow sandbar and, during low tide, it may be possible to walk between the two. **Scawfell Island** is the largest in the group; on its northern side, Refuge Bay has a safe anchorage and a camping ground.

Camp-site availability, bookings and permits for the Cumberland Islands and the nearby Sir James Smith Island group can be found online at www.nprsr.qld.gov.au or at the Mackay visitor centre (p199).

Facilities on all islands are limited and access can be difficult unless you have your own boat or can afford to charter one (or a seaplane); ask for more info at the Mackay visitor centre.

Cape Hillsborough National Park

Despite being so easy to get to, this small coastal park, 50km north of Mackay, feels like it's at the end of the earth. Ruggedly beautiful, it takes in the rocky, 300m-high Cape Hillsborough and Andrews Point and Wedge Island, which are joined by a causeway at low tide. The park features rough cliffs, a broad beach, rocky headlands, sand dunes, mangroves, hoop pines and rainforest. Kangaroos, wallabies, sugar gliders and turtles are common, and the roos are likely to be seen on the beach in the evening and early morning. There are also the remains of Aboriginal middens and stone fish traps, accessible by good walking tracks. On the approach to the foreshore area there's also an interesting boardwalk leading out through a tidal mangrove forest.

Smalleys Beach Campground (www.nprsr.qld.gov.au; site per person/family $5.45/21.80) is a small, pretty and grassed camping ground hugging the foreshore and absolutely jumping with kangaroos. There's no self-registration here; book permits online.

Cape Hillsborough Nature Resort (07-4959 0152; www.capehillsboroughresort.com.au; 51 Risley Pde; unpowered/powered site $29/34, fishing hut $65-75, cabin $65-135;) is in a quiet spot on a long stretch of beach. There's nothing fancy about the joint, but once you see kangaroos on their magical morning beach hops, things like shiny surrounds somehow matter less.

THE WHITSUNDAYS

The Whitsunday group of islands off the northeast Queensland coast is, as the cliché goes, a tropical paradise. The 74 islands that make up this arresting archipelago are really the tips of mountain tops jutting out from the Coral Sea, and from their sandy fringes the ocean spreads towards the horizon in beautiful shades of crystal, aqua, blue and indigo. Sheltered by the Great Barrier Reef, there are no crashing waves or deadly undertows, and the waters are perfect for sailing.

Of the numerous stunning beaches and secluded bays, Whitehaven Beach stands out for its pure white silica sand. It is undoubtedly the finest beach in the Whitsundays, and possibly one of the finest in the world.

Airlie Beach, on the mainland, is the coastal hub and major gateway to the islands. Only seven of the islands have tourist resorts, catering to every budget and whim: choose from the basic accommodation at Hook Island to the exclusive luxury of Hayman Island. Most of the Whitsunday Islands are uninhabited, and several offer back-to-nature beach camping and bushwalking.

Activities

Sailing

What could be better than sailing from one island paradise to another? There are plenty of **sailing tours** itching to get your landlubber feet on deck, but if you've got salt water in your veins, a **bareboat charter** might be more your style. A bareboat charter lets you rent a boat without skipper, crew or provisions. You don't need formal qualifications, but you (or one of your party) have to prove you can competently operate a vessel.

Expect to pay between $500 to $1000 a day in the high season (September to January) for a yacht sleeping four to six people. A booking deposit of $500 to $750 and a security bond of between $200 and $2000 is payable before departure and refunded after the boat is returned undamaged. Bedding is usually supplied and provisions can be provided at extra cost. Most companies have a minimum hire period of five days.

It's worth asking if the company belongs to the Whitsunday Bareboat Operators Association, a self-regulatory body that guarantees certain standards. Also check that the latest edition of David Colfelt's *100 Magic Miles of the Great Barrier Reef* is stowed on board.

There are a number of bareboat charter companies around Airlie Beach: **Charter Yachts Australia** (1800 639 520; www.cya.com.au; Abel Point Marina); **Cumberland Charter Yachts** (1800 075 101; www.ccy.com.au; Abel Point Marina); **Queensland Yacht Charters** (1800 075 013; www.yachtcharters.com.au; Abel Point Marina); **Whitsunday Escape** (1800 075 145; www.whitsundayescape.com; Abel Point Marina); and **Whitsunday Rent A Yacht** (1800 075 000; www.rentayacht.com.au; 6 Bay Terrace, Shute Harbour).

If you want to know why those old salts at the bar keep smiling into their drinks, learn to sail at the **Whitsunday Marine Academy** (07-4946 5782; www.explorewhitsundays.com; 4 The Esplanade), run by Explore Whitsundays, or the **Whitsunday Sailing Club** (07-4946 6138; www.whitsundaysailingclub.com.au; Airlie Point).

Diving

Dreamy diving experiences abound at spectacular sites such as Black, Knuckle, Fairy, Bait and Elizabeth Reefs. However, the fringing reefs around the islands (especially on their northern tips) are often more colourful and abundant than most of the walls on the outer reef, and there's usually a greater variety of softer coral.

Costs for open-water courses with several ocean dives start at around $600 and generally involve two or three days' tuition on the mainland, with the rest of the time diving the reef. Check that the Great Barrier Reef Marine Park levy and any other additional costs are included in the price. **Whitsunday Dive Adventures** (07-4948 1239; www.whitsundaydivecentre.com; 16 Commerce Close, Cannonvale; PADI course $599) is a good place to start.

A number of **sailing cruises** include diving as an optional extra. Prices start from $75 for introductory or certified dives. Ferry operator **Cruise Whitsundays** (07-4946 4662; www.cruisewhitsundays.com; intro dive from $119) offers dives on day trips to the reef.

Most of the **island resorts** also have dive schools and free snorkelling gear.

Kayaking

Paddling with dolphins and turtles is one of the best ways to experience the Whitsundays. **Salty Dog Sea Kayaking** (07-4946 1388; www.saltydog.com.au; Shute Harbour; half-/full-day trip $80/130) offers guided tours and kayak rental ($50/70 per half-/full day), plus a brilliant six-day kayak/camping expedition ($1490) that's suitable for beginners.

The **Ngaro Sea Trail** combines kayaking trails with island bushwalks for a modern-day walk (and paddle) in the local Ngaro people's footsteps. Visit www.nprsr.qld.gov.au/parks/whitsunday-ngaro-sea-trail for info and itinerary ideas.

Tours

Not everyone has the time or the money to sail, and must rely on the faster catamarans to whisk them around the islands on a day trip.

Most day trips include activities such as snorkelling or boom-netting with scuba diving as an optional extra. Most of the cruise operators run out of Abel Point Marina but those that run from Shute Harbour do coach pick-ups from Airlie Beach and Cannonvale. You can take a public bus to Shute Harbour.

Following are some of the day trips on offer; bookings can be made at any Airlie Beach tour agent:

Cruise Whitsundays CRUISE
(07-4946 4662; www.cruisewhitsundays.com; Shingley Dr, Abel Point Marina; full-day cruise from $99) As well as operating as a ferry, Cruise Whitsundays offers trips to Hardy Reef, Whitehaven Beach and various islands including Daydream and Long. Or you can grab a daily Island Hopper pass (adult/child $120/59) and make your own itinerary. It also operates a popular day trip aboard the Camira (adult/child $189/99 including lunch and all drinks), a catamaran that takes in Whitehaven Beach.

Voyager 4 Island Cruise BOAT TOUR
(07-4946 5255; www.wiac.com.au; adult/child $140/80) A good-value day cruise that in-

Whitsunday Islands

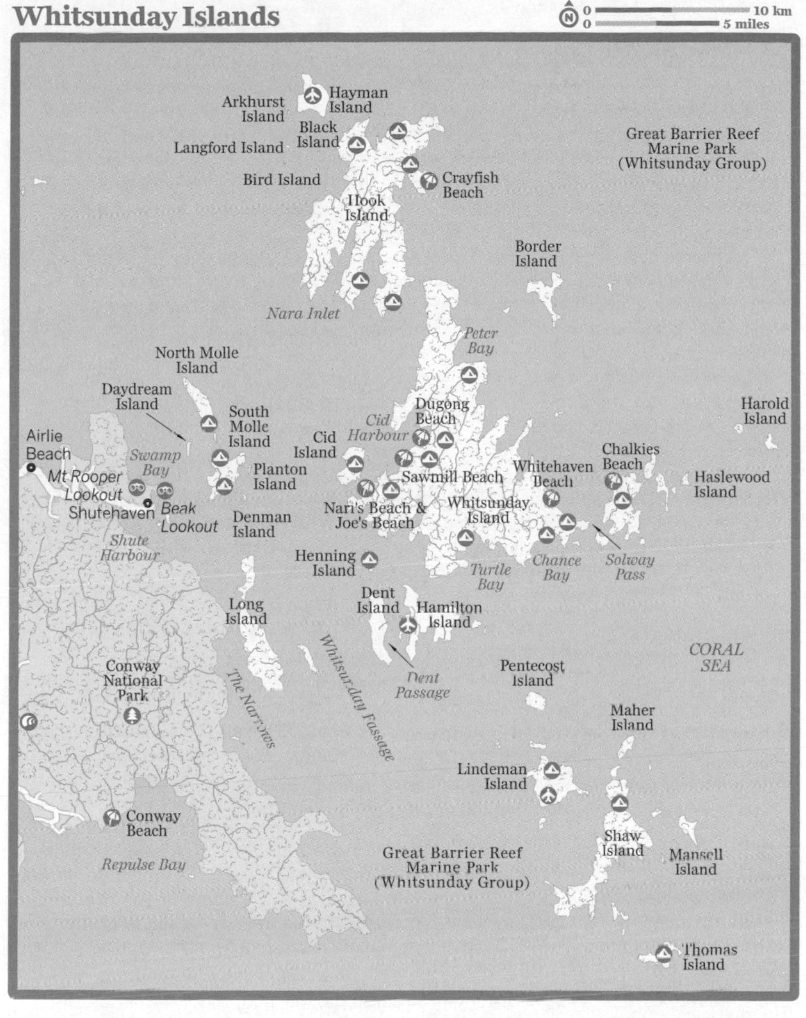

cludes snorkelling at Hook Island, beachcombing and swimming at Whitehaven Beach, and checking out Daydream Island. Add a scenic flight for $60.

Ecojet Safari TOUR
(☎07-4948 2653; www.ecojetsafari.com.au; per person $190, 2 people per jet ski) Explore the islands, mangroves and marine life of the northern Whitsundays on these three-hour, small group jet-ski safaris.

Ocean Rafting BOAT TOUR
(☎07-4946 6848; www.oceanrafting.com.au; adult/child/family $129/81/384) Visit the 'wild' side of the islands in a very fast, big yellow speedboat. Swim at Whitehaven Beach, regain your land legs with a guided national park walk or snorkel the reef at Mantaray Bay and Border Island.

Big Fury BOAT TOUR
(☎07-4948 2201; adult/child/family $130/70/350) Speeds out to Whitehaven Beach on an open-air sports boat followed by lunch and snorkelling at a secluded reef nearby.

Air Whitsunday SCENIC FLIGHTS
(☎07-4946 9111; www.airwhitsunday.com.au; Terminal 1, Whitsunday Airport) Offers a range of

SAILING THE WHITSUNDAYS

Daydreams of an island holiday almost always feature a white sailboat skimming the fantasy-blue seas. In the Whitsundays, it isn't hard to put yourself in that picture, but with the plethora of charters, tours and specials on offer, deciding how to go about it can be confusing. Before booking, compare what you'll get for the price you'll pay. Cheaper companies can have crowded boats, bland food and cramped quarters. If you're flexible with dates, last-minute stand-by rates can considerably reduce the price and you'll also have a better idea of weather conditions.

Most overnight sailing packages are for three days and two nights or two days and two nights. Again, check what you'll pay for. Some companies set sail in the afternoon of the first day and return by mid-morning of the last, while others set out early and return late. Also be sure about what you're committing to – don't set sail on a party boat if you're after a chilled-out cruise.

Most vessels offer snorkelling on the fringing reefs (around the islands), where the softer coral is often more colourful and abundant than on the outer reef. Check if snorkel equipment, stinger suits and reef taxes are included in the package. Diving usually costs extra.

Once you've decided, book at one of the many booking agencies in Airlie Beach such as **Whitsundays Central Reservation Centre** (☎1800 677 119; www.airliebeach.com; 259 Shute Harbour Rd) or a management company such as **Whitsunday Sailing Adventures** (☎07-4946 4999; www.whitsundaysailing.com; The Esplanade) or **Explore Whitsundays** (☎07-4946 5782; www.explorewhitsundays.com; 4 The Esplanade).

Some recommended sailing trips:

Camira (www.cruisewhitsundays.com; day trip $189) One of the world's fastest commercial sailing catamarans is now a lilac-coloured Whitsunday icon. This good-value day trip includes Whitehaven Beach, snorkelling, morning and afternoon tea, a barbecue lunch and all refreshments (including wine and beer).

Solway Lass (www.solwaylass.com; 3-day/3-night trip from $559) You get a full three days on this 28m tallship – the only authentic tallship in Airlie Beach. Popular with backpackers.

Prima Sailing (www.primasailing.com.au; 2-day/2-night tour from $360) Fun tours with a 12-person maximum. Ideal for couples chasing style and substance.

Atlantic Clipper (www.atlanticclipper.com.au; 2-day/2-night trip from $455) Young, beautiful and boozy crowd...and there's no escaping the antics. Snorkelling (or recovering) on Langford Island is a highlight.

Derwent Hunter (www.tallshipadventures.com.au; day trip $175) A very popular sailing safari on a timber gaff-rigged schooner. Good option for couples and those more keen on wildlife than the wild life.

Whitehaven Xpress (www.whitehavenxpress.com.au; day trip $160) Locally owned and operated for over a decade, the Xpress rivals the bigger operators for its Hill Inlet and Whitehaven tours.

SV Domino (www.aussieyachting.com; day trip $150) Takes a maximum of eight guests to Bali Hai island, a little-visited 'secret' of the Whitsundays. Includes lunch and a good two-hour snorkel.

Crewing

Adventurous types might see the 'Crew Wanted' ads posted in hostels or at the marina and dream of hitching a ride on the high seas. In return for a free bunk, meals and a sailing adventure, you get to hoist the mainsail, take the helm and clean the head. You could have the experience of a lifetime – whether good or bad depends on the vessel, skipper, other crew members (if any) and your own attitude. Think about being stuck with someone you don't know on a 10m boat several kilometres from shore before you actually find yourself there. Be sure to let someone know where you're going, with whom and for how long.

tours, including day trips to Hayman Island ($245) and Whitehaven ($240).

Sleeping

Resorts

Rates quoted are standard, but hardly anyone pays them. Most travel agents will put together a range of discounted package deals combining air fares, transfers, accommodation and meals.

Camping

NPRSR (www.nprsr.qld.gov.au) manages the **Whitsunday Islands National Park** camping grounds on several islands for both independent campers as well as groups on commercial trips. Camping permits (per person/family $5.45/21.80) are available online or at the NPRSR booking office in Airlie Beach.

You must be self-sufficient and are advised to take 5L of water per person per day plus three days' extra supply in case you get stuck. You should also have a fuel stove as wood fires are banned on all islands.

Get to your island with **Whitsunday Island Camping Connections – Scamper** (☎07-4946 6285; www.whitsundaycamping.com.au). It leaves from Shute Harbour and can drop you at South Molle, Denman or Planton Islands ($65 return); Whitsunday Island ($105 return); Whitehaven Beach ($155 return); and Hook Island ($160 return). Camping transfers include complimentary 5L water containers. You can also hire camp kits ($40 first night; $20 subsequent nights) which include a tent, gas stove, Esky and more.

Information

Airlie Beach is the mainland centre for the Whitsundays, with a bewildering array of accommodation options, travel agents and tour operators. Shute Harbour, about 12km east of Airlie, is the port for some day-trip cruises and island ferries, while most of the yachts and other cruise companies berth at Abel Point Marina about 1km west of Airlie Beach.

David Colfelt's *100 Magic Miles of the Great Barrier Reef – The Whitsunday Islands* has been referred to as the 'bible to the Whitsundays'. It contains an exhaustive collection of charts with descriptions of boat anchorages in the area, articles on the islands and resorts and features on diving, sailing, fishing, camping and natural history.

Visit the NPRSR (p211) in Airlie Beach for camping permits and info.

Whitsundays Region Information Centre (☎1300 717 407; www.whitsundaytourism.com; ⊙10am-5pm) On the Bruce Hwy at the southern entry to Proserpine.

Getting There & Around

AIR

The two main airports for the Whitsundays are at Hamilton Island and Proserpine (Whitsunday Coast). Airlie Beach is home to the small Whitsunday Airport, about 6km from town.

BOAT

Cruise Whitsundays (☎07-4946 4662; www.cruisewhitsundays.com; one-way adult/child from $36/24) provides ferry transfers to Daydream, Long and South Molle Islands and to the Hamilton Island Airport.

BUS

Greyhound (☎1300 473 946; www.greyhound.com.au) and **Premier** (☎13 34 10; www.premierms.com.au) detour off the Bruce Hwy to Airlie Beach. **Whitsunday Transit** (☎07-4946 1800; www.whitsundaytransit.com.au) connects Proserpine, Cannonvale, Abel Point, Airlie Beach and Shute Harbour.

Whitsundays 2 Everywhere (☎07-4946 4940; www.whitsundaytransfers.com) operates airport transfers from both Whitsunday Coast (Proserpine) and Mackay Airports to Airlie Beach.

Proserpine

POP 3390

There's no real reason to linger in this industrial sugar-mill town, which is the turn-off point for Airlie Beach and the Whitsundays. However, it's worth stopping at the helpful Whitsundays Region Information Centre (p207) just south of town for information about the Whitsundays and surrounding region.

If you do find yourself in Proserpine with time to spare, head to **Colour Me Crazy** (☎07-4945 2698; 2b Dobbins Lane; ⊙8.30am-5.30pm Mon-Fri, to 3.30pm Sat, 9.30am-2.30pm Sun), an eye-popping labyrinth of out-there jewellery, clothing and homewares.

Proserpine's Whitsunday Coast Airport is 14km south of town, serviced from Brisbane and some other capitals by **Jetstar** (☎13 15 38; www.jetstar.com.au) and **Virgin Blue** (☎13 67 89; www.virginblue.com.au).

In addition to meeting all planes and trains, **Whitsunday Transit** (☎07-4946 1800; www.whitsundaytransit.com.au) has eight scheduled bus services running daily from Proserpine to Airlie Beach. One way/return from the airport costs $18/36, and from the train station it's $12.10/24.20.

Airlie Beach

POP 7868

Like olives, oysters and Vegemite, Airlie Beach is a love-or-hate affair. A good-time town of the highest order, the mainland gateway to the Whitsundays is loud, brash and busy, a total contrast to the tranquil ocean glittering just metres offshore. Despite a backdrop of jungle-clad hills and Airlie's proximity to obvious natural wonders, those in search of serenity will find it only once anchors are aweigh; those after wildlife need look no further than the frenzied backpacker bars lining the recently renovated main drag. That said, the town does offer some respite from the party pace in the form of a lovely swimming lagoon and the amble-worthy landscaped foreshore.

Abel Point Marina, where the Cruise Whitsundays ferries depart from and where many of the cruising yachts are moored, is about 1km west along a pleasant boardwalk, while many other vessels leave from Shute Harbour (about 12km east); most cruise companies run courtesy buses into town.

Activities

There are seasonal operators in front of the Airlie Beach Hotel that hire out jet skis, catamarans, windsurfers and paddle skis.

Lagoon SWIMMING
(Shute Harbour Rd) FREE Take a dip year-round in the stinger-croc-tropical-nasties-free lagoon in the centre of town.

Tandem Skydive Airlie Beach SKYDIVING
(07-4946 9115; www.skydiveairliebeach.com.au; from $249) Jump out of a plane from 8000, 10,000, 12,000 or 14,000ft up.

Fishing FISHING
Grab a cheap handline and have a go at catching your own dinner. Popular spots in Airlie include the rock walls by the sailing club in Cannonvale, the Airlie Beach Marina and the fishing pontoon in Shute Harbour.

Tours

See the Whitsundays Tours section (p204) for details of tours throughout the islands.

Whitsunday Crocodile Safari TOUR
(07-4948 3310; www.proserpineecotours.com; adult/child $120/60) Spy on wild crocs, explore secret estuaries and eat bush tucker.

Festivals & Events

Airlie Beach Race Week SAILING
(www.airlieraceweek.com) Sailors from across the world descend on Airlie for the town's annual regatta, held in August.

Sleeping

Airlie Beach is a backpacker haven, but with so many hostels, standards vary and bedbugs are a common problem. Most of the resorts have package deals and stand-by rates that are much cheaper than those advertised. Try the **Whitsundays Central Reservation Centre** (1800 677 119; www.airliebeach.com; 259 Shute Harbour Rd) for accommodation ideas and specials, or the usual suspects online.

★ **Kipara** RESORT $
(www.kipara.com.au; 2614 Shute Harbour Rd; private room/cabin/villa from $60/95/105;) Tucked away in lush, green environs, this budget resort makes it easy to forget you're only 2km from the frenzy of town. Mega-clean, outstanding value, helpful staff and regular wildlife visits make this one of Airlie's best options. Long-term rates also available.

Bush Village Budget Cabins HOSTEL $
(1800 809 256; www.bushvillage.com.au; 2 St Martins Rd; dm from $32, d $80;) Among the best budget accommodation options in town. Dorms and doubles are in 17 self-contained cabins set in leafy gardens. There's off-street parking and it's close to the supermarket.

Nomads Backpackers HOSTEL $
(07-4999 6600; www.nomadsairliebeach.com; 354 Shute Harbour Rd; dm/d $23/88;) Set on a 3-hectare leafy lot with volleyball and a pool, Nomads feels a bit more 'resorty' than many of the other hostels in town. Accommodation is nothing special, though tent sites are nice and shady, and private rooms have TV, fridge and kitchenette.

Seabreeze Tourist Park CARAVAN PARK $
(07-4946 6379; www.theseabreezepark.com.au; 234 Shute Harbour Rd; camp site $14, caravan site from $30, cabin/villa from $90/130;) Grassy and sprawling with fresh

Airlie Beach

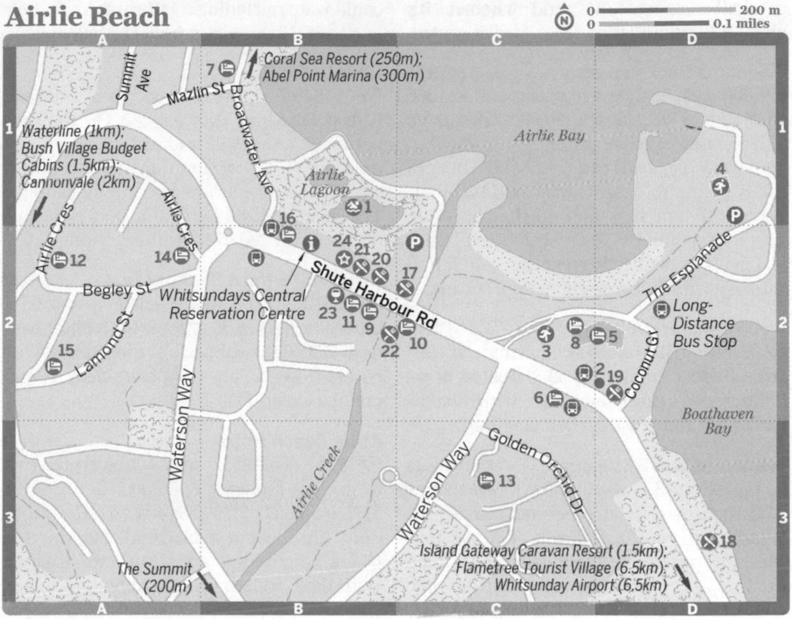

Airlie Beach

Activities, Courses & Tours

1 Lagoon ... B1
2 Whitsunday Dive Adventures ... D2
3 Whitsunday Marine Academy ... C2
4 Whitsunday Sailing Club ... D1

Sleeping

5 Airlie Beach Hotel ... D2
6 Airlie Beach YHA ... C2
7 Airlie Waterfront B&B ... B1
8 Airlie Waterfront Backpackers ... C2
9 Beaches Backpackers ... B2
10 Magnums Backpackers ... C2
11 Nomads Backpackers ... B2
12 Sunlit Waters ... A2
13 Water's Edge Resort ... C3
14 Waterview ... A2
15 Whitsunday Organic B&B ... A2
16 Whitsundays Central Reservation Centre ... B2

Eating

17 Airlie Supermarket ... C2
Deja Vu ... (see 13)
18 Denman Cellars Beer Cafe ... D3
19 Fish D'vine ... D2
20 Harry's Corner ... B2
21 Mr Bones ... B2
22 Village Cafe ... B2
Whitsunday Sailing Club ... (see 4)

Drinking & Nightlife

23 Paddy's Shenanigans ... B2
Phoenix Bar ... (see 6)

Entertainment

24 Mama Africa ... B2

ocean views and a nice kicked-back feel. Camp sites are shady, while the new timber Bali Villas offer an exoticism most caravan parks are decidedly lacking.

Beaches Backpackers HOSTEL $
(☎07-4946 6244; www.beaches.com.au; 356 Shute Harbour Rd; dm/d $22/70;) You must at least enjoy a drink at the big open-air bar, even if you're not staying here. If you do choose to hang your hat, bring earplugs and your biggest party boots. Not one for the serenity set.

Backpackers by the Bay HOSTEL $
(☎07-4946 7267; www.backpackersbythebay.com; 12 Hermitage Dr; dm/d & tw $25/68;) A low-key alternative to the seething party-hostel cluster downtown, with tidy rooms, hammocks, a good pool and a distinct lack

of skull-clanging tunes and whoops. It's about a 10-minute walk from Airlie's centre.

Magnums Backpackers HOSTEL **$**
(☎1800 624 634; www.magnums.com.au; 366 Shute Harbour Rd; camp site/van site $22/24, dm/d $22/56, share cabin per person $24; ❄@📶) A loud party bar, loads of alcohol and a bevy of pretty young things…it must be Magnums. Forget the tent sites close to the bar – you won't sleep unless you're comatose. Once you get past the hectic reception, you'll find simple dorms in a tropical garden setting.

Airlie Beach YHA HOSTEL **$**
(☎07-4946 6312; airliebeach@yha.com.au; 394 Shute Harbour Rd; dm $26.50, d $69; ❄@≋) Central and reasonably quiet with a sparkling pool and great kitchen facilities.

Flametree Tourist Village CARAVAN PARK **$**
(☎07-4946 9388; www.flametreevillage.com.au; 2955 Shute Harbour Rd; unpowered/powered site $21/27, cabin from $79; ❄@≋🐾) The spacious sites are scattered through lovely, bird-filled gardens and there's a good camp kitchen and barbecue area. It's 6.5km west of Airlie.

Waterview APARTMENT **$$**
(☎07-4948 1748; www.waterviewairliebeach.com.au; 42 Airlie Cres; studio/1-bedroom unit from $135/150; ❄📶) An excellent choice for location and comfort, this boutique accommodation overlooks the main street and has gorgeous views of the bay. The rooms are modern, airy and spacious and have kitchenettes for self-caterers.

Coral Sea Resort RESORT **$$**
(☎1800 075 061; www.coralsearesort.com; 25 Ocean View Ave; d/1-bedroom apt/2-bedroom apt from $185/330/410; ❄@📶≋) At the end of a low headland overlooking the water, just west of the town centre, Coral Sea Resort has one of the best positions around. Many rooms have stunning views.

Whitsunday Organic B&B B&B **$$**
(☎07-4946 7151; www.whitsundaybb.com.au; 8 Lamond St; s/d $155/185-210) 🍃 Rooms are comfortable, but it's the organic-everything (garden, walks, breakfasts, wines) that everyone comes here for. You can book a healing essential-oil massage, meditate in the garden tepee or just indulge in all things *om*.

Sunlit Waters APARTMENT **$$**
(☎07-4946 6352; www.sunlitwaters.com; 20 Airlie Cres; studios from $92, 1-bedroom apt $115; ❄≋) These large studios have everything you could want, including a self-contained kitchenette and great views from the balconies.

Club Crocodile HOTEL **$$**
(☎07-4946 7155; www.clubcroc.com.au; 240 Shute Harbour Rd; d from $110; P❄≋) On the road between Cannonvale and Airlie Beach is this excellent budget option that's really popular with domestic tourists and young families. The Olympic-sized swimming pool is the hub of the action and even features a waterfall.

Airlie Waterfront Backpackers HOSTEL **$$**
(☎1800 089 000; www.airliewaterfront.com; 6 The Esplanade; dm $25-33, d & tw with/without bathroom $130/60) Flashpackin' good-times, with coveted ocean views, squeaky-clean rooms and flatscreen TVs.

Airlie Beach Hotel HOTEL **$$**
(☎1800 466 233; www.airliebeachhotel.com.au; cnr The Esplanade & Coconut Gr; motel s/d $135/145, hotel r $179-289; ❄📶≋) The motel units are looking a bit tired, but the sea-facing hotel rooms are clean and spacious. With three restaurants and a bottle shop on site and a perfect downtown location, you could do far worse than stay here.

Water's Edge Resort APARTMENT **$$$**
(☎07-4948 2655; www.watersedgewhitsundays.com.au; 4 Golden Orchid Dr; 1-bedroom apt $225-275, 2-bedroom apt $275-350; ❄≋) Its Balinese theme, wet-edge pools and languid tropical vibe (gently) scream 'Holidays!' Cool, creamy pastel rooms, top-notch facilities and fecund gardens keep up the dreamy feel; you'll easily forget you're just minutes from town.

Airlie Waterfront B&B B&B **$$$**
(☎07-4946 7631; www.airliewaterfrontbnb.com.au; cnr Broadwater Ave & Mazlin St; d $242-285; ❄@) Absolutely gorgeous views and immaculately presented from top to toe, this sumptuously furnished B&B oozes class and is a leisurely five-minute walk into town along the boardwalk. Some rooms have a spa.

Eating

The **Airlie supermarket** (277 Shute Harbour Rd) is the main self-catering option in the centre of town.

Fish D'vine SEAFOOD **$**
(☎07-4948 0088; 303 Shute Harbour Rd; mains $14-28; ⏰5pm-late) Pirates were definitely onto something: this fish-and-rum bar is shiploads of fun, serving up all things nib-

bly from Neptune's realm and lashings and lashings of rum (over 200 kinds of the stuff).

Harry's Corner CAFE $
(☎07-4946 7459; 273 Shute Harbour Rd; mains $6.70-17.50; ⏰7am-3pm) Come for the all-day breakfasts, giant in scope and mammoth in portion. Harry's also serves up open Danish sandwiches, filled bagels and good salads.

Denman Cellars Beer Cafe TAPAS $
(☎07-4948 1333; Shop 15, 33 Port Dr; mains $12-26; ⏰11am-10pm Mon-Fri, 8am-11pm Sat & Sun) Solid mod-Oz food including lamb meatballs, very small shared seafood tapas and a stock breakfast menu pales in comparison to the beer menu (over 700 brews!).

Whitsunday Sailing Club PUB $
(☎07-4946 6138; Airlie Point; mains $14-32; ⏰noon-2.30pm & 5.30-8.30pm Mon-Fri, 11am-2.30pm & 5.30-8.30pm Sat & Sun) Sit outside on the terrace for a substantial meal, a drink and wonderful ocean views. Steak, schnitzel and seafood choices offer few surprises.

Marino's Deli DELI $
(Whitsunday Shopping Centre, Cannonvale; dishes $8-23.50; ⏰7.30am-8pm Mon-Sat) Great takeaway pasta and antipasto offerings.

★ **Mr Bones** PIZZERIA, TAPAS $$
(☎0416 011 615; Lagoon Plaza, 263 Shute Harbour Rd; shared plates $12-17, pizza $15-23; ⏰9am-9pm Tue-Sat) Mr Bones is the new standard bearer in Airlie Beach for hip, affordable dining. It's rightfully gaining repute for its perfect thin-based pizzas – try the prawn and harissa – while the 'not pizzas' (appetisers including the lip-licking blackened fish skewers with pineapple and mint salsa) are also spectacular.

Village Cafe CAFE $$
(☎07-4946 5745; 366 Shute Harbour Rd; mains $19.95-29.50; ⏰7.30am-9pm) Village Cafe is always busy with hungover backpackers and those chasing good coffee, and the breakfasts at this place are just the tonic to get the day started. Order a 'hot rock' and cook your protein of choice to perfection on a sizzling volcanic slab that's been heated for 12 hours.

Deja Vu FUSION $$
(☎07-4948 4309; Golden Orchid Dr; lunch $19-25, dinner $27.50-34.50; ⏰noon-2.30pm & 6-9pm Wed-Sat, noon-2.30pm Sun) Rated as one of Airlie's best, this Polynesian-themed restaurant concocts dishes with all kinds of international influences. Aim to be in town for weekly gastro-event The Long Sunday Lunch (eight courses per person costs $44.50). Bookings are required here.

Drinking & Nightlife

It's said that Airlie Beach is a drinking town with a sailing problem. The bars at **Magnums** and **Beaches**, the two big backpackers in the centre of town, are always crowded, and are popular places to kick off a ribald evening.

Phoenix Bar BAR
(390 Shute Harbour Rd; ⏰7pm-3am) Dance'n'DJ hotspot with drink specials and free pizzas nightly (from 6pm to 8pm).

Paddy's Shenanigans IRISH PUB
(352 Shute Harbour Rd; ⏰5pm-3am) As one would expect.

Mama Africa CLUB
(263 Shute Harbour Rd; ⏰10pm-5am) Just a stumble across the road from the main party bars, this African-style safari nightclub throbs a beat that both hunter and prey find hard to resist.

Information

The main drag is stacked with privately run tour agencies. Check out their noticeboards for stand-by rates on sailing tours and resort accommodation. Internet and wi-fi access is widely available.

NPRSR (☎13 74 68; www.nprsr.qld.gov.au; cnr Shute Harbour & Mandalay Rds; ⏰9am-4.30pm Mon-Fri) For camping permits and info.

Getting There & Away

AIR

The closest major airports are Whitsunday Coast (Proserpine) and Hamilton Island.

Whitsunday Airport (☎07-4946 9180), a small airfield 6km east of Airlie Beach, is midway between Airlie Beach and Shute Harbour.

BOAT

Transfers between Abel Point Marina and Daydream and Long Islands are provided by **Cruise Whitsundays** (☎07-4946 4662; www.cruise-whitsundays.com), as are airport transfers from Abel Point Marina to Hamilton Island.

See the Getting There & Away sections of individual islands for more details.

BUS

Greyhound (☎1300 473 946; www.greyhound.com.au) and **Premier Motor Service** (☎13 34 10; www.premierms.com.au) buses detour off the Bruce Hwy to Airlie Beach. There are buses between Airlie Beach and all the major centres along the coast, including Brisbane ($232, 19 hours), Mackay ($30, two hours), Townsville ($46, 4 hours) and Cairns ($92, 9 hours).

Long-distance buses stop on The Esplanade, between the sailing club and the Airlie Beach Hotel.

Whitsunday Transit (☎07-4946 1800; www.whitsundaytransit.com.au) connects Proserpine (Whitsunday Airport), Cannonvale, Abel Point, Airlie Beach and Shute Harbour. Buses operate from 6am to 10.30pm.

Getting Around

Airlie Beach is small enough to cover by foot. Most cruise boats have courtesy buses that will pick you up from wherever you're staying and take you to either Shute Harbour or Abel Point Marina. To book a taxi, call **Whitsunday Taxis** (☎13 10 08).

Most of the major car-rental agencies are repesented here: offices line Shute Harbour Rd.

Conway National Park

The mountains of this national park and the Whitsunday Islands are part of the same coastal mountain range. Rising sea levels following the last ice age flooded the lower valleys, leaving only the highest peaks as islands, now cut off from the mainland.

The road from Airlie Beach to Shute Harbour passes through the northern section of the park. Several **walking trails** start from near the picnic and day-use area. About 1km past the day-use area, there's a 2.4km walk up to the **Mt Rooper lookout**, with good views of the Whitsunday Passage and islands. Further along the main road, towards Coral Point and before Shute Harbour, there's a 1km track leading down to **Coral Beach** and **The Beak lookout**. This track was created with the assistance of the Giru Dala, the traditional custodians of the Whitsunday area, and a brochure available at the start of the trail explains how the local Aborigines use plants growing in the area.

To reach the beautiful **Cedar Creek Falls**, turn off the Proserpine–Airlie Beach road on to Conway Rd, 18km southwest of Airlie Beach. It's then about 15km to the falls; the roads are well signposted.

Long Island

Long Island has some of the prettiest beaches in the Whitsundays and 13km of walking tracks. The island stretches 9km long by 1.5km wide; a 500m-wide channel separates it from the mainland. Day-trippers can use the facilities at Long Island Resort.

Sleeping

National Park Camp Site CAMPGROUND **$**
(www.nprsr.qld.gov.au; per person/family $5.45/21.80) Basic camping at Long Island's Sandy Bay (not to be confused with the Sandy Bay camping ground at nearby South Molle).

Paradise Bay BUNGALOW **$$$**
(☎07-4946 9777; www.paradisebay.com.au; 3-night packages, d from $1500) This secluded eco-friendly lodge comprises 10 spacious bungalows made from Australian hardwood. In the name of peace and tranquillity, no children or motorised water sports are allowed, and there's no internet either. The tariff is inclusive of sailing tours, food and house wines; helicopter transfers are an extra $760 per bungalow.

Long Island Resort RESORT **$$$**
(☎1800 075 125; www.oceanhotels.com.au/longisland; d incl all meals $230-380;) A resort for everyone – yep, the kids are more than welcome here. Sitting on Happy Bay at the north of the island, Long Island Resort is a comfortable place with three levels of accommodation, the best being those on the beachfront. There are some fabulous short walks and plenty of activities to keep all age groups busy: who doesn't love mini-golf?

Getting There & Around

Cruise Whitsundays (☎07-4946 4662; www.cruisewhitsundays.com) connects Long Island Resort to Shute Harbour by frequent daily services. The direct trip takes about 20 minutes, and costs adult/child $36/24.

Hook Island

The 53-sq-km Hook Island, second-largest of the Whitsundays, is predominantly national park and rises to 450m at Hook Peak. There are a number of good beaches dotted around the island, and some of the region's best diving and snorkelling locations. Many travellers come here enticed by the low prices and have left disappointed because it's not what they expected. If you want luxury, don't come to Hook Island...try Hayman instead!

There are national-park **camping grounds** (www.nprsr.qld.gov.au; per person/

family $5.45/21.80) at Maureen Cove, Steen's Beach, Curlew Beach and Crayfish Beach. Although basic, they provide some wonderful back-to-nature opportunities.

Hook Island Wilderness Resort (07-4946 5255; www.hookislandresort.com; camp site per person $10, dm $35, d with/without bathroom $150/100;) is an extremely basic place: the only stars it rates are the ones twinkling overhead. But if you don't mind roughing it and value snorkelling (and a wonderful beachfront location) over style, give it a go. The resort is open erratically: be sure to check the website before making plans.

Transfers are arranged when you book your accommodation. Otherwise, **Whitsunday Island Camping Connections – Scamper** (07-4946 6285; www.whitsundaycamping.com.au) can organise drop offs to the camping grounds (minimum four people) for around $160 per person return.

South Molle Island

The largest of the Molle group of islands at 4 sq km, South Molle is virtually joined to Mid Molle and North Molle Islands. Apart from the resort area and golf course at Bauer Bay in the north, the island is all national park and is crisscrossed by 15km of walking tracks, with some superb lookout points. The highest point is Mt Jeffreys (198m), but the climb up **Spion Kop** will reward you with fantastic sunset views. The track to Spion Kop passes an ancient Ngaro stone quarry – look out for an area of shattered rock spilling down the hillside.

There are national park **camping grounds** (13 74 68; www.nprsr.qld.gov.au; per person/family $5.45/21.80) at Sandy Bay in the south and at Paddle Bay near the resort.

Adventure Island Resort (1800 466 444; www.koalaadventures.com; 2 nights/3 days Sail and Stay package $379;) is *the* party place to stay, but there are plenty of daytime activities to keep you busy too, including archery, bushwalking, fish feeding, sailing, paddling and snorkelling. The resort is the sole domain of those cruising on the *Pride of Airlie*, which stops at South Molle for two nights on its three-day 'Sail and Stay' trip. The journey also includes Whitehaven Beach.

Day-trippers and campers can get to South Molle with Whitsunday Island Camping Connections ($65 return; p213).

Daydream Island

Daydream Island, just over 1km long and 200m wide, would live up to its name a bit more if it wasn't quite so busy; one could be forgiven for mistaking it for a floating theme park. The closest resort to the mainland, it's a very popular day-trip destination suitable for everybody, especially busy families, swinging singles and couples looking for a romantic island wedding.

The large **Daydream Island Resort & Spa** (1800 075 040; www.daydreamisland.com; d from $310;) is surrounded by beautifully landscaped tropical gardens, with a stingray-, shark- and fish-filled lagoon running through it. It has tennis courts, a gym, catamarans, windsurfers, three swimming pools and an open-air cinema all included in the tariff. There are five grades of accommodation and most package deals include a buffet breakfast. There's also a club with constant activities to keep children occupied, and they'll love the **stingray splash** ($38) and fish-feeding sessions. The resort occupies the entire island, so it's not the place to head if you're seeking isolation.

Cruise Whitsundays (07-4946 4662; www.cruisewhitsundays.com; one-way adult/child $36/24) connects Daydream Island to Abel Point Marina and Shute Harbour with frequent daily services.

Hamilton Island

POP 1209

Hamilton can come as a shock for the first-time visitor, with swarms of people and heavy development making it more like a busy town rather than a castaway island. Though not everyone's idea of a perfect getaway, it's hard not to be impressed by the sheer range of accommodation options, restaurants, bars and activities – there's something for everyone. Day-trippers can use some resort facilities, including tennis courts, squash courts, a gym, a golf driving range and a mini-golf course.

From **Catseye Beach**, in front of the resort, you can hire windsurfers, catamarans, jet skis and other equipment, and go parasailing or waterskiing.

A few shops by the harbour organise dives and certificate courses; you can take a variety of cruises to other islands and the outer reef. Half-day fishing trips cost around $190 per person with fishing gear supplied.

There are a few **walking trails**, the best being the clamber up to Passage Peak (239m) on the northeastern corner of the island. Hamilton also has day care and a Clownfish Club for kids.

Sleeping

Hamilton Island Resort RESORT **$$$**
(13 73 33; www.hamiltonisland.com.au; d from $340;) Hamilton Island Resort has options ranging from hotel rooms to self-contained apartments and penthouses. The rates listed in the following reviews are for one night, although almost everyone stays for at least three when the cheaper package deals come into effect.

Qualia RESORT **$$$**
(1300 780 959; www.qualia.com.au; d from $975;) The ultra-luxe Qualia is set on 12 hectares, with modern villas materialising like heavenly tree houses in the leafy hillside. The resort has a private beach, two restaurants, a spa and two swimming pools.

Beach Club RESORT **$$$**
(www.hamiltonisland.com.au/BeachClub; d from $595;) Flanking the main resort complex, the Beach Club has terraced rooms with absolute beachfront positions.

Whitsunday Holiday Homes APARTMENT **$$$**
(13 73 33; www.hihh.com.au; from $288;) Private accommodation ranging from three-star apartments to family-friendly houses and five-star luxury digs. Rates include your own golf buggy for highbrow hooning. There's a four-night minimum stay in some properties.

BEST WHITSUNDAY ISLAND RESORTS...

Only seven of the islands have resorts, but each has its own unique flavour and style. Do you want partying or pampering? Eco or extravagant? Check the list below...

...for ecotourism

- Paradise Bay (p212) is an exclusive ecoresort with a conscience. It has just 10 simple hardwood bungalows and implements 'Earth-kind' sustainable operations without compromising on luxury.

...for luxury

- Qualia (p214) on Hamilton Island is divine. Guests stay in luxurious pavilions among the trees and feast on Coral Sea views from their own private plunge pool.
- Hayman Island Resort (p215) epitomises old-fashioned luxury with a focus on sensory/gustatory indulgence and impeccable service. It also has a whopping big pool.

...for families

- Daydream Island Resort & Spa (p213) is always buzzing with activity. There's fun stuff for all age groups on and off the water. With a kiddies club, an open-air cinema and plenty of restaurants, cafes and a pool bar, neither you or your young charges will be bored.
- Long Island Resort (p212) may be less glitzy than others, but still has plenty of activities to keep the kids busy while you laze on the beach or lounge beside the pool with pink cocktail in hand.

...for romance

- Paradise Bay (p212) is not only an ecoresort, it's a honeymoon hotspot. It's exclusive and intimate but don't expect glitzy-glam – this is simple, nature-based elegance.

...for fun

- Adventure Island Resort (p213) on South Molle Island carries the Airlie Beach party crowd into the wee hours, with DJs, hot bands and nightly shenanigans. The island has fantastic bushwalks to cure those nasty hangovers so, come nightfall, you can start all over again. The resort is for those on a 'Sail and Stay' package (travelling on the *Pride of Airlie*).

Palm Bungalows CABIN $$$
(www.hamiltonisland.com.au/palm-bungalows; d from $340;) These attractive individual units behind the resort complex are closely packed but buffered by lush gardens. Each has a double and single bed and a small patio.

Reef View Hotel HOTEL $$$
(www.hamiltonisland.com.au/reef-view-hotel; d from $360;) Four-star hotel popular with families.

Eating

The main resort has a number of restaurants, but the marina also offers plenty of choice. There's also a supermarket for self-caterers.

Manta Ray Cafe CAFE $$
(07-4946 8213; Marina Village; mains $17-30; 10.30am-9pm) Wood-fired gourmet pizzas are a favourite here.

Marina Tavern PUB $$
(07-4946 8839; Marina Village; mains from $17.50; 11am-midnight) Drop in for a decent pub feed or a drink.

Bommie Restaurant MODERN AUSTRALIAN $$$
(07-4948 9433; mains $38-50; 6pm-midnight Tue-Sat) Upmarket Mod-Oz cuisine with water views as exclusive as the prices. It's within the resort complex.

Romano's ITALIAN $$$
(07-4946 8212; Marina Village; mains $33-40; 6pm-midnight Thu-Mon) Popular Italian restaurant with a deck jutting over the water.

Mariners Seafood Restaurant SEAFOOD $$$
(07-4946 8628; Marina Village; mains $38-48; 6pm-late Sat-Wed) While the emphasis is on seafood, grills are also available.

Drinking & Nightlife

Some of the bars in the resort and harbourside offer nightly entertainment; try the popular **Boheme's Nightclub** (Marina Village; 9pm-late Thu-Sat).

Getting There & Away

AIR

Hamilton Island Airport is the main arrival centre for the Whitsundays, and is serviced by **Qantas** (13 13 13; www.qantas.com.au), **Jetstar** (13 15 38; www.jetstar.com.au) and **Virgin Blue** (13 67 89; www.virginblue.com.au).

BOAT

Cruise Whitsundays (07-4946 4662; www.cruisewhitsundays.com) connects Hamilton Island Airport and the marina with Abel Point Marina and Shute Harbour in Airlie Beach ($48).

Getting Around

There's a free shuttle-bus service operating around the island from 7am to 11pm.

You can hire a golf buggy (per one/two/three/24 hours $45/55/60/85) to whiz around the island.

Hayman Island

The most northern of the Whitsunday group, little Hayman is just 4 sq km in area and rises to 250m above sea level. It has forested hills, valleys and beaches and a five-star resort.

An avenue of stately date palms leads to the main entrance of the recently refurbished **One&Only Hayman Island Resort** (07-4940 1838; www.hayman.com.au; r incl breakfast $590-8000;), one of the most gilded playgrounds on the Great Barrier Reef with its hectare of swimming pools, landscaped gardens and exclusive boutiques.

Resort guests must first fly to Hamilton's Great Barrier Reef Airport before being escorted to Hayman's fleet of luxury cruisers (one way adult/child $145/72.50) for a pampered transfer to the resort.

Lindeman Island

Lovely little Lindeman was once home to a busy Club Med resort; these days, it's only nature photographers and hikers who provide any semblance of bustle, making independent treks for the varied island tree life and the sublime view from Mt Oldfield (210m). Lindeman is mostly national park, with empty bays and 20km of impressive walking trails. **Boat Port** is the best spot for camping.

Whitsunday Island

Whitehaven Beach, on Whitsunday Island, is a pristine 7km-long stretch of blinding sand (at 98% pure silica, said sand is some of the whitest in the world), bounded by lush tropical vegetation and a brilliant blue sea. From Hill Inlet at the northern end of the beach, the pattern of dazzling sand through the turquoise and aquamarine water paints a magical picture. There's excellent snorkelling from its southern end. Whitehaven is one of Australia's most beautiful beaches.

There are national-park **camping grounds** (☎13 74 68; www.nprsr.qld.gov.au; adult/family $5.45/21.80) at Dugong, Nari's and Joe's Beaches in the west; at Chance Bay in the south; at the southern end of Whitehaven Beach; and Peter Bay in the north.

Whitsunday Island Camping Connections (p207) can get you there from $105 return.

Other Whitsunday Islands

The northern islands are undeveloped and seldom visited by cruise boats. Several of these – Gloucester, Saddleback and Armit Islands – have national-park camping grounds. The NPRSR (p211) office in Airlie Beach can issue camping permits and advise you on which islands to visit and how to get there.

Bowen

POP 10,260

Bowen is a classic reminder of the typical small Queensland coastal towns of the 1970s: wide streets, low-rise buildings, wooden Queenslander houses and laid-back, friendly locals. What makes Bowen stand out from other similar northern towns is its 24 colourful murals, all depicting various events and facets of the region's history. The large, detailed artworks are scattered on walls throughout the centre of town; grab a walking map and more info at the visitor centre.

The foreshore, with its landscaped esplanade, picnic tables and barbecues is a focal point, and there are some truly stunning beaches and bays northeast of the town centre.

Bowen gets busy during fruit-picking season (April to November). The famous Bowen mango unsurprisingly hails from here.

Keep an eye out for the 'Bowenwood' sign on the town's water tower; Baz Luhrmann's epic movie *Australia* was shot here in 2007 and the locals are still a little star-struck.

Sleeping & Eating

Bowen Backpackers HOSTEL $
(☎07-4786 3433; www.bowenbackpackers.net; Herbert St; dm from $20; ❄@) Located at the beach end of Herbert St (past the Grandview Hotel), this is the place to stay if you're working in the surrounding fruit farms. Rooms are neat and reasonably spacious. Ring ahead, as it sometimes closes in the off-season.

Barnacles Backpackers HOSTEL $
(☎07-4786 4400; www.barnaclesbackpackers.com; 18 Gordon St; dm from $30; 📶) Clean, hostel that can help with fruit-picking jobs.

Bowen Arrow Motel MOTEL $$
(☎07-4786 2499; www.bowenarrowmotel.com.au; 18512 Bruce Hwy; d $115; 📶🏊) Come for the wordplay, stay for the friendly service. Intimate (there are only 12 rooms) and clean with free wi-fi and a great little pool/spa.

Rose Bay Resort RESORT $$
(☎07-4786 9000; www.rosebayresort.com.au; 2 Pandanus St; r $150-300; ❄@🏊) In a beautiful location right on the beach, these spacious studios and comfy units will ensure plenty of quiet time. Minimum two-night stay.

Jochheims Pies BAKERY $
(49 George St; pies $4.60; ⏰5.30am-3.30pm Mon-Fri, to 12.30pm Sat) They've been keeping Bowen bellies full of homemade pies and baked treats since 1963; try a Hugh Jackman ('hunky beef') pie; the actor was a regular here during the filming of *Australia*.

Cove CHINESE, MALAY $$
(☎07-4791 2050; Coral Cove Apartments, Horseshoe Bay Rd; mains $17-28.50; ⏰lunch & dinner Tue-Sun) The spectacular views of the Coral Sea from the timber deck demand a long lunch, or at least a sunset drink before dinner. The menu features an interesting fusion of Chinese and Malay dishes.

Information

Tourism Bowen (☎07-4786 4222; www.tourismbowen.com.au; ⏰8.30am-5pm Mon-Fri, 10.30am-5pm Sat & Sun) Just look for the humongous mango about 7km south of Bowen on the Bruce Hwy.

There's also an **information booth** (Santa Barbara Pde; ⏰10am-5pm Mon-Fri, open sporadically Sat & Sun) in town.

Getting There & Away

BUS

Long-distance bus services stop outside **Bowen Travel** (☎07-4786 1611; 40 Williams St) where you can book tickets for bus journeys. **Greyhound Australia** (☎1300 473 946; www.greyhound.com.au) and **Premier** (☎13 34 10; www.premierms.com.au) are two companies that have frequent buses running to/from Airlie Beach ($23, 1½ hours) and Townsville ($26, four hours).

Townsville to Mission Beach

Includes ➡

Best Places to Eat

- Wayne & Adele's Garden of Eating (p224)
- Sweatshop (p222)
- Monsoon Cruising (p240)
- Benny's Hot Wok (p223)
- Fish Bar (p238)

Best Places to Stay

- Shambhala Retreat (p228)
- Noorla Heritage Resort (p231)
- Jackaroo Hostel (p237)
- Bungalow Bay Koala Village (p228)
- Coral Lodge (p222)

Why Go?

In between the tourist magnets of Cairns and Airlie Beach, Townsville is a 'real' city with a pulse. Although North Queensland's largest urban centre is often bypassed by visitors, it has a surprising number of attractions: a palm-lined beachfront promenade, gracious 19th-century architecture and a host of cultural and sporting venues and events. Magnetic Island's national park, beaches, walking trails and wildlife are a quick ferry ride away.

North of Townsville, the Great Green Way wends past small sugar towns including Ingham, Cardwell, Tully and Innisfail; a stop offers the chance to experience true far northern country hospitality. Mission Beach, about half an hour east of Tully, is a laid-back village that ironically attracts thrillseekers by the busload, all keen on the region's skydiving, white-water rafting and water sports. Forested Hinchinbrook Island and the lovely Dunk Island are top choices for the less adrenaline-addled.

When to Go

Townsville

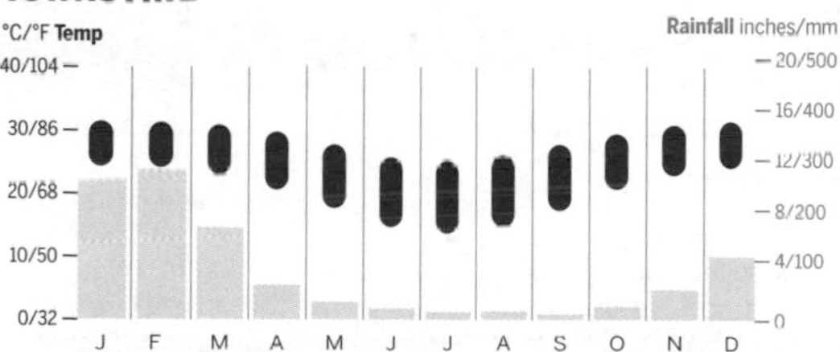

May Celebrate all things wet and wonderful at Tully's Golden Gumboot Festival.

Aug Townsville shows off its cultural side during the Australian Festival of Chamber Music.

Oct Let your dreads down at Mission Beach's Mission Evolve Music Fest.

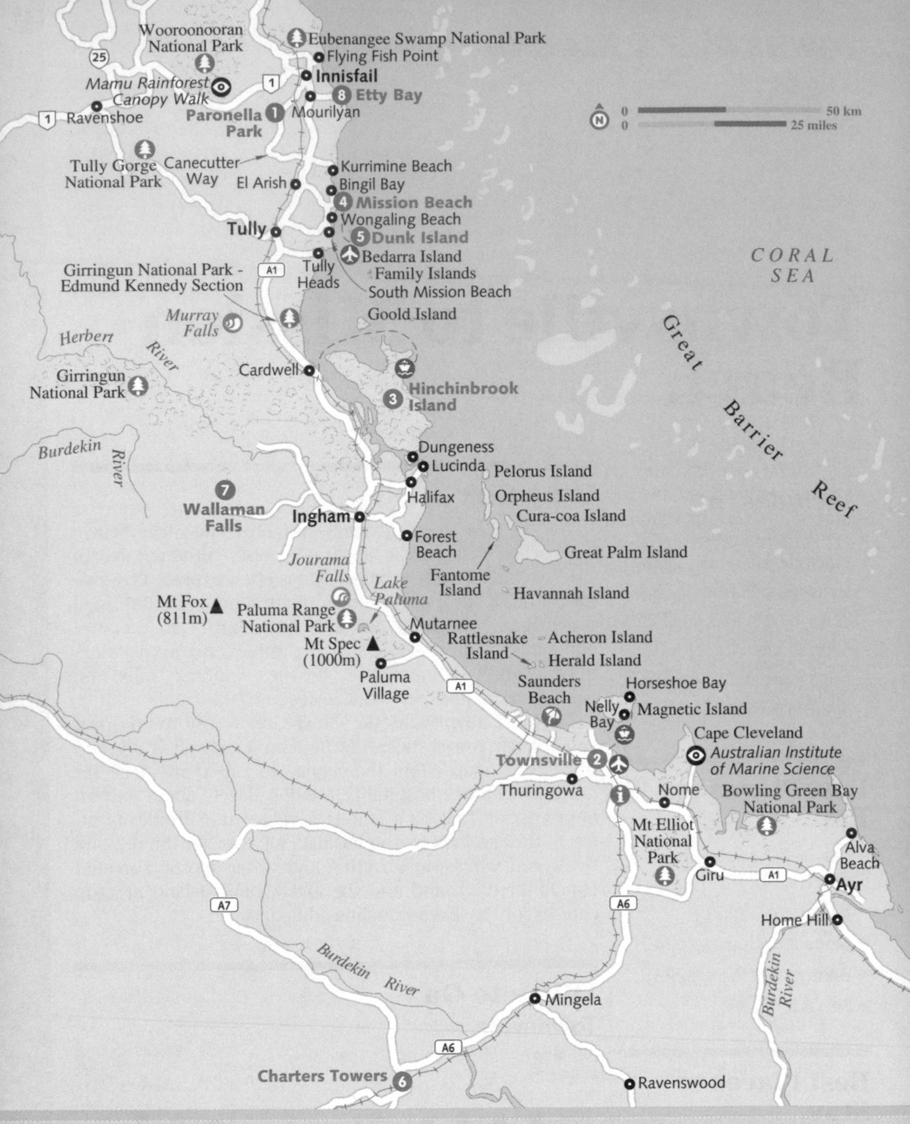

Townsville to Mission Beach Highlights

1 Hearing the story behind the ruined castles of **Paronella Park** (p239) on a day or night tour.

2 Cheering on the Cowboys, North Queensland's National Rugby League team, or National Basketball League team, the Crocodiles, in **Townsville** (p219).

3 Tackling the 32km-long Thorsborne Trail on pristine **Hinchinbrook Island** (p232).

4 Skydiving onto a sandy landing at **Mission Beach** (p235).

5 Having a secluded beach to yourself on **Dunk Island** (p239).

6 Watching a *Ghosts After Dark* outdoor film screening in the gold-rush town of **Charters Towers** (p226).

7 Slipping, sliding and schlepping down to Australia's highest single-drop waterfall, **Wallaman Falls** (p231).

8 Watching wild cassowaries wander along the beach at picturesque **Etty Bay** (p239).

TOWNSVILLE & AROUND

North Queensland's largest city is an ideal base for coastal, inland and offshore day trips.

Townsville

POP 189,931

Sprawling beneath a brooding red hill, Townsville is an underrated spot with a lot to offer: excellent museums, a huge aquarium, world-class diving, two major sporting teams, vibrant nightlife and an endless esplanade. A pedestrian-friendly city, it's easy to take in its sights on foot: grand, refurbished 19th-century buildings offer loads of landmarks, and if you get lost the friendly locals will be only too happy to lend a hand... or shout you a beer. Townsville has a lively, young populace, with thousands of students and armed forces members intermingling with old-school locals, fly-in-fly-out mine workers and summer-seekers lapping up the average 320 days of sunshine per year.

Townsville is only 350km from Cairns, but is much drier than its tropical rival: if 'Brownsville' is baking your bones, the splendid beaches of Magnetic Island are but a ferry jaunt away.

Sights & Activities

The compact city centre is easy to get about on foot.

★Reef HQ Aquarium AQUARIUM
(www.reefhq.com.au; Flinders St E; adult/child $26.50/12.80; 9.30am-5pm) Townsville's excellent aquarium is a living reef on dry land. A staggering 2.5 million litres of water flow through the coral-reef tank, home to 130 corals and 120 fish species. The backdrop of the predator exhibit is a replica of the bow of the SS *Yongala*, which sank in 1911 off the coast of Townsville during a wild cyclone, killing all 122 passengers onboard; it wasn't located until 1958. Kids will love seeing, feeding and touching turtles at the **turtle hospital**. Talks and tours throughout the day focus on different aspects of the reef and the aquarium.

Castle Hill LOOKOUT
Hoof it up this striking 286m-high red hill (an isolated pink granite monolith) that dominates Townsville's skyline for stunning views of the city and Cleveland Bay. Walk up via the rough 'goat track' (2km one way) from Hillside Cres. Otherwise, drive via Gregory St up the narrow, winding 2.6km Castle Hill Rd. A signboard up top details short trails leading to various lookout points.

Museum of Tropical Queensland MUSEUM
(www.mtq.qm.qld.gov.au; 70-102 Flinders St E; adult/child $15/8.80; 9.30am-5pm) Not your everyday museum, the Museum of Tropical Queensland reconstructs scenes using detailed models with interactive displays. At 11am and 2.30pm, you can load and fire a cannon, 1700s-style; galleries include the kid-friendly MindZone science centre and displays on North Queensland's history from the dinosaurs to the rainforest and reef.

Billabong Sanctuary WILDLIFE RESERVE
(www.billabongsanctuary.com.au; Bruce Hwy; adult/child $30/19; 9am-4pm) Just 17km south of Townsville, this eco-certified wildlife park offers up-close-and-personal encounters with Australian wildlife – from dingoes to cassowaries – in their natural habitat. You could easily spend all day at the 11-hectare park, with feedings, shows and talks every half-hour or so.

Botanic Gardens GARDENS
(sunrise-sunset) FREE Townsville's botanic gardens are spread across three locations: each has its own character, but all have tropical plants and are abundantly green. Closest to the centre, the formal, ornamental **Queens Gardens** (cnr Gregory & Paxton Sts) are 1km northwest of town at the base of Castle Hill.

Cultural Centre CULTURAL CENTRE
(07-4772 7679; www.cctownsville.com.au; 2-68 Flinders St E; 9.30am-4.30pm) Showcases the history, traditions and customs of the Wulgurukaba and Bindal people. Call for guided-tour times.

Perc Tucker Regional Gallery GALLERY
(www.townsville.qld.gov.au/facilities/galleries/perc-tucker; cnr Denham & Flinders Sts; 10am-5pm Mon-Fri, to 2pm Sat & Sun) Contemporary art gallery in a stately 1885-built former bank. Exhibitions focus on North Queensland artists.

Maritime Museum of Townsville MUSEUM
(www.townsvillemaritimemuseum.org.au; 42-68 Palmer St; adult/child $6/3; 10am-3pm Mon-Fri, noon-3pm Sat & Sun) One for the boat buffs, with a gallery dedicated to the wreck of the *Yongala* and exhibits on North Queensland's naval industries. Tours of decommissioned patrol boat HMAS *Townsville* are available.

Townsville

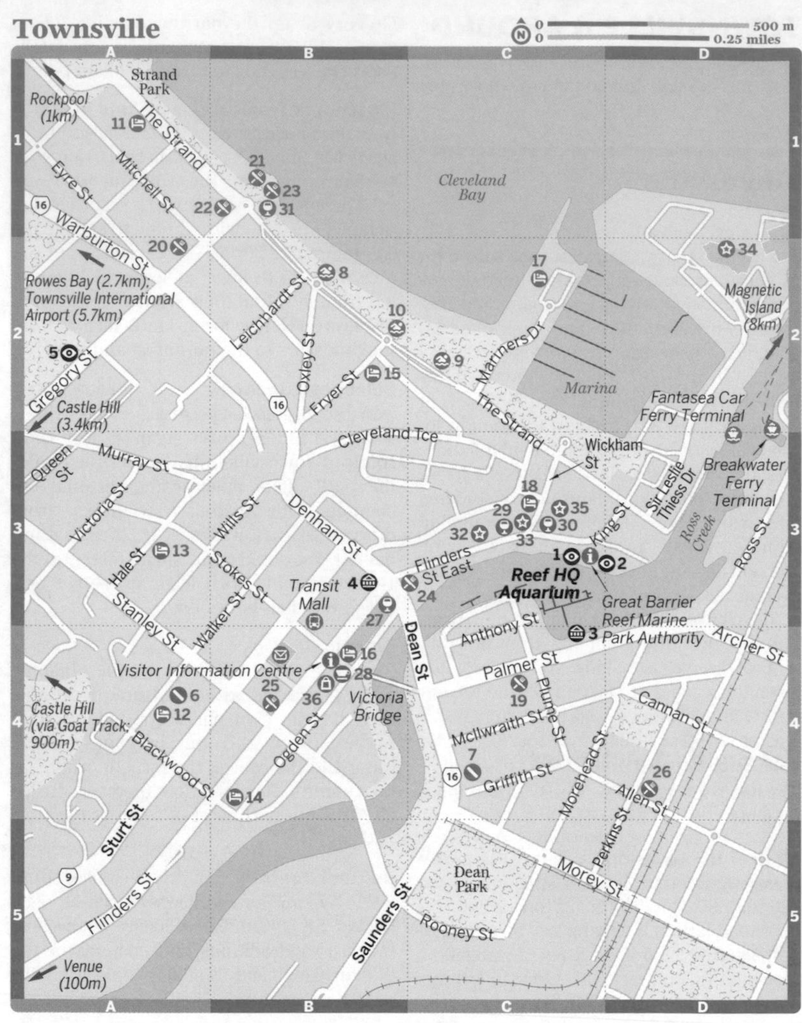

Strand SWIMMING, OUTDOORS

Stretching 2.2km, Townsville's waterfront is interspersed with parks, pools, cafes and playgrounds – with hundreds of palm trees providing shade. Walkers and joggers take to the path from first light while beachgoers take over by mid-morning, and evening strollers are at it by late afternoon. Its golden-sand beach is patrolled and protected by two stinger enclosures.

At the northern tip is the **rock pool** (24hr) FREE, an enormous artificial swimming pool surrounded by lawns and sandy beaches. Alternatively, head to the chlorinated safety of the heritage-listed, Olympic-sized swimming pool, **Tobruk Memorial Baths** (www.townsville.qld.gov.au; adult/child $5/3; 5.30am-7pm Mon-Thu, to 6pm Fri, 7am-4pm Sat, 8am-5pm Sun). There's also a fantastic **water playground** (10am-8pm Dec-Mar, to 6pm Sep-Nov, Apr & May, to 5pm Jun-Aug) FREE for the kids.

Skydive Townsville SKYDIVING

(07-4721 4721; www.skydivetownsville.com.au; tandem jump from $395) Hurl yourself from a perfectly good plane and land right on the Strand.

Townsville

Top Sights

1 Reef HQ Aquarium C3

Sights

2 Cultural Centre D3
3 Maritime Museum of Townsville C4
Museum of Tropical Queensland .... (see 2)
4 Perc Tucker Regional Gallery B3
5 Queens (Botanic) Gardens A2

Activities, Courses & Tours

6 Adrenalin Dive A4
7 Remote Area Dive C4
8 Strand B2
9 Tobruk Memorial Baths C2
10 Water Playground B2

Sleeping

11 Aquarius on the Beach A1
12 Civic Guest House A4
13 Coral Lodge A3
14 Grand Northern Hotel B4
15 Historic Yongala Lodge Motel B2
16 Holiday Inn B4
17 Mariners North C2
Orchid Guest House .... (see 13)
18 Reef Lodge C3

Eating

Absolute Tea .... (see 4)
19 Benny's Hot Wok C4
20 Cafe Bambini A2
21 Cbar B1
22 Harold's Seafood B1
23 Longboard Bar & Grill B1
Souvlaki Bar .... (see 22)
24 Summerie's Thai Cuisine C3
25 Sweatshop B4
26 Wayne & Adele's Garden of Eating D4

Drinking & Nightlife

27 Brewery B3
28 Coffee Dominion B4
29 Heritage Bar C3
30 Molly Malones C3
31 Seaview Hotel B1

Entertainment

32 Consortium C3
33 Flynns C3
34 Jupiters Casino D2
35 The Shed C3

Shopping

36 Cotters Market B4

Woodstock Trail Rides HORSE RIDING
(☎07-4778 8888; www.woodstocktrailrides.com.au; Jones Rd; 90min/half-day ride $80/100, cattle muster $175) Situated 43km south of Townsville, this huge property has full- and half-day horse-riding trips as well as **cattle musters** for aspiring cowboys and cowgirls. Transfers for full-day rides and cattle musters are included from Townsville. Bookings essential.

Tours

Kookaburra Tours GUIDED TOUR
(☎0448 794 798; www.kookaburratours.com.au) Highly recommended day trips in Townsville and further afield, with enthusiastic, informed commentary. Options include 'Heritage and Highlights' city tours (adult/child $40/18), Wallaman Falls (adult/child $125/55), rainforest tours (adult/child $125/55) and Aboriginal cultural tours (adult/child $140/65).

Townsville Ghost Tours GUIDED TOUR
(☎0404 453 354; www.townsvilleghosttours.com.au) Five spooky options, from city haunts aboard the 'ghost bus' (from $65) to an overnight trip to Ravenswood ($250 including meals and accommodation).

Festivals & Events

The city has a packed calendar of festivals and events, including home games of its revered sporting teams, the **North Queensland Cowboys** (www.cowboys.com.au; season Mar-Sep) National Rugby League team and the **Crocodiles** (www.crocodiles.com.au; season mid-Oct–Apr) National Basketball League team. If you don't believe how popular basketball can be in Australia, you will when you see locals driving around with croc tails hanging out of their car boots.

Townsville 400 MOTOR SPORTS
(www.v8supercars.com.au) V8 Supercars roar through a purpose-built street circuit each July during the V8 Supercar Championship.

Australian Festival of Chamber Music MUSIC
(www.afcm.com.au) Townsville gets cultural during this internationally renowned festival each August.

Sleeping

Townsville fills to capacity during festivals and events, so it's wise to book ahead. Midrange motels and self-catering units stretch along the Strand, while international chains and backpacker places cluster in the city centre and around Palmer St.

Reef Lodge HOSTEL $
(☎07-4721 1112; www.reeflodge.com.au; 4 Wickham St; dm $22-26, d with/without bathroom $80/62; ❄@📶) The cruisy atmosphere at Townsville's best – and most central – hostel extends from Buddhist sculptures and hammocks strewn through the garden to a nerdishly compelling '80s video-game room.

Coral Lodge B&B $
(☎07-4771 5512; www.corallodge.com.au; 32 Hale St; s/d without bathroom $70/90, units from $85; ❄) If you're looking to stay in a charming, old-fashioned Aussie home (with a three-legged cat), this century-old property can't be beat. Upstairs self-contained units are like having your own apartment while downstairs guest rooms share bathrooms. The welcoming owners will pick you up from the bus, train or ferry.

Civic Guest House HOSTEL $
(☎07-4771 5381; www.civicguesthousetownsville.com.au; 262 Walker St; dm from $24, d from $58; @📶) Recently renovated, and oh how it sparkles. A contender for cleanest hostel on earth, the Civic lives up to its name with friendly staff and a laid-back clientele. Free transport to/from the ferry or bus station.

Rowes Bay Caravan Park CARAVAN PARK $
(☎07-4771 3576; www.rowesbaycp.com.au; Heatley Pde; unpowered/powered site $26/36, cabin with/without bathroom from $98/65, villa $105; ❄@📶🏊) Leafy park directly opposite Rowes Bay's beachfront. Brand-new villas are smaller than cabins but spiffier.

Orchid Guest House GUESTHOUSE $
(☎07-4771 6683; www.orchidguesthouse.com.au; 34 Hale St; dm $27, s with/without bathroom $75/55, d $85/65; ❄) Not one for the party set, but a godsend to those looking for somewhere cheap and cheerful to lay their head. Weekly rates available for working backpackers.

Grand Northern Hotel HOTEL $
(☎07-4771 6191; www.gnhotel.com.au; 500 Flinders St; s with/without air-con $70/60, d & tw with/without air-con $80/70; P❄) Swill and sleep at this historic 1901 pub in Townsville's bustling centre. It's not exactly a tranquil haven, but for those who like to be in the thick of it all, the GN can't be beat. All rooms share facilities.

Historic Yongala Lodge Motel MOTEL $$
(☎07-4772 4633; www.historicyongala.com.au; 11 Fryer St; motel r $99-105, 1-bedroom apt $115-120; ❄📶🏊) Built in 1884, this lovely historic building is but a short stroll from the Strand and city centre. The rooms and apartments are small but good value. The excellent **restaurant** (mains $20 to $38, open for dinner Monday to Saturday) is long-loved by locals.

Holiday Inn HOTEL $$
(☎07-4729 2000; www.townsville.holiday-inn.com; 334 Flinders St; d $110-189; ❄📶🏊) Nicknamed the 'sugar shaker', this 20-storey, 1976-built circular building (the city's tallest) is a Townsville icon. Its rooms are much more contemporary than the exterior suggests, and there's a great rooftop pool with unrivalled views over the city.

Aquarius on the Beach HOTEL $$
(☎1800 622 474; www.aquariusonthebeach.com.au; 75 The Strand; d $110-150; ❄@📶🏊) The spectacular balcony views impress almost as much as the size of this place, the tallest building on the Strand. Don't be put off by the dated facade – this is one of the better places around, and the service is faultless.

Mariners North APARTMENT $$$
(☎07-4722 0777; www.marinersnorth.com.au; 7 Mariners Dr; 2-/3-bedroom apt from $259/405, min stay two nights; ❄📶🏊) Self-contained, absolute oceanfront apartments have generous living areas, big bathrooms and brilliant balconies overlooking Cleveland Bay and out to Maggie. Free gym use.

Eating

Palmer St is Townsville's premier dining strip, offering a diverse range of cuisines: wander along and take your pick. Perpendicular to the Strand, Gregory St has a clutch of cafes and takeaway joints. Many of Townsville's bars and pubs also serve food.

★**Sweatshop** CAFE $
(☎0435 845 237; www.thesweatshop.com.au; 181 Flinders St; jaffles $7, burgers $12; ⏰7.30am-4pm Mon-Wed, to 8pm Thu, to midnight Fri & Sat, 9am-3pm Sun) Hipsters in Townsville? Who'd a-thunk it? This tongue-in-cheek art space serves simple, high-quality food and the best coffee ($3.50) in Townsville. Chow down on fresh-baked treats and gawk at an ever-evolving gallery showcasing local talent.

Benny's Hot Wok ASIAN $$
(☎07-4724 3243; 17-21 Palmer St; mains $14-32; ⊙5pm-late daily, yum cha 10.30am -2.30pm Sun) Famous in FNQ for its staggering range of pan-Asian options – from freshly made sushi and sashimi to Peking duck rolls, steaming laksas and sizzling Mongolian lamb – Benny's is also a top spot for a cocktail and a catch-up.

Cafe Bambini CAFE $
(46 Gregory St; mains $11.50-20; ⊙5.30am-5pm Mon-Fri, 6.30am-4pm Sat & Sun;) With four locations strewn around town, this local success story cooks up some of the best (all-day!) breakfasts in Townsville, while lunches are fresh and filling.

Summerie's Thai Cuisine THAI $
(☎07-4420 1282; 232 Flinders St; lunch special $12.50, dinner mains from $17; ⊙11.30am-2.30pm & 5.30-10pm) Authentic Thai food that gets the thumbs up from coconut-curry-crazed locals. The name of specialty dish 'Heaven on Earth' (slow-cooked coconut prawns with crunchy greens) is definitely not false advertising.

Souvlaki Bar GREEK $
(Shops 3 & 4, 58 The Strand; mains $6.50-17.50; ⊙10.30am-9pm Mon-Fri, to 10pm Sat & Sun) Hellenic heaven, with juicy gyros, meze galore and home-made honey puffs all vying for tummy space.

BLOWIN' IN THE WIND

Queensland is The Sunshine State, known for its sultry climate and year 'round holiday weather; an old slogan went as far as claiming it was 'Beautiful one day, perfect the next'. But up in the far north, a dark cloud looms – literally – on the horizon between November and April each year. Cyclones – known elsewhere as hurricanes or typhoons – are a part of life in the tropics, with an average of four or five forming each season. While it's rare for these cyclones to escalate into full-blown destructive storms, big ones do come a'crashing: in February 2011, Cyclone Yasi smashed into the coast around Mission Beach with winds estimated at up to 300km/h, ripping through the towns of Tully and Cardwell and islands including Dunk, Bedarra and Hinchinbrook. Hundreds of homes along the coast between Innisfail and Ingham were severely damaged, banana plantations and cane fields flattened and areas of national park rainforest pummelled. Amazingly, there were no deaths or serious injuries.

Here are a few cyclonic facts to blow your hair back:

➡ Tropical cyclones are rated by their intensity in categories. A Category 1 storm blows gales of less than 125km/h, a Category 2 has destructive winds of 125km/h to 164km/h, cyclones from Category 3 (165km/h to 224km/h) to Category 5 (over 280km/h) are unsurprisingly billed as 'severe'.

➡ During the season, keep a sharp ear out for cyclone predictions and alerts. If a cyclone watch or warning is issued, stay tuned to local radio and monitor the **Bureau of Meteorology** website (www.bom.gov.au) for updates and advice. Locals tend to be complacent about cyclones, but will still buy out the bottle shop when a threat is imminent!

➡ Cyclone names are given in alphabetical order, alternating between male and female, from a seasonal list of 104 names compiled by the Bureau of Meteorology Tropical Cyclone Warning Centre. Names must not offend or be controversial, but it was a different story in the old days, when storms were frequently named after irksome politicians, mythological creatures and mothers-in-law.

➡ Yasi was a shocker, but the worst cyclone to hit the far northern coast was Category 5 Cyclone Mahina, which hit Bathurst Bay on Cape York in March 1899. More than 400 people were killed, including 100 Indigenous Australians and hundreds of workers on pearler fleet vessels. Mahina still holds the record for the world's greatest-ever storm surge (between 13m and 14.6m); on a nearby island, dolphins were found atop 15m-high cliffs!

Harold's Seafood SEAFOOD **$**
(cnr The Strand & Gregory St; meals $4-10; ⌚lunch & dinner) This takeaway joint has bug burgers of the Moreton Bay variety.

Wayne & Adele's Garden of Eating MODERN AUSTRALIAN **$$**
(☎07-4772 2984; 11 Allen St; mains from $19; ⌚6.30-10pm Mon, 6.30-11pm Thu-Sat, noon-3pm Sun) For those who like a side serving of quirky with their grub, you can't miss mains like 'Don't Lose Your Tempeh' (curried vego tempeh fritter with kaffir-lime gado-gado salad) or 'Goat in a Boat' (Moroccan goat pie on date dahl). The purple courtyard is as flamboyant as the menu.

Absolute Tea TEAHOUSE **$$**
(☎07-4721 2311; 269 Flinders St; tea per pot from $4.90, high tea $25; ⌚9.30am-3.30pm Wed-Sun) Ignore the sweat trickling down your neck and imagine yourself a lady (or gentleman) at this refined tropical tea-room. Take High or Devonshire Tea, opt for an elegant luncheon or just sip your way through 100 types of tea.

Longboard Bar & Grill MODERN AUSTRALIAN **$$**
(☎07-4724 1234; The Strand, opposite Gregory St; mains $15-34; ⌚11.30am-3pm & 5.30pm-late) This waterfront eatery plies a lively crowd with grillhouse favourites such as sticky barbecue pork ribs, steaks and buffalo wings. Ignore the incongruous surf theme and be sure to pack a bib.

Cbar CAFE **$$**
(The Strand, opposite Gregory St; mains $16-32; ⌚7am-10pm; 🅥) Dependable and delicious, with an all-day dining menu that caters to the grazers (antipasto $18) and the gluttons (huge battered fish burgers $17).

> **DANGER: STINGERS & CROCS**
>
> From around late October to May, swimming in coastal waters is inadvisable due to the presence of box jellyfish, irukandji and other marine stingers. Only swim where there is a patrolled stinger net.
>
> Saltwater crocodiles inhabit the mangroves, estuaries and open water. Warning signs are posted around the waterways where crocodiles might be present. Pay heed, as these signs are not just quirky props for your holiday snaps: crocs are faster and more clever than you might think!

Drinking & Nightlife

It must be the sunny climate because Townsville sure loves a sip. Most nightlife concentrates around Flinders St East, while Palmer St and the Strand offer lower-key spots. Check listings in Thursday's edition of the *Townsville Bulletin*. Opening hours tend to vary according to the season and the crowds, and nightclubs generally stay open until 5am.

Heritage Bar BAR
(www.heritagebar.com.au; 137 Flinders St E; ⌚5pm-2am Tue-Sat) A surprisingly chic craft bar with suave 'mixologists' delivering creative cocktails to a cool crowd looking for something more than a beer-barn swillfest. Also has a sophisticated bar menu for tipsy nibbles: don't miss Oyster Overdose ($11.50 per dozen) on Monday to Thursday afternoons.

Brewery BREWERY
(252 Flinders St; ⌚11.30am-midnight Mon-Sat) Brews are made on-site at this stunningly restored 1880s former post office. Soak up a Townsville Bitter or Bandito Loco with a meal at its refined **restaurant** (mains $17 to $36).

Coffee Dominion CAFE
(cnr Stokes & Ogden Sts; ⌚6am-5pm Mon-Fri, 7am-1pm Sat & Sun) 🌿 Eco-conscious establishment roasting beans from the Atherton Tableland to Zambia. If you don't find a blend you like, invent your own and they'll grind it fresh.

Seaview Hotel PUB
(cnr The Strand & Gregory St; ⌚10am-midnight) Renowned for its Sunday beer-garden sessions and prime position on the Strand, the Seaview serves ice-cold schooners and has live music and entertainment. Its immense **restaurant** (mains $21 to $44) serves steaks on a par with the size of the premises.

Molly Malones PUB, CLUB
(87 Flinders St E; ⌚11.30am-1am Mon & Tue, to 2am Wed, to 3am Thu, to 5am Fri, 5pm-5am Sat, 5pm-1am Sun) This boisterous Irish pub stages live music on Friday and Saturday nights, or you can shake it on the dance floor at its adjacent nightclub, **The Shed** (⌚8pm-3am Sun-Thu, to 5am Fri & Sat).

GREAT BARRIER REEF TRIPS FROM TOWNSVILLE

The Great Barrier Reef lies further offshore than from Cairns and Port Douglas, hence fuel costs push up the prices. On the upside, it's less crowded (and suffers fewer effects from crowds). Trips from Townsville are dive-oriented; if you just want to snorkel, take a day trip that just goes to the reef – the *Yongala* is for diving only. The *Yongala* is considerably closer to Alva Beach near Ayr, so if your main interest is wreck diving, you may want to consider a trip with Alva Beach–based Yongala Dive (p230).

The visitor centre has a list of Townsville-based operators offering Professional Association of Diving Instructors (PADI)–certified learn-to-dive courses with two days' training in the pool, plus at least two days and one night living aboard the boat. Prices start at about $615; you'll need to obtain a dive medical (around $60). A couple of popular options:

Adrenalin Dive (07-4724 0600; www.adrenalinedive.com.au; 252 Walker St) Day trips to the *Yongala* (from $220) and Wheeler Reef (from $280), both including two dives. Also offers snorkelling (from $180) on Wheeler Reef as well as live-aboard trips and dive-certification courses.

Remote Area Dive (RAD; 07-4721 4424; www.remoteareadive.com.au; 16 Dean St) Runs day trips (from $220) to Orpheus and Pelorus Islands. Also live-aboard trips and dive courses.

Entertainment

Flynns LIVE MUSIC
(101 Flinders St E; 5pm-late Tue-Sun) A jolly Irish pub that doesn't try too hard to be Irish. Wildly popular for its $8 jugs and live music every night except Wednesdays, when karaoke takes over.

Consortium CLUB
(159 Flinders St E; 9pm-5am Tue & Thu-Sun) Resident DJs, DJ comps and events like foam parties and RNB bashes make this big city-style venue Townsville's brashest nightclub.

Jupiters Casino CASINO
(www.jupiterstownsville.com.au; Sir Leslie Thiess Dr; 10am-2am Sun-Thu, to 4am Fri & Sat) For a waterside flutter.

Shopping

Cotters Market MARKET
(www.townsvillerotarymarkets.com.au; Flinders St Mall; 8.30am-1pm Sun) Around 200 craft and food stalls, as well as live entertainment.

Strand Night Market MARKET
(www.townsvillerotarymarkets.com.au; The Strand; 5-9.30pm 1st Fri of month May-Dec) Browse the stalls on the Strand for curios, crafts and knick-knacks.

Information

Australia Post (Shop 1, Post Office Plaza, Sturt St; 8.30am-5.30pm Mon-Fri)

Internet Den (277 Flinders St; per 90min $5; 8am-10pm) Full-service internet cafe with super-fast computers.

Visitor Information Centre (07-4721 3660; www.townsvilleholidays.info; cnr Flinders & Stokes Sts; 9am-5pm Mon-Fri, to 1pm Sat & Sun) Extensive visitor information on Townsville, Magnetic Island and nearby national parks. There's another branch on the Bruce Hwy 10km south of the city.

Getting There & Away

AIR

From **Townsville Airport** (www.townsvilleairport.com.au), **Virgin Blue** (13 67 89; www.virginblue.com.au), **Qantas** (13 13 13; www.qantas.com.au) and **Jetstar** (13 15 38; www.jetstar.com.au) fly to Cairns, Brisbane, the Gold Coast, Sydney, Melbourne, Mackay and Rockhampton, with connections to other major cities.

BUS

Greyhound Australia (1300 473 946; www.greyhound.com.au) has three daily services to Brisbane ($270, 23 hours), Rockhampton ($136, 12 hours), Airlie Beach ($45, 4½ hours), Mission Beach ($41, 3¾ hours) and Cairns ($60, six hours). Buses pick up and drop off at the Breakwater Ferry Terminal.

Premier Motor Service (13 34 10; www.premierms.com.au) has one service a day to/from Brisbane and Cairns, stopping in Townsville at the Fantasea car ferry terminal.

CAR

Major car-rental agencies are represented in Townsville and at the airport.

TRAIN

Townsville's **train station** (Charters Towers Rd) is 1km south of the centre.

The Brisbane–Cairns *Sunlander* travels through Townsville three times a week. Journey time between Brisbane and Townsville is 24 hours (one-way from $140); contact **Queensland Rail** (☎1800 872 467; www.traveltrain.com.au).

 Getting Around

TO/FROM THE AIRPORT

Townsville Airport is 5km northwest of the city centre in Garbutt. A taxi to the centre costs about $20. The **Airport Shuttle** (☎1300 266 946; www.con-x-ion.com; one way/return $10/18) services all arrivals and departures, with pick-ups and drop-offs throughout the central business district (bookings essential).

BUS

Sunbus (☎07-4771 9800; www.sunbus.com.au) runs local bus services around Townsville. Route maps and timetables are available at the visitor information centre and online.

TAXI

Taxis congregate at ranks across town, or call **Townsville Taxis** (☎13 10 08; www.tsvtaxi.com.au).

Magnetic Island

POP 2500

'Maggie', as she's affectionately called, is a 'real' island. Permanent residents live and work here and some even make the daily commute to Townsville. Over half of this mountainous, triangular-shaped island's 52

RAVENSWOOD & CHARTERS TOWERS

You don't have to venture too far inland for a taste of the dry, dusty Queensland outback – a stark contrast to the verdant coast. This detour is easily accessible on a day trip from Townsville, but it's worth staying overnight if you can.

Along the Flinders Hwy, a turn-off at Mingela, 88km southwest of Townsville, leads 40km south to the tiny gold-mining village of **Ravenswood** (population 350), with a couple of gorgeous turn-of-the-20th-century pubs with basic (shared-bathroom) accommodation.

A further 47km west along the Flinders Hwy from Mingela is the historic gold-rush town of **Charters Towers** (population 8234). The 'towers' are its surrounding tors (hills). William Skelton Ewbank Melbourne (WSEM) Charters was the gold commissioner during the rush, when the town was the second-largest, and wealthiest, in Queensland. With almost 100 mines, some 90 pubs and a stock exchange, it became known simply as 'the World'.

Today, a highlight of a visit to the Towers is strolling past its glorious facades recalling the grandeur of those heady days, and listening to locals' ghost stories.

History oozes from the walls of the 1890 **Stock Exchange Arcade**, next door to the **Charters Towers visitor centre** (☎07-4761 5533; www.charterstowers.qld.gov.au; 74 Mosman St; ⏲9am-5pm). The visitor centre has a free brochure outlining the **One Square Mile Trail** of the town centre's beautifully preserved 19th-century buildings. The centre books all tours in town, including those to the reputedly haunted **Venus Gold Battery**, where gold-bearing ore was crushed and processed from 1872 to 1973.

Come nightfall, panoramic **Towers Hill**, the site where gold was first discovered, is the atmospheric setting for a free **open-air cinema** showing the 20-minute film *Ghosts After Dark* – check seasonal screening times with the visitor centre.

In-town accommodation includes the period-furniture-filled former pub, the **Royal Private Hotel** (☎07-4787 8688; www.royalprivate-hotel.com; 100 Mosman St; d without bathroom $55, d with bathroom from $95; ❄📶). A venture to Charters Towers is incomplete without scoffing one of the award-winning pies at **Towers Bakery** (114 Gill St; pies from $4; ⏲5am-3pm Mon-Fri, to 1pm Sat).

Greyhound Australia (☎1300 473 946; www.greyhound.com.au) has four weekly services between Townsville and Charters Towers ($38, 1¾ hours).

The **Queensland Rail** (☎1800 872 467; www.traveltrain.com.au) *Inlander* train runs twice weekly between Townsville and Charters Towers ($35, three hours).

sq km is national park, with scenic walks and abundant wildlife, including one of Australia's largest concentrations of wild koalas. Inviting beaches offer adrenalin-pumping water sports or just the chance to bask in the sunshine, and the granite boulders, hoop pines and eucalypts are a fresh change from the clichéd tropical-island paradise.

Sights & Activities

There's one main road across the island, which goes from Picnic Bay, past Nelly and Geoffrey Bays, to Horseshoe Bay. Local buses ply the route regularly.

Picnic Bay

Picnic Bay was once home to the ferry terminal (now at Nelly Bay), and its erstwhile hustle and bustle has been replaced by serenity-seekers and the elegant curlew, whose spooky cries seem to carry all the way to Townsville (which there are great views of from here). There's a stinger net during the season (November to May) and the swimming is superb.

Nelly Bay

Your time on Maggie will begin and end here if you come by ferry. There's a wide range of eating and sleeping options and a decent beach. There's a children's playground towards the northern end of the beach and good snorkelling on the fringing coral reef.

Arcadia

Arcadia village has the island's major concentration of shops, eateries and accommodation. Its main beach, **Geoffrey Bay**, has a reef at its southern end (reef walking at low tide is discouraged). By far its prettiest beach is **Alma Bay cove**, with huge boulders tumbling into the sea. There's plenty of shade, along with picnic tables and a children's playground here.

If you head to the end of the road at **Bremner Point**, between Geoffrey Bay and Alma Bay, at 5pm you can have wild rock wallabies – accustomed to being fed at the same time each day – literally eating out of your hand.

Radical Bay & the Forts

Townsville was a supply base for the Pacific during WWII, and the forts were designed to protect the town from naval attack. If you're going to do just one walk, then the **forts walk** (2.8km, 1½ hours return) is a must. It starts near the Radical Bay turn-off, passing lots of ex-military sites, gun emplacements and false 'rocks'. At the top of the walk is the observation tower and command post, which have spectacular coastal views, and you'll almost certainly spot **koalas** lazing about in the treetops. Return the same way or continue along the connecting paths, which deposit you at Horseshoe Bay (you can catch the bus back).

Nearby **Balding Bay** is Maggie's unofficial nudie beach.

Horseshoe Bay

Horseshoe Bay, on the north coast, is the best of Maggie's accessible beaches. You'll find water-sports gear for hire, a stinger net, a row of cafes and a fantastic pub.

Bungalow Bay Koala Village has a **wildlife park** (www.bungalowbay.com.au; adult/child $19/12; ⏲2hr tours 10am, noon & 2.30pm), where you can cuddle crocs and koalas.

Pick up local arts and crafts at Horseshoe Bay's **market** (⏲9am-2pm second and last Sun of month), which sets up along the beachfront.

Tours

Pleasure Divers DIVING
(☎07-4778 5788; www.pleasuredivers.com.au; 10 Marine Pde, Arcadia; open-water course per person $349) Three-day PADI open water courses, as well as advanced courses and *Yongala* wreck dives.

Tropicana Tours DRIVING TOUR
(☎07-4758 1800; www.tropicanatours.com.au; full day adult/child $198/99) If you're time-poor, this full-day tour with guides takes in the island's best spots in its stretch 4WD. Price includes close encounters with wildlife, lunch at a local cafe and a sunset cocktail. Shorter tours are also available.

Horseshoe Bay Ranch HORSE RIDING
(☎07-4778 5109; www.horseshoebayranch.com.au; 38 Gifford St, Horseshoe Bay; 2hr ride $100) Gallop dramatically into the not-so-crashing surf on this popular bushland-to-beach two-hour tour. Pony rides for littlies are available too (20 minutes, $20).

Magnetic Island Sea Kayaks KAYAKING
(☎07-4778 5424; www.seakayak.com.au; 93 Horseshoe Bay Rd, Horseshoe Bay; tours from $60)

Join an eco-certified morning or sunset tour, or go it alone on a rented kayak (single/double per day $75/150).

Providence V CRUISE
(☎0427 882 062; www.providencesailing.com.au) Snorkel, boom-net and simply indulge sailing-off-into-the-sunset fantasies on Maggie's only tallship. Two-hour sails from $65 per person.

Sleeping

Picnic Bay

Tropical Palms Inn MOTEL $$
(☎07-4778 5076; www.tropicalpalmsinn.com.au; 34 Picnic St; unit from $100;) With a terrific little swimming pool right outside your front door, the self-contained motel units here are bright and comfortable. Reception rents 4WDs (from $75 per day).

Nelly Bay

Base Backpackers HOSTEL $
(☎1800 242 273; www.stayatbase.com; 1 Nelly Bay Rd; camping per person $12, dm $25-30, d with/without bathroom from $120/70;) If sleep is a dirty word, then step right up. Base is famous for wild full-moon parties, but things can get raucous any time, thanks to the infamous on-site Island Bar. Sleep/food/transport package deals are available.

★**Shambhala Retreat** RETREAT $$
(☎0448 160 580; www.shambhala-retreat-magnetic-island.com.au; 11 Barton St; d from $105;) Serenity now. This green-powered property consists of three tropical units complete with Buddhist wall hangings and tree-screened patios for spying on local wildlife. Two have outdoor courtyard showers; all have fully-equipped kitchens, large bathrooms and laundry facilities. Minimum stay is two nights.

Island Leisure Resort RESORT $$
(☎07-4778 5000; www.islandleisure.com.au; 4 Kelly St; d buré from $189/f buré from $229;) Self-contained, Polynesian-style cabins (*burés*) give this by-the-beach spot an extra-tropical feel. Private patios allow guests to enjoy their own piece of paradise: a lagoon pool and barbie area beckon social souls.

Arcadia

Hotel Arcadia HOTEL $
(☎07-4778 5177; www.hotelarcadia.com.au; 7 Marine Pde; r $99-145;) Formerly Magnums, the Hotel Arcadia has been upgraded from salacious to surprisingly swish. It hasn't lost its fun feel, though, and its on-site bistro and bar, the **Island Tavern** (mains $19.50-28; bistro 11am-8pm, bar noon-3am), keeps punters happy with cheap jugs, live music and cane-toad races every Wednesday night. Two awesome pools.

Arcadia Beach Guest House GUESTHOUSE $$
(☎07-4778 5668; www.arcadiabeachguesthouse.com.au; 27 Marine Pde; dm $35-40, safari tent $55, d without bathroom $85-100, d with bathroom $130-160;) So much to choose from! Will you stay in a bright, beachy room (named after Magnetic Island's bays), a safari tent or dorm? Go turtle-spotting from the balcony, rent a canoe, a Moke or a 4WD…or all of the above? Free ferry pick-ups.

Horseshoe Bay

Bungalow Bay Koala Village HOSTEL $
(☎07-4778 5577, 1800 285 577; www.bungalowbay.com.au; 40 Horseshoe Bay Rd; unpowered/powered site per person $12.50/15, dm $28, d with/without bathroom $90/74;) Not only a resort-style, YHA-associated hostel but a nature wonderland with its own wildlife park. Less than five minutes' walk from the beach, A-frame bungalows are strewn throughout leafy grounds backing onto national park. Cool off at the breezy outdoor bar, go coconut bowling on Thursdays, or tuck into a curry at the on-site **restaurant** (mains $15.50-24; lunch & dinner).

Shaws on the Shore APARTMENT $$$
(☎07-4778 1900; www.shawsontheshore.com.au; 7 Pacific Dr; 1-/2-/3-bedroom apt $175/265/320;) These great-value, self-contained apartments are just a literal stagger from the beach. Private balconies overlook the bay, and inside, they're cool, clean and welcoming.

Eating & Drinking

Several hotels and hostels have restaurants and bars that are at least as popular with locals as they are with guests and visitors. Opening hours can fluctuate according to the season and the crowds.

Seafood is, unsurprisingly, the chomp of choice on Maggie.

Picnic Bay

Picnic Bay Hotel PUB $

(The Esplanade; mains $11-26; R&R Cafe Bar 9am-late) Settle in for a drink, with Townsville's city lights sparkling across the bay. Its **R&R Cafe Bar** has an all-day grazing menu and huge salads, including Cajun prawn.

Nelly Bay

Man Friday MEXICAN, INTERNATIONAL $$

(07-4778 5658; 37 Warboy St; mains $14-39; dinner Wed-Mon;) Chow down on classy Mexican favourites in an incongruous but idyllic fairy-lit garden. Bring your own wine, and be sure to book ahead.

Le Paradis FRENCH $$

(07-4778 5044; cnr Mandalay Ave & Sooning St; restaurant mains $23-40; restaurant from 6pm, cafe from 11am) This fully-licenced restaurant offers a range of French-inspired eats, including divine garlic butter escargot. The attached cafe sells fresh baguettes and the usual burgery/fish-and-chipsy fare.

Arcadia

Arcadia Night Market MARKET $

(RSL Hall, Hayles Ave; 5.30-8pm Fri) Small but lively night market, with licenced bar and plenty of cheap eats to chow through.

Caffè dell' Isola ITALIAN $$

(7 Marine Pdc; mains from $15; breakfast & lunch Tue, Thu & Sun, breakfast, lunch & dinner Wed, Fri & Sat (& daily during school holidays)) Order pineapple on your pizza at your peril at this authentic Italian cafe, where the crust is crispy and the tastes are traditional. Or indulge your sweet tooth with a gelato instead: there are more than 20 fruity flavours to choose from.

Horseshoe Bay

Noodies on the Beach MEXICAN $

(07-4778 5786; 2/6 Pacific Dr; from $10; 10am-10pm Mon-Wed & Fri, 8am-10pm Sat, 8am-3pm Sun; P) You can't help but love a joint which hands out free sombreros with jugs of margarita. Noodies dishes up fine Mexican food, but is arguably more famous for its coffee – reputedly the best on Maggie – and has a book exchange to boot.

Marlin Bar PUB $$

(3 Pacific Dr; mains $16-24; lunch & dinner) You can't leave Maggie without enjoying a cold one by the window as the sun sets across the bay at this popular seaside pub. The meals are on the large side and (surprise!) revolve around seafood.

Barefoot MODERN AUSTRALIAN $$

(07-4758 1170; www.barefootartfoodwine.com.au; 5 Pacific Dr; mains from $20; lunch & dinner Thu-Mon) Sophisticated without being standoffish, this restaurant/art gallery has an extensive wine list, fresh seafood platters and gourmet desserts.

Information

There's no official visitor information centre on Magnetic Island, but Townsville's visitor information centre has info and maps, and can help find accommodation. Maps are also available at both ferry terminals in Townsville and at the terminal at Nelly Bay.

Most businesses take EFTPOS, and ATMs are scattered throughout the island, including one at the **post office** (Sooning St, Nelly Bay; 9am-5pm Mon-Fri, to 11am Sat).

Getting There & Away

All ferries arrive and depart Maggie from the terminal at Nelly Bay.

Sealink (07-4726 0800; www.sealinkqld.com.au) operates a frequent passenger ferry between Townsville and Magnetic Island (adult/child return $32/16), which takes around 20 minutes. Ferries depart Townsville from the Breakwater Terminal on Sir Leslie Thiess Dr.

Fantasea (07-4796 9300; www.magneticislandferry.com.au; Ross St, South Townsville) operates a car ferry crossing eight times daily (seven on weekends) from the south side of Ross Creek, taking 35 minutes. It costs $178 (return) for a car and up to three passengers, and $29/17 (adult/child return) for foot passengers only. Bookings are essential and bicycles are transported free.

Both Townsville terminals have car parking.

Getting Around

BICYCLE

Magnetic Island is ideal for cycling, although some of the hills can be hard going. Most places to stay rent bikes for around $20 per day, though many offer them free to guests.

BUS

Sunbus (www.sunbus.com.au/sit_magnetic_island) ploughs between Picnic Bay and Horseshoe Bay, meeting all ferries and stopping at

WORTH A TRIP

ORPHEUS ISLAND

Forget about Orpheus in the Underworld: here, it's all about the underwater. Part of the Palm Islands group, Orpheus is surrounded by magnificent fringing reef that's home to a mind-blowing collection of fish (1100 species) and a mammoth variety of both hard and soft corals. While the island is great for snorkellers and divers year 'round (pack a stinger suit in summer), seasonal treats like manta-ray migration (August to November) and coral spawning (mid-November) make the trip out here all the more worthwhile.

The island itself is mostly national park, and is formed out of ancient volcanic rock. There is scattered rainforest, but Orpheus is mainly blanketed in dry woodland trees such as Moreton Bay ash and acacias. While the island shelters a miscellany of birds and reptiles, it is also home to a surprising number of goats; the animals were released on Orpheus in the 19th century as part of a madcap scheme to provide food for potential shipwreck survivors. At one stage, the hardy ruminants numbered more than 4000; these days, QPWS keep the numbers down with regular control programs.

Accommodation on Orpheus comes in two flavours: splurge or scrimp. The luxurious **Orpheus Island Resort** (07-4777 7377; www.orpheus.com.au; d $900-2800) offers minimalistic island-chic in the form of ultra-classy suites and villas; gourmet meals, water-sports equipment and some tours are included in the price. Otherwise, pitch your tent at any of the island's three bush camping sites at Yank's Jetty, Pioneer Bay or South Beach. The first two have toilets and picnic tables; the last is totally without facilities. You'll need to be self-sufficient, so bring all water and a fuel stove. Get permits from **NPRSR** (www.nprsr.qld.gov.au).

The resort offers helicopter transfers (ex-Townsville/Cairns $275/550); otherwise, ask around the town of Lucinda to arrange a boat ride over.

major accommodation places. A day pass covering all zones is $7.20.

MOKE & SCOOTER

Moke and scooter rental places abound. You'll need to be over 21, have a current international or Australian driver's licence and leave a credit-card deposit. Scooter hire starts at around $35 per day, Mokes about $75. Try **MI Wheels** (07-4758 1111; www.miwheels.com.au; 138 Sooning St, Nelly Bay) for a classic Moke or 'topless' car, or **Roadrunner Scooter Hire** (07-4778 5222; 3/64 Kelly St, Nelly Bay) for scooters and trail bikes.

Ayr & Around

POP 8885

On the delta of the mighty Burdekin River 90km southeast of Townsville, Ayr is the commercial centre for the rich farmlands of the Burdekin Valley. The town and its surrounds are devoted to the production and harvesting of sugar cane, melons and mangoes. Find out more at the **Burdekin visitor centre** (07-4783 5988; www.burdekintourism.com.au; Plantation Park, Bruce Hwy; 9am-4pm) on the southern side of town.

Yongala Dive (07-4783 1519; www.yongaladive.com.au; 56 Narrah St, Alva Beach) does dive trips ($259 including gear) out to the *Yongala* wreck from Alva Beach, 17km northeast of Ayr. It only takes 30 minutes to get out to the wreck from here, instead of a 2½-hour boat trip from Townsville. Book ahead for backpacker-style accommodation at its onshore **dive lodge** (dm/d $25/60; @), with free pick-ups from Ayr.

NORTH OF TOWNSVILLE

As you leave Townsville, you also leave the Dry Tropics. The scorched-brown landscape slowly gives way to sugar-cane plantations lining the highway and tropical rainforest shrouding the hillsides.

Waterfalls, national parks and small villages hide up in the hinterland, including **Paluma Range National Park** (part of the Wet Tropics World Heritage Area); visitor centres in the area have leaflets outlining walking trails, swimming holes and camping grounds.

The region north of Townsville was hardest hit by Cyclone Yasi in February 2011 (and by Cyclone Larry in 2006), with damage to the coastline, islands, national parks and farmland. Much of the damage has been cleaned up, while some areas are still recovering.

Ingham & Around

POP 4767

Ingham is the proud guardian of the 120-hectare **Tyto wetlands** (Tyto Wetlands Information Centre; 07-4776 4792; www.tyto.com.au; cnr Cooper St & Bruce Hwy; 8.45am-5pm Mon-Fri, 9am-4pm Sat & Sun), which has 4km of walking trails and attracts around 230 species of birds, including far-flung guests from Siberia and Japan. The locals – hundreds of wallabies – love it too, converging at dawn and dusk. There's an art gallery and library on-site.

The poem which inspired the iconic Slim Dusty hit 'Pub With No Beer' (1957) was written in the **Lees Hotel** (07-4776 1577; www.leeshotel.com.au; 58 Lannercost St; s/d from $88/105, meals from $12; meals lunch & dinner Mon-Sat;) by Ingham canecutter Dan Sheahan, after American soldiers drank the place dry. You'll spot the pub – which today has rooms, meals and even beer – by the mounted horseman on the roof.

Noorla Heritage Resort (07-4776 1100; www.hotelnoorla.com.au; 5-9 Warren St; s $69-169, d $79-179;) was once the domain of Italian canecutters. These days, Ingham's wonderful 1920s art deco guesthouse has magnificently restored high-ceilinged rooms, plus cheaper container-style rooms in the garden. A photo montage of local stories lines the walls, bringing its history to life, as do the stories told around its aqua-tiled, guest-only bar.

The **Australian Italian Festival** (www.australianitalianfestival.com.au) celebrates the fact that 60% of Ingham residents are of Italian descent, with pasta flying, wine flowing and music playing over three days. Check the website for festival dates.

Ingham is the jumping-off point for the majestic **Wallaman Falls**, the longest single-drop waterfall in Australia at 305m. Located in **Girringun National Park**, 51km south-west of the town (the road is sealed except for the last 10km), the falls look their best in the Wet, though they are spectacular at any time. A steep but very worthwhile walking track (2km) takes you to the bottom. The **camping ground** (www.nprsr.qld.gov.au; per person/family $5.45/21.80) has barbecues and showers, plus regular wildlife visits, including – for those who can sit quietly and still – the occasional bobbing platypus in the swimming hole. Pick up a leaflet from the Tyto Wetlands Information Centre.

Mungalla Station (07-4777 8718; www.mungallaaboriginaltours.com.au; 2hr tour adult/child $52/30), 15km east of Ingham, runs insightful Aboriginal-led tours, including boomerang throwing and stories from the local Nywaigi culture. It's worth the extra cash to experience the traditional **Kupmurri** (adult/child incl tour $102.50/60) lunch of meat and vegies that are wrapped in banana leaves and cooked underground in an earth 'oven'. If you have a self-contained caravan or a campervan, you can **camp** (per van $10) overnight.

Cute little **Lucinda**, 27km northeast of Ingham, attracts happy-snappers gawking at the town's 5.76km-long jetty. The roofed structure, with a continuous conveyor belt running its length, is the world's longest bulk sugar-loading jetty, allowing enormous carrier ships to dock. Public access is off limits but it's an impressive sight nonetheless. **Hinchinbrook Marine Cove** (07-4777 8377; www.hinchinbrookmarinecove.com.au; 1 Denney St; d $125, bungalow $150, townhouse $195, cafe dishes $7-18, restaurant mains $22-32; cafe 7am-6pm, restaurant dinner Wed-Sat;) overlooks a busy little fishing port, and has the area's best accommodation, plus a cafe and restaurant. Lucinda is also a top fishing spot: ask locals for the best place to wet your line.

Greyhound Australia (1300 473 946; www.greyhound.com.au; Townsville/Cairns $39/52) and **Premier** (13 34 10; www.premierms.com.au; Townsville/Cairns $26/34) buses stop in Ingham on their Cairns–Brisbane runs.

Ingham sits along the **Queensland Rail** (1800 872 467; www.traveltrain.com.au) Brisbane–Cairns train line.

Cardwell & Around

POP 1250

Most of the Bruce Hwy runs several kilometres inland from the coast, so it comes as something of a shock to see the sea lapping right next to the road as you pull into the small town of Cardwell – the closest access point to Hinchinbrook Island. Poor Cardwell took a beating from Cyclone Yasi, with many of the town's older homes smashed and the new marina switched to spin cycle.

Sights & Activities

Cardwell Forest Drive OUTDOORS

From the town centre, this scenic 26km round trip through the national park is chockas with lookouts, walking tracks and picnic areas signposted along the way. There are super swimming opportunities at **Attie Creek Falls**, as well as the aptly named **Spa Pool**, where you can sit in a rock hollow as water gushes over you.

Cardwell's visitor centre has brochures detailing other walking trails and swimming holes in the park.

Historic Cardwell Post Office & Telegraph Station MUSEUM
(53 Victoria St; ⏲10am-1pm Mon-Fri, 9am-noon Sat) FREE Check out the original postal room and old telephone exchange at this wooden building (built in 1870), which has survived cyclones and termites.

Girringun Aboriginal Art Centre GALLERY
(www.art.girrungun.com.au; 235 Victoria St; ⏲8.30am-5pm Mon-Thu, to 2pm Fri) Traditional woven baskets are among the works for sale at this corporation of Aboriginal artists.

Sleeping & Eating

Cardwell Beachcomber Motel & Tourist Park CARAVAN PARK $
(☎07-4066 8550; www.cardwellbeachcomber.com.au; 43a Marine Pde; unpowered/powered site $27/34, motel d $98-125, cabins & studios $95-115;) This large park took a thrashing in Yasi, but is back in action with new poolside cabins, cute studios and modern ocean-view villas. A surprisingly swish **restaurant** (mains from $25; ⏲breakfast daily, lunch & dinner Mon-Sat) dishes up seafood, steaks and whiz-bang pizzas.

Kookaburra Holiday Park CARAVAN PARK $
(☎07-4066 8648; www.kookaburraholidaypark.com.au; 175 Bruce Hwy; unpowered/powered site $22/29, dm/s/d without bathroom $25/45/50, cabin without bathroom $65, unit $85-105;) Well-run park that lends guests fishing rods, prawn nets and crab pots to catch dinner.

Cardwell Central Backpackers HOSTEL $
(☎07-4066 8404; www.cardwellbackpackers.com.au; 6 Brasenose St; dm $20;) Friendly hostel catering mostly to seasonal workers (management can help find jobs), but accepts overnighters. Free internet and pool table.

Mudbrick Manor B&B $$
(☎07-4066 2299; www.mudbrickmanor.com.au; Lot 13, Stony Creek Rd; s/d $90/120;) As the name suggests, this family home is hand-built from mud bricks (and timber and stone). Huge, beautifully appointed rooms congregate around a fountained courtyard. Rates include hot breakfast; book at least a few hours ahead for delicious three-course dinners (per person $30).

Seaview Cafe FAST FOOD $
(87 Victoria St; ⏲24hr) A famous stopover for hungry drivers, the cavernous Seaview dishes up local flavours in the form of crab sangas ($11), barra burgers ($9.90) and a mammoth all-day breakfast ($16.80). It ain't fancy, but it gets the job done nicely.

Information

The **Rainforest & Reef Centre** (☎07-4066 8601; www.greatgreenwaytourism.com/rainforestreef.html; 142 Victoria St; ⏲8.30am-5pm Mon-Fri, 9am-1pm Sat & Sun), next to Cardwell's jetty, has a truly brilliant interactive rainforest display and detailed info on Hinchinbrook Island and other nearby national parks.

Getting There & Away

Greyhound Australia (☎1300 473 946; www.greyhound.com.au) and **Premier** (☎13 34 10; www.premierms.com.au) buses on the Brisbane–Cairns route stop at Cardwell. Fares to Cairns are $48, to Townsville $36.

Cardwell is on the Brisbane–Cairns train line; contact **Queensland Rail** (☎1800 872 467; www.traveltrain.com.au) for details.

Boats depart for Hinchinbrook Island from Port Hinchinbrook Marina, 2km south of town.

Hinchinbrook Island

Australia's largest island national park is a holy grail for walkers and those wanting to spend a bit of alone time with nature. Granite mountains rise dramatically from the sea; rugged Mt Bowen (1121m) is the 399-sq-km island's highest peak. The mainland side is dense with lush tropical vegetation, while long sandy beaches and tangles of mangrove curve around the eastern shore. Hinchinbrook's rainforest sustained considerable damage during Cyclone Yasi.

Hinchinbrook's highlight is the **Thorsborne Trail** (also known as the East Coast Trail), a 32km coastal track from Ramsay Bay past Zoe Bay, with its beautiful waterfall, to George Point at the southern tip. **NPRSR camp sites** (☎13 74 68; www.nprsr.qld.gov.au; per person $5.45) are interspersed along the route. It's recommended that you take three nights to complete the challenging trail; return walks of individual sections are

WORTH A TRIP

PALUMA RANGE NATIONAL PARK

As the southern gateway to the Wet Tropics World Heritage Area, Paluma Range National Park and the little village of Paluma offer a leafy respite from the tedium of the Bruce Hwy. Running almost all the way from Ingham to Townsville, the park is divided in two parts, the Mt Spec section and the northern Jourama Falls section.

Mt Spec

The Mt Spec part of the park (61km north of Townsville or 40km south of Ingham) is a misty Eden of rainforest and eucalypt trees crisscrossed by a variety of walking tracks. This range of habitats houses an incredibly diverse population of birds, from golden bowerbirds to black cockatoos.

From the northern access route of the Bruce Hwy, take the 4km-long partially-sealed Spiegelhauer Rd to **Big Crystal Creek**; from there, it's an easy 100m walk from the car park to **Paradise Waterhole**, a popular spot with a sandy beach and lofty mountain views. There's an **NPRSR camping ground** (www.nprsr.qld.gov.au; per person/family $5.45/ 21.80) here with gas barbecues, toilets and drinking water; be quick, as sites get snapped up quickly.

The southern access route (Mt Spec Rd) is a sealed, albeit twisty, road that writhes up the mountains to **Paluma village**. Beware: though you may have come up here 'just for a drive', the village's cool air and warm populace may change your mind. Stay overnight at the **Paluma Rainforest Inn** (☎07-4770 8688; www.rainforestinnpaluma.com; 1 Mt Spec Rd; d $125; ❄), a true rainforest haven that sports 50 varieties of rhododendrons in its gardens.

En route to Paluma, be sure to stop off at **Little Crystal Creek**, a picturesque swimming hole with a cute stone bridge, picnic area and waterfalls.

Jourama Falls

Waterview Creek tumbles down these eponymous falls and other cascades past palms and umbrella trees, making this section a fine place for a picnic and a perambulation. It's a steep climb to the lookout; keep your eyes peeled for kingfishers, freshwater turtles and endangered mahogany gliders on the way up. The **NPRSR camping ground** (www.nprsr.qld.gov.au; per person/family $5.45/ 21.80) has cold showers, gas barbecues, water (treat before drinking) and composting toilets.

This part of the park is reached via a 6km sealed road (though the creek at the entrance can be impassable in the Wet), 91km north of Townsville and 24km south of Ingham. Be sure to fuel up before veering off the highway.

also possible. This is no tiptoe through the tulips, but a real-life wilderness adventure, with hungry native beasts (including crocs), saber-toothed mossies, and very rough patches. You'll have to draw your own water.

As only 40 walkers are allowed to traverse the trail at any one time, NPRSR recommends booking a year ahead for a place during the high season and six months ahead for other dates. Cancellations are not unheard of, so it's worth asking if you've arrived without a booking.

Hinchinbrook Island Cruises (☎07-4066 8601; www.hinchinbrookislandcruises.com.au) runs a service from Cardwell to Hinchinbrook's Ramsay Bay boardwalk (one way $90, one hour). It also operates a cruise to Zoe Bay as well as water taxis for the region and island transfers: book through Cardwell's Rainforest & Reef Centre (p232).

Thorsborne Trail walkers can pick up a one-way transfer back to the mainland with **Hinchinbrook Wilderness Safaris** (☎07-4777 8307; www.hinchinbrookwildernesssafaris.com.au; $50), from George Point at the southern end of the trail.

Tully

POP 2500

It may look like just another sleepy sugarcane village, but Tully is a burg with a boast, calling itself the 'Wettest town in Australia'. A gigantic **golden gumboot** at Tully's entrance is as high as the waters rose (7.9m) in 1950: climb the spiral staircase to the viewing

DON'T MISS

TULLY RIVER RAFTING

The Tully River provides thrilling white water year-round thanks to Tully's trademark bucket-downs and the river's hydroelectric floodgates. Rafting trips are timed to coincide with the daily release of the gates, resulting in grade-four rapids foaming against a backdrop of stunning rainforest scenery.

Day trips with **Raging Thunder Adventures** (☎07-4030 7990; www.ragingthunder.com.au; standard/'xtreme' trip $189/215) or **R'n'R White Water Rafting** (☎07-4041 9444; www.raft.com.au; $189) include a barbecue lunch and transport from Tully or nearby Mission Beach. Transfers from Cairns are an extra $10.

platform up top to get a sense of just how much that is! The **Golden Gumboot Festival** (www.tullygumbootfestival.com), held each May, celebrates the soak with a parade and lashings of entertainment. And while boggy **Babinda** challenges Tully's claim, the fact remains that all that rain ensures plenty of raftable rapids on the nearby Tully River.

The **Tully Visitor & Heritage Centre** (☎07-4068 2288; Bruce Hwy; ⊙8.30am-4.45pm Mon-Fri, 9am-2pm Sat & Sun) has a brochure outlining a self-guided **heritage walk** around town, with 17 interpretative panels (including one dedicated to Tully's UFO sightings), and **walking trail** maps for the nearby national parks. The centre also has free internet and a book exchange.

Book at the visitor centre for 90-minute **Tully Sugar Mill Tours** (adult/child $17/11; ⊙daily late Jun-early Nov). Tour times depend on seasonal conditions; wear closed shoes and a shirt with sleeves.

The Indigenous operators of **Ingan Tours** (☎1300 728 067; www.ingan.com.au; adult/child $120/60) visit 'sacred story places' on their full-day 'Spirit of the Rainforest' tours (Tuesdays, Thursdays and Saturdays).

Practically all accommodation in Tully is geared for banana workers, with cheap weekly rates and help finding farm work – try the excellent **Banana Barracks** (☎07-4068 0455; www.bananabarracks.com; 50 Butler St; dm with/without bathroom $28/24, bungalows $30-40; @🛜🏊) bang in the town centre, which is also the hub of Tully's nightlife, with an on-site **nightclub** (⊙Thu-Sat).

Tully's pubs serve hearty meals (except Sundays), while **Joe's Pizza Parlour** (☎07-4068 1996; 46 Butler St; pizzas from $12; ⊙dinner, days vary) has thick-crust old-school pizzas.

Greyhound Australia (☎1300 473 946; www.greyhound.com.au) and **Premier** (☎13 34 10; www.premierms.com.au) buses stop in town on the Brisbane–Cairns route; fares to Cairns/Townsville are $29/$39. Tully is also on the **Queensland Rail** (☎1800 872 467; www.traveltrain.com.au) Brisbane–Cairns train line.

Mission Beach

POP 4000

Less than 30km east of the Bruce Hwy's rolling sugar-cane and banana plantations, the hamlets that make up greater Mission Beach are hidden amongst World Heritage rainforest. The rainforest extends right to the Coral Sea, giving this 14km-long palm-fringed stretch of secluded inlets and wide, empty beaches the castaway feel of a tropical island.

The frightfully powerful Cyclone Yasi made landfall at Mission Beach in 2011, stripping much of the rainforest and vegetation bare. However, the communities here recovered quickly – within two weeks, water and power was restored and most businesses and tourist operators were running normally.

Although collectively referred to as Mission Beach or just 'Mission', the area comprises a sequence of individual villages strung along the coast. **Bingil Bay** lies 4.8km north of **Mission Beach proper** (sometimes called North Mission). **Wongaling Beach** is 5km south; from here it's a further 5.5 kilometres south to **South Mission Beach**. Most amenities are in Mission proper and Wongaling Beach; South Mission Beach and Bingil Bay are mainly residential.

Mission is one of the closest access points to the Great Barrier Reef, and the gateway to Dunk Island. There are plenty of opportunities for on-foot exploring here: walking tracks fan out around Mission Beach, with Australia's highest density of cassowaries (around 40) roaming the rainforest. While Mission's coastline seems to scream 'toe dip!', don't just fling yourself into the water any old where: stick to the swimming enclosures, lest you have a nasty encounter with a marine stinger…or croc.

Activities

Adrenalin junkies flock to Mission Beach for extreme and water-based sports, including white-water rafting on the nearby Tully River. If you've got your own board, Bingil Bay is one of the rare spots inside the reef where it's possible to surf, with small but consistent swells of around 1m.

Stinger enclosures at Mission Beach and South Mission Beach provide safe year-round swimming.

The visitor centre has heaps of information on the many superb walking tracks in the area.

Skydiving SKYDIVING
Mission Beach is rightfully one of the most popular spots in Queensland for skydiving. Two outfits will take you up: **Jump the Beach** (☎1300 800 840; www.jumpthebeach.com.au; 9000/11,000/14,000ft tandem jump $284/345/369) and **Skydive Mission Beach** (☎1300 800 840; www.skydivemissionbeach.com; 9000/11,000/14,000ft tandem dive $249/310/334). Both use the beach to cushion your landing.

Big Mama Sailing SAILING
(☎0437 206 360; www.bigmamasailing.com; adult/child from $65/40) Hit the water on an 18m ketch with passionate boaties Stu, Lisa and Fletcher. Choose from a 2.5hr sunset tour, barbecue lunch cruise or full day on the reef.

Calypso Dive DIVING
(☎07-4068 8432; www.calypsodive.com.au) Calypso runs reef dives (from $264, including gear), wreck dives of the *Lady Bowen* ($225), and PADI open-water courses ($625). Otherwise, snorkel the reef ($169) or take a jet-ski tour around Dunk Island (from $224).

Mission Beach Adventure Centre WATER SPORTS
(☎0429 469 330; Seaview St, Mission Beach) This little rainbow hut by the beach runs the gamut of water and beach sports, from kayak (single/double per hour $15/30) to stand-up board hire (per hour $15). Its **cafe** (dishes $5-8) is famed for its hot dogs.

Coral Sea Kayaking KAYAKING
(☎07-4068 9154; www.coralseakayaking.com; half-/full-day tour $80/128) Knowledgable full-day guided tours to Dunk Island; easygoing bob-arounds on the half-day option.

Fishin' Mission FISHING
(☎0427 323 469; www.fishinmission.com.au; half-/full-day trip $140/230) Chilled-out reef-fishing charters with local pros.

Mission Beach Tropical Fruit Safari FOOD TASTING
(☎07-4068 7099; www.missionbeachtourism.com; Mission Beach Visitor Centre, Porter Promenade; adult/family $8/20; ⊙1-2pm Mon & Tue) Get to know (and taste) weird and wonderful local tropical fruits.

Festivals & Events

Markets MARKET
Local arts, crafts, jewellery, tropical fruit, home-made gourmet goods and more overflow from stalls at the **Mission Beach Markets** (Porter Promenade; ⊙8am-1pm 1st & 3rd Sun of month). Even more wonderful stuff, including hand-made log furniture, is up for grabs at the **Mission Beach Rotary Monster Market** (Marcs Park, Cassowary Dr, Wongaling Beach; ⊙8am-12.30pm last Sun of month Apr-Nov).

Mission Evolve Music Fest MUSIC
(www.missionevolve.com.au) Two days of live music in October featuring blues, roots, soul, funk and DJs from around Far North Queensland.

Sleeping

The visitor centre has a list of booking agents for holiday rentals. Hostels have courtesy bus pick-ups.

South Mission Beach

Sea-S-Ta GUESTHOUSE $$$
(☎07-4088 6699; www.sea-s-ta.com.au; 38 Kennedy Esplanade; per night $350, 2-night min stay) Awkward name, amazing place. This self-contained holiday house is a great option for groups looking to stay and play in Mission. The bright, Mexico-inspired hacienda sleeps six, and comes with *mucho* extras, from juicers to his'n'hers slippers. Rates go down the longer you stay.

Wongaling Beach

★**Scotty's Mission Beach House** HOSTEL $
(☎1800 665 567; www.scottysbeachhouse.com.au; 167 Reid Rd; dm $25-29, d $71; ❄@📶🏊) Clean, comfy rooms (including girls-only dorms

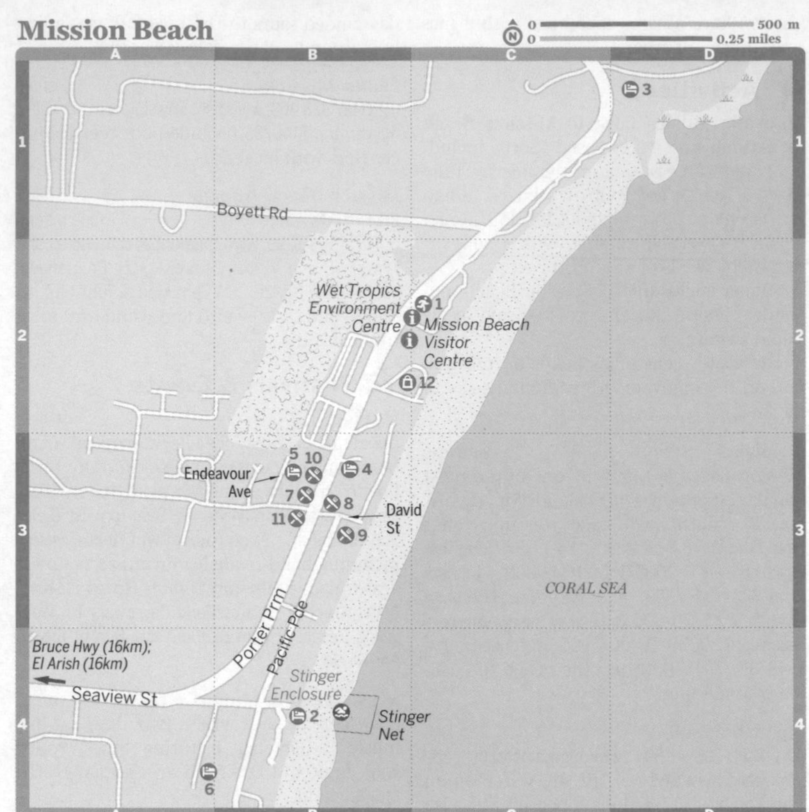

Mission Beach

Activities, Courses & Tours

Mission Beach Adventure Centre .... (see 2)
1 Mission Beach Tropical Fruit Safari C2

Sleeping

2 Castaways Resort & Spa B4
3 Mission Beach Ecovillage D1
4 Mission Beach Retreat B3
5 Rainforest Motel B3
6 Sejala on the Beach A4

Eating

7 Early Birds Cafe B3
8 Fish Bar B3
9 Garage Bar & Grill B3
10 New Deli B3
11 Zenbah B3

Shopping

12 Mission Beach Markets B2

with Barbie-pink sheets!) are grouped around Scotty's grassy, social pool area. Out front, **Scotty's Bar & Grill** (mains $10-30; dinner), open to nonguests, has something happening virtually every night, from fire-twirling shows to pool comps and live music. Classic backpackery good times, ahoy!

Dunk Island View Caravan Park CARAVAN PARK $
(07-4068 8248; www.dunkislandviewcaravanpark; 21 Webb Rd; unpowered/powered site $28/38, 1-/2-bedroom unit $98/128;) Wake to fresh sea breezes at this clean and congenial spot just 50m from the beach. Everything you'd want from a caravan park, with the bonus of a new on-site cafe (fish and chips $8).

Hibiscus Lodge B&B B&B $$
(07-4068 9096; www.hibiscuslodge.com.au; 5 Kurrajong Cl; r $115-155; P) Wake to the sound of birds chirping and, more than likely, spot a cassowary or two during breakfast (an

absolute must) on the rainforest-facing deck of this lovely B&B. With only three (very private) rooms, bookings are essential. No kids.

Licuala Lodge B&B **$$**
(07-4068 8194; www.licualalodge.com.au; 11 Mission Circle; s/d/t incl breakfast $99/135/185;) Chummy B&B with a guest kitchen, wonderful verandah and cassowary gatecrashers. Don't be alarmed by the teddy bears in your bedroom.

Mission Beach

Mission Beach Retreat HOSTEL **$**
(07-4088 6229; www.missionbeachretreat.com.au; 49 Porter Promenade; dm $22-25, d $56;) Bang in the centre of town with the bonus of being beachfront, this is an easy, breezy backpacker spot that's hard not to like.

Mission Beach Ecovillage CABIN **$$**
(07-4068 7534; www.ecovillage.com.au; Clump Point Rd; d $135-220;) With its own banana and lime trees scattered around its tropical gardens and a direct path through the rainforest to the beach, this 'ecovillage' makes the most of its environment. Bungalows cluster around a rocky pool, and deluxe cottages have private spas. There's a licensed **restaurant** (mains $18.50; dinner Wed-Sat).

Rainforest Motel MOTEL **$$**
(07-4068 7556; www.missionbeachrainforestmotel.com.au; 9 Endeavour Ave; s/d $98/119;) A charming little gem, this motel is not only great value, but friendly and well-appointed to boot. Close to the shops but tucked away behind lush greenery. Free bikes available.

Castaways Resort & Spa RESORT **$$$**
(07-4068 7444; www.castaways.com.au; Pacific Pde; d $165-215, 1-/2-bedroom unit $265/345;) Castaways' cheapest rooms don't have balconies, so it's worth splashing out a bit more for one of the 'Coral Sea' rooms with an extended deck and day bed. The units are small, but perks include two elongated pools, a luxurious **spa** (www.driftspa.com.au) and stunning beach views from its tropical-style **bar/restaurant** (mains $12-32; breakfast, lunch & dinner). Come on Tuesdays for tropical high tea.

Sejala on the Beach CABIN **$$$**
(07-4088 6699; www.sejala.com.au; 26 Pacific Pde; d $260;) Three huts (request one facing the beach) with rainforest showers, decks with private BBQs and loads of character. Romance central.

Bingil Bay

★ **Jackaroo Hostel** HOSTEL **$**
(07-4068 7137; www.jackaroohostel.com; 13 Frizelle Rd; camp site $15, dm/d incl breakfast $24/58;) Run by globetrotting brothers Robert and Jade, this timber pole-frame retreat high in the rainforest has it all, and then some. Jungly surrounds, a sparkling pool, airy rooms and the breezy terrace tempt you to linger longer; the outdoor cinema and free surfboard hire cement the deal.

Sanctuary CABIN **$$**
(1800 777 012, 07-4088 6064; www.sanctuaryatmission.com; 72 Holt Rd; dm $35, s/d hut $65/70, cabin $145/165; mid-Apr–mid-Dec;) Reached by a steep 600m-long rainforest walking track from the car park (4WD pick-up available), you can sleep surrounded only by flyscreen on a platform in simple huts, or opt for en suite cabins whose showers have floor-to-ceiling rainforest views. Tramp the walking tracks, take a yoga class ($15), indulge in a massage (per hour $80), and cook in the self-catering kitchen or dine on wholesome fare at the **restaurant** (mains $19-33; 7.30am-8.30pm;). Eco-initiatives include its own sewerage system, rainwater harvesting and biodegradable detergents. Not suitable for kids under 11.

Eating & Drinking

The majority of bars and/or restaurants are clustered in Mission Beach proper along Porter Promenade and its adjoining spider's web of tiny walkways and arcades. There's a small supermarket here, and a huge Woolworths supermarket at Wongaling Beach (look for the giant cassowary), which also has a handful of eateries, bars and bottle shops.

Wongaling Beach

Millers Beach Bar & Grill PUB **$**
(07-4068 8177; 1 Banfield Pde; $10-38; 3pm-late Tue-Fri, noon-late Sat & Sun) So close to the beach you'll be picking sand out of your beer, Millers has a rockin' little courtyard custom-made for lazy loitering. Graze on $10 pizzas (4pm to 6pm daily), attack a giant steak, or just devour the view of Dunk Island over a cocktail.

★Cafe Rustica ITALIAN $$
(07-4068 9111; 24 Wongaling Beach Rd; mains $18-25; 5pm-late Wed-Sat, 10am-late Sun;) This contemporary corrugated-iron beach shack is home to delicious home-made pastas and crispy-crust pizzas; they also make their own gelato and sorbet. Be sure to book ahead.

Mission Beach

★Fish Bar SEAFOOD $
(07-4088 6419; Porter Promenade; $10-17; 10am-midnight) For socialising and scarfing, this place is tough to top. It's laid-back yet lively, with an equally zingy menu that includes buckets of prawns (lunch $10) and pig on a spit ($13). Live music on Sundays.

New Deli CAFE, DELI $
(Shop 1, 47 Porter Promenade; mains $8-16; 9.30am-6pm Mon-Fri;) Stock up on goodies for a gourmet picnic at this aromatic gourmet deli/cafe where most produce is organic and everything is home-made, including scrumptious biscuits.

Zenbah INTERNATIONAL $
(07-4088 6040; 39 Porter Promenade; mains $9-25; 10am-1.30am Fri & Sat, to midnight Sun-Thu) The colourful chairs on the sidewalk mark Zenbah as the vibrant little eatery/hangout it is. The food ranges from Middle Eastern to Asian all the way back to pizza, and you can digest it all to a backdrop of live tunes on Fridays and Saturdays. Free courtesy bus.

Early Birds Cafe CAFE $
(Shop 2, 46 Porter Promenade; mains $6-15; 6am-3pm Thu-Tue;) Early Birds' all-day tropical Aussie Brekkie ($13.50) of bacon and eggs, grilled tomato and banana, toast, and tea or coffee is perfect after a morning swim.

Garage Bar & Grill MODERN AUSTRALIAN $$
(07-4088 6280; 41 Donkin Lane; meze plate $17; 9am-late;) This super-social spot on Mission's 'Village Green' serves delicious 'sliders' (mini burgers), free-pour cocktails ($14), good coffee, cakes and tapas. Wash it all down with some toe-tappin' live music.

Bingil Bay

Bingil Bay Cafe CAFE $$
(29 Bingil Bay Rd; mains $14-23; 6.30am-10pm;) Everything is groovy at this lavender landmark, from the eclectic menu to the mellow vibes emanating from the porch. Breakfast is a highlight, or just grab a coldie and immerse yourself in the art displays, live music and hey-dude buzz.

THE CASSOWARY: ENDANGERED NATIVE

Looking like something out of *Jurassic Park*, a flightless prehistoric bird struts through the rainforest. It's as tall as a grown man, has three razor-sharp, dagger-style clawed toes, a bright-blue head, red wattles (the lobes hanging from its neck), a helmet-like horn and shaggy black feathers similar to an emu's. Meet the cassowary, an important link in the rainforest ecosystem. It's the only animal capable of dispersing the seeds of more than 70 species of trees whose fruit is too large for other rainforest animals to digest and pass (which acts as fertiliser). You're most likely to see cassowaries in the wild around Mission Beach, Etty Bay and the Cape Tribulation section of the Daintree National Park. They can be aggressive, particularly if they have chicks. Do not approach them; if one threatens you, don't run – give the bird right-of-way and try to keep something solid between you and it, preferably a tree.

It is estimated that there are 1000 or less cassowaries in the wild north of Queensland. An endangered species, the cassowary's biggest threat is loss of habitat, and most recently the cause has been natural. Tropical Cyclone Yasi stripped much of the rainforest around Mission Beach bare, threatening the struggling population with starvation. The birds are also exposed to the elements and more vulnerable to dog attacks and being killed by cars as they venture out in search of food.

Next to the Mission Beach visitor centre, there are cassowary conservation displays at the **Wet Tropics Environment Centre** (07-4068 7197; www.wettropics.gov.au; Porter Promenade; 10am-4pm), staffed by volunteers from the **Community for Cassowary & Coastal Conservation** (C4; www.cassowaryconservation.asn.au). Proceeds from gift-shop purchases go towards buying cassowary habitat. The website www.savethecassowary.org.au is also a good source of info.

Information

The efficient **Mission Beach visitor centre** (☎07-4068 7099; www.missionbeachtourism.com; Porters Promenade; ⏲9am-4.45pm Mon-Sat, 10am-4pm Sun) has reams of info in multiple languages.

The **Mission Beach Information Station** (www.missionbeachinfo.com; 4 Wongaling Shopping Centre, Cassowary Dr, Wongaling Beach; internet 20min/hr $2/5; ⏲9am-7pm) can also help with tour bookings, and has internet booths.

Getting There & Around

Greyhound Australia (☎1300 473 946; www.greyhound.com.au) and **Premier** (☎13 34 10; www.premierms.com.au) buses stop in Wongaling Beach next to the 'big cassowary'. Fares with Greyhound/Premier are $23/19 to Cairns, $41/46 to Townsville.

Sugarland Car Rentals (☎07-4068 8272; www.sugarland.com.au; 30 Wongaling Beach Rd, Wongaling Beach; ⏲8am-5pm) rents small cars from $35 per day.

Mission Beach Adventure Centre (p235) rents bikes ($10/20 for a half-/full day).

Or call a **taxi** (☎13 10 08).

Dunk Island

Dunk Island is known to the Djiru Aboriginal people as Coonanglebah (the island of peace and plenty). They're not wrong: this is pretty much your ideal tropical island, with lush jungle, white sand beaches and blue water.

Walking trails crisscross (and almost circumnavigate) Dunk: the circuit track (9.2km) is the best way to have a proper stickybeak at the island's interior and abundant wildlife. There's good snorkelling over bommies at Muggy Muggy and great swimming at Coconut Beach.

The island's resort is closed due to cyclone damage, though **camping** (Map p278; ☎0417 873 390; per person $5.15) has reopened.

Mission Beach Dunk Island Water Taxi (☎07-4068 8310; www.missionbeachwatertaxi.com; Banfield Pde, Wongaling Beach; adult/child return $35/18), departing from Wongaling Beach, makes the 20-minute trip to Dunk Island.

Mission Beach to Innisfail

The road north from Mission Beach rejoins the Bruce Hwy at **El Arish** (population 442), home to not much bar a golf course and the memorabilia- and character-filled **El Arish Tavern** (38 Chauvel St), built in 1927.

From El Arish, you can take the more direct route north by continuing straight along the Bruce Hwy, with turn-offs leading to beach communities including exquisite **Etty Bay**, with its wandering cassowaries, rocky headlands, rainforest, large stinger enclosure and a superbly sited caravan park.

Alternatively, detour west via the Old Bruce Hwy, also known as **Canecutter Way** (www.canecutterway.com.au). **Mena Creek** is home to the enchanting ruins of two once-grand castles at the five-hectare **Paronella Park** (☎07-4065 0000; www.paronellapark.com.au; Japoonvale Rd; adult/child $40/20; ⏲9am-7.30pm). Built in the 1930s as a whimsical entertainment centre for the area's hard-working folk, the mossy Spanish ruins now have an almost medieval feel, and walking trails lead through rambling gardens past a waterfall and swimming hole. Take the 45-minute daytime tour and/or one-hour night tour to hear the full, fascinating story. Admission includes both tours, as well as one night at its powered **camping ground**; otherwise book in to one of the sweet little **cabins** (d shared bathroom $85; ❄). Tickets to Paronella Park are valid for one year.

Innisfail & Around

POP 8262

Sitting pretty just 80km south of the Cairns tourism frenzy, Innisfail is a textbook example of a laid-back, far northern country town. Fisherfolk ply the wide Johnstone River, tractors trundle down the main street, and locals are equally proud of their magnificent art deco architecture and born-and-bred footy (rugby league) hero Billy Slater.

Beachside Flying Fish Point is 8km northeast of Innisfail's town centre, while national parks, including the Mamu Rainforest Canopy Walkway, are within a short drive.

Sights & Activities

Mamu Rainforest Canopy Walkway VIEWPOINT
(www.nprsr.qld.gov.au/parks/mamu; Palmerston Hwy; adult/child $20/10; ⏲9.30am-5.30pm, last entry 4.30pm) About 27km along the Palmerston Hwy (signposted 4km northwest of Innisfail), this canopy-level rainforest walkway gives you eye-level views of the fruits, flowers and birds, and a bird's-eye perspective from its 100-step, 37m-high tower.

Allow at least an hour to complete the 2.5km, wheelchair-accessible circuit.

The Palmerston Hwy continues west to Millaa Millaa, passing the entrance to the Waterfalls Circuit.

Wooroonooran National Park PARK

The **Palmerston (Doongan) section** of this national park is home to some of the oldest surviving rainforest in Australia; **NPRSR** (www.nprsr.qld.gov.au) has details of camping grounds and walking trails.

Art Deco Architecture ARCHITECTURE

(www.artdeco-innisfail.com.au) Following a devastating 1918 cyclone, Innisfail rebuilt in the art deco style of the day, and 2006's Cyclone Larry resulted in many of these striking buildings being refurbished. Pick up a free, comprehensive **town walk brochure** from the visitor centre, detailing over two dozen key points of interest.

Festivals & Events

Foodie fun during the **Feast of the Senses** (www.feastofthesenses.com.au) in March includes food stalls, farm tours and markets.

Sleeping & Eating

Innisfail's hostels primarily cater to banana pickers who work the nearby plantations; weekly rates average about $185 (dorm). The **Backpackers Shack** (07-4061 7760; www.backpackersshack.com; 7 Ernest St;) and **Codge Lodge** (07-4061 8055; www.codgelodge.com; 63 Rankin St; dm $30;) are good options. The visitor centre has a full list.

Drop by the **Innisfail Fish Depot** (51 Fitzgerald Esplanade; 8am-6pm Mon-Fri, 9am-4pm Sat, 10am-4pm Sun) for fresh-as-it-gets fish to throw on the barbie and organic cooked prawns by the bagful ($18 to $20 per kilo).

Flying Fish Tourist Park CARAVAN PARK $

(07-4061 3131; www.ffpvanpark.com.au; 39 Elizabeth St, Flying Fish Point; unpowered/powered site $28/33, cabin $60-95, villa $105-115;) Fish right off the beach across the road from this first-rate park, or organise boat rental through the friendly managers.

Barrier Reef Motel MOTEL $$

(07-4061 4988; www.barrierreefmotel.com.au; Bruce Hwy; s/d $110/120, unit $150-170;) The best place to stay in Innisfail, this comfortable motel next to the visitor centre has airy, tiled rooms with large bathrooms. Self-caterers should nab one of the units with kitchenettes; otherwise head to the **restaurant** (mains $28-30.50; breakfast & dinner;) or just have a drink at the bar.

Monsoon Cruising SEAFOOD $

(0427 776 663; 1 Innisfail Wharf; mains $12-17.50; 10am-5pm Wed-Sat Mar-Dec;) Everything is locally sourced and/or organic aboard this moored cruiser – from bread baked fresh to black tiger prawns straight off the trawlers.

Flying Fish Point Cafe CAFE $

(9 Elizabeth St, Flying Fish Point; mains $12-21; 7.30am-8pm) Come hungry to finish the huge seafood baskets of battered and crumbed fish, barbecued calamari, wonton prawns, tempura scallops and more.

Oliveri's Continental Deli DELI $

(www.oliverisdeli.com.au; 41 Edith St; sandwiches $8-9; 8.30am-5.15pm Mon-Fri, to 12.30pm Sat;) An Innisfail institution offering goodies like 60-plus varieties of European cheese, ham and salami, and scrumptious sandwiches.

Roscoe's ITALIAN $$

(07-4061 6888; 3b Ernest St; mains $22-36, buffets $18-42; 11.30am-1.30pm & 5.30-9.30pm) Popular local haunt for its buffets, complete with home-made desserts like tiramisu.

Information

The **visitor centre** (07-4061 2655; www.cassowarycoasttourism.com.au; cnr Eslick St & Bruce Hwy; 9am-5pm Mon-Fri, 10am-12.30pm Sat & Sun) gives out discount vouchers for many of the area's attractions.

Getting There & Away

Bus services operate once daily with **Premier** (13 34 10; www.premierms.com.au) and several times daily with **Greyhound Australia** (1300 473 946; www.greyhound.com.au) between Innisfail and Townsville (4½ hours) and Cairns (1½ hours).

Innisfail is on the Cairns–Brisbane train line; contact **Queensland Rail** (1800 872 467; www.traveltrain.com.au) for information.

PATRICK DANCEL / GETTY IMAGES ©

The Great Barrier Reef

Each year, more than 1.5 million visitors come to this World Heritage–listed area that stretches across 2000km of coastline. Diving and snorkelling are just some of the ways to experience this wonderful and rich ecosystem. There's also sailing, scenic flights and idyllic days exploring the reef's gateway towns and stunning islands.

Contents

Above Aerial view of the Great Barrier Reef

Gateways to the Reef

There are numerous ways to approach Australia's massive undersea kingdom. You can head to a popular gateway town and join an organised tour, sign up for a multiday sailing or diving trip exploring less-travelled outer fringes of the reef, or fly out to a remote island, where you'll have the reef largely to yourself.

The Whitsundays

Home to turquoise waters, coral gardens and palm-fringed beaches, the Whitsundays offer many options for reef-exploring: base yourself on an island, go sailing, or stay on Airlie Beach and island-hop on day trips.

Cairns

The most popular gateway to the reef, Cairns has dozens of boat operators offer day trips with snorkelling, as well as multiday reef explorations on live-aboard vessels. For the uninitiated, Cairns is a good place to learn to dive.

Port Douglas

An hour's drive north of Cairns, Port Douglas is a laid-back beach town with dive boats heading out to over a dozen sites, including more pristine outer reefs, such as Agincourt Reef.

Townsville

Australia's largest tropical city is far from the outer reef (2½ hours by boat) but has some exceptional draws: access to Australia's best wreck dive, an excellent aquarium, marine-themed museums, plus multiday live-aboard dive boats departing from here.

Southern Reef Islands

For an idyllic getaway off the beaten path, book a trip to one of several remote reef-fringed islands on the southern edge of the Great Barrier Reef. You'll find fantastic snorkelling and diving right off the island.

1. Clownfish **2.** Airlie Beach (p208) **3.** Reef HQ Aquarium (p219), Townsville

2

ULLA LOHMANN / GETTY IMAGES ©

1

2

TANYA PUNTTI / GETTY IMAGES ©

1. Whitehaven Beach (p215) 2. Helicopter scenic flight over Whitsunday Islands (p203) 3. Snorkelling, Cairns (p250)

Top Reef Encounters

Donning a mask and fins and getting an up-close look at this marine wonderland Is one of the best ways to experience the Great Barrier Reef. You can get a different take aboard a glass-bottomed boat tour, on a scenic flight or on a land-based reef walk.

Diving & Snorkelling

The classic way to see the Great Barrier Reef is to board a catamaran and visit several different coral-rich spots on a long day trip. Nothing quite compares to that first underwater glimpse, whether diving or snorkelling.

Semi-submersibles & Boats

A growing number of reef operators (especially around Cairns) offer semi-submersible or glass-bottomed boat tours, which give cinematic views of coral, rays, fish, turtles and sharks – without you ever having to get wet.

Sailing

You can escape the crowds and see some spectacular reef scenery aboard a sailboat. Experienced mariners can hire a bareboat, others can join a multiday tour – both are easily arranged from Airlie Beach or Port Douglas.

Reef Walking

Many reefs of the southern Great Barrier Reef are exposed at low tide, allowing visitors to walk on the reef top (on sandy tracks between living coral). This can be a fantastic way to learn about marine life, especially if accompanied by a naturalist guide.

Scenic Flights

Get a bird's-eye view of the vast coral reef and its cays and islands from a scenic flight. You can sign up for a helicopter tour or a seaplane tour (particularly memorable over the Whitsundays).

Marine life

Nature's Theme Park

Home to some of the greatest biodiversity of any ecosystem on earth, the Great Barrier Reef is a marine wonderland. You'll find 30-plus species of marine mammals along with countless species of fish, coral, molluscs and sponges. Above the water, 200 bird species and 118 butterfly species have been recorded on reef islands and cays.

Common fish species include dusky butterfly fish, which are a rich navy blue with sulphur-yellow noses and back fins; large graphic turkfish, with luminescent pastel coats; teeny neon damsels, with darting flecks of electric blue; and six-banded angelfish, with blue tails, yellow bodies and tiger stripes. Rays, including the spotted eagle ray, are worth looking out for.

The reef is also a haven to many marine mammals, such as whales, dolphins and dugongs. Dugongs are listed as vulnerable, and a significant number of them live in Australia's northern waters; the reef is home to around 15% of the global population. Humpback whales migrate from Antarctica to the reef's warm waters to breed between May and October, and minke whales can be seen off the coast from Cairns to Lizard Island in June and July. Porpoises and killer and pilot whales also make their home here.

One of the reef's most-loved inhabitants is the sea turtle. Six of the world's seven species (all endangered) live on the reef and lay eggs on the islands' sandy beaches in spring or summer.

Cairns & the Daintree Rainforest

Includes ➡

Best Places to Eat

- Ochre (p257)
- Lillypad (p257)
- Flames of the Forest (p273)
- Sassi Cucina e Bar (p273)
- Mocka's Pies (p273)

Best Places to Stay

- Tropic Days (p256)
- Pink Flamingo (p272)
- QT Resort (p272)
- Mungumby Lodge (p280)
- Cape Trib Exotic Fruit Farm Cabins (p279)

Why Go?

Tropical, touristy Cairns is an unmissable stop on any East Coast traveller's itinerary. Experienced divers and first-time toe-dippers swarm to the steamy city for its easy access to the Great Barrier Reef, while those more interested in submerging themselves in boozy good times are well-served by a barrage of bars and clubs. For day-trippers, the Atherton Tableland – home to cooler climes, volcanic-crater lakes, jungly waterfalls and gourmet food producers – is just a short and scenic drive away.

The winding road from Cairns to ritzy Port Douglas offers spectacular coastal vistas, but it's north of the Daintree River that the adventure really begins. The magnificent Daintree National Park stretches up the coast, with rainforest tumbling right onto white-sand beaches; don't be so awestruck by the stunning surrounds that you forget to keep an eye out for crocs! Further up, the Bloomfield Track from Cape Tribulation to Cooktown is one of Australia's great 4WD journeys.

When to Go

Cairns

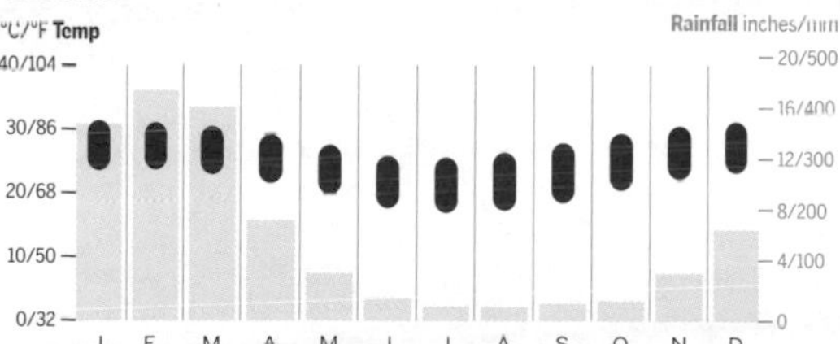

May Port Douglas turns on the pizazz for Carnivale.

June A costumed re-enactment of Cook's landing is the centrepiece of the Cooktown Discovery Festival.

November The reef's annual coral spawning is a delight for divers.

Cairns & the Daintree Rainforest Highlights

1 Diving, snorkelling and swimming among the fish, turtles and anemones in the multicoloured corals of the **Great Barrier Reef**, from Cairns (p251) or Port Douglas (p269).

2 Taking an Aboriginal-guided walk and swimming in the crystal-clear waters of **Mossman Gorge** (p274).

3 Riding the Skyrail cable car through the rainforest to the market town of **Kuranda** (p264) and returning to Cairns by scenic railway.

4 Barra fishing, barbecuing or watching the sunset

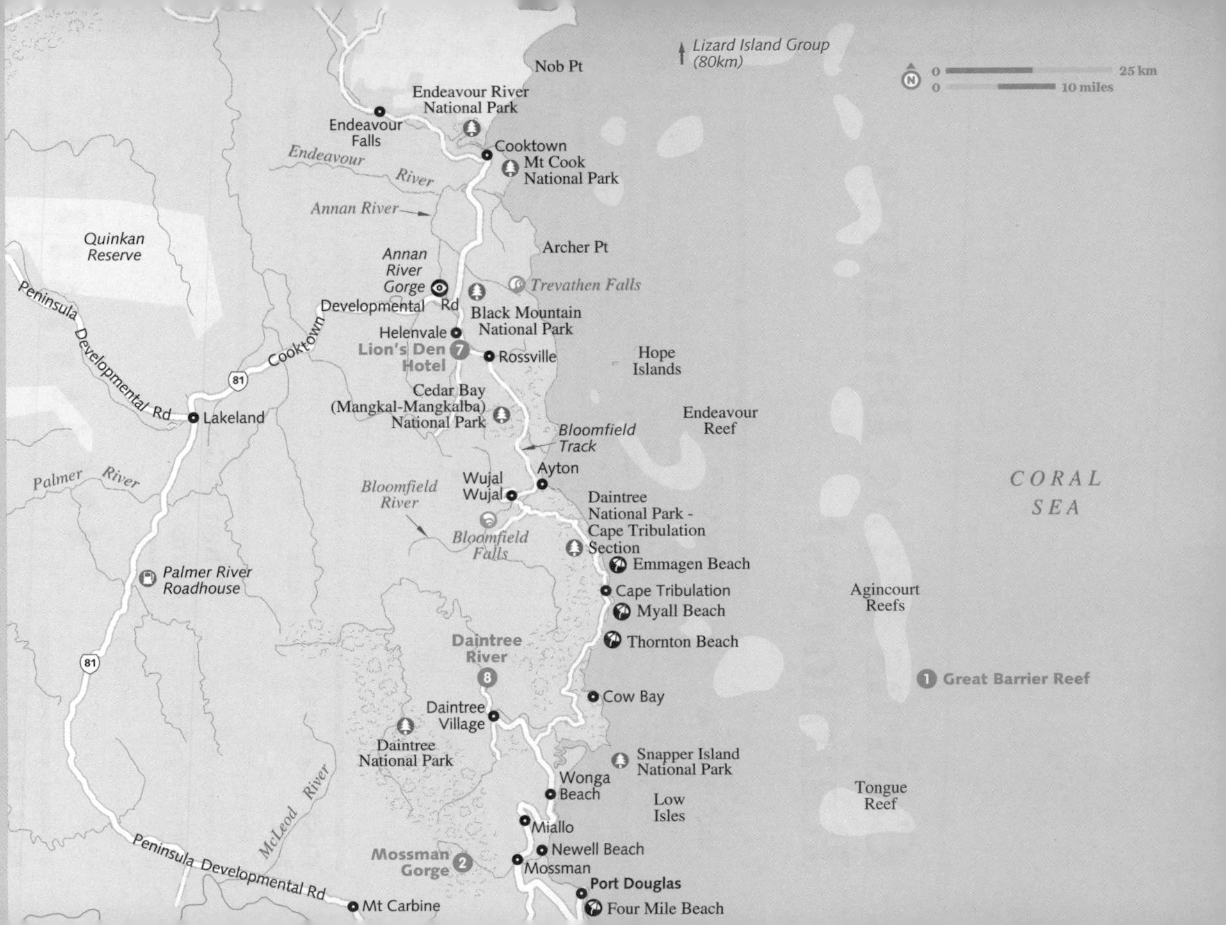

during a cruise on **Lake Tinaroo** (p268).

5 Drifting up and away over the patchwork quilt–like Atherton Tableland in a hot-air balloon from **Mareeba** (p254).

6 People-watching from a cafe on the esplanade at **Palm Cove** (p262).

7 Toasting the completion of the 4WD Bloomfield Track at the iconic **Lion's Den Hotel** (p280).

8 Scanning for saltwater crocs on a cruise along the **Daintree River** (p275).

CAIRNS

POP 165,860

Cairns has come a long way since its beginnings as a boggy swamp and rollicking goldfields port. Heaving under the weight of countless resorts, tour agencies, souvenir shops and a million reminders of its proximity to the reef, Cairns is unabashedly geared towards tourism. The city's scores of hostels and hotels ring to a jumble of hellos and goodbyes: for many, Cairns is the end of the road after a long East Coast jaunt; for others flying into the international airport, it's just the start of the adventure. Whichever way you're going, it's a perfect place to meet other travellers.

Old salts claim Cairns (pronounced 'Cans') has sold its soul, but it does have an infectious holiday vibe. The city centre is more boardshorts than briefcases, and you'll find yourself throwing away all notions of speed and schedules here, thanks to humidity and a hearty hospitality that can turn a short stroll into an impromptu social event. Fittingly, Cairns is awash with bars, nightclubs, eateries and cafes suiting all budgets. There's no beach in town, but the magnificent Esplanade Lagoon more than makes up for it; otherwise, the northern beaches are but a local bus ride or easy drive away.

Sights

★Cairns Esplanade & Lagoon WATERFRONT
(www.cairnsesplanade.com.au; lagoon 6am-10pm Thu-Tue, noon-10pm Wed) FREE Sunbathers flock to Cairns' shallow but spectacular saltwater swimming lagoon on the city's reclaimed foreshore. The artificial 4800-sq-metre lagoon is patrolled by lifeguards and illuminated at night.

Northwest from the lagoon, the boardwalk promenade, stretching for almost 3km, has picnic areas, free barbecues and playgrounds lining the foreshore.

From markets to live gigs, free fitness classes to festivals, there's always something happening on the Esplanade. Check the website for updates on events.

Flecker Botanic Gardens GARDENS
(www.cairns.qld.gov.au; Collins Ave; 7.30am-5.30pm Mon-Fri, 8.30am-5.30pm Sat & Sun, information centre 9am-4.30pm Mon-Fri, 10am-2.30pm Sat & Sun; 131) FREE These beautiful tropical gardens are an explosion of greenery and rainforest plants. Pick up a walks brochure from the information centre or ask about free guided walks. There's a great cafe and a new, well-camouflaged visitor centre (it's made of mirrors!).

Across the road, the **Rainforest Boardwalk** leads to **Saltwater Creek** and **Centenary Lakes**, a birdwatcher's delight. Uphill from the gardens, **Mt Whitfield Conservation Park** has two walking tracks through rainforest, climbing to viewpoints over the city; follow joggers up the **Red Arrow circuit** (1.5km, one hour) or the more demanding **Blue Arrow circuit** (6.6km, four to five hours).

Tanks Arts Centre GALLERY, THEATRE
(www.tanksartscentre.com; 46 Collins Ave; gallery 10am-4pm Mon-Fri) Three gigantic, ex-WWII fuel-storage tanks have been transformed into studios, galleries showcasing local artists' work and an inspired performing-arts venue. There's a lively **market day**.

Cairns Regional Gallery GALLERY
(www.cairnsregionalgallery.com.au; cnr Abbott & Shields Sts; adult/child under 16 $5/free; 9am-5pm Mon-Fri, 10am-5pm Sat, 10am-2pm Sun) In a colonnaded heritage building (1936), exhibitions at this acclaimed gallery have an emphasis on local and Indigenous works, plus excellent visiting exhibitions.

Tjapukai Cultural Park CULTURAL CENTRE
(07-4042 9999; www.tjapukai.com.au; Kamerunga Rd; adult/child $40/25, Tjapukai by Night adult/child $109/59; 9am-5pm, Tjapukai by Night 7pm-9.30pm) Allow at least three hours at this Indigenous-owned cultural extravaganza. It incorporates the Creation Theatre, where the story of creation is told using giant holograms and actors, a Dance Theatre, gallery, boomerang- and spear-throwing demonstrations and turtle-spotting canoe rides. The fireside corroboree is the centrepiece of the **Tjapukai by Night** dinner-and-show deal.

The park is about 15km north of the city centre, just off the Captain Cook Hwy near the Skyrail terminal; transfers are available (extra charge).

Mangrove Boardwalk BOARDWALK
(Airport Avenue) FREE Explore the swampier side of Cairns on this revelatory wander into the wetlands. Eerie snap-crackle-slop noises provide a fitting soundtrack to the spooky surrounds, which are signposted with informative guides to the weird lifeforms scurrying in the mud below you. Bring mosquito repellant. It's just before the Cairns Airport.

Crystal Cascades & Lake Morris WATERFALL, LAKE

About 14km from Cairns, the Crystal Cascades are a series of beautiful waterfalls and (croc-free) pools. The area is accessed by a 1.2km (30-minute) pathway. Crystal Cascades is linked to Lake Morris (the city's reservoir) by a *steep* rainforest **walking trail** (allow three hours return); it starts near the picnic area.

Reef Teach INTERPRETIVE CENTRE

(07-4031 7794; www.reefteach.com.au; 2nd fl, Main Street Arcade, 85 Lake St; adult/child $18/9; lectures 6.30-8.30pm Tue-Sat) Before heading out to the reef, take your knowledge to greater depths at this excellent and informative centre, where marine experts explain how to identify specific types of coral and fish and how to treat the reef with respect.

Centre of Contemporary Arts GALLERY, THEATRE

(CoCA; www.centre-of-contemporary-arts-cairns.com.au; 96 Abbott St; 10am-5pm Mon-Sat) FREE CoCA houses the **KickArts** (www.kickarts.org.au) galleries of local contemporary visual art, as well as the **JUTE Theatre** (www.jute.com.au; CoCA, 96 Abbott St) and the **End Credits Film Club** (www.endcredits.org.au). Their wonderful gift shop is full of local artworks and jewellery.

Activities

Innumerable tour operators run adventure-based activities from Cairns, most offering transfers to/from your accommodation.

★NQ Watersports WATERSPORTS

(0411 739 069; www.nqwatersports.com.au; B-finger, Pier Marina; jet-ski croc tours solo/tandem $190/260) It's a world first: croc-spotting tours...on a jet ski! Zip down Trinity Inlet to cop an eyeful of salties up-close, while nesting eagles soar dramatically overhead. The company also offers parasailing ($90), jetskiing sans-crocs ($90) and bumper tubing ($35).

AJ Hackett Bungee & Minjin BUNGEE JUMPING

(1800 622 888; www.ajhackett.com; McGregor Rd; bungee jumps $169, minjin swings $89, bungee & minjin swing combos $225; 10am-5pm) Bungee jump from the purpose-built tower or swing from the trees on the minjin (a harness swing).

DANGER: STINGERS & CROCS

From around late October to May, swimming in coastal waters is inadvisable due to the presence of box jellyfish, irukandji and other marine stingers. Only swim where there is a patrolled stinger net.

Saltwater crocodiles inhabit the mangroves, estuaries and open water. Warning signs are posted around the waterways where crocodiles might be present. Pay heed, as these signs are not just quirky props for your holiday snaps: crocs are faster and cleverer than you might think!

Fishing Cairns FISHING

(0448 563 586; www.fishingcairns.com.au) Arranges river, reef and game fishing trips.

Cable Ski WATERSPORTS

(07-4038 1304; www.cableskicairns.com.au; Captain Cook Hwy; adult/child per hr $39/34, per day $69/64; 10am-6pm) Learn to waterski, wakeboard or kneeboard without the boat at this water-sports park near the Skyrail.

Tours

An astounding 600-plus tours drive, sail and fly out of Cairns each day. You can book at any of the zillions of agencies lining the city streets.The following is but a small taste of what's on offer.

Great Barrier Reef

Reef trips generally include transport, lunch and snorkelling gear. Many have diving options including introductory dives requiring no prior experience. When choosing a tour, consider the vessel (catamaran or sailing ship), its capacity (from six to 300 people), what extras are offered and the destination. The outer reefs are more pristine; inner reef areas can be patchy, showing signs of damage from humans, coral bleaching and crown-of-thorns starfish. In most cases you get what you pay for. Some operators offer the pricier option of a trip in a glass-bottomed boat or semi-submersible.

The majority of boats depart from the Pier Marina and Reef Fleet Terminal at about 8am, returning at around 6pm. A number of operators also offer multiday liveaboard trips, which include specialised dive

Cairns

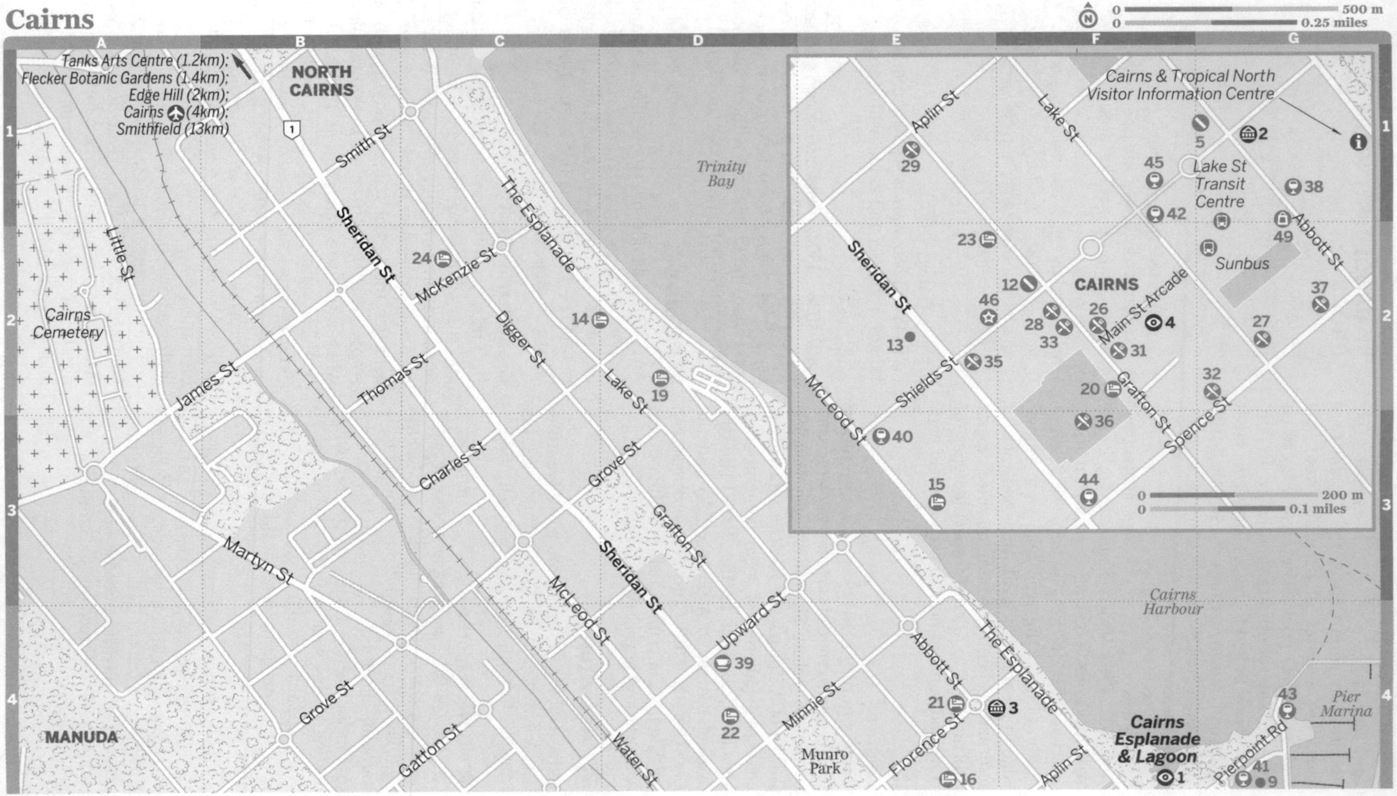

0 500 m
0 0.25 miles

Tanks Arts Centre (1.2km); Flecker Botanic Gardens (1.4km); Edge Hill (2km); Cairns (4km); Smithfield (13km)

NORTH CAIRNS
Smith St
Sheridan St
The Esplanade
Trinity Bay
Little St
24
McKenzie St
14
Cairns Cemetery
Digger St
James St
Thomas St
Lake St
19
Charles St
Grove St
Grafton St
Martyn St
McLeod St
Sheridan St
Upward St
39
Abbott St
The Esplanade
Grove St
Minnie St
21
3
22
MANUDA
Gatton St
Water St
Munro Park
Florence St
16
Aplin St
Cairns Esplanade & Lagoon
1
Cairns Harbour
Pierpoint Rd
41
9
43
Pier Marina

Aplin St
Lake St
Cairns & Tropical North Visitor Information Centre
5
2
29
45
Lake St Transit Centre
38
42
Abbott St
49
23
Sunbus
Sheridan St
12
CAIRNS
Main St Arcade
37
46
26
4
27
28
33
31
13
35
Shields St
32
McLeod St
20
Grafton St
36
40
Spence St
15
44

0 200 m
0 0.1 miles

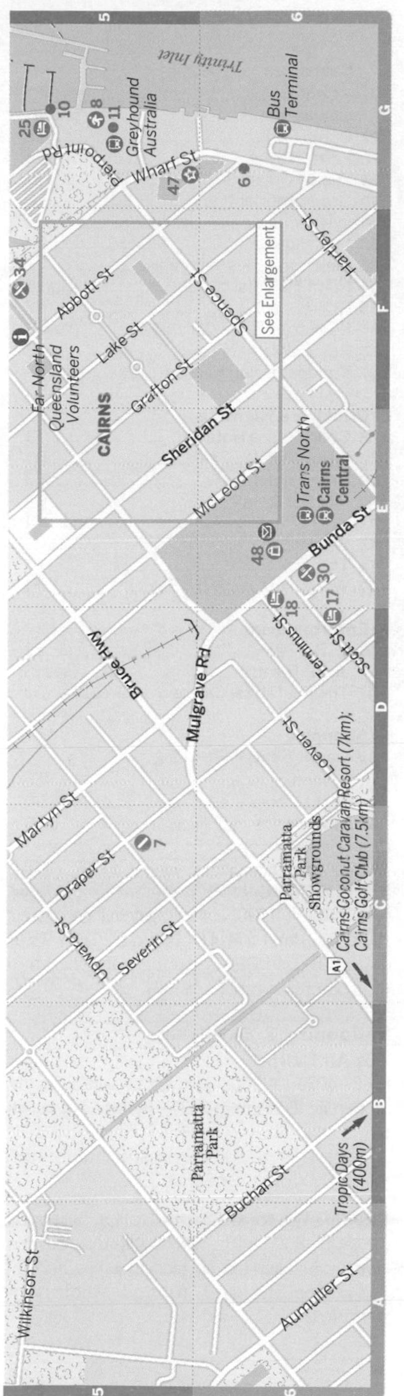

opportunities such as night diving. Dive-course companies also offer tours.

Cod Hole, near Lizard Island, is one of Australia's premier diving locations; extended live-aboard trips are mainly for keen certified divers.

Coral Princess CRUISE
(☎1800 079 545, 07-4040 9999; www.coralprincess.com.au) Three- to seven-night cruises between Cairns, Pelorus Island and Lizard Island return (from $1347 per person, twin share).

Reef Daytripper SAILING
(☎07-4036 0566; www.reefdaytripper.com.au; adult/child/family from $139/100/425) Small-group, personalised catamaran trips to Upolu Reef on the outer Great Barrier Reef.

Passions of Paradise DIVING, SNORKELLING
(☎1800 111 346, 07-4041 1600; www.passions.com.au; adult/child $139/89) Sexy catamaran taking you to Michaelmas Cay and Paradise Reef for snorkelling or diving.

Great Adventures BOAT TOUR
(☎07-4044 9944; www.greatadventures.com.au; 1 Spence St, Reef Fleet Terminal; adult/child trips from $84/42) Runs half and full day trips to Green Island and the outer Great Barrier Reef on fast catamarans. Diving add-ons, glass-bottomed boat and semi-submersible tours available.

Silverswift DIVING, SNORKELLING
(☎07-4044 9944; www.silverseries.com.au; adult/child from $196/146) Popular catamaran trips that offer snorkelling/diving on three outer reefs.

Sunlover DIVING, SNORKELLING
(☎07-4050 1333; www.sunlover.com.au; adult/child/family $190/80/460) Fast family-friendly catamaran rides to a snorkelling pontoon on the outer Moore Reef. Options include semi-submersible trips and helmet diving.

Scenic Flights

Great Barrier Reef Helicopters SCENIC FLIGHTS
(☎07-4081 8888; www.gbrhelicopters.com.au; flights from $159-599) Huge range of helicopter flights, including a 10-minute soar above Cairns city ($159), a 15-minute flight from Green Island ($239) and an hour-long reef and rainforest trip ($599, ex-Cairns).

Cairns

Top Sights
1 Cairns Esplanade & Lagoon ... F4

Sights
2 Cairns Regional Gallery ... G1
3 Centre of Contemporary Arts ... E4
4 Reef Teach ... F2

Activities, Courses & Tours
5 Cairns Dive Centre ... G1
6 Cairns Seaplanes ... G6
7 Deep Sea Divers Den ... C5
8 Great Adventures ... G5
9 Great Barrier Reef Helicopters ... G4
10 NQ Watersports ... G5
11 Passions of Paradise ... G5
12 Pro-Dive ... F2
Raging Thunder ... (see 11)
13 Skydive the Reef Cairns ... E2

Sleeping
14 Acacia Court ... D2
15 Cairns Central YHA ... E3
16 Cairns Girls Hostel ... E4
17 Cairns Sharehouse ... D6
18 Dreamtime Travellers Rest ... E6
19 Floriana Guesthouse ... D2
20 Gilligan's ... F2
21 Hotel Cairns ... E4
22 Njoy Travellers Resort ... D4
23 Northern Greenhouse ... E2
24 Reef Palms ... C2
25 Shangri-La ... G5

Eating
26 Caffiend ... F2
Cairns Central Shopping Centre ... (see 48)
Charlie's ... (see 14)
27 Corea Corea ... G2
28 Fetta's Greek Taverna ... F2
29 Fusion Organics ... E1
30 Green Ant Cantina ... E6
31 Lillypad ... F2
32 Marinades ... G2
33 Meldrum's Pies in Paradise ... F2
34 Night Markets ... F5
35 Ochre ... E2
Perrotta's at the Gallery ... (see 2)
36 Rusty's Markets ... F3
37 Voodooz Cajun Kitchen ... G2

Drinking & Nightlife
38 Court House Hotel ... G1
39 Flying Monkey Cafe ... D4
40 Grand Hotel ... E3
41 Pier Bar & Grill ... G4
42 PJ O'Briens ... F1
43 Salt House ... G4
44 The Jack ... F3
45 Woolshed Chargrill & Saloon ... F1

Entertainment
46 12 Bar Blue ... E2
JUTE Theatre ... (see 3)
47 The Reef Hotel Casino ... G5

Shopping
48 Cairns Central Shopping Centre ... E6
Night Markets ... (see 34)
49 Woolworths ... G1

Cairns Seaplanes SCENIC FLIGHTS
(☎07-4031 4307; www.cairnsseaplanes.com; 2/3 Abbott St; 30-minute flights from $269) Scenic reef flights, including to Green Island.

White-Water Rafting

The thrill level of white-water rafting down the Barron, Russell and North Johnstone Rivers is hitched to the season: the wetter the weather, the whiter the water. The Tully River has rapids year-round.

Trips are graded according to the degree of difficulty, from armchair rafting (Grade 1) to white-knuckle (Grade 5).

Foaming Fury RAFTING
(☎07-4031 3460, 1800 801 540; www.foamingfury.com.au) Full-day trips on the Russell River ($200) or half-day on the Barron ($124); family rafting options available.

Raging Thunder RAFTING
(☎07-4030 7990; www.ragingthunder.com.au; adult/child from $74/47) Full-day Tully trips (standard trip $199, 'xtreme' trip $229) and half-day Barron trips ($133).

Ballooning & Skydiving

Hot Air Cairns BALLOONING
(☎07-4039 9900; www.hotair.com.au/cairns; 30-minute flights from $235) Balloons take off from Mareeba to take in dawn over the Atherton Tablelands. Prices include return transfers from Cairns.

Skydive the Reef Cairns SKYDIVING
(☎1800 800 840; www.skydivethereefcairns.com.au; 51 Sheridan St; tandem jumps 14,000ft $334) See the reef from a whole new perspective.

City Tours

Cairns Discovery Tours GUIDED TOUR
(☎07-4028 3567; www.cairnsdiscoverytours.com; adult/child $69/35; ⊙Mon-Sat) Half-day afternoon tours run by horticulturists; they includes the botanic gardens and Palm Cove. Northern-beaches transfers are an extra $5.

Atherton Tableland

Food Trail Tours FOOD TOUR
(☎07-4041 1522; www.foodtrailtours.com.au; adult/child from $159/80; ⊙Mon-Sat) Taste your way around the Tableland visiting farms producing macadamias, tropical-fruit wine, cheese, chocolate and coffee.

On the Wallaby OUTDOORS
(☎07-4033 6575; www.onthewallaby.com; day/overnight tours $99/169) Excellent activity-based tours including cycling, hiking and canoeing.

Uncle Brian's Tours OUTDOORS
(☎07-4033 6575; www.unclebrian.com.au; tours $119; ⊙Mon-Wed, Fri & Sat) Lively small-group day trips covering forests, waterfalls and lakes.

Captain Matty's Barefoot Tours OUTDOORS
(☎07-4055 9082; www.barefoottours.com.au; tours $85) Fun full-day jaunt around the Tablelands with swimming stops at waterfalls and a natural waterslide.

Cape Tribulation & the Daintree

After the Great Barrier Reef, Cape Trib is the region's next most popular day trip – usually including a cruise on the Daintree River. Access is via a well-signposted sealed road, so don't discount hiring your own vehicle, especially if you want to take your time.

Billy Tea Bush Safaris ECOTOUR
(☎07-4032 0077; www.billytea.com.au; day trips adult/child $185/135) Exciting day ecotours to Cape Trib.

Tropics Explorer OUTDOORS
(☎1800 801 540, 07-4031 3460; www.tropicsexplorer.com.au; day tours from $99) Fun Cape Trib trips; overnight tours available.

Cape Trib Connections OUTDOORS
(☎07-4032 0500; www.capetribconnections.com; day trips adult/child $119/99) Includes Mossman Gorge, Daintree River, Cape Tribulation Beach and Port Douglas. Also runs overnight tours.

Cooktown & Cape York

Adventure North Australia DRIVING TOUR
(☎07-4028 3376; www.adventurenorthaustralia.com; 1-day tours adult/child $250/200) Has 4WD trips to Cooktown via the coastal route, returning via the inland route. Also two- and three-day tours, fly-drive and Aboriginal cultural tours.

DIVE COURSES

Cairns is the scuba-diving capital of the Great Barrier Reef and a popular place to attain Professional Association of Diving Instructors (PADI) open-water certification. There's a staggering number of courses to choose from, from budget four-day courses that combine pool training and reef dives to five-day courses that include two days' pool theory and three days' living aboard a boat, diving less-frequented parts of the reef. Many operators are multilingual.

All operators require you to have a dive medical certificate, which they can arrange (around $60). A reef tax ($40 to $80) is payable as well. Many operators also offer advanced courses for certified divers. Dive schools include the following:

Cairns Dive Centre (☎07-4051 0294; www.cairnsdive.com.au; 121 Abbott St) A long-running operator affiliated with Scuba Schools International (SSI) rather than PADI. There are live-aboard courses (four/five days $640/780) and day tours ($180).

Deep Sea Divers Den (☎07-4046 7333; www.diversden.com.au; 319 Draper St) Long-established school running multiday live-aboard courses and trips from $445.

Pro-Dive (☎07-4031 5255; www.prodivecairns.com; cnr Grafton & Shields St) One of Cairns' most experienced operators, offering a comprehensive, five-day learn-to-dive course incorporating a three-day live-aboard trip ($825).

Festivals & Events

Cairns Festival FESTIVAL
(www.festivalcairns.com.au; Aug-Sept) The Cairns Festival takes over the city with a packed program of performing/visual arts, music and family events.

Sleeping

Cairns is a backpacker hotspot, with around 40 hostels ranging from intimate converted houses to hangar-sized resorts. Dozens of midrange, virtually identical motels line up along Sheridan St.

For families or groups, it's worth checking out **Cairns Holiday Homes** (www.cairnsholidayhomes.com.au). Workers and backpackers sticking around for a while will be well-served by **Cairns Sharehouse** (07-4041 1875; www.cairns-sharehouse.com; 17 Scott St; s per week from $155, d per person per week from $120;), with almost 200 long-stay rooms strewn across the city. The **Accommodation Centre** (1800 807 730, 07-4051 4066; www.accomcentre.com.au) has information on a wide range of options.

Most tour operators also pick up and drop off at accommodation at Cairns' northern beaches.

★ Tropic Days HOSTEL $
(1800 421 521, 07-4041 1521; www.tropicdays.com.au; 26-38 Bunting St; camp sites $12, tents $16, dm $26-27, d without bathroom $64-74;) Tucked behind the Showgrounds (with a courtesy bus into town), Cairns' best hostel has a tropical garden with hammocks, pool table, bunk-free dorms and a relaxed feel. Nonguests can book for Monday night's croc, emu and roo barbecue ($12 including a didgeridoo show).

Gilligan's HOSTEL $
(07-4041 6566; www.gilligansbackpackers.com.au; 57-89 Grafton St; dm $25-37, d $130;) The 'G spot' is pricey, impersonal and very loud, but all rooms at this flashpacker resort have en suites and most have balconies; higher-priced rooms come with fridges and TVs. It has several bars plus nightly entertainment, a beauty salon and a gym to work off all that beer.

Cairns Girls Hostel HOSTEL $
(07-4051 2016; www.cairnsgirlshostel.com.au; 147 Lake St; dm/tw $20/48;) Sorry lads! This white-glove-test-clean, female-only hostel is one of the most accommodating budget stays in Cairns.

Njoy Travellers Resort HOSTEL $
(07-4031 1088; www.njoy.net.au; 141 Sheridan St; dm/s/d from $19/40/56;) Fun and easygoing spot with a lagoon pool and licensed communal areas. Also offers free shuttle buses to the marina every morning and free dinner vouchers.

Cairns Central YHA HOSTEL $
(07-4051 0772; www.yha.com.au; 20-26 McLeod St; dm $25-30, s/d/f $40/80/117;) Bright, spotless and professionally staffed. Free pancakes for breakfast!

Dreamtime Travellers Rest HOSTEL $
(07-4031 6753, 1800 058 440; www.dreamtime-hostel.com; cnr Bunda & Terminus Sts; dm $24-26, s/d from $55/60;) This hostel at the edge of the city combines friendly staff with cosy rooms in an old Queenslander. Cheap pizza, fire twirling and barbecue nights make your stay all the sweeter.

Lake Placid Tourist Park CARAVAN PARK $
(07-4039 2509; www.lakeplacidtouristpark.com; Lake Placid Rd; powered sites $31, cabins from $50, cottage with en suite from $110;) Close enough to enjoy the spoils of the Big Smoke (it's a 15-min drive from the CBD) but far enough to revel in rainforesty repose, this spot overlooks the aptly named Lake Placid. Easy access to Skyrail, Kuranda Scenic Railway and the northern beaches.

Floriana Guesthouse GUESTHOUSE $
(07-4051 7886; www.florianaguesthouse.com; 183 The Esplanade; s/d/studio $69/79/130;) Cairns-of-old still exists at this enchanting guesthouse, which retains its original polished floorboards and art deco fittings. The swirling staircase leads to 10 individually decorated rooms; all have en suites.

Northern Greenhouse HOSTEL $$
(07-4047 7200; www.northerngreenhouse.com.au; 117 Grafton St; dm/tw/apt $28/95/140;) It fits into the budget category with dorm accommodation and a relaxed attitude, but this friendly place is a cut above, with neat studio-style apartments with kitchens and balconies. The central deck, pool and games room are great for socialising. Free breakfast and Sunday barbie.

Reef Palms APARTMENTS $$
(1800 815 421; www.reefpalms.com.au; 41-7 Digger St; apt $120-180;) The crisp, white interiors of Reef Palms' apartments will have you wearing your sunglasses

inside. All rooms have kitchen facilities; larger ones include a lounge area and a spa. Good for couples and families.

Acacia Court HOTEL **$$**
(☎07-4051 1501; www.acaciacourt.com; 223-227 The Esplanade; d $120-170; P❄📶🏊) A stroll along the Esplanade from town, this waterfront high-rise's beachy touches and a choice of ocean or mountain views make it great value for money. Most rooms have private balconies and its famous buffet restaurant Charlie's is downstairs.

Shangri-La HOTEL **$$$**
(☎07-4031 1411; www.shangri-la.com/cairns; Pierpoint Rd; r from $270; P❄@📶🏊) In an unbeatable waterfront setting towering over the marina, Shangri-La is Cairns' top hotel, a super-swish five-star that ticks all the boxes for views, facilities (including a gym and pool bar) and service. Off-season rates available online.

Hotel Cairns HOTEL **$$$**
(☎07 4051 6188; www.thehotelcairns.com; cnr Ab bott & Florence Sts; d $195-265; ❄📶🏊) There's a true tropical charm to this sprawling bone-white hotel, built in traditional Queenslander 'plantation' style. Rooms have an understated elegance and the huge 'tower' rooms and suites offer luxury touches including private balconies. Check the website for special deals.

Eating

There's something to tickle every tastebud here: pubs dish up some surprisingly fab (and cheap) fare; the Esplanade has an overwhelming variety of chowhouses; the Pier Marketplace's boardwalk is lined with international restaurants and a random wander around the city streets (Grafton Street especially) throws up everything from Indian to Bavarian to hipster cuisine. Check the *Cairns Post* every Wednesday for restaurant coupons and specials.

Lillypad CAFE **$**
(☎07-4051 9565; 72 Grafton St; dishes $10-14; ⏲7am-3pm; 🌿) With humungous feasts from crepes to wraps and a truckload of vegetarian options, this is one of the best-value options in town. It's a little bit hippy, and a whole lot busy: you'll probably have to wait a while. Don't miss the fresh juices.

Caffiend CAFE **$**
(78 Grafton St; dishes from $12; ⏲Tues-Sat 7.30am-3pm, Sunday 8am-2pm; 📶) Down the graffitied alleyway and bang! You're in Melbourne! Superb coffee, all-day breakfast, gourmet lunches, art galore and the occasional live gig: what's not to love?

Corea Corea KOREAN **$**
(upstairs, Orchid Plaza, 58 Lake St; dishes from $9.50; ⏲10am-9pm) Disregard the empty-mall atmosphere at Orchid Plaza and dig into the spicy, sizzling Korean dishes at this massively popular haunt.

Voodooz Cajun Kitchen CAJUN **$**
(☎07-4051 3493; 5/12 Spence St; dishes from $9.50; ⏲noon-midnight, closed Tues) A little bit of the South up north, Voodooz serves up bewitching belly-busters including Po-Boy sandwiches, Creole jambalaya and seafood gumbo. Live music and cocktails (including The Hurricane) add to the N'Orleans feel.

Fusion Organics CAFE **$**
(www.fusionorganics.com.au; cnr Aplin & Grafton Sts; dishes $4-19.50; ⏲7am-3pm Mon-Fri, to 2pm Sat; 🌿) In the courtyard of a 1921 redbrick former ambulance station, Indian chefs spice up Fusion's organic, allergy-free fare, including quiches, frittata, filled breads and 'detox' juices.

Meldrum's Pies in Paradise BAKERY **$**
(97 Grafton St; pies $4.70-5.90; ⏲7am-5pm Mon-Fri, to 2.30pm Sat; 🌿) A Cairns institution, Meldrum's bakes 40 inventive varieties of the humble Aussie pie – from chicken and avocado to pumpkin gnocchi or tuna mornay.

Night Markets FOOD COURT **$**
(The Esplanade; dishes $10-15; ⏲5-11pm daily) The Night Markets have a cheap, busy Asian-style food court.

Ochre MODERN AUSTRALIAN **$$**
(☎07-4051 0100; www.ochrerestaurant.com.au; 43 Shields St; mains $23-37; ⏲noon-3pm & 6-10pm Mon-Fri, 3-10pm Sat & Sun; 🌿) The menu at this innovative restaurant utilises native Aussie fauna (such as croc with native pepper, or roo with quandong-chilli glaze) and flora (like wattle-seed damper loaf or lemon myrtle panacotta). Can't decide? Try a tasting plate.

Green Ant Cantina MEXICAN **$$**
(☎07-4041 5061; www.greenantcantina.com; 183 Bunda St; mains $15-40; ⏲6pm-late daily; 🌿)

Behind the railway station, this little slice of alternative Mexico is worth seeking out for its homemade quesadillas, enchiladas and Corona-battered tiger prawns. Stick around after eating and try the Green Ant brews (there are seven). Open-mic night on Sundays.

Charlie's SEAFOOD **$$**
(☎07-4051 5011; 223-227 The Esplanade; buffet $23.50; ⏲6-10.30pm daily) It's not the fanciest place in town, but Charlie's (at Acacia Court) is famous for its nightly all-you-can-eat seafood buffet. Fill your plate over and over with prawns, oysters, clams or hot food, and shamelessly scoff it all on the poolside terrace.

Fetta's Greek Taverna GREEK **$$**
(☎07-4051 6966; www.fettasgreektaverna.com.au; 99 Grafton St; dishes $13-25; ⏲11.30am-3pm Mon-Fri, 5.30pm-late daily) The white walls and blue-accented windows do a great job evoking Santorini. But it's the classic Greek dishes that are the star of the show here. The $35 set menu goes the whole hog – dip, saganaki, mousakka, salad, grilled meats, calamari, baklava AND coffee. Yes, you can break your plate.

Marinades INDIAN **$$**
(☎07-4041 1422; 43 Spence St; mains $14-30, lunch sets $10-12; ⏲11am-2.30pm, 6-10pm Tue-Sun; ✎) The pick of Cairns' Indian restaurants for its *long* menu of aromatic dishes, such as lobster marinated in cashew paste and Goan prawn curry.

Perrotta's at the Gallery MEDITERRANEAN **$$**
(☎07-4031 5899; 38 Abbott St; mains $14-36; ⏲8.30am-11pm daily; ✎) This chic spot adjoining the Cairns Regional Gallery tempts you onto its covered deck for tasty breakfasts, good coffees, and an inventive Med-inspired menu.

Self-Catering

For fresh fruit, veg and other local treats, hit the frenzied, multicultural **Rusty's Markets** (www.rustysmarkets.com.au; 57 Grafton St; ⏲5am-6pm Fri-Sat, to 3pm Sun), or for groceries, try the **Cairns Central Shopping Centre** (www.cairnscentral.com.au; McLeod St; ⏲9am-5.30pm Mon-Wed, Fri & Sat, to 9pm Thu, 10am-4.30pm Sun).

 Drinking & Entertainment

Cairns has a reputation as the party capital of the north, and there are loads of going-out options available. Many venues are multipurpose, offering food, alcohol and some form of entertainment, and you can always find a beer garden or terrace to enjoy balmy evenings.

The website www.entertainmentcairns.com and the *Time Out* section in Thursday's *Cairns Post* list the hotspots and gig guides. Can't decide? Try **Cairns Ultimate Party** (☎07-4041 0332; www.ultimatepartycairns.com; per person $35; ⏲Tues & Sat nights), a wild-n-crazy bus tour that takes in five suitably frenetic venues over six hours.

★ **Salt House** BAR
(www.salthouse.com.au; 6/2 Pierpoint Rd; ⏲9am-2am Fri-Sun, noon-midnight Mon-Thu) Next to Cairns' yacht club, Salt House is the city's most sought-after bar. Killer cocktails are paired with occasional live music or DJs hitting the decks. Its restaurant serves up excellent modern Australian food.

Flying Monkey Cafe CAFE
(☎0411 084 176; 154 Sheridan St; coffee $3.50; ⏲6.30am-3.30pm Mon-Fri, 7am-noon Sat) Fantastic coffee, ever-changing local art exhibitions, colourful buskers and a beyond-affable staff make the Monkey a must-do for caffeine-and-culture hounds.

Court House Hotel PUB
(38 Abbott St; ⏲9am-late) Housed in Cairns' gleaming-white former courthouse (1921), this pub is now a buzzing watering hole with polished timber bar and heaps of outdoor nooks. Live music in the beergarden all weekend.

Pier Bar & Grill BAR
(www.pierbar.com.au; Pier Marketplace; ⏲11.30am-late) A local institution for its waterfront location and well-priced meals. The Sunday session is a must, at the very least for the $5 wood-fired pizzas.

Grand Hotel PUB
(www.grandhotelcairns.com; 34 McLeod St; ⏲10am-10pm Mon-Thu, 10am-midnight Fri & Sat, 11am-8pm Sun) This laidback haunt is worth a visit just so that you can rest your beer on the bar – an 11m-long carved crocodile! Great place to loiter with the locals.

The Jack BAR
(☎07-4051 2490; www.thejack.com.au; cnr Spence & Sheridan Sts; ⏲til late daily) The huge beer garden with barrels for tables, big screens and a music stage is the stand-out at this vaguely Irish-themed pub attached to a hostel (dorms from $19).

Woolshed Chargrill & Saloon BAR
(www.thewoolshed.com.au; 24 Shields St; ⌚til late daily) An eternal backpacker magnet, where young travellers, dive instructors and the occasional locals get hammered and dance on tables.

PJ O'Briens IRISH PUB
(cnr Lake & Shields Sts; ⌚til late daily) It has sticky carpets and reeks of stale Guinness, but Irish-themed PJ's packs 'em in with party nights, pole dancing and dirt-cheap meals.

The Reef Hotel Casino CASINO, BAR
(www.reefcasino.com.au; 35-41 Wharf St; ⌚9am-5am Fri & Sat, to 3am Sun-Thu) In addition to table games and pokies, Cairns' casino has three restaurants and four bars, including Vertigo Cocktail Bar & Lounge, with free live music, ticketed shows and a massive sports bar (free movies twice a week). Check out the upstairs wildlife dome.

12 Bar Blue JAZZ
(☎07-4041 7388; 62 Shields St; ⌚7pm-late Wed-Sun) Intimate bar with jazz, blues and swing. Songwriter open-mic night takes place on Thursdays, and general jam-a-thon on Sundays.

Shopping

Cairns offers the gamut of shopping, from high-end boutiques to garish souvenir barns.

The huge **Cairns Central Shopping Centre** (www.cairnscentral.com.au; McLeod St; ⌚9am-5.30pm Mon-Wed, Fri & Sat, to 9pm Thu, 10am-4.30pm Sun) has a couple of supermarkets plus a huge range of speciality stores selling everything from books to bikinis. **Woolworths** (103 Abbott St; ⌚9am-9pm daily) is another CBD option for items such as sunscreen and SIM cards.

Head to the **Night Markets** (www.nightmarkets.com.au; The Esplanade; ⌚4.30pm-midnight) if your supply of 'Cairns Australia' T-shirts is running low, or you need your name on a grain of rice.

Information

INTERNET ACCESS

Dedicated internet cafes are clustered along Abbott St between Shields and Aplin Sts.

POST

Post Office (☎13 13 18; www.auspost.com.au; Shop 115, Cairns Central Shopping Centre; ⌚9am-5pm Wed-Fri, to noon Sat)

THE BAMA WAY

From Cairns to Cooktown, you can see the country through Aboriginal eyes along the **Bama Way** (www.bamaway.com.au). Bama (pronounced Bumma) means 'person' in the Kuku Yalanji and Guugu Yimithirr languages, and highlights include tours with Aboriginal guides, such as the Walker Family tours on the Bloomfield Track, and Willie Gordon's enlightening Guurrbi Tours in Cooktown. Pick up a Bama Way map from visitor centres.

TOURIST INFORMATION

The government-run **Cairns & Tropical North Visitor Information Centre** (☎1800 093 300; www.cairns-greatbarrierreef.org.au; 51 The Esplanade; ⌚8.30am-6pm Mon-Fri, 10am-6pm Sat & Sun) offers impartial advice, books accommodation and tours and houses an interpretive centre.

Other useful contacts:

Cairns Discount Tours (☎07-4055 7158; www.cairnsdiscounttours.com.au) Knowledgeable booking agent specialising in last-minute deals.

Far North Queensland Volunteers (☎07-4041 7400; www.fnqvolunteers.org; 68 Abbott St) Arranges volunteer positions with nonprofit community groups.

Royal Automobile Club of Queensland (RACQ; ☎07-4042 3100; www.racq.com.au; 537 Mulgrave Rd, Earlville) Maps and information on road conditions state-wide, including Cape York. For 24-hour recorded road-report service, call 1300 130 595.

Getting There & Away

AIR

QANTAS (☎13 13 13; www.qantas.com.au), **Virgin Australia** (☎13 67 89; www.virginaustralia.com) and **Jetstar** (☎13 15 38; www.jetstar.com.au) arrive and depart the **Cairns Airport** (www.cairnsairport.com) with flights to/from all Aussie capital cities and large regional centres. There are international flights to/from places including China, Papua New Guinea and New Zealand.

Skytrans (☎1300 759 872; www.skytrans.com.au) services Cape York with regular flights to Coen, Bamaga and Lockhart River, as well as Burketown and Normanton in the Gulf and Mount Isa.

Hinterland Aviation (☎07-4040 1333; www.hinterlandaviation.com.au) has one to four flights daily to/from Cooktown (one-way from $125, 40 minutes).

BUS

Cairns is the hub for Far North Queensland buses.

Greyhound Australia (☎1300 473 946; www.greyhound.com.au) Has four daily services down the coast to Brisbane (from $300, 29 hours) via Townsville ($60, six hours), Airlie Beach ($93, 11 hours) and Rockhampton ($195, 18 hours). Departs from Reef Fleet Terminal, at the southern end of The Esplanade.

Premier (☎13 34 10; www.premierms.com.au) Runs one daily service to Brisbane ($205, 29 hours) via Innisfail ($19, 1½ hours), Mission Beach ($19, two hours), Tully ($26, 2½ hours), Cardwell ($30, three hours), Townsville ($55, 5½ hours) and Airlie Beach ($90, 10 hours). Cheaper bus passes are available. Departs from Cairns Central Rail Station.

Trans North (☎07-4095 8644; www.transnorthbus.com; Cairns Central Rail Station) Has five daily bus services connecting Cairns with the Tablelands, including Kuranda ($8, 30 minutes, four daily), Mareeba ($18, one hour, one to three daily) and Atherton ($23.40, 1¾ hours, one to three daily). Departs from Cairns Central Rail Station; buy tickets when boarding.

John's Kuranda Bus (☎0418 772 953) Runs a service ($5, 30 minutes) between Cairns (departs Lake St Transit Centre) and Kuranda two to five times daily.

Sun Palm (☎07-4087 2900; www.sunpalmtransport.com.au) Runs northern services from Cairns to Port Douglas ($40, 1½ hours) via Palm Cove and the northern beaches (from $20). Departs from the airport and CBD.

Country Road Coachlines (☎07-4045 2794; www.countryroadcoachlines.com.au) Runs a daily bus service between Cairns and Cooktown ($81) and Cape Tribulation ($50) on either the coastal route (Bloomfield Track via Port Douglas/Mossman) or inland route (via Mareeba), depending on the day of departure and the condition of the track. Departs from the Reef Fleet Terminal.

CAR & MOTORCYCLE

All major car-rental companies have branches in Cairns and at the airport, with discount car and campervan-rental companies proliferating throughout town and on the Cook Highway just north of the airport turn-off. Daily rates start at around $45 for a late-model small car and around $80 for a 4WD. The big operators like Hertz and Europcar are located in Cairns Square (cnr Shields & Abbott Sts), or try the cheaper **Cairns Older Car Hire** (☎07-4053 1066; www.cairnsoldercarhire.com; 410 Sheridan St; per day from $35) or **Rent-a-Bomb** (☎07-4031 4477; www.rentabomb.com.au; 144 Sheridan St; per day from $30).

Wicked Campers (☎07-4031 1387; www.wickedcampers.com.au; 75 Sheridan St) and **Hippie Camper Hire** (☎1800 777 779; www.hippiecamper.com; 432 Sheridan St) have Cairns branches.

If you're in for the long haul, check hostels, www.gumtree.com.au and the big noticeboard on Abbott St for used campervans and ex-backpackers' cars.

Alternatively, hire a Harley ($190 to $260) from **Choppers Motorcycle Tours & Hire** (☎0408 066 024; www.choppersmotorcycles.com.au; 150 Sheridan St), or smaller bikes/scooters from $95/$75 a day. Also offers motorcycle tours, from one hour to a full-day ride to Cape Trib.

TRAIN

The *Sunlander* departs Cairns' **train station** (Bunda St) on Tuesday, Thursday and Saturday for Brisbane (one-way from $200, 31½ hours): contact **Queensland Rail** (☎1800 872 467; www.traveltrain.com.au).

The Kuranda Scenic Railway (p266) runs daily services.

Getting Around

TO/FROM THE AIRPORT

The airport is about 7km north of central Cairns; many accommodation places offer courtesy pick-ups. Sun Palm (p260) meets all incoming flights and runs a shuttle bus (adult/child $12/6) to the CBD. You can also book airport transfers with them to/from Cairns' northern beaches ($20), Palm Cove ($20) and Port Douglas ($40). A trip to the CBD with **Black & White Taxis** (☎13 10 08; www.blackandwhitetaxis.com.au) is around $25.

BICYCLE & SCOOTER

Bike Man (☎07-4041 5566; www.bikeman.com.au; 99 Sheridan St; per day/week $15/60) Hire, sales and repairs.

Cairns Scooter & Bicycle Hire (☎07-4031 3444; www.cairnsbicyclehire.com.au; 47 Shields St; scooters/bikes per day from $85/25) Zip around on a nifty-fifty or take it slow on a pushie. Also sells used scooters.

BUS

Sunbus (☎07-4057 7411; www.sunbus.com.au) runs regular services in and around Cairns from the Lake Street Transit Centre, where schedules are posted. Useful routes include: Flecker Botanic Gardens/Edge Hill (bus 131), Holloways Beach and Yorkeys Knob (buses 112, 113, 120), and Trinity Beach, Clifton Beach and Palm Cove (buses 110, 111). Most buses heading north go via Smithfield. All are served by the late-running night service (N). Heading south, Bus 140 runs as far south as Gordonvale. Single tickets from $2.30.

TAXI

Black & White Taxis (p260) have a rank near the corner of Lake and Shields Sts, and one outside Cairns Central Shopping Centre.

AROUND CAIRNS

The city and its northern beaches have plenty to keep you entertained, but nearby islands and highlands make great side trips.

Babinda & Around

South of Cairns, a lush pocket of rainforest offers a rewarding trip for walkers and wildlife watchers. The surrounding towns and settlements also provide enchanting glimpses into the area's heritage.

Babinda

POP 1069

On the Bruce Hwy, 60km south of Cairns, Babinda is a small working-class town that leads 7km inland to a rainforest park called the **Babinda Boulders**, where a photogenic creek rushes between 4m-high granite rocks. It's croc-free, but here lurks an equal danger: highly treacherous waters. Legend has it that a young Aboriginal woman threw herself into the then-still waters after being separated from her love; her anguish caused the creek to rise up, becoming the surging, swirling torrent it is today. Almost 20 visitors have lost their lives at the Boulders. Swimming is permitted in calm, well-marked parts of the creek, but pay heed to signs where even thoughts of a toe-dip are prohibited. Walking tracks give you the close – but safe – access you need for obligatory gasps and photographs.

The free **Babinda Boulders Camping Ground** (two-night maximum) has toilets, cold showers and free barbecues.

Nearby, you can kayak the clear waters of Babinda Creek with **Babinda Kayak Hire** (☎07-4067 2678; www.babindakayakhire.com.au; 330 Stager Rd; half-/full-day including pick-ups $42/63).

Drop into Babinda's little blue **visitor centre** (☎07-4067 1008; www.babindainfocentre.com.au; cnr Munro St & Bruce Hwy; ⏲9am-4pm) for more info.

Wooroonooran National Park

Part of the Wet Tropics World Heritage Area, the rugged rainforest in the **Josephine Falls** section of Wooroonooran National Park creeps to the peak of Queensland's highest mountain, Mt Bartle Frere (1622m). It provides an exclusive environment for a number of plant and animal species. The car park for Josephine Falls – a spectacular series of waterfalls and pools – is signposted 6km off the Bruce Hwy, about 10km south of Babinda, followed by a steep paved 600m walk through the rainforest and along a mossy creek.

The falls are at the foot of the Bellenden Ker Range. The **Mt Bartle Frere Summit Track** (15km, two days return) leads from the Josephine Falls car park to the summit. The ascent is for fit and well-equipped walkers only; rain and cloud can close in suddenly. Get a trail guide from the info centre or contact the **NPRSR** (☎13 74 68; www.nprsr.qld.gov.au). **Camping** (per person $5.45) is permitted along the trail; book ahead.

Cairns' Northern Beaches

Despite what some brochures may infer, Cairns city is sans-beach. But just 15 minutes, a Sunbus ticket or a foot on the gas will bring you to a string of lovely beach communities, all with their own distinct character: Yorkeys Knob is popular with sailors (though a proposed mega-casino could change that vibe), Trinity is big with families and Palm Cove is a swanky honeymoon haven.

All beaches can be reached via well-marked turnoffs on the Cook Highway.

Yorkeys Knob

Yorkeys Knob is a low-key settlement that's known for its Half Moon Bay, home to 200 bobbing boats. The 'Knob' part of the name still elicits nudges and chortles from easily amused locals; others wonder where the apostrophe went.

Kite Rite (☎07-4055 7918; www.kiterite.com.au; Shop 9, 471 Varley St; per hr $79) offers kite- and windsurfing instruction, including gear hire, and a two-day certificate course ($499).

A block or so back from the beach, **Villa Marine** (☎07-4055 7158; www.villamarine.com.au; 8 Rutherford St; d $89-159; ❄📶🏊) is the best-value spot in Yorkeys. Friendly owner Peter makes you feel at home in the retro-style, single-storey self-contained apartments arranged around a pool.

Yorkeys Knob Boating Club (☎07-4055 7711; www.ykbc.com.au; 25-29 Buckley St; mains $17-29.50; ⊙noon-3pm & 6-9pm daily, 8-10am Sat & Sun;) is a diamond find: try the fresh seafood basket ($22.50) or the local catch of the day ($24); oysters are $10 a dozen on Saturdays.

Trinity Beach

Trinity Beach, with its many dining and drinking options and long stretch of sheltered sands, make it a favourite for holidaymakers.

Self-contained apartments are just footsteps from the beach at **Castaways** (☎07-4057 6699; www.castawaystrinitybeach.com.au; cnr Trinity Beach Rd & Moore St; 1-/2-bedroom apt $132/165;), which has three pools, spas, tropical gardens and good stand-by rates.

The beachside **L'Unico Trattoria** (☎07-4057 8855; www.lunico.com.au; 75 Vasey Esplanade; mains $16-44; ⊙noon-late daily;) serves stylish Italian cuisine, including bugs with garlic, chilli and white wine, homemade four-cheese gnocchi and wood-fired pizzas.

Fratelli on Trinity (☎07-4057 5775; 47 Vasey Esplanade; mains from $15; ⊙7-11.30am & noon-4.30pm Thu-Sun, 5.30pm-late daily) is a cute little beach shack, but don't let its easy-breezy feel fool you into thinking the food is anything less than top-class: the pastas are superb and dishes like slow-cooked lamb shoulder and garlic, and rosemary rolled pork belly roast might even distract you from the million-dollar views.

Palm Cove

More intimate than Port Douglas and more upmarket than its southern neighbours, Palm Cove is essentially one big promenade along the paperbark-lined Williams Esplanade, with a gorgeous stretch of white-sand beach and top-notch restaurants luring sunlovers out of their luxury resorts.

Activities

Beach strolls, shopping and leisurely swims will be your chief activities here, but there's no excuse for not getting out on the water.

Palm Cove Watersports KAYAKING
(☎0402 861 011; www.palmcovewatersports.com; kayak hire per hour $33) Organises 1½-hour early-morning sea-kayaking trips ($56) and half-day paddles to nearby Double Island (adult/child $96/74).

Beach Fun & Co WATERSPORTS
(☎0411-848 580; www.tourismpalmcove.com; Williams Esplanade) Hires catamarans ($50 per hour), jet skis (per 15 minutes single/double $60/80), paddle boats ($30) and SUP boards ($30), and organises jet-ski tours around Double Island and Haycock – aka Scout's Hat – Island (single/double from $140/200). Fishing boats start from $100 for two hours.

Sleeping

Most of Palm Cove's accommodation has a minimum two-night stay.

Palm Cove Camping Ground CAMPGROUND $
(☎07-4055 3824; 149 Williams Esplanade; unpowered/powered sites $19/27) The only way to do Palm Cove on the cheap, this council-run beachfront camping ground is right near the jetty, and has a barbecue area and laundry.

Silvester Palms APARTMENTS $$
(☎07-4055 3831; www.silvesterpalms.com.au; 32 Veivers Rd; 1-/2-/3-bedroom apt from $100/140/150;) These bright self-contained apartments are an affordable alternative to Palm Cove's city-sized resorts.

★**Reef House Resort & Spa** BOUTIQUE HOTEL $$$
(☎07-4080 2600; www.reefhouse.com.au; 99 Williams Esplanade; d from $279;) Once the private residence of an army brigadier, Reef House is more intimate and understated than most of Palm Cove's resorts. The whitewashed walls, wicker furniture and big beds romantically draped in muslin all add to the air of refinement. The Brigadier's Bar works on a quaint honesty system; complimentary punch is served by candlelight at twilight.

Peppers Beach Club & Spa HOTEL $$$
(☎1300 737 444, 07-4059 9200; www.peppers.com.au; 123 Williams Esplanade; d from $200;) Step through the opulent lobby at Peppers and into a wonder-world of swimming pools – there's the sand-edged lagoon pool and the leafy rainforest pool and swim-up bar – tennis courts and spa treatments. Even the standard rooms have private balcony spas, and the penthouse suites (from $550) have their own rooftop pool.

Eating & Drinking

Palm Cove has some fine restaurants and cafes strung along the Esplanade. All resorts have swish dining options open to non-guests.

Surf Club Palm Cove LICENSED CLUB $$
(07-4059 1244; 135 Williams Esplanade; meals $14-30; 6pm-late) A great local for a drink in the sunny garden bar and bargain-priced seafood, plus decent kids' meals.

El Grecko GREEK $$
(07-4055 3690; www.elgrekostaverna.com.au; level 1, Palm Cove Shopping Village, Williams Esplanade; meze from $14, mains $24-30; 5.30-10.30pm;) Souvlaki, spanakopita and moussaka are among the staples at this lively taverna. Good meze platters; belly dancing Friday and Saturday nights.

Apres Beach Bar & Grill BAR, BISTRO $$
(07-4059 2000; www.apresbeachbar.com.au; 119 Williams Esplanade; mains $23-39; 7.30am-late daily) The most happening place in Palm Cove, with a zany interior of old motorcycles, racing cars and a biplane hanging from the ceiling, and regular live music. Big on steaks of all sorts, too.

Beach Almond ASIAN $$$
(07-4059 1908; www.beachalmond.com; 145 Williams Esplanade; mains $28-59; 11am-3pm Sat & Sun, 6-10pm daily) A rustic beach house near the jetty is the setting for Palm Cove's most inspired dining. Black-pepper prawns, Singaporean mud crab and Balinese barra are among the fragrant, fresh innovations.

Nu Nu MODERN AUSTRALIAN $$$
(07-4059 1880; www.nunu.com.au; 123 Williams Esplanade; mains $24-80; 11.30am-late Thurs-Mon) With one of the highest profiles on the coast, you'll need to book way ahead at the designer Nu Nu. Try something from the Mod Oz/Asian/Med menu, or throw in the towel and let the chef decide (six-course tasting menu $110, $175 with paired wines).

Information

Commercially run tour-booking companies are strung along Williams Esplanade; the Cairns & Tropical North Visitor Information Centre (p259) in Cairns can help with bookings.

Paradise Village Shopping Centre (113 Williams Esplanade) has a post office (with internet access, $4 per hour), small supermarket and newsagent.

Ellis Beach

Ellis Beach is the last (and possibly best) of the northern beaches and the closest to the highway, which runs right past it. The long sheltered bay is a stunner, with a palm-fringed, patrolled swimming beach and stinger net in summer.

Daily events at **Hartley's Crocodile Adventures** (07-4055 3576; www.crocodileadventures.com; adult/child $33/17.50; 8.30am-5pm daily) include tours of this croc farm, along with feedings, 'crocodile attack' shows, and boat cruises on its lagoon. The park is just up the highway in Wangetti Beach.

Ellis Beach Oceanfront Bungalows (1800 637 036, 07-4055 3538; www.ellisbeach.com; Captain Cook Hwy; unpowered sites $32, powered sites $35-41, cabins without bathroom $95-115, bungalows $155-190;) is a beachfront slice of paradise, with camping, cabins and contemporary bungalows, all of which enjoy widescreen ocean views.

Ellis Beach Bar 'n' Grill (Captain Cook Hwy; mains $15-28; 8am-8pm daily) has good food, great views, live music Sundays from 1pm and pinball.

Islands off Cairns

Green Island

This beautiful coral cay is only 45 minutes from Cairns and has a rainforest interior with interpretive walks, a fringing white-sand beach and snorkelling just offshore. You can walk around the island in about 30 minutes.

The island and its surrounding waters are protected by their national- and marine-park status. **Marineland Melanesia** (07-4051 4032; www.marinelandgreenisland.com.au; adult/child $18/8) has an aquarium with fish, turtles, stingrays and crocodiles, plus a collection of Melanesian artefacts.

Luxurious **Green Island Resort** (07-4031 3300, 1800 673 366; www.greenislandresort.com.au; ste $650-750;) has stylish split-level suites, each with a private balcony. Island transfers are included. It is partially open to day trippers, meaning anyone can enjoy the restaurants, bars, ice-cream parlour and watersports facilities.

Great Adventures (p253) and **Big Cat** (07-4051 0444; www.greenisland.com.au; adult/child from $84/42) run day trips, with optional glass-bottomed boat and semi-submersible tours.

Alternatively, hop aboard **Ocean Free** (☎07-4052 1111; www.oceanfree.com.au; adult/child from $140/95), spending most of the day offshore at Pinnacle Reef, with a short stop on the island.

Fitzroy Island

A steep mountaintop rising from the sea, Fitzroy Island has coral-strewn beaches, woodlands and walking tracks, one of which ends at a now-inactive lighthouse. The most popular snorkelling spot is around the rocks at Nudey Beach, which, despite its name, is not officially clothing-optional. Unlike the rest of the island, Nudey actually has some sand on it.

The **Fitzroy Island Turtle Rehabilitation Centre** (www.saveourseaturtles.com.au; adult/child $5.50/2.20; ⏲tours 2pm daily) looks after sick and injured sea turtles before releasing them back into the wild. Daily educational tours (maximum 15 guests) visit the new turtle hospital. Book through the Fitzroy Island Resort.

You can pitch a tent at the **Fitzroy Island Camping Ground** (☎07-4044 6700; camp sites $32), run by the Fitzroy Island Resort. It has showers, toilets and barbecues; advance bookings essential.

Tropi-cool accommodation at the **Fitzroy Island Resort** (☎07-4044 6700; www.fitzroyisland.com; studio/cabin $195/369, 1 & 2 bedroom ste $350-515; ❄🏊) ranges from sleek studios and beachfront cabins through to a luxurious self-contained apartment ($650). Its restaurant, bar and kiosk are open to day trippers.

Raging Thunder (p254) runs day trips from Cairns. Bounce off the ocean trampoline!

Frankland Islands

If the idea of hanging out on one of five uninhabited coral-fringed islands with excellent snorkelling and stunning white sandy beaches appeals – how can it not? – cruise out to the Frankland Group National Park.

Camping is available on the rainforesty High and Russell Islands; contact the **NPRSR** (☎13 74 68; www.nprsr.qld.gov.au; permit $5.45) for advance reservations and seasonal restrictions.

Frankland Islands Cruise & Dive (☎07-4031 6300; www.franklandislands.com.au; adult/child from $149/79) run excellent day trips which include a cruise down the Mulgrave River, snorkelling gear and tuition and lunch. Guided snorkelling tours with a marine biologist and diving packages are also offered. Transfers for campers to/from Russell Island are available. Boats depart from Deeral; transfers from Cairns and the northern beaches cost $16 per person.

You'll need to organise your own boat or charter to reach High Island.

Atherton Tableland

Climbing back from the coast between Innisfail and Cairns is the fertile food bowl of the far north, the Atherton Tableland. Quaint country towns, eco-wilderness lodges and luxurious B&Bs dot greener-than-green hills between patchwork fields, pockets of rainforest, spectacular lakes and waterfalls, and Queensland's highest mountains: Bartle Frere (1622m) and Bellenden Ker (1593m).

Four main roads lead in from the coast: the Palmerston Hwy from Innisfail, the Gillies Hwy from Gordonvale, the Kennedy Hwy from Cairns, and Rex Range Rd between Mossman and Port Douglas.

ℹ Getting There & Around

There are bus services to the main towns from Cairns (generally three services on weekdays, two on Saturday and one on Sunday), but not to the smaller towns or all the interesting areas *around* the towns, so it's worth hiring your own wheels.

Trans North (p260) has regular bus services connecting Cairns with the Tableland, departing from Cairns Central Rail Station and running to Kuranda ($8, 30 minutes), Mareeba ($18, one hour), Atherton ($23.40, 1¾ hours) and Herberton/Ravenshoe ($31/36, two/2½ hours, Mondays, Wednesdays, Fridays).

John's Kuranda Bus (☎0418 772 953) runs a service between Cairns and Kuranda two to five times daily ($5, 30 minutes).

Kuranda

POP 3000

Hidden in the rainforest, the artsy, alternative market town of Kuranda is the Tableland's most popular day trip.

👁 Sights & Activities

Walking trails wind around the village – the visitor centre has maps, or just get Kuranda-zen with it all and go with the flow. During the Wet, the mighty, must-see **Barron Falls** are in full thunder; they're just a quick tootle down Barron Falls Road (Skyrail and the railway have lookouts too).

Markets MARKETS

Follow the clouds of incense down to the **Kuranda Original Rainforest Markets** (www.kurandaoriginalrainforestmarket.com.au; Therwine St; ⏲9.30am-3pm). Operating since 1978, they're still the best place to see artists at work and hippies at play. Pick up everything from avocado ice cream to organic lingerie and sample local produce like honey and fruit wines.

Across the way, the more touristy **Heritage Markets** (www.kurandamarkets.com.au; Rob Veivers Dr; ⏲9.30am-3.30pm) overflow with souvenirs and crafts, such as ceramics, emu oil, jewellery, clothing and bottles of incredibly hot sauce.

Rainforestation ZOO

(☎07-4085 5008; www.rainforest.com.au; Kennedy Hwy; adult/child $44/22; ⏲9am-4pm) An enormous tourist park west of town with a wildlife section, rainforest/river tours aboard an amphibious WWII Army Duck and an interactive Aboriginal experience.

Wildlife Sanctuaries & Zoos WILDLIFE SANCTUARIES

Kuranda's rainforest twitters, growls and snaps with all manner of creatures, and the town itself is home to a handful of zoos and sanctuaries. The visitor centre has a full list; try these ones for starters.

If you can wake 'em from their gum leaf coma, you can cuddle a koala (there are wombats and wallabies too) at the **Koala Gardens** (☎07-4093 9953; www.koalagardens.com; Heritage Markets, Rob Veivers Dr; adult/child $17/8.50, koala photos extra; ⏲9.45am-4pm daily). The **Australian Butterfly Sanctuary** (☎07-4093 7575; www.australianbutterflies.com; 8 Rob Veivers Dr; adult/child/family $19/9.50/47.50; ⏲9.45am-4pm daily) is Australia's largest butterfly aviary: you can see butterflies being bred in the lab on a half-hour tour. **Birdworld** (☎07-4093 9188; www.birdworldkuranda.com; Heritage Markets, Rob Veivers Dr; adult/child $17/8.50; ⏲9am-4pm) is home to 80 species of free-flying native and exotic birds. Combination tickets for all three cost $46/23 per adult/child.

Kuranda Riverboat CRUISE

(☎07-4093 7476; www.kurandariverboat.com; adult/child/family $15/7/37; ⏲hourly 10.45am-2.30pm) Hop aboard for a 45-minute calm-water cruise along the Barron River. Located behind the train station; buy tickets on board.

DON'T MISS

WATERFALLS CIRCUIT

Take in four of the Tableland's most picturesque waterfalls on this leisurely 15km circuit. Start by swinging on to Theresa Creek Rd, 1km east of Millaa Millaa on the Palmerston Hwy. Surrounded by tree ferns and flowers, the **Millaa Millaa Falls**, 1.5km along, are easily the best for swimming and have a grassy picnic area. Almost ridiculously picturesque, the spectacular 12m falls are reputed to be the most photographed in Australia. **Zillie Falls**, 8km further on, are reached by a short walking trail that leads to a lookout peering down (with some vertigo) on the falls from above. The next, **Ellinjaa Falls**, have a 200m walking trail down to a rocky swimming hole at the base of the falls. A further 5.5km down the Palmerston Hwy there's a turn-off to **Mungalli Falls**.

Sleeping

Kuranda Rainforest Park CARAVAN PARK $

(☎07-4093 7316; www.kurandarainforestpark.com.au; 88 Kuranda Heights Rd; unpowered/powered sites from $28/30, s/d without bathroom $30/60, cabins $95-105;) This well-tended park lives up to its name, with grassy camping sites enveloped in rainforest. The basic but cosy 'backpacker rooms' open onto a tin-roofed timber deck, cabins come with poolside or garden views, and there's a restaurant serving local produce on site. It's a 10-minute walk from town via a forest trail.

★ **Cedar Park Rainforest Resort** ECO RESORT $$

(☎07-4093 7892; www.cedarparkresort.com.au; 250 Cedarpark Road; s/d from $125/145; @) Set deep in the bush (a 20-minute drive from Kuranda), this unusual property is part Euro-castle, part Aussie-bush-retreat. In lieu of TV, visitors goggle at wallabies, peacocks and dozens of native birds; there's also a spa, creek access, fireplace, a gourmet restaurant and free port wine.

Kuranda Hotel Motel MOTEL $$
(07-4093 7206; www.kurandahotel.com.au; cnr Coondoo & Arara Sts; s/d $95/100;) Locally known as the 'bottom pub', the back of the Kuranda Hotel Motel has spacious '70s-style motel rooms. Open for lunch daily and dinner Thursday to Saturday.

Eating

★**Petit Cafe** CREPERIE $
(www.petitcafekuranda.com; Shop 35, Kuranda Original Rainforest Markets; crepes $10-17) Duck out the back of the original markets for a mouth-watering range of crepes with savoury or sweet fillings. Winning combinations such as macadamia pesto and feta cheese will entice *le* drool.

Kuranda Coffee Republic CAFE $
(10 Thongon St; coffee $3.50-5.50; 8am-4pm Mon-Fri, 9am-4pm Sat & Sun) Food is basically limited to biscotti, but who cares when the coffee's this good? You can see – and smell – the locally grown beans being roasted on site.

Annabel's Pantry BAKERY $
(Therwine St; pies $4.50-5; 10am-3pm daily;) With around 25 pie varieties, including kangaroo and veggo.

Frogs CAFE $$
(Heritage Markets; mains $14-36; 9.30am-4pm daily;) Frogs has been a stayer on the Kuranda eat-scene since 1980: even the local water dragons hang out here. Relaxed and casual with a menu including gourmet salads and tasting platters of roo, emu, croc, barra and tiger prawns (the eponymous frogs get a reprieve).

Information

The **Kuranda visitor centre** (07-4093 9311; www.kuranda.org; Centenary Park; 10am-4pm) is centrally located in Centenary Park.

Getting There & Away

Those who believe in the journey as much as the destination are in luck here.

Winding 34km from Cairns to Kuranda through picturesque mountains and 15 tunnels, the **Kuranda Scenic Railway** (07-4036 9333; www.ksr.com.au) line was built between 1886-91: workers dug tunnels by hand, and battled sickness, steep terrain and hostile Aboriginals. Today, the 1¾-hour pleasure trip costs $49/25 per adult/child one way, and $79/37 return. Trains depart from Cairns at 8.30am and 9.30am daily, returning from the pretty Kuranda station at 2pm and 3.30pm.

At 7.5km, **Skyrail Rainforest Cableway** (07-4038 5555; www.skyrail.com.au; Cnr Cook Hwy & Cairns Western Arterial Rd; adult/child one way $47/23.50, return $71/35.50; 9am-5.15pm) is one of the world's longest gondola cableways, skimming the jungle canopy for a true bird's-eye view of the rainforest. There are two stops on the 90-minute ride; both offer spectacular views and interpretive panels.

Combination Scenic Railway and Skyrail deals are available.

You can also get to Kuranda with **Trans North** (07-4095 8644; www.transnorthbus.com; one way $8) and **John's Kuranda Bus** (0418 772 953; one way $5).

Mareeba

POP 10,181

This town revels in a 'wild west' atmosphere, with local merchants selling leather saddles, handcrafted bush hats and the oversized belt buckle of your bronco-bustin' dreams. July's **Mareeba Rodeo** (www.mareebarodeo.com.au) is one of Australia's biggest and best, with bull riding, a 'beaut ute' muster and boot scootin' country music.

Once the heart of Australia's largest tobacco growing region, Mareeba now turns its soil to more wholesome produce, with organic coffee plantations, distilleries, a mango winery, and abundant fruit and nut crops. **Food Trail Tours** (www.foodtrailtours.com.au; adult/child $159/80 from Cairns) visits food and wine producers in and around Mareeba; alternatively, self-drive to **Mt Uncle Distillery** (07-4086 8008; www.mtuncle.com; 1819 Chewko Rd, Walkamin; 10am-4.30pm daily) to wet your whistle with local liqueurs.

The **Mareeba Wetlands** (07-4093 2514; www.mareebawetlands.org; adult/child $15/7.50; 10am-4.30pm April-Jan) is a 20-sq-km sanctuary harbouring more than 200 bird species: over 12km of walking trails criss-cross the park. Safari tours (from $38) depart during the week, or you can take a 30-minute eco-cruise (adult/child $15/7.50) or paddle in a canoe ($15 per hour). The on-site **Jabiru Safari Lodge** (07-4093 2514; www.jabirusafarilodge.com.au; cabins per person incl breakfast $109-179, all inclusive $215-285) has solar-powered tented cabins and a spa. Take the Pickford Rd turn-off from Biboohra, 7km north of Mareeba.

The **Mareeba Heritage Museum & Tourist Information Centre** (07-4092 5674; www.mareebaheritagecentre.com.au; Centenary Park, 345 Byrnes St; 8am-4pm) FREE has heaps of info.

Atherton

POP 7288

Atherton is a spirited country town that makes a decent base for exploring the delights of the southern Tablelands. It also offers year-round picking jobs: the **Atherton Tableland Information Centre** (07-4096 7405; www.athertontablelands.com.au; cnr Main & Silo Rds) has work info.

Thousands of Chinese migrants came to the region in search of gold in the late 1800s, but all that's left of Atherton's Chinatown is the corrugated iron **Hou Wang Temple** (www.houwang.org.au; 86 Herberton Rd; adult/child $10/5; 11am-4pm Wed-Sun). Admission includes a guided tour.

Crystal Caves (07-4091 2365; www.crystalcaves.com.au; 69 Main St; adult/child $22.50/10; 8.30am-5pm Mon-Fri, to 4pm Sat, 10am-4pm Sun, closed Feb) is a gaudy mineralogical museum that houses the world's biggest amethyst geode (more than 3m high and weighing 2.7 tonnes). Crack a geode and take home your own glittery, gazillion-year-old souvenir.

The **Barron Valley Hotel** (07-4091 1222; www.bvhotel.com.au; 53 Main St; s/d without bathroom $40/60, s/d with bathroom $60/85;) is a Heritage-listed art deco beauty, with tidy rooms and a restaurant serving hearty meals (mains $18 to $35).

Millaa Millaa

POP 600

The dairy community of Millaa Millaa is the gateway to the Tablelands from the south and the closest village to the Waterfalls Circuit. Information is available at www.millaamillaa.com.au.

The village's heart is its only pub, **Millaa Millaa Hotel** (07-4097 2212; 15 Main St; s/d $80/90, mains $15-27; 10am-9pm), which serves mountain-sized meals and has six spick-and-span motel units.

At the **Falls Teahouse** (07-4097 2237; www.fallsteahouse.com.au; Palmerston Hwy; bunks from $35, d incl breakfast $120; teahouse 10am-5pm daily), you might like to warm your bones by the fireplace, or soak up rolling farmland views on the back verandah as you hoe into dishes like pan-fried barra and local beef pies (meals $7 to $23). It's at the intersection of the Millaa Millaa Falls turn-off.

About 6km southeast of the village, the biodynamic **Mungalli Creek Dairy** (07-4097 2232; www.mungallicreekdairy.com.au; 254 Brooks Rd; meals $18; 10am-4pm, closed Feb) serves up tasting platters of creamy yoghurt and cheese.

Malanda & Around

POP 2053

Round these parts, 'Malanda' has been a byword for 'milk' ever since 560 cattle made the 16-month overland journey from New South Wales in 1908. There's still a working dairy here, and the town is surrounded by rainforest. Locals cool off in the shady, croc-free **Malanda Falls**.

Guided rainforest walks (per person $16; 9.30am, 11.30am Sat & Sun; bookings essential), led by members of the Ngadjonji community, can be organised through Malanda's **visitor centre** (07-4096 6957; www.malandafalls.com; Malanda-Atherton Rd, across from Malanda Falls; 9.30am-4.30pm daily). Or head on up to the **Malanda Dairy Centre** (07-4095 1234; www.malandadairycentre.com; 8 James St; tours adult/child $10.50/6.50; tours at noon Thu-Tue, call to confirm) for 40-minute factory tours, which include a cheese platter or a milkshake. If you're not yet languishing in a lacto-haze, its licenced **cafe** (mains from $15;) has great grub.

About 10km from Malanda, tiny Tarzali has accommodation options including the wonderful **Canopy** (07-4096 5364; www.canopytreehouses.com.au; Hogan Rd, Tarzali, via Malanda; d $229-379;) , with timber pole-houses tucked into a patch of old-growth rainforest and loads of inquisitive wildlife to watch. Two-night minimum stay.

Yungaburra

POP 1150

Home to a colony of platypuses, tiny Yungaburra is one of the unassuming gems of the Tableland. Queensland's largest National Trust village with 18 Heritage-listed buildings, its boutique accommodation and stunning surrounds have made it a popular weekend retreat for those in the know.

The 500-year-old **Curtain Fig** tree, signposted 3km out of town, is a must-see for its gigantic, otherworldly aerial roots that hang down to create an enormous 'curtain'.

Day trippers descend on the village to hunt through crafts and produce at the vibrant **Yungaburra Markets** (www.yungaburramarkets.com; Gillies Hwy; 7.30am-12.30pm, 4th Saturday of the month). In late October, the

Tablelands Folk Festival (www.tablelandsfolkfestival.org; tickets $55, camping $22.50) features music, workshops and poetry readings.

If you're very quiet, you might be lucky enough to catch a glimpse of a timid monotreme at the **platypus viewing platform** on Peterson Creek. Dusk and dawn give you your best chance, but it's worth stopping any time.

★**On the Wallaby** (07-4095 2031; www.onthewallaby.com; 34 Eacham Rd; camping $10, dm/d with shared bathroom $24/55; @) is a homey hostel with handmade timber furniture and mosaics, spotless rooms – and no TV! Nature-based **tours** ($40) include night canoeing; tour packages and transfers (one-way $30) are available from Cairns.

Nick's Restaurant (07-4095 9330; www.nicksrestaurant.com.au; 33 Gillies Hwy; mains $8.50-36.50; 11.30am-3pm Sat & Sun, 5.30-11pm Tue-Sun) has been serving it up Swiss-style since 1986. Costumed staff, piano-accordion serenades and impromptu yodelling provide an apt backdrop for a menu that spans schnitzels to smoked pork loin. Vegos are catered for, too.

Yungaburra's **visitor centre** (07-4095 2416; www.yungaburra.com; Maud Kehoe Park; 9am-5pm) has a complete list of B&Bs, including beautiful retreats in the nearby countryside.

Lake Tinaroo

Tinaroo was allegedly named after a prospector stumbled across a deposit of alluvial tin there and, in a fit of excitement, shouted 'Tin! Hurroo!'. The excitement hasn't died down since, with locals fleeing the swelter of the coast for boating, waterskiing and lazy shoreline lolling.

Barramundi fishing is permitted year-round, though you'll need to pick up a permit (weekly $7.45), available from local businesses and accommodation. Or you might like to head out for a fish, a barbie or glass of wine during a sunset cruise aboard a super-comfy 'floating lounge room' skippered by **Lake Tinaroo Cruises** (0457 033 016; www.laketinaroocruises.com.au; 2/4hr boat charters $200/300).

The 28km **Danbulla Forest Drive** winds its way through rainforest and softwood plantations along the north side of the lake. There are five **Queensland Parks camping grounds** (13 74 68; www.nprsr.qld.gov.au; permits $5.45) in the Danbulla State Forest. All have water, barbecues and toilets; advance bookings are essential. Otherwise, **Lake Tinaroo Holiday Park** (07-4095 8232; www.laketinaroohholidaypark.com.au; 3 Tinaroo Falls Dam Rd; unpowered/powered sites $27/31, cabins $89-129;) has mod-cons, rents out boats ($90 per half-day) and canoes ($10 per hour) AND has a giant jumping pillow!

Crater Lakes National Park

Part of the Wet Tropics World Heritage Area, the two mirror-like, croc-free crater lakes of **Lake Eacham** and **Lake Barrine** are easily reached by sealed roads off the Gillies Hwy. Camping is not permitted.

Lake Barrine is the largest of the lakes, and is cloaked in thick old-growth rainforest; a 5km walking track around its edge takes about 1½ hours. The **Lake Barrine Rainforest Tea House** (07-4095 3847; www.lakebarrine.com.au; Gillies Hwy; mains $7.50-18; 9am-3pm daily) sits out over the lakefront; book downstairs for 45-minute **lake cruises** (adult/child $16/8; 9.30am, 11.30am, 1.30pm). A quick scarper from the teahouse brings you to the grand **twin Kauri Pines**, 1000-year-old giants over 45m tall.

Lake Eacham's clear waters are ideal for swimming and turtle-spotting. There are sheltered picnic areas, a pontoon and boat ramp. The 3km lake-circuit track is an easy one hour walk. Stop by the **Rainforest Display Centre** (McLeish Rd; 9am-1pm Mon, Wed & Fri) for information on the history of the timber industry and replanting of the rainforest.

Crater Lakes Rainforest Cottages (07-4095 2322; www.craterlakes.com.au; Lot 17, Eacham Close, Lake Eacham; d $240; @) has four themed timber cottages, each in their own private patch of rainforest and filled with romantic treats. For something a little more earthy, the **Lake Eacham Tourist Park** (07-4095 3730; www.lakeeachamtouristpark.com; Lakes Dr; unpowered/powered sites $22/25, cabins $90-110; @) has shady campsites and cute cabins.

PORT DOUGLAS TO THE DAINTREE

Be pampered in Port Douglas, explore the wilderness of the Daintree Rainforest, or journey to rough-and-ready Cooktown.

Port Douglas

POP 4772

Back in the 1960s, Port Douglas was a sleepy fishing village with a laidback population of 100; come the '80s and the construction of the Sheraton Mirage mega-resort, and 'Port' morphed into a flashy playground for the big-hair, big-money set. These days, the town has settled somewhere between the two extremes: unhurried yet upmarket, it's a sophisticated alternative for those looking to escape Cairns' hectic tourist scene. Port's white-sand beach, Four Mile, is mere steps away from the main streets (Macrossan and Davidson), and the Great Barrier Reef is less than an hour offshore.

Sights & Activities

Four Mile Beach BEACH

Backed by palms, this broad stretch of squeaky sand reaches as far as you can squint. There's a swimming enclosure in front of the surf life-saving club. In ye olde days, planes used to land on Four Mile, so firm is its sand.

For a fine view over the beach, follow Wharf St and the steep Island Point Rd to **Flagstaff Hill Lookout**.

★**Wildlife Habitat Port Douglas** ZOO

(07-4099 3235; www.wildlifehabitat.com.au; Port Douglas Rd; adult/child $32/16; 8am-5pm) There's no shortage of wildlife tourist parks in north Queensland, but this one is up there with the best. The sanctuary endeavours to keep and showcase native animals in enclosures that mimic their natural environment, while allowing you to get up close to koalas, kangaroos, crocs, cassowaries and more. Tickets valid for three days. It's 4km from town; head south along Davidson St.

Come early to have **Breakfast with the Birds** (adult/child breakfast incl admission $47/23.50; 8-10.30am) or book in for **Lunch with the Lorikeets** (adult/child incl admission $47/23.50; noon-2pm).

St Mary's by the Sea CHURCH

(6 Dixie St) FREE Worth a peek inside (when it's not overflowing with wedding parties), this quaint, nondenominational, white timber church was built in 1911.

Ballyhooley Steam Railway MINIATURE TRAIN

(www.ballyhooley.com.au; adult/child day pass $10/5; Sun) Kids will get a kick out of this cute miniature steam train. Every Sunday (and some public holidays), it runs from the little station at Marina Mirage to St Crispins station. A round trip takes about one hour; discounts are available for shorter sections.

Port Douglas Yacht Club SAILING

(07-4099 4386; www.portdouglasyachtclub.com.au; 1 Spinnaker Cl) Free sailing with club members every Wednesday afternoon (WAGS): sign on from 4pm.

Diving Courses DIVING

Several companies offer PADI open-water certification as well as advanced dive certificates, including **Blue Dive** (0427 983 907; www.bluedive.com.au; 4- to 5-day open-water courses from $760). For one-on-one instruction, learn with **Tech Dive Academy** (07-3040 1699; www.tech-dive-academy.com; 4-day open-water courses from $1090).

Port Douglas Boat Hire BOATING

(07-4099 6277; Berth C1, Marina Mirage) Rents dinghies (per hour $33) and canopied, family-friendly pontoon boats (per hour $43) plus fishing gear.

Wind Swell WATERSPORTS

(0427 498 042; www.windswell.com.au; 6 Macrossan St) Kite surfing and stand-up paddle boarding for everyone from beginners to high flyers: lessons begin at $50. Find them in action at the southern end of Four Mile Beach at the park or drop into their shop on Macrossan St.

Golf GOLF

The **Sheraton Mirage** (www.miragecountryclub.com.au) and **Paradise Links** (www.paradiselinks.com.au) resorts have prestigious, pricey, golf courses. The **Mossman Golf Club** (www.mossmangolfclub.com.au), 20 minutes north of Port, is considerably cheaper.

Historical Walks WALKING

Download DIY historical walks through Port Douglas, Mossman and Daintree from the **Douglas Shire Historical Society** (www.douglashistory.org.au).

Tours

Port Douglas is a hub for tours, and many based out of Cairns also pick up from here, including some white-water rafting and hot-air ballooning trips. Conversely, many of the following tours departing from Port Douglas also offer pick-ups from Cairns and Cairns' northern beaches.

Port Douglas

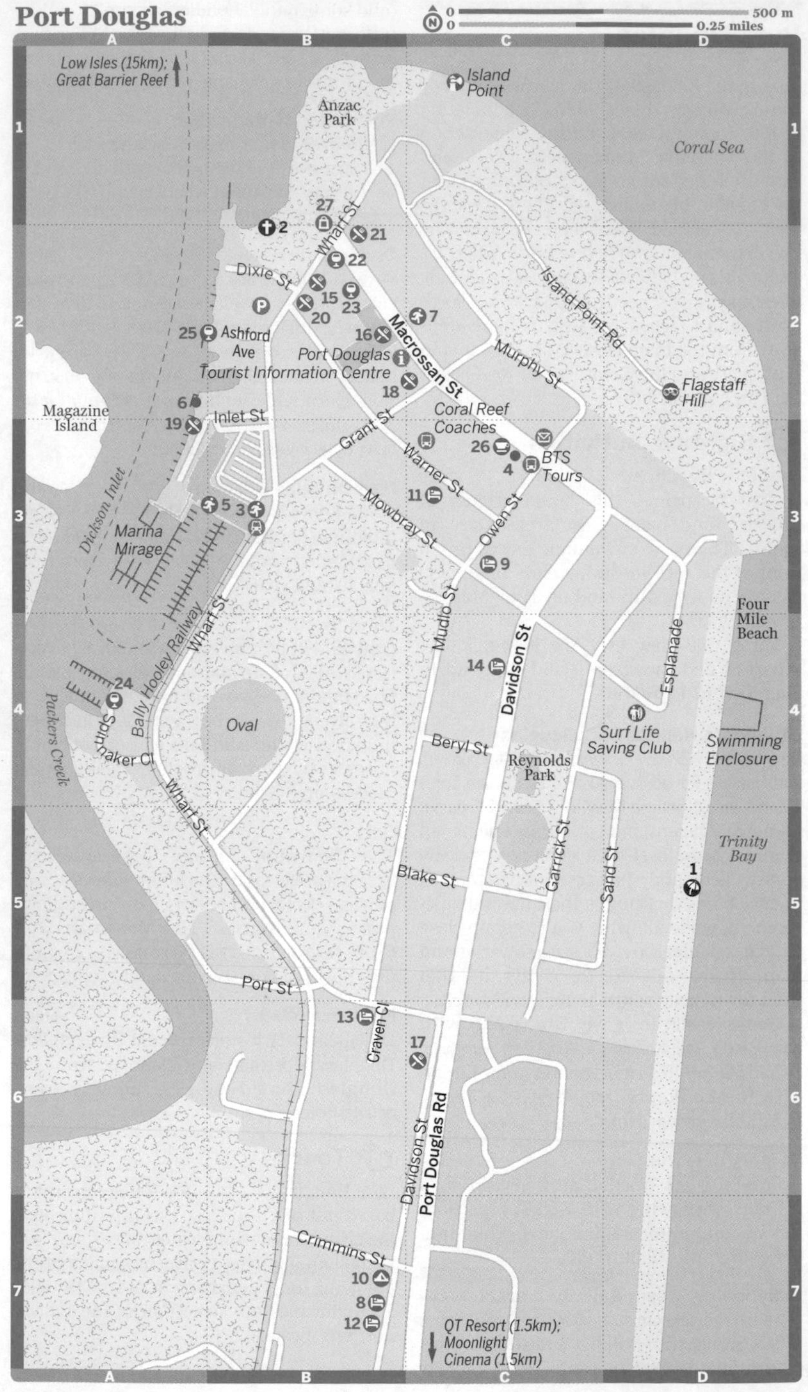

Port Douglas

Sights

1 Four Mile Beach D5
2 St Mary's by the Sea B2

Activities, Courses & Tours

3 Ballyhooley Steam Railway B3
4 BTS Tours C3
5 Port Douglas Boat Hire B3
Port Douglas Yacht Club .... (see 24)
6 Reef Sprinter A2
7 Wind Swell C2

Sleeping

8 Dougies B7
9 Hibiscus Gardens C3
10 Pandanus Caravan Park B7
11 ParrotFish Lodge C3
12 Pink Flamingo B7
13 Port O' Call Lodge B6
14 Tropic Sands C4

Eating

15 2 Fish B2
16 Coles Supermarket B2
17 Han Court C6
18 Mocka's Pies C2
19 On the Inlet A3
20 Salsa Bar & Grill B2
21 Sassi Cucina e Bar B2

Drinking & Nightlife

22 Court House Hotel B2
23 Iron Bar B2
24 Port Douglas Yacht Club A4
25 Tin Shed B2
26 Whileaway Bookshop Cafe C3

Shopping

27 Port Douglas Markets B1

Great Barrier Reef

The outer reef is closer to Port Douglas than it is to Cairns, and the unrelenting surge of visitors has had a similar impact on its condition here. You will still see colourful corals and marine life, but it is patchy in parts.

Most day tours depart from Marina Mirage. Tour prices usually include reef tax, snorkelling, transfers from your accommodation, lunch and refreshments.

An introductory, controlled scuba dive, with no certification or experience necessary, costs around $250, with additional dives around $50; certified divers will pay around $260 for two dives with all gear included.

Several operators visit the Low Isles, a small group of islands surrounded by beautiful coral reef just 15km offshore; you've got a great chance for spotting turtles here.

Quicksilver CRUISE
(☎07-4087 2100; www.quicksilver-cruises.com; adult/child $219/110) Major operator with fast cruises to Agincourt Reef. Try an 'ocean walk' helmet dive ($155) on a submerged platform. Also offers scenic helicopter flights from the pontoon on the reef ($159, minimum two passengers).

Sailaway SAILING, SNORKELLING
(☎07-4099 4772; www.sailawayportdouglas.com; adult/child $215/130) Popular sailing and snorkelling trip to the Low Isles that's great for families. Also offers 90-minute twilight sails ($50) off the coast of Port Douglas.

Sail Tallarook SAILING
(☎07-4099 4070; www.sailtallarook.com.au; adult/child half-day sail $99/75) Historic 30-metre yacht. Sunset cruises ($50, Tuesday and Thursday) include cheese platters; BYO drinks.

Reef Sprinter SNORKELLING, BOATING
(☎07-4099 6127; www.reefsprinter.com.au; adult/child $120/100) Superfast 15-minute trip to the Low Isles for snorkelling (and no seasickness!).

The Daintree & Around

There are 4WD tours from Cairns via Port Douglas to Cooktown and Cape York.

Reef & Rainforest Connections ECOTOUR
(☎07-4035 5566; www.reefandrainforest.com.au; adult/child from $177/115) Runs a flagship, 12-hour Cape Trib and Mossman Gorge trip.

BTS Tours OUTDOORS
(☎07-4099 5665; www.btstours.com.au; 49 Macrossan St; Daintree adult/child $160/115, Mossman Gorge $72/40) Tours to the Daintree Rainforest and Cape Trib, including canoeing, swimming and rainforest walks.

Fishing

Reef-, river- and land-based fishing charters operate regularly out of Port Douglas. Fishing gear and bait is included.

Tropical Fishing & Eco Tours FISHING, TOURS
(☎07-4099 4272; www.fishingecotours.com; fishing trips from $100, inlet tours from $40) For fishing, inlet tours or charter.

Fishing Port Douglas FISHING
(☎0409 610 869; www.fishingportdouglas.com.au; share/sole charter per half day from $90/320) Fishing on the river and reef.

River Cruises & River Snorkelling

Back Country Bliss Adventures SNORKELLING
(☎07-4099 3677; www.backcountryblissadventures.com.au; trips $80) Drift-snorkel down the Mossman River. Expect to see turtles and freshwater fish. Kid-friendly.

Lady Douglas RIVER CRUISES
(☎07-4099 1603; www.ladydouglas.com.au; 1½hr cruises adult/child $30/20) Paddlewheeler running four daily croc-spotting tours (including sunset cruise) along the Dickson Inlet.

Bike Tours

Bike N Hike Adventure Tours BIKE TOUR
(☎0416 339 420; www.bikenhiketours.com.au; tours from $88) Bounce down the aptly named Bump Track (an old Aboriginal trail) on a cross-country tour ($128, 7.30am to 11.30am Tuesday and Thursday, 1.30pm to 5.30pm Sunday) or a berserk night tour ($88, 6.30pm to 8.30pm nightly).

Festivals & Events

Port Douglas Carnivale CARNIVAL
(www.carnivale.com.au; May) This 10-day festival includes a colourful street parade, live music, and lashings of good food and wine.

Porttoberfest BEER FESTIVAL
(Port Douglas Marina; late October) The tropical take on Octoberfest, with live music, German food and beer. See www.visitportdouglasdaintree.com.au/events for annual updates.

Sleeping

Port Douglas is swimming in accommodation, mainly in self-contained apartments or upmarket resorts just out of town.

ParrotFish Lodge HOSTEL $
(☎07-4099 5011; www.parrotfishlodge.com; 37-39 Warner St; dm $25-32, d with/without bathroom $110/80;) Energetic backpackers with a bar, live tunes and lots of freebies, including breakfast, bikes and pick-ups from Cairns.

Dougies HOSTEL $
(☎07-4099 6200; www.dougies.com.au; 111 Davidson St; campsites per person $15, dm $26, d $68;) It's easy to hang about Dougies' sprawling grounds in a hammock by day and move to the bar at night. If you can summon the energy, bikes and fishing gear are available for rent. Free pick-up from Cairns on Monday, Wednesday and Saturday.

Pandanus Caravan Park CARAVAN PARK $
(☎07-4099 5944; www.pandanuscp.com.au; 97-107 Davidson St; 2-person unpowered/powered sites $38/44, 2-person cabins $80-110;) Five minutes' stroll from the beach, this park has a good range of cabins and free gas barbecues.

Port O' Call Lodge HOSTEL $
(☎07-4099 5422; www.portocall.com.au; cnr Port St & Craven Cl; dm $38, d $85-129;) Low-key hostel on solar/wind energy with en suite rooms and a good-value bar/bistro.

Tropic Sands APARTMENTS $
(☎07-4099 6166; www.tropicsands.com.au; 21 Davidson St; d from $89;) Schmick open-plan rooms with fully equipped kitchens and private balconies in a beautiful colonial-style building. No kids; two-night minimum.

★**Pink Flamingo** BOUTIQUE HOTEL $$
(☎07-4099 6622; www.pinkflamingo.com.au; 115 Davidson St; r $125-195;) Flamboyantly painted rooms, private courtyards (with hammocks, outdoor baths and outdoor showers) and an al fresco bar make the Pink Flamingo Port Douglas' hippest digs. Outdoor movie nights, gym and bike rental on offer.

Birdsong Bed & Breakfast B&B $$
(☎07-4099 1288; www.portdouglasbnb.com; 6188 Captain Cook Hwy; d/apt from $135/249; P) Posh open-plan B&B set on sprawling tropical grounds. Induce delusions of grandeur as you ogle the private heli-pad and gawp at the in-house movie theatre. Rates go down the longer you stay.

Turtle Cove Beach Resort GAY RESORT $$
(☎07-4059 1800; www.turtlecove.com; Captain Cook Hwy; d/suite from $154/277; P@) Mega-popular gay/lesbian resort with absolute beach frontage and a clothing-optional beach. Located 15 minutes south of Port. No kids.

★**QT Resort** RESORT $$$
(☎07-4099 8900; www.qtportdouglas.com.au; 87-109 Port Douglas Rd; d $240-260, villa $290-410;) Upmarket retro-kitsch decor and a DJ spinning lounge beats in the bar may make you forget you're in Queensland. Restaurant, **Bazaar**, serves up a quality buffet spread and stylish rooms have flat-screen TVs and plush beds.

Hibiscus Gardens RESORT $$$
(07-4099 5995; www.hibiscusportdouglas.com.au; 22 Owen St; d $155-385;) Balinese influences of teak furnishing and fixtures and plantation shutters give this stylish resort an exotic ambience. Their day spa is renowned as one of the best in town.

Eating

For a town its size, Port Douglas has some incredibly sophisticated dining options. Advance reservations are recommended and essential for really popular places. For self-catering, there's a large **Coles** (11 Macrossan St) supermarket in the Port Village shopping centre.

Mocka's Pies BAKERY $
(07-4099 5295; 9 Grant St; pies $4.50-6; 8am-4pm) Institution serving amazing Aussie pies with exotic ingredients such as crocodile, kangaroo and barra.

The Beach Shack MODERN AUSTRALIAN $$
(07-4099 1100; www.the-beach-shack.com.au; 29 Barrier St, Four Mile Beach; mains $16.50-29; 11.30am-3pm & 5.30-10pm;) There'd be an outcry if this locals' favourite took its macadamia-crumbed eggplant (with grilled and roast veggies, goat's cheese and wild rocket) off the menu. But it's the setting that makes it really worth heading to the southern end of Four Mile: a lantern-lit garden with sand underfoot. Good fish, sirloins and blackboard specials, too.

On the Inlet SEAFOOD $$
(07-4099 5255; www.portdouglasseafood.com; 3 Inlet St; mains $24-40; noon-11.30pm) Jutting out over Dickson Inlet, tables spread out along a huge deck where you can await the 5pm arrival of George the 250kg groper, who comes to feed most days. Take up the bucket-of-prawns-and-a-drink deal ($18 from 3.30pm to 5.30pm).

Salsa Bar & Grill MODERN AUSTRALIAN $$
(07-4099 4922; www.salsaportdouglas.com.au; 26 Wharf St; mains $20-37; noon-3pm & 5.30-9.30pm;) Salsa is a stayer on Port's fickle scene. Try the Creole jambalaya (rice with prawns, squid, crocodile and smoked chicken) or the roo with tamarillo marmalade. Also has outstanding cocktails.

Han Court CHINESE $$
(07-4099 5007; 85 Davidson Street; mains from $16) If Port's fancy fusion/Mod Oz/culinary-buzzword-du-jour menus are wearing you out, head to Han for good comfort food. They've been in town forever, and dish up familiar, tasty staples, such as honey chicken and black-bean beef, on a candlelit deck.

★ **Sassi Cucina e Bar** ITALIAN $$$
(07-4099 6744; cnr Wharf & Macrossan Sts; mains $26-49; noon-10pm) Scrimp, save, steal to splurge on an authentic Italian feast at this legendary local. Owner-chef Tony Sassi's spin on seafood is world-renowned, but the taste of absolutely anything off the menu will linger longer than your Four Mile tan.

2 Fish SEAFOOD $$$
(07-4099 6350; www.2fishrestaurant.com.au; 7/20 Wharf St; mains $29-40; 11.30am-3pm & 5.30-10pm daily) There's a lot more seafood here than the modest name would infer: over a dozen types of fish, from coral trout to red emperor and wild barramundi, are prepared in a variety of innovative ways.

Flames of the Forest FINE DINING $$$
(07-4099 5983; www.flamesoftheforest.com.au; Mowbray River Rd; dinner with show, drinks & transfers from $180) This unique experience goes way beyond the traditional concept of 'dinner and a show', with diners escorted deep in to the rainforest for a truly immersive night of theatre, culture and gourmet cuisine. Bookings essential.

Drinking & Nightlife

Drinking and dining go hand in hand in Port Douglas and the local clubs and hotels all serve up inexpensive pub-style meals.

Tin Shed LICENSED CLUB
(www.thetinshed-portdouglas.com.au; 7 Ashford Ave; 10am-10pm) Port Douglas' Combined Services Club is a rare find: bargain dining on the waterfront, and even the drinks are cheap.

Iron Bar PUB
(07-4099 4776; www.ironbarportdouglas.com.au; 5 Macrossan St; 11am-3am) Incongruous, wacky outback decor sets the scene for a wild night out: after polishing off a slab o'steak (mains $17 to $30), head upstairs for a flutter on the cane-toad races ($5) or dance to the live tunes.

Court House Hotel PUB
(07-4099 5181; cnr Macrossan & Wharf Sts; 11am-late) Commanding a prime corner location, the 'Courty' is a lively local, with bands on weekends. Meals ($20 to $30) available.

Whileaway Bookshop Cafe CAFE
(2/43 Macrossan St; 6am-6pm) For smart coffees in literary surrounds.

Port Douglas Yacht Club LICENSED CLUB
(www.portdouglasyachtclub.com.au; 1 Spinnaker Cl; bar 4-10pm Mon-Fri, noon-10pm Sat & Sun) There's a spirited nautical atmosphere at the PDYC. Inexpensive meals are served nightly.

Entertainment

Moonlight Cinema CINEMA
(www.moonlight.com.au/port-douglas/; 87-109 Port Douglas Rd, QT Resort, Port Douglas; tickets adult/child $16/12; Jun-Oct) Bring a picnic or hire a bean bag for outdoor movie screenings.

Shopping

Port Douglas Markets MARKET
(Anzac Park, Macrossan St; 8am-1pm Sun) These markets are treasure without the trash, with handmade arts, crafts and jewellery, plus local tropical fruits and produce.

Information

The **Port Douglas Tourist Information Centre** (07-4099 5599; www.infoportdouglas.com.au; 23 Macrossan St; 8am-6.30pm) has maps and makes tour bookings.

The *Port Douglas & Mossman Gazette* comes out every Thursday, and has heaps of local info, gig guides and more.

Getting There & Away

The 70km coast-hugging drive between Cairns and Port Douglas is one of the loveliest in the whole country. For those sans-wheels, there are many bus options, including the following:

Coral Reef Coaches (07-4098 2800; www.coralreefcoaches.com.au) connects Port Douglas with Cairns ($40, 1¼ hours) via Cairns airport and Palm Cove.

Sun Palm (p274) has frequent daily services between Port Douglas and Cairns ($40, 1½ hours) via the northern beaches and the airport.

Country Road Coachlines (07-4045 2794; www.countryroadcoachlines.com.au) has a bus service between Port Douglas and Cooktown on the coastal route via Cape Tribulation three times a week ($70), weather permitting.

Getting Around

Port Douglas Bike Hire (07-4099 5799; www.portdouglasbikehire.com.au; cnr Wharf & Warner Sts; per day from $19) Has high-performance bikes for hire as well as tandems ($32 per day). Free delivery and pick-up.

Sun Palm (07-4087 2900; www.sunpalmtransport.com.au) Runs in a continuous loop every half-hour (7am to midnight) between Wildlife Habitat and Marina Mirage.

For vehicle hire, the major international rental chains are represented here, or try a local company like **Paradise Wheels** (07-4099 6625; www.paradisewheels.com.au) or **Port Douglas Car Hire** (07-4099 4999; www.portdouglascarhire.com). Many places don't let you take cars off-road: check before hiring. It's the last place before Cooktown where you can hire a 4WD.

Mossman

POP 1733

Mossman – only 20km north of Port – is a pleasant, unpretentious town with a sugar mill and cane trains. Mossman is an obligatory stop on a visit to Mossman Gorge, and it's also a good place to stock up on petrol and supplies if you're heading north.

Sights & Activities

★ **Mossman Gorge** GORGE
(07-4099 7000; www.mossmangorge.com.au; Mossman Gorge Centre; Dreamtime walk adult/child $50/25; 8am-6pm) In the southeast corner of Daintree National Park, 5km west of Mossman town, Mossman Gorge forms part of the traditional lands of the Kuku Yalanji Indigenous people. Carved by the Mossman River, the gorge is a boulder-strewn valley where sparkling water washes over ancient rocks. **Walking tracks** loop along the river to a refreshing **swimming hole** – take care, as the currents can be swift. There's a picnic area here but no camping. The complete circuit back to the entrance takes about an hour.

Book in for one of the 1½-hour Indigenous **Kuku-Yalanji Dreamtime Walks** through the slick new on-site centre, which also houses an art gallery and bush-tucker restaurant.

Janbal Gallery GALLERY
(07-4098 3917; www.janbalgallery.com.au; 5 Johnston Rd; 10am-5pm Tue-Sat) Browse and buy the art at this Aboriginal-run gallery, or create your own masterpiece (canvas, boomerang or didgeridoo) under the guidance of artist-in-residence, Binna.

Sleeping & Eating

Mossman Motel Holiday Villas VILLAS $$
(07-4098 1299; www.mossmanmotel.com.au; 1-9 Alchera Drive; villas $120-210; P ❄ @ ☎ ≋) Fantastic-value villas on landscaped grounds complete with rock waterfall and pool.

Silky Oaks Lodge LUXURY RESORT $$$
(07-4098 1666; www.silkyoakslodge.com.au; Finlayvale Rd; studio treehouse/garden treehouse/deluxe treehouse/riverhouse $400/500/630/800;) This international resort woos honeymooners and stressed-out execs with hammocks, rejuvenation treatments and polished-timber cabins complete with spa baths. Its stunning **Treehouse Restaurant & Bar** (mains $36-44; breakfast 7-10am, lunch noon-2.30pm, dinner 6-8.30pm) is open to interlopers.

Mojo's MODERN AUSTRALIAN $$
(07-4098 1202; www.mojosbarandgrill.com.au; 41 Front St; mains $18-45; 11.30am-2pm Mon-Fri, 6pm-late Mon-Sat;) Mojo's has a menu that's more Montmartre than Mossman – elegant fare includes fried brie with truffle-honey walnuts and pork-belly spring rolls.

Information

NPRSR (13 74 68; www.nprsr.qld.gov.au) has information on the Daintree National Park up to and beyond Cape Tribulation.

Getting There & Away

BTS (07-4099 5665; www.portdouglasbus.com; 49 Macrossan St, Port Douglas) has return shuttles from Port Douglas to Mossman Gorge (adult/child return $26/16, 8.30am and 11.30am).

THE DAINTREE

The Daintree represents many things: a river, a rainforest national park, a reef, a village, and the home of its traditional custodians, the Kuku Yalanji people. It encompasses the coastal lowland area between the Daintree and Bloomfield Rivers, where the rainforest meets the coast. It's an ancient but fragile ecosystem, once threatened by logging and development but now largely protected as a World Heritage Area.

Daintree River to Cape Tribulation

Part of the Wet Tropics World Heritage Area, the region from the Daintree River north to Cape Tribulation is extraordinarily beautiful and famed for its ancient rainforest, sandy beaches and rugged mountains.

The length of Cape Tribulation Rd is scattered with places to stay and eat. There's no mains power north of the Daintree River – electricity is supplied by generators or, increasingly, solar power. Shops and services are limited, and mobile-phone reception is largely nonexistent.

The **Daintree River ferry** (car/motorcycle/bicycle & pedestrian one way $13/5/1; 6am-midnight, no bookings) carries people and their cars across the river about every 15 minutes.

Cow Bay & Around

Sights & Activities

On the steep, winding road between Cape Kimberley and Cow Bay is the **Walu Wugirriga Lookout** (Alexandra Range Lookout), with an information board and sweeping views over the range and the Daintree River inlet that are especially breathtaking at sunset.

Not far beyond the lookout, the award-winning **Daintree Discovery Centre** (07-4098 9171; www.daintree-rec.com.au; Tulip Oak Rd; adult/child/family $32/16/78, valid seven days; 8.30am-5pm) takes you high into the forest canopy with its aerial walkway, including climbing up a 23m tower used to study carbon levels. A small theatre runs films on cassowaries, crocodiles, conservation and climate change. The (included) audio guide offers an excellent Aboriginal tour.

The white-sand **Cow Bay Beach** lies at the end of the sealed Buchanan Creek Rd (also called Cow Bay Rd, or simply 'the road to the beach') and rivals any coastal paradise.

Also known as Jungle Bugs & Butterflies, the **Daintree Entomological Museum** (07-4098 9045; www.daintreemuseum.com.au; Turpentine Rd; adult/child $10/5; 10am-5pm) displays a large private collection of local and exotic bugs, butterflies and spiders.

Book ahead for a walk with **Cooper Creek Wilderness** (07-4098 9126; www.ccwild.com; Cape Tribulation Rd; guided walks $55-250). Bring your togs for the day walks (departing 9am, 2pm and 3pm), which take you through Daintree rainforest and include a dip in Cooper Creek. Night walks (departing at 8pm) focus on spotting nocturnal wildlife. There's also a full day tour including lunch and a river cruise ($130).

Cape Tribulation Wilderness Cruises (0457 731 000; www.capetribcruises.com; Cape Tribulation Rd; adult/child from $28/20) has one-hour mangrove cruises where you can go in search of crocodiles.

Sleeping & Eating

The best-value accommodation in the area is at **Daintree Rainforest Bungalows**

WORTH A TRIP

DAINTREE VILLAGE

You may be racing to the beaches of Cape Trib, but for lovers of local wildlife, it's worth taking the 20km detour to tiny Daintree village (population 146).

Croc-spotting and birdwatching cruises on the Daintree River are the village's main attraction. Numerous operators run trips – try **Crocodile Express** (07-4098 6120; www.crocodileexpress.com; 1hr cruises adult/child $25/13; daily from 8.30am), or **Daintree River Wild Watch** (07-4098 7068; www.daintreeriverwildwatch.com.au; 2hr cruises adult/child $55/35), which has informative sunrise bird-watching cruises and sunset photography nature cruises. Those short on time can take a one-hour cruise on a covered boat with **Bruce Belcher's Daintree** (07-4098 7717; www.daintreerivercruises.com; 1hr cruises adult/child $27/12).

The 15 boutique 'banyans' (treehouses) of **Daintree Eco Lodge & Spa** (07-4098 6100; www.daintree-ecolodge.com.au; 20 Daintree Rd; banyans from $215-598;) sit high in the rainforest a few kilometres south of the village. Nonguests are welcome at its superb **Julaymba Restaurant** (mains $26.50-40; breakfast, lunch & dinner), where the menu makes tasty use of local produce, including bush tucker ingredients.

Daintree Riverview (0409 627 434; www.daintreeriverview.com; 2 Stewart St; unpowered/powered sites per person $10/15, cabins $99-130) is a less pricey option, with waterside camping, good-value cabins and a lovely deck overlooking the river.

Tick off another of Australia's 'Big Things' – and try a Barra Burger – at the **Big Barra** (07-4098 6186; 12 Stewart St; mains $18, burgers from $7; 9am-5pm). Their homemade ice cream ($5.50) comes in exotic local flavours including soursop and black sapote.

No fuel is available in Daintree village.

(07-4098 9229; www.daintreerainforestbungalows.com; Lot 40, Spurwood Rd; d $110). Its free-standing wooden cabins are simple but stylish, with en suites and covered decks overlooking the rainforest. Minimum stay is two nights.

Also in the Cow Bay area, **Epiphyte B&B** (07-4098 9039; www.rainforestbb.com; 22 Silkwood Rd; s/d/cabins from $75/110/135) is situated on a 3.5-hectare property with individually styled rooms with en suites and their own verandahs. The spacious cabin has a patio, kitchenette and sunken bathroom. From the front deck of the house you can kick back with views of imposing Thornton Peak (1975m). Rates include breakfast.

The boutique motel rooms at **Daintree Rainforest Retreat Motel** (07-4098 9101; www.daintreeretreat.com.au; 1473 Cape Tribulation Rd; r $110-240, cabin $550;) have tropical colour schemes and glossy woodwork. Some have kitchenettes, or guests can dine at its restaurant **Tree Frogs** (mains $15-40; dinner Mon-Sat).

The **Cow Bay Hotel** (07-4098 9011; Cape Tribulation Rd; mains $14-30; 11am-3pm & 6-9.30pm), adjacent to the turn-off to the beach, is the only real pub in the whole Daintree region. Down towards the beach on Buchanan Creek Rd, the jungly **Crocodylus Village** (07-4098 9166; www.crocodyluscapetrib.com; Buchanan Creek Rd; dm $25 d $75-110;) hostel also has a restaurant and bar that are open to the public. It organises activities including half-day kayaking trips and two-day sea-kayaking tours to Snapper Island.

There are no agonising decisions at **Daintree Ice Cream Company** (07-4098 9114; Lot 100, Cape Tribulation Rd; ice creams $6; 11am-5pm), an all-natural ice-cream producer – you get a cup of four exotic flavours that change daily. Hustle it off on a 20-minute orchard walk.

Just south of Cooper Creek, **Rainforest Village** (07-4098 9015; www.rainforestvillage.com.au; 7am-7pm) sells groceries, ice and fuel, and has a small **camping ground** (unpowered/powered sites $22/28) with hot showers and a camp kitchen.

At the crescent-shaped **Thornton Beach**, the licensed **Cafe on Sea** (07-4098 9118; Cape Tribulation Rd; mains $12-25; 9am-4pm) is only a towel-length back from the sand.

Cape Tribulation

This little piece of paradise retains a frontier quality, with low-key development, road signs alerting drivers to cassowary crossings and crocodile warnings.

The rainforest tumbles right down to two magnificent, white-sand beaches – Myall and Cape Trib – separated by a knobby cape. The village of Cape Tribulation marks the end of the road and the beginning of the 4WD-only coastal route along the Bloomfield Track.

Sights & Activities

Beaches & Waterholes SWIMMING

Long walks on the swathes of **Cape Tribulation Beach** or **Myall Beach** are a favourite pastime and you can swim safely outside stinger season, though heed warning signs and local advice about croc sightings. A couple of boardwalks run through the mangroves.

If you're a bit wary, take a dip in the clear, croc-free **swimming hole** (admission by gold coin donation) next to Mason's Store.

Bat House WILDLIFE CENTRE

(07-4098 0063; www.austrop.org.au; Cape Tribulation Rd; admission $5; 10.30am-3.30pm Tue-Sun) A nursery for injured or orphaned fruit bats (flying foxes), run by conservation organisation Austrop, which also welcomes forest rehabilitation and planting volunteers for a minimum of one week.

Mt Sorrow HIKING

Fit walkers should start early for the Mt Sorrow Ridge walk (7km, five to six hours return, start no later than 10am); it's strenuous but worth it. The start of the marked trail is 150m north of the Kulki picnic area car park.

Tours

Most tours offer free pick-ups from local accommodation.

Jungle Surfing ZIPLINE, HIKING

(07-4098 0043; www.junglesurfing.com.au; zipline $90, night walks $40, combo $120; night walks 7.30pm) Get right up into the rainforest on an exhilarating flying fox (zipline) zoom through the canopy, stopping at five tree platforms. Guided night walks follow zany biologist-guides, who shed light on the dark jungle. Rates include pick-up from Cape Trib accommodation (self-drive not allowed).

Cape Trib Exotic Fruit Farm FARM TOUR

(07-4098 0057; www.capetrib.com.au; Lot 5, Nicole Dr; tour adult/child $25/12.50; 2pm Sun, Tue & Thu Jun-Oct) Bookings are essential for tours of these magnificent tropical orchards and a tasting of 10 of the 100-plus seasonal organic fruits grown here. It also has a couple of stunning private cabins.

Cape Trib Horse Rides HORSE RIDING

(07-4098 0030; www.capetribhorserides.com.au; per person $89; 8am & 1.30pm) Leisurely rides along the beach.

D'Arcy of the Daintree DRIVING

(07-4098 9180; www.darcyofdaintree.com.au; tours adult/child from $129/77) Entertaining 4WD trips up the Bloomfield Track to Wujal Wujal Falls and as far as Cooktown and down Cape Tribulation Rd.

Mason's Tours WALKING, DRIVING

(07-4098 0070; www.masonstours.com.au; Mason's Store, Cape Tribulation Rd) Longtimer Lawrence Mason conducts interpretive walks (groups up to five people two hours/half day $300/500) through the rainforest; 4WD tours up the Bloomfield Track to Cooktown are also available (groups up to five people half/full day $800/1250).

Ocean Safari SNORKELLING

(07-4098 0006; www.oceansafari.com.au; adult/child $123/79; 9am & 1pm) Ocean Safari leads

DAINTREE NATIONAL PARK: THEN & NOW

The greater Daintree Rainforest is protected as part of Daintree National Park. The area has a controversial history: despite conservationist blockades, in 1983 the Bloomfield Track was bulldozed through lowland rainforest from Cape Tribulation to the Bloomfield River, and the ensuing international publicity led indirectly to the federal government nominating Queensland's wet tropical rainforests for World Heritage listing. The move drew objections from the Queensland timber industry and the state government but, in 1988, the area was inscribed on the World Heritage List, resulting in a total ban on commercial logging in the area.

World Heritage listing doesn't affect land ownership rights or control and, since the 1990s, efforts have been made by the Queensland Government and conservation agencies to buy back and rehabilitate freehold properties, adding them to the Daintree National Park and installing visitor interpretation facilities. Sealing the road to Cape Tribulation in 2002 opened the area to rapid settlement, triggering the buy-back of hundreds more properties. Coupled with development controls, these efforts are now bearing the fruits of forest regeneration. Check out **Rainforest Rescue** (www.rainforestrescue.org.au) for more information.

Cape Tribulation Area

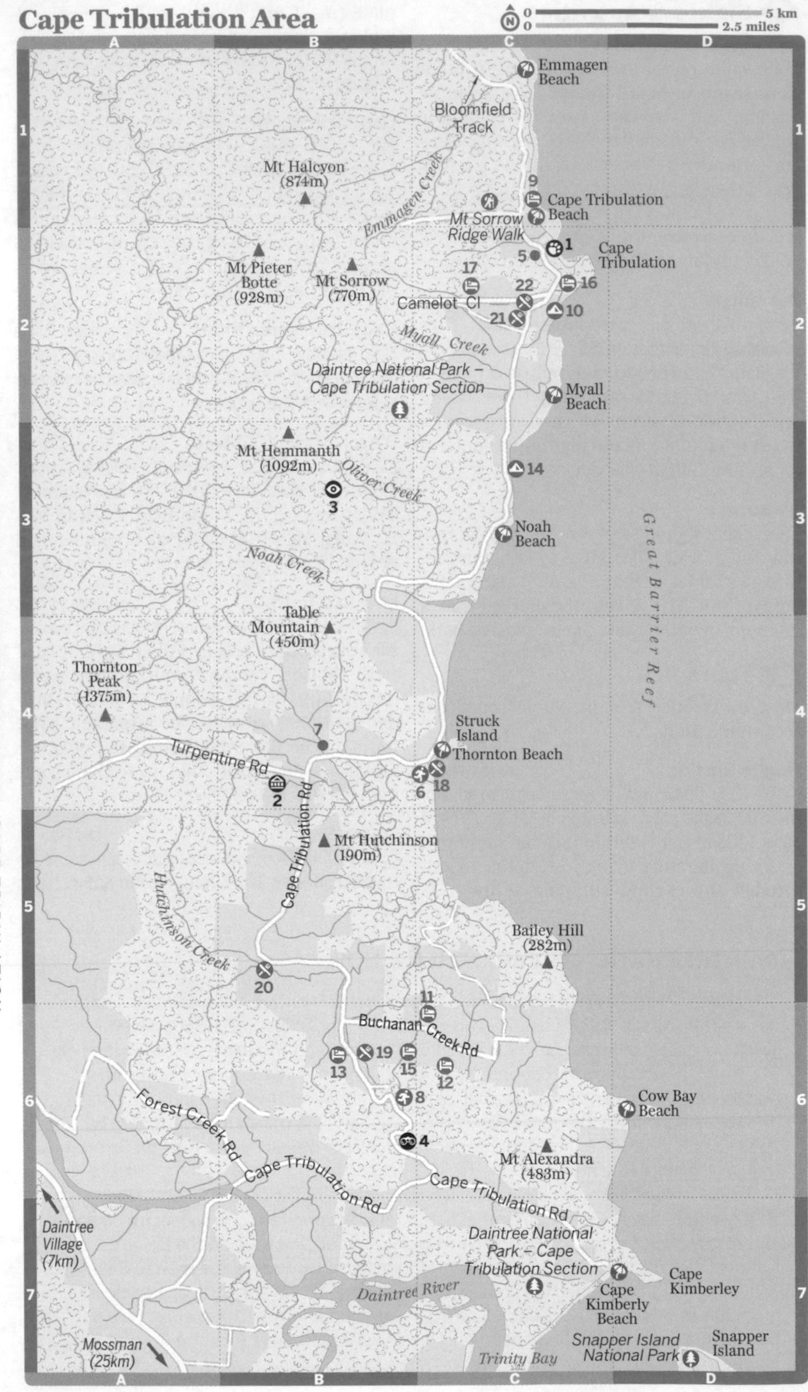

Cape Tribulation Area

Sights

1 Bat House C2
2 Daintree Entomological Museum B4
3 Daintree Rainforest B3
4 Walu Wugirriga Lookout B6

Activities, Courses & Tours

5 Cape Trib Exotic Fruit Farm C2
6 Cape Tribulation Wilderness Cruises C4
7 Cooper Creek Wilderness B4
8 Daintree Discovery Centre B6
Mason's Tours .... (see 21)

Sleeping

9 Cape Trib Beach House C1
Cape Trib Exotic Fruit Farm Cabins .... (see 5)
10 Cape Tribulation Camping C2
11 Crocodylus Village C6
12 Daintree Rainforest Bungalows C6
13 Daintree Rainforest Retreat Motel B6
14 Dunk Island Campground C3
15 Epiphyte B&B B6
16 PK's Jungle Village C2
17 Rainforest Hideaway C2

Eating

18 Cafe on Sea C4
19 Cow Bay Hotel B6
20 Daintree Ice Cream Company B5
IGA Supermarket .... (see 16)
21 Mason's Store & Cafe C2
22 Whet Restaurant & Cinema C2

small groups (25 people maximum) on snorkelling cruises to the Great Barrier Reef, just half an hour offshore.

Paddle Trek Kayak Tours KAYAKING
(07-4098 0062; www.capetribpaddletrek.com.au; kayak hire per hour $16-55, trips $69-79) Guided sea-kayaking trips and kayak hire.

Sleeping & Eating

Cape Trib Beach House HOSTEL $
(07-4098 0030; www.capetribbeach.com.au; Lot 7, Rykers Rd; dm $26-32, d $80, cabins $130-230;) Rainforest huts house dorms through to en suite timber cabins. There's a tidy communal kitchen as well as an open-deck licensed restaurant and bar.

PK's Jungle Village HOSTEL $
(07-4098 0040; www.pksjunglevillage.com; Cape Tribulation Rd; unpowered sites per person $15, dm $25-28, d $95-125;) PK's is a long-standing backpacker hub. You can reach Myall Beach by boardwalk, and its Jungle Bar is the entertainment epicentre of Cape Trib.

Cape Tribulation Camping CAMPGROUND $
(07-4098 0077; www.capetribcamping.com.au; Cape Tribulation Rd; unpowered & powered sites from $40; @) Beachfront spot with a nightly communal fire and friendly managers and kayaking guides (kayak hire from $20 per hour).

★ **Cape Trib Exotic Fruit Farm Cabins** CABIN $$
(07-4098 0057; www.capetrib.com.au; Lot 5, Nicole Dr; d $190) Amid the orchards of Cape Trib Exotic Fruit Farm, these two pole cabins have timber floors, ceilings and decks, and electric Eskies. Rates include breakfast hampers filled with tropical fruit from the farm. Minimum stay two nights; book in advance.

Rainforest Hideaway B&B $$
(07-4098 0108; www.rainforesthideaway.com; 19 Camelot Cl; d $130-140) This B&B was single-handedly built by its owner, artist and sculptor 'Dutch Rob' – even the furniture is handmade. A sculpture trail winds through the property; rates include breakfast.

Mason's Store & Cafe CAFE, SELF-CATERING $
(Cape Tribulation Rd; mains $15; 10am-4pm Sun-Thu, to 7pm Fri & Sat) Dishes up good fish and chips and huge steak sandwiches. The store sells some groceries and takeaway alcohol.

Whet Restaurant & Cinema AUSTRALIAN, INDIAN $$
(07-4098 0007; www.whet.net.au; 1 Cape Tribulation Rd; mains $17.50-33; 11.30am-3pm & 5.30-9.30pm) Cape Trib's coolest address, offering trendy Mod-Oz and Indian (Fridays) cuisine. Movies ($10) are at 2pm, 4pm and 8pm.

IGA Supermarket SUPERMARKET
(07-4098 0015; PK's Jungle Village; 8am-6pm) The Daintree's largest supermarket.

Information

Stop in at **Mason's Store** (07-4098 0070; Cape Tribulation Rd; 8am-6pm) for info on the region, including Bloomfield Track conditions.

NORTH TO COOKTOWN

There are two routes to Cooktown from the south: the coastal route from Cape Tribulation via the 4WD-only Bloomfield Track, and the inland route, which is sealed all the way via Peninsula Developmental Rd and Cooktown Developmental Rd.

Inland Route

The inland route runs along the western side of the Great Dividing Range for 332km (about 4½ hours' drive) from Cairns to Cooktown.

The historical township of **Mt Molloy** (population 274) marks the start of the Peninsula Developmental Rd, about 40km north of Mareeba. Since its mining heyday, the town centre has shrivelled to comprise a pub, bakery, post office and a cafe that serves up jaw-crackingly massive burgers that have twice been recognised as the 'world's best'. The road continues north via **Mt Carbine** to the **Palmer River Roadhouse**, where you'll find fuel, camping and meals. The Palmer River gold rush (1873–83) occurred about 70km west of here; there are still pockets of miners trying their luck in them thar hills.

It's another 15km to **Lakeland** at the junction of the Peninsula Developmental Rd and the Cooktown Developmental Rd. Head west and you're on your way to Laura and Cape York (4WD and forward planning essential); continue straight northeast and it's another 80km to Cooktown.

Some 30km shy of Cooktown, the spooky **Black Mountain National Park**, with thousands of stacked, square, black granite boulders formed 260 million years ago, marks the northern end of the Wet Tropics World Heritage Area. The eerie mountain is cloaked in mystery and legend: ask a local for their take on the place!

Coastal Route

The legendary 4WD-only Bloomfield Track connecting Cape Tribulation to Cooktown traverses creek crossings, diabolically steep climbs and patchy surfaces. It can be impassable for weeks on end during the Wet, and even in the Dry you should check road conditions, as creek crossings are affected by tide times. It's unsuitable for trailers.

The track is a contentious one: bulldozed through pristine forest in the early '80s, it was the site of battles between environmental protestors and police. Some locals still seek a staged closure over the next decade or so.

It's 8km from Cape Trib to **Emmagen Creek**, from where the road climbs and dips steeply and turns sharp corners. This is the most challenging section of the drive. The road then follows the broad Bloomfield River before crossing it 30km north of Cape Trib.

Turn left immediately after the bridge to see the **Bloomfield Falls**. Crocs inhabit the river and the site is significant to the Indigenous Wujal Wujal community, just north of the river. The local **Walker Family** (07-4040 7500; www.bamaway.com.au; adult/child $25/12.50; by reservation) runs highly recommended half-hour **walking tours** of the falls and surrounding forest.

About 5km north of Wujal Wujal, the **Bloomfield Track Takeaway & Middleshop** (07-4060 8174; dishes from $10; 8am-10pm Tue-Sat, to 8pm Sun & Mon) serves food and has fuel, fishing tackle and groceries.

North of Bloomfield, several walks begin from **Home Rule Rainforest Lodge** (07-4060 3925; www.home-rule.com.au; Rossville; unpowered sites per adult/child $10/5, r adult/child $25/15), at the end of a bumpy 3km driveway. Spotless facilities include a communal kitchen; meals are available as well as canoe hire. Home Rule is ground zero for the weekend-long **Wallaby Creek Festival** (www.wallabycreekfestival.org.au; Sep), with roots, blues and Indigenous music on two stages.

It's only another 9km to the welcoming **Lion's Den Hotel** (07-4060 3911; www.lionsdenhotel.com.au; 398 Shiptons Flat Rd, Helenvale; unpowered/powered sites per person $12/28, s/d $45/65, d safari tents $80;). This iconic watering hole with genuine corrugated, graffiti-covered decor dates back to 1875 and still attracts a steady stream of travellers and local characters. There's fuel and ice-cold beer, and its **restaurant** (mains from $20; breakfast, lunch & dinner) serves up excellent pub grub.

David Attenborough has spent time at the **Mungumby Lodge** (07-4060 3158; www.mungumby.com; Helenvale; s/d $260/279;) – you'll see why as you explore its rainforest walks and nearby waterfall. En suite bungalows are scattered among the lawns and mango trees. Rates include breakfast; lunch, dinner and nature tours are available.

About 4km north, the Bloomfield Track meets the sealed Cooktown Developmental Rd, from where it's 28km to Cooktown.

Cooktown

POP 2339

At the southeastern edge of Cape York Peninsula, Cooktown is a small place with a big history: for thousands of years, Waymbuurr was the place the local Guugu Yimithirr and Kuku Yalanji people used as a meeting ground, and it was here that on 17 June 1770,

Lieutenant (later Captain) Cook beached the *Endeavour*. The *Endeavour* had earlier struck a reef offshore from Cape Tribulation, and Cook and crew spent 48 days here while they repaired the damage – making it the site of Australia's first, albeit transient, non-Indigenous settlement.

Cooktown is a hotspot for history hounds, those looking to work on banana plantations and folks who believe that happiness is a fishing rod and an Esky full of beer.

Sights

Cooktown hibernates during the Wet, and many attractions and tours close or have reduced hours. The main street, Charlotte St, has some beautiful 19th-century buildings.

Grassy Hill LOOKOUT
Be sure you get to the top of this 162m-high knoll come dusk/dawn: with 360-degree views of the town, river and ocean, the view is spectacular! Cook himself climbed this hill looking for a passage out through the reefs. Drive up or walk via a steep path from town or bush trail via Cherry Tree Bay: walkers need minimum 20 minutes to ascend.

Nature's Powerhouse INTERPRETIVE CENTRE
(☎07-4069 6004; www.naturespowerhouse.com.au; off Walker St; admission by donation; ⌚9am-5pm) This environmental centre is home to two excellent galleries: the **Charlie Tanner Gallery**, with pickled and preserved creepy-crawlies, and the **Vera Scarth-Johnson Gallery**, displaying botanical illustrations of the region's native plants.

The centre doubles as Cooktown's official visitor centre and is at the entry to Cooktown's 62-hectare **Botanic Gardens** (off Walker St; ⌚24hr) FREE, one of Australia's oldest.

James Cook Museum MUSEUM
(☎07-4069 5386; cnr Helen & Furneaux Sts; adult/child $10/3; ⌚9.30am-4pm) Built as a convent in 1889, Cooktown's finest historical building houses well-preserved relics from Cook's time in the area, including journal entries and the cannon and anchor from the *Endeavour*, retrieved from the sea floor in 1971, plus displays on local Indigenous culture.

Bicentennial Park PARK
Bicentennial Park is home to the much-photographed bronze **Captain Cook statue**. Nearby, the **Milbi Wall** is a 12m-long mosaic that spans creation stories to European contact with the local Gungarde (Guugu Yimithirr) people, to recent attempts at reconciliation. Sitting just out in the water from Bicentennial Park is the **rock** marking the spot where Cook ran aground and tied up to a tree (part of the original tree is on display at the James Cook Museum).

Cooktown's **wharf** is one of Queensland's sweetest fishing spots.

TOURS FROM COOKTOWN

Although the reef is not far away, there are no regularly scheduled dive or snorkelling trips. Water-based tours depart from the wharf.

★**Guurrbi Tours** (☎07-4069 6043; www.guurrbitours.com; tours 2/4hr $95/120, self-drive $65/85; ⌚Mon-Sat) Nugal-warra family elder Willie Gordon runs revelatory tours that use the physical landscape to describe the spiritual landscape. The morning Rainbow Serpent tour involves some walking, bush tucker and rock-art sites, including a birthing cave. The afternoon Great Emu tour is shorter and visits three rock-art sites. Self-drivers meet near the Hopevale Aboriginal Community.

Maaramaka Walkabout Tours (☎07-4060 9389; irenehammett@hotmail.com; tours 1/2hr $84/42) Aboriginal cultural stories, rainforest walks and bush tucker in a gorgeous setting near Hopevale.

Cooktown Barra Fishing Charters (☎0408 036 887; half-/full day $120/220, minimum two people) Fishing and heli-fishing trips, plus croc-spotting, bird watching, mud-crabbing and eco tours.

Cooktown Tours (☎1300 789 550; www.cooktowntours.com) Two-hour town tours (adult/child $55/33) and half-day trips to Black Mountain and the Lion's Den Hotel (adult/child $110/77).

Saratoga Fishing & Hunting Adventures (☎07-4069 6697; www.capeyorksafaris.com) Fishin' and piggin' up the Cape York Peninsula.

Festivals & Events

Cooktown Discovery Festival HISTORICAL
(www.cooktowndiscoveryfestival.com.au; Queen's birthday weekend) Commemorates Cook's landing in 1770 with costumed re-enactment, grand parade and Indigenous events.

Sleeping & Eating

Cooktown has plenty of accommodation, including several caravan parks, but book ahead in the Dry. See www.tourismcapeyork.com for more options, including B&Bs.

Pam's Place Hostel & Cooktown Motel HOSTEL, MOTEL $
(07-4069 5166; www.cooktownhostel.com; cnr Charlotte & Boundary Sts; dm/s/d $27.50/55/60, motel d $100;) Cooktown's YHA-associated hostel offers the cheapest sleeps in town. Friendly managers can help find harvest work.

Seaview Motel MOTEL $$
(07-4069 5377; www.cooktownseaviewmotel.com.au; 178 Charlotte St; d $99-175, townhouses $235;) A great location opposite the wharf, with modern rooms (some with private balconies). Includes breakfast.

Sovereign Resort Hotel HOTEL $$$
(07-4043 0500; www.sovereign-resort.com.au; cnr Charlotte & Green Sts; d $180-220, tr & q $210-280;) Nicknamed 'the Half-Sovereign' following cyclone damage in 1949, these are now Cooktown's swishest digs, with tropical-style rooms and gorgeous gardens. Dine fine at the smart **Balcony Restaurant** (07-4069 5400; Sovereign Resort , cnr Charlotte & Green Sts; mains $25-33; 7-9.30am & 6-10pm) or kick back at the low-key **Cafe-Bar** (mains $11-23; 11am-8pm;).

Verandah Cafe CAFE $
(Walker St; mains $8-18; 10am-2.30pm;) Attached to Nature's Powerhouse at the entrance to the botanic gardens, the deck of this cafe is a serene setting for tea and scones or dishes like gado gado with coconut damper.

Gill'd & Gutt'd FISH & CHIPS $
(07-4069 5863; Fisherman's Wharf, Webber Esplanade; mains $7-12; 11.30am-9pm) Fish and chips on the waterside wharf.

Cooktown Bowls Club LICENSED CLUB $$
(07-4069 5819; Charlotte St; mains $15-25; 11.30am-2.30pm Wed-Fri, 5.30-10pm daily;) Big bistro meals. Join the locals in social bowls Wednesday and Saturday afternoons.

Restaurant 1770 MODERN AUSTRALIAN $$$
(07-4069 5440; 7 Webber Esplanade; breakfast $19, lunch & dinner mains $30-39; 7.30-9.30am, 11.30am-2pm & 6-9.30pm Tue-Sat;) Opening on to a waterside deck, try the fresh local fish but save space for mouth-watering desserts.

Information

Cooktown Travel Centre (07-4069 5446; 113 Charlotte St) Information and bookings for tours, transport and accommodation.

Tourist Information Centre (07-4069 6004; www.naturespowerhouse.com.au; Walker St; 9am-5pm) Housed in the Nature's Powerhouse complex.

Getting There & Around

Cooktown's airfield is 7.5km west of town along McIvor Rd. **Hinterland Aviation** (07-4040 1333; www.hinterlandaviation.com.au) has one to four flights daily to/from Cairns (one-way from $125, 40 minutes).

Country Road Coachlines (07-4045 2794; www.countryroadcoachlines.com.au) runs a daily bus service between Cairns and Cooktown ($81) on either the coastal route (Bloomfield Track, via Port Douglas) or inland route (via Mareeba), depending on the day of departure and the condition of the track.

Lizard Island

The five islands of the Lizard Island Group cluster just 33km off the coast about 100km north from Cooktown. The continental main island, Lizard Island, has a dry, rocky, mountainous terrain and spectacular fringing reef for snorkelling and diving. Most of the island is national park, with plenty of wildlife – including 11 different species of lizard – and 24 glistening white beaches.

Accommodation is either five-star luxury at *ultra*-exclusive **Lizard Island Resort** (1300 863 248; www.lizardisland.com.au; Anchor Bay; d from $1520;), or bush camping at the island's **camping ground** (13 74 68; www.nprsr.qld.gov.au; per person $5.45). Bring all supplies as there are no shops on the island.

Flying is the easiest way to reach Lizard Island; book all air transfers to/from Cairns (return $650, $590 for resort guests) through the resort. Flight time is one hour.

Daintree Air Services (1800 246 206, 07-4034 9400; www.daintreeair.com.au) has full-day tours from Cairns at 8am ($750). The trip includes gourmet lunch, snorkelling gear, transfers and a local guide.

Understand Queensland

Queensland Today

Queensland has always been a land of boom, bust and opportunity, a pattern played out over and over again on economic, political and environmental fronts. Western Australia has taken over as Australia's fastest growing state, but the sun still shines on Queensland: Brisbane can rightly claim its mantle of 'Australia's New World City', and the Great Barrier Reef remains a gorgeous technicolour vision.

Best on Film

Praise (director John Curran; 1998) Two mismatched 20-something lovers in down-and-out Brisbane.

Muriel's Wedding (director PJ Hogan; 1994) Comedic misadventures of socially awkward dreamer Muriel (Toni Collette).

Australia (director Baz Luhrmann; 2008) Sweeping epic filmed around Bowen on the Whitsunday Coast..

Dead Calm (director Phillip Noyce; 1989) Nicole Kidman gets nervous on a yacht in the Great Barrier Reef.

The Coolangatta Gold (director Igor Auzins; 1984) Critically derided '80s Gold Coast surf-lifesaving saga.

Best in Print

It's Raining in Mango (Thea Astley; 1987) Fortunes and failures of a pioneer family in Cooktown.

Carpentaria (Alexis Wright; 2006) Indigenous writer Alexis Wright's tale of the fictional town of Desperence.

Johnno (David Malouf; 1975) Coming-of-age tale set in 1940s Brisbane.

He Died with a Felafel in his Hand (John Birmingham; 1994) Grungy share-house life in Brisbane and beyond.

Reminiscences of Early Queensland (Tom Petrie; 1904) A bushman's story of life with Aboriginal peoples.

The Big Wet Continues

Much of eastern Australia was wracked by drought for the first decade of this century: this ended in 2011 with record rainfalls across Queensland. The drought was over, but floods inundated dozens of towns, affecting one million sq km – roughly the size of France and Germany combined. The Brisbane River broke its banks, flooding vast stretches of Brisbane and destroying the city's prized network of riverside walkways.

Then, in 2013, southeast Queensland was again inundated, this time by the tail-end of Tropical Cyclone Oswald, which immersed Bundaberg and parts of Brisbane in river water again. Residents of low-lying suburbs wrung themselves dry and started rebuilding (again).

Meanwhile, Out on the Reef

Many climatologists believe these floods are yet more evidence of climate change wreaking havoc on Queensland's weather. Climate change remains a hot topic here (no pun intended) – particularly when it comes to Queensland's biggest tourist attraction, the Great Barrier Reef. As sea temperatures rise, marine researchers predict disastrous consequences for the reef. Some estimates place the near-total devastation of the reef within the next 50 years. This destruction is unthinkable on many fronts – not least of which is the catastrophic economic consequences: the Great Barrier Reef generates an estimated $4 billion in annual tourism revenue.

Good Times, Bad Times

When the 2008 global financial crisis erupted, Queensland was ready to weather the storm. An ongoing economic boom fuelled by tourism and mining was luring about 1000 Aussies per week into southeast Queensland in 2007. But the boom went bust: the global economy stuttered and Queensland's growth slumped to just 0.2% in 2011. A depressed housing market, downturns in manufacturing and construction, and falling tourism hit the state. The soaring Australian dollar meant more spending power for Aussies overseas, but hurt Queensland tourism and exports.

Things soon picked up though, with southeast Queensland in particular booming again from 2012: growth promptly bounced back to around 4%. In other good news, the Gold Coast's fledgling Australian Football League (AFL) team (the aptly named 'Suns') seems to be dragging itself off the bottom of the AFL ladder, and the Gold Coast has been announced as the host of the 2018 Commonwealth Games. With a bit of luck, the new Gold Coast Light Rail system will be up and running by then. And, if the hospitality and arts sectors are any measure, Brisbane is also kicking goals, with a slew of new cafes, galleries and small bars opening their doors in recent times.

Political Challenges

After 20-plus years of left-wing Labor government, Queenslanders elected conservative Campbell Newman's Liberal National Coalition to office in 2012. Newman brought a new swagger and confidence to the top job, befitting a state on the rise, but he has since been causing ructions: a 42% pay rise for members of parliament; the decision not to introduce daylight savings time in Queensland (country voters – comprising much of the Coalition's supporter base – largely oppose daylight savings); and his plans to introduce Optional Preferential Voting in Queensland for federal elections (at odds with the way the rest of Australia votes, this system grants voters the ability to vote for a single candidate rather than distributing preferences from most to least preferred). Newman's wind-back of laws protecting the Wild Rivers area in Far North Queensland has also alarmed many, but despite his abrasive style, Newman remains popular amongst the proletariat.

Meanwhile, renegade north Queensland federal MP Bob Katter has been ruminating about north Queensland seceding from Queensland proper and becoming Australia's seventh state – interesting times!

POPULATION: **4.61 MILLION**

AREA: **1,852,642 SQ KM**

GDP: **AUD$284 BILLION**

GDP GROWTH: **3.5%**

INFLATION: **2.2%**

UNEMPLOYMENT: **6%**

if Queensland were 100 people

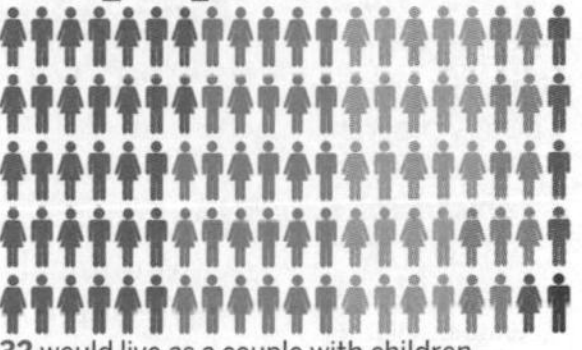

32 would live as a couple with children
28 would live as a couple with no children
23 would live alone
11 would be a one-parent family
5 would live as a group household
1 would be other family household

belief systems

(% of population)

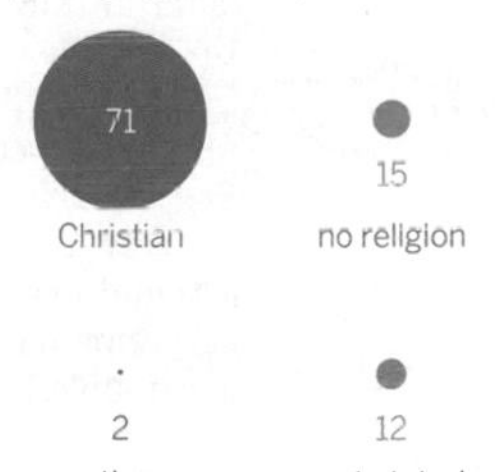

population per sq km

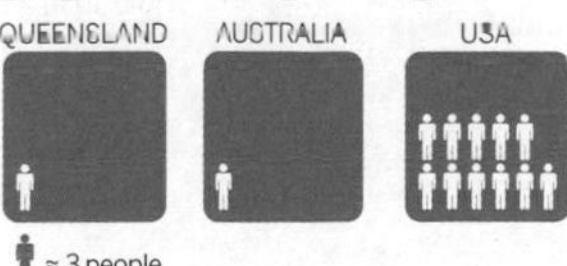

History

by Dr Michael Cathcart & Regis St Louis

Human settlement in Queensland dates back 60,000 years, though historians know little of its inhabitants prior to Captain Cook's arrival in 1770. Since then, the state has been shaped by pastoral expansion, gold rushes, workers strikes, wars, depression, mining booms, a rise in nationalism and, most recently, a growing global outlook and landmark legal recognition of Australia's first peoples.

Dr Michael Cathcart presents history programs on ABC TV, is a broadcaster on ABC Radio National and teaches history at the Australian Centre, University of Melbourne.

Arrival of the British

In April 1770, Aboriginal people standing on a beach in southeastern Australia saw an astonishing spectacle out at sea. It was an English ship, the *Endeavour,* under the command of then-Lieutenant James Cook. His gentleman passengers were English scientists visiting the Pacific to make astronomical observations and to investigate 'new worlds'. As they sailed north along the edge of this new-found land, Cook began drawing the first British chart of Australia's east coast. This map heralded the beginning of conflicts between European settlers and indigenous peoples.

A few days after that first sighting, Cook led a party of men ashore at a place known to the Aboriginal people as Kurnell. Though the Kurnell Aboriginal people were far from welcoming, the *Endeavour's* botanists were delighted to discover that the woods were teeming with unfamiliar plants. To celebrate this profusion, Cook renamed the place Botany Bay.

As his voyage northwards continued, Cook strewed English names the entire length of the coastline. In Queensland, these included Hervey Bay (after an English admiral), Dunk Island (after an English duke), Cape Upstart, the Glass House Mountains and Wide Bay.

One night, in the seas off the great rainforests of the Kuku Yalanji Aboriginal people, in what is now known as Far North Queensland, the *Endeavour* was inching gingerly through the Great Barrier Reef when the crew heard the sickening sound of ripping timbers. They had run aground near a cape which today is a tourist paradise. Cook was in a glowering mood: he named it Cape Tribulation, 'because here began all our troubles'. Seven days later Cook managed to beach the wounded ship

TIMELINE

60,000 BC

Although the exact start of human habitation in Australia is still uncertain, according to most experts this is when Aboriginal people settled on the continent.

6000 BC

Rising water levels due to global warming force many indigenous groups off their fertile flatland homes along the coast. Vast sections of land disappear into the sea.

3000 BC

The last known large migration to the continent from Asia occurs (at least until about 1970). Humans introduce the dingo which, along with hunting, drives some native species to extinction.

in an Aboriginal harbour named Charco (Cook renamed it Endeavour), where his carpenters patched the hull.

Back at sea, the *Endeavour* finally reached the northern tip of the Cape York Peninsula. On a small, hilly island (Possession Island), Cook raised the Union Jack and claimed the eastern half of the continent for King George III. His intention was not to dispossess the indigenous peoples, but to warn off other European powers – notably the Dutch, who had already charted much of the coastline.

European Settlement

In 1788 the English were back. On 26 January, 11 ships sailed into a harbour just north of Botany Bay. The First Fleet was under the command of a humane and diligent officer named Arthur Phillip. Under his leadership, the settlers cut down trees, built shelters and laid out roadways. They were building a prison settlement in the lands of the Eora people. Phillip called the place Sydney.

In the early years of the settlement, both the convicts and the free people of Sydney struggled to survive. Their early attempts to grow crops failed and the settlement relied on supplies brought by ship. Fortunate or canny prisoners were soon issued with 'tickets of leave', which gave them the right to live and work as free men and women on the condition that they did not attempt to return home before their sentences expired.

The convict system could also be savage. Women (who were outnumbered five to one) lived under constant threat of sexual exploitation. Female convicts who offended their jailers languished in the depressing 'female factories' (women's prisons). Male offenders were cruelly flogged and could be hanged even for such crimes as stealing. In 1803, English officers established a settlement to punish reoffenders at Port Arthur, on the wild southeast coast of Tasmania.

The impact of these settlements on the Aboriginal people was devastating. Multitudes were killed by unfamiliar diseases such as smallpox and, in the years that followed European settlement, many others succumbed to alcoholism and despair as they felt their traditional lands and way of life being wrenched away.

A classic biography is *The Life of Captain James Cook* (1974), by JC Beaglehole. Another fascinating read is Tony Horwitz's *Blue Latitudes: Boldly Going Where Captain Cook Has Gone Before* (2002), both travelogue and biography.

Convicts to Queensland

By the 1820s Sydney was a busy port, teeming with soldiers, merchants, children, schoolmistresses, criminals, preachers and drunks. The farms prospered, and in the streets children were chatting in a new accent that we would probably recognise today as 'Australian'.

The authorities now looked north to the lands of the Yuggera people, where they established another lonely penal colony at Redcliffe. Here, men laboured under the command of the merciless Captain Patrick

AD 1607

Spanish explorer Luis Torres manages to sail between Australia and New Guinea and not discover the rather large continent to the south. The strait bears his name today.

1770

English Captain James Cook maps Australia's east coast in the scientific ship *Endeavour*. He runs aground on the Great Barrier Reef near a place he names Cape Tribulation.

1823

Government explorer John Oxley surveys Redcliffe for a convict settlement. It is established the following year and becomes known as a place of blood, sweat and tears.

1844–45

The first guidebook to Australia is written in the form of a journal by Ludwig Leichhardt. It chronicles his party's exploration from Brisbane almost to Darwin. In 1848 he vanishes without a trace.

Logan, building their own prison cells and sweating on the farms they had cleared from the bush. These prisoners suffered such tortures that some welcomed death, even by hanging, as a blessed release.

Logan himself met a brutal end when he was bashed and speared while riding in the bush. Shortly after his murder, a group of soldiers reported that they had seen him on the far bank of a river, screaming to be rescued. But as they rowed across to investigate, his tormented ghost melted into the heat...

Logan's miserable prison spawned the town of Brisbane, which soon became the administrative and supply centre for the farmers, graziers, loggers and miners who occupied the region. But the great hinterland of Queensland remained remote and mysterious – in the firm control of its Aboriginal owners.

Vestiges of a Convict Past

St Helena Island, Moreton Bay

Commissariat Store Museum (p52), Brisbane

Old Windmill & Observatory (p53), Brisbane

The Barracks (p80) (former Petrie Terrace Gaol), Brisbane

Explorers & Settlers

The hinterland frontier was crossed in 1844, when an eccentric Prussian explorer named Ludwig Leichhardt led a gruelling 15-month trek from Brisbane to Port Essington (near today's Darwin). His journal – the first European travel guide to Australia's Top End – would have secured his place in Australian history, but today he is remembered more for the manner of his death. In 1848 his entire party vanished in the desert during an attempt to cross the continent. Journalists and poets wrote as if Leichhardt had been received into a silent mystery that lay at the heart of Australia. It might seem strange that Australians should sanctify a failed explorer, but Leichhardt – like two other dead explorers, Burke and Wills – satisfied a Victorian belief that a nation did not come of age until it was baptised in blood.

As Queensland formally separated from NSW in 1859, graziers, miners and small farmers were pushing further west and north. Some European settlers established cooperative relations with local tribes, sharing the land and employing Aboriginal people as stockmen or domestics. Conversely, others saw settlement as a tough Darwinian struggle between the British race and a primitive Stone Age people – a battle the Europeans were destined to win. Indeed, settlers who ran sheep on the vast grasslands of the Darling Downs sometimes spoke as if they had taken possession of a great park where no other humans had ever lived. Today, Aboriginal people across the country tell stories of how European settlers shot whole groups of their people or killed them with poisoned food. Some Aboriginal tribes fought back, but the weapons of the white people were formidable – including the notorious Native Police, a government-backed squad made up of Aboriginal people recruited from distant tribes who violently suppressed any uprisings.

1846

Sole survivor of a shipwreck off Queensland, Jemmy Morrill is rescued by Aboriginal people. He lives with them for 17 years, and later plays a key role in improving European–Aboriginal relations.

1859

Queen Victoria gives approval to establish the new colony of Queensland, which formally separates from New South Wales and is named in her honour (rather than 'Cooksland', another proffered option).

1872

The gold rush sweeps into Charters Towers, funding the construction of magnificent homes and public buildings. Queensland is connected to Europe by telegraph.

1884

In a tragic last stand, the defiant Kalkadoon Indigenous nation is defeated in a massacre at Battle Mountain, near Mt Isa.

Meanwhile, on the tropical coast, growers were developing a prosperous sugar-cane industry that relied on the sweat of thousands of labourers from the Solomon Islands, Vanuatu and other Pacific islands. Known as 'kanakas', these workers endured harsh and sometimes cruel conditions that were considered intolerable for white workers.

Gold & Revolution

In 1871 an Aboriginal stockman named Jupiter spotted gold glinting in a waterhole near Charters Towers. His find triggered a gold rush that attracted thousands of prospectors, publicans, traders, prostitutes and quacks to the diggings. For a few exhilarating years, any determined miner, regardless of class, had a real chance of striking it rich. By the 1880s, Brisbane itself had grown prosperous on wool and gold but, by then, life on the goldfields was changing radically. The easy gold was gone. The free-for-all had given way to an industry in which the company boss called the shots.

As displaced prospectors searched for work, the overheated economy of eastern Australia collapsed, throwing thousands of labouring families into the miseries of unemployment and hunger. The depression of the 1890s exposed stark inequalities as barefoot children scavenged in the streets. But this was Australia, 'the working man's paradise' – the land where the principle of 'a fair day's pay for a fair day's work' was sacred. As employers tried to drive down wages, a tough Queensland working class began to assert itself. Seamen, factory workers, miners, loggers and shearers organised themselves into trade unions to take on Queensland's equally tough bosses and shareholders.

A LAST STAND

The Kalkadoon (also known as Kalkatungu) people of the Mt Isa region in western Queensland were known for their fierce resistance to colonial expansion. As pastoralism and mining concerns pushed into their country in the 1860s, some of the Kalkadoon initially worked for the settlers as labourers and guides. However, competition for land and resources eventually led to conflict, and the Kalkadoon waged guerrilla-style warfare against settlers and their stock. They soon gained a reputation as ferocious warriors who seemingly melted away into the bush. In 1883 they killed five Native Police and a prominent pastoralist – an incident that turned the tide of the conflict against them.

In September 1884, some 600 Kalkadoon retreated to a defensive site known as Battle Mountain, where they fought one last battle against the Native Police and armed settlers. Despite heroic resistance, which included a charge against cavalry positions, the Kalkadoon warriors were mercilessly slain, their spears and clubs no match for guns. In all, an estimated 900 Kalkadoon were killed between 1878 and 1884.

1891

A violent shearers' strike around Barcaldine, where 1000 men camp around the town, establishes a labour legend. The confrontation leads to the birth of the Australian Labor Party.

1901

The new federal government removes kanakas from Queensland, in line with the White Australia policy. Mortality figures for these Pacific Islanders were almost five times those of whites.

1902

The first trans-Pacific cable between Australia and Canada is completed, terminating on the Gold Coast. The cable also allows Australia to join the England cable link.

1908

Queensland's first national park is established on the western slope of Tamborine Mountain. Today, the national park stretches onto the Tamborine plateau and into surrounding foothills.

The result was a series of violent strikes. The most famous of these erupted in 1891 after angry shearers proclaimed their socialist credo under a great gum tree, known as the 'Tree of Knowledge', at Barcaldine in central Queensland. As the strike spread, troopers, right-wing vigilantes and union militants clashed in bitter class warfare. The great radical poet Henry Lawson expected revolution: *'We'll make the tyrants feel the sting/O' those that they would throttle;/They needn't say the fault is ours/If blood should stain the wattle!'*

The striking shearers were defeated and their leaders jailed by a government determined to suppress the unrest. Despite this loss, trade unions remained a powerful force in Australia and the Barcaldine strike contributed to the formation of a potent new force in Australian politics: the Australian Labor Party.

Nationalism

Whatever their politics, many Queenslanders still embody the gritty, independent outlook that was so potent in colonial thinking. At the end of the 19th century, Australian nationalist writers and artists idealised the people of 'the bush' and their code of 'mateship'. The most popular forum for this 'bush nationalism' was the *Bulletin* magazine, whose pages were filled with humour and sentiment about daily life, written by a swag of writers, most notably Henry Lawson and AB 'Banjo' Paterson.

While these writers were creating national legends, the politicians of Australia were forging a national constitution.

Robert Hughes' bestseller *The Fatal Shore* (1987) is a highly readable if sometimes harrowing portrait of Australian history, told through the experience of convicts, free settlers and the Indigenous peoples they displaced.

Federation & WWI

On 1 January 1901, Australia became a federation. When the bewhiskered members of the new national parliament met in Melbourne, their first aim was to protect the identity and values of a European Australia from an influx of Asians and Pacific Islanders. Their solution was the infamous White Australia policy. Its opposition to nonwhite immigrants would remain a core Australian value for the next 70 years.

For European settlers, this was to be a model society, nestled in the skirts of the British Empire. Just one year later, in 1902, white women won the right to vote in federal elections. In a series of radical innovations, the government introduced a broad social-welfare scheme and protected Australian wage levels with import tariffs. This mixture of capitalist dynamism and socialist compassion became known as the 'Australian Settlement'.

When war broke out in Europe in 1914, thousands of Australian men rallied to the Empire's call. They had their first taste of death on 25 April 1915, when the Anzacs (the Australian and New Zealand Army Corps) joined an Allied assault on the Gallipoli Peninsula in Turkey. Eight

1915

In line with Australia's close ties to Britain, Australian and New Zealand troops (the Anzacs) join the Allied invasion of Turkey at Gallipoli.

1923

Vegemite, a savoury, yeasty breakfast spread, is invented. Given it is a byproduct of brewing that had gone to waste, it is a modern marketing triumph.

1928

Reverend John Flynn starts the Royal Flying Doctor Service in Cloncurry – an invaluable service that now has networks around the country.

1929

The Great Depression: thousands go hungry and one in three households experiences unemployment. Irene Longman becomes the first woman elected to Queensland's parliament.

months later, the British commanders acknowledged that the tactic had failed. By then, 8141 young Australians were dead. Soon, Australians were fighting in the killing fields of Europe. When the war ended, 60,000 Australian men had died. Ever since, on 25 April, Australians have gathered at the country's many war memorials for the sad and solemn services of Anzac Day.

Turbulent '20s

Australia careered wildly into the 1920s, continuing to invest in immigration and growth. In Queensland, breathtakingly rich copper, lead, silver and zinc deposits were discovered at Mt Isa, setting in motion a prosperous new chapter in the history of Queensland mining.

ONCE A JOLLY SWAGMAN

Written in 1895 by AB 'Banjo' Paterson (1864–1941), *Waltzing Matilda* is widely regarded as Australia's unofficial national anthem. While not many can sing the entire official anthem, *Advance Australia Fair*, without a lyric sheet, just about every Aussie knows the words to the strange ditty about a jolly swagman who jumped into a billabong and drowned himself rather than be arrested for stealing a jumbuck (sheep). But what does it mean?

For the song's origins to be understood, it has to be seen in the political context of its time. The 1890s was a period of political change in Queensland. Along with nationalistic calls for Federation, economic crisis, mass unemployment and severe droughts dominated the decade. An ongoing battle between pastoralists and shearers led to a series of strikes that divided the state and led to the formation of the Australian Labor Party to represent workers' interests.

In 1895 Paterson visited his fiancée in Winton, and together they travelled to Dagworth Station south of Kynuna, where they met Christina Macpherson. During their stay they went on a picnic to the Combo Waterhole, a series of billabongs on the Diamantina River, where Paterson heard stories about the violent 1894 shearers' strike on Dagworth Station. During the strike rebel shearers burnt seven woolsheds to the ground, leading the police to declare martial law and place a reward of £1000 on the head of their leader, Samuel Hoffmeister. Rather than be captured, Hoffmeister killed himself near the Combo Waterhole.

Paterson later wrote the words to *Waltzing Matilda* to accompany a tune played by Christina Macpherson on a zither. While there is no direct proof he was writing allegorically about Hoffmeister and the shearers' strikes, a number of prominent historians have supported the theory and claimed the song was a political statement. Others maintain it is just an innocent but catchy tune about a hungry vagrant, but the song's undeniable anti-authoritarianism and the fact that it was adopted as an anthem by the rebel shearers weigh heavily in favour of the historians' argument.

1937

Thousands of cane toads are released into the wild in an effort to control pests damaging Queensland's sugar cane fields. The action proves disastrous to Australian biodiversity.

1941

The Japanese bomb Townsville – a strategic centre for defence, with a major base for US and Australian military forces.

1962

Indigenous Australians gain the right to vote in federal elections – but they have to wait until 1967 to receive full citizenship.

1965

Merle Thornton and Rosalie Bogner chain themselves to a Brisbane bar to protest public bars being open to men only. Their action marks the beginnings of the feminist movement in Australia.

This was also the decade in which intrepid aviators became international celebrities. For Queensland, a state that felt its isolation profoundly, the aeroplane was a revolutionary invention. The famous airline Qantas (an acronym for Queensland and Northern Territory Aerial Services) was founded at Longreach, in the centre of the state, in 1920. Eight years later, veteran Queensland aviator Bert Hinkler flew solo from England to Darwin in just 16 days.

It was not just aeroplanes that linked Australia to the rest of the world. Economics, too, was a global force. In 1929 the Wall St crash and high foreign debt caused the Australian economy to collapse into the abyss of the Great Depression. Once again, unemployment brought shame and misery to one in three households, but for those who were wealthy or employed, the Depression made less of a dent in day-to-day life. In the midst of this hardship, sport diverted a nation in love with games and gambling.

Delving into History

Newstead House (p61), Brisbane

Queensland Maritime Museum (p57), Brisbane

Cobb & Co Museum (p110), Toowoomba

Jondaryan Woolshed Complex (p114), Darling Downs

Queensland Museum (p57), Brisbane

WWII & Growth

As the economy began to recover, the whirl of daily life was hardly dampened when Australian servicemen and -women sailed off to Europe to fight in a new war in 1939. Though Japan was menacing, Australians took it for granted that the British navy would keep them safe. In December 1941, Japan bombed the US fleet at Pearl Harbor. Weeks later, the 'impregnable' British naval base in Singapore crumbled, and soon thousands of Australians and other Allied troops were enduring the savagery of Japan's prisoner-of-war camps.

As the Japanese swept through Southeast Asia and into Papua New Guinea, the British announced that they could not spare any resources to defend Australia. But the legendary US general Douglas MacArthur saw that Australia was the perfect base for US operations in the Pacific and established his headquarters in Brisbane. As the fighting intensified, thousands of US troops were garrisoned in bases the length of Queensland: Australians and Americans got to know each other as never before. In a series of savage battles on sea and land, Australian and US forces gradually turned back the Japanese advance. The days of the Australian–British alliance were numbered.

As the war ended, a new slogan rang through the land: 'Populate or Perish!' The Australian government embarked on an ambitious scheme to attract thousands of immigrants. With government assistance, people flocked from Britain and from non-English-speaking countries. They included Greeks, Italians, Slavs, Serbs, Croatians, Dutch and Poles, followed by Turks, Lebanese and others.

This was the era when Australian families basked in the prosperity of a 'long boom' created by skilful government management of the

1968

Setting the political scene in Queensland for the next 19 years, Joh Bjelke-Petersen becomes premier. His political agenda was widely described as development at any price.

1970s

Inflation, soaring interest rates and rising unemployment bring the golden postwar days to an end. As house prices skyrocket, home ownership slips out of reach for many.

1974

The audacious Beerburrum mail robbery is pulled off in southeast Queensland – the most lucrative mail robbery in Australian history at the time.

1975

The Great Barrier Reef Marine Park is proclaimed, protecting 2000km of reef – the most extensive reef system in the world.

economy. Manufacturing companies such as General Motors and Ford operated with generous tariff support. The social-welfare system became more extensive and now included generous unemployment benefits. The government owned many key services, including Qantas, which it bought in 1947. This, essentially, was the high point of the 'Australian Settlement' – a partnership of government and private enterprise designed to share prosperity as widely as possible.

At the same time, there was growing world demand for the type of primary products produced in Queensland: metals, coal, wool, meat and wheat. By the 1960s mining dominated the state's economy and coal was the major export. That same decade, the world's largest bauxite mine roared into life at Weipa on the Cape York Peninsula.

This era of postwar growth and prosperity was dominated by Robert Menzies, the founder of the modern Liberal Party of Australia, and Australia's longest-serving prime minister. Menzies had an avuncular charm, but he was also a vigilant opponent of communism. As the Cold War intensified, Australia and New Zealand entered a formal military alliance with the USA – the 1951 Anzus security pact. It followed that when the USA became involved in a civil war in Vietnam more than a decade later, Menzies committed Australian forces to the conflict. In 1966 Menzies retired, leaving his successors a bitter legacy: an antiwar movement that divided Australia.

A Question of Tolerance

In the 1960s, increasing numbers of Australians saw that Indigenous Australians had endured a great wrong that needed to be put right. From 1976 until 1992 Aboriginal people won major victories in their struggle for land rights. As Australia's imports from China and Japan increased, the White Australia policy became an embarrassment. It was officially abolished in the early 1970s, and soon thereafter Australia was a little astonished to find itself leading the campaign against the racist apartheid policies of white South Africa.

By the 1970s more than one million migrants had arrived from non-English-speaking countries, filling Australia with new languages, cultures, food and ideas. At the same time, China and Japan far outstripped Europe as Australia's major trading partners. As Asian immigration increased, Vietnamese communities became prominent in Sydney and Melbourne. In both those cities a new spirit of tolerance known as multiculturalism became a particular source of pride.

The impact of postwar immigration was never as great in Queensland, and the values of multiculturalism made few inroads into the state's robustly old-time sense of what it means to be Australian. This Aussie insularity was well understood by the rough-hewn and irascible Joh Bjelke-

Avian Cirrus, Bert Hinkler's tiny plane that made the first England-to-Australia solo flight, is on display at the Queensland Museum in Brisbane.

1980

Queensland wins the first of the annual all-star 'State of Origin' rugby league series against southern rivals New South Wales. As of 2013, the ledger stands at 20 wins to Queensland, 12 to NSW, with two drawn series.

1981

The Great Barrier Reef becomes a Unesco World Heritage Site, a move furiously opposed by Queensland Premier Joh Bjelke-Petersen, who intended to do exploratory mining for oil on the reef.

1982

Brisbane hosts the Commonwealth Games. Australia tops the medal tally, winning 107 medals overall. Matilda, a 13m-high winking kangaroo, was the mascot for the Games.

1990s

Queensland experiences rapid population growth – mostly from domestic migration – even while a full-blown recession is underway, with high unemployment and huge bank and corporate collapses.

Petersen, premier of Queensland for 19 years from 1968. New Zealand-born Johannes Bjelke-Petersen was the longest-serving (1968–1987) and longest-lived (1911–2005) premier of Queensland. He was described as a paradox of piety, free enterprise and political cunning or, more succinctly, as 'a Bible-bashing bastard' by Prime Minister Gough Whitlam in 1975.

Kept in office by malapportionment (which gave more voting power to his rural base – he never won more than 39% of the popular vote), he established a policy of development on the state. Under his tenure, forests were felled to make way for dams, coal mines, power stations and other burgeoning infrastructure projects.

Bjelke-Petersen's administration strongly encouraged the development of the Gold Coast. There were few environmental restrictions as hotels and high-rise apartment blocks transformed quiet seaside towns into burgeoning holiday resorts. Among many projects under his term was the building of a highway through the Daintree rainforest and the demolition of historic or heritage buildings to make way for new developments (Brisbane's Bellevue Hotel, dating from the 1880s, was demolished – in the middle of the night – despite public attempts to save it). His plans to drill for oil in the Great Barrier Reef came to nothing when the reef was declared a World Heritage Site in 1981. Meanwhile, Queensland spent less on social infrastructure than any other state in Australia.

TERRA NULLIUS TURNED ON ITS HEAD

In May 1982 Eddie Mabo led a group of Torres Strait Islanders in a court action to have traditional title to their land on Mer (Murray Island) recognised. Their argument challenged the legal principle of *terra nullius* (literally 'land belonging to no one') and demonstrated their unbroken relationship with the land over a period of thousands of years. In June 1992 the High Court of Australia found in favour of Eddie Mabo and the islanders, rejecting the principle of *terra nullius* – this became known as the Mabo decision. The result has had far-reaching implications in Queensland and the rest of Australia, including the introduction of the Native Title Act in 1993.

Eddie Mabo accumulated more than 20 years' experience as an Indigenous leader and human-rights activist. He had 10 children, was often unemployed, established a Black Community School – the first institution of its kind in Australia – and was involved in Indigenous health and housing. In the late 1960s he worked as a gardener at James Cook University, returning there in 1981 for a conference on land rights, where he delivered a historic speech that culminated in the landmark court case.

Eddie Mabo died of cancer six months before the decision was announced. After a customary period of mourning he was given a king's burial ceremony on Mer, reflecting his status among his people – such a ritual had not been performed on the island for some 80 years.

1992

After 10 years in the courts, the landmark Mabo decision is delivered by the High Court. Effectively, this gives recognition to Indigenous land rights across the country.

1997

Warning of being 'swamped by Asians', Queenslander Pauline Hanson founds the anti-immigration One Nation party. Popularity wanes following a 2003 fraud conviction.

2006

The legendary 'Crocodile Hunter' Steve Irwin is killed by a stingray while shooting the wildlife documentary *Ocean's Deadliest*. His conservation work continues via the Steve Irwin Foundation.

2007

Peter Beattie, the longest-serving Labor premier in Queensland history, retires. His deputy, Anna Bligh, becomes the state's first female premier. She is ousted by conservative Campbell Newman in 2012.

In the 1970s there were widespread reports of police brutality against student demonstrations at the University of Queensland, a well-known haven for anti–Bjelke-Petersen sentiment. In 1977 street marches were banned.

Things took a turn in the late 1980s, when a series of investigations revealed that Bjelke-Petersen presided over a compromised system. His police commissioner was jailed for graft (bribery), and in 1991 Bjelke-Petersen faced his own criminal trial (for perjury; allegations of corruption were also incorporated into the trial). Although the jury was deadlocked and didn't return a verdict, the tides had turned against him, and most Queenslanders were eager to put the Bjelke-Petersen days behind them.

For more on one of Queensland's most controversial politicians, read Hugh Lunn's *Joh: The Life and Political Adventures of Johannes Bjelke-Petersen* (1978).

Recent Challenges

Since the 1970s, Australia has been dismantling the protectionist scaffolding that allowed its economy to develop. Wages and working conditions, which used to be fixed by an independent authority, are now much more uncertain. Two centuries of development have also placed great strains on the environment – on water supplies, forests, soil, air quality and the oceans. Australia is linked more closely than ever to the USA (exemplified by its involvement in the 21st century's Afghanistan and Iraq wars). Some say this alliance protects Australia's independence; others insist that it reduces Australia to a fawning 'client state'.

In Queensland, old fears and prejudices continue to struggle with tolerance and an acceptance of Asia, and Indigenous issues seem as intractable as ever. Indigenous leaders acknowledge that poverty, violence and welfare dependency continue to blight the lives of too many Indigenous communities. In the Cape York Peninsula, Aboriginal leaders, cattle ranchers, the government and mining companies displayed a new willingness to work with each other on land issues when they signed the Cape York Heads of Agreement in 2001. In late 2007, worrying newspaper reports (such as those appearing in *The Australian* and *New York Times*) of child sexual abuse in the Cape York Aboriginal communities highlighted the enormous social problems within Indigenous communities in Queensland and across the country.

In 2008 an official apology to the stolen generations (Aboriginal children taken from their parents and placed with white families during the 19th and 20th centuries) delivered by the Australian government was an important step on the road to addressing long-standing grievances afflicted on Australia's first peoples.

2008

On behalf of parliament, Australian prime minister Kevin Rudd (a Queenslander) delivers a moving apology to Indigenous Australians for laws and policies that 'inflicted profound grief, suffering and loss'.

2011

Powerful floods inundate vast areas of Queensland (including Brisbane), killing 35 people and causing billions of dollars in damages. Cyclone Yasi follows weeks later, devastating parts of north Queensland.

2011

The Gold Coast wins its bid to host the 2018 Commonwealth Games, beating the Sri Lankan city of Hambantota for the privilege 43 votes to 27.

2013

The Brisbane River again swells with floodwaters. Locals watch nervously as the waters rise, flooding riverside restaurants and several suburbs – but the damage is not as extreme as in 2011.

Climate Change & the Great Barrier Reef

By Dr Terry Done & Paul Marshall

The Great Barrier Reef (GBR) is one of the world's most diverse coral-reef ecosystems. It is also the world's largest, an archipelagic edifice so vast that it can be viewed from space. But, like coral reefs all around the world, the GBR is facing some big environmental challenges.

The Reef

The reef's ecosystem includes the sea-floor habitats between the reefs, hundreds of continental islands and coral cays, and coastal beaches, headlands and estuaries. The 2900 reefs (ranging from less than 1km to 26km in length) that make up the GBR system support truly astounding biological diversity, with over 1500 species of fish, over 400 species of reef-building coral, and hundreds of species of mollusc (clams, snails, octopuses), echinoderm (sea stars, bêches-de-mer, sea urchins), sponge, worm, crustacean and seaweed. The GBR is also home to marine mammals (dolphins, whales, dugongs), dozens of species of bird, and six of the planet's seven species of sea turtle. The GBR's 900 or so islands range from ephemeral, unvegetated or sparsely vegetated sand cays to densely forested cays and continental islands.

At the Crossroads

These are tough times in which to be a coral reef. In the last three decades the GBR has endured more severe cyclones than in the whole of the last century (and more can be expected in the changed climate of the 21st century); recurrent outbreaks of coral-devouring crown-of-thorns starfish; two major coral-bleaching events caused by unusually hot water temperatures; and record-breaking floods that washed huge volumes of fresh water, sediments, fertilisers and other farm chemicals into the sea, triggering blooms of light-blocking plankton and disrupting the ecological relationships that keep coral reefs vibrant and resilient.

With all this going on, it's no surprise that a bit of web surfing could give the impression that the GBR is suffering more than other reefs around the world. But the plethora of information about risks to the reef simply reflects the amount of research, government investment and national commitment to tackling the challenge rather than pretending that everything is OK. It is an unfortunate reality that damaged reefs are easier to find now than they were 30 years ago. But the GBR is still one of the best places in the world to see coral reefs, especially if you have one of the hundreds of accredited tourism operators show you around. A recent study by the volunteer reef-monitoring group Reef Check Australia found that the amount of coral at 70% of dive sites monitored between 2001 and 2011 either remained the same or increased. Like every reef around the world, the GBR is in trouble – but in this case scientists, reef managers, coastal residents and even visitors are joining forces to help the reef through the challenges of the century ahead.

Eroding the Foundations

Overshadowing the future of coral reefs is climate change. Global warming is a serious problem for these iconic ecosystems, even though they have evolved in warm water, and thrive in clear, shallow seas along the equator and as far north and south as the Tropics of Cancer and Capricorn.

The main building blocks of coral reefs are 'stony' or 'hard' corals, and about 400 of the world's 700 or so species occur on the GBR. The secret of their success as reef builders – and their Achilles heel in a warming world – is symbiosis between the coral and tiny single-celled plants called zooxanthellae that live within their tissues. Thanks to bright sunlight and warm waters, the zooxanthellae are photosynthetic powerhouses that produce sugars and other carbohydrates needed by the coral (a colony of polyps) to grow its tissues, produce sperm and eggs, and build the colony's communal limestone skeletons. These skeletons – occupied by thousands of polyps and capable of growing several metres high and across in many different shapes – are an evolutionary bonanza in that they provide a rigid framework to orient the polyps to best utilise the sunlight and to use their stinging tentacles to catch passing pinhead-sized crustaceans that corals need nutritionally. Over thousands of years, the corals produce the reef framework, lagoon sands, coral beaches and coral islands that are the foundation for the entire coral-reef ecosystem. But now, as temperatures approach levels not seen for thousands of years, these foundations are at risk.

Changing Environments & Coral Bleaching

The idyllic symbiosis between coral and zooxanthellae evolved to perfectly match the environmental conditions of the past. But corals don't like change, and they are currently being hit with rates of change unparalleled for at least 400,000 years.

Bright sunlight and warm waters are required to support coral reefs, but it's a fine line between warm enough and too warm. Around the turn of the last century (mainly 1998 and 2002 for the GBR, as late as 2010 elsewhere), spikes in water temperatures caused the densely packed zooxanthellae to go into metabolic overdrive, producing free radicals and other chemicals that are toxic to the coral host. The corals' response was to expel their zooxanthellae, to rid themselves of the

THE GREAT BARRIER REEF MARINE PARK

Established in 1975, the 360,000-sq-km Great Barrier Reef Marine Park (about the same size as Italy) is one of the best-protected large marine systems on the planet. About 30% of the park is closed and the remainder is open to commercial and recreational fishing. There are a handful of coastal cities along the reef's southern half (notably Cairns, Townsville, Mackay and Gladstone), some with ports to service cattle and sugar export, and mineral export and import. Shipping lanes traverse its length and breadth, and ore carriers, cargo ships and cruise liners must use local marine pilots to reduce the risk of groundings and collisions.

Australia is internationally recognized for its leading management and protection of the Great Barrier Reef: the marine park is inscribed on the World Heritage List and has an envied program of management led by the Great Barrier Reef Marine Park Authority. But there is an aura of pessimism across the reef-science world, and the elephant in the room is climate change. For comprehensive information and educational tools at all levels, see www.gbrmpa.gov.au and www.coralwatch.org.

REEF GEOLOGY

Unlike mainland Australia, today's Great Barrier Reef (GBR) is relatively young, geologically speaking. Its foundations formed around 500,000 years ago, northern Australia was by then surrounded by tropical waters, as Australia drifted gradually northward from the massive South Pole land mass that was Gondwana. The GBR grew and receded several times in response to changing sea levels. Coastal plains that are now the sea floor were occupied by Indigenous Australians only 20,000 years ago, when the ice-age sea level was 130m lower than it is today. As the icecaps contracted, seas flooded continental shelves and stabilised near their current levels about 6000 to 8000 years ago. Corals settled atop high parts of the Queensland shelf, initiating the unique combination of biological and geological processes that have built the reef ecosystem we see today.

damaging toxins. Water temperatures must return to normal before the small numbers of remaining zooxanthellae start to reproduce and thus reinstate the corals' live-in food factory. But if the heat wave persists for more than a few weeks, the highly stressed corals succumb to disease and die, their skeletons soon becoming carpeted with fine, shaggy algal turfs. A 2013 study found that about 10% of GBR coral deaths over the last three decades followed these episodes, known as coral bleaching. And an important reality is that climate change isn't occurring in isolation: this study also highlighted that storm waves and outbreaks of the coral-eating crown-of-thorns starfish are big killers of corals (each around 40%). The effects are cumulative, and with projections of an increase in the severity of cyclones and the frequency of coral-bleaching events, we are likely to see more incidents of broad-acre coral death under a changing climate.

It takes one to two decades for a healthy coral reef to bounce back after being wiped out. So far, damaged GBR sites have shown remarkable resilience to damaging events, but the future might not be so rosy, as more frequent events driven by climate change repeatedly decimate reefs before they can fully recover. In other parts of the world, some reefs have suffered the added insults of decades of pollution and overfishing. By those means, former coral areas have become persistent landscapes of rubble and seaweed.

Worry Globally, Act Locally

Floating in the warming waters of the GBR, feeling the immensity of the reef and the problem that is climate change, it's easy to feel that action is futile. But science is showing that local efforts can make a difference. Reducing the amount of nutrients (from fertilisers) that enter GBR waters may increase the tolerance of corals to warmer seas, decrease crown-of-thorns outbreaks and help corals maintain dominance over seaweeds. State and federal governments are therefore working with farmers to improve practices and reduce the losses of chemicals and valuable soil into the reef, and their efforts have already begun to deliver encouraging results.

Science also suggests that those fishing practices that maintain abundant herbivorous fish on the reefs may also be vital in keeping corals in the ascendancy. Fishing is carefully regulated, making the GBR a rare example of a coral-reef system that maintains a healthy coral-seaweed balance while still delivering sustainable seafood. There is no commercial use of fish traps or spears, and responsible fishing practices adopted by most fishers in the GBR also mean that sharks are still a common sight (although more work needs to be done to secure the future of these important predators). Bottom trawling for prawns (shrimp) has been dramatically scaled back over recent decades, with associated improvements in the health of the soft-seabed communities between reef outcrops. Other issues on the radar for the GBR include ship groundings, dredging and port expansion.

The GBR tourism industry is a world leader in sustainable, eco-friendly and climate-friendly practices. Visiting the reef with an eco-accredited tourism business is not only a great way to experience the beauty and wonder of coral reefs; it's also one of the best things you can do to help the GBR, a small part of your fare directly supporting reef research and management.

Beyond the Corals...

Coral reefs are more than just corals, and our worries about a warming climate extend to the multitude of critters that call these ecosystems home. Green and loggerhead turtles bury their eggs at the back of coral-island beaches, the warm sand incubating the developing embryos. The sex of the hatchlings is determined by the temperature the eggs experience: cooler temperatures cause eggs to develop into male hatchlings; warmer eggs become females. Turtle researchers are worried that a warmer world could create an imbalance in the sex ratio, putting extra strain on already depleted turtle populations. For turtles the risks don't stop there. Rising sea levels (predictions are as much as 1.1m higher by the end of this century) put many nesting areas at greater risk of deadly flooding. Turtles will need to find higher ground for nesting, but in many coastal areas natural barriers or urban development limit their options.

For coral-reef fish, sea-level change might not be a big issue, but changes in ocean temperature have the potential to affect the timing and success of important processes such as reproduction. There is also growing evidence that fish might be prone to the effects of ocean acidification, which is the direct result of increased absorption of CO_2 by the world's seas. The upside to this process is that it has kept the atmosphere from warming even faster. But the pH of seawater is important to a wide range of chemical and biological processes, including the ability of fish to find their home reef and to avoid predators.

Climate change is also altering ocean currents, making life difficult for animals that rely on the timing and location of water movements for their survival. Scientists have already observed mass deaths of seabird chicks on remote islands as a result of their parents having to travel too far to find the schools of fish they need to feed their flightless young. Plankton, too, are vulnerable to changing chemistry and currents, with potential flow-on effects through entire food chains. Corals don't escape the effects of ocean acidification, either. More-acidic water makes it more

GET INVOLVED

You can help the reef in practical ways during your visit. You can report sightings of important reef creatures or send in information about any problems you encounter directly to the Great Barrier Reef Marine Park Authority by contributing to the Eye on the Reef Program (go to www.gbrmpa.gov.au or get the free Eye on the Reef smartphone app). If you're around for long enough (or time your visit right), you could undertake some training and become a Reef Check volunteer (see www.reefcheckaustralia.org). If turtles are your passion, see www.seaturtlefoundation.org for opportunities to volunteer with them. If you're a resident, look out for www.seagrasswatch.org, and if you like fishing, combine your fishing with research at www.info-fish.net.

difficult for corals to build their skeletons, leading to slower growth or more fragile structures.

The Future

In the best traditions of good science, its practitioners are a sceptical lot, but you won't find a credible coral-reef expert who will say that climate change isn't a serious issue. Where scientists may differ is about the rate at which and the extent to which reefs and their mind-boggling biodiversity may adjust or adapt.

You might have heard it said that 'the climate has changed before and we still have corals'. While this has a grain of truth, the reality is that previous episodes of rapid climate change caused mass extinctions that took millions of years to get over. Playing on the Australian tendency to believe that 'she'll be right, mate', those who deny that climate change is happening have tried to portray the science as uncertain, biased and even wrong. But the solid body of science indicates that climate change is real, it is already under way, and coral reefs are right in the firing line. Certainly we should energetically debate the best ways of tackling this problem, but there can be no room for equivocation: we have to act with urgency and decisiveness at local, national and global levels if we are to give coral reefs a fighting chance of providing future generations with the wonderful experiences we can still enjoy.

If humans continue to pollute the atmosphere with greenhouse gases at present rates, we will likely overtax any realistic capacity of coral-reef ecosystems to cope. All around the world, coral reefs are proving themselves to be the 'canary in the coalmine' of climate change. The worldwide reduction in reef assets that occurred when heat waves swept equatorial regions in 1998 was unprecedented in scale, providing a wake-up call to reef scientists, reef managers and the community at large about what the future holds. Like polar zones, coral reefs are sentinel systems that will continue to show us the impacts of climate change on the natural world (and the millions of humans who depend on these ecosystems). But the ending to the climate-change story is still being written. Concerted action can yet avoid the worst-case scenario for reefs. And when visitors and residents choose to avoid and reduce sources of pressure on corals and other reef creatures, they buy coral reefs important time to adapt – and, hopefully, to cope – until society takes the necessary action to control its impacts on the climate.

The Arts in Queensland

Melbourne has long hailed itself as Australia's arts capital, a claim that Sydney has never seemed too fussed about contesting (there's too much going on down at the beach...). But artists from Queensland – and Brisbane in particular – can certainly claim a substantial contribution to Australia's artistic heritage.

The Arts: Brisbane & Beyond

Following the fall of the National Party in the 1990s, the new Labor government did much to stimulate and encourage artistic and cultural development. Brisbane in particular has experienced a cultural renaissance with the building of world-class art museums and exhibition spaces. Home to one of Australia's biggest arts festivals – the Brisbane Festival in September – it's also a town where you can get your artistic rocks off every night of the week: live music, theatre, opera, art-house and international cinema and poetry readings are all accessible and affordable.

For a dose of 100% Australian music talent, tune in to the national radio station Triple J (www.abc.net.au/triplej) for 'Home and Hosed', from 9pm Monday to Thursday.

Outside of the capital, you'll find simmering arts scenes in Cairns and Townsville, both of which have a mix of galleries and cultural centres that showcase the best of north Queensland and beyond. Cairns also has a lively arts and culture festival to rival Brisbane's, though on a smaller scale – the Cairns Festival in August.

The Aboriginal art scene in Queensland is quite vibrant, though you have to know where to look. The state has some captivating rock-art sites, where you can connect to ancient art traditions dating back tens of thousands of years. You can also encounter fine works by living Aboriginal artists at galleries scattered around the state, though Brisbane is still the best place to begin the cultural journey.

Music

Indigenous music has been one of the Australian music industry's great success stories of recent years, and Queensland has produced some outstanding Indigenous musicians. Christine Anu is a Torres Strait Islander who was born in Cairns. Her debut album, *Stylin' Up* (1995), blends Creole-style rap, Islander chants and traditional languages with English, and was followed by the interesting *Come My Way* (2000) and *45 Degrees* (2003) – highly recommended listening. Ever evolving, she even released a colourful children's album *Chrissy's Island Family* (2007).

Brisbane's pub rock scene has produced a couple of Australia's all time greatest bands. The Saints, considered by many to be one of the seminal punk bands (and oft quoted as a founding inspiration for the Seattle grunge movement of the 1990s), began performing in Brisbane in the mid-1970s before moving on to bigger things in Sydney and, later, London. Their 1976 single, *I'm Stranded,* was a high-water mark for the band.

More recently, the iconic Brisbane band Powderfinger – a five-piece melodic rock outfit – played a dominant role in the Australian music industry from the 1990s until their breakup in 2010. Sing-along anthems and angelic-but-grunty guitar riffs define their classic albums such as the breakthrough *Double Allergic* (1996); *Odyssey Number Five* (2000); *Vulture Street* (2003); their best-of album, *Fingerprints* (2004); and their last hurrah, *Golden Rule* (2009). They played their final concert in Brisbane in late 2010 before a crowd of 10,000. Critics were left scratching their heads as to why the band failed to harness a broader international audience. Lead singer Bernard Fanning has also released two solo albums, *Tea and Sympathy* (2005) and *Departures* (2013).

The Australian Record Industry Association (ARIA) award-winning debut album *Polyserena* (2002) by Queensland band George is deliciously haunting. Katie Noonan (George's acclaimed lead singer) went on to release her first solo album *Skin* in 2007. She's worked on myriad collaborative recordings and performances since then, including projects with jazzy trio Elixir.

Best Art Galleries

Gallery of Modern Art (p57), Brisbane

Stanthorpe Regional Art Gallery (p105)

Institute of Modern Art (p277), Brisbane

Perc Tucker Regional Gallery (p219), Townsville

Another star hailing from the Sunshine State is Pete Murray. He looks more like a rugby player than a sensitive lyricist, but his beachy acoustic licks and chocolate-smooth voice have earned him national and international acclaim. His debut, *Feeler* (2003), and more recent offerings *See the Sun* (2005), *Summer at Eureka* (2008) and *Blue Sky Blue* (2013) are all summer-sweet listens.

Another Queensland success story is The Veronicas, made up of twins of Sicilian descent whose pop style is a hit with teenagers. More interesting is Kate Miller-Heidke, a classically trained singer, who channels the likes of Björk, Kate Bush and Cyndi Lauper in her works. Chase down a copy of *Little Eve* (2007), *Curiouser* (2008) or *Night Flight* (2012). *The Last Day on Earth,* from *Curiouser,* was a top-10 single.

Flying the flag for Far North Queensland, the McMenamins are a talented brother-and-sister folk duo who are receiving increasing airplay and have performed around the country. Their self-titled debut (released in 2003), as well as *In this Light* (2006), *Long Time Gone* (2010) and *Sand and Stone* (2013) are all worth a spin.

Painting & Photography

Queensland's art scene was slow to emerge, with paintings by early settlers first appearing in the second half of the 19th century. In the 20th century a few seminal figures helped put Queensland on the map.

Ian Fairweather (1891–1974) is described by some critics and fellow artists as Australia's greatest painter. He used muted colours and shied away from typical Australian themes (such as gum trees, and pastoral and rugged landscapes), instead incorporating Asian elements (gouaches of villages and market scenes), influenced by his years living in China from 1930 to 1933. An enigmatic figure, he spent the last years of his life as a recluse on Bribie Island.

ROCK 'N' ROLL BRISBANE

It's a long way from Hollywood Blvd, but Fortitude Valley has its very own (comparatively modest) **Valley Walk of Fame** honouring the city's most successful musicians. At the top end of Brunswick St Mall are 10 plaques celebrating artists that have called Brisbane home (at least for their formative years): the pre–Saturday Night Fever **Bee Gees**; punk legends **The Saints**; New Zealand–born, but Queensland-raised **Keith Urban**; and 15-time ARIA award–winning rockers **Powderfinger**, just to name a few. Nineties electro-rockers **Regurgitator** and indie band **Custard** also get a mention. Brisbane rocks!

DAVID MALOUF

Lebanese–Australian author and poet David Malouf (b 1934 in Brisbane) is one of Queensland's most internationally recognised writers, having been nominated for the Booker Prize in 1993 and winning the Neustadt International Prize for Literature in 2000. Among other titles, he is well known for his evocative tales of an Australian boyhood in Brisbane – *Johnno* (1975); as well as his memoir *12 Edmondstone Street* (1985); and for *The Great World* (1990), his Australian epic that spans two world wars. Set on the Gold Coast, his 1982 novel *Fly Away Peter* tells the poignant story of a returned soldier struggling to come to terms with ordinary life and the unjust nature of social hierarchy. His collection of short stories *Every Move You Make* (2006) dissects Australian life across the continent, including Far North Queensland. His most recent novel is *Ransom* (2009), an ambitious recount of books 16 to 24 of Homer's epic *Iliad*.

The long-lived Lloyd Rees (1895–1988) has an impressive body of work and is one of Queensland's best-known artists of the 20th century. A master of light and texture, he was obsessed with capturing a spiritual element in the landscapes he painted. He was born in Brisbane and painted right up until his death in Hobart in 1988.

One of Queensland's most successful living artists is William Robinson (b 1936). He has worked in a variety of styles and completed some of his most successful work after moving from Brisbane to a large property in the Gold Coast hinterland. His paintings capture the magical quality of the rainforest and the awe-inspiring power of the mountains near Springbrook. His work is on display in Brisbane's Old Government House.

Brisbane-based Richard Bell (b 1953) is an Aboriginal artist who creates provocative works that touch on politics, religion and Aboriginal relations (words over one controversial but prize-winning piece read, 'Aboriginal art – it's a white thing'). He also explores black–white relations in large Lichtenstein-like cartoon tableaus.

Tracey Moffatt (b 1960), who also hails from Brisbane, blends cinema, photography and visual arts in carefully constructed 'film stills' with underlying themes of poverty and violence. Her work hangs in galleries all over the world and she has been described as one of Australia's '50 most collectable artists'.

For a first hand look at some of the best contemporary painting and photography being produced in Queensland, swing by Brisbane's deliciously subversive Institute of Modern Art (p86) in Fortitude Valley, and the Queensland Centre for Photography (p57) near South Bank.

Tina Cooper, one of Australia's leading glass-blowing artists, creates exquisite and richly textured works. Her gallery, Tina Cooper Glass (p154) in Eumundi, on the Sunshine Coast, showcases her sculptures and colourful pieces.

Aboriginal Rock Art

Rock art – engravings, stencils, drawings and paintings, often found in broad cave or cliff galleries – is a diary of human activity by Australia's indigenous peoples stretching over tens of thousands of years. Queensland has plenty of sites, especially hidden around the Far North. Try to see some while you're here – the experience of viewing rock art in the surroundings in which it was painted is far more profound than seeing it in a gallery.

Carnarvon Gorge, in Carnarvon National Park, houses rock engravings, freehand drawing and over 2000 mouth-sprayed stencils, which are of deep spiritual significance to the present-day Bidjarra people of the area.

The Kuku Yalanji sites, in Mossman Gorge, feature Dreaming legends depicted in cave paintings. The Kuku Yalanji community offers excellent guided walks to see and understand the art.

QUEENSLAND ON THE SILVER SCREEN

Although Australia's film industry was founded in Victoria and New South Wales (with no small input from South Australia), Queensland has made significant inroads in recent decades, which in turn has fostered new growth in the artistic wing of the industry.

The commercial industry here is based around the Village Roadshow Studios at Warner Bros Movie World on the Gold Coast – one of two world-class movie studios in Australia (the other being Fox Studios Australia in Sydney). Village Roadshow has produced a string of films targeting the family market including *Scooby Doo* (2002), *Peter Pan* (2003) and *The Chronicles of Narnia: The Voyage of the Dawn Treader* (2011). Other commercial films produced here include the horror thriller *Ghost Ship* (2002) and *The Great Raid* (2002), which tells the story of a WWII rescue mission of American prisoners in a Japanese prisoner-of-war camp in the Philippines. In the horror genre, *Undead* (2002), shot in southeast Queensland, is about a town that becomes infected with a zombie virus. In 2013, Village Roadshow Studios announced it would be the site for the filming of Angelina Jolie's WWII epic *Unbroken*.

Other titles filmed in the state include the following:

- *Australia* (2008) – Baz Luhrmann's epic was partly filmed in Bowen. The second-highest-grossing Australian film of all time (after *Crocodile Dundee*) relates the adventure of an English aristocrat (played by Nicole Kidman) in northern Australia against the backdrop of WWII.
- *Ocean's Deadliest* (2007) – The last documentary Steve Irwin made before his untimely death features Philippe Cousteau, grandson of oceanographer Jacques Cousteau.
- *Gettin' Square* (2003) – Directed by Jonathan Teplitzky is this exquisitely funny and dark story about two low-grade criminals trying to extricate themselves from their past.
- *Swimming Upstream* (2002) – The autobiographical story of Anthony Fingleton, a Queensland swimmer. It captures the hardship of his life with his alcoholic father (played by Geoffrey Rush) in gritty 1960s Brisbane.
- *The Thin Red Line* (1998) – Terrence Malick's critically acclaimed tale of WWII soldiers in the Pacific.
- *Praise* (1998) – Adapted from the novel by Andrew McGahan, this is a toothy, honest tale of mismatched love in down-and-out Brisbane.
- *Muriel's Wedding* (1994) – A hit comedy that strips the lino off the suburban dream as Muriel attempts to escape a monotonous life.
- *Dead Calm* (1989) – A taut, underrated thriller-on-a-yacht starring Nicole Kidman, Sam Neill and Billy Zane, filmed around the Great Barrier Reef.
- *Crocodile Dundee* (1986) – Paul Hogan's record-breaking vehicle to stardom, as well as its two sequels, were partially shot in Queensland.

The Split Rock and Guguyalangi Galleries, on the Cape York Peninsula, have some of the best-known examples of Quinkan art, a painting style in northern Australia that's named after human-like spirit figures with oddly shaped heads. There are hundreds of ancient rock-art sites displaying this style around Laura in Cape York. The most accessible is the Split Rock site; tours are led by Aboriginal guides from Laura. Check out the **Quinkan & Regional Cultural Centre site** (www.quinkancc.com.au) for information about Cape York Peninsula rock art and how to access it.

Wangaar-Wuri sites, near Cooktown, depict different aspects of local society and Aboriginal culture, including family stories, mythical figures, spiritual beliefs and practical guidance. Difficult to find on your own, they are best visited with local guides on **Guurrbi Tours** (☎07-4069 6043; www.guurrbitours.com; tours 2/4hr $95/120, self-drive $65/85; ⌚Mon-Sat), who can help explain the fascinating works.

Survival Guide

Deadly & Dangerous

If you're the pessimistic type, you might focus on the things that can bite, sting, burn or drown you in Queensland: bushfires, treacherous surf, blazing heat, jellyfish, snakes, spiders, sharks, crocodiles, ticks, mosquitoes... But chances are the worst you'll encounter are a few pesky flies and mosquitoes. So splash on some insect repellent and boldly venture forth!

OUT & ABOUT

At the Beach

Around 80 people per year drown on Australia's beaches, where pounding surf and rips (strong currents) can create serious hazards. If you happen to get caught in a rip and are being taken out to sea, swim parallel to the shore until you're out of the rip, then head for the beach – don't try to swim back against the rip, you'll only tire yourself.

Bushfires

Bushfires happen regularly in Queensland. In hot, dry and windy weather and on total-fire-ban days, be extremely careful with naked flames (including cigarette butts) and don't use camping stoves, campfires or barbecues. Bushwalkers should delay trips until things cool down. If you're out in the bush and you see smoke, take it seriously: find the nearest open space (downhill if possible). Forested ridges are dangerous places to be. Always heed the advice of authorities.

Coral Cuts

Coral can be extremely sharp: you can cut yourself by merely brushing against the stuff. Make sure to clean cuts thoroughly and douse with antiseptic to avoid infection.

Heat Sickness & Dehydration

Hot weather is the norm in Queensland and can lead to heat exhaustion or more severe heatstroke (resulting from extreme fluid depletion). When arriving from a temperate or cold climate, remember that it takes two weeks to acclimatise.

Unprepared travellers die from dehydration each year in remote areas. Always carry sufficient water for any trip (driving or hiking), and let someone know where you're going and when you expect to arrive. Carry communications equipment and if in trouble, stay with your vehicle rather than walking for help.

Sunburn & Skin Cancer

Australia has one of the highest rates of skin cancer in the world. Monitor exposure to direct sunlight closely. Ultraviolet (UV) radiation is greatest between 10am and 4pm, so avoid skin exposure during these times. Wear a wide-brimmed hat and a long-sleeved shirt with a collar. Always use SPF 30+ sunscreen, and apply it 30 minutes before exposure and repeat regularly to minimise sun damage.

THINGS THAT BITE & STING

Crocodiles

The risk of a crocodile attack in tropical Far North Queensland is real, but with some common sense it is entirely avoidable. 'Salties' are estuarine crocodiles that can grow to 7m. They inhabit coastal waters and are mostly seen in the tidal reaches of rivers, though on occasion they're spotted on beaches and in freshwater lagoons. Always heed any advice, such as crocodile warning signs, that you might come across. Don't assume it's safe to swim if there are no signs: if you're not sure, don't swim.

If you're away from popular beaches anywhere north of Mackay, avoid swimming in rivers, waterholes and in the sea near river outlets. Don't clean fish or prepare food near the water's edge, and camp at least 50m away from waterways. Crocodiles are particularly mobile and dangerous during the breeding season (October to March).

Jellyfish

Jellyfish – including the potentially deadly box jellyfish and Irukandji – occur in Australia's tropical waters. It's unwise to swim north of Agnes Water between November and May unless there's a stinger net. 'Stinger suits' (full-body Lycra swimsuits) prevent stinging, as do wetsuits. Swimming and snorkelling are usually safe around Queensland's reef islands throughout the year; however, the rare (and tiny) Irukandji has been recorded on the outer reef and islands.

Wash stings with vinegar to prevent further discharge of remaining stinging cells, followed by rapid transfer to a hospital. Don't attempt to remove the tentacles.

Marine Animals

Marine spikes and poisonous spines – such as those found on sea urchins, catfish, stingrays, scorpion fish and stonefish – can cause severe local pain. If you're stung, immediately immerse the affected area in hot water (as hot as can be tolerated) and seek medical care.

Contact with blue-ringed octopuses and Barrier Reef cone shells can be fatal, so don't pick them up. If someone is stung, apply a pressure bandage, monitor breathing carefully and conduct mouth-to-mouth resuscitation if breathing stops. Seek immediate medical care.

Mosquitoes

'Mozzies' can be a problem just about anywhere in Queensland. Malaria isn't present, but dengue fever is a danger in northern Queensland, particularly during the wet season (November to April). Most people recover in a few days, but more severe forms of the disease can occur. To minimise bites:

- Wear loose, long-sleeved clothing.
- Apply repellent with minimum 30% DEET on exposed skin.
- Use mosquito coils.
- Sleep under fast-spinning ceiling fans.

Sharks

Despite extensive media coverage, the risk of shark attack in Australia is no greater than in other countries with extensive coastlines. Check with surf life-saving groups about local risks.

Snakes

There's no denying it: Australia has plenty of venomous snakes, but few species are aggressive. Unless you are messing with or accidentally stand on one, you're unlikely to be bitten. About 80% of bites occur on the lower limbs: wear protective clothing (such as gaiters) when bushwalking.

If bitten, apply an elastic bandage (or improvise with a T-shirt). Wrap firmly around the entire limb – but not so tightly that you cut off the circulation – and immobilise with a splint or sling; then seek medical attention. Don't use a tourniquet, and don't try to suck out the poison.

Spiders

Australia has poisonous spiders, although the only species to have killed anyone recently, the Sydney funnel-web, isn't a Queenslander. Common species include the following:

- Redback – Bites cause increasing pain followed by profuse sweating. Apply ice and transfer to hospital.
- Whitetail – Blamed for causing slow-healing ulcers. If bitten, clean bite and seek medical assistance.
- Huntsman – A disturbingly large spider that's harmless, though seeing one can affect your blood pressure (and/or underpants).

Ticks

Common bush ticks can be dangerous if lodged in the skin and undetected. If walking in tick-prone areas, check your body every night (and those of children and dogs). Remove a tick by dousing with methylated spirits or kerosene and levering it out intact. See a doctor if bites become infected (tick typhus cases have been reported in Queensland).

A BIT OF PERSPECTIVE

Australia's plethora of poisonous and biting critters is impressive, but don't let it put you off. There's approximately one shark-attack and one croc-attack fatality per year here. Blue-ringed-octopus deaths are rarer – only two in the last century. Jellyfish do better – about two deaths annually – but you're still more than 100 times more likely to drown. Spiders haven't killed anyone in the last 20 years. Snake bites kill one or two people per year, as do bee stings, but you're about a thousand times more likely to perish on the nation's roads.

Directory A–Z

Accommodation

Queensland has an excellent range of sleeping options, including guesthouses and B&Bs, high-end seaside resorts, party-prone hostels, camping grounds and cabins, as well as no-fuss hotels and motels.

B&Bs

Bed and breakfast options include restored miners' cottages, converted barns, rambling old houses, upmarket country manors, beachside bungalows and simple bedrooms in family homes. Tariffs are typically in the midrange bracket, but can be much higher.

Local tourist offices can usually give you a list of local B&Bs. Online, try the following:

Bed & Breakfast and Farmstay Association of Far North Queensland (www.bnbnq.com.au)

Bed & Breakfast Site (www.babs.com.au)

OZ Bed and Breakfast (www.ozbedandbreakfast.com)

Camping & Caravanning

If you want to explore Queensland on a shoestring, camping is the way to go.

Camping in national parks can cost from nothing to $15 per person. Tent sites at private camping and caravan parks cost around $20 to $30 per couple per night (slightly more with electricity). Many of these outfits also hire out cabins with kitchenettes, running from $60 to $170 per night sleeping one to six people.

National parks and their camping areas are administered state-by-state, with bookings handled online through Queensland's **Department of National Parks, Recreation, Sport & Racing** (www.nprsr.qld.gov.au).

If you intend to do a lot of caravanning or camping, joining a major chain will save you some money:

Big 4 (www.big4.com.au)

Discovery Holiday Parks (www.discoveryholidayparks.com.au)

Top Tourist Parks (www.toptouristparks.com.au)

Farmstays

Many coastal and hinterland farms offer a bed for the night and the chance to see rural Australia at work. At some you sit back and watch other people raise a sweat, while others like to get you involved in day-to-day activities.

Regional and town tourist offices should be able to tell you what's available in their area. Also check out:

Bed & Breakfast Site (www.babs.com.au) Look under family holidays/farmstays.

Willing Workers on Organic Farms (WWOOF; www.wwoof.com.au).

Hostels

Backpackers are highly social, low-cost Queensland fixtures. There are staggering numbers of them, ranging from family-run places in converted houses to huge, custom-built resorts replete with bars, nightclubs and party propensity. Standards range from outstanding to awful, and management from friendly to scary.

Dorm beds typically cost $25 to $35, with single rooms sometimes available (around $60) and doubles costing $70 to $100.

Useful organisations with annual memberships (around $45) that yield lodging and other discounts:

BOOK YOUR STAY ONLINE

For more accommodation reviews by Lonely Planet authors, check out http://lonelyplanet.com/hotels. You'll find independent reviews, as well as recommendations on the best places to stay. Best of all, you can book online.

Base Backpackers (www.stayatbase.com)

Nomads (www.nomadsworld.com)

VIP Backpackers (www.vipbackpackers.com)

YHA (www.yha.com.au)

Hotels

Hotels along the east coast are generally of the business or luxury-chain variety (midrange to top end): comfortable, anonymous, mod-con filled rooms in multistorey blocks.

Motels

Drive-up motels offer comfortable midrange accommodation and are found all over Queensland. They rarely offer a cheaper rate for singles, so are better value for couples or groups of three. You'll mostly pay between $100 and $150 for a simple room with a kettle, fridge, TV, air-con and bathroom.

Pubs

Hotels along the east coast – ones that serve beer – are commonly known as pubs (from the term 'public house'). Generally, rooms are small and weathered, with a long amble down the hall to the bathroom. They're usually central and cheap – singles/doubles with shared facilities from $50/80, more if you want a private bathroom – but if you're a light sleeper, avoid booking a room above the bar and check whether a band is playing downstairs that night.

Rental Accommodation

If you're on the east coast for a while, then a rental property or room in a shared flat or house will be an economical option. Delve into the classified advertisement sections of the daily newspapers; Wednesday and Saturday are usually the best days. Noticeboards in universities, hostels, bookshops and cafes are also useful. Resources include the following:

City Hobo (www.cityhobo.com) Matches your personality with your ideal big-city suburb.

Couch Surfing (www.couchsurfing.com) Connects spare couches with new friends.

Flatmate Finders (www.flatmatefinders.com.au) Long-term share-accommodation listings.

Stayz (www.stayz.com.au) Holiday rentals.

SLEEPING PRICE RANGES

The following price indicators refer to the cost of a double room with bathroom in high season (summer in southern Queensland, winter in Far North Queensland) per night:

$ less than $100

$$ $100–200

$$$ more than $200

Expect to pay $20 to $50 more during school and public holidays, and during the high seasons.

Customs Regulations

For comprehensive information on customs regulations, contact the **Australian Customs & Border Protection Service** (☎02-6275 6666, 1300 363 263; www.customs.gov.au).

➡ There's a duty-free quota of 2.25L of alcohol, 50 cigarettes, and dutiable goods up to the value of $900 per person.

➡ Prohibited goods include drugs (all medicines must be declared), wooden items and food – Australia is very strict on this, so declare all food items, even leftover edibles taken from the plane.

Discount Cards

➡ The International Student Identity Card (ISIC; www.isic.org), available to full-time students worldwide, yields discounts on accommodation, transport and admission to various attractions.

➡ Travellers over 60 with some form of identification (eg a Seniors Card – www.seniorscard.com.au) are often eligible for concession prices.

Electricity

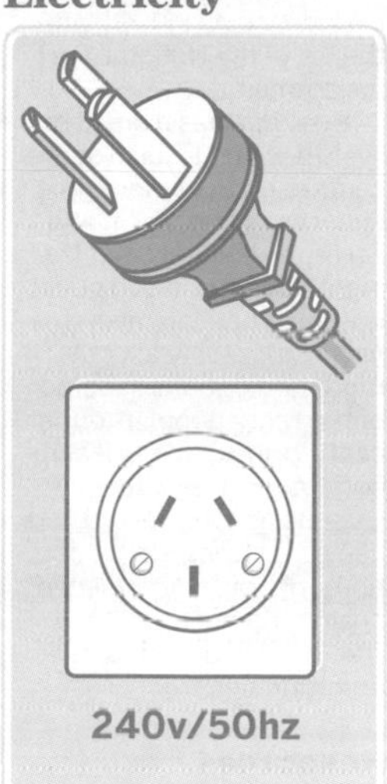

Food

Eating in Queensland, with its endless coastline and swathes of farming country, often involves seafood and steak (or a combination of the two, known as 'surf 'n' turf' or 'reef 'n' beef'). You'll find

EATING PRICE RANGES

The following price indicators refer to a standard main course:

$ less than $15

$$ $15–32

$$$ more than $32

cafes and restaurants almost everywhere, with vegetarians well catered for in the cities and larger towns.

Gay & Lesbian Travellers

Historically, Queensland has a poor reputation when it comes to acceptance of gays and lesbians. Homosexuality was only decriminalised in Queensland in 1991, after the fall of the National Party government.

Brisbane has a small but lively gay and lesbian scene centred on the inner-city suburbs of New Farm and Fortitude Valley, with a few nightclubs, pubs and guesthouses. There are also gay- and lesbian-only accommodation options in some of the more popular tourist centres, including Brisbane and Cairns. Elsewhere in Queensland, however, there can be a strong streak of homophobia, and violence against homosexuals is a risk, particularly in rural communities.

Resources

Gay & Lesbian Counselling Brisbane (☎1800 877 924; www.gayandlesbiancounselling.com) Counselling appointments.

Gay & Lesbian Tourism Australia (www.galta.com.au)

Same Same (www.samesame.com.au) News, events and lifestyle features.

Health

Although there are plenty of hazards in Queensland, few travellers will experience anything worse than an upset stomach or a bad hangover. If you do fall ill, the standard of hospitals and health care is high.

Availability & Cost of Health Care

Australia has an excellent health-care system. It's made up of privately run medical clinics and hospitals, as well as a system of public hospitals funded by the Australian government.

- The Medicare system covers Australian residents for some health-care costs. Visitors from countries with which Australia has a reciprocal health-care agreement are eligible for benefits specified under the Medicare program. Agreements are currently in place with Finland, Italy, Malta, the Netherlands, Norway, Sweden and the UK – check the details before departing these countries. For further details, visit www.humanservices.gov.au/customer/enablers/medicare/medicare-card/new-arrivals-and-visitors-to-australia.
- Painkillers, antihistamines for allergies, and skincare products are widely available at chemists throughout Australia. You may find that medications readily available over the counter in some countries are only available in Australia by prescription. These include the oral contraceptive pill, some medications for asthma and all antibiotics.
- In remote locations there may be a significant delay in emergency services reaching you. Don't underestimate the vast distances between most major outback towns; an increased level of self-reliance and preparation is essential. Consider taking a wilderness first-aid course, such as those offered by **Wilderness First Aid Consultants** (www.equip.com.au). Take a comprehensive first-aid kit and ensure that you have adequate means of communication. Australia has extensive mobile-phone coverage, but additional radio communication is important for remote areas. The **Royal Flying Doctor Service** (RFDS; www.flyingdoctor.net) provides a back-up for remote communities.

Health Insurance

Health insurance is essential for all travellers. While health care in Queensland is of a high standard and not overly expensive by international standards, considerable costs can build up if you require medical care, and repatriation is expensive.

Recommended Vaccinations

The **World Health Organization** (WHO; www.who.int/wer) recommends that all travellers should be covered for diphtheria, tetanus, measles, mumps, rubella, chicken pox and polio, as well as hepatitis B, regardless of their destination.

If you're entering Australia within six days of having stayed overnight or longer in a yellow-fever-infected country, you'll need proof of yellow-fever vaccination. For a full list of these countries visit **Centers for Disease Control & Prevention** (www.cdc.gov/travel).

Resources

Lonely Planet's *Travel with Children* includes advice on travel health for younger children.

There's a wealth of travel health advice on the internet:

Lonely Planet (www.lonelyplanet.com) A good place to start.

World Health Organization (WHO; www.who.int/wer) Publishes *International Travel* *and Health,* revised annually and available for free online.

MD Travel Health (www.mdtravelhealth.com) Provides complete travel health recommendations for every country, updated daily.

Tap Water

Tap water in Queensland is generally safe to drink. Water taken from streams, rivers and lakes should be treated before drinking.

Insurance

Worldwide travel insurance is available at www.lonelyplanet.com/travel_services. You can buy, extend and claim online anytime – even if you're already on the road.

- A good travel insurance policy covering theft, loss and medical problems is essential. Some policies specifically exclude 'dangerous activities' such as scuba diving, white-water rafting and even bushwalking. Make sure your policy covers you for your activity of choice.
- You should check if your insurer will pay doctors or hospitals directly rather than requiring you to pay on the spot and claim later. If you have to claim later, keep all documentation. Check that the policy covers ambulances and emergency medical evacuations by air.

Internet Access

There are fewer internet cafes in Queensland these days than there were five years ago (thanks to the advent of iPhones/iPads and wi-fi) but you'll still find them in most sizeable towns. Hourly costs range from $6 to $10. Most youth hostels have internet machines and wi-fi, as do many hotels and caravan parks. Most public libraries have internet access (but generally it's provided for research, not to check Facebook).

If you're going to be in Queensland for a while, check with your Internet Service Provider (ISP) for access numbers you can dial into in Australia. Some major Australian ISPs:

Dodo (☎13 36 36; www.dodo.com)

iinet (☎13 19 17; www.iinet.net.au)

iPrimus (☎13 17 89; www.iprimus.com.au)

Optus (☎1800 780 219; www.optus.com.au)

Telstra BigPond (☎13 76 63; www.bigpond.com)

Wi-fi

It's still rare in remote Queensland, but wireless internet access is increasingly the norm in city accommodation, with cafes, bars, libraries and even some public gardens also providing wi-fi access (often free for customers/guests). For locations, visit www.freewifi.com.au.

Telstra, Optus, Vodafone and other big carriers sell mobile broadband devices with a USB connection that work with most laptops and allow you to get online just about anywhere in the country. Prices are around $80 for 30 days of access (cheaper for long-term fixed contracts).

Legal Matters

- Most travellers will have no contact with Queensland's police or legal system; if they do, it's most likely to be while driving. There's a significant police presence on Queensland roads. Police have the power to stop your car, see your licence (you're required to carry it), check that your vehicle is roadworthy, and insist that you take a breath test for alcohol (and sometimes illicit drugs). The legal limit is 0.05 blood alcohol content. If you're over you'll be facing a court appearance, fine and/or suspension of your licence.
- First-time offenders caught with small amounts of illegal drugs are likely to receive a fine rather than go to jail, but the recording of a conviction against you may affect your visa status.

PRACTICALITIES

- **Currency** The Australian dollar comprises 100 cents. There are 5c, 10c, 20c, 50c, $1 and $2 coins, and $5, $10, $20, $50 and $100 notes.
- **DVDs** Australian DVDs are encoded for Region 4, which includes Mexico, South America, Central America, New Zealand, the Pacific and the Caribbean.
- **Newspapers** Leaf through Brisbane's *Courier-Mail* or the national *Australian* newspapers.
- **Radio** Tune in to ABC radio; check out www.abc.net.au/radio.
- **Smoking** Banned on public transport, in pubs, bars and eateries, and in some public outdoor spaces.
- **TV** The main free-to-air TV channels are the government-sponsored ABC, multicultural SBS and the three commercial networks – Seven, Nine and Ten – plus numerous additional channels from these main players.
- **Weights and measures** Australia uses the metric system.

➡ If you remain in Australia beyond the life of your visa, you'll officially be an 'overstayer' and could face detention and then be prevented from returning to Australia for up to three years.

➡ If you're arrested, it's your right to telephone a friend, lawyer or relative before questioning begins. Legal aid (www.nationallegalaid.org) is available only in serious cases. However, many solicitors do not charge for an initial consultation.

Money

All prices in this guide are listed in Australian dollars.

ATMs & Eftpos

➡ ATMs proliferate in cities, but don't expect to find them everywhere, certainly not off the beaten track or in small towns. Most ATMs accept cards issued by other banks (for a fee) and are linked to international networks.

➡ Most service stations, supermarkets, restaurants, cafes and shops have Electronic Funds Transfer at Point of Sale (Eftpos) facilities, allowing you to make purchases and even withdraw cash with your credit or debit card. Just don't forget your PIN (Personal Identification Number)!

➡ Remember that withdrawing cash via ATMs or Eftpos may incur significant fees – check the costs with your bank first.

Credit Cards

Credit cards such as Visa and MasterCard are widely accepted for everything from a hostel bed or a restaurant meal to an adventure tour, and are essential for hiring a car. They can also be used for cash advances at banks and from ATMs, though these transactions incur immediate interest. Diners Club and American Express (Amex) are not as widely accepted.

Lost credit-card contact numbers:

American Express (☎1300 132 639; www.americanexpress.com.au)

Diners Club (☎1300 360 060; www.dinersclub.com.au)

MasterCard (☎1800 120 113; www.mastercard.com.au)

Visa (☎1800 450 346)

Debit Cards

A debit card allows you to draw money directly from your home bank account using ATMs, banks or Eftpos machines. Any card connected to the international banking network – Cirrus, Maestro, Plus and Eurocard – should work with your PIN. Expect substantial fees.

Companies such as Travelex offer debit cards (Travelex calls them 'Cash Passport' cards) with set withdrawal fees and a balance you can top up from your personal account while on the road.

Exchanging Money

Changing foreign currency or travellers cheques is usually no problem at banks throughout Queensland, or at licensed moneychangers such as Travelex or AmEx in big cities.

Tipping

Tipping isn't traditionally part of Australian etiquette, but it's increasingly the norm to tip around 10% for good service in restaurants, and a few dollars for porters (bellhops) and taxi rides.

Travellers Cheques

The ubiquity and convenience of internationally linked credit and debit card facilities in Queensland means that travellers cheques are virtually redundant – but AmEx and Travelex will cash travellers cheques, as will major banks.

Opening Hours

Business hours sometimes vary from season to season, but use the following as a guide:

Banks 9.30am-4pm Mon-Fri; some also 9am–noon Sat

Cafes 8am-5pm

Nightclubs 10pm-4am Thu-Sat

Post Offices 9am-5pm Mon-Fri; some also 9am–noon Sat

Pubs & Bars noon-midnight; bars often later

Restaurants noon-2.30pm & 6.30-9pm

Shops 9am-5pm Mon-Sat

Supermarkets 7am-8pm

Photography

➡ Digital cameras, memory sticks and batteries are sold prolifically in cities and urban centres. Try electronics stores (Dick Smith, Tandy) or the larger department

TAX REFUNDS FOR TRAVELLERS

If you purchase new or second-hand goods with a total minimum value of $300 from any one supplier no more than 30 days before you leave Australia, you are entitled under the Tourist Refund Scheme (TRS) to a refund of any Goods & Services Tax paid (GST, which is one-eleventh of the purchase price). The scheme only applies to goods you take with you as hand luggage or wear onto the plane or ship. The refund is valid for goods bought from more than one supplier, but only if at least $300 has been spent at each. For more information, contact the **Australian Customs & Border Protection Service** (☎02-6275 6666, 1300 363 263; www.customs.gov.au).

stores. Many internet cafes, camera stores and large stationers (Officeworks, Harvey Norman) have printing and CD-burning facilities. Cheap, disposable underwater cameras are available at most beach towns.

- As in any country, politeness goes a long way when taking photographs; ask before taking pictures of people. For Indigenous Australians, photography can be highly intrusive: photographing cultural places, practices and images, sites of significance and ceremonies may also be a sensitive matter. Always ask first.
- Check out Lonely Planet's *Travel Photography* guide.

Post

Australia Post (www.auspost.com.au) is efficient and reliable. Posting standard letters or postcards within the country costs 60c. International rates for airmail letters up to 50g cost $2.60. Postcards cost $1.70.

Public Holidays

New Year's Day 1 January

Australia Day 26 January

Easter (Good Friday to Easter Monday inclusive) March or April

Anzac Day 25 April

Labour Day First Monday in May

Queen's Birthday Second Monday in June

Royal Queensland Show Day (Brisbane only) Second or third Wednesday in August

Christmas Day 25 December

Boxing Day 26 December

School Holidays

Key times when prices are highest and many accommodation options are booked out in advance:

- Christmas holiday season (mid-December to late January)
- Shorter (two-week) school-holiday periods generally fall in mid-April, late June to mid-July, and late September to mid-October

> **GOVERNMENT TRAVEL ADVICE**
>
> The following government websites offer travel advisories and information on current hot spots.
>
> - **Australian Department of Foreign Affairs & Trade** (DFAT; www.smarttraveller.gov.au)
> - **British Foreign & Commonwealth Office** (www.gov.uk/fco)
> - **Government of Canada** (www.travel.gc.ca)
> - **US State Department** (www.travel.state.gov)

Safe Travel

Queensland is a relatively safe place to visit, but take reasonable precautions. The Gold Coast and Cairns get dishonourable mentions when it comes to theft: don't leave hotel rooms or cars unlocked or valuables visible through car windows.

Floods, cyclones and bushfires regularly decimate parts of the state, but pay attention to warnings from local authorities and you'll be fine.

Telephone

Australia's main telecommunication companies:

Telstra (13 22 00; www.telstra.com.au) The main player.

Optus (1800 780 219; www.optus.com.au) Telstra's main rival.

Vodafone (1300 650 410; www.vodafone.com.au) Mobile phone services.

Virgin (1300 555 100; www.virginmobile.com.au) Mobile phone services.

Mobile Phones

- Local numbers with the prefix 04xx belong to mobile phones.
- Australia's digital network is compatible with GSM 900 and 1800 (used in Europe), but generally not with networks in the USA or Japan.
- Queensland generally gets good mobile-phone reception, but service can be haphazard or non-existent in the interior and far north (eg the Daintree Rainforest)
- To get connected, buy a starter kit, which may include a phone or, if you have your own phone, a SIM card (under $10) and a prepaid charge card. Pick up starter kits and SIM cards at airport mobile-phone shops or outlets in the big cities. Purchase recharge vouchers at convenience stores and newsagents.

Phone Codes

To call overseas from Australia, dial 0011 or 0018, the country code, then the area code (without the initial 0). So, for a London number you'd dial 0011-44-171, then the number.

If dialling Queensland from overseas, the country code is 61, and drop the zero in the 07 area code.

Area codes within Australia:

STATE/ TERRITORY	AREA CODE
Queensland	07
New South Wales, Australian Capital Territory	02
South Australia, Western Australia, Northern Territory	08
Victoria, Tasmania	03

Phonecards & Public Phones

You can purchase phonecards at newsagents and post offices. Use them with public or private phones by dialling a toll-free access number and then the PIN on the card. Some public phones also accept credit cards (most are coin-free these days).

Toll-Free & Reverse-Charges Calls

Toll-free numbers (prefix ☎1800) can be called free of charge. Calls to numbers beginning with ☎13 or ☎1300 are charged at the rate of a local call.

To make a reverse-charge (collect) call within Australia, dial ☎1800-REVERSE (☎1800 738 3773) from any public or private phone.

Time

Australia is divided into three time zones:

Eastern Standard Time (Greenwich Mean Time + 10 hours) Queensland, New South Wales, Victoria and Tasmania

Central Standard Time (30 minutes behind Eastern Standard Time) Northern Territory, South Australia

Western Standard Time (two hours behind Eastern Standard Time) Western Australia

Note that Queensland remains on Eastern Standard Time all year, while most of Australia switches to daylight-saving time over the summer (October to early April) when clocks are wound forward one hour.

Toilets

Toilets in Queensland are sit-down Western style (though you mightn't find this prospect too appealing in some remote pitstops). See www.toiletmap.gov.au for public toilet locations throughout the state.

Tourist Information

Tourist information is provided in Queensland by regional and local offices – often volunteer-staffed info centres in key tourist spots. Note that some tourist info outlets are also booking agents and will steer you towards the tour/accommodation that pays them the best commission.

Resources

Australian Tourist Commission (ATC; www.australia.com) National organisation charged with luring foreign visitors.

Department of National Parks, Recreation, Sport & Racing (www.nprsr.qld.gov.au) Has information on national parks throughout Queensland, including campsite bookings.

Tourism Queensland (www.queenslandholidays.com.au) Official Queensland government-run website stacked with information, from accommodation to diving the Great Barrier Reef.

Travellers with Disabilities

Disability awareness in Queensland is reasonably high. Legislation requires new accommodation to meet accessibility standards and tourist operators must not discriminate. Facilities for wheelchairs are improving in accommodation, but there are still many older establishments where the necessary upgrades haven't been made.

Resources

Accessible Tourism (www.australiaforall.com) Good site for accessibility information.

Deaf Australia (www.deafau.org.au)

Disability Information Service (www.communities.qld.gov.au/disability) Queensland government's Department for Communities, Child Safety & Disability Services; support throughout Queensland.

National Disability Services (www.nds.org.au) The national industry association for disability services.

Spinal Injuries Association (www.spinal.com.au) In Brisbane.

Vision Australia (www.visionaustralia.org.au)

Wheelie Easy (www.wheelieeasy.com.au) Runs specialised tours in Far North Queensland for travellers with impaired mobility.

Visas

All visitors to Australia need a visa. Only New Zealand nationals are exempt: they sheepishly receive a 'special category' visa on arrival. The main visa categories for travellers are as follows:

eVisitor (651) A free three-month visa for many European passport holders.

Electronic Travel Authority (ETA; 601) A free three-month visa for citizens of 34 countries, including Brunei, Canada, Hong Kong, Japan, Malaysia, Singapore, South Korea and the USA .

Tourist Visa (600) A three-, six- or 12-month visa ($115) for citizens of countries other than those listed above, or for people from the above countries who want to stay longer than three months.

Detailed information (including info on visa extensions) and application forms are available on the website of the **Department of Immigration and Citizenship** (www.immi.gov.au). .

Volunteering

Lonely Planet's *Volunteer: A Traveller's Guide to Making a Difference Around the World* has useful information. Also check out these resources:

Conservation Volunteers Australia (www.conservationvolunteers.com.au) Nonprofit organisation involved in tree planting, walking-track construction and surveys.

Go Volunteer (www.govolunteer.com.au) National website listing volunteer opportunities.

i to i Volunteering (www.i-to-i.com) Conservation-based volunteer holidays in Australia.

Lizard Island Research Station (www.australianmuseum.net.au/lizard-island-research-station) Opportunities to help researchers studying marine ecology and seabirds.

Reef Check (www.reefcheckaustralia.org) Train to monitor the health of the reef.

Sea Turtle Foundation (www.seaturtlefoundation.org) Volunteer opportunities in sea-turtle conservation.

Volunteering Australia (www.volunteeringaustralia.org) Support, advice and volunteer training.

Volunteering Qld (www.volunteeringqld.org.au) Volunteering info and advice.

Willing Workers on Organic Farms (WWOOF; www.wwoof.com.au) 'WWOOFing' is where you do a few hours' work each day on a farm in return for bed and board, often in a family home. The farms are supposed to be organic (including permaculture and biodynamic growing), but that isn't always so. Some places aren't even farms – you might help out at pottery or do the books at a seed wholesaler. Whether participants have a farm or just a veggie patch, most are concerned to some extent with alternative lifestyles. Most places have a minimum stay of two nights. You can join online or through various WWOOF agents for a fee of $65. You'll get a membership number and a booklet that lists participating enterprises. Add $5 for overseas postage.

Women Travellers

Queensland is generally a safe place for women travellers, although the usual sensible precautions apply. Sexual harassment is rare, although the Aussie male culture does have its sexist elements. Avoid hitch-hiking and walking alone late at night – and if you are out on the town, always keep enough money aside for a taxi back to your accommodation. Solo women should be wary of staying in basic pub accommodation unless it looks safe and well managed.

Work

Finding Work

- If you're in Brisbane and happy with bar work or waiting on tables, the best advice is to go knocking on doors in Fortitude Valley or New Farm. Many places want staff for longer than three months, though, so it may take a bit of footwork to find a willing employer. The *Courier-Mail* newspaper has daily employment listings – Wednesday and Saturday are the best days to look.
- Backpacker magazines and hostel noticeboards are good options for sourcing local work. Casual work can often be found during peak season in tourist hubs such as Cairns, the Gold Coast and the resort towns along the Queensland coast.
- Harvest work is popular elsewhere in Queensland. The main spots are Bundaberg, Childers, Stanthorpe, Bowen, Tully and Innisfail, where everything from avocados to zucchinis are harvested throughout the year, and hostels specialise in finding travellers work.
- People with computer, secretarial, nursing and teaching skills can often find work temping in the cities (via employment agencies).

Working Visas

If you come to Australia on a tourist visa you are not allowed to work for pay. To work, you'll need one of the following visas:

Work and Holiday Visa (462) – for citizens of Argentina, Bangladesh, Chile, Indonesia, Iran, Malaysia, Thailand, Turkey, the USA and Uruguay.

Working Holiday Visa (417) – for citizens of Belgium, Canada, Republic of Cyprus, Denmark, Estonia, Finland, France, Germany, Hong Kong, Republic of Ireland, Italy, Japan, Republic of Korea, Malta, Netherlands, Norway, Sweden, Taiwan and the UK.

Both visas cost $365; visit www.immi.gov.au for more info (including your options if you're not from one of the countries listed here).

Resources

Australian Job Search (www.jobsearch.gov.au) Government-run website listing myriad jobs around the country.

Grunt Labour (www.gruntlabour.com) Specialises in mining, manufacturing and agricultural-based recruitment, plus seasonal fruit-picking.

Harvest Trail (www.jobsearch.gov.au/harvesttrail) Harvest jobs around Australia.

Seek (www.seek.com.au) General employment site; good for metropolitan areas.

Travellers at Work (www.taw.com.au) Excellent site for working travellers in Australia.

Workabout Australia (www.workaboutaustralia.com.au) Gives a state-by-state breakdown of seasonal work opportunities.

Taxes

If you're earning money in Australia, you'll be paying tax, and will have to lodge a tax return. See the website of the **Australian Taxation Office** (ATO; www.ato.gov.au) for info on how to do this, including getting a Payment Summary from your employer, timing/dates for lodging returns, and receiving your Notice of Assessment.

You'll need to apply for a **Tax File Number** (TFN) to give to your employer. Without it, tax will be deducted at the maximum rate from your wages. Apply online via the ATO; it takes up to four weeks to be issued.

Transport

GETTING THERE & AWAY

Unless you're travelling from within Australia, getting to Queensland usually involves a long-haul flight. Flights, tours and rail tickets can be booked online at lonelyplanet.com/bookings.

Entering Australia

Arrival in Australia is usually straightforward and efficient, with the usual customs declarations. There are no restrictions for citizens of any particular foreign countries entering Australia – if you have a current passport and visa, you should be fine.

Air

High season (with the highest prices) for flights into Australia is roughly over the country's summer (December to February); low season generally tallies with the winter months (June to August), though this is actually peak season in tropical Far North Queensland.

Many international flights head to Sydney or Melbourne before flying to Queensland, but Brisbane receives a growing number of direct international flights. Cairns and the Gold Coast also receive some international flights.

Australia's international carrier is **Qantas** (www.qantas.com.au), which has an outstanding safety record (...as Dustin Hoffman said in *Rainman*, 'Qantas never crashed').

International Airports

Brisbane Airport (www.bne.com.au)

Cairns Airport (www.cairnsairport.com)

Land

Travelling overland to Queensland from elsewhere in Australia is an education in how big this country is. The journey from Brisbane to the nearest state capital, Sydney, is a torturous 1030km; while the journey from Brisbane to Cairns in Queensland's north covers 1700km!

The Pacific Hwy is the main access point into Queensland from the south, crossing the New South Wales (NSW) border at Tweed Heads. A lesser-used route from the south is the New England Hwy, crossing the border at Tenterfield. The Newell Hwy is the most direct route to Brisbane from Melbourne or Adelaide.

The other major route into southern Queensland is the Mitchell Hwy. It crosses the border at Barringun and links Bourke in outback NSW with Charleville in outback Queensland.

The main road from the west is the Barkly Hwy, which crosses the Northern Territory–Queensland border around 15km west of Camooweal and cuts across to Mt Isa.

Sea

It is possible (if not straightforward) to travel between Queensland and Papua New Guinea, Indonesia, New Zealand and the Pacific islands by hitching rides or crewing on yachts – usually you have to at least contribute towards food. Ask around at marinas and sailing clubs in places like Great Keppel Island,

QANTAS AIRPASS

Qantas offers a discount-fare **Walkabout Air Pass** for passengers flying into Australia from overseas with Qantas or American Airlines. The pass allows you to link up around 80 domestic Australian destinations for less than you'd pay booking flights individually. See www.qantas.com.au for more information.

Airlie Beach, the Whitsundays and Cairns.

Alternatively, **P&O Cruises** (www.pocruises.com.au) operates holiday cruises between Brisbane and destinations in New Zealand and the Pacific. Even more alternatively, some freighter ships allow passengers to travel on-board as they ship cargo to/from Australia: see websites such as www.freighterexpeditions.com.au and www.freightercruises.com for options.

BRISBANE BIKE-SHARE

Brisbane has an inexpensive public bike-sharing scheme that allows speedy access to bikes across town. Basically you subscribe online and can then borrow a bike for up to 24 hours, and return it to any of the dozens of bike stations around the city. Sometimes a helmet will accompany the bike, but it's a good idea to have your own (and a lock). For details see **CityCycle** (www.citycycle.com.au).

GETTING AROUND

Air

Queensland is well serviced by airlines, big and small.

Hinterland Aviation (www.hinterlandaviation.com.au) Flies between Cairns and Cooktown.

Jetstar (www.jetstar.com.au) Flies between Brisbane and many coastal destinations, as well as Hamilton Island.

Qantas (www.qantas.com.au) Flies to many locations in Queensland, including Brisbane, Cairns, Townsville, Mt Isa and Hamilton Island.

Regional Express (REX; www.rex.com.au) Connects Townsville with small regional airports.

Skytrans (www.skytrans.com.au) Serves northern Queensland, flying from Cairns to Bamaga (tip of Australia) and Mt Isa, among other obscure locations.

Tiger Airways (www.tigerairways.com) Budget offshoot of Singapore Airlines. Services Brisbane, the Gold Coast and a few other Queensland destinations.

Virgin Australia (www.virginaustralia.com.au) Flies between Brisbane and many coastal destinations, including Hamilton Island.

Bicycle

Queensland can be a good place for cycling, although you need to choose your areas: roads such as the Bruce Hwy between Brisbane and Cairns can be long and hot with limited verges and heavy traffic. The best areas for touring are the Gold Coast hinterland, the Sunshine Coast secondary roads, and the area north of Cairns. Many touring cyclists carry camping equipment but it's feasible to travel from town to town staying in hostels, hotels or caravan parks.

➡ Summer in Queensland isn't a great time for cycling. It can get very hot and incredibly humid, with daily torrential downpours. Drink plenty of water: dehydration can be life-threatening.

➡ Bicycle helmets are compulsory, as are front and rear lights for night riding.

➡ Within Australia you can load your bike onto a bus or train to skip the boring bits of road. Note that some bus companies require you to dismantle your bike, and don't guarantee that it will travel on the same bus as you. Trains are easier: supervise the loading if you can.

➡ See Lonely Planet's *Cycling Australia* or contact **Bicycle Queensland** (www.bq.org.au) for detailed information. Additionally, the Queensland government has an informative website, including road rules, maps and other resources: www.tmr.qld.gov.au/travel-and-transport/cycling.

Hire

Rates charged by most rental outfits for road or mountain bikes range from $10 to $15 per hour and $25 to $50 per day. Security deposits can range from $50 to $200, depending on the rental period.

Purchase

For a new road or mountain bike in Queensland, your bottom-level starting price will be around $600. With all the requisite on-the-road equipment (panniers, helmet, lights etc) you're looking at upwards of $1700.

To sell your bike (or buy a second-hand one), try hostel noticeboards or online:

Bike Exchange (www.bikeexchange.com.au).

Gumtree (www.gumtree.com.au)

Trading Post (www.tradingpost.com.au)

Boat

There are no scheduled ferry services along the Queensland coast (other than those out to various islands), but cruising the coastline on a yacht is certainly an idyllic way to explore the state. Ask about the possibility of crewing on board a yacht at marinas in places like Cairns, Airlie Beach, Great Keppel Island, the Whitsundays and Manly in Brisbane.

Bus

Queensland's bus network is reliable, but not the cheapest for long hauls. Most buses have air-con and toilets; all are smoke-free. There are no separate classes on buses (very democratic). Book seats at least a day ahead (a week or two during summer). Small towns eschew formal bus terminals for an informal drop-off/pick-up point, usually outside a post office or shop.

Bus Companies

Coachtrans (www.coachtransonline.com.au) Connects Brisbane with the Gold Coast and Sunshine Coast.

Coral Reef Coaches (www.coralreefcoaches.com.au) Runs between Cairns and Port Douglas.

Country Road Coachlines (www.countryroadcoachlines.com.au) Cairns to Cooktown via inland (via Mareeba) or coastal (via Port Douglas and Cape Tribulation) routes.

Crisps Coaches (www.crisps.com.au) Services inland from Brisbane to Toowoomba, Stanthorpe and south to Tenterfield in NSW.

Greyhound (www.greyhound.com.au) Extensive network across Queensland, continuing interstate.

Paradise Coaches (www.paradisecoaches.com.au) Runs from Rockhampton to Emerald and Longreach, and between Emerald and Mackay.

Premier Motor Service (www.premierms.com.au) Greyhound's main competitor: has fewer daily services but usually costs a little less.

Sun Palm (www.sunpalmtransport.com.au) Services between Cairns and Port Douglas.

Bus Passes

Bus passes are a good option if you plan on multiple stopovers. Book online or phone at least a day ahead to reserve a seat.

Greyhound (☎1300 473 946; www.greyhound.com.au) offers myriad money-saving passes – check the website for comprehensive info. A few options:

- **Kilometre Pass** Gives you go-anywhere flexibility, plus the choice to backtrack. Choose from 1000km ($188) up to 25,000km ($2499). Valid for 12 months.
- **Mini Traveller Pass** Up to 90 days of one-direction travel along a dozen popular routes – including Brisbane to Cairns ($339) and Hervey Bay to Cairns ($261) – stopping as often as you like.

Premier Motor Service (☎13 34 10; www.premierms.com.au) offers several passes for one-way travel along the east coast, including three-month passes between Byron Bay and Cairns ($215) or Sydney and Cairns ($313).

TYPICAL ONE-WAY BUS FARES

ROUTE	FARE ($)	DURATION (HR)
Airlie Beach–Townsville	45	4½
Brisbane–Cairns	300	29
Brisbane–Hervey Bay	69	5½
Cairns–Mt Isa	230	19
Hervey Bay–Rockhampton	88	6½
Mackay–Airlie Beach	30	2
Rockhampton–Mackay	60	5
Townsville–Cairns	60	5½

Car & Motorcycle

Queensland is a big, sprawling state – for the locals, driving is the accepted means of getting from A to B. For travellers too, the best way to explore much of the state is by car – it's certainly the only way to access interesting, out-of-the-way places without taking a tour.

Motorcycles are also popular here: between April and November the climate is ideal for bikes. A fuel range of 350km will easily cover fuel stops along the coast. The long, open roads here are really made for large-capacity machines above 750cc.

The **Department of Transport and Main Roads** (www.tmr.qld.gov.au) is the Queensland government body responsible for roads. It provides a wealth of free information on Australian road rules and conditions, and downloadable brochures including the extremely useful *Guide to Queensland Roads*, which includes distance charts, road maps and other helpful information.

Driving Licence

To drive in Australia you'll need to hold a current driving licence issued in English from your home country. If the licence isn't in English, you'll also need to carry an International Driving Permit, issued in your home country.

Automobile Associations

The national **Australian Automobile Association** (AAA; ☎02-6247 7311; www.aaa.asn.au) is the umbrella organisation for the various state associations. In Queensland, the **Royal Automobile Club of Queensland** (RACQ; www.racq.com.au) holds sway, and offers reciprocal service arrangements (such as emergency breakdown assistance) with other states and with similar organisations overseas – including AAA in the USA and RAC or AA in the

CLIMATE CHANGE & TRAVEL

Every form of transport that relies on carbon-based fuel generates CO_2, the main cause of human-induced climate change. Modern travel is dependent on aeroplanes which might use less fuel per kilometre per person than most cars but travel much greater distances. The altitude at which aircraft emit gases (including CO_2) and particles also contributes to their climate change impact. Many websites offer 'carbon calculators' that allow people to estimate the carbon emissions generated by their journey and, for those who wish to do so, to offset the impact of the greenhouse gases emitted with contributions to portfolios of climate-friendly initiatives throughout the world. Lonely Planet offsets the carbon footprint of all staff and author travel.

UK. Bring proof of membership with you.

The RACQ also produces a useful set of Queensland maps, can book tours and accommodation, and can provide advice on weather, road conditions and buying a car. Also on offer is additional insurance on top of your compulsory third-party personal liability cover.

Hire

There are plenty of car-rental companies in Queensland, big and small, ready to put you behind the wheel. The main thing to remember is distance – if you want to travel far, you'll need unlimited kilometres.

Larger car-rental companies have drop-offs in major cities and towns; smaller local firms are sometimes cheaper but may have restrictions. The big firms sometimes also offer one-way rentals, which may not cost extra. Most companies require drivers to be over the age of 21, though in some cases it's 18 and in others 25. Typical rates are from $40/60/80 per day for a small/medium/large car.

The usual big international companies all operate in Queensland (Avis, Budget, Europcar, Hertz, Thrifty), but smaller companies often have better deals.

Abel Rent A Car (www.abel.com.au) Based in Brisbane.

Apex Car Rentals (☎1800 121 029; www.apexrentacar.com.au; 400 Nudgee Rd, Hendra) Outlets at Brisbane, Cairns and Gold Coast airports.

Bargain Wheels (www.bargainwheels.com.au) Searches local hire companies for the best deals.

East Coast Car Rentals (www.eastcoastcarrentals.com.au) Some of Queensland's best prices; offices in Brisbane, Cairns and the Gold Coast.

4WDS

Having a 4WD enables you to get away from the touristy routes and out to some of the natural wonders and wilderness areas that most travellers don't see. Something middle-sized like a Nissan X-Trail costs around $100 to $150 per day; for a Toyota Land Cruiser you're looking at around $150 up to $200, which should include unlimited kilometres. Check insurance conditions carefully, especially the excess, as they can be onerous (in Queensland $4000 excess is typical, although this can often be reduced to around $1000 on payment of an additional daily charge of around $30).

The major car-hire companies have 4WD rentals, or try **Apollo** (☎1800 777 779; www.apollocamper.com) or **Britz** (☎1800 331 454; www.britz.com.au).

CAMPERVANS

Once the preserve of meandering grey nomads, campervanning has exploded in Australia in recent years, and nowhere more so than in Queensland. The advantages are obvious: a weather-proof home on wheels, providing transport, accommodation, cooking gear (usually), and no mucking around with tents. Most towns have at least one caravan park where you can park and plug into power. National parks usually have self-registration or pre-booked campsites.

Campervan hire rates are from around $90 (two-berth) or $150 (four-berth) per day, usually with minimum five day hire and unlimited kilometres.

Apollo (☎1800 777 779; www.apollocamper.com)

Britz (☎1800 331 454; www.britz.com.au)

Camperman Australia (☎1800 216 223; www.campermanaustralia.com.au)

Jucy Rentals (☎1800 150 850; www.jucy.com.au)

Maui (☎1300 363 800; www.maui.com.au)

Mighty Cars & Campers (☎1800 670 232; www.mightycampers.com)

Spaceships (☎1300 132 469; www.spaceshipsrentals.com.au)

Travelwheels (☎1800 289 222; www.travelwheels.com.au)

Wicked Campers (☎1800 246 869; www.wickedcampers.com.au)

ONE-WAY RELOCATIONS

Relocations (where you pick up a vehicle in one location and return it to another) are usually cheap deals, although they usually don't allow much time flexibility. Most of the large hire companies offer deals, or try the following operators:

Drive Now (☎1300 547 214; www.drivenow.com.au)

imoova (☎1300 789 059; www.imoova.com)

Relocations2Go (☎1800 735 627; www.relocations2go.com)

Transfercar (☎02-8011 1870; www.transfercar.com.au)

RIDE-SHARING

Ride-sharing is a good way to split costs and environmental impact with other travellers. As with hitching, there are potential risks involved: meet in a public place before hitting the road, and if anything seems off, don't hesitate to back out. Hostel noticeboards are good places to find ads, or check these online classifieds:

Catch a Lift (www.catchalift.com)

Coseats (www.coseats.com)

Jayride (www.jayride.com.au)

Need A Ride (www.needaride.com.au)

Insurance

➡ Throughout Australia, third-party personal injury insurance is included in the vehicle-registration cost, ensuring that every registered vehicle carries at least minimum insurance. We recommend extending that minimum to at least third-party property insurance – minor collisions can be amazingly expensive.

➡ When it comes to hire cars, understand your liability in the event of an accident. You can pay an additional daily amount to the rental company which will reduce your liability from upwards of $3000 to a few hundred dollars in the event of an accident.

➡ Be aware that if you're driving on dirt roads you may not be covered by insurance (even if you have a 4WD): if you have an accident you'll be liable for all costs. Also, many insurance policies don't cover damage to windscreens or tyres – always read the small print.

Purchase

Australian cars are not cheap, but if you plan to stay several months and do plenty of driving, buying a car will probably work out to be cheaper than renting one. You can buy from a car dealer or a private vendor (private sales are often cheaper). Hostel noticeboards are good places to start looking. Online, have a look at **Car Sales** (www.carsales.com.au) and **Trading Post** (www.tradingpost.com.au).

REGISTRATION & LEGALITIES

➡ When you buy a vehicle in Queensland, you need to contact the Queensland government's **Department of Transport & Main Roads** (www.tmr.qld.gov.au) to transfer the registration into your own name within 14 days. Similarly, when selling a vehicle you need to advise the Department of the sale and change of name. To facilitate this, the buyer and seller need to complete and sign a Transfer of Vehicle

ROAD DISTANCES (KM)

	Airlie Beach	Brisbane	Bundaberg	Cairns	Cape York	Hervey Bay	Mackay	Mission Beach	Mt Isa	Noosa Heads	Rockhampton	Surfers Paradise
Brisbane	1114											
Bundaberg	770	362										
Cairns	633	1699	1356									
Cape York	1580	2648	2304	949								
Hervey Bay	877	291	124	1463	2411							
Mackay	149	968	623	735	1683	730						
Mission Beach	520	1588	1244	139	1087	1351	623					
Mt Isa	1131	1827	1612	1111	1492	1719	1234	1137				
Noosa Heads	1011	138	259	1598	2545	188	865	1485	1821			
Rockhampton	482	633	288	1068	2016	395	336	956	1333	529		
Surfers Paradise	1197	79	445	1784	2731	374	1051	1671	1881	221	715	
Townsville	288	1356	1011	349	1297	1118	391	237	905	1253	724	1439

These are the shortest distances by road; other routes may be considerably longer. For distances by coach, check the companies' leaflets.

Registration Application form. Note that it's much easier to sell a car in the same state in which it's registered, otherwise you (or the buyer) must re-register it in the new state, which can be a hassle.

➡ In Queensland, sellers are required to provide a safety certificate when transferring registration; a gas certificate is also required for vehicles running on gas. If the vehicle you're considering doesn't have these certificates, it's worth having a roadworthy check done by a mechanic before you buy it. Contact the **RACQ** (☎13 19 05; www.racq.com.au) for a list of licensed vehicle testers.

➡ It's the buyer's responsibility to ensure the car isn't stolen and that there's no money owing on it: check the car's details with the **Personal Property Securities Register** (☎1300 007 777; www.ppsr.gov.au).

➡ For full details on processes and costs, see www.tmr.qld.gov.au/registration/transferring-registration.

BUY-BACK DEALS

One way of bypassing the hassles of buying/selling a vehicle privately is to enter into a buy-back arrangement with a dealer. Beware: many dealers will find ways of knocking down the price when you return the vehicle – even if a price has been agreed upon in writing – by pointing out repairs that allegedly will be required to gain a safety certificate. The cars on offer have usually been driven around Australia several times, often with minimal servicing, and are generally pretty tired.

Road Hazards & Precautions

➡ Be wary of driver fatigue; driving long distances (particularly in hot weather) can be utterly exhausting. Falling asleep at the wheel is not uncommon. On a long haul, stop and rest every two hours or so – do some exercise, change drivers or find a decent coffee.

➡ Unsealed road conditions vary wildly and cars perform differently when braking and turning on dirt. Don't exceed 80km/h on dirt roads; if you go faster you won't have time to respond to a sharp turn, stock on the road or an unmarked gate or cattle grid. If you're in a rental car, check your contract to ensure you're covered for driving on unsealed roads.

➡ Queensland has few multi-lane highways, although there are stretches of divided road (four or six lanes) in busy areas such as the toll roads and freeways around Brisbane. Two-lane roads however, are the only option for many routes. Be aware that you can only overtake other vehicles when there is a dotted white line down the middle or on your side of the road. Never overtake on full double lines as these are placed along high-risk, low-visibility stretches of road.

➡ Many rural Queenslanders avoid travelling after dark because of the risks posed by nocturnal animals on the roads. Kangaroos are common on country roads, as are cows and sheep in the unfenced outback. Kangaroos are most active around dawn and dusk and often travel in groups: if you see one hopping across the road, slow right down, as its friends may be just behind it. If you hit and kill an animal, pull it off the road, preventing the next car from having a potential accident. If the animal is injured, wrap it in a towel or blanket and contact the **Department of Environment & Heritage Protection** (☎1300 130 372; www.ehp.qld.gov.au).

➡ With Queensland's heavy tropical rains, flooding can occur with little warning, especially in outback areas and the Far North (and, more recently, in downtown Brisbane!). Roads can be cut off for days during floods, and floodwaters sometimes wash away whole sections of road.

Road Rules

➡ Australians drive on the left-hand side of the road; all cars are right-hand drive.

➡ At unmarked intersections (unusual) and at roundabouts, you must give way to vehicles entering the intersection from your right.

➡ The general speed limit in built-up and residential areas is 50km/h (sometimes 60km/h). Near schools, the limit is usually 25km/h in the morning and afternoon. On the highway it's 100km/h or 110km/h. Police have speed radar guns and cameras, and are fond of using them in strategic locations.

➡ Seatbelt usage is compulsory. Children up to the age of seven must be belted into an approved safety seat.

TOLL ROADS

There are a handful of toll roads around Brisbane with electronic toll-pass detection. Regardless of whether you're travelling in your own vehicle or in a rental, you'll be in for a hefty fine if you don't pay the tolls (all of which are under $5). You can organise a toll pass ahead of time (most rental companies can supply you with one for a daily charge), or you can pay tolls online within three days of driving on the toll roads: see **go via** (www.govia.com.au) for payment and pass details.

➡ Random breath tests are common. If you're caught with a blood alcohol level of more than 0.05%, expect a court appearance, a fine and the loss of your licence. Police can randomly pull any driver over for a breathalyser or drug test.

➡ Using a mobile phone while driving is illegal (excluding hands-free technology).

Fuel

Diesel and unleaded fuel are available from all service stations. LPG (gas) is also available in populated areas but not always at more remote service stations. On main Queensland highways there's usually a small town or petrol station every 50km or so.

Prices vary from place to place, but at the time of writing unleaded was hovering between $1.40 and $1.60 per litre in the cities. Out in the country, prices soar – in outback Queensland you can pay as much as $2.20 per litre.

Parking

Brisbane, Cairns and parts of the Gold Coast present the usual hassles with parking – limited spaces, tight time restrictions and hefty fines – but elsewhere in Queensland, parking is rarely a problem.

Outback Driving

If you really want to see remote outback Queensland, you need to be prepared for harsh weather and to tackle dirt roads in unpredictable states of repair: a 4WD is the way to go. The **RACQ** (☎13 19 05; www.racq.com.au) can advise on preparation, supplies, maps and track notes, and runs a 24-hour telephone service with a pre-recorded reports on road conditions throughout the state (dial ☎1300 130 595). Local police are your best bet once you're on the road.

➡ Apart from being stocked with spare parts and tyres, plenty of water (5L per person per day and extra for the radiator) and a basic knowledge of outback driving (such as deflating tyres to get through deep sand), an extra safety precaution is to carry a high-frequency (HF) radio transceiver or satellite phone to contact Royal Flying Doctor Service bases, a Global Positioning System (GPS) unit and/or an emergency position-indicating radio beacon (EPIRB).

➡ It's wise not to attempt tough outback tracks during the heat of summer (November to March) when the dust can be severe and water scarce, making a breakdown more dangerous. Travel during the Wet (November to April) in the north may be hindered by flooding and impassable mud.

➡ There are still many unsealed roads in Queensland where the official recommendation is that you report to the police before you leave, and again when you arrive at your destination. If not the police, tell friends, family and/or your car-hire company what you're up to.

➡ If you do run into trouble in the back of beyond, always stay with your car. It's easier to spot a car than a human being from the air, and you wouldn't be able to carry a heavy load of water very far anyway. Police suggest that you carry two spare tyres (for added safety) and, if stranded, set fire to one of them (let the air out first) – the pall of smoke will be seen for miles.

Hitching

Hitching is never entirely safe in any country in the world, and we don't recommend it. Travellers who decide to hitch should understand that they are taking a small but potentially serious risk. People who do choose to hitch will be safer if they travel in pairs and let someone know where they are planning to go.

Local Transport

Bus, Train & Ferry

Brisbane has a comprehensive public transport networks with buses, trains and river ferries, run by **Translink** (☎13 12 30; www.translink.com.au), with services extending to the Sunshine Coast, Gold Coast and parts of the Darling Downs.

Larger cities such as Toowoomba, Mt Isa, Bundaberg, Rockhampton, Mackay, Townsville and Cairns all have local bus services. There are also local bus services throughout the Gold Coast and Sunshine Coast.

Taxi

Brisbane, Cairns and the Gold Coast have plenty of taxis, but outside of these centres taxi numbers diminish. Taxi fares vary throughout the state, but shouldn't differ much from those in Brisbane, where a 5km cross-town jaunt costs about $25.

Black & White (☎13 32 22; www.blackandwhitecabs.com.au) In Brisbane.

Cairns Taxis (☎13 10 08; www.blackandwhitetaxis.com.au)

Gold Coast Cabs (☎13 10 08; www.gccabs.com.au)

Suncoast Cabs (☎13 10 08; www.suncoastcabs.com.au) On the Sunshine Coast.

Townsville Taxis (☎13 10 08; www.tsvtaxi.com.au)

Yellow Cab Co (☎13 19 24; www.yellowcab.com.au) In Brisbane.

Tram

By the time you read this, the shiny new **Gold Coast Rapid Transit** (www.goldlinq.com.au) tram system might be operational, linking 16 stops over 13km between Southport and Broadbeach. Until then, local buses are your best bet.

Tours

Several backpacker and tour bus companies operate along the Queensland coast. These trips are economically priced and can be more fun than conventional tour buses: the buses are usually smaller and you'll meet other travellers.

AAT Kings (☎1300 556 100; www.aatkings.com) Big coach company (popular with the older set) with myriad tours all around Australia.

Adventure Tours Australia (☎1800 068 886; www.adventuretours.com.au) Affordable, young-at-heart tours in all states.

Oz Experience (☎1300 300 028; www.ozexperience.com) Backpacker buses covering central, northern and eastern Australia.

Train

Queensland has a sizeable rail network that services the coast between Brisbane and Cairns, with several routes heading inland to Mt Isa, Longreach and Charleville. There are nine main service routes, including the Kuranda Scenic Railway, which is primarily a tourist route in northern Queensland. All services are operated by **Queensland Rail** (☎1800 872 467; www.queenslandrail.com.au).

Additionally, **NSW TrainLink** (☎13 22 32; www.nswtrainlink.info) has a daily XPT (express passenger train) service between Brisbane and Sydney (economy seat/1st-class seat $95/130, 15 hours).

Classes & Costs

Travelling by rail within Queensland is generally slower and more expensive than bus travel, although some economy fares are comparable. Where sleeping berths are available they cost from around $70 extra per night in economy (cheaper for triple-bunk cabins than singles or twins), and approximately $230 more for 1st class. The *Sunlander* from Brisbane to Cairns also has 'Queenslander Class', which includes comfortable berths, meals in the restaurant car and historical commentary en route.

Half-price concession fares are available to kids under 16 years of age, and students with an International Student Identity Card (ISIC) can get discounts of up to 40%. There are also discounts for seniors and pensioners.

Reservations

Book online or by phone via **Queensland Rail** (☎1800 872 467; www.queenslandrail.com.au). There are also Queensland Rail travel centres throughout the state. These booking offices can advise on rail travel, sell tickets and put together rail-holiday packages: see the website for locations.

Train Services

GULFLANDER

The *Gulflander* is a strange, snub-nosed little train that travels once a week along the 152km line connecting the remote Gulf of Carpentaria towns of Normanton and Croydon – a unique and memorable five-hour journey. Fares are $69/115 one-way/return. Departs Normanton on Wednesday; departs Croydon on Thursday.

INLANDER

The *Inlander* runs from Townsville 977km east to Mt Isa (economy seat $179, single/twin/triple sleeper per person $375/375/250, 20 hours) on Sunday and Thursday. Returns from Mt Isa Monday and Friday.

KURANDA SCENIC RAILWAY

One of the most popular tourist trips out of Cairns is the **Kuranda Scenic Railway** (☎07-4036 9333; www.ksr.com.au) – a spectacular 1½-hour trip on a historic steam train through the rainforest to Kuranda, 34km west of Cairns. Fares from $49/79 one-way/return; runs daily.

SAVANNAHLANDER

A classic 1960s train, the **Savannahlander** (www.savannahlander.com.au) makes the two-day, 229km trip between Cairns (departs Wednesday) and Forsayth (departs Friday). Trains run between March and December. The journey costs $227/381 for a single/return trip.

SPIRIT OF QUEENSLAND

Introduced in 2013, this service runs 1681km from Brisbane to Cairns (25 hours, Monday and Friday), with flashy reclining 'railbed' seats and premium economy seats. Fares are $369/519 premium economy seat/railbed. Railbed fares include food. Returns from Cairns Wednesday and Saturday.

SPIRIT OF THE OUTBACK

The *Spirit of the Outback* travels the 1325km northwest from Brisbane to Longreach via Rockhampton (economy seat $235, triple/1st-class sleeper per person $315/569, 24 hours) on Tuesday and Saturday. A connecting bus service operates between Longreach and Winton. Returns from Longreach Monday and Thursday.

SUNLANDER

The *Sunlander* travels the 1681km from Brisbane to Cairns three times a week (economy seat $219, single/twin/triple sleeper per person $499/499/349, Queenslander class $899, 31 hours) on Tuesday, Thursday and Sunday. Returns from Cairns Tuesday, Thursday and Saturday.

TILT TRAIN

The *Tilt Train*, a high-speed, business-class train, makes the 1681km trip from Brisbane to Cairns (business seat $369, 24 hours) on Monday and Friday. Returns from Cairns Tuesday, Thursday and Saturday.

There are also shorter *Tilt Train* trips along the 351km route from Brisbane and Bundaberg (economy/business seat $89/115, 4½ hours) and the 639km route from Brisbane to Rockhampton (economy/business seat $135/185, 7½ hours).

WESTLANDER

The *Westlander* heads 777km inland from Brisbane to Charleville via Toowoomba (economy seat $149, twin/triple sleeper per person $327/219, 17 hours) on Tuesday and Thursday. From Charleville there are connecting bus services to Cunnamulla and Quilpie. Return from Charleville is on Wednesday and Friday.

Behind the Scenes

SEND US YOUR FEEDBACK

We love to hear from travellers – your comments keep us on our toes and help make our books better. Our well-travelled team reads every word on what you loved or loathed about this book. Although we cannot reply individually to your submissions, we always guarantee that your feedback goes straight to the appropriate authors, in time for the next edition. Each person who sends us information is thanked in the next edition – the most useful submissions are rewarded with a selection of digital PDF chapters.

Visit **lonelyplanet.com/contact** to submit your updates and suggestions or to ask for help. Our award-winning website also features inspirational travel stories, news and discussions.

Note: We may edit, reproduce and incorporate your comments in Lonely Planet products such as guidebooks, websites and digital products, so let us know if you don't want your comments reproduced or your name acknowledged. For a copy of our privacy policy visit lonelyplanet.com/privacy.

OUR READERS

Many thanks to the travellers who used the last edition and wrote to us with helpful hints, useful advice and interesting anecdotes:

Ross Arnold, Michelle Blanchard, Daniel Fishman, Pam Ganley, Mary Gough, Terry Marshall, Ian McHaffie, Kerry McIlroy, Bob Stocker, Daniel Ziegler

AUTHOR THANKS

Charles Rawlings-Way

Huge thanks to Maryanne for the gig, and to my highway-addled co-authors, who covered a helluva lot of kilometres in search of the perfect review. Thanks also to the all-star in-house Lonely Planet production staff, and in Brisbane thanks to Christian, Lauren, Rachel, Brett and all the kids. Special thanks as always to Meg, my road-trippin' sweetheart, and our daughters Ione and Remy who provided countless laughs, unscheduled pit-stops and ground level perspectives along the way.

Meg Worby

Thanks to Maryanne for this one and for all the gigs: it's been a pleasure working with you. More than ever, thanks to the in-house team at Lonely Planet: you guys are great at what you do. In Brisbane, a massive thank you to Lauren, Christian, Orlando, Ilaria and the Goodies for your generosity, soulful company and high-rollin' insider tips on Brisvegas. To our little daughters, Ione and Remy, thanks for crawling over every inch of South Bank with us! And to Charles: 'proper job' (Brisbane's a long way from Devon, but you made it seem like home).

Tamara Sheward

Backslapping g'days and goodonyas to the multitude of Queenslanders (and a few non-Smart State ring-ins) who helped with the large but lovely challenge of covering the almost-2000km from FNQ to the Sunshine Coast. Everyone from visitor info centre staff to pub-propper-uppers proved that with sunny climes come equal dispositions. Extra big shout-out to 1770: we'll be back, and we will be annexing. *Dušan moj ljubav, ti si najbolji avanturista i muž na svetu;* Masha, are you ready for this?

ACKNOWLEDGMENTS

Climate map data adapted from Peel MC, Finlayson BL & McMahon TA (2007) 'Updated World Map of the Köppen-Geiger Climate Classification', Hydrology and Earth System Sciences, 11, 1633–44.

Cover photograph: Frankland Islands, Steve Parish/Corbis ©

THIS BOOK

This 7th edition of Lonely Planet's *Queensland & the Great Barrier Reef* guidebook was researched and written by Charles Rawlings-Way, Meg Worby and Tamara Sheward. The previous edition was written by Regis St Louis, Sarah Gilbert, Catherine Le Nevez and Olivia Pozzan. This guidebook was commissioned in Lonely Planet's Melbourne office, and produced by the following:

Commissioning Editor Maryanne Netto
Destination Editor Tasmin Waby
Product Editor Dianne Schallmeiner
Senior Cartographer Julie Sheridan
Book Designer Wibowo Rusli
Senior Editor Karyn Noble
Assisting Editors Sarah Bailey, Nigel Chin, Bruce Evans, Lauren Hunt, Rosie Nicholson
Assisting Cartographer Alison Lyall
Cover Researcher Naomi Parker
Thanks to Anita Banh, Imogen Bannister, David Carroll, Laura Crawford, Ryan Evans, Larissa Frost, Nóirín Hegarty, Genesys India, Jouve India, Indra Kilfoyle, Trent Paton, Martine Power, Averil Robertson, John Taufa, Angela Tinson, Juan Winata

Index

Map Legend

Sights

- Beach
- Bird Sanctuary
- Buddhist
- Castle/Palace
- Christian
- Confucian
- Hindu
- Islamic
- Jain
- Jewish
- Monument
- Museum/Gallery/Historic Building
- Ruin
- Sento Hot Baths/Onsen
- Shinto
- Sikh
- Taoist
- Winery/Vineyard
- Zoo/Wildlife Sanctuary
- Other Sight

Activities, Courses & Tours

- Bodysurfing
- Diving
- Canoeing/Kayaking
- Course/Tour
- Skiing
- Snorkelling
- Surfing
- Swimming/Pool
- Walking
- Windsurfing
- Other Activity

Sleeping

- Sleeping
- Camping

Eating

- Eating

Drinking & Nightlife

- Drinking & Nightlife
- Cafe

Entertainment

- Entertainment

Shopping

- Shopping

Information

- Bank
- Embassy/Consulate
- Hospital/Medical
- Internet
- Police
- Post Office
- Telephone
- Toilet
- Tourist Information
- Other Information

Geographic

- Beach
- Hut/Shelter
- Lighthouse
- Lookout
- Mountain/Volcano
- Oasis
- Park
- Pass
- Picnic Area
- Waterfall

Population

- Capital (National)
- Capital (State/Province)
- City/Large Town
- Town/Village

Transport

- Airport
- Border crossing
- Bus
- Cable car/Funicular
- Cycling
- Ferry
- Metro station
- Monorail
- Parking
- Petrol station
- Subway station
- Taxi
- Train station/Railway
- Tram
- Underground station
- Other Transport

Note: Not all symbols displayed above appear on the maps in this book

Routes

- Tollway
- Freeway
- Primary
- Secondary
- Tertiary
- Lane
- Unsealed road
- Road under construction
- Plaza/Mall
- Steps
- Tunnel
- Pedestrian overpass
- Walking Tour
- Walking Tour detour
- Path/Walking Trail

Boundaries

- International
- State/Province
- Disputed
- Regional/Suburb
- Marine Park
- Cliff
- Wall

Hydrography

- River, Creek
- Intermittent River
- Canal
- Water
- Dry/Salt/Intermittent Lake
- Reef

Areas

- Airport/Runway
- Beach/Desert
- Cemetery (Christian)
- Cemetery (Other)
- Glacier
- Mudflat
- Park/Forest
- Sight (Building)
- Sportsground
- Swamp/Mangrove

Contributing Authors

Dr Michael Cathcart wrote the History chapter. Michael presents history programs on ABC TV, is a broadcaster on ABC Radio National and teaches history at the Australian Centre, University of Melbourne. His most recent book is *Starvation in a Land of Plenty* (2013), an illustrated account of the life and death of the explorer William Wills.

Dr Terry Done co authored the Climate Change & the Great Barrier Reef chapter. Terry is a coral-reef researcher, and was formerly a research scientist at the Australian Institute of Marine Science (AIMS). He has written more than 80 scientific papers and book chapters with a focus on coral reefs, including their ecology, processes of reef growth, and the effects of fishing, pollution and climate change. Terry lives in Townsville, and in his free time is an avid hiker, fly-fisher, traveller and grandfather of three.

Paul Marshall co-authored the Climate Change & the Great Barrier Reef chapter. Paul has spent his life diving on, researching and writing about coral reefs and the issues they face. He works with the Great Barrier Reef Marine Park Authority and University of Queensland, leading Australian and international efforts to understand the implications of climate change for the conservation and management of coral reefs. He lives with his wife and two daughters in Townsville.

OUR STORY

A beat-up old car, a few dollars in the pocket and a sense of adventure. In 1972 that's all Tony and Maureen Wheeler needed for the trip of a lifetime – across Europe and Asia overland to Australia. It took several months, and at the end – broke but inspired – they sat at their kitchen table writing and stapling together their first travel guide, *Across Asia on the Cheap*. Within a week they'd sold 1500 copies. Lonely Planet was born.

Today, Lonely Planet has offices in Franklin, London, Melbourne, Oakland, Beijing and Delhi, with more than 600 staff and writers. We share Tony's belief that 'a great guidebook should do three things: inform, educate and amuse'.

OUR WRITERS

Charles Rawlings-Way

Coordinating Author, Brisbane & Around, The Gold Coast As a likely lad, Charles suffered in shorts through Tasmanian winters and dreamed of far-away tropical Queensland. At 24 he threw a surfboard and guitar into the back of his 1973 HQ Holden panel van and hit the road: an epic dash from Hobart to Cape Tribulation that stalled in Gympie with an imploding gear box. More recently he's spent time mooching around Brisbane's bookshops, bars and band rooms, cementing his love for the Sunshine State. An underrated guitarist, sometime architect and proud father of daughters, Charles has penned 20-something guidebooks for Lonely Planet. Charles also co-wrote the Plan Your Trip section, plus Queensland Today, the Arts feature and the Survival Guide.

Meg Worby

Coordinating Author, Brisbane & Around, The Gold Coast Meg's first foray into Queensland introduced her to a green turtle, face-to-face underwater. Twenty-eight years and six trips later, Queensland's inhabitants are still naturally charming and a shell-load more cosmopolitan. A former member of Lonely Planet's languages, editorial and publishing teams, this is Meg's eighth Australian guidebook for Lonely Planet. Meg also co-wrote the Plan Your Trip section, plus Queensland Today, the Arts feature and the Survival Guide.

Tamara Sheward

Noosa & the Sunshine Coast, Fraser Island & the Fraser Coast, Capricorn Coast & the Southern Reef Islands, Whitsunday Coast, Townsville to Mission Beach, Cairns & the Daintree Rainforest Despite a hearty dislike of heat and humidity, Tamara has nevertheless spent years living all over the Sunshine State, from the torrid Torres Strait on down. An off-and-on Cairns resident since 1989, Tamara has a fine appreciation of cyclone parties and hand-reel fishing, and shudders at the merest whisper of cane toads. Going from snow to swelter – Tamara's usual Lonely Planet stomping grounds are Serbia and Russia – made for a whole new style of research, one that may or may not have involved lots of icy Queensland ales and inappropriate bikini flouncing. Tamara also wrote Your Reef Trip and the Great Barrier Reef colour section.

Published by Lonely Planet Publications Pty Ltd
ABN 36 005 607 983
7th edition – August 2014
ISBN 978 1 74220 576 2

10 9 8 7 6 5 4 3 2 1
Printed in China